THE
GREAT
THOUGHTS

THE
GREAT
THOUGHTS

COMPILED BY

GEORGE SELDES

Foreword by Henry Steele Commager

BALLANTINE BOOKS

NEW YORK

Library of Congress Catalog Card Number: 84-45673

ISBN: 0-345-29887-X

Text design by Ann Gold
Cover design by Ray Barber
Manufactured in the United States of America
First Edition: April 1985

10 9 8 7 6 5 4 3

This book is dedicated to the memory of my wife, Helen Larkin Seldes, who helped me for many years gather and evaluate the great thoughts which rule the world; and to my neighbor Edna Belisle, the Woodstock Ambulance, and Dr. Hugh P. Hermann, who together saved me from death one morning, when the final draft was only half completed. . . .

And to twenty-six friends, my neighbors in Hartland and nearby towns who make living here possible, and to whom I have dedicated my birthday parties ever since I was ninety. . . .

And to everyone who made publication possible, including editors Joëlle Delbourgo and Elizabeth Sacksteder at Ballantine Books, and Mary Lee Coughlin, who struggled with every one of the thousands of paragraphs for many months, until *The Great Thoughts* achieved its final form.

George Seldes
Hartland-4-Corners, Vermont

CONTENTS

FOREWORD

Because Americans have had, from the beginning, a "free" press, we have had a longer tradition of the congenital nay-sayer, the contrary-minded, and the "come-outer" than most other nations. That tradition began with *Common Sense*, and with *The Crisis* (written as a series of newspaper articles) It was continued by William Lloyd Garrison and his anti-slavery *Liberator*, which insured that he "would be heard"; by Theodore Parker, the Great American Preacher, who dissented from the Dissenters and preached to the largest congregation in the country; and by Frederick Douglass, who published his own paper to carry on the work that Parker left unfinished. In the next century the tradition was carried on by Bryan, whose *Commoner* was his private organ; by Fighting Bob LaFollette, who gave his *Weekly* his own name; by William Allen White, who made his Emporia *Gazette* a national newspaper; and by I.F. Stone, whose *Weekly Newsletter* is alas no more with us.

It is to this tradition that George Seldes belongs. He had, from the beginning—that was way back in the first decade of this century—the right credentials. His father had set an example: a failed pharmacist, he was not at all a failed radical, what with his admiration for Tolstoy and Kropotkin and Thoreau, and for Henry George, whose name his own son bore (the son was forced by his *Chicago Tribune* service chief to drop the "Henry"). Young George blundered into journalism, as it were. He was the star reporter for the Pittsburg *Post* and the Chicago *Tribune*, then a member of Pershing's press corps of war correspondents, eventually becoming head of the *Tribune* bureau in Rome and Berlin. As a correspondent he discovered a knack—almost a genius—for being *there* at the right time. He was there in Lenin's Moscow, there in Mussolini's Rome, there in Hitler's Berlin, there when the French stormed Damascus, there when Franco conquered Spain; sooner or later he met almost everyone and took their measure—usually one that fitted a bit tightly.

But twenty years of journalism disillusioned him—not with life, not with the American people, but with journalism—all except his own. So, in 1940—could he have picked a worse time?—he launched his own private newsletter, called quite simply *In fact*. Ever sanguine, he hoped to reach a million readers—working people, mostly, and intellectuals. That hope was doomed, but in fact *In fact* did pretty well—not far from two hundred thousand, which was more than all the major liberal weeklies combined. The time was not, after all, propitious for either independence or candor.

From the beginning, Seldes boasted that he "belonged to no party, no organization, no group, society, or faction." He might have added "to no nation," for with Tom Paine he could say, "My country is mankind." Better yet, he might have said with Paine that while "moderation in temper is always a virtue, moderation in principle is always a vice."

The accuracy of that depends, to be sure, upon the principle. In Seldes' case the principle was quite simply that the truth shall make men free.

After the war Seldes returned to his home in Vermont, where he could cultivate his garden and at the same time cultivate philosophy. Out of that retreat came, some twenty years ago, his compendium of Great Quotations. Since then he has been collecting and—we may be sure—assimilating Great Thoughts.

The Great Thoughts is a tribute not only to those thinkers who have influenced George Seldes, but to Seldes himself, who lived with them and by them, who has found them comforting, stimulating, and challenging. Clearly it is his hope that they will serve this purpose for others.

Henry Steele Commager
Amherst, Massachusetts
December 1984

INTRODUCTION

"Great men are they who see that spiritual
is stronger than any material force, that thoughts
rule the world."

—Emerson, *Progress of Culture*

No one, so far as I know, has ever challenged the Rev. Mr. Ralph Waldo Emerson's impressive dictum. The philosopher-king Marcus Aurelius Antoninus (120–180 A.D.) believed that the "universe is change," and that "our life is what our thoughts make it." Paracelsus (1493–1541) wrote that "thoughts are free and are subject to no rule. On them rests the freedom of man, and they tower above the light of nature . . . create a new heaven, a new firmament, a new source of energy from which new arts flow." In the seventeenth century the French mathematician–philosopher Blaise Pascal (who indeed may have influenced Mr. Emerson) wrote that "man's greatness lies in the power of thought," and in my own lifetime the English mathematician-philosopher Bertrand Russell, whom I once met, confirmed these views on my present subject:

> Men fear thought as they fear nothing else on earth—more than ruin—more even than death . . .
> Thought is subversive and revolutionary, destructive and terrible, thought is merciless to privilege, established institutions, and comfortable habit. Thought looks into the pit of hell and is not afraid. Thought is great and swift and free, the light of the world, and the chief glory of man.

A hundred notable men and women, from A to W, from Henry Adams to Sir Henry Wotton, have similarly expressed themselves. Nor are these sentiments confined to great men or intellectuals.

On reading the paragraphs above, one of my native Vermont neighbors who frequently helps me with my manuscripts, recently remarked, "Words are weapons." (My friend assures me that he had never read Hazlitt's *Table Talk* nor any Hazlitt commentator who quoted the famous remark, "Great thoughts reduced to a practice become great acts.")

My own efforts to record the greatest thoughts of the ages began some fifty years ago, in the 1930s. At that time I was writing a great deal on freedom of the press, and often needed suitable epigraphs for books or chapters on the subject. Although a number of collections of quotations were then available, I could find in them nothing of John Stuart Mill, whose *On Liberty* I had read not once but perhaps five times, nor anything I needed from Milton's *Areopagitica: A Speech for the Liberty of Unlicensed Printing,* one of the great landmarks not only of freedom of the press but freedom of mankind. I became convinced that a book of not merely familiar but of truly *great* quotations would be welcomed by many people. After many years of work on the project, *The Great Quotations* was published, and my feeling was almost immediately justified by sales—which have now passed the 1,100,000 mark, clothbound and paperback.

Yet from the day in 1960 when I held the first printed copy in my hand, I began to think of improvement, of additions and eliminations, and when technical difficulties prevented them, I had a vague idea—this vagueness was twenty years ago—that I could abandon "quotations" altogether and gather from the literature of the world, and perhaps even the morning newspapers, only the great thoughts which Mr. Emerson told me rule the world.

Further food for thought came from an unexpected source. In preparing *The Great Quotations* (as well as the volume you hold in your hand) I had written to scores, perhaps a hundred, notable persons of my time, asking them to verify the accuracy of the quotations that I had selected from their work. Curiously enough, the world famous with whom I corresponded—Einstein in 1954, Shaw in 1937, and Freud in 1924, for example—all replied, whereas many others who never achieved greatness ignored the matter of correcting their proofsheets. All were asked for suggestions, and the most notable reply was a 2-page holograph letter from Aldous Huxley which cost me weeks of work but was nevertheless of utmost value. Mr. Huxley seems to have sensed or suspected that I had been working for many years under the impression that "great" thoughts must necessarily mean "good" thoughts, that I was not including the great and powerful and most important evil thoughts of princes, kings, dictators, and demagogues who had, not only in ancient times but only yesterday, ruled a large part, in fact a major part, of the self-styled civilized world. Mr. Huxley concluded:

> It might be interesting to have a short section in your book devoted to what may be called negative quotations—utterances of pure nonsense, pollyanna uplift, anti-intelligence and anti-liberty—all drawn from the speeches or writings of the eminent. E.g. passages in praise of the executioner as the main pillar of civilized society from Joseph de Maistre's "Soirées de St. Petersbourg." Passages from Louis Veuillot's "Parfums de Rome," holding up the papal pre-1870 government as the best in the world. Passages on infant damnation from St. Augustine and from the Calvinists. Passages on Jesus as a salesman from Bruce Barton. And so forth. A few pages of these wd constitute a stimulating Chamber of Horrors—or, divided up, might serve as a preface to the various sections of your book.

Although several of our century's greatest evil thinkers had already gone to their rewards at the time Mr. Huxley wrote this letter—Hitler by his own hand and Mussolini shot by his own people then hanged by his feet from the rafters of a gas station—Stalin was still murdering dissenters by the tens of thousands; the nation which boasted one billion inhabitants, China, was still an absolute dictatorship; and their little imitators were ruling countries by force, by imprisonment, torture, and death, and at best by brain-washing and mind-manipulation, while addressing their populations and the world with words, good or evil, important enough to be recorded. While Mr. Huxley's suggestion changed substantially the content of *The Great Quotations,* it has had perhaps an even greater effect on this book. I have endeavored throughout to represent the evil and destructive ideas of the ages that have periodically made the world a worse place in which to live.

Some fifty years ago I began underlining passages and making notes in the margins of my books—never the first editions, never the well-printed, well-bound copies, but the early dollar reprints and the later paperbacks. It made the work of years later much easier, and today, it is just one year short of a quarter of a century since I began copying, on ten thousand filing cards, the collected *great* thoughts, and some eight or nine years since I began the actual preparation of this manuscript.

Although the marked pages and passages have been a great help, I have had to read or reread many of the books which have moved or changed or ruled the world, and almost every day has been worthwhile—whether it involved rereading all or parts of *War and Peace,* or *Moby Dick,* or *Walden,* or perhaps Plato's *Republic* or the *Nichomachean Ethics* of Aristotle, or even Theodore Dreiser's turgid masterpiece, *Sister Carrie* (which Sinclair Lewis insisted honestly should have won the Nobel Prize years before he got his).

Most of the world's masterpieces are read because they are required reading in high schools and colleges; they make little impression on young minds and are immediately forgotten by almost everyone. Except one day the graduate may read somewhere a list of "the ten best novels" or "the hundred greatest books of all time" and can contentedly say, "I have read every one of them." How many people read a great book again in their mature years? How many of the millions who do read books realize they are missing one of the truly great pleasures of life by not *re-reading* books?

One of the real purposes of this collection is to recall to the reader one or more of the great thoughts he or she found in the great books years and years ago, and to stir the reader's imagination to the point of finding the book in the library and reading it again. Not only the *Nichomachean Ethics* but *Sister Carrie* will take on new dimensions of greatness—as the present writer found out only recently.

In addition to the extensive reading that I have done in preparing this collection, I have also actually talked to a number of men who have given us thoughts that changed the world in our lifetime—or, having now passed my 94th year, I should perhaps say, my lifetime. Among them are Lenin and Einstein, and I missed meeting Freud in Vienna only through the trickery of a journalistic colleague. I did become an intimate visitor, if not a personal friend, of another great man who in the course of history will be recognized: I am referring to the Vienna psychiatrist Alfred Adler, "the father of individual psychiatry"—a man big enough to open his home every Wednesday afternoon to a score or two of foreigners, psychiatrists, Americans studying medicine, and even a journalist or two.

The only words Hitler spoke during the two-and-a-half hour reception the Baron von Maltzan gave for the foreign press and the leaders of all seven political parties in 1925 were "*Guten Tag*" and "*Guten Abend.*" But later, in Nürnberg in the 1930s, I heard him rant and rage and roar for hours without adding anything to his two previous profound remarks. (It is my view, based on considerable information I had during my years as a correspondent in Berlin, that the great if evil thoughts in *Mein Kampf* are not Hitler's but those of his cell companion, Rudolf Hess, to whom, the story goes, Hitler "dictated" his book.) On the other hand, while I lived in Italy I heard Mussolini denounce the Goddess of Liberty and proclaim the "profoundly moral values of violence"—and incidentally, in an interview he granted me, try to pass off Nietzsche's famous or notorious views as his own. Lenin, in one interview, and the three or four times I heard him speak, said nothing especially noteworthy, but unlike his fellow dictators, Lenin did smile on many occasions, and even at times illustrated his views with a little commonplace humor. Like many great men, these historic figures were in many ways banal; it is not (except possibly in Lenin's case) the greatness of their thoughts but the thoroughness of their execution of them that changed history—illustrating again the truth of Hazlitt's famous remark.

In the literary world, it has been my good fortune to know Sinclair Lewis and Theodore Dreiser very well, Thomas Wolfe slightly; and during the Spanish Civil War my wife and I lived in the same little hotel as Hemingway (and scores of war correspondents from all parts of the world). But I cannot remember a phrase spoken by Lewis, Dreiser, Wolfe, Hemingway, or any other notable writers I have met worth reporting—whereas in their books they demonstrate their great worth, whether recognized by the Nobel committee or not.

Although I never met him personally, Freud serves as the best illustration of the work which has occupied most of my past decade. For a good six months of that time, forsaking all others, I read and copied out from the complete British edition of his works what has now become known as the Freudian philosophy. When finally assembled and edited and typed cleanly, there were just 40 pages or about 12,000 words, all of which I valued and could not destroy. (In conventional collections of quotations Freud is represented by a few short selections—if anything at all.) Obviously 40 pages is an impossibility in a volume seeking to encompass the whole world in say 1500 manuscript pages—but what are editors for? In the end I had to thank them humbly for reducing Freud to twenty, perhaps eighteen pages—which is still, I believe, the largest section devoted to one human being, living or dead, and representative of his lasting importance as a great thinker.

CENSORSHIP AND SUPPRESSION

"Every burned book enlightens the world." —Emerson, "Compensation"

One of the first impressions received from reading the original works—books, letters, contemporary reports—of thinking men and women on all important subjects must be that censorship and suppression have always existed. Incredible as it may seem, especially to professional patriots, not only the military leaders who established this Republic but the politico-philosophical leaders who guided the course of the American Revolution were both victims of contemporary and later witch hunters. As late as 1956, before the Senate Judiciary Committee, when a representative of Americans for Democratic Action read a statement of Thomas Jefferson's, one of the Senators from the State of Washington, A. V. Watkins, denounced it as false and unbelievable. Confronted with the evidence—a letter from Jefferson to Madison in 1787, available in most history books in most of the nation's libraries—Senator Watkins declared: "If Jefferson were here and advocated such a thing, I would move that he be prosecuted."

What Jefferson had written to Madison was simply this: "I hold that a little rebellion, now and then, is a good thing."*

---

*Mr. Jefferson also wrote in 1787 to Colonel W.S. Smith: "What country can preserve its liberties, if its rulers are not warned from time to time, that its people preserve the spirit of resistance?"

The reader will not find Jefferson's views on an occasional "little rebellion" keeping his country on the course originally planned for it in any of the popular, conventional, safe, and harmless compendiums of the thoughts of the Founders of our country. It may also come as a surprise to Conservatives to learn that their idol, the First President of the United States, wrote in 1789 of mankind becoming more "liberal" and expressed the hope of seeing America "among the foremost nations in examples of justice and liberality"—one of his many similar remarks. The world "Liberal" has not changed its meaning throughout the centuries, and this is why Mussolini proclaimed that "Fascism . . . does not hesitate to call itself illiberal and anti-liberal" and "Fascism now throws the noxious theories of so-called Liberalism upon the rubbish heap," and again, "Communism and Fascism have nothing to do with Liberalism."

On the other hand, President Eisenhower was generally hailed for his Conservatism, "Dynamic Conservatism," and "Progressive Dynamic Conservatism"—if one can imagine such a political policy—and Gladstone once referred to the American uprising of 1775 as "a conservative revolution." If one is fair-minded in quoting FDR's 1939 radio address in which he said that "A Conservative is a man with two perfectly good legs who, however, has never learned to walk," one must also quote the preceding definition: "A Radical is a man with both feet firmly planted in the air." Conservatism is equally a part of the American tradition although not always given equal time in literary and academic circles.

Modern bookburning and censorship have especially interested me since the day in 1924 when the English writer William Bolitho, hearing that I had been assigned to Rome, suggested I make it my first business to collect everything extant on Mussolini's past. The Italian dictator was then suppressing all documentary evidence of his former political incarnations as a radical, communist, socialist, and atheist, notably his own youthful writings, including a 1904 pamphlet entitled, *Dieu n'existe pas.* Forty years later, revisiting Russia secretly, I was able to investigate Stalin's success in censoring and destroying every printed word about his past which did not make him the Soviet hero and leader, next only to Lenin. He had suppressed Jack Reed's *Ten Days That Shook the World* and had it rewritten, substituting his name and eliminating Trotsky's as co-founder of the R.S.F.S.R. in 1917. Stalin actually succeeded in withdrawing the Great Soviet Encyclopedia and eliminating Trotsky from its pages. There is no mention of the great Russian famine of 1922 when American help saved the lives of between six and ten million Russians—several of them now the rulers of the country. Every day for a week I questioned fifty or sixty of the 70,000 students in Moscow University, the brightest young minds in the country, and never in my life have I heard so many falsifications and distortions believed in as "the true history of our country."

As for Hitler, if one were to search for something to say in his favor, it might be the fact that he destroyed books in a public bonfire and published their titles throughout the world rather than eliminating them by stealth or having them forged.

Nor can the United States escape censure in the matter of censorship and suppression. The State Department not only purged its Army libraries abroad after World War II but in several cities burned the censored books secretly.* When, shortly afterwards, for-

---

*In 1953 Senator Joe McCarthy subpoenaed no less than 100 authors, myself included, whose books were found in overseas libraries. Those who refused to take an oath saying they were not communists were held for public hearings, Hollywood style, with cameras and voice recorders, and held up to public ridicule. Several were thereby deprived of a livelihood.

eign correspondents were able to publish the news, public opinion was so aroused that President Eisenhower concluded his 1953 Dartmouth College commencement oration with the memorable words, "Don't join the book burners"—words which may outlive all the others spoken or written by him.

It is unfortunate, however, that in the three decades following the Dartmouth Declaration there has not been a year or two without headlines reporting censorship. And, for the first time, the nation has become aware of the disgraceful pressures which have been brought to bear upon publishers by the buyers of books for the vast public school system, with the result that books have been withdrawn and expurgated—*Huckleberry Finn* one of the many victims.

As for this volume, it must speak for itself. No subject called "controversial" by those who want to censor or suppress it has been omitted, no Ism because it was a "sacred cow"; throughout the following pages the reader will find, whether he approves of them or not, subjects generally omitted elsewhere. For example:

Libertarianism, Liberalism
Conservatism, Toryism, the status quo
Democracy vs. Fascism
Radicalism, Socialism, Communism, Anarchism
Atheism, Agnosticism, Deism, Freethought
Capitalism, Free Enterprise, Laissez-faire
Individualism, Collectivism, Totalitarianism
Sex, Love, Passion, Lust

Even before the present era, when "Liberal" has become a dirty word in the dull lexicon of narrow-minded people, the word "Libertarian" has always been suspect—although Liberty is a subject sacred to every American school child, and perhaps even to many who have grown up. But call yourself a "Libertarian" and perhaps a majority of those who hear you immediately grow suspicious, and sometimes even angry.

As for "Individualism" and "Non-conformity," one has only to compare the writings of such men as Jefferson, Monroe, Madison, Ethan Allen, and Tom Paine with the almost daily propaganda of the new Conservatives to realize how far backwards from the time of the founders of the nation and its first thinkers we have gone in recent times. The great waves of censorship in the past few years, most notably in the schools of the generation soon to reach its maturity and eventually to run the country, are the latest example of modern thought control in America. (At the same time we are far from the totalitarian Soviet regime, where everything is censored, everyone is brainwashed, the vast masses of people are mind-manipulated; in non-dictatorial countries like our own, despite censorship and all attempts at thought control, one is still free to speak, to publish, to form a political party, to vote according to conscience, and to change everything.)

The honest compiler of great quotations or great thoughts, working for honest readers, must of necessity leave his own prejudices, convictions, and perhaps stupidities, behind; he must never omit or even consider omitting anything important in his chosen field—even at the risk of the enmity of the narrow-minded and the prejudiced, many of them in powerful positions, who can censor and distort and falsify and suppress without ever being found out.

BOOKS RULE THE WORLD

"Books rule the world, or at least those nations which
have a written language; the others do not matter."
                                              —Voltaire

Long before picture-writing was superceded by an alphabet, long before illuminated manuscripts, and even before Gutenberg "did use at an early period in his career a mechanical press of some kind," important thoughts in the form of laws to be obeyed by the populace—for example, the Babylonian code of Hammurabi—were cut into stone pillars and displayed in the public squares. Centuries later the most civilized of all people, the Greeks, could read not laws, regulations of property ownership, threats of imprisonment, but the greatest words of their Seven Sages cut into marble pillars of the temple of Apollo at Delphi. My Britannica tells me that the first inscriptions in history were the cuneiform characters on clay tablets dating "as early as 2400 B.C.," and that Gutenberg printed the Bible before 1456—the first printed book.

If books have ruled the world for some 4400 years, the question logically arises, which books? This question has intrigued the literary and educational world for a long time. According to Dr. Robert B. Downs, onetime president of the American Library Association and head of the University of Illinois Library, in 1935 *Publishers Weekly* asked three of the most noted literary men of the time which books published in the past fifty years they thought had had the greatest influence on the American people. John Dewey, Charles A. Beard, and Edward Weeks each prepared a list of fifty titles, but only four of them appeared on all three lists:

Marx: *Das Kapital*
Bellamy: *Looking Backward*
Frazer: *The Golden Bough*
Spengler: *The Decline of the West*

In 1939 Malcolm Cowley and Bernard Smith polled the leading educators, critics, and littérateurs of the day to find out which were "Books That Changed Our Minds." From the 134 entries they received, they selected the following to discuss in their book on the subject:

Freud: *The Interpretation of Dreams*
Adams: *The Education of Henry Adams*
Turner: *The Frontier in American History*
Sumner: *Folkways*
Veblen: *Business Enterprise*
Dewey: *Studies in Logical Theory*
Beard: *Economic Interpretation of the Constitution*
Parrington: *Main Currents in American Thought*

Lenin: *The State and the Revolution*
Spengler: *The Decline of the West*

Numerous literary men and women, most notably in England and America, have engaged in this fascinating business of list-making. Of the dozen or more that I have come upon in the past half century, the majority place the Bible first, and several include not only the Koran but St. Augustine's *City of God* and Bunyan's *Pilgrim's Progress*. Shakespeare is of course a popular choice. Those compilers who have limited themselves to modern times usually agree on Darwin, Marx, Freud, Einstein, and Harvey's *De Motu Cordis*. Only one modern work of fiction crops up on these lists of great books, and even it is not generally mentioned: *Uncle Tom's Cabin* by Harriet Beecher Stowe, which every school child in my time was forced to read because, teacher said, it was a powerful attack upon slavery and helped justify the Civil War which ended it.

All in all, there are so many repetitions among the lists that the total number of titles is probably no more than a hundred. Although all are credited with having "ruled," "changed," or "moved" the world, or having had a great influence on the rather small minority of civilized people who read books, several titles have been censored and burned in public—and in more cruel ancient times not only have great books been burned but their authors have been reduced to ashes along with their works.

Dr. Mortimer J. Adler, one of the best minds of our time, to whom I have already paid tribute in my introduction to *The Great Quotations,* once engaged in a more unusual list-making project. With the assistance of a large research staff, he spent eight years judging no less than 700 possible candidates for the answer to the questions, "What is an idea?" and "What are the great ideas?"

In answering the latter question, Adler came up with an "irreducible minimum of 102." In the six years that followed the publication of this list, Dr. Adler wrote that he had received no suggestions for additions of comparable magnitude to his original items. Inasmuch as the original list includes Liberty, Justice, Labor, Life and Death, Love, Man, Opinion, Philosophy, Progress, Religion, Truth, War and Peace, Wealth, Will, Wisdom, World, and 83 similarly all-embracing ideas, the reason no one proposed an addition is obvious.

If Dissent and all modern Isms—Socialism, Communism, Naziism, Fascism, even Republicanism and Liberalism are not named among the 102, most of them are probably included under other headings. Dr. Adler has stated that some great ideas—God, State, Man, Knowledge, and Wealth—involve as many as forty or fifty different topics. He does not list either Rebel or Radical, neither Agnosticism nor Non-Conformity, but here again they may be covered by such general ideas as Government, Politics, and Religion.

It is my hope that in this volume none of Dr. Adler's great ideas have been neglected. They are, however, arranged by thinker, rather than subject, as my aim has been not only to record the great thoughts, but to provide an overview of the thought of particular great thinkers. Readers who want to achieve a basic understanding of the entire work of, say, Aristotle or Freud or Marx or Proust will, I hope, find this book suited to the purpose. Those who prefer to explore a variety of thinkers' approaches to a particular idea will find the index helpful.

Certain of the absolutely greatest ideas have, however, been intentionally omitted—specifically, those found in the Bible, as well as the Koran, the various books of the Sayings of Confucius, and the sacred books of Buddhism, which have shaped the lives of not a few great thinkers, but millions, probably billions of people. The reasons for this omission are, first, the technical impossibility of the task—a hundred times more impossible than devoting a mere 20 pages to Dr. Freud—and, second, my desire not to duplicate the efforts of others. In the case of the Bible, in almost every library in the country one can find concordances which list every thought, every idea, almost every word, not once but several times; and there are guides and quotation books for every religion that survives today, as well as most of the forgotten ones. Similarly, Shakespeare is not quoted in these pages; not only are concordances readily available, but he is relatively well represented in the conventional quotation books. Nor have I included proverbs and other sayings of anonymous origin. Not only are these recorded elsewhere, but, in my view, few qualify as great thoughts; whatever greatness they may once have had has been lost through over-familiarity. "A stitch in time saves nine" may be a good idea, but it's also a cliché. I have preferred to stress the fresh, not the stale; the unfamiliar, not the hackneyed; the profound, not the glib.

GREAT THOUGHTS: A BOOK, A PAGE, A PHRASE

As we have seen, the qualified persons who have made this subject their study have agreed that books have changed the world, moved the world, and in fact ruled the world. Yet many of us who read books have limited leisure for reading and cannot begin to determine for ourselves exactly which books (or portions of books), out of the millions in our bookstores and libraries, will reward us with the most insight into the world we live in. Fortunately for us, learned men have for centuries devoted years of study to providing us with this kind of guidance. The Oxford University Press, for example, has succeeded in producing in two volumes of some 4500 pages its *Anthology of English Literature,* covering the Middle Ages through the twentieth century; and Dr. Mary Warnock, Fellow of St. Hugh's College, Oxford, has produced for the New American Library a volume on Jeremy Bentham and John Stuart Mill in a mere 352 pages.

And yet, the biographies of many notable men tell us that one great thought in one paragraph, or on one page, or, in an amazing case, one great phrase, was enough to change the career of its reader, a great man. In this way one thought can be said to have influenced many persons for many years—and will continue to do so, perhaps for centuries.

One example of this phenomenon is Mr. Bernard Shaw. Anyone who ever heard him speak in public with his strong Irish accent, as I once did at the Albert Hall in London, may have heard him say, "Henry George made a man of me."* He had been accustomed to going from book shop to book shop in the Charing Cross Road, picking up a shilling volume and reading a paragraph or a page before deciding whether or not to buy. He does not name the book by Henry George that he found on that fateful day when he achieved manhood, but it could have been none other than *Progress and Poverty.*

I myself was brought up on this book. My father, without knowing Mr. Shaw's views on the subject, told his sons that his whole life changed when, as a very young man work-

---

*Shaw frequently also said in public, "Karl Marx made a man of me." But, as the anecdote will show, I have a personal reason for preferring the former statement.

ing for a living in New York City, he stumbled upon a parade one day in 1886 and joined it. He heard Henry George, candidate for mayor, the favorite of the whole population, expound the Single Tax, and my father immediately offered his services on Sunday, his free day, at George's headquarters.

I have always wondered what page it was that Mr. Shaw read which made a convert of him, what great idea he came upon in his youth which so influenced him. Could it have been these few paragraphs which were underlined in the copy my father gave me:

> This association of poverty with progress is the great enigma of our time. It is the central fact from which spring industrial, social and political difficulties that perplex the world, and with which statesmanship and philanthropy and education grapple in vain. . . . it is the riddle which the Sphinx of Fate puts to our civilization, and which not to answer is to be destroyed.
>
> So long as all the increased wealth which modern progress brings goes but to build up great fortunes, to increase luxury and make sharper the contrast between the House of Have and the House of Want, progress is not real and cannot be permanent. . . .
>
> This then is the remedy for the unjust and unequal distribution of wealth in modern civilization, and for all the evils which rise from it:
>
> *We must make land common property.*

Henry Steele Commager, in his *Living Ideas in America,* says of *Progress and Poverty:* "Few other American books and certainly no other American economic treatise exercised a comparable influence in the world at large." Although younger Americans may today be unfamiliar with this work, it lives on in the ideas of others, as readers of the excerpts quoted in this book cannot fail to recognize.

Mark Twain (or Samuel L. Clemens, as his living relatives inform me they want him to be known), in his *What Is Man?,* states that "the chance reading of a book or of a paragraph in a newspaper, can start a man on a new track and make him renounce his old associations and seek new ones that are in sympathy with his new ideal; and the result for that man, can be an entire change of his way of life."

As for Eugene V. Debs, whom a generation knew as the perpetual Socialist candidate for President of the United States, it was not until he was sent to jail for the first time that he began to read Karl Marx and so became the Socialist leader of his time. He had been brought up on Hugo and Voltaire, whose books he had found in his father's library, but it was his reading in prison that changed his life.

The most amazing conversion, it seems to me, is that of the English philosopher and jurist Jeremy Bentham, whose lifework was the result of reading not one great book or even one page of a great book, but of a single phrase.

"In 1768, when he came back to Oxford to record his vote at the University parliamentary election," writes Dr. Warnock, Bentham "happened to go into a circulating library attached to the coffeehouse near Queen's, and there he found a copy of Joseph Priestley's new pamphlet, 'Essay on Government.' In it he found the phrase 'The greatest happiness of the greatest number.' On this discovery he says: 'It was by that pamphlet and this phrase in it that my principles on the subject of morality, public and private, were determined. It was from that pamphlet and that page of it that I drew the phrase, the words and the import of which have been so widely diffused over the civilized world.' "

"Upon certain ideas derived from Helvetius and Beccaria," continues Dr. Warnock, "and upon this phrase of Priestley's he decided that he would build a foundation for scientific jurisprudence and for legislation; in fact he devoted the whole of his life to this task."

While it is unlikely that any of my readers will experience a conversion comparable to Bentham's as a result of reading a phrase or a paragraph collected in *The Great Thoughts,* the example does serve to illustrate the potential value of my approach. Quotations lifted out of context in a compilation like this one obviously cannot replace the experience of reading a great thinker's work in its entirety. But sometimes an isolated phrase or paragraph will work on the reader's imagination more forcefully than it might when buried in a possibly difficult text. Each time a quotation in this book makes a reader think about a problem in a new way, I shall have achieved my aim.

Of course not every thought contained herein will speak to every reader in this way. To some readers, the greatness of certain quotations may in fact seem obscure. I confess that I am unable to answer the pertinent question: What constitutes a *great* thought? As we have already seen, when the most competent persons of the time were engaged to choose the great books, it was found that all agree in very few instances. Nevertheless I am sure that every reader of the great Greek philosophers, coming upon the following from the "Aphorisms" of Epicurus, will agree with me that it is a great thought, probably one of the greatest, for it aims directly at one of the vital problems which has afflicted man since he began to think, the problem of good and evil. Epicurus wrote, circa 300 B.C.:

> The gods can either take away evil from the world and will not, or, being willing to do so cannot; or they neither can nor will, or lastly, they are both able and willing. If they have the will to remove evil and cannot, then they are not omnipotent. If they can, but will not, then they are not benevolent. If they are neither able nor willing, then they are neither omnipotent nor benevolent. Lastly, if they are both able and willing to annihilate evil, how does it exist?

Any judgment as to "greatness" must inevitably be subjective. In making my selections I have looked for profundity, the excitement, the clarity, the lasting influence exemplified by the above from Epicurus.

I have also been guided by all my predecessors, some of whom have devoted the best part of a literary lifetime to one great man or one great cultural idea. Lists made by persons in whom one has faith are invaluable. Certainly one must have faith in the Britannica, which has proved to be an indispensable source in preparing this collection.

Whether or not this compiler has produced a worthwhile volume which does justice to the great thoughts that rule the world—and which have interested me from the day exactly fifty-one years ago when I needed epigraphs from Mill and Milton—is for the reader to say. The compiling of, first, quotations whose greatness was without question but which nevertheless had been censored and popularly omitted, and later on, the great thoughts of all ages, has occupied the best part of my lifetime. The purpose, above all, has been to produce a book which will be read for a lifetime.

George Seldes
Hartland-4-Corners, Vermont
October 1984

THE
GREAT
THOUGHTS

PETER ABELARD (Pierre Abailard) (1079–1142)
French priest, scholastic philosopher*

Ethics

God considered not action, but the spirit of the action. It is the intention, not the deed, wherein the merit or praise of the doer consists.

The sin, then, consists not in desiring a woman, but in consent to the desire, and not the wish for whoredom, but the consent to the wish is damnation.

LORD ACTON (John E.E. Dalberg) (1834–1902)
English historian

Historic responsibility has to make up for the want of legal responsibility. Power tends to corrupt, and absolute power corrupts absolutely.

Great men are almost always bad men, even when they exercise influence and not authority; still more when they superadd the tendency of the certainty of corruption of authority.

---

*"Abelard was not only the greatest philosopher of his time but a crucial moment in the evolution of the humanitarian mind."—Kenneth Rexroth.

There is no worse heresy than that the office sanctifies the holder of it. That is the point at which the negation of Catholicism and the negation of Liberalism meet and keep high festival, and the end learns to justify the means.
> Letter from Acton to Creighton, April 3, 1887, quoted in *Life and Letters of Mandell Creighton* (1904)

Lectures on Modern History (1906)

Modern history teaches us so nearly, it is so deep a question of life and death, that we are bound to find our own way through it, and to owe our insight to ourselves.

Property is not the sacred right. When a rich man becomes poor it is a misfortune, it is not a moral evil. When a poor man becomes destitute, it is a moral evil, teeming with consequences and injurious to society and morality.
> "The Study of History," Inaugural lecture, June 11, 1895

The History of Freedom and Other Essays (1907)

Liberty, next to religion, has been the motive of good deeds and the common pretext of crime, from the sowing of the seed at Athens, two thousand four hundred and sixty years ago, until the ripened harvest was gathered by men of our race.

In every age its [liberty's] progress has been beset by its natural enemies, by ignorance and superstition, by lust of conquest and by love of ease, by the strong man's craving for power, and the poor man's craving for food.

The most certain test by which we judge whether a country is really free is the amount of security enjoyed by minorities.
> Ch.1

It is bad to be oppressed by a minority, but it is worse to be oppressed by a majority. . . .

from the absolute will of an entire people there is no appeal, no redemption, no refuge but treason.
"The History of Freedom in Antiquity" (1877)

Letters to Mary Gladstone (1904)

Almost all that has been done for the good of the people has been done since the rich lost the monopoly of power, since the rights of property were discovered to be not unlimited.
April 24, 1881

———

Whenever a single definite object is made the supreme end of the State, be it the advantage of a class, the safety or the power of the country, the greatest happiness of the greatest number, or the support of any speculative idea, the State becomes for the time inevitably absolute.

History is not a web woven with innocent hands. Among all the causes which degrade and demoralize men, power is the most constant and the most active.
Contribution, *The Home and Foreign Review,* July 1862, "Essays on Freedom and Power"

Everything secret degenerates; nothing is safe that does not bear discussion and publicity.
Quoted in *Time,* August 22, 1969

ABIGAIL (SMITH) ADAMS
(1744–1818)
American writer, wife of John Adams

The Book of Abigail and John: Selected Letters of the Adams Family, 1762–1784

I am more and more convinced that man is a dangerous creature; and that power, whether vested in many or a few, is ever grasping, and, like the grave, cries, "Give, give!"
Letter to John Adams, November 27, 1775

I long to hear that you have declared an independency. And, by the way, in the new code of laws which I suppose it will be necessary for you to make, I desire you would remember the ladies and be more generous and favourable to them than your ancestors.

Do not put such unlimited power into the hands of the husbands. Remember, all men would be tyrants if they could.

If particular care and attention is not paid to the ladies, we are determined to foment a re-

bellion, and will not hold ourselves bound by any laws in which we have no voice or representation.
Letter to John Adams, March 31, 1776

BROOKS ADAMS
(1848–1927)
American historian

The Law of Civilization and Decay (1897)

Thought is one of the manifestations of human energy, and among the earlier and simpler phases of thought two stand conspicuous—Fear and Greed. Fear, which by stimulating the imagination, creates a belief in an invisible world, and ultimately develops a priesthood; and Greed, which dissipates energy in war and trade.

The Emancipation of Massachusetts (1887)

The power of the priesthood lies in the submission to a creed. In their onslaughts on rebellion they have exhausted human torments; nor, in their lust for earthly dominion, have they felt remorse, but rather joy, when slaying Christ's enemies and their own.

HENRY (BROOKS) ADAMS
(1838–1918)
American historian

The Education of Henry Adams (1907)

Women have, commonly, a very positive moral sense; that which they will, is right; that which they reject, is wrong; and their will, in most cases, ends by settling the moral.
Ch. 6

A friend in power is a friend lost.
Ch. 7

Chaos often breeds life when order breeds habit.
Ch. 16

A teacher affects eternity; he can never tell where his influence stops.
Ch. 20

The study of history is useful to the historian by teaching him his ignorance of women. . . . The woman who is known only through a man is known wrong.
Ch. 23

Practical politics consists in ignoring facts.

The historian must not try to know what is truth, if he values his honesty; for, if he cares for his truths, he is certain to falsify his facts.

Ch. 24

Images are not arguments, rarely even lead to proof, but the mind craves them, and, of late more than ever, the keenest experimenters find twenty images better than one, especially if contradictory; since the human mind has already learned to deal in contradictions.

A stone arrowhead is as convincing as a steam-engine. . . . To evolutionists may be left the processes of evolution; to historians the single interest is the law of reaction between forces and force—between mind and nature—the law of progress.

Ch. 34

The Degradation of the Democratic Dogma (1919)

The world is made up of a few immense forces, each with an organization that corresponds with its strength. The church stands first; and at the outset we must assume that the church will not and cannot accept any science of history, because science by its definition, must exclude the idea of a personal and active providence. The state stands next and the hostility of the state would be assumed toward any system or science that might not strengthen its arm. Property is growing more and more timid and looks with extreme jealousy on any new idea that might weaken its vested rights. Labor is growing more and more self-confident and looks with contempt on all theories that do not support its own. Yet we cannot conceive of a science of history that would not, directly or indirectly, affect all these vast social forces.

If, finally, the science should prove that society at a certain time revert to the church and recover its old foundation of absolute faith in a personal providence and a revealed religion, it commits suicide.

A science cannot be played with. If an hypothesis is advanced that obviously brings into direct sequence of cause and effect all the phenomena of human history, we must accept it, and if we accept we must teach it. The mere fact that it overthrows social organizations cannot affect our attitude. The rest of society can accept or ignore, but we must follow the new light no matter where it leads.

Presidential address, sent from Mexico as a message to the American Historical Association, by its president, 1894

Mont-Saint-Michel and Chartres (1904)

True it was, although one should not say it jestingly, that the Virgin embarrassed the Trinity; and perhaps this was the reason behind all the other excellent reasons, why men loved and adored her with a passion such as no other deity has ever inspired. . . . Mary concentrated in herself the whole rebellion of man against fate; the contempt for human law as its outcome; the whole unutterable fury of human nature beating itself against the walls of its prison-house, and suddenly seized by a hope that in the Virgin man had found a door of escape. . . . She cared not a straw for conventional morality, and she had no notion of letting her friends be punished, to the tenth or any other generation, for the sins of their ancestors or the peccadilloes of Eve.

The Puritans abandoned the New Testament and the Virgin in order to go back to the beginning, and renew the quarrel with Eve.

Man is an imperceptible atom always trying to become one with God.

The two poles of social and political philosophy seem necessarily to be organization or anarchy; man's intellect or the forces of nature.

Absolute liberty is absence of restraint; responsibility is restraint; therefore, the ideally free individual is responsible only to himself. This principle is the philosophical foundation of anarchism, and, for anything that science has yet proved, may be the philosophical foundation of the universe; but it is fatal to all society and is especially hostile to the State.

Letters of Henry Adams

Man has mounted science, and is now run away . . . science will be the master of man. . . . Some day science may have the existence of man in its power, and the human race may commit suicide by blowing up the world.

1862

The press is the hired agent of a monied system, and set up for no other purpose than to tell lies where their interests are involved. One can trust nobody and nothing.

We shall some day catch an abstract truth by the tail, and then we shall have our religion and our immortality.

Quoted in Ernest Samuels, *Henry Adams: The Middle Years* (1958)

JOHN ADAMS
(1735–1826)
Second President of the United States

Diary and Autobiography

The Church of Rome has made it an article of faith that no man can be saved out of their church, and all other religious sects approach this dreadful opinion in proportion to their ignorance, and the influence of ignorant or wicked priests.

February 16, 1756

Constitution of Massachusetts: Declaration of Rights (1780)

The right of a nation to kill a tryant in case of necessity can no more be doubted than to hang a robber, or kill a flea.

A government of laws and not of men.

The Life and Works of John Adams (1851)

The priesthood have, in all ancient nations, nearly monopolized learning. . . . And ever since the Reformation, when or where has existed a Protestant or dissenting sect who would tolerate A FREE INQUIRY? The blackest billingsgate, the most ungentlemanly insolence, the most yahooist brutality, is patently endured, countenanced, propagated, and applauded. But touch a solemn truth in collision with a dogma of a sect, though capable of the clearest proof, and you will soon find you have disturbed a nest, and the hornets will swarm about your eyes and hand, and fly into your face and eyes.

Letter to John Taylor

Dissertation on the Canon and the Feudal Law (1765)

Liberty cannot be preserved without a general knowledge among the people.

The preservation of the means of knowledge among the lowest ranks is of more importance to the public than all the property of all the rich men in the country.

Let us dare to read, think, speak and write.

Let the pulpit resound with the doctrines and sentiments of religious liberty. Let us hear the dangers of thralldom of our consciences from ignorance, extreme poverty, and dependence; in short, from civil and political slavery.

"A Defense of the Constitution of the United States Against the Attacks of M. Turgot" (1787–1788)

The way to secure Liberty is to place it in the people's hands, that is, to give them a power at all times to defend it in the legislature and in the courts of justice. . . .

It is agreed that "the end of all government is the good and ease of the people, in a secure enjoyment of their rights without oppression;" but it must be remembered that the rich are *people* as well as the poor; that they have rights as well as others; that they have as clear and as sacred a right to their large property as others have to theirs which is smaller; that oppression of them is as possible and as wicked as to others.

Property is surely a right of mankind as real as liberty.

The proposition that the people are the best keepers of their own liberties is not true. They are the worst conceivable, they are no keepers at all; they can neither judge, act, think, or will, as a political body.

My country has in its wisdom contrived for me the most insignificant office that ever the invention of man contrived or his imagination conceived.

Letter, written as Vice-President, 1789

The Hebrews have done more to civilize men than any other nation. If I were an atheist, and believed in blind eternal fate, I should still believe that fate had ordained the Jews to be the most essential instrument for civilizing the nations.

Letter to F. A. Vanderkemp, July 13, 1815

The question before the human race is, whether the God of nature shall govern the world by his own laws, or whether priests and kings shall rule it by fictitious miracles?

Letter to Jefferson, June 20, 1815 (Quoted by Jefferson in a letter.)

. . . this would be the best of all possible worlds, if there were no religion in it.

Letter to Jefferson, 1816 (Quoted by Jefferson in a letter.)

Power must never be trusted without a check.
> Letter to Jefferson, February 2, 1816

The Revolution was effected before the war commenced. The Revolution was in the minds and hearts of the people; a change in their religious sentiments, their duties and obligations. *This radical change in the principles, opinions, sentiments and affections of the people, was the real American Revolution.*
> Letter to Hezekiah Niles, February 15, 1818

SAMUEL ADAMS
(1722–1803)
American revolutionary leader

Independent Advertiser (1748)

I believe that no people ever yet groaned under the heavy yoke of slavery but when they deserved it.

JOSEPH ADDISON
(1672–1719)
English essayist, poet

Cato (1713)

A day, an hour, of virtuous liberty
Is worth a whole eternity in bondage.

The Guardian, No. 3

Knowledge is, indeed, that which, next to virtue, truly and essentially raises one man above another.

The Spectator, 239 (March 8, 1711)

Gold is a wonderful clearer of the understanding; it dissipates every doubt and scruple in an instant, accommodates itself to the meanest capacities, silences the loud and clamorous, and brings over the most obstinate and inflexible.

For as it is the chief concern of wise men to retrench the evils of life by the reasonings of philosophy; it is the employment of fools to multiply them by the sentiments of superstition.

To be an atheist requires an infinitely greater measure of faith than to receive all the great truths which atheism would deny.

ALFRED ADLER
(1870–1937)
Austrian pioneer of individual psychology

The Individual Psychology of Alfred Adler (1956, ed. Heinz and Rowena Ansbacher)

To be human means to feel inferior.

To be a human being means to possess a feeling of inferiority which constantly presses towards its own conquest. . . . The greater the feeling of inferiority that has been experienced, the more powerful is the urge for conquest and the more violent the emotional agitation.

What Life Means to You (1931)

All failures—neurotics, psychotics, criminals, drunkards, problem children, suicides, perverts, and prostitutes—are failures because they are lacking in social interest.

If ever we hear of a case of lying, we must look for a severe parent. A lie would have no sense unless the truth were felt as dangerous.

Problems of Neurosis (1929)

The truth is often a terrible weapon of aggression. It is possible to lie, and even to murder, with the truth.
It is easier to fight for principles than to live up to them.

The tests of one's behavior pattern: relationship to society, relationship to one's work, relationship to sex.*
Vienna interview with George Seldes, *N.Y. World,*
1926

MORTIMER J. ADLER
(1902–   )
American philosopher, educator

Every idea is a source of life and light which animates and illuminates the words, facts, examples, and emotions that are dead—or deadly—and dark without them.

Not to engage in this pursuit of ideas is to live like ants instead of like men.
> Quoted in *Saturday Review,* November 22, 1958

*This is the gist of Adlerian thinking, he said.—G.S.

In Aristotelian terms, the good leader must have *ethos, pathos* and *logos.* The *ethos* is his moral character, the source of his ability to persuade. The *pathos* is his ability to touch feelings, to move people emotionally. The *logos* is his ability to give solid reasons for an action, to move people intellectually.

Quoted in *Time,* June 15, 1974

AESCHYLUS
(525–456 B.C.)
Greek dramatist

The Libation Bearers

High fortune,
this in man's eye is god and more than god
    is this.

Lines 59–60

Prometheus Bound

For only Zeus is free.

Line 50

. . . against necessity,
against its strength, no one can fight and
    win.

Lines 105–106

Words are healers of the sick tempered.

Line 380

Agamemnon

Chorus:
    Zeus, who guided men to think
    who laid it down that wisdom
    comes alone through suffering.
    Still there drips in sleep against the heart
    grief of memory; against
    our pleasure we are temperate.

Lines 176–180

Fear is stronger than arms.

Seven Against Thebes

it is yours [women's] to be silent and stay
    within doors.

Line 232

The Suppliant Maidens

Honor modesty more than your life.

Line 1012

Fragment 162

God is not averse to deceit in a holy cause.

AESOP
(620–560 B.C.)
Greek fabulist

Aesop's Fables

Better to die once for all, than live in continual terror.

Any excuse will serve a tyrant.

"The Wolf and the Lamb"

United we stand, divided we fall.

"The Four Oxen and the Lion"

(Jean) LOUIS (Rodolphe) AGASSIZ
(1807–1873)
Swiss-born, American naturalist

Agassiz at Penikese

The study of Nature is intercourse with the highest Mind. You should never trifle with Nature.

I cannot afford to waste my time making money.

Letter refusing lecture course offer

Every great scientific truth goes through three states: First, people say it conflicts with the Bible; next, they say it has been discovered before; lastly, they say they always believed it.

Attributed

AGATHON*
(448–400 B.C.)
Athenian tragic poet

Even the gods cannot change history.

Quoted in Aristotle, *Nicomachean Ethics,*
Bk, VI, Ch. 2, 1139b 10

JAMES AGEE
(1909–1955)
American writer

Let Us Now Praise Famous Men (1941)

In every child who is born, under no matter what circumstances, and of no matter what parents, the potentiality of the human race is

---

*Remembered chiefly because he was quoted by Aristotle and Plato.

born again: and in him, too, once more, and of each of us, our terrific responsibility toward human life; toward the utmost idea of goodness, of the horror of terror, and of God.

LEOPOLDO ALAS Y UREÑA ("Clarín")
(1852–1901)
Spanish novelist and critic

The Cock of Socrates (1901)

He who would prove all life, leaves it empty. To know the way of everything is to be left with the geometry of things and with the substance of nothing. To reduce the world to an equation is to leave it without head or feet.

EDWARD ALBEE
(1928–   )
American dramatist

Good writers define reality; bad ones merely restate it. A good writer turns fact into truth; a bad writer will, more often than not, accomplish the opposite.
Quoted in *The Saturday Review,* May 4, 1966.

ALCUIN (Flaccus Albinus Alcuinus) OF YORK
(735–804)
English scholar

Works

Nor should we listen to those who say "The voice of the people is the voice of God," for the turbulence of the mob is always close to insanity.
Epistle 127, letter to Charlemagne, 800 A.D.

ALEXANDER III (Alexander the Great)
(356–323 B.C.)
King of Macedonia

I will not steal a victory.

The end and perfection of our victories is to avoid the vices and infirmities of those whom we subdue.
Quoted in Plutarch, *The Lives of The Noble Grecians and Romans,* "Alexander"

ETHAN ALLEN
(1738–1789)
American officer, Revolutionary War

"Reason the Only Oracle of Man," pamphlet, Bennington, Vermont, 1784 (first freethought publication in America)

Reason the Only Oracle of Man.
Title

For mankind to hate truth as it may bring their evil deeds to light and punishment, is very easy and common, but to hate truth as truth, or God as God, which is the same as to hate goodness for its own sake, unconnected with any other consequences, is impossible even to a (premised) diabolical nature itself.
Page 31

There is not any thing, which has contributed so much to delude mankind in religious matters, as mistaken apprehensions concerning supernatural inspiration or revelation; not considering, that all true religion originates from reason, and can not otherwise be understood, but by the exercise and improvement of it.
Page 200

THOMAS J. J. ALTIZER
(1927–   )
Professor of Religion, Emory University

Theology itself is coming to confess that ours is a time in which God is dead. *

We are not simply saying that modern man is incapable of believing in God, or even that we exist in a time in which God has chosen to be silent. . . . A theological statement that proclaims the death of God must mean that God is not present in the Word of faith. . . . He is truly absent, he is not simply hidden from view, and therefore he is truly dead.
Contribution, *The Christian Century,* July 7, 1965

It is not possible for any responsible person to think that he can any longer know or experience God in nature, in history, in the eco-

*The phrase, "God is dead," was used by Nietzsche in *The Gay Science.*

nomic or political areas, or in anything which is genuinely modern, whether in thought or in experience.

Contribution, *The Journal of Religion,*
April, 1963

God has died in His transcendent form and reality and is now fully incarnate in every human face and hand. It is a way of saying that Christ lives more fullly and more comprehensively now than He has ever lived before.

Contribution, *Saturday Review,*
June 25, 1966

ST. AMBROSE
(340–397)
Bishop of Milan

Letters

The wise man is always free; he is always held in honor; he is always master of the laws. The law is not made for the just, but for the unjust. The just man is a man unto himself, and he does not need to summon the law from afar, for he carries it enclosed in his heart. . . .

The wise man is free, since one who does as he wishes is free. . . . Because he does what he wishes, the free man is wise. . . . One who acts with wisdom has nothing to fear, for fear lives in sin. Where there is no fear there is liberty; where there is liberty there is the power of doing what one wishes. Therefore, only the wise man is free.

Letter to Simplicianus, c. 386

Let a woman show deference, not being a slave to her husband; let her show she is ready to be guided, not coerced.

Adam was deceived by Eve, not Eve by Adam. . . . it is right that he whom that woman induced to sin should assume the role of guide lest he fall again through feminine instability.

Letter 63, 396

Hexameron

There is nothing evil save that which perverts the mind and shackles the conscience.

I, 31

Flight from the World

Law is twofold—natural and written. The natural law is in the heart, the written law on tables. All men are under the natural law.

3. 15

On the Duties of the Clergy

Nature has poured forth all things for the common use of all men. And God has ordained that all things should be produced that there might be food in common for all, and that the earth should be the common possession of all. Nature created common rights, but usurpation has transformed them into private rights.

I, 132

AMERICAN ANTHROPOLOGICAL ASSOCIATION

Resolution

Race involves the inheritance of similar physical variations by large groups of mankind, but its psychological and cultural connotations, if they exist, have not been ascertained by science.

The terms "Aryan" and "Semitic" have no racial significance whatsoever. They simply denote linguistic families.

Anthropology provides no scientific basis for discrimination against any people on the ground of racial inferiority, religious affiliation, or linguistic heritage.

December 1938

AMERICAN CIVIL LIBERTIES UNION

Annual Report, 1955–56

Liberty is always unfinished business.

Title

AMERICAN LEGION
(Founded 1919)
Society of veterans of U.S. armed forces

Constitution

For God and Country, we associate ourselves together for the following purposes: To uphold and defend the Constitution of the United States of America; to maintain law and order; to foster and perpetuate a 100% Americanism. . . .

Preamble

FISHER AMES
(1758–1808)
American statesman

The Dangers of American Liberty (1805)

A government by the passions of the multitude, or, no less correctly, according to the vices and ambitions of their leaders, is a democracy. We have heard so long of the indefeasible sovereignty of the people, and have admitted so many specious theories of the rights of man, which are contradicted by his nature and experience, that few will dread at all, and fewer still will dread as they ought, the evils of an American democracy.

The people as a body cannot deliberate. Nevertheless, they will feel an irresistible impulse to act, and their resolutions will be dictated to them by their demagogues. . . . and the violent men, who are the most forward to gratify those passions, will be their favourites. What is called the government of the people is in fact too often the arbitrary power of such men. Here, then, we have the faithful portrait of democracy. . . .

The truth is, and let it humble our pride, the most ferocious of all animals, when his passions are roused to fury and are uncontrolled, is man; and of all governments, the worst is that which never fails to excite, but was never found to restrain their passions, that is, democracy. It is an illuminated hell, that in the midst of remorse, horror, and torture, rings with festivity; for experience shews, that one joy remains to this most malignant description of the damned, the power to make others wretched.

Liberty has never yet lasted long in a democracy, nor has it ever ended in anything better than despotism. With the change of our government, our manners and sentiments will change.

                                        Attributed

HENRI FREDERIC AMIEL
(1821–1881)
Swiss philosopher

Amiel's Journal 1849–1872 (pub. 1883, tr. Mrs. Humphrey Ward)

Heroism is the brilliant triumph of the soul over the flesh—that is to say, over fear: fear of poverty, of suffering, of calumny, of sickness, of isolation, and of death. There is no serious piety without heroism. Heroism is the dazzling and glorious concentration of courage.
                                        October 1, 1849

Action is but coarsened thought—thought becomes concrete, obscure and unconscious.
                                        December 30, 1850

Man defends himself as much as he can against truth, as a child does against a medicine, as the man of the Platonic cave did against the light. He does not willingly follow his path, but has to be dragged along backward.

The natural liking for the false has several causes: the inheritance of prejudices, which produces an unconscious habit, a slavery; the predominance of the imagination over reason, which affects the understanding; the predominance of the passions over the conscience, which depraves the heart; the predominance of the will over the intelligence, which vitiates the character.

A lively, disinterested, persistent liking for truth is extraordinarily rare. Action and faith enslave thought, both of them in order not to be troubled or inconvenienced by reflection, criticism and doubt.

Truth is not only violated by falsehood; it may be outraged by silence.

Without passion man is a mere latent force and possibility, like the flint which awaits the shock of the iron before it can give forth its spark.

Self-interest is but the survival of the animal in us. Humanity only begins for man with self-surrender.
                                        December 17, 1856

The great artist is the simplifier.
                                        November 25, 1861

We are always making God our accomplice, that so we may legalize our own iniquities. Every successful massacre is consecrated by a Te Deum, and the clergy have never been wanting in benedictions for any victorious enormity.
                                        October 6, 1866

The efficacy of religion lies precisely in what is not rational, philosophic, nor eternal; its efficacy lies in the unforeseen, the miraculous, the extraordinary. Thus religion attracts more devotion according as it demands more faith—that is to say, as it becomes more incredible to the profane mind.
                                        June 5, 1870

In order to see Christianity, one must forget almost all the Christians.

Philosophy means, first, doubt; and afterwards the consciousness of what knowledge means, the consciousness of uncertainty and of ignorance, the consciousness of limit, shade, degree, possibility. The ordinary man doubts nothing and suspects nothing.

Emancipation from error is the condition of real knowledge.

August 30, 1872

The philosopher aspires to explain away all mysteries, to dissolve them into light. Mystery, on the other hand, is demanded and pursued by the religious instinct; mystery constitutes the essence of worship.

To know how to grow old is the master-work of wisdom, and one of the most difficult chapters in the great art of living.

September 21, 1874

A belief is not true because it is useful.

November 15, 1876

ANACHARSIS
(fl. c. 600 B.C.)
Scythian philosopher

Written laws are like spiders' webs, and will like them only entangle and hold the poor and weak, while the rich and powerful easily break through them.

Quoted in Plutarch, *The Lives of The Noble Grecians and Romans,* "Solon"

The market-place is a place set aside where men may deceive and overreach each other.

Quoted in Diogenes Laërtius, *Sententiae*

What is man's chief enemy? Each man is his own.

Quoted in Stobaeus, Flor., II, 43

ANACREON
(c. 568–478 B.C.)
Greek lyric poet

Fragment (c. 500 B.C.)

Nature has given hearts to bulls, hoofs to horses, swiftness to hares, the power of swimming to fishes, of flying to birds, understanding to men. She had nothing more for women save beauty. Beauty is proof against spears and shields. She who is beautiful is more formidable than fire and iron.

Odes

Cursed he be above all others
Who's enslaved by love of money.

Money takes the place of brothers,
Money takes the place of parents,
Money brings us war and slaughter.

XLVI

ANAXANDRIDES
(died c. 520 B.C.)
Spartan ruler

Fragments

To be a slave to pleasure is the life of a harlot, not of a man.

It is good to die before one has done anything deserving of death.

ANAXIMANDER OF MILETUS
(fl. c. 545 B.C.)
Greek philosopher

Living creatures arose from the moist element as it was evaporated by the sun. Man was like another animal, namely a fish, in the beginning.

The Presocratic Philosophers, ed. G.S. Kirk and J.E. Raven, 1957; Fragment 139, Hippolytus, Ref. I,6,6

SHERWOOD ANDERSON
(1876–1941)
American writer

Winesburg, Ohio (1919)

Everyone in the world is Christ and they are all crucified.

"The Philosopher"

LEONID ANDREYEV
(1871–1919)
Russian writer

Savva (1914)

What do I want? To free the earth, to free mankind.

I want to do away with everything behind man, so that there is nothing to see when he looks back. I want to take him by the scruff of his neck and turn his face toward the future!

ST. ANSELM
(c. 1033–1109)
Archbishop of Canterbury

Proslogion

Nor do I seek to understand that I may believe, but I believe that I may understand. For this too I believe, that unless I first believe, I shall not understand.

SUSAN B(rownell) ANTHONY
(1820–1906)
American women's suffrage advocate

Women's Rights to Suffrage (address, 1873)

It was we, the people; not we, the white male citizens; nor yet we, the male citizens; but we, the whole people, who formed the Union.

For any state to make sex a qualification that must ever result in disenfranchisement of an entire half of the people is to pass a bill of attainder, or an *ex post facto* law, and is therefore in violation of the supreme law of the land.

. . . this oligarchy of sex, which makes fathers, brothers, husband and sons, the oligarchs over the mother and sisters, the wife and daughters of every household—which ordains all men sovereigns, all women subjects, carries dissension, discord, and rebellion into every house of the nation.

Men, their rights and nothing more; women, their rights and nothing less.
                                   Conclusion

ANTIPHANES
(388–311 B.C.)
Greek comic dramatist

Fragment

I trust only one thing in a woman: that she will not come to life again after she is dead. In all other things I distrust her.

ANTISTHENES
(c. 445–365 B.C.)
Founder, Cynic School of Philosophy

The most useful piece of learning for the uses of life is to unlearn what is untrue.
                Quoted in Noyes, *Views of Religion*

GUILLAUME APPOLINAIRE (né Kostrowitsky)
(1880–1918)
Italian-born French poet

Surrealism
                                   Invented word

Alcools (1913)
                      Perdre
          La vie pour trouver la Victoire.
          Lose Life to find Victory.

ST. THOMAS AQUINAS (Thomas of Aquin)
(1225–1274)
Scholastic philosopher

Summa Theologica, Pt. I, First Part

Human salvation demands the divine disclosure of truths surpassing reason.
                Q. 1, art. 1, "I answer that. . . ."

Whether God Exists?
Objection 1. It seems that God does not exist, because if one of two contraries be infinite, the other would be altogether destroyed. But the name "God" means that He is infinite goodness. If, therefore, God existed, there would be no evil discoverable; but there is evil in the world. Therefore God does not exist.

I answer that, The existence of God can be proved in five ways.

The first and the more manifest way is the argument from motion. It is certain, and evident to our senses, that in the world some things are in motion. Now whatever is moved is moved by another, for nothing can be in motion except it is in potentiality to that towards which it is moved; whereas a thing moves inasmuch as it is in act. . . . It is therefore impossible that in the same respect and in the same way a thing could be both mover and moved, i.e., that it should move itself. Therefore, whatever is moved must be moved by another. . . . But this cannot go on to infinity, because then there would be no first mover, and consequently, no other mover. . . . Therefore it is necessary to arrive at the first mover, moved by no other; and this everyone understands to be God.
                                   Q. 2, art. 3

. . . we attribute to Him some things known by divine revelation, to which natural reason cannot reach, as, for instance, that God is Three in One.

Q. 12, art. 13, Reply Obj. 1

God wills all men to be saved by His antecedent will, which is to will not absolutely, but relatively; and not by his consequent will, which is to will absolutely.

Q. 23, art. 5, Reply Obj. 3

God can remove all corruption of the mind and body from a woman who has been seduced; but the fact that she has been seduced cannot be removed from her. In the same way, it is impossible that the fact of having sinned and lost charity can be removed from the sinner.

Q. 25, art. 4, Reply Obj. 3

Man should not consider his material possessions his own, but as common to all, so as to share them without hesitation when others are in need.

For things which are generated and corrupted, in which alone there can be natural evil, are a very small part of the whole universe. Then again, defects in nature are found in every species only in a small number of cases. In man alone does evil manifest itself in the majority of cases. For the good of man as regards the senses of the body is not the good of man as man, but the good according to the reason. More men, however, follow the sense rather than the reason.

Q. 49, art. 3, Reply Obj. 5

And therefore the Philosopher [Aristotle] says in *Metaphysics vi* that good and evil, which are objects of the will, are in things, but truth and error, which are objects of the intellect, are in the mind.

Q. 82, art. 3, "I answer that . . ."

Man has free choice, or otherwise counsels, exhortations, commands, prohibitions, rewards and punishments would be in vain.

Q. 83, "I answer that . . ."

As regards the individual nature, woman is defective and misbegotten, for the active power in the male seed tends to the production of a perfect likeness in the masculine sex; while the production of woman comes from defect in the active power, or from some material indisposition, or even from some external influence, such as that of a south wind, which is moist, as the Philosopher [Aristotle] observes. On the other hand, as regards universal hu-

man nature, woman is not misbegotten, but is included in nature's intention as directed to the work of generation. Now the universal intention of nature depends on God, Who is the Author of nature.

Q. 92, art. 1, Reply Obj. 1

It was right for woman to be made from a rib of man. First, to signify the social union of man and woman, for the woman should neither use authority over man, and so she was not made from his head; nor was it right for her to be subject to man's contempt as his slave, and so she was not made from his feet. . . .

Q. 92, art. 3, "I answer that . . . "

Perfection of moral virtue does not wholly take away the passions, but regulates them. . . .

Q. 95, art. 3, Reply Obj. 3

Good can exist without evil, whereas evil cannot exist without good. . . .

Q. 109, art. 2, Reply Obj. 1

Summa Theologica, Pt. I, Second Part

And if we wish to know the order of all the passions in the way of generation, love and hatred are first; desire and aversion second; hope and despair third; fear and daring fourth; anger, fifth; sixth and last, joy and sadness, which follow from all the passions. . . . yet so that love precedes hatred, desire precedes aversion, hope precedes despair, fear precedes daring, and joy precedes sadness.

To suffer ecstasy is a means to be placed outside oneself.

Summa Theologica, Pt. II, Second Part

When a thing is done again and again, it seems to proceed from a deliberate judgment of reason. Accordingly, custom has the force of a law, abolishes law, and is the interpreter of law.

Q. 97, art. 3, "I answer that . . ."

The light of faith makes us see what we believe.

Q. 1, art. 4, Reply Obj. 3

For it is a much graver matter to corrupt the faith which quickens the soul, than to forge money, which supports temporal life. Therefore forgers of money and other evil-doers are condemned to death at once by the secular authority, much more reason is there for heretics, as soon as they are convicted of heresy, to be not only condemned to excommunication but even to be put to death.

Community of goods is ascribed to the natural law, not that the natural law dictates that all things should be possessed in common and that nothing should be possessed as one's own; but because the division of possessions is not according to the natural law, but rather arose from human agreements which belong to positive law. . . . Hence the ownership of possessions is not contrary to the natural law, but an addition thereto devised by human reason.

Q. 94, art. 5, Reply Obj. 3

Some say that when pleasure is the chief motive of the marriage act It is a mortal sin; that when it is an indirect motive it is a venial sin; and that when it spurns the pleasure altogether, and is displeasing, it is wholly void of venial sin; so that it would be a mortal sin to take pleasure when it is offered, but that perfection requires one to detest it. But this is impossible since . . . the same judgment applies to pleasure as to action, because pleasure in a good action is good, and in an evil action, evil; therefore as the marriage act is not evil in itself, neither will it be always a mortal sin to seek pleasure therein.

Consequently the right answer to this question is that if pleasure is sought in such a way as to exclude the honesty of marriage, so that it is not as a wife but as a woman that a man treats his wife, and that he is ready to use her in the same way if she were not his wife, it is a mortal sin . . . if, however, he seek pleasure within the bounds of marriage, so that it is not to be sought in another than his wife, it is a venial sin.

The Summa Contra Gentiles III

If God had deprived the world of all these things which proved an occasion of sin, the universe would have been imperfect. Nor was it fitting for the common good to be destroyed in order that individual evil might be avoided, especially as God is so powerful that He can direct any evil to a good end.

Ch. LXXI

Two Precepts of Charity

Three things are necessary for the salvation of man: to know what he ought to believe; to know what he ought to desire; and to know what he ought to do.

That the saints may enjoy their beatitude and the grace of God more abundantly, they are permitted to see the punishment of the damned in Hell.

Quoted in Nietzsche, *On the Geneology of Morals*, I, 5.

JOHN ARBUTHNOT
(1667–1735)
Scottish writer, physician

All political parties die at last of swallowing their own lies.

Epigram; quoted in Garnett, *Life of Emerson*

The History of John Bull (1712)

Law is a bottomless pit, it is a cormorant, a Harpy that devoures everything.

ARCHIMEDES
(c. 287–212 B.C.)
Greek mathematician

Give me a place to stand and I will move the world.

Pappus, *Synagoge*, VIII, 10, xi

ARCHYTAS OF TARENTUM
(fl. c.400–350 B.C.)
Pythagorean mathematician, philosopher

No more deadly curse has ever been given by nature to man than carnal pleasure. There is no criminal purpose and no evil deed which the lust for pleasure will not drive man to undertake.

Quoted in Cicero, *De Senectute*, Ch. 12

ROBERT ARDREY
(1908–   )
American writer

The Social Contract (1970)

Aggressiveness is the principal guarantor of survival.

HANNAH ARENDT
(1906–1975)
German-born American political philosopher

The Life of the Mind, unfinished trilogy

Thinking, willing and judging are the three basic fundamental activities. They cannot be derived from each other and although they have certain common characteristics, they cannot be reduced to a common denominator.

Contributions to *The New Yorker*

The most radical revolutionary will become a conservative the day after the revolution.
September 12, 1970

. . . the way God has been thought of for thousands of years is no longer convincing; if anything is dead, it can only be the traditional *thought* of God.
November 21, 1970

Mathematics, the non-empirical science par excellence . . . the science of sciences, delivering the key to those laws of nature and the universe which are concealed by appearances.

Nothing we use or hear or touch can be expressed in words that equal what is given by the senses. . . . Was it not precisely the discovery of a discrepancy between words, the medium in which we think, and the world of appearances, the medium in which we live, that led to philosophy and metaphysics in the first place?

Fear is an emotion indispensable for survival.

What science and the quest for knowledge are after is *irrefutable* truth; that is, propositions that human beings are not free to reject—that are compelling. They are of two kinds, as we have known since Leibnitz: truths of reasoning and truths of fact.

It is more than likely that if men were ever to lose the appetite for meaning which we call thinking, and cease to ask unanswerable questions, they would lose not only the ability to produce those thought-things which we call works of art but also the capacity for asking all the unanswerable questions upon which every civilization is founded.
November 21, 1977

Absence of thought is indeed a powerful factor in human affairs—statistically speaking the most powerful.

Every thought is an afterthought.

. . . the intramural warfare between philosophy and common sense.
November 28, 1977

. . . with the rise of Christianity, faith replaced thought as the bringer of immortality.

. . . Nietzsche reversed Plato, forgetting that a reversed Plato is still Plato. . . . Marx . . . turned Hegel upside down, producing a very Hegelian system of history in the process.

There are no dangerous thoughts; thinking itself is dangerous.

The sad truth is that most evil is done by people who never make up their minds to be either good or evil.

Unthinking men are like sleepwalkers.
December 5, 1977

PIETRO ARETINO
(1492–1556)
Italian writer

"La Talanta"

He who is not impatient is not in love.

LUDOVICO ARIOSTO
(1474–1533)
Italian poet

Orlando Furioso (1532)

Nature made him—then broke the mold.

We soon believe the things we would believe.

They think they have God Almighty by the toe.

ARISTOPHANES
(c. 450–385 B.C.)
Athenian poet, dramatist

The Birds (411 B.C.)

The wise learn many things from their foes.
Line 375

By words the mind is winged.
Line 1447

The Knights (424 B.C.)

The qualities necessary for a demagogue are these: to be foul-mouthed, base-born, a low, mean fellow.

Line 217

To plunder, to lie, to show your arse, are three essentials for climbing high.

Line 180

Lysistrata (411 B.C.)

How true is the saying, "It is impossible to live with the tormentors [women], impossible to live without them."

Line 1038

The Clouds (423 B.C.)

Old men are twice children.

Line 1417

ARISTOTLE
(384–322)
Greek philosopher

De Anima

To perceive is to suffer.

Nicomachean Ethics

Every art and every inquiry, and similarly every action and pursuit, is thought to aim at some good; and for this reason the good has rightly been declared to be that at which all things aim.

Bk.I, ch. 1, 1094a, lines 1–3

. . . most men, and men of the most vulgar type, seem (not without some ground) to identify the good, or happiness, with pleasure; which is the reason why they love the life of enjoyment.

Bk.I, ch. 5, 1095b, lines 14–17

The mass of mankind are evidently slavish in their tastes, preferring a life suitable to beasts. . . .

Bk.I, ch. 5, 1095b, lines 19–20

. . . people of superior refinement and of active disposition identify happiness with honour; for this is, roughly speaking, the end of the political life.

Bk.I, ch. 5, 1095b, lines 22–23

The life of money-making is one undertaken under compulsion, and wealth is evidently not the good we are seeking; for it is merely useful for the sake of something else.

Bk. I, ch. 5, 1096a, lines 5–7

. . . as sight is in the body, so is reason in the soul. . . .

Bk. I, ch. 6, 1096b, lines 29–30

. . . the self-sufficient we now define as that which when isolated makes life desirable and lacking in nothing; and such we think happiness* to be; and further we think it most desirable of all things.

Bk. I, ch. 7, 1097b, lines 15–17

For one swallow does not make a summer, nor does one day; and so too one day, or a short time, does not make a man blessed or happy.

Bk. I, ch. 7, 1098a, lines 18–19

For the man who flies from and fears everything and does not stand his ground against anything becomes a coward, and the man who fears nothing at all but goes to meet every danger becomes rash; and similarly the man who indulges in every pleasure and abstains from none becomes self-indulgent, while the man who shuns every pleasure, as boors do, becomes in a way insensible; temperance and courage, then, are destroyed by excess and defect, and preserved by the mean.

Bk.II, ch. 2, 1104a, lines 20–25

But not every action nor every passion admits of a mean; for some have names that already imply badness, e.g. spite, shamelessness, envy, and in the case of actions adultery, theft, murder . . . . Nor does goodness or badness with regard to such things depend on committing adultery with the right woman, at the right time, and in the right way, but simply to do any of them is to go wrong.

Bk.II, ch. 6, 1107a, lines 10–18

With regard to honour and dishonour the mean is proper pride, the excess is known as a sort of empty vanity, and the deficiency undue humility.

Bk.II, ch. 7, 1107b, lines 22–25

By passions I mean appetite, anger, fear, confidence, envy, joy, friendly feelings, hatred, longing, emulation, pity, and in general the feelings that are accompanied by pleasure or pain.

Bk.II, ch. 5, 1105b, lines 21–23

---

*The Greek word usually translated as "happiness" as used by Aristotle (as well as by Plato and the Stoics) should, according to noted scholars, be translated as "well-being."

Now death is the most terrible of things; for it is the end, and nothing is thought to be any longer either good or bad for the dead.
Bk.III, ch. 5, 1115a, line 26

The man, then, who faces and who fears the right things and from the right motive, in the right way and at the right time, and who feels confidence under the corresponding conditions, is brave.
Bk.III, ch. 7, 1115b, lines 16–18

But to die to escape from poverty or love or anything painful is not the mark of a brave man, but rather of a coward; for it is softness to fly from what is troublesome, and such a man endures death not because it is noble but to fly from evil.
Bk.III, ch. 7, 1116a, lines 12–15

. . . for the lesser evil is reckoned a good in comparison with the greater evil, since the lesser evil is rather to be chosen than the greater. . . .
Bk.V, ch. 3, 1131b, lines 20–22

What creates the problem is that the equitable is just, but not legally just but a correction of legal justice. The reason is that all law is universal but about some things it is not possible to make a universal statement which shall be correct.
Bk.V, ch. 10, 1137b, lines 11–15

Truth . . . is the work of everything intellectual.
[The attainment of truth indeed is the function of every part of the intellect. (Loeb tr.)]
Bk. VI, ch. 2, 1139a, line 30

. . . the states of virtue by which the soul possesses truth by way of affirmation or denial are five in number, i.e., art, scientific knowledge, practical wisdom, philosophic wisdom, intuitive reason; we do not include judgment and opinion because in these we may be mistaken.
Bk.VI, ch. 2, 1139b, lines 15–19

All art is concerned with coming into being.
Bk. VI, ch. 4, 1140a, line 11

. . . man is not the best thing in the world.
Bk.VI, ch. 7, 1141a, line 22

Surely it is strange, too, to make the supremely happy man a solitary; for no one would choose the whole world on condition of being alone, since man is a political creature and one whose nature is to live with others.
Bk.IX, ch. 8, 1169b, lines 16–19

The happy life is thought to be virtuous; now a virtuous life requires exertion, and does not consist in amusement.
Bk.X, ch. 6, 1177a

. . . the activity of God, which surpasses all others in blessedness, must be contemplative; and of human activities, therefore, that which is most akin to this must be most of the nature of happiness.
Bk.X, ch. 8, 1178b, line 23

Metaphysics

All men by nature desire to know.
Bk.I, ch. 1, 980a, line 23

. . . we do not know a truth without knowing its cause.
Bk.I, ch. 1, 9936b, line 22

It is right also that philosophy should be called knowledge of the truth.
Bk.II, ch. 1, 993b, line 20

Poetics

Tragedy is an imitation not of human beings but of action, life, happiness, and unhappiness.

Comedy aims at representing men as worse, Tragedy as better than in actual life.
Bk.II, ch. 2, 1448a, line 18

A tragedy, then, is the imitation of an action that is serious and also, as having magnitude, complete in itself; in language with pleasurable accessories, each kind brought in separately in the parts of the work; in a dramatic, not in a narrative form; with incidents arousing pity and fear, wherewith to accomplish its catharsis of such emotions.
Bk.II, ch. 6, 1449b, lines 25–30

. . . a whole is that which has a beginning, a middle, and an end . . . . A well-constructed Plot, therefore, cannot either begin or end at any point one likes; beginning and end in it must be of the forms just described.
Bk.II, ch. 7, 1450b, lines 26–34

Character must be true to life; for this is a distinct thing from goodness and propriety. . . .
Bk.XV, ch. 15, 1454a, line 25

Politics

. . . man is . . . a political animal.
Bk.I, ch. 2, 1253a, line 1

And it is characteristic of man that he alone has any sense of good and evil, of just and unjust, and the like, and the association of living beings who have this sense makes a family and a state.
Bk.I, ch. 2, 1253a, lines 15–18

. . . the state is by nature clearly prior to the family and to the individual, since the whole is of necessity prior to the part. . . .
Bk.I, ch. 2, 1253a, line 20

But he who is unable to live in society, or who has no need because he is sufficient for himself, must be either a beast or a god.
Bk.I, ch. 2, 1253a, lines 27–29

Life is doing things, not making things.
Bk.I, ch. 4, 1254a, line 7

He is by nature a slave who is capable of belonging to another.
Bk.I, ch. 4, 1254a, line 15

Also, as regards male and female, the former is superior, the latter is inferior; the male is ruler, the female is subject.
Bk.I, ch. 4, 1254b, lines 10–15

One would have thought that it was even more necessary to limit population than property. . . . The neglect of this subject, which in existing states is so common, is a never-failing cause of poverty among the citizens; and poverty is the parent of revolution and crime.
Bk. II, ch. 6, 1265b, lines 6–12

The law is reason unaffected by desire
Bk. III, ch. 16, 1287a, line 32

There exists in nature a principle of leadership and rulership, as also of social union based on justice and expediency. But there is no natural principle of dictatorship or another constitution which is a perversion. All the latter are contrary to nature.
Bk. III, ch. 16, 1287b

Now, to judge at least from what has been said, it is manifest that, where men are alike and equal, it is neither expedient nor just that one man should be lord of all, whether there are laws, or whether there are no laws, but he himself is in the place of law. Neither should a good man be lord over good men, nor a bad man over bad; nor, even if he excels in virtue, should he have a right to rule, unless on a particular case, at which I have already hinted, and to which I will once more recur.
Bk. III, ch. 16, line 1288a, lines 1–5

If liberty and equality, as is thought by some, are chiefly to be found in democracy, they will be best attained when all persons alike share in the government to the utmost.

. . . good laws, if they are not obeyed, do not constitute good government.
Bk.IV, ch. 8, 1294a, line 4

. . . for the principle of an aristocracy is virtue, as wealth is of an oligarchy, and freedom of a democracy.
Bk. IV, ch. 8, 1294a, line 10

Thus it is manifest that the best political community is formed by citizens of the middle class, and that those states are likely to be well-administered in which the middle class is large, and stronger if possible than both the other classes. . . .
Bk. IV, ch. 11, 1295b, lines 35–37

Revolutions in democracies are generally caused by the intemperance of demagogues, who either in their private capacity lay information against rich men until they compel them to combine (for a common danger unites even the bitterest enemies), or coming forward in public stir up the people against them.
Bk. V, ch. 5, 1304b, lines 20–24

We cannot learn without pain.

The only stable state is the one in which all men are equal before the law.

Democracy, for example, arises out of the notion that those who are equal in any respect are equal in all respects; because men are equally free, they claim to be absolutely equal.
Bk. V, ch. 1, 1301a, lines 28–30

Equality consists in the same treatment of similar persons, and no government can stand which is not founded on justice.
Bk. VII

Rhetoric

The intention makes the crime.
Bk.I

. The type of character produced by wealth lies on the surface for all to see. Wealthy men are insolent and arrogant; their possession of wealth affects their understanding; they feel as if they had every good thing that exists; wealth becomes a standard of value for everything else, and therefore they imagine there is nothing they cannot buy. They are luxurious and ostentatious; . . . ostentatious and vulgar.

In a word, the type of character produced by wealth is that of a prosperous fool.

The forms of Virtue are: justice, courage, magnificence, magnanimity, liberality, gentleness, prudence, wisdom.

Every action must be due to one or other of seven causes: chance, nature, compulsion, habit, reasoning, anger, or appetite.

Reason is a light that God has kindled in the soul.

The end of democracy is freedom; of oligarchy, wealth; of aristocracy the maintenance of education and national institutions; of tyranny, the protection of the tyrant.

Bk. II

There was never a genius without a tincture of madness.

Quoted in Seneca, *De Tranquilitate Anima*

When the people is master of the vote it becomes master of the government.

Quoted in *The Constitution of Athens*

Beauty is the gift of God.

Quoted by Diogenes Laërtius

I count him braver who overcomes his desires than him who conquers his enemies; for the hardest victory is the victory over self.

Quoted in Stobaeus, *Floritegium*

The end of art is to figure the hidden meaning of things and not their appearance; for in this profound truth lies their true reality, which does not appear in their external outlines.

Quoted in Malraux, *Metamorphosis of the Gods*, 1957

NEIL ARMSTRONG
(1930–   )
American astronaut

First words spoken on the moon

That's one small step for a man, one great leap for mankind.

July 20, 1969, 4:17:40 P.M. EST

MATTHEW ARNOLD
(1822–1888)
English poet, critic, essayist

Culture and Anarchy (1869)

The people who believe most that our greatness and welfare are proved by our being very rich, and who most give their lives and thoughts to becoming rich, are just the very people whom we call Philistines.

In the same way let us judge the religious organizations which we see all around us. Do not let us deny the good and the happiness which they have accomplished, but do not let us fail to see clearly that their idea of human perfection is narrow and inadequate; and that the Dissidence of Dissent and the Protestantism of the Protestant religion will never bring humanity to its goal.

. . . we call ourselves, in the sublime and aspiring language of religion which I have before noticed, *children of God.* Children of God;—it is an immense pretension!—and how are we to justify it? By the works that we do, and the words which we speak.

The pursuit of perfection, then, is the pursuit of sweetness and light. . . . He who works for sweetness and light, works to make reason and the will of God prevail. He who works for machinery, he who works for hatred, works only for confusion. Culture looks around machinery and beyond machinery, culture hates hatred, culture has a great passion, the passion for sweetness and light. It has one yet even greater!—the passion for making them *prevail.*

The great men of culture are those who have had a passion for diffusing, for making prevail, for carrying from one end of society to the other, the best knowledge, the best ideas of their time; who have labored to divest knowledge of all that was harsh, uncouth, difficult, abstract, professional, exclusive; to humanize it, to make it efficient outside the clique of the cultivated and learned, yet still remain the best knowledge and thought of the time, and a true source, therefore, of sweetness and light.

Culture is then properly described not as having its origin in curiosity, but as having its origin in the love of perfection: it is a study of perfection.

The uppermost idea with Hellenism is to see things as they really are; the uppermost idea with Hebraism is conduct and obedience.

Philistine gives the notion of something particularly stiffnecked and perverse in the resistance to light and its children; and therein it especially suits our middle-class.

Thus we have got three distinct terms, Barbarians, Philistines and Populace, to denote roughly the three classes into which our society is divided.

Essays in Criticism

. . . home* of lost causes, and forsaken beliefs, and unpopular names, and impossible loyalties!

Preface

Discourses in America

To have the sense of creative activity is the great happiness and the great proof of being alive.

"The Functions of Criticism," 1864

Masses make movements, individualities explode them.

"Literature and Science," 1865

"The Buried Life" (1852)

—Alas, is even Love too weak
To unlock the heart, and let it speak?
Are even lovers powerless to reveal
To one another what indeed they feel?
I knew the mass of men conceal'd
Their thoughts, for fear that if reveal'd
They would by other men be met
With blank indifference, or with blame reprov'd:
I knew they liv'd and mov'd
Trick'd in disguises, alien to the rest
Of men, and alien to themselves—and yet
The same heart beats in every human breast.

St. 2

"The Scholar Gypsy" (1853)

Thou waitest for the spark from Heaven: and we,
Vague half-believers of our casual creeds,
Who never deeply felt, not clearly will'd,
Whose insight never has borne fruit in deeds,
Whose weak resolves never have been fulfill'd,
For whom each year we see
Breeds new beginnings, disappointments new;
Who hesitate and falter life away,
And lose to-morrow the ground won to-day—
Ah, do not we, Wanderer, await it too?

St. 18

"Rugby Chapel" (1857)

Most men eddy about
Here and there—eat and drink,

Chatter and love and hate,
Gather and squander, are raised
Aloft, are hurl'd in the dust,
Striving blindly, achieving
Nothing; and then they die—

St. 6

"Written in Emerson's Essays" (1849)

The will is free:
Strong is the Soul, and wise, and beautiful:
The seeds of godlike power are in us still:
Gods are we, Bards, Saints, Heroes, if we will.—

"Dover Beach" (1867)

Ah, love, let us be true
To one another! for the world, which seems
To lie before us like a land of dreams,
So various, so beautiful, so new,
Hath really neither joy, nor love, nor light,
Nor certitude, nor peace, nor help for pain;
And we are here as on a darkling plain
Swept with confused alarms of struggle and flight,
Where ignorant armies clash by night.

St. 3–4

"To a Friend" (1849)

Who saw life steadily, and saw it whole:

Sonnet 2

The Bible is no longer dogma, it is literature.

Quoted by Noyes, *Views of Religion*

RAYMOND ARON
(1905–   )
French political philosopher, journalist

The Great Debate, The Opium of the Intellectuals (1965)

The Left is dominated by three ideas, which are not necessarily contradictory, but usually divergent: *liberty,* against arbitrary power and for the rights of the individual; *organization,* for the purpose of substituting a rational order in place of tradition or the anarchy of private enterprise; and *equality,* against the privileges of birth and wealth.

Page 32

The myth of the Revolution serves as a refuge for utopian intellectuals; it becomes the mysterious, unpredictable intercessor between the real and the ideal.

Page 65

---

*A reference to Oxford.

Far from being the science of working-class misfortune, Marxism is an intellectualist philosophy which has seduced certain groups of the proletariat; far from being the immanent philosphy of the Proletariat, Communism merely makes use of this pseudo-science in order to attain its own end, the seizure of power.

Page 83

Left, Revolution, Proletariat—these fashionable concepts of the later-day counterpart of the great myths which once inspired political optimism: Progress, Reason, the People.

Page 94

Marxism now plays little part in the culture of the West. . . . It is true, of course, that no modern historian or economist would think exactly as he does if Marx never existed. . . . The historian no longer dares shut his eyes to the humble realities which rule the lives of millions of human beings.

Page 105

In search of hope in an age of despair, the philosopher settles for an optimism based on catastrophe.

Page 106

People fight for luxuries, for power, or for ideas with just as much passion as they fight for money. Interests may be reconciled, but not philosophies. . . . The desire for power is no less basic than the desire for wealth.

Pages 153–154

It is not absurd to prefer the authority of a single party to the slow deliberations of the parliamentary system, but anyone who counts on the dictatorship of the proletariat to accomplish freedom misjudges human nature and ignores the inevitable results of the concentration of power in a few hands. . . . anyone who wonders why philosophers who are prisoners of dialectical materialism or novelists enslaved by socialist realism are lacking in genius misjudges the very essence of the creative process. The idolators of history cause more and more intellectual havoc, not because they are inspired by good or bad sentiments, but because they have wrong ideas.

Page 159

It is true that Communism is all the more attractive where the throne of God is empty. . . . The intellectual who no longer feels attached to anything is not satisfied with opinions merely; he wants certainty, he wants a system. The Revolution provides him with his opium.

Page 257

Communist faith justifies the means. Communist faith forbids the fact that there are many roads towards the Kingdom of God. Communist charity does not even allow its enemies to die an honorable death.

Page 269

Marx called religion the opium of the people. Whether it wants to or not, the Church consolidates and establishes injustice. It helps men to forget their ills instead of curing them. Obsessed with the hereafter, the believer is indifferent to temporal things.

Page 291

The Christian opium makes the people passive, the Communist opium incites them to revolt.

Page 292

On War

Science not only makes war insane because the havoc caused would be out of all proportion with any conceivable issue at stake; it also eliminates most of the economic causes of wars and brings countries together willy-nilly.

The men and the nations sharing the benefits of modern industrial civilization are divided chiefly by ideological prejudices and human passions. The power of false ideas condemn all hope of world unity in the immediate future, but not the hope of gradual reconciliation of the human race.

Marxism is the opium of the intellectuals.

Quoted in *Time*, July 9, 1979

ASOKA
(died 238 B.C.)
Buddhist Emperor of India

Decree (inscription on a pillar)

It is forbidden to decry other sects; the true believer gives honor to whatever in them is worthy of honor.

ATHANASIAN CREED
Written between 381–428

Now the Catholic faith is this: that we worship one God in Trinity, the Trinity in Unity, neither confounding the Persons, nor dividing the substance, for there is one Person of the Father, another of the Son, and another of the Holy Ghost; but the Godhead of the Father, of the Son, and of the Holy Ghost is one, the glory equal, the majesty co-eternal.*

SAINT ATHANASIUS
(293–373)
Bishop of Alexandria

If the world goes against truth, then Athanasius goes against the world.

All things are pure to the pure. . . . Man is the handwork of God. There is certainly nothing in us that is impure.
Letter to Amun (a monk), quoted by Migne in
Patrologia Graeca

W(ystan) H(ugh) AUDEN
(1907–1973)
British-born American poet

Henry James: An American Scene

It is just as true as it ever was that man is born in sin, that the majority are always, relatively, in the wrong, the minority sometimes, relatively, in the right (every one, of course, is free at any time to belong to either), and all before God, absolutely in the wrong, that all of the people some of the time and some of the people most of the time will abuse their liberty and treat it as the license of an escaped slave.

. . . realizing that, since people will never cease trying to interfere with the liberties of others in pursuing their own, the State can never wither away.
Introduction

Nothing I wrote saved a single Jew from being gassed . . . it's perfectly all right to be an *engagé* writer as long as you don't think you're changing things. Art is our chief means of breaking bread with the dead.
Statement in *The New York Times,* August 7, 1971

The Age of Anxiety (Pulitzer Prize, 1948)

We would rather be ruined than changed
We would rather die in our dread
Than climb the cross of the moment
And let our illusions die.
Epilogue

---

*The Athanasian Creed, so-called because in many manuscripts it bears the title "The Faith of Saint Athanasius," is more accurately designated by its first words *Quicunque Vult.* Its history has been the subject of much controversy.

"September 1, 1939"

There is no such thing as the State
And no one exists alone;
Hunger allows no choice
To the citizen or the police;
We must love one another or die.

"City Without Walls" (1970)

"Post coitum homo tristis"
What nonsense! If he could,
he would sing.

BERTHOLD AUERBACH
(1812–1882)
German novelist

On the Heights (1865)

What will people say—in these words lies the tyranny of the world, the whole destruction of our natural disposition, the oblique vision of our minds. These four words hold sway everywhere.

EMILE AUGIER
(1820–1889)
French writer

Le Mariage d'Olympe (1855)

La nostalgie de la boue.
A longing for the gutter.
Act 1

SAINT AUGUSTINE
(354–430)
Numidian-born Christian convert, Bishop of Hippo

On Christian Doctrine (396–427)

We are ensnared by the wisdom of the serpent; we are set free by the foolishness of God.

The City of God (413–426)

To confess that God exists, and at the same time to deny that he has foreknowledge of future things, is the most manifest folly.

He that is good is free, though he is a slave; he that is evil is a slave, though he be a king.

Whatever the physical or seminal causes that play their part in the production of living things, by the activities of angels or of men, or by the intercourse of male and female in animals and human beings, whatever effect the longings or emotions in the mother's consciousness may have on the child in her womb, in its susceptible state, leaving some traces in its features or complexion, it remains true that only God most high can create the actual natures which are thus affected in different ways, each in its own kind.

Justice being taken away, then, what are kingdoms but great robberies. For what are robberies themselves, but little kingdoms.

Book IV

The purpose of all war is peace.

Book XV

Although, therefore, lust may have many objects, yet when no object is specified, the word lust usually suggests to the mind the lustful excitement of the organs of generation. And this lust not only takes possession of the whole body and outward members, but also makes itself felt within, and moves the whole man with a passion in which mental emotion is mingled with bodily appetite, so that the pleasure which results is the greatest of bodily pleasures.

So possessing indeed is this pleasure, that the moment of time in which it is consummated, all mental activity is suspended.

What friend of wisdom and holy joys, who being married, but knowing, as the apostle says, "how to possess this vessel in sanctification and honor, not in the disease of desire, as the Gentiles who know not God," would not prefer if this were possible, to beget children without that lust, so that in this function of begetting offspring the members created for this purpose should not be animated by the heat of lust, but should be actuated by his volition, in the same way as his other members serve him for their respective ends.

Book XVI

Lust requires for its consummation darkness and secrecy; and this not only when unlawful intercourse is desired, but even such fornication as the earthly city has legalized. Where there is no fear of punishment, these permitted pleasures still shrink from the public eye.

Book XVIII

The chief cause of slavery, then, is sin— that a man should be put in bonds to another; and this happens only by the judgment of God, in whose eyes it is no crime.

Book XIX

The standing miracle of this visible world is little thought of, because always before us. . . . For man himself is a greater miracle than any miracle done through his instrumentality.

Book XIX

If the thing believed is incredible, it is also incredible that the incredible should have been so believed.

Book XXII

Why, they ask, do not those miracles which you preach of as past events, happen nowadays? I might reply that they were necessary before the world believed, to bring the world to believe; but whoever is still looking for prodigies to make him believe is himself a good prodigy for refusing to believe where the world believes.

Book XXII

There are some who think that in the resurrection all will be men, and that women will lose their sex. . . . For myself I think that both sexes will remain in the resurrection.

Book XXII

Woman is as much the creation of God as man is. If she was made from man, this was to show her oneness with him; and if she was, this was to pre-figure the oneness of Christ and the Church.

Book XXII

As in Paradise there was no excessive heat or cold, so its inhabitants were exempt from the vicissitudes of fear and desire. . . .

In such happy circumstances and general human well-being we should be far from suspecting that offspring could have been begotten without the disease of lust, but those parts, like all the rest, would be set in motion by the command of the will; and without the seduction stimulus of passion, with calmness of mind and without the corrupting of the integrity of the body, the husband would lie upon the bosom of his wife. Nor ought we not to believe this because it cannot be proved by experiment.

Book XXVI

Confessions (397–398)

Poetry is devil's wine.

The greatest virtues are only splendid sins.

But, behold, out of my memory I bring it, when I say there are four perturbations of the mind, desire, joy, fear, sorrow. . . .

Hidden is the good heart, hidden is the evil heart, an abyss is in the good heart and in the evil heart.

Free curiosity is of more value than harsh discipline.

Every disorder of the soul is its own punishment.

Thus doth the soul commit fornication, when she turns from Thee, seeking without Thee, what she findeth not pure and untainted, till she returns to Thee.

Book I

And I enquired what the iniquity was, and found it to be no substance, but the perversion of the will, turned aside from Thee, O God, the Supreme, toward these lower things, and casting out its bowels and puffed up outwardly.

Book VII

But I, wretched, most wretched, in the very commencement of my early youth, had begged chastity of Thee, and said, "Give me chastity, and continency, only not yet."

Book VIII

The pleasures of this life for which I would weep are in conflict with the sorrows of this life in which I would rejoice, and I know not on which side stands the victory.

Why does truth call forth hatred?

Book X

Just as in the human soul there is one element which takes thought and dominates another which is subjected to obedience, so woman has been created corporeally for man; for although she has indeed a nature like that of man in her mind and rational intelligence, yet by her bodily sex she is subjected to the sex of her husband, much as an appetite, which is the source of action, must be subjected to reason.

Book XIII

"The Problem of Free Choice" (tr. Don Mark Pontifex)

Passion is the evil in adultery. If a man has no opportunity of living with another man's wife, but if it is obvious for some reason that he would like to do so, and would do so if he could, he is no less guilty than if he was caught in the act.

A law which is not just does not seem to be a law.

We are certainly in a common class with the beasts; every action of animal life is concerned with seeking bodily pleasure and avoiding pain.

Meanwhile the passions rage like tyrants, and throw into confusion the whole soul and life of men with storms from every quarter, fear on one side, desire on another, on another anxiety, or false empty joy, here pain for the thing which was loved and lost, there eagerness to win what was not possessed, there grief for an injury received, here burning desire to avenge it. Wherever he turns, avarice can confine him, self-indulgence dissipate him, ambition master him, pride puff him up, envy torture him, sloth drug him, obstinacy rouse him, oppression afflict him, and the countless other feelings which crowd and exploit the power of passion.

In Ioannis Evangelium

What is faith save to believe what you do not see?

Understanding is the reward of faith. Therefore seek not to understand that thou mayest believe, but believe that thou mayest understand.

Against Lying

All sin is a form of lying.

Lying is forbidden even for the salvation of heretics.

Since, then, eternal life is lost by lying, a lie may never be told for the preservation of the temporal life of another.

Lying is wrong even to save chastity.

On the Good of Marriage

Obedience is in a way the mother of all virtues.

Marriage is not a good, but it is a good in comparison with fornication.

Continence is a greater good than marriage. But I am aware of some that murmur: if all men should abstain from intercourse, how will the human race exist? Would that all would abstain; much more speedily would the City of God be filled, and the end of the world hastened.

Total abstinence is easier than perfect moderation.

Continence is an angelic exercise.

Of Continence

There are three unions in this world: Christ and the Church, husband and wife, spirit and flesh.

No one ever hated his own flesh.

Contra Julian

There is no possible source of evil except good.

I, 9

Of Baptism

There is no salvation outside the Church.

IV

On Patience

Parricide is more wicked than homicide, but suicide is most wicked of all.

Soliloquies

Nothing so much casts down the mind of man from its citadel as do the blandishments of women, and that physical contact without which a wife cannot be possessed.

De Sybolo

He cannot have God for his father who refuses to have the Church for his mother.

Bk. XIII

Heretics

None save great men have been the authors of great heresies.

De Trinitate (400–416)

God always is, nor has He been and is not, nor is but has not been, but as He never will not be; so He never was not.

14, 15, 2

Soliloquium Animae ad Deum

Necessity has no law.

AVICENNA (Ibn Sina)
(980–1037)
Persian philosopher, physician, scientist

Avicenna on Theology (tr. Arberry)

Man was thus equipped with these (three) souls out of all the world. . . . By virtue of the animal soul he shares with the animals; his physical soul links him with the plants; his human soul is a bond between him and the angels.

The function of the human, rational soul is the noblest function of all, for it is itself the noblest of spirits. Its function consists of reflecting upon things of art and meditating upon the things of beauty: its gaze being turned towards the higher world, its loves not this lower abode and meaner station. Belonging as it does to the higher side of life and to primal substances, it is not its business to eat and drink, neither does it require luxury and coition; rather its function is to wait for the revelation of truths.

Man's relation to the world of Spirit is established by reasoning; speech follows after it. If a man possesses no knowledge of reasoning, he is incapable of expressing truth.

"Katib al-Najat"

FRANCOIS-NOËL ("Gracchus") BABEUF
(1760–executed 1797)
French journalist, revolutionist

Poster, "Analyse de la doctrine de Baboeuf (sic), *Le tribun du peuple*" (1796; summary of Sylvain Maréchal's Manifesto of Equals)

All work and the enjoyment of its fruits must be in common.

Article 4

In a true society there should be neither rich nor poor.

Article 7

Defense (trial for treason, Vendôme, 1797)

The ends justify the means. To reach a certain goal, one must vanquish everything that stands in the way.

Nothing has been better proven than this maxim: *that one succeeds in having too much only by causing others not to have enough.*

Everything owned by those who have more than their individual due of society's goods, is theft and usurpation.

. . . to establish a *common administration;* to suppress private property. . . . This form of government will bring about the disappearance of all boundary lines, fences, walls, locks on doors, trials, thefts, and assassinations; of all crimes, tribunals, prisons, gibbets, and punishments; of the despair that causes all calamity; and of greed, jealousy, insatiability, pride, deception, and duplicity,—in short, of all vices. . . . It will put an end to the gnawing worm of perpetual inquietude . . . about what the morrow will bring, or at least what next year will bring, in our old age, for our children and for their children.

BABYLONIAN TALMUD

Old age hurries upon him who commits adultery.

Shabbath, c. 450 A.D.

FRANCIS BACON (Lord Verulam) (1561–1626)
English essayist, philosopher

Advancement of Learning (1605)

Liberty of speech inviteth and provoketh liberty to be used again, and so bringeth much to a man's knowledge.

. . . that knowledge may not be as a courtesan, for pleasure and vanity only, or as a bondswoman, to acquire and gain to her master's use, but as a spouse, for generation, fruit, and comfort.

Philosophers should diligently inquire into the powers and energy of custom, imitation, emulation, company, friendships, praise, reproof, exhortation, reputation, laws, books, studies, etc.; for these are the things that reign in men's morals; by these agents the mind is formed and subdued.

Out of monuments, names, words, proverbs, traditions, private records and evidences, fragments of stories, passages of books, and the like, we do save and recover somewhat from the deluge of time.

There was never a miracle wrought by God to convert an atheist, because the light of nature might have led him to confess a God.

To say that a blind custom of obedience should be a surer obligation than duty taught and understood . . . is to affirm that a blind man may tread surer by a guide than a seeing man by a light.

The pleasure and delight of knowledge and learning, it far surpasseth all other in nature. . . . We see in all other pleasures there is satiety, and after they are used their verdure departeth; which showeth well they be but the deceits of pleasure, and not pleasure: and that it was the novelty that pleasured, not the quality.

As for the narrations touching the prodigies and miracles of religions, they are either not true, or not natural; therefore impertinent for the story of nature.

Bk. 2

The sum of behaviour is to retain a man's own dignity, without intruding upon the liberty of others.

But men must know, that in this theater of man's life it is reserved only for God and the angels to be lookers on.

If a man will begin with certainties, he shall end in doubts; but if he will be content to begin with doubts, he shall end in certainties.

Bk. 5, Ch. 8

De Dignitate et Augmentis Scientiarum, enlarged version of *The Advancement of Learning* (1623)

Hurl calumnies boldly, something is sure to stick.

To know truly is to know by causes.

Nothing is terrible, except fear itself.

It is due to Justice that man is a God to man and not a wolf.

Great hypocrites are the true atheists.

The Essays or Counsels, Civill and Morall (1625)*

The virtue of Prosperity is temperance; the virtue of Adversity is fortitude; which in morals is the more heroical virtue. Prosperity is the blessing of the Old Testament; Adversity is the blessing of the New; which carrieth the greater benediction, and the clearer revelation of God's favor.

*The text used here is that of James Spedding, *The Works of Francis Bacon,* v. XII, 1857–1874, ed. Professor Mary Augusta Scott, Scribners, 1908.

Certain virtue is like precious odours, most fragrant when they are incensed or crushed: for Prosperity doth best discover vice, but Adversity doth best discover virtue.

"Of Adversity"

To seek to extinguish Anger is but a bravery of the Stoics. We have better oracles: *Be angry, but sin not. Let not the sun go down upon your anger.*

"Of Anger"

It is true, that a little philosophy inclineth man's mind to atheism; but depth in philosophy bringeth men's mind about to religion.

The causes of atheism are: divisions in religion, if they be many . . . scandal of priests . . . custom of profane scoffing in holy matters . . . and lastly, learned times, specially with peace and prosperity; for troubles and adversities do more bow men's minds to religion. They that deny a God destroy men's nobility; for certainly man is of kin to the beasts by his body; and, if he be not of kin to God by his spirit, he is a base and ignoble creature.

"Of Atheism"

Virtue is like a rich stone, best plain set.

"Of Beauty"

Custom is the principal magistrate of man's life.

"Of Custom and Education"

Men fear Death, as children fear to go in the dark. . . .

Revenge triumphs over death; Love slights it; Honour aspireth to it; Grief flieth to it; Fear pre-occupateth it.

A man would die, though he were neither valiant, nor miserable, only upon a weariness to do the same thing so oft, over and over.

"Of Death"

For it is the solecism of power, to think to command the end, and yet not endure the mean[s].

"Of Empire"

It had been hard for him that spake it to have put more truth and untruth together in few words, than in that speech, *whosoever is delighted in solitude is either a wild beast or a god.* *

---

* "But he who is unable to live in society, or who has no need because he is sufficient for himself, must be either a beast or a god: he is no part of a state."—Aristotle, *Politics,* Bk. 1 (Jowett tr.)

For a crowd is not company; and faces are but a gallery of pictures; and talk but a tinkling cymbal, where there is no love.

Certainly, if a man would give it a hard phrase, those that want friends to open themselves unto are cannibals of their own hearts. . . . this communicating of a man's self to his friends works two contrary effects; for it redoubleth joys, and cutteth griefs in halfs.

. . . it was a sparing speech of the ancients, to say that *a friend is another himself.*

"Of Friendship"

The desire of power in excess caused the angels to fall: but in charity there is no excess; neither can angel or man come in danger by it.

"Of Goodness and Goodness of Nature"

Men in great place are thrice servants: servants of the sovereign or state; servants of fame; and servants of business. So as they have no freedom; neither in their persons, nor in their actions, nor in their times. It is a strange desire, to seek power and to lose liberty: or to seek power over others and to lose power over a man's self.

"Of Great Place"

As the births of living creatures at first are ill-shapen, so are all Innovations, which are the births of time. . . . Surely every medicine is an innovation; and he that will not apply new remedies must expect new evils; for time is the greatest innovator.

"Of Innovations"

Judges ought to remember that their office is *jus dicere,* and not *jus dare;* to interpret law, and not to make law, or give law.

Nuptial love maketh mankind; friendly love perfecteth it; but wanton love corrupteth and embaseth it.

"Of Judicature"

He that hath wife and children hath given hostages to fortune; for they are impediments to great enterprises; either of virtue or mischief.

Unmarried men are best friends, best masters, best servants; but not always best subjects. . . . A single life doth well with churchmen; for charity will hardly water the ground where it must first fill a pool.

Chaste women are often proud and forward, as presuming upon the merit of their chastity. . . . Wives are young men's mistresses; companions for middle age; and old men's nurses. . . . But yet he was reputed one of the wise men, that made answer to the question when a man should marry? *A young man not yet, an older man not at all.*

"Of Marriage and Single Life"

Children sweeten labours; but they make misfortunes more bitter. They increase the care of life; but they mitigate the remembrance of death. The perpetuity by generation is common to beasts; but memory, merit, and noble works, are proper to men. And surely a man shall see the noblest works and foundations have proceeded from childless men; which have sought to express the images of their minds, where those of their bodies have failed.

"Of Parents and Children"

Revenge is a kind of wild justice; which the more man's nature runs to, the more ought law to weed it out. . . . Certainly, in taking revenge a man is but even with his enemy; but in passing it over, he is superior; for it is a prince's part to pardon.

This is certain, that man that studieth revenge keeps his own wounds green, which otherwise would heal and do well.

"Of Revenge"

I cannot call Riches better than the baggage of virtue. The Roman word is better, *impedimenta.* . . . Of great riches there is no real use, except it be in the distribution; the rest is but conceit.

The ways to enrich are many, and most of them foul.

"Of Riches"

Above all things, good policy is to be used that the treasure and monies in a state be not gathered into few hands. . . . And money is like muck, not good except it be spread.

"Of Seditions and Troubles"

To spend too much time in studies is sloth; to use them too much for ornament, is affectation; to make judgment wholly by their rules, is the humour of a scholar. . . . Read not to contradict and confute; nor to believe and take for granted; nor to find talk and discourse; but to weigh and consider. Some books are to be tasted, others to be swallowed, and some few to be chewed and digested. . . . Reading maketh a full man; conference a ready man; and writing an exact man. . . . Histories make men wise; poets witty; the mathematics subtile;

natural philosophy deep; moral grave; logic and rhetoric able to contend.

"Of Studies"

Atheism leaves a men to sense, to philosophy, to natural piety, to laws, to reputation, all which may be guides to an outward moral virtue, though religion were not; but superstition dismounts all these, and erecteth an absolute monarchy in the minds of man.

The master of superstition is the people; and in all superstition wise men follow fools; and arguments are fitted to practice, in a reversed order.

"Of Superstition"

. . . a just and honourable war is the true exercise. A civil war indeed is like the heat of a fever; but a foreign war is like the heat of exercise, and serveth to keep the body in health; for in slothful peace, both courage will effeminate and manners corrupt.

"Of the True Greatness of Kingdoms and Estates"

What is truth? said jesting Pilate; and would not stay for an answer.

A mixture of a lie doth ever add pleasure.

"Of Truth"

Young men are fitter to invent than to judge; fitter for execution than for counsel; and fitter for new projects than for settled business. . . . Young men, in the conduct and manage of actions, embrace more than they can hold; stir more than they can quiet; fly to the end, without consideration of the means and degrees; pursue some new principles which they have chanced upon absurdly; care not to innovate, which draws unknown inconveniences; use extreme remedies at first; and that which doubleth all errors, will not acknowledge or retract them; like an unready horse, that will neither stop nor turn. Men of age object too much, consult too long, adventure too little, repent too soon, and seldom drive business home to the full period but content themselves with a mediocrity of success.

"Of Youth and Age"

The New Organon (1620), "Aphorisms"

There are four classes of idols which beset men's minds. To these for distinction's sake I have assigned names,—calling the first class *Idols of the Tribe;* the second, *Idols of the Cave;* the third, *Idols of the Market-Place;* the fourth, *Idols of the Theater.*

XXXIX

The human understanding is no dry light, but receives infusion from the will and affections; whence proceed sciences which may be called "sciences as one would." For what a man had rather were true he more readily believes. Therefore he rejects difficult things from impatience of research; sober things, because they narrow hope; the deeper things of nature, from superstition; the light of experience, from arrogance and pride; things not commonly believed, out of deference to the opinion of the vulgar. Numberless in short are the ways, and sometimes imperceptible, in which the affections color and infect the understanding.

XLIX

Again, men have been kept back as by a kind of enchantment from progress in the sciences by reverence for antiquity, by the authority of men counted great in philosophy, and then by general consent.

LXXXIV

For whatever deserves to exist deserves also to be known, for knowledge is the image of existence; and things mean and splendid exist alike.

CXX

. . . so assuredly the very contemplation of things, as they are, without superstition or imposture, error or confusion, is in itself more worthy than all the fruits of inventions.

CXXIX

Apothegms

I am of his mind who said, "Better it is to live where nothing is lawful, than where all things are lawful."

69

"De Natura Rerum"

It is sufficiently clear that all things are changed, and nothing really perishes, and that the sum of matter remains absolutely the same.

I have taken all knowledge to be my province.

Letter to Lord Burghley, 1592

The punishing of wits enhances their authority, and a forbidden writing is thought to be a certain spark of truth, that flies up in the faces of them who seek to tread it out.

Quoted in Milton, *Aeropagitica*

ROGER BACON
(c. 1220–1292)
English philosopher, scientist

Opus Majus (1266–67)

There are in fact four very significant stumbling-blocks in the way of grasping the truth, which hinder every man however learned, and scarcely allow anyone to win a clear title to wisdom, namely, the example of weak and unworthy authority, longstanding custom, the feeling of the ignorant crowd, and the hiding of our own ignorance while making a display of our apparent knowledge.

tr. Brownlee Haydn

There are two modes of acquiring knowledge, namely by reasoning and experience. Reasoning draws a conclusion and makes us grant the conclusion, but does not make the conclusion certain, nor does it remove doubt so that the mind may rest on the intuition of truth, unless the mind discovers it by the path of experience.

tr. R.B. Burke

GEORGE F. BAER
(1842–1914)
American railroad industrialist

The rights and interests of the laboring man will be protected and cared for, not by labor agitators, but by the Christian men to whom God in His infinite wisdom has given the control of the property interests of the country.

Letter to Rev. W.F. Clark, July 17, 1902

WALTER BAGEHOT
(1826–1877)
English economist

The English Constitution (1873)

The tyranny of the commonplace, which seems to accompany civilization.

The whole history of civilization is strewn with creeds and institutions which were invaluable at first, and deadly afterwards.

Physics and Politics (1869)

One of the greatest pains to human nature is the pain of a new idea.

It was government by discussion that broke the bond of ages and set free the originality of mankind.

Quoted by Adlai Stevenson, *Harper's,*
February 1956

BAHA'U'LLÁH ("The Splendour of God")
(1817–1892)
Persian religious sect leader

Truths for a new day:
1. The oneness of mankind.
2. The foundation of all religion is one.
3. Religion must be in accord with science and reason.

Promulgated in the United States by 'Abdu'l-Baha,
lecture trip, 1912

PHILIP JAMES BAILEY
(1816–1902)
English poet

"Festus"

Evil and good are God's right hand and left.

Who never doubted never half believed.
Where doubt, there truth is—'tis her shadow.

MIKHAIL A. BAKUNIN*
(1814–1876)
Russian writer, anarchist

Le Progrès (1869)

No one at all interested in the study of history could have failed to see that there was always some great material interest at the bottom of even the most abstract, the most sublime and idealistic theological and religious struggles.

Religion has always sanctified violence and transformed it into right. It has whisked away humanity, justice and fraternity into a ficti-

---

*Chief opponent of Karl Marx, an influence on both Lenin and Mussolini; appears in fiction in Turgenev and probably is Dostoyevski's Prince Stavrogin in *The Possessed.*

tious heaven, so as to leave room on earth for the reign of iniquity and brutality. It has blessed successful brigands, and, in order to increase their fortune even further, has preached obedience and resignation to their innumerable victims, the people.

It is the State, the altar of political religion, upon which the natural society is always immolated: a devouring universatility, living upon human sacrifices, like the Church. The State, I repeat, is the younger brother of the Church.

Both [Church and State] have the same principle as their point of departure: that of the natural wickedness of man, which can be vanquished, according to the Church, only by divine grace and the death of the natural man in God; and according to the State, only by law and the immolation of the individual upon the altar of the State. Both strive to transform men, the one into a saint, the other into a citizen. But the natural man must die, for the religions of the Church and of the State unanimously pronounce his sentence.

God and the State (1871)

The liberty of man consists in this, that he obeys the laws of nature, because he has himself recognized them as such, and not because they have been imposed upon him externally by any foreign will whatsoever, human or divine, collective or individual.

Christianity is the complete negation of common sense and sound reason.

There are but three ways for the populace to escape its wretched lot. The first two are by the route of the wine-shop or the church; the third is by that of the social revolution.

All law has for its object to confirm and exalt into a system the exploitation of the workers by a ruling class.

Our first work must be the annihilation of everything as it now exists.

The old world must be destroyed and replaced by a new one. When you have freed your mind from the fear of God, and that childish respect for the fiction of right, then all the remaining chains that bind you—property, marriage, morality, and justice—will snap asunder like threads.

Reaction in Germany (Ruge's *Deutsche Yahrbücher*, 1842)

The passion for destruction (is) a creative
passion. *

Gesammelte Werke [*Complete Works*] (ed. Golos
Trude, Moscow)

Man has liberated himself (by breaking the
divine commandment not to eat of the tree of
knowledge), he has divided himself from animal nature and made himself man; he began
his history and his human development with
this act of disobedience and knowledge, i.e.,
with rebellion and thought.

If there is a State, then there is domination,
and in turn, there is slavery.

They [the Marxists] say that such a yoke, the
dictatorship of the state, is the inevitable but
transitional remedy for achieving the maximum liberation of the people. . . . We answer
that any dictatorship can have only one aim:
self-perpetuation.

I

Collective property and individual property,
these two banners will be the standards under
which, from now on, the great battles of the
future will be fought.

If there is a human being who is freer than
I, then I shall necessarily become his slave. If I
am freer than any other, then he will become
my slave. Therefore equality is an absolutely
necessary condition of freedom.

The first duty . . . is that of making every
effort for the triumph of equality. . . .

This is the entire program of revolutionary
socialism, of which equality is the first condition, the first word. It admits freedom only
after equality, in equality and through equality, because freedom outside of equality can
only create privilege.

From the naturalistic point of view, all men
are equal. There are only two exceptions to
this rule of naturalistic equality: geniuses and
idiots.

II

Freedom is the absolute right of all adult
men and women to seek permission for their
actions only from their own conscience and

reason, and to be determined in their actions
only by their own will, and consequently to be
responsible only to themselves, and then to the
society to which they belong, but only insofar
as they have made a free decision to belong to
it.

It is necessary to abolish completely, in
principle and in practice, everything which
may be called political power. As long as political power exists there will always be rulers and
ruled, masters and slaves, exploiters and exploited.

If one would make a thorough revolution,
one must attack things and relationships, destroy property and the State. Then there would
be no need to destroy men.

No revolution can count on success if it
does not speedily spread beyond the individual
nation to all other nations.

To my utter despair I have discovered, and
discover every day anew, that there is in the
masses no revolutionary idea or hope or passion.

III

Revolutions are not improvised. They are
not made at will by individuals. They come
through the force of circumstances, and are
independent of any deliberate will or conspiracy. They can be foreseen, but their explosion
can never be accelerated.

IV

Oeuvres (Paris)

All temporal and human power proceeds directly from spiritual or divine authority.

But authority is the negation of liberty.
God, or rather the fiction of God, is thus the
sanction and the intellectual and moral cause
of all the slavery on earth, and the liberty of
men will not be complete unless it will have
completely annihilated the inauspicious fiction of a heavenly master.

Vol. I

Polnoye Sobraniye Sochinenii

The real and complete liberation of mankind is the great aim, the sublime end of history.

The State is force; nay, it is the silly parad-
ing of force. However many pains it may take,
it cannot conceal the fact that it is the legal
maimer of our will, the constant negation of

---

*"The desire to destroy is also a creative desire" (tr.
Edmund Wilson). "The urge to destroy is a creative
urge" (another translation).

our liberty. Even when it commands good, it makes this valueless by commanding it, for every command slaps liberty in the face.

I

Catechism of the Revolution (The Nachaev Catechism)

The revolutionist is a doomed man. He has no personal interests, no affairs, sentiments, attachments, property, not even a name of his own. Everything in him is absorbed by one exclusive interest, one thought, one passion—the revolution.

Article 1

To him [the revolutionist] whatever aids the triumph of the revolution is ethical; all that which hinders it is unethical and criminal.

Article 1

The revolutionist despises every sort of doctrinairism and has renounced the peaceful scientific pursuits, leaving them to future generations. He knows only one science, the science of destruction.

Article 5

He is not a revolutionist if he is attached to anything in this world, if he cannot stop before the annihilation of any situation, relation or person belonging to this world—everybody and everything must be equally hateful for him.

Article 13

Selected Works

Powerful states can maintain themselves only by crime, little states are virtuous only by weakness.

The State . . . will become nothing more than a simple business office, a sort of central bookkeeping department, devoted to the service of Society.

The subordination of labor to capital is the source of all slavery: political, moral and material.

In a word, we object to all legislation, all authority, and all influence, privileged, patented, official and legal, even when it has proceeded from universal suffrage, convinced that it must always turn to the profit of a dominating and exploiting minority, against the interests of the immense majority enslaved.

Throw theory into the fire; it only spoils life.
Letter to his sisters, November 1842

Declaration (signed with 46 others)

From each according to his faculties; to each according to his needs.

If God existed, it would be necessary to abolish him.
Quoted by Benjamin R. Tucker, Address, Unitarian Ministers Association, October 14, 1890

Religion is a collective insanity.
Quoted in Noyes, *Views of Religion*

I shall die and the worms will eat me, but I want our idea to triumph. I want the masses of humanity to be truly emancipated from all authorities and from all heroes, present and to come.

You are mistaken if you think I do not believe in God. . . . I seek God in man, in human freedom, and now I seek God in revolution.
Quoted in Eugene Pyziur, *The Doctrine of Anarchism of Mikhail A. Bakunin* (1955)

It is the peculiarity of privilege and of every privileged position to kill the intellect and heart of man. The privileged man, whether he be privileged politically or economically, is a man depraved in intellect and heart.
Quoted in *Britannica*, 11th ed., vol. III

JAMES BALDWIN
(1924–   )
American writer

Notes of a Native Son (1955)

A devotion to humanity . . . is too easily equated with a devotion to a Cause, and Causes, as we know, are notoriously bloodthirsty.

At the root of the American Negro problem is the necessity of the American white man to find a way of living with the Negro in order to be able to live with himself.

The world is white no longer, and it will never be white again.

Nobody Knows My Name (1961)

Freedom is not something that anybody can be given, freedom is something people take.

No Name in the Street (1972)

. . . the Western party is over, and the white man's sun has set. Period.

If the concept of God has any validity or any use, it can only be to make us larger, freer, and more loving. If God cannot do this, then it is time we got rid of Him.
> Contribution, *The New Yorker*,
> November 17, 1962

The price of the liberation of the white people is the liberation of the Blacks—the total liberation, in the cities, in the towns, before the law, and in the mind.
> Speech, quoted in *Time*, May 17, 1963.

If you are born under the circumstances in which Black people are born, the destruction of the Christian churches may not only be desirable but necessary.
> Address, World Council of Churches, Uppsala,
> Sweden, July 7, 1968

ROGER BALDWIN
(1884–1982)
Founder, American Civil Liberties Union

Credo for ACLU

. . . the goal of a society with a minimum of compulsion, a maximum of individual freedom and of voluntary association, and the abolition of exploitation and poverty.

JOHN BALL
(?–hanged 1381)
English priest, social agitator

Whan Adam dalf and Eve span
Who was thanne a gentil man?
> From text for sermon to rebels at Blackheath

John Balle, seynte Marye prist, gretes wele alle maner men and byddes them in the name of the Trinity, Fadur, and Sone, and Holy Gost, stonde Manyliche togedyr in trewth, and helpeth trewthe and trewthe shal helpe yowe.
> Quoted in "Prima Epistola Johannis Balle"

"How the Commons of England Rebelled Against the Noblemen" (1381)

Ah, ye good people, the matters goeth not well to pass in England, nor shall not do till everything be common, and there shall be no villeins nor gentlemen, but that we may be all united together, and that the lords be no greater masters than we be.
> Quoted in *Chronicles of Froissart* (1583)

HOSEA BALLOU
(1771–1852)
American theologian

Weary the path that does not challenge. Doubt is an incentive to truth and patient inquiry leadeth the way.

A religion that requires persecution to sustain it is of the devil's propagation.
> Universalist publications, c. 1819

HONORÉ DE BALZAC
(1799–1850)
French writer

La Comédie humaine.
    The Human Comedy.
> General title for his series of novels

The Physiology of Marriage (1830)

Marriage should war incessantly with that monster that is the ruin of everything. This is the monster of habit.

GEORGE BANCROFT
(1800–1891)
American historian

"To the Workingmen of Northampton"

The feud between the capitalists and the laborer, the House of Have and the House of Want, is as old as social union, and can never be entirely quieted . . .
> Contribution, *Boston Courier*, October 22, 1834

The Office of the People in Art, Government, and Religion (1835)

The best government rests on the people, and not on the few, on persons and not on property, on the free development of public opinion and not on authority.

Address, Historical Society, New York (1854)

The exact measure of the progress of civilization is the degree in which the intelligence of the common mind has prevailed over wealth and brute force; in other words, the measure of the progress of civilization is the progress of the people.

BERTRAND BARÈRE DE VIEUZAC
(1755–1841)
French revolutionary

The tree of liberty will grow only when watered by the blood of tyrants.
> Address, National Assembly, 1792; quoted in *Le Moniteur*, January 13, 1793

JOEL BARLOW
(1754–1812)
American diplomat, libertarian

Treaty with Tripoli (signed 1797)*

As the government of the United States is not in any sense founded on the Christian religion. . . .

PIO BAROJA Y NESSI
(1872–1956)
Spanish writer

The Tree of Knowledge (1911)

A curiosity to surprise life.

JEAN-LOUIS BARRAULT
(1910–   )
French producer and actor

Art is permanent revolution.
> Contribution, *Atlas*, December 1968

*The full title of the treaty was: "Treaty of Peace and Friendship Between the Bey and Subjects of Tripoli of Barbary." The foregoing statement is from Article II. It can be found in *Treaties and Other International Acts of the United States*, edited by Hunter Miller, vol. 2, 1776–1818. U.S. Government Printing Office, 1931, p. 365.

Barlow wrote the treaty. Inasmuch as President George Washington approved it as written, the quotation "The government of the United States is not in any sense founded on the Christian Religion" has been attributed to him and widely publicized. When the Senate ratified the treaty, President John Adams signed it, adding this statement: "Now, be it known, that I, John Adams, President of the United States of America, having seen and considered the said treaty, do, by and within the consent of the Senate, accept, ratify and confirm the same, and every clause and article thereof." (See p. 383 of *Treaties*.)

My thanks are due Miss Virginia Close of Baker Library, Dartmouth, for tracing the source after many years of failure by others.—G.S.

BERNARD M. BARUCH
(1870–1965)
American financier and statesman

Let us not be deceived—we are today in the midst of a cold war.
> Speech, Columbia, S.C., April 16, 1947*

ST. BASIL (The Great)
(330–379)
Bishop of Caesarea

"Homilies"

The bread that you store up belongs to the hungry; the cloak that lies in your chest belongs to the naked; the gold that you have hidden in the ground belongs to the poor.

FULGENCIO BATISTA Y ZALDIVAR
(1901–1973)
Dictator of Cuba

A government needs one hundred soldiers for every guerrilla it faces.
> Quoted in *El Caribe*, New York, January 1, 1959

CHARLES (Pierre) BAUDELAIRE
(1821–1867)
French poet

Mon Coeur mis à nu (1887)

There is in every man at all times two simultaneous tendencies, one toward God, the other toward Satan.
> xix

Le Spleen de Paris (1863)

It is the hour for drunkenness! If you would not be the martyred slave of Time, drink without stopping! Drink wine, drink poetry, drink virtue, drink as you wish.

This life is a hospital in which every patient is possessed with a desire to change his bed.

Fusées I; also *Journal intime*

Even if God did not exist, religion would still be holy and divine . . . God is the only being who does not have to exist in order to reign.

*Ghost-written by Herbert Bayard Swope, editor, *New York World*.

Les Fleurs du Mal (1861)

Hypocritical reader—my double—my brother.

Preface

FRANCIS BEAUMONT
(1584–1616)
and
JOHN FLETCHER
(1579–1625)
English dramatists

The Scornful Lady (c. 1614)

There is no other purgatory but a woman.

Act III: i

SIMONE DE BEAUVOIR
(1908–   )
French writer

The Coming of Age (1970)

And indeed it is old age, rather than death, that is to be contrasted with life. Old age is life's parody, whereas death transforms life into a destiny. In a way, death preserves life by giving it the absolute dimension—"As unto himself eternity changes him at last." Death does away with time.

There is only one solution if old age is not to be an absurd parody of our former life, and that is to go on pursuing ends that give our existence a meaning—devotion to individuals, to groups or to causes, social, political, intellectual or creative work. . . . One's life has value so long as one attributes value to the life of others, by means of love, friendship, indignation, compassion.

Society cares about the individual only in so far as he is profitable.

The old tend to join the ranks of the conservatives. They do their utmost to preserve the status quo.

A Very Easy Death

There is no such thing as a natural death: nothing that happens to a man is ever natural, since his presence calls the world into question. . . . All men must die but for every man his death is an accident and, even if he knows it and consents to it, an unjustifiable violation.

The Prime of Life (American ed.)

Hatred can at times be a positively joyous emotion.

The Second Sex (1949; tr. H. M. Parshlay)

One is not born, but rather becomes a woman. No biological, psychological or economic fate determines the figure that the human female presents in society; it is civilization as a whole that produces this creature, intermediate between male and eunuch, which is described as feminine.

In all civilizations and still in our day woman inspired man with horror: the horror of his own carnal contingence, which he projects upon her.

The two essential traits that characterize woman, biologically speaking, are the following: her grasp upon the world is less extended than man's, and she is more closely enslaved to the species.

The aversion of Christianity in the matter of the feminine body is such that while it is willing to doom its God to an ignominious death, it spares him the defilement of being born: the Council of Ephesus of the Eastern Church and the Lateran Council of the West declared the virgin birth of Christ. The first Fathers of the Church—Origen, Tertullian and Jerome—thought that Mary had been brought to bed in blood and filth like other women; but the opinion of St. Ambrose and St. Augustine was the one that prevailed. The body of the Virgin remained closed. Since the Middle Ages the fact of having a body has been considered, in woman, an ignominy.

p. 156

Women's homosexuality is one attempt among others to reconcile her autonomy with the passivity of her flesh. And if Nature is to be invoked, one can say that all women are naturally homosexual. The lesbian, in fact, is distinguished by her refusal of the male and her liking for feminine flesh; but every adolescent female fears penetration and masculine domination, and she feels a certain repulsion for the male body; on the other hand the female body is for her as for the male, an object of desire.

pp. 301–382

Marriage is obscene in principle in so far as it transforms into rights and duties the mutual relations which should be founded on a spontaneous urge; it gives an instrumental and therefore degrading character to the two bodies in dooming them to know each other in their general aspect as bodies, not as persons. The husband is often chilled by the idea that he is doing a duty, and the wife is ashamed to find herself given to someone who is exercising a right over her.

pp. 418–419

This complex mixture of affection and resentment, hate, constraint, resignation, dullness, and hypocrisy called conjugal love is supposedly respected only by way of extenuation, whitewash. But the same is true of affection as of physical love: for it to be genuine, authentic, it must first of all be free.

p. 446

Marriage . . . is directly correlated to prostitution, which, it has been said, follows humanity from ancient to modern times like a dark shadow over the family.

p. 523

Religion sanctions woman's self-love; it gives her the guide, father, lover, divine guardian she longs for nostalgically; it feeds her day-dreams; it fills her empty hours. But, above all, it confirms the social order, it justifies her resignation, by giving her the hope of a better future in a sexless heaven. This is why women today are still a powerful trump in the hand of the Church; it is why the Church is notably hostile to all measures liable to help in women's emancipation. There must be religion for women; and there must be women, "true women," to perpetuate religion.

pp. 487–488

Love has been assigned to woman as her supreme vocation, and when she directs it toward a man, she is seeking God in him; but if human love is denied her by circumstance, if she is disappointed or overparticular she may choose to adore divinity in the person of God Himself.

p. 630

Christianity gave eroticism its savor of sin and legend when it endowed the human female with a soul. . . .

p. 688

—————

. . . marriage is a very alienating institution, for men as well as for women. . . . It's a very

dangerous institution—dangerous for men who find themselves trapped, saddled with a wife and children to support; dangerous for women, who aren't financially independent and end up depending on men who can throw them out when they are 40, and dangerous for children because their parents vent all their frustrations on them.

Interview, *New York Times Magazine,*
June 2, 1974

It is easier to think of the world without a creator than of a creator loaded with all the contradictions of the world.

Quoted in *Time,* April 8, 1966

AUGUST BEBEL
(1840–1913)
German socialist leader

Antisemitismus und Socialdemokratie (October 27, 1893)

Anti-Semitism is the Socialism of fools.

—————

All political parties, all matters of right, are at bottom only questions of might.

Speech, Reichstag, July 3, 1871

The nature of business is swindling.

Speech, Zurich, December 1892

When Socialism comes into power, the Roman Church will advocate Socialism with the same vigor it is now favoring feudalism and slavery.

Address, Social Democratic Party Congress, Jena, 1906

CESARE BONESANA, MARCHESE DI BECCARIA
(1735–1794)
Italian economist, penologist

"On Crimes and Punishments" (1764)

The greatest happiness for the greatest number.

It is better to prevent crimes than to punish them.

There are three sources of the moral and political principles which govern mankind, namely, revelation, natural law, and social conventions. . . . There are, then, three distinct kinds of virtue and vice—the religious, the natural, and the political.

Happy is the nation without a history.

(cf. Carlyle)

HENRY WARD BEECHER
(1813–1887)
American clergyman

Proverbs from Plymouth Pulpit (1867)

Law represents the effort of men to organize society; governments, the efforts of selfishness to overthrow liberty.

The worst thing in the world next to anarchy, is government.

The ignorant classes are the dangerous classes. Ignorance is the womb of monsters.

The Negro is superior to the white race. If the latter do not forget their pride of race and color, and amalgamate with the purer and richer blood of the Blacks, they will die out and wither away in unprolific skinniness.

Speech, New York, 1866

LUDWIG VAN BEETHOVEN
(1770–1827)
German composer

Music is a higher revelation than philosophy.

Letter to Bettina von Arnim, 1810

EDWARD BELLAMY
(1850–1898)
American sociologist

As political equality is the remedy for political tyranny, so is economic equality the only way of putting an end to the economic tyranny exercised by the few over the many through the superiority of wealth.

From the masthead of his weekly, *The New Nation*

ST. ROBERT BELLARMINE
(1542–1621)
Italian cardinal

The Pope may act outside the law, above the law, and against the law.

Freedom of belief is pernicious, it is nothing but the freedom to be wrong.

Quoted in *The Life and Works of Blessed Robert Cardinal Bellarmine* (1928), ed. J. Brodrick

HILAIRE (Joseph) BELLOC
(1870–1953)
English poet

Epigrams

The accursed power which stands on Privilege
(And goes with Women, and Champagne, and Bridge)
Broke—and Democracy resumed her reign:
(Which goes with Bridge, and Women, and Champagne).

"On a General Election"

When I am dead, I hope it may be said:
"His sins were scarlet, but his books were read."

"On His Books"

Lines to a Don

Don poor at Bed and worse at Table,
Don pinched, Don starved, Don miserable;
Don stuttering, Don with roving eyes,
Don nervous, Don of crudities. . . .
Don middle-class, Don sycophantic,
Don dull, Don brutish, Don pedantic;
Don hypocritical, Don bad,
Don furtive, Don three-quarters mad;
Don (since a man must make an end),
Don that shall never be my friend.

The Servile State (1912)

At its first inception all Collectivist Reform is necessarily deflected, and evolves, in the place of what it had intended, a new thing: a society wherein the owners remain few and wherein the proletarian mass accept a security at the expense of servitude.

JULIEN BENDA
(1867–1956)
French philosopher, psychologist

*Le Trahison des Clercs** (1927)

The State, Country, Class, are now frankly God; we may even say that for many people (and some are proud of it) they alone are god.

---

*The Richard Aldington translation is entitled *The Great Betrayal in England;* the Beacon Press title is *The Betrayal of the Intellectuals.* This work has also been referred to as *The Treason of the Cultured Classes.* "Clerc" was originally a man of learning. According to Herbert Read, distinguished clercs who

Peace is only possible if men cease to place their happiness in the possession of things "which cannot be shared," and if they raise themselves to a point where they adopt an abstract principle superior to their egotisms. In other words, it can only be obtained by a betterment of human morality.

ST. BENEDICT OF NURSIA
(480?–554)
Patriarch of Western monks

Motto of Benedictine Order

> Laborare est orare.
> To labor is to pray.

RUTH BENEDICT
(1887–1948)
and
GENE WILTFISH
(1902–   )
American anthropologists

The Races of Mankind

Aryans, Jews, Italians are not races. Aryans are people who speak Indo-European, "Aryan" languages. . . . As Hitler uses it, the term has no meaning, racial, linguistic or otherwise.

Jews are people who practice the Jewish religion. They are of all races, Negro and Mongolian. European Jews are of many different biological types; physically they resemble the populations among whom they live.

DAVID BEN-GURION (né Gryn)
(1886–1973)
Polish-born Israeli prime minister

It is a world cooperative commonwealth at which we ought to aim, built on freedom. A single country—or a group of countries—with this peaceful cooperative aim can make its impact on the whole world. The best way of teaching is by example, and our goal here is to build a cooperative commonwealth of free men.

Contribution, *New York Times Magazine*, September 24, 1961

have betrayed their trust include: Momsen, Treitschke, Brunetière, Lemaître, D'Annunzio, and Kipling.

JEREMY BENTHAM
(1748–1832)
English philosopher

The Commonplace Book

The greatest happiness of the greatest number is the foundation of morals and legislation.
(*Works* X, 142)

Principles of Morals and Legislation (1789)

All punishment is mischief; all punishment in itself is evil.
Ch. 16, Sec. 2

Every law is an infraction of liberty. *
Quoted in Isaiah Berlin,
"Two Concepts of Liberty"

Constitutional Code (1827)

But in truth, in no instance has a system in regard to religion been ever established, but for the purpose, as well as with the effect of its being made an instrument of intimidation, corruption, and delusion, for the support of depredation and oppression in the hands of government.

BEOWULF**

> Wyrd oft nereth
> Unfaegne eorl, thone his ellen deah.
> Fate often saves an undoomed warrior when his courage endures.
> (tr. George Metes)

NICHOLAI ALEKSANDROVICH BERDYAYEV (Nicholas Berdyaev)
(1874–1948)
Russian religious philosopher

The End of Our Times (tr. 1933)

The worship of Mammon instead of God is a characteristic of Socialism as well as Capitalism.

Socialism is no longer an Utopia or a dream: it is an objective threat, and a warning

---

*Cf. Bentham, *Anarchical Fallacies: Preamble.* See 2 *Works* (1843 Bowring ed.) 493.
**"The epic of *Beowulf*, the most precious relic of old English . . . has come down to us in a single ms., written about A.D. 1000."—*Britannica*, 11th ed., vol. III.

to Christians to show them unmistakably that they have not fulfilled the word of Christ.

Christianity and Anti-Semitism

Perhaps the saddest thing to admit is that those who rejected the Cross have to carry it, while those who welcomed it so often engaged in crucifying others.

BERNARD BERENSON
(1865–1959)
American art critic

Aesthetics and History (1948)

Only works of art can be life-enhancing, for merely visible things are not. . . . Art history is the history of art as an experience, and is indifferent to questions of beauty.

. . . the fundamental truth that lies at the bottom of spiritual values—the truth, namely, that human life, consciously lived, rests on tragic foundations.

[Definition of culture]: The effort to build a House of Life where man will be able to attain the highest development that his animal nature will permit, taking him ever further away from the jungle and the cave, and bringing him nearer and nearer to that humanistic society which under the name of Paradise, Elysium, Heaven, City of God, Millennium, has been the craving of all good men these last four thousand years and more.

Except as its clown and jester, society does not encourage individuality, and the State abhors it.

Art as art, not art for art, must be life-enhancing.

Essays in Appreciation (1958)

The ultimate justification of the work of art is to help the spectator to become a work of art himself.

Between truth and the search for truth, I opt for the second.

HENRI BERGSON
(1859–1941)
French philosopher, Nobel Prize 1927

Creative Evolution (1907)

Élan vital. [Vital ardor—or to glow, or burst.]

Intelligence is characterized by a natural incomprehension of life.

. . . for a conscious being, to exist is to change, to change is to mature, to mature is to go on creating oneself endlessly.

Les deux sources de la morale et de la religion [*The Two Sources of Morality and Religion*] (1932)

The universe . . . is a machine for creating gods.

Sex-appeal is the keynote to our civilization.

Homo sapiens, the only creature endowed with reason, is also the only creature to pin its existence on things unreasonable.

American edition, 1935

GEORGE BERKELEY
(1685–1753)
Irish-born, English bishop, philosopher

Dialogues Between Hylas and Philoneos (1713)

I have no reason for believing the existence of matter. I have no immediate intuition thereof: neither can I immediately, from any sensations, ideas, notions, actions or passions infer an unthinking, unperceiving, inactive substance—either by probable deduction or necessary consequence.

The Principles of Human Knowledge (1710)

. . . that all the choir of heaven and furniture of the earth, in a word all those bodies which compose the mighty frames of the world, have any substance without a mind, that their being (*esse*) is to be perceived or known; that consequently so long as they are not actually perceived by me, or do not exist in my mind or that of any other *created spirits,* they must either have no existence at all *or else exist in the mind of some eternal spirit.*

I, vi

SIR ISAIAH BERLIN
(1909–   )
Fellow of All Souls, Oxford

"Two Concepts of Liberty," Inaugural lecture, October 31, 1958, Oxford

But to manipulate men, to propel them towards goals which you—the social reformers—see, but they may not, is to deny their human essence, to treat them as objects without wills of their own, and therefore to degrade them.

In the ideal society, composed of wholly responsible human beings, laws, because I should scarcely be conscious of them, would gradually wither away. Only one social movement was bold enough to render this assumption quite explicit and accepts its consequences—that of the Anarchists.

ST. BERNARD OF CLAIRVAUX
(1090–1153)
Abbot of Clairvaux

*Meditations Piissimae et Cogitione Humanae Conditionis**

Man is nothing else than fetid sperm, a sack of dung, the food for worms. . . . You have never seen a viler dunghill.

On Consideration

Both swords therefore belong to the Church, the spiritual and the material. The material sword is to be drawn in defense of the Church, the spiritual by the Church; the spiritual by the hand of the priest, the material by the soldier but at a sign from the priest, and on the order of the emperor.

4, 3

CLAUDE BERNARD
(1813–1878)
French scientist

Leçons de pathologie expérimentale

Science does not permit exceptions.

Pensées

Hatred is the most clear-sighted, next to genius.

Introduction à l'étude de la medicine expérimentale (1865)

Great men have been compared to giants upon whose shoulders pygmies have climbed, who nevertheless see further than they.

FRIEDRICH A. J. VON BERNHARDI
(1849–1930)
German general

Germany and the Next War (1912)

War is a biological necessity of the first importance, a regulative element in the life of mankind which cannot be dispensed with.

But it [war] is not only a biological law but a moral obligation, and, as such, an indispensable factor in civilization.

THE BHAGAVAD-GITA (The Song of God)
(2nd century B.C.)

The Blessed Lord's Song (tr. Swami Paramananda, 1944)

Knowledge is indeed better than blind practice; meditation excels knowledge; surrender of the fruits of action is more esteemed than meditation. Peace immediately follows surrender.

He who hates no creature and is friendly and compassionate to all, who is free from attachment and egotism, equal-minded in pleasure and pain, and forgiving. . . .
He to whom the world is not afflicted and who is not afflicted by the world, who is free from elation, envy, fear and anxiety, he is dear to me. . . .
He who neither rejoices, nor hates, nor sorrows, nor desires and who has renounced good and evil, he who is thus full of devotion, is dear to me.

Lust, anger and greed, these three are the soul-destroying gates of hell.

Forsaking egoism, power, pride, lust, anger and possession; freed from the notion of "mind," and tranquil; one is thus fit to become one with Brahman.

As in this body the embodied soul passes through childhood, youth and old age, in the same manner it goes from one body to another; therefore the wise are never deluded regarding it.

For that which is born death is certain, and for the dead birth is certain. Therefore grieve not over that which is unavoidable.

BHARITIHARI
(died c. 650)
Indian grammarian

The Sringa Satak (c. 625)

Nothing enchants the soul so much as young women. They alone are the cause of evil, and there is no other.

Woman is the chain by which man is attached to the chariot of folly.

*The full text, in Latin, is given in Havelock Ellis, *Studies in the Psychology of Sex*, vol. 4, p. 119.

BIAS OF PRIENE IN IONIA
(fl. c. 570 B.C.)
One of the Seven Sages of Greece

Truth breeds hatred.

Maxim

Bias used to say that men sought to calculate life both as if they were fated to live a long and a short time, and that they ought to love one another as if at a future time they would come to hate one another; for that most men were bad.

Quoted in Diogenes Laërtius, *Bias,* v

AMBROSE BIERCE
(1842–disappeared in Mexico 1914)
American writer

The Enlarged Devil's Dictionary (1906)

BIBLE, n. A collection of fantastic legends without any scientific support. . . . full of dark hints, historical mistakes and contradictions.

BIRTH, n. The first and direst of all disasters.

CARTESIAN, adj. Relating to Descartes, a famous philosopher, author of the celebrated dictum, *Cogito, ergo sum.* . . . The dictum might be improved, however, thus: *Cogito cogito ergo cogito sum*—"I think that I think, therefore I think that I am"; as close an approach to certainty as any philosopher has ever yet made.

CHRISTIAN, n. One who believes that the New Testament is a divinely inspired book admirably suited to the spiritual needs of his neighbor. One who follows the teachings of Christ so far as they are not inconsistent with a life of sin.

DECALOGUE, n. A series of commandments. . . . Following is the revised edition . . .

Thou shalt no God but me adore:
'Twere too expensive to have more.

Don't steal; thou'lt never thus compete
Successfully in business. Cheat.

HISTORY, n. An account mostly false, of events mostly unimportant, which are brought about by rulers mostly knaves, and soldiers mostly fools.

IRRELIGION, n. The principal one of the great faiths of the world.

LABOR, n. One of the processes by which A acquires property for B.

LAND, n. A part of the earth's surface, considered as property. The theory that land is property subject to private ownership and control is the foundation of modern society. . . . Carried to its logical conclusion, it means that some have the right to prevent others from living; for the right to own implies the right exclusively to occupy. . . .

MAMMON, n. The god of the world's leading religion.

PHILOSOPHY, n. A route of many roads leading from nowhere to nothing.

PRAY, v. To ask that the laws of the universe be annulled in behalf of a single petitioner confessedly unworthy.

RELIGION, n. A daughter of Hope and Fear, explaining to Ignorance the nature of the Unknowable.

REVOLUTION, n. A bursting of the boilers which usually takes place when the safety valve of public discussion is closed.

SAINT, n. A dead sinner revised and edited.

UN-AMERICAN, adj. Wicked, intolerable, heathenish.

PRINCE OTTO VON BISMARCK
(1815–1898)
Prussian Chancellor

Not by speeches and majority decisions will the greatest problem of the time be decided— that was the mistake of 1848—but by Blood and Iron.

Impromptu speech to ministers and deputies, Prussian House of Delegates, September 30, 1862

Nothing should be left to an invaded people except their eyes for weeping.

Quoted in Paul Loyson, *The Gods in the Battle*

All treaties between great states cease to be binding when they come in conflict with the struggle for existence.

Attributed

HUGO L. BLACK
(1886–1971)
U.S. Supreme Court Justice

Majority Opinion, Everson v. Board of Education, 330 U.S. 1 (1947)

The "establishment of religion" clause of the First Amendment means at least this: Neither a state nor the Federal Government can set up a church. Neither can pass laws which aid one religion, aid all religions, or prefer one religion over another.

The First Amendment has erected a wall between church and state. That wall must be kept high and impregnable. We could not approve the slightest breach.

Conclusion

Address, New York University School of Law, 1960

The Framers [of the Constitution] knew that free speech is the friend of change and revolution. But they also knew that it is always the deadliest enemy of tyranny.

Opinion, *New York Times v.* U.S., June 30, 1971 (the Pentagon Papers case)

In the First Amendment the Founding Fathers gave the free press the protection it must have to fulfill its essential role in our democracy. The press was to serve the governed, not the governors. The Government's power to censor the press was abolished so that the press would remain forever free to censure the government. The press was protected so that it could bare the secrets of Government and inform the people.

SIR WILLIAM BLACKSTONE
(1723–1780)
English writer on law

Commentaries on the Laws of England (1765)

That the King can do no wrong, is a necessary and fundamental principle of the English constitution.

III, 17

It is better that ten guilty escape than that one innocent suffer.

IV, 27

The liberty of the press is indeed essential to the nature of a free state, but this consists in laying no previous restraints upon publication, and not in freedom from censure for criminal matter when published.

1769 edition, IV, 151

Husband and wife are one person in the law; that is, the very being or legal existence of the woman is suspended during the marriage.

1789 edition

To deny the possibility, nay, actual existence of witchcraft and sorcery is at once flatly to contradict the revealed word of God in various passages of both the Old and New Testament. . . .

1850 edition

Democracies are usually the best calculated to direct the end of law; aristocracies to invent the means by which that end shall be obtained; and monarchies to carry those means into execution.

The most universal and effectual way of discovering the true meaning of law, when the words are dubious, is by considering the reason and spirit of it; or the cause which moved the legislator to enact it. For when this reason ceases, the law itself ought likewise to cease with it.

To make a particular custom good, the following are necessary requisites: That it has been used so long that the memory of man runneth not to the contrary.

The only true and natural foundations of society are the wants and fears of individuals.
Quoted in J. W. Ehrlich, *Ehrlich's Blackstone* (1959)

WILLIAM BLAKE
(1757–1827)
English poet, artist

America: A Prophecy (1793)

For every thing that lives is holy, life delights in life;
Because the soul of sweet delight can never be defil'd.

Plate 8

Annotations to Bacon's "Essays" (1798)

Self Evident Truth is one Thing and Truth the result of Reasoning is another Thing. Rational Truth is not the Truth of Christ, but of Pilate. It is the Tree of the Knowledge of Good & Evil.

"Truth"

Annotation to Watson's "Apology for The Bible"
(1798)

All Penal Laws court Transgression & therefore are cruelty & Murder. The laws of the
Jews were (both ceremonial & real) the basest
& most oppressive of human codes, & being
like all other codes given under the pretence of
divine command were what Christ pronounced them, the Abomination that maketh
desolation, i.e. State Religion, which is the
source of all Cruelty.

Page 251

The Everlasting Gospel (c. 1818)

The vision of Christ that thou dost see
Is my Vision's Greatest Enemy:
a. 1–2

Both read the Bible day & night,
But thou read'st black where I read white.
a. 13–14

Thou art a Man, God is no more,
Thine own humanity learn to Adore
c. 41–42

If Moral Virtue was Christianity,
Christ's Pretensions were all Vanity. . . .
Supplementary Passage (1818), I. 1

"Milton" (1804–08)

I will not cease from Mental Fight,
Nor shall my Sword sleep in my hand
Till we have built Jerusalem
In England's green & pleasant Land.
Preface, 15

"Jerusalem" (1804–1820)

I care not whether Man is Good or Evil; all
that I care
Is whether he is a Wise Man or a Fool. Go,
put off Holiness
And put on Intellect . . .
Ch. 4, plate 91

"Auguries of Innocence" (1787)

To See a World in a Grain of Sand
And a Heaven in a Wild Flower,
Hold Infinity in the palm of your hand
And Eternity in an hour.
Lines 1–4

A Robin Red breast in a Cage
Puts all Heaven in a Rage.
Lines 5–6

A Horse misus'd upon the Road
Calls to Heaven for Human blood.
Lines 10–11

He who mocks the Infant's Faith
Shall be mock'd in Age & Death.
He who shall teach the Child to Doubt
The rotting Grave shall ne'er get out.
He who respects the Infant's Faith
Triumphs over Hell & Death.
Lines 85–90

The Strongest Poison ever known
Came from Caesar's Laurel Crown.
Lines 95–96

The Whore & Gambler, by the State
Licenc'd, build that Nation's Fate.
The Harlot's cry from Street to Street
Shall weave Old England's winding Sheet.
Lines 110–114

Songs of Experience (1794)

In every cry of every Man,
In every Infant's cry of fear,
In every voice, in every ban,
The mind-forg'd manacles I hear.
"London," st. 2

But most thro' midnight streets I hear
How the Youthful Harlot's curse
Blasts the new born Infant's tear,
And blights with plagues the Marriage
hearse.
"London," st. 4

Love seeketh not Itself to please,
Nor for itself hath any care,
But for another gives its ease,
And builds a Heaven in Hell's despair.
"The Clod & the Pebble," st. 1

Tyger! Tyger! burning bright
In the forests of the night,
What immortal hand or eye
Could frame thy fearful symmetry?
"The Tyger," st. 1

I was angry with my friend:
I told my wrath, my wrath did end.
I was angry with my foe:
I told it not, my wrath did grow.
"A Poison Tree," st. 1

Cruelty has a Human Heart,
And Jealousy a Human Face;
Terror the Human Form Divine,
And Secrecy the Human Dress.
"A Divine Image," st. 1

Poems and Fragments From the Notebook (1793–1818)

> He who binds to himself a joy
> Does the winged life destroy;
> But he who kisses the joy as it flies
> Lives in eternity's sun rise.
> "Eternity"

The Marriage of Heaven and Hell (1790–93)

Without Contraries is no progression. Attraction and Repulsion, Reason and Energy, Love and Hate, are necessary to Human existence.

From these contraries spring what the religious call Good & Evil. Good is the passive that obeys Reason. Evil is the active springing from Energy.
Plate 3

All Bibles or sacred codes have been the causes of the following Errors:
1. That Man has two real existing principles. Viz: a Body & a Soul.
2. That Energy, call'd Evil, is alone from the Body; & that Reason, call'd Good, is alone from the Soul.
3. That God will torment Man in Eternity for following his Energies.

But the following Contraries to these are True:
1. Man has no Body distinct from his Soul; . . .
2. Energy is the only life, and is from the Body; and Reason is the bound . . . of Energy.
Plate 4

Those who restrain desire, do so because theirs is weak enough to be restrained; . . .
Plate 5

He who desires but acts not, breeds pestilence.

If the fool would persist in his folly he would become wise.
Plate 7

The man who never alters his opinion is like standing water, & breeds reptiles of the mind.
Plate 19

"Jah & His Two Sons, Satan & Adam" (1820)

Art is the Tree of Life. Science is the Tree of Death. God is Jesus.

"A Memorable Fancy"

. . . the voice of honest indignation is the voice of God.

"To the Jews" (1804–1820)

If Humility is Christianity, you, O Jews, are the true Christians. . . . The return of Israel is a Return to Mental Sacrifice & War. Take up the Cross, O Israel & follow Jesus.

"Note-book" (1793)

> In a wife I would desire
> What in whores is always found—
> The lineaments of gratified desire.

The road to excess leads to the palace of wisdom.

Joys impregnate, sorrows bring forth.

Everything possible to be believed is an image of truth.

One law for the lion and ox is oppression.

Exuberance is beauty.

Truth can never be told so as to be understood and not be believed.

To generalize is to be an idiot.
Written on margin, Joshua Reynolds' *Discourses*

LOUIS BLANC
(1811–1882)
French Socialist, journalist

The Organization of Labor (1848 edition, tr. Ronald Sanders)

. . . a day will come when a strong and active government will no longer be needed, because there will no longer be inferior and subordinate classes in society. . . . The seedbed of Socialism can be fertilized only by the wind of politics.

LOUIS AUGUSTE BLANQUI
(1805–1881)
French radical, journalist

La Patrie en Danger!

The homeland in danger!
Title of his journal; French slogan.

Critique sociale (1834–1850)

A few individuals seized upon the common earth by ruse or by violence and, claiming possession of it, have established by laws that it is to be their property forever. . . . This right to property logically extended itself from the soil to other instruments, namely the accumulated products of labor, designated by the generic term, capital.

Humanity never stands still; it advances or retreats.

PAUL EUGEN BLEULER
(1857–1939)
Swiss psychiatrist

Schizophrenia [divided mind—or split soul]
    Word coined in *Dementia Praecox* (1911)

GIOVANNI BOCCACCIO
(1313–1375)
Italian author

Il meglio è l'inimico del bene.
Better is the enemy of good.
    Quoting a common Italian phrase

LUDWIG BOERNE
(1786–1837)
German political writer

Der ewige Jude [The Eternal Jew] (1821)

To want to be free is to be free.

If you must hate, if hatred is the leaven of your life, which alone can give flavor, then hate what should be hated: falsehood, violence, selfishness.

Kritiken, No. 21 (1823)

There is nothing to fear but fear.

Fragmente und Aphorismen (1840)

The difference between Liberty and liberties is as great as between God and gods.

The Holy Roman Empire—neither holy, nor Roman, nor an empire.

BOETHIUS, ANICUS MANLIUS SEVERINUS
(c. 480–524)
Roman philosopher, statesman

De Consolatione Philosophiae (c. 524)

If there is a God, whence proceed so many evils? If there is no God, whence cometh any good?
                                                I

As faintness is a disease of the body, so is vice a sickness of the mind. Wherefore, since we judge those who have corporal infirmities to be rather worthy of compassion than hatred, much more are they to be pitied, and not abhorred, whose minds are oppressed with idleness, the greatest malady that may be.
                                                IV

For often in desperate circumstances the will embraces death, which nature shuns, and, on the other hand, the will sometimes restrains the act of propagation on which alone the continuation of mortal things depends, which nature always desires.
                                                XIV

Then she [Philosophy, personified] said . . . I assert that there is no such thing as chance, and I declare that chance is just an empty word [*inanem vocem*] with no real meaning. For what place can be left for purposelessness when God puts all things in order?
There is [free will] she said, for there can be no rational nature that is not endowed with free will. . . .
                                                XV

ALEXANDER A. BOGOMOLETZ
(1881–1946)
Ukrainian physician, scientist

The Prolongation of Life (1946)

The fundamental precept of the fight for longevity is avoidance of satiety. One must not lose desires. They are mighty stimulants to creativeness, to love, and to long life.

The scorn of death is again one of the methods of prolonging life. . . The best way not to die too soon is to cultivate the duties of life and the scorn of death.

Man is as old as his connective tissues.

NIELS BOHR
(1885–1962)
Danish physicist

There are trivial truths and the great truths. The opposite of a trivial truth is plainly false. The opposite of a great truth is also true.
    Contribution, *New York Times,* October 20, 1957

NICOLAS BOILEAU-DESPÉREAUX
(1636–1711)
French poet and critic

Epistles

The painful burden of having nothing to do.

XI

L'Art poétique (1674)

Who cannot limit himself can never be able to write.

HENRY ST. JOHN, VISCOUNT BOLINGBROKE
(1678–1751)
English statesman

Letters on the Study of History (pub. posthumously 1752)

It is a very easy thing to devise good laws; the difficulty is to make them effective. The great mistake is that of looking upon men as virtuous, or thinking that they can be made so by laws, and consequently the greatest art of the politician is to render vices serviceable to the cause of virtue.

SIMON BOLIVAR
(1783–1830)
South American liberator

If Nature is against us, we will fight Nature.

Quoted by Waldo Frank

Those who have served the cause of the revolution have plowed the seas.

Attributed

JOSEPH BONAPARTE
(1768–1844)
French barrister, King of Naples

Gold is, in the last analysis, the sweat of the poor, and the blood of the brave.

Attributed

NAPOLEON BONAPARTE, *see* Napoleon

DIETRICH BONHOEFFER
(1906–executed 1945)
German theologian

I fear that Christians who stand with only one leg upon earth, also stand with only one leg in heaven.

Letter to fiancée, August 12, 1943

BONIFACE VIII
(1235–1303)
Pope from 1294

Unam Sanctam (November 18, 1302)

The true faith compels us to believe there is one holy Catholic Apostolic Church and this we firmly believe and plainly confess. And outside of her there is no salvation or remission from sins.

Now, therefore, we declare, say, determine and pronounce that for every human creature it is necessary for salvation to be subject to the authority of the Roman pontiff.

BOOK OF COMMON PRAYER
Liturgy of the Anglican Church, first published in 1650, with periodic additions and revisions*

The Litany (1662)

From all inordinate and sinful affection; and from all the deceits of the world, the flesh, and the devil, Good Lord, deliver us.

The Burial of the Dead (1662)

In the midst of life we are in death.

Earth to earth, ashes to ashes, dust to dust; in sure and certain hope of the Resurrection unto eternal life. . . .

THE BOOK OF GOOD COUNSELS
(c. 300 B.C.)
Sanscrit

Wealth is friends, home, father, brother,
  title to respect and fame;
Yes, wealth is held for wisdom—that it
    should be
  so is shame.

*These quotations from the 1928 edition.

EVANGELINE CORY BOOTH
(1865–1950)
Salvation Army Commander

Drink has drained more blood . . .
Plunged more people into bankruptcy . . .
Slain more children . . .
Dethroned more reason,
Wrecked more manhood,
Dishonored more womanhood . . .
Blasted more lives . . .
Driven more to suicide, and
Dug more graves than any other poisoned
    scourge
    that ever swept the death-dealing waves
    across the world.
> Quoted in biography by P.W. Wilson

CESARE BORGIA
(1476?–1507)
Italian cardinal, military leader

Aut Caesar, aut nihil.
Either Caesar or nothing.
> Motto

MARTIN BORMANN
(1900–1945)
German Nazi leader

Education is a danger. . . . At best an education which produces useful coolies for us is admissible. Every educated person is a future enemy.
> Letter to his wife, Gerda

MAX BORN
(1882–1970)
German-born British physicist
Nobel Prize, 1954

My Life and My Views (1968)

. . . science . . . is so greatly opposed to history and tradition that it cannot be absorbed by our civilization.

The human race has today the means for annihilating itself—either in a fit of complete lunacy, i.e., in a big war, by a brief fit of destruction, or by careless handling of atomic technology, through a slow process of poisoning and of deterioration in its genetic structure.
> Contribution, *Bulletin of the Atomic Scientists,*
> June, 1957

JAMES BOSWELL
(1740–1795)
Scottish biographer of Samuel Johnson

Concubinage is almost universal. If it was morally wrong why was it permitted to the most pious men under the Old Testament? Why did our Saviour never say a word against it?
> Letter to William Temple, March 18, 1775

ANTOINE, COMTE BOULAY DE LA MEURTHE
(1761–1840)
French politician

C'est pire qu'un crime, c'est une faute.
It is worse than a crime, it is a blunder.
> Comment on Napoleon's execution of the Duke of
> Enghien; frequently attributed to Talleyrand

THOMAS BOWDLER
(1754–1825)
English physician, editor

Family Shakespeare (1818)*

I acknowledge Shakespeare to be the world's greatest dramatic poet, but regret that no parent could place the uncorrected book in the hands of his daughter, and therefore I have prepared the Family Shakespeare. . . . Many words and expressions occur which are of so indecent a nature as to render it highly desirable that they should be erased. . . . Expressions are omitted which can not with propriety be read aloud in the family.
> Preface

CLAUDE G. BOWERS
(1878–1958)
American historian, diplomat

History is the torch that is meant to illuminate the past, to guard us against the repetition of our mistakes of other days. We cannot join

---

*"The words "bowdlerize" and "bowdlerism" derive from this doctor's name. Among the parts censored by him were: Hamlet's speeches to Ophelia, Act III, sc. 2; the third scene of Act II of *Macbeth,* the porter's description of drinking; Scene 4 of *Henry V,* Act III, during which Katharine of Anjou attempts to learn English, which was written in old French.

in the rewriting of history to make it conform to our comfort and convenience.
> Introduction, F. Jay Taylor, *The U.S. and the Spanish Civil War*, 1956

CHARLES BRADLAUGH
(1833–1891)
English reformer

Speeches (1890)

Liberty's chief foe is theology.

Without free speech no search for truth is possible . . . no discovery of truth is useful. . . . Better a thousandfold abuse of free speech than denial of free speech. The abuse dies in a day, but the denial slays the life of the people, and entombs the hope of the race.

OMAR N. BRADLEY
(1893–1983)
American general

We have grasped the mystery of the atom and rejected the Sermon on the Mount.
> Address, Armistice Day, 1948

LOUIS D. BRANDEIS
(1856–1941)
U.S. Supreme Court Justice

The Employer and Trades Unions (1904)

Industrial democracy should ultimately attend political democracy.

Concurring opinion, Whitney v. California, 274 U.S. 357 (1927)

Fear of serious injury cannot alone justify oppression of free speech and assembly. Men feared witches and burnt women. It is the function of speech to free men from the bondage of irrational fears.

Those who won our independence . . . valued liberty both as an end and as a means. They believed liberty to be the secret of happiness and courage to be the secret of liberty . . . that without free speech and assembly discussion would be futile; that with them, discussion affords ordinarily adequate protection against the dissemination of noxious doctrine; that the greatest menace to freedom is an inert people; that public discussion is a political duty; and that this should be a fundamental principle of the American government.

But they knew that order cannot be secured merely through fear of punishment for its infraction; that it is hazardous to discourage thought, hope and imagination; that fear breeds repression; that repression breeds hate; that hate menaces stable government; that the path of safety lies in the opportunity to discuss freely supposed grievances and proposed remedies; and that the fitting remedy for evil counsels is good ones. . . . Those who won our independence by revolution were not cowards. They did not fear political change. They did not exalt order at the cost of liberty.

Dissent, Olmstead v. U.S., 277 U.S. 438 (1928)

To declare that in the administration of criminal law the end justifies the means—to declare that the Government may commit crimes in order to secure conviction of a private criminal—would bring terrible retribution.

The makers of our Constitution sought to protect Americans. . . . They conferred, as against the government, the right to be let alone—the most comprehensive of rights and the right most valued by civilized men.

The function of the press is very high. It is almost holy. To misstate or suppress the news is a breach of trust.
> Contribution, *Collier's*, March 23, 1912

While there are many contributing causes of unrest . . . there is one which is fundamental. That is the necessary conflict—the contrast between our political liberty and our industrial absolutism.
> Testimony, U.S. Commission on Industrial Relations, 1915

GEORGES BRAQUE
(1882–1963)
French painter

Pensées sur l'Art

Art was made to disturb, science reassures.

There is only one valuable thing in art: the thing you cannot explain.
> Quoted in *Saturday Review,* May 28, 1966

BERTHOLD BRECHT
(1898–1956)
German playwright

The Caucasian Chalk Circle (1944–45)

Terrible is the temptation to be good.

Diaries (1920–1922)

. . . the essence of art is simplicity, grandeur and sensitivity, and that of form is coolness.

Happy is the country which requires no heroes.
Quoted in *New Republic,* September 23, 1976

GERALD BRENAN
(fl. 1899)
British writer

Thoughts in a Dry Season

Religions are kept alive by heresies, which are really sudden explosions of faith. Dead religions do not produce them.

When the coin is tossed either Love or Lust will fall uppermost. But if the metal is right, under the one will always be the other.

WILLIAM J. BRENNAN
(1906–   )
U.S. Supreme Court Justice

The American system of criminal prosecution is accusatorial, not inquisitorial, and the Fifth Amendment is its essential mainstay.
Malloy v. Hogan, 378 U.S. 1 (1964)

LEONID ILYICH BREZHNEV
(1906–1982)
Russian engineer, politician,
General Secretary of Soviet Communist party
from 1964

Communism is mankind's tomorrow.
Fiftieth Anniversary speech, Red Square, Moscow,
November 3, 1967

ROBERT BRIFFAULT
(1876–1948)
British surgeon, anthropologist, novelist

Rational Evolution (1930)

No myth of miraculous creation is so marvelous as the fact of man's evolution.

The empire of the warrior, built by the sword, perishes by the sword. The dominion of the priest, established over the minds of men, endures.

The oppressed are always morally in the right.

And holders of power are always morally in the wrong . . . power is, of its intrinsic nature, an injustice.

Democracy is the worst form of government. It is the most inefficient, the most clumsy, the most unpractical. . . . It reduces wisdom to impotence and secures the triumph of folly, ignorance, clap-trap and demagogy. . . . Yet democracy is the only form of social order admissable, because it is the only one consistent with justice.

Sin and Sex (1931)

Puritan tradition, combined with Christian management of adolescence, has converted the sexual life of civilized men and women into a neurosis.

The Mothers (1927)

The sexual instincts are the most malleable of any instincts. Let them be repressed, let their direct aim be denied them, and they will soon assume unrecognizable forms, from the depth of vice to the highest exaltation of art and religion.
Ch. 13

Women are innately conservative and, if it is true that a man learns nothing after forty, it may be said that a woman learns nothing after twenty-five.
Ch. 29

A(braham) A(rden) BRILL
(1874–1948)
American psychoanalyst

The Super-Ego is the highest mental evolution attainable by man, and consists of a precipitate of all prohibitions, all the rules of conduct which are impressed on the child by his parents and parental substitutes. The feeling of *conscience* depends altogether on the development of the Super-Ego.
Quoted in Downs, *Books that Changed the World*

EMILY BRONTË
(1818–1848)
English writer

Last Lines (1846)

No coward soul is mine,
No trembler in the world's storm-troubled
    sphere:

I see Heaven's glories shine,
And faith shines equal, arming me from
  fear.
St. 1

Vain are the thousand creeds
That move men's hearts; unutterably
  vain . . .
St. 3

RUPERT BROOKE
(1887–1915)
British poet

Sonnet (1908)

Oh! Death will find me long before I tire
  Of watching you; and swing me suddenly
Into the shade and loneliness and mire
  Of the last land!
St. 1

"The Dead" (1914)

Honour has come back, as a king, to earth,
And paid his subjects with a royal wage;
And Nobleness walks in our ways again;
And we have come into our heritage.
St. 2

"The Soldier" (1914)

If I should die, think only this of me:
That there's some corner of a foreign field
That is forever England.

PHILLIPS BROOKS
(1835–1893)
American religious leader

Sermons (1883)

In the best sense of the word, Jesus was a radical. . . . His religion has so long been identified with conservatism . . . that it is almost startling sometimes to remember that all the conservatives of his own times were against him; that it was the young, free, restless, sanguine, progressive part of the people who flocked to him.

HENRY PETER, LORD BROUGHAM
(1778–1868)
Scottish statesman, historian

The Present State of the Law (February 7, 1828)

Education makes people easy to lead, but difficult to drive; easy to govern, but impossible to enslave.

Practical Observations upon the Education of the People (1825)

To tyrants, indeed, and bad rulers, the progress of knowledge among the mass of mankind is a just object of terror; it is fatal to them and their designs.

The great Unwashed.
Attributed

CHARLES BROCKDEN BROWN
(1771–1810)
First American libertarian writer

Alcuin: A Dialogue (c. 1798)

Of all the forms of injustice, that is the most egregious which makes the circumstances of sex a reason for excluding one half of mankind from all those paths which lead to usefulness and honor.

H. RAP BROWN
American Black leader

I consider myself neither legally nor morally bound to obey the laws made by a body in which I have no representation.

We stand on the eve of a Black Revolution.
Statement written in 1967

JOHN BROWN
(1800–hanged 1859)
American abolitionist

. . . had I so interfered in behalf of the rich, the powerful, the intelligent, the so-called great, or in behalf of their children, or any of that class, and suffered and sacrificed what I have in this interference, it would have been all right, and every man in this court would have deemed it an act worthy of reward rather than punishment.
Verbatim report of hearing, New York Herald,
November 3, 1859; from last speech,
November 2, 1859

I, John Brown, am now quite certain that the crimes of this guilty land: will never be purged away; but with Blood.
Last written statement, handed to a guard
(December 2, 1859)

SIR THOMAS BROWNE
(1605–1682)
English physician, writer

Religio Medici (1643)

No man can justly censure or condemn another, because indeed no man truly knows another.

Further, no man can judge another, because no man knows himself.

Charity begins at home, is the vice of the World; yet is every man his own greatest enemy, and, as it were, his own Executioner.

Section iv

Every man is not a proper Champion for Truth, nor fit to take up the Gauntlet in the cause of Verity: Many, from the ignorance of these Maximes, and an inconsiderate Zeal unto Truth, have too rashly charged the Troops of Error, and remain as Trophies unto the enemies of Truth: A man may be in as just possession of Truth as of a City, and yet be forced to surrender; 'tis therefore far better to enjoy her with peace, than to hazard her in battle . . .

For indeed Heresies perish not with their Authors, but, like the river *Arethusa,* though they lose their currents in one place, they rise up again in another. . . . For as though there were a *Metempsychosis,* and the soul of one man passed into another; Opinions do find, after certain Revolutions, men and minds like those that first begat them.

Section vi

I could be content that we procreate like trees, without conjunction, or that there were any way to perpetuate the World without this trivial and vulgar way of coition; it is the foolishest act a wise man commits in all his life; nor is there any thing that will more deject his cool'd imagination, when he shall consider what an odd and unworthy piece of folly he hath committed.

Section ix

There is no man alone, because every man is a Microcosm, and carries the whole World about him.

Section x

Natura nihil agit frustrar (Nature does nothing in vain) is the only indisputed Axiome in Philosophy. . . .

Section xv

As Reason is a Rebel unto Faith, so Passion unto Reason: As the Propositions of Faith seem absurd unto Reason, so the Theorems of Reason unto Passion, and both unto Reason.

Section xix

It is a brave act of valour to contemn death; but where life is more terrible than death, it is then the truest valour to dare to live.

Section xliv

There is no such thing as solitude, nor any thing that can be said to be alone and by itself, but God.

Part ii, Section x

*Hydriotaphia; Urne Burial** (1658)

But the long habit of living indisposeth us for dying.

But the iniquity of oblivion blindly scattereth her poppy, and deals with the memory of men without distinction of merit of perpetuity. . . . Who knows whether the best of men be known, or whether there be not more remarkable persons forgot than any that stand remembered in the known account of time?

The Egyptian mummies, which Cambyses or time hath spared, avarice now consumeth. Mummy is become merchandise, Mizraim cures wounds, and Pharoah is sold for balsame.

There is nothing strictly immortal but immortality.

But man is a noble animal, splendid in ashes, and pompous in the grave, solemnizing nativities and deaths with equal luster nor omitting ceremonies of bravery in the infamy of his nature.

Christian Morals (pub. posthumously 1716)

Offer not only peace-offerings, but holocausts unto God; where all is due make no reserve, and cut not a cumin seed with the Almighty.

1, i

He that is chaste and continent not to impair his strength, or honest for fear of contagion, will hardly be heroically virtuous.

1, iii

---

*The full title: Hydriotaphia; Urne Burial, or a Discourse of the Sepulchral Urnes Lately Found in Norfolk.

Live not by old ethics and the classical rules of honesty. Put no new names nor notions upon authentic virtues and vices. Think not that morality is ambulatory; that vices in one age are not vices in another; or that virtues, which are under the everlasting seal of right reason, may be stamped by opinion.

1,xii

Guide not the hand of God, nor order the finger of the Almighty unto thy will and pleasure.

Pt. 3, v

Be able to be alone. Lose not the advantage of solitude, and the society of thyself.

3, ix

If length of days be thy portion, make it not thy expectation. Reckon not upon a long life: think every day the last, and live always beyond thy account. He that so often surviveth his expectations lives many lives.

3, xxx

Pseudodoxia Epidemica (Enquiries into Vulgar and Common Errors) (1646)

As for popular errors, they are more nearly founded upon an erroneous inclination of the people, as being the most deceptible part of mankind, and ready with open arms to receive the encroachments of error. . . .
Again, their individual imperfections being great, they are moreover enlarged by their aggregation; and being erroneous in their single numbers, once huddled together they will be error itself. For being a confusion of knaves and fools, and a farraginous concurrence of all conditions, tempers, sexes, and ages, it is but natural if their determinations be monstrous and many ways inconsistent with truth. And therefore wise men have always applauded their own judgment in the contradiction of that of the people.

'Tis as dangerous to be sentenced by a Physician as a Judge.

Letter to a friend

ELIZABETH BARRETT BROWNING
(1806–1861)
English poet

Aurora Leigh (1857)

Earth's fanatics make
Too frequently heaven's saints.

And we all have known
Good critics, who have stamped out poets'
hopes;
Good statesmen, who pulled ruin on the
state;
Good patriots, who for a theory, risked a
cause;
Good kings, who disembowelled for a tax;
Good popes, who brought all good to jeopardy;
Good Christians, who sat still in easy chairs,
And damned the general world for standing
up.—
Now, may the good God pardon all good
men!

Bk. IV

Since when was genius found respectable?

Bk. VI

ROBERT BROWNING
(1812–1889)
English poet

"Bishop Blougram's Apology" (1855)

You call for faith:
I show you doubt, to prove that faith exists.
The more of doubt, the stronger faith, I say,
If faith overcomes doubt.

"The Bishop Orders His Tomb at St. Praxed's Church" (1845)

And then how I shall lie through centuries,
And hear the blessed mutter of the mass,
And see God made and eaten all day long,
And feel the steady candle-flame, and taste
Good strong thick stupefying insense-smoke!

The Ring and the Book (1868–69)

Mothers, wives, and maids,
There are the tools wherewith priests manage men.

iv

. . . it is the glory and good of Art,
That Art remains the one way possible
Of speaking truth, to mouths like mine, at least.

xii

There's a new tribunal now,
Higher than God's—the educated man's.

xiii

The Two Poets of Croisic

What I call God,
And fools call Nature.

"The Inn Album" (1875)

Ignorance is not innocence but sin . . .

"Easter Day" (1850)

How very hard it is to be
A Christian!
'Tis well averred,
A scientific faith's absurd . . .

"Pippa Passes (1841)

God's in his Heaven—
All's right with the world!

"Andrea del Sarto" (1855)

Ah, but a man's reach should exceed his
grasp,
Or what's a Heaven for?

"A Death in the Desert" (1864)

. . . progress, man's distinctive mark alone,
Not God's, and not the beasts': God is, they
are,
Man partly is and wholly hopes to be.

Paracelsus (1835)

Progress is the law of life; man is not man as
yet.

ORESTES A. BROWNSON
(1803–1876)
American Unitarian, Catholic convert, founder Workingmen's Party

"The Laboring Classes"

Wages is a cunning devise of the devil for
the benefit of tender consciences, who would
retain all the advantages of the slave system,
without the expense, trouble, and odium of
being slave-holders.

Following the destruction of the Banks,
must come that of the Monopolies, of all
PRIVILEGE. . . . the greatest of them all, the
privilege which some have of being born rich
while others are born poor. It will be seen at
once that we allude to the hereditary descent
of property, an anomoly in our American system, which must be removed or the system itself will be destroyed.

The most dreadful of all wars, the war of the
poor against the rich, a war which, however

long it may be delayed, will come and come
with all its horrors.
Contribution, *Boston Quarterly,* 1840

GUIDO (Giordano) BRUNO
(1548–burned at stake, 1600)
Italian philosopher*

Heroic Furies

. . . religion is needed for restraining rude
populations, which have to be ruled, whereas
rational demonstration is for such, of a contemplative nature, as know how to rule themselves and others.

It is proof of a base and low mind for one to
wish to think with the masses or majority,
merely because the majority is the majority.
Truth does not change because it is, or is not,
believed by a majority of the people.
Quoted in Mason, *Great and Mind Liberating*
Thoughts

WILLIAM JENNINGS BRYAN
(1860–1925)
American politician, fundamentalist

Speech, 1896 Democratic Convention, won Bryan
the nomination for President

Having behind us the producing masses of
this nation and the world, supported by the
commercial interests, the laboring interests,
and the toilers everywhere, we will answer
their demand for a gold standard by saying to
them: "You shall not press down upon the
brow of labor this crown of thorns; you shall
not crucify mankind upon a cross of gold."
Quoted in *The Memoirs of William Jennings Bryan*
(1925)

Scopes trial speech (1925)

There is no more reason to believe that man
descended from an inferior animal than there
is to believe that a stately mansion has descended from a small cottage.

Man is not a mammal.**

---

*"He turned his face away from the proffered cruci-
fix and died in silence."—Santillana, *The Age of*
Adventure
**Attorney Darrow forced Bryan to repeat this incre-
dible statement several times.

If we have to give up either religion or education, we should give up education.
                    Contribution, *The Commoner,* January 1923

All the ills from which America suffers can
be traced to the teaching of evolution.
                    Address, Seventh Day Adventists, 1924

WILLIAM CULLEN BRYANT
(1794–1878)
American poet, editor

The Newspaper Press

The press, important as is its office, is but
the servant of human intellect and its ministry
is for good or evil, according to the character
of those who direct it. The press is a mill that
grinds all that is put into its hopper. Fill the
hopper with poisoned grain and it will grind it
to meal, but there is death in the bread.
                    "Prose Writings," II

Can anything be imagined more abhorrent
to every sentiment of generosity or justice than
the law which arms the rich with the legal
right to fix, by assize, the wages of the poor? If
this is not SLAVERY, we have forgotten the
definition. . . . If it be not in the colour of his
skin, and in the poor franchise of naming his
own terms in a contract for work, what advantage has the labourer of the North over the
bondman of the South?
                    Editorial on the rights of workingmen to organize
                    and strike, June 13, 1836

MARTIN BUBER
(1878–1965)
Austrian-born Israeli theologian, philosopher

Paths in Eutopia (1950)

Power abdicates only under the stress of
counter-power.

"The Listener" (1962)

I don't like religion much, and I am glad
that in the Bible the word is not to be found.
                    BBC broadcast

On Judaism (1967)

The prophet is appointed to oppose the
king, and even more: history.

ROBERT BUCHANAN
(1841–1901)
Scottish poet, novelist, playwright

The New Rome

The gods are dead, but in their name
Humanity is sold in shame.
While (then as now!) the tinsel'd Priest
Sitteth with robbers at the feast,
Blesses the laden blood-stain'd board,
Weaves garlands round the butcher's sword,
And poureth freely (now as then)
The sacramental blood of men.

PEARL S. BUCK
(1892–1973)
American writer, Nobel Prize 1938

What America Means to Me (1947)

It may be that religion is dead, and if it is,
we had better know it and set ourselves to try
to discover other sources of moral strength before it is too late.

George Villiers, 2nd DUKE OF
BUCKINGHAM
(1628–1687)
English satirist, poet, dramatist

The world is made up, for the most part, of
fools or knaves, both irreconcilable foes to
truth; the first being slaves to a blind credulity,
which we may properly call bigotry, and the
last too jealous of that power they have
usurped over the folly and ignorance of the
others, which the establishment of the empire
of reason would destroy.
                    Letter to Mr. Clifford

HENRY THOMAS BUCKLE
(1821–1862)
English historian

History of Civilization in England (1857)

Every new truth which has ever been pro-
pounded has, for a time caused mischief; it has
produced discomfort, and often unhappiness;
sometimes disturbing social and religious arrangements. . . . And if the truth is very great
as well as very new, the harm is serious. Men
are made uneasy; they flinch; they cannot bear

the sudden light; a general restlessness supervenes; the face of society is disturbed, or perhaps convulsed; old interests and old beliefs have been destroyed before new ones have been created. These symptoms are the precursors of revolution; they have preceded all the great changes through which the world has passed.

BUDDHA (Siddhārtha Guatama)
(c. 563 B.C.—483 B.C.)
The last historical Buddha*

The Sermon at Benares

These two extremes, monks, are not to be practiced by one who has gone forth from the world. What are the two? That conjoined with the passions and luxury, low, vulgar, common, ignoble, and useless. Avoiding the two extremes the Tathagata [the Perfect One, or the Buddha] has gained the enlightenment of the Middle Path, which produces insight and knowledge, and tends to calm, to higher knowledge, enlightenment, Nirvana.

This is the noble Eightfold way: namely, right view, right intention, right speech, right action, right livelihood, right effort, right mindfulness, right concentration. This, monks, is the Middle Path, of which the Taghagata has gained enlightenment, which produces insight and knowledge, and tends to calm, to higher knowledge, enlightenment, Nirvana.

Now this, monks, is the noble truth of pain: Birth is painful, old age is painful, sickness is painful, death is painful, sorrow, lamentation, dejection, and despair are painful. Contact with unpleasant things, not getting what one wishes is painful. In short, the five groups of grasping [skandhas] are painful.

Now this, monks, is the noble truth of the cause of pain: the craving, which tends to rebirth, combined with pleasure and lust, finding pleasure here and there; namely, the

---

*". . . the last historical Buddha, whose family name was Gotama . . . son of Suddhotana, one of the chiefs of the tribe of Sakiyas." *Britannica,* 11th ed., IV, p. 737, ed. E. A. Burt. *The Compassionate Buddha* gives date of birth 544 B.C., family name Gautama, given name Siddhārtha. According to this source, the Buddhist Scriptures were "first committed to writing several generations after his death."

craving for passion, the craving for existence, the craving for nonexistence.

Georges Louis Leclerc, COMTE DE BUFFON
(1707–1788)
French naturalist

Le style est l'homme même.
Style is the man himself.
Discourse, *Académie Française,* August 25, 1753

Le Génie, c'est la patience.
Genius is patience.
Attributed by H. de Seychelles

NIKOLAI IVANOVICH BUKHARIN
(1888–1939)
Soviet Russian theoretician

The ABC of Communism

Religion was and continues to be one of the most powerful instruments in the hands of the oppressors, for the maintenance of inequality, for the exploitation and for the servile obedience of the workers. . . . Religion and Communism are incompatible theoretically as well as practically. . . . A Communist who rejects the commandments of religion and acts according to the orders of the party, ceases to be a believer. On the contrary, a believer who pretends to be a Communist, but who breaks the orders of the party in the name of the commandments of religion, ceases to be a Communist.

Faith in God and the devil, in good and evil spirits, in a word, in religion, is a means of confusing the national consciousness. . . . Science has shown that religion began with the worship of dead ancestors. . . . Man began first by worshipping them; the worship of dead rich men is thus the basis of religion. . . . When the Hebrews were ruled by their princes, who punished and tortured them in every way, there arose the doctrine of a severe and wrathful God, the God of the Old Testament. He was a cruel old man who mercilessly chastised his subjects. . . .

Faith in God is thus a reflection of loathsome earthly conditions; it is faith in a slavery which exists, presumably, not only on earth but throughout the Universe.

Works (Steklov edition)

Where there is no religion, no state can exist. Religion is the substance and essence of the life of any state.

II

Bukharin and Preobrazhensky

Socialism is Communism in course of construction; it is incomplete Communism.

BULWER-LYTTON, *see* **Lytton**

RALPH J. BUNCHE
(1904–1971)
American diplomat

There are no warlike people—just warlike leaders.

Address, United Nations

LUIS BUÑUEL
(1900–1983)
Spanish movie maker

The sexual act cannot be reduced to a chapter on hygienics; it is an exciting, dark, sinful, diabolical experience. Sex is a black tarantula and sex without religion is like an egg without salt. . . . Sex multiplies the possiblities of desire.

A writer or painter cannot change the world. But they can keep an essential margin of nonconformity alive. Thanks to them the powerful can never affirm that everyone agrees with their acts. That small difference is very important. When power feels itself totally justified and approved it immediately destroys whatever freedom we have left; and that is Fascism.

Quoted by Carlos Fuentes, contribution, *New York Times Magazine,* March 11, 1973.

JOHN BUNYAN
(1628–1688)
English writer, allegorist

Instructions for the Ignorant (1675)

Question: What kind of sins are the greatest? Answer: Adultery, fornication, murder, theft, swearing, lying, covetousness, witchcraft, sedition, heresies, or any of the like.

Pilgrim's Progress (1678)

When they were got out of the wilderness, they presently saw a town before them, and the name of that town is Vanity; and at the town there is a fair kept, called Vanity Fair. At this fair are all such merchandise sold as houses, lands, trades, places, honors, preferments, titles, countries, kingdoms, lusts, pleasures and delights of all sorts, as whores, bawds, wives, husbands, children, masters, servants, lives, blood, bodies, souls, silver, gold, pearls, precious stones, and what not.

Then went the jury out, whose names were, Mr. Blind-man, Mr. No-good, Mr. Malice, Mr. Love-lust, Mr. Live-loose, Mr. Heady, Mr. High-mind, Mr. Enmity, Mr. Liar, Mr. Cruelty, Mr. Hate-light, and Mr. Implacable; who everyone gave in his private verdict against him among themselves, and afterwards unanimously concluded to bring him in guilty before the judge.

. . . a man who could look no way but downward, with a muck-rake in his hand. *

One leak will sink a ship; and one gin will destroy a sinner.

Grace Abounding to the Chief of Sinners (1666)

If all the fornicators and adulterers in England were hanged by the neck till they be dead, John Bunyan, the object of their envy, would be still alive and well.

LUTHER BURBANK
(1849–1926)
American horticultural scientist

Science is knowledge arranged and classified according to truth, facts, and the general laws of nature.

The lure of happiness and the fear of pain are fundamental qualities possessed by all living things and are the two forces which have through untold millenniums kept what we usually call life from destruction by the ever encroaching outside forces of destruction.

Life is heredity plus environment.

---

*The original use of the word, which inspired Theodore Roosevelt in his criticism of muckrakers, q.v.

The God within us is the only available God we know and the clear light of science teaches us that we must be our own saviours.
Quoted in San Francisco Bulletin, January 22, 1926

JAKOB CHRISTOPH BURCKHARDT
(1818–1897)
Swiss historian

Reflections on History (1943)

Lasting peace not only leads to enervation; it permits the rise of a mass of precarious, fear-ridden, distressful lives which would not have survived without it and which nevertheless clamour for their "rights," cling somehow to existence, bar the way to genuine ability, thicken the air and as a whole degrade the nation's blood. War restores real ability to honour. As for these wretched lives, war may at least reduce them to silence.

Further, war, which is simply the subjection of all life and property to one momentary aim, is morally vastly superior to the mere violent egoism of the individual; it develops power in the service of a supreme general idea and under a discipline which nevertheless permits supreme heroic virtue to unfold. Indeed, war alone grants to mankind the magnificent spectacle of a general submission to a general aim.
Ch. 4

FRANK GELETT BURGESS
(1866–1951)
American writer

Without bigots, eccentrics, cranks and heretics the world would not progress.
Attributed

EDMUND BURKE
(1729–1797)
British statesman, political writer

A Vindication of Natural Society (1756)*

A man is allowed sufficient freedom of thought, provided he knows how to choose his

*"This essay is little known as he was compelled by the storm of opposition it met to withdraw it from publication. The reader will not find it in 'Burke's Complete (?) Works.' "—Sprading, *Liberty and the Great Libertarians,* 1913, p. 60.

subject properly. . . . But the scene is changed as you come homeward, and atheism or treason may be the names given in Britain to what would be reason and truth if asserted in China.

The miseries derived to mankind from superstition under the name of religion, and of ecclesiastical tyranny under the name of church government, have been clearly and usefully exposed. We begin to think and to act from reason and from nature alone. This is true of several, but still is by far the majority in the same old state of blindness and slavery; and much is to be feared that we shall perpetually relapse, while the real productive cause of all this superstitious folly, enthusiastical nonsense, and holy tyranny hold a reverend place in the estimation even of those who are otherwise enlightened.

But whoever is a genuine follower of Truth keeps his eye steady upon his guide, indifferent whither he is led, provided that she is his leader.

Where mystery begins religion ends.

All writers on the science of policy are agreed, and they agree with experience, that all governments must frequently infringe the rules of justice to support themselves; that truth must give way to dissimulation, honesty to convenience, and humanity itself to the reigning of interest. The whole of this mystery of iniquity is called the reason of state.

Ask of politicians the ends for which laws were originally designed, and they will answer that the laws were designed as a protection for the poor and the weak, against the oppression of the rich and powerful. . . .

The most obvious division of society is into rich and poor, and it is no less obvious that the number of the former bear a great disproportion to those of the latter. The whole business of the poor is to administer to the idleness, folly, and luxury of the rich, and that of the rich, in return, is to find the best methods of confirming the slavery and increasing the burdens of the poor. In a state of nature it is an invariable law that a man's acquisitions are in proportion to his labors. In a state of artificial society it is a law as constant and as invariable that those who labor must enjoy the fewest things, and that those who labor not at all have the greatest number of enjoyments. A constitution of things this, strange and ridiculous beyond expression!

Power gradually extirpates from the mind every human and gentle virtue. Pity, benevolence, friendship, are things almost unknown in high stations.

We are indebted for all our miseries to our distrust of that guide which Providence thought sufficient for our condition,—our own reason, which rejecting, both in human and Divine things, we have given our necks to the yoke of political and theological slavery.

We first throw away the tales along with the rattles of our nurses; those of the priest keep their hold a little longer; those of the government the longest of all.

From the earliest dawnings of policy to this day, the invention of man has been sharpening and improving the mystery of murder, from the first rude essays of clubs and stones, to the present perfection of gunnery.

Thoughts on the Cause of the Present Discontents (1770)

When bad men combine, the good must associate; otherwise they will fall, one by one, an unpitied sacrifice in a contemptible struggle.

Speeches

Falsehood is a perennial spring.

To tax and to please, no more than to love and to be wise, is not given to men.
On American Taxation, April 19, 1774

Depend upon it, that the lovers of freedom will be free.
To the electors of Bristol, 1774

Abstract liberty, like other mere abstractions, is not to be found.

All government, indeed every human benefit and enjoyment, every virtue, and every prudent act, is founded on compromise and barter. . . . Man acts from motives relative to his interests; and not on metaphysical speculations.

The concessions of the weak are the concessions of fear.
On Conciliation with the American Colonies, March 22, 1775

All wealth is power, so power must infallibly draw wealth to itself by some means or other.
Commons, February 11, 1780

The people never give up their liberties but under some delusion.
1784

There is one thing and one thing only, which defies all mutation: that which existed before the world, and will survive the fabric of the world itself—I mean justice.
On the impeachment of Warren Hastings

Reflections on the Revolution in France (1790)

Make the Revolution a parent of settlement, and not a nursery of future revolutions.

The power of perpetuating our property in our families is one of the most valuable and interesting circumstances belonging to it, and that which tends the most to the perpetuation of society itself.

We know . . . that man is by his constitution a religious animal; that atheism is against, not only our reason, but our instincts; that it cannot prevail long.

I love a manly, moral, regulated liberty.

Of this I am certain, that in a democracy the majority of the citizens is capable of exercising the most cruel oppressions upon the minority . . . and that oppression of the minority will extend to far greater numbers, and will be carried on with much greater fury, than can almost ever be apprehended from the dominion of a single sceptre.

Kings will be tyrants from policy, when subjects are rebels from principle.

An enlightened self-interest. . . .

But the age of chivalry is gone. That of the sophisters, economists, and calculators has succeeded; and the glory of Europe is extinguished forever.

A State without the means of some change is without the means of its conservation.

A perfect democracy is therefore the most shameless thing in the world. As it is the most shameless, it is the most fearless.

Superstition is the religion of feeble minds.

Letters on a Regicide Peace (1797)

Manners are of more importance than laws. Upon them, in a great measure, the laws depend. The law touches us but here and there, and now and then. Manners are what vex or smooth, corrupt or purify, exalt or debase, barbarize or refine us, by a constant, steady, uniform, insensible operation, like that of the air we breathe in. They give their whole form and color to our lives. According to their quality, they aid morals, they support them, or they totally destroy them.

The blood of man should have never been shed but to redeem the blood of man. It is well shed for our family, for our friends, for our God, for our country, for our kind. The rest is vanity; the rest is crime.

War never leaves where it found a nation.

Among a people generally corrupt, liberty cannot long exist.
Letter to the Sheriffs of Bristol, April 3, 1777

The tyranny of the multitude is a multiplied tyranny.
Letter to Thomas Mercer, February 26, 1790

The only thing necessary for the triumph of evil is for good men to do nothing.
Attributed*

ROBERT BURNS
(1756–1796)
Scottish poet

Letters of Robert Burns (1831), Vol. 1

. . . a certain delicious Passion, which in spite of acid disappointment, gin-house Prudence and bookworm Philosophy, I hold to be the first of human joys, our dearest pleasure here below.
Memorandum for Dr. John Moore, August 1787

I have a hundred times wished that one could resign life as an officer resigns a commission. . . .
to Mrs. Dunlop, January 21, 1788

O, what a peacemaker is a guid weel-willy p--le.** It is the mediator, the guarantee, the umpire, the bond of union, the solemn league

and covenant, the plenipotentiary, the Aaron's rod, the Jacob's staff, the prophet Elisah's pot of oil, the Ahaseurus' sceptre, the sword of mercy, the philosospher's stone, the horn of plenty, the Tree of Life between man and woman.
to Robert Ainslie, March 3, 1788

Man is naturally a kind, benevolent animal, but he is dropt into such a damn'd needy situation here in this vexatious world, and has such a whoreson, hungry, growling, multiplying Pack of Necessities, Appetites, Passions & Desires about him, ready to devour him, for want of other food; that in fact he must lay aside his cares for others that he may look properly to himself.—Every One, more or less, in the words of the old Scots Proverb, "Has his cods in a cloven stick, and maun wyse them out the best way he can."—
June 30, 1788

All my fears and cares are of this world; if there is another, an honest man has nothing to fear from it.

"Epistle to the Rev. John McMath"
The upright, honest-hearted man
Who strives to do the best he can,
Need never fear the church's ban
Or hell's damnation.

"Ode for General Washington's Birthday"

But come, ye sons of Liberty
Columbia's offspring, brave as free,
In danger's hour still flaming in the van,
Ye know, and dare maintain, the Royalty of
Man.

"The Author's Earnest Cry and Prayer"
Freedom and whiskey gang thegither.

"The Rights of Woman" (1792)
While Europe's eye is fix'd on mighty
things,
The fate of empires and the fall of kings;
While quacks of state must each produce his
plan,
And even children lisp the Rights of Man;
Amid this mighty fuss just let me mention,
The Rights of women merit some attention.

"Robert Bruce's March to Bannockburn"
By oppression's woes and pains,
By our sons in servile chains,
We will drain our dearest veins,
But we shall be free.

---

*This quotation is probably the best known of all Burke's remarks, credited to him in many books, anthologies, etc. It is not to be found in the eight volumes of Burke letters, although it is frequently listed as part of a letter to William Smith dated 9 January 1795, nor is it in any letter to Mr. Smith. The quotation has been used for many years as a public service just before national or state elections by a leading advertising agency, Young & Rubicam. It occupied whole pages of the *New York Times,* but neither Young & Rubicam nor the *Times* was able to give the source when requested by G.S.
**This word censored by Burns or his publisher, not the present compiler.

Lay the proud usurper low!
Tyrants fall in every foe!
Liberty's in every blow!
Forward! let us do, or die!

[second version]

"The Cotter's Saturday Night"

Princes and lords are but the breath of
kings.
"An honest man's the noblest work of God."

"A Dedication to Gavin Hamilton"

Morality, thou deadly bane,
Thy tens o'thousands thou hast slain!

"Man was Made to Mourn"

Man—whose heaven-erected face
The smiles of love adorn—
Man's inhumanity to man
Makes countless thousands mourn.

"Second Epistle to Mr. Graham of Fintry" (1791)

Critics—appalled, I venture on the name,
Those cut-throat bandits in the paths of
fame:

JOHN BURROUGHS
(1837–1921)
American naturalist and author

The Light of Day

The deeper our insight into the methods of
nature . . . the more incredible the popular
Christianity seems to me.

Science has done more for the development
of western civilization in one hundred years
than Christianity did in eighteen hundred
years.

ROBERT BURTON (Democritus Jr.)
(1577–1640)
English clergyman

The Anatomy of Melancholy (1621)

One religion is as good as another.

As the saying is, *homo solus aut deus, aut
daemon:* a man alone is either a Saint or a
devil.*

---

*See Aristotle, *Politics*, Bk. 1, and Bacon *Essays*,
"Of Friendship."

Love indeed (I may not deny) first united
provinces, built cities, and by a perpetual generation makes and preserves mankind; but if it
rage it has no more love, but burning lust, a
disease, frenzy, madness, hell. . . .

It subverts kingdoms, overthrows cities,
towns, families; mars, corrupts and makes a
massacre of men; thunder and lightning, wars,
fires, plagues, have not done the mischief as
this burning lust, this brutish passion.

The greatest enemy to man is man.

It is believable because incredible.

If there is hell upon earth, it is to be found
in a melancholy man's heart.

If adversity hath killed his thousands, prosperity hath killed his ten thousands; therefore
adversity is to be preferred. The one deceives,
the other instructs; the one is miserably happy,
the other happily miserable; and therefore
many philosophers have voluntarily sought adversity and commend it in their precepts.

He who goes to law . . . holds a wolf by the
ear.

One man has never married, and that's his
hell; another is, and that's his plague.

I say with Didacus Stella, a dwarf standing
on the shoulders of a giant may see farther
than a giant himself.

BISHOP RICHARD DE BURY
(1287–1345)
Chancellor of England

Philobiblion (1345)

All the glory of the world would be buried
in oblivion, unless God had provided mortals
with the remedy of books.

HERMANN BUSENBAUM (or
Busembaum)
(1600–1688)
German Jesuit priest, writer

Medulla Theologiae Moralis (1645)*

When the end is lawful, the means are also
lawful.

---

*Researchers deny that either Machiavelli or the So-
ciety of Jesus is the author of the common saying,
"The end justifies the means." Lord Chief Justice
Wilmot wrote (Collins v. Blantern, 1767), "The end
directs and sanctifies the means."

SAMUEL BUTLER
(1612–1680)
English poet, satirist

Miscellaneous Thoughts

Opinion governs all mankind,
Like the blind's leading of the blind . . .

Authority intoxicates,
And makes mere sots of magistrates;
The fumes of it invade the brain,
And make men giddy, proud, and vain . . .

The souls of women are so small,
That some believe they've none at all . . .
                          I, 386 (c. 1680)

SAMUEL BUTLER
(1835–1902)
English writer

Note-Books

All progress is based upon a universal innate desire on the part of every organism to live beyond its income.

Is life worth living? That is a question for an embryo, not a man.

The three most important things a man has are, briefly, his private parts, his money, and his religious opinions.

Life is the art of drawing sufficient conclusions from insufficient premises.
                          I

Virtue is, as it were, the repose of sleep or death. Vice is the awakening of knowledge of good and evil—without which there is no life worthy of the name.
                          II

God and man are powerless without one another.

Genius is a nuisance, and it is the duty of schools and colleges to abate it by setting genius-traps in its way.

It is curious that money, which is the most valuable thing in life, *excepis excipiendis,* should be the most fatal corrupter of music, literature, painting and all the arts. As soon as any art is pursued with a view of money, then farewell, in ninety-nine cases out of a hundred, all hope of genuine good work.

. . . genius . . . is no respecter of time, trouble, money or persons, the four things around which human affairs turn most persistently.
                          XI

An honest God's the noblest work of man.

To live is like to love—all reason is against it, and all healthy instinct for it.

Independence is essential for permanent but fatal to immediate success.

An Apology to the Devil. It must be remembered that we have heard only one side of the case. God has written all the books.
                          XIV

God and the Devil are an effort after specialization and division of labor.

As long as there will be an unknown there will be a God. . . .
                          XX

Christianity is a woman's religion, invented by women and womanish men for themselves. The Church's one foundation is not Christ, as is commonly said, it is woman; and calling the Madonna the Queen of Heaven is only a poetical way of acknowledging that women are the main support of the priests.
                          XXI

Theist and Atheist
The fight between them is as to whether God shall be called God or shall have some other name.

Life is not an exact science, it is an art.
                          XXII

To himself everyone is an immortal; he may know that he is going to die, but he can never know that he is dead.

If life is an illusion, then so is death—the greatest of all illusions. If life must not be taken too seriously—then neither must death.
                          XXIII

George Gordon, LORD BYRON
(1788–1824)
English poet

"Childe Harold's Pilgrimage" (1809–17)

Hereditary bondsmen! know yet not
Who would be free *themselves* must strike
    the blow?
                          Canto II, lxxvi

He who surpasses or subdues mankind,
Must look down on the hate of those below.

Canto III, xlv

'Tis solitude should teach us how to die;
It hath no flatterers; vanity can give
No hollow aid; alone—man with his God
must strive.

Canto IV, xxxiii

Yet, Freedom! yet the banner, torn, but
flying,
Streams like the thunderstorm *against* the
wind!

Canto IV, xcvii

"The Prisoner of Chillon" (1816)

Eternal Spirit of the Chainless Mind!
—Brightest in dungeons, Liberty! thou art:
—For there thy habitation is the heart—
The heart which love of thee alone can
bind. . . .

"Marino Faliero" (1820)

They never fail who die
In a great cause: the block may soak their
gore;
Their heads may sodden in the sun; their
limbs
Be strung to city gates and castle walls—
But still their spirit walks abroad.

"Don Juan" (1821)

All tragedies are finish'd by a death
All comedies are ended by a marriage.

Pleasure's a sin, and sometimes
Sin's a pleasure.

'Tis melancholy, and a fearful sign
Of human frailty, folly, also crime,
That love and marriage rarely can combine,
Although they both are born in the same
clime.

Adversity is the first path to truth.

. . . the spouseless virgin *Knowledge* . . .

What men call gallantry, and gods adultery,
Is much more common where the climate's
sultry.

Christians have burned each other quite
persuaded

That all the Apostles would have done as
they did.

"Let there be light!" said God, "and there
was light."
"Let there be blood!" said man, and there's
a sea.

Let us have wine and women, mirth and
laughter,
Sermons and soda-water the day after.

In her first passion woman loves her lover,
In all the others all she loves is love.

"The Giaour" (1813)

For Freedom's battle, once begun
Bequeath'd by bleeding Sire to Son,
Though baffled oft, is ever won.

"English Bards and Scotch Reviewers" (1809)

Shrink not from blasphemy—it will pass for
wit.

Diary

What is democracy?—an aristocracy of
blackguards.

May, 1821

I wish men to be free, as much from mobs
as from kings—from you as me.

Byron's Letters and Journals, ed. Marchand

The grand *primum mobile* of England is
cant; cant political, cant poetical, cant religious, cant moral, but always cant, multiplied
through all the varieties of life.

To John Murray

Those who swallow their Deity, really and
truly, in transubstantiation, can hardly find
anything else otherwise than easy of digestion.

To Thomas Moore, March 8, 1822

They say that knowledge is power. I used to
think so, but I now know that they mean
money.

To Douglas Kinnaird

PIERRE J. G. CABANIS
(1757–1808)
French physician, writer

Epigrams

A man is as old as his arteries.
(cf. Bogomoletz)

CAIUS JULIUS CAESAR
(100–44 B.C.)
Roman general, statesman, historian*

The Gallic Wars

Fere libenter homines id quod volunt, credunt.
Men willingly believe what they wish.
"De Bello Gallico," III, 18

In his Pontic triumph he displayed among the show-pieces of the procession an inscription of but three words, "I came, I saw, I conquered," (*Veni, vidi, vici*), not indicating the events of the war, as the others did, but the speed with which it was finished.

Then Caesar cried: "Take we the course which the signs of the Gods and the false dealings of our foes point out! The die is cast," said he. (*Iacta alea est.*)

Et tu Brute. **
Quoted in Suetonius, The Lives of the Caesars: The Deified Julius

. . . all men who deliberate upon difficult questions ought to be free from hatred and friendship, anger and pity.
Quoted in Crispus C. Sallustius, "The War with Catiline" (tr. J. C. Rolphe) I, 1.

---

*Aulus Hirtius is credited with writing parts of Caesar's Commentaries, and the eighth book of *The Gallic Wars*.
**Suetonius writes that Caesar, speaking Greek, said *"Kai su teknon"* ["You too, my child?"] (Rolphe tr., p. 111).

When the swords flash, let no idea of love, piety, or even the face of your fathers move you. If they oppose you, let the blood of your own fathers flow from your blade.
Attributed by Lucan; quoted by Montaigne

PEDRO CALDERON DE LA BARCA
(1600–1681)
Spanish dramatist, poet

La Vida es Sueño [Life is a Dream]

It is man's greatest crime to have been born.

CALGACUS
(c. 85 A.D.)
Caledonian tribal chief

Atque ubi colitudinum faciunt pacem appellant.
They create a desolation and call it peace.
Quoted in Tacitus, Agricola (tr. H. Mattingly p. 80)

JOHN C. CALHOUN
(1782–1850)
American statesman

Speeches

A power has risen up in the government greater than the people themselves, consisting of many, and various, and powerful interests, combined into one mass, and held together by the cohesive power of the vast surplus in the banks.
On the Public Deposits, May 28, 1836*

There never has yet existed a wealthy and civilized society in which one portion of the community did not, in point of fact, live on the labour of the other.
On the Reception of Abolition Petitions, February, 1837

Many in the South once believed that it (slavery) was a moral and political evil. That folly and delusion are gone. We see it now in its true light and regard it as the most safe and stable basis for free institutions in the world.
January 12, 1838

---

*Frequently but falsely attributed to Lincoln.

CALLIMACHUS*
(fl. 250 B.C.)
Greek poet, grammarian

Still are thy pleasant voices, thy nightingales, awake; for death, he taketh all away, but them he cannot take.

Epigram 80

A good man never dies.

Epigram 451

A great book, a great evil.**
Quoted in Athenaeus, *The Doctors at Dinner*, 72ᵃ

JOHN CALVIN
(né Jean Chauvin or Caulvin)
(1509–1564)
French protestant reformer

Institutes of the Christian Religion (1536)

God foreordained, for His own glory and the display of His attributes of mercy and justice, a part of the human race, without any merit of their own, to eternal salvation, and another part, in just punishment of their sin, to eternal damnation.

The interdiction of marriage to priests was an act of impious tyranny, not only contrary to the word of God, but at war with every principle of justice.

God, who is perfect righteousness, cannot love the iniquity which He sees in all. All of us, therefore, have that within us which deserves the hatred of God.

And therefore the very infants themselves, since they bring with them their own damnation from their mother's womb, are bound not by another's but by their own fault. For although they have not as yet brought forth the fruits of their own iniquity, yet they have the seeds thereof inclosed within them; yea, their whole nature is a certain seed of sin.

---

*From *Greek Anthologies*, Book 7, tr. W. J. Cory.
**The word "great" is interpreted as "large" or "long" by critics.

CHARLES PRATT, 1st Earl Camden
(1714–1794)
Lord Chancellor of England

The great end for which men entered into society was to preserve their property. That right is preserved sacred and incommunicable in all instances where it has not been taken away or abridged by some public law for the good of the whole.

Judgment, Entick *v.* Carrington, 1765

TOMMASO CAMPANELLA
(1568–1639)
Italian philosopher

"The People"

The people is a beast of muddy brain
That knows not its own strength.

(cf. Alexander Hamilton)

ALBERT CAMUS
(1913–1960)
Algeria-born French novelist, Nobel Prize 1957

The Fall (1957)

Don't wait for the last judgment—it takes place every day.

We cannot assert the innocence of anyone, whereas we can state with certainty the guilt of all. Every man testifies to the crime of all the others—that is my faith and hope.

Truth, like light, blinds. Falsehood, on the contrary, is a beautiful twilight that enhances every object.

Summer in Algiers (1938)

If there is a sin against life, it consists perhaps not so much in despairing of life as in hoping for another life and in eluding the implacable grandeur of this life.

The Myth of Sisyphus (1955)

I want everything to be explained to me or nothing. . . . The absurd springs from this confrontation between the human call and the unreasonable silence of the world.

The absurd is the essential concept of the first truth.

There is but one truly serious philosophical problem, and that is suicide. Judging whether life is or is not worth living amounts to answering the fundamental question of philosophy.

There exists an obvious fact that seems utterly moral: namely, that a man is always a prey to his truths. Once he has admitted them, he cannot free himself from them.

It was previously a question of finding out whether or not life had to have a meaning to be lived. It has now become clear, on the contrary, that it will be lived all the better if it has no meaning.

To think is first of all to create a world (or to limit one's own world, which comes to the same thing).

But crushing truths perish from being acknowledged.

Notebooks I (1935–42)

A guilty conscience needs to confess. A work of art is a confession.

Turning its back to skepticism . . . humanity strives to find a truth. It will relax when society has found an error that is livable.

Beauty is unbearable . . . offering us for a minute the glimpse of an eternity that we should like to stretch over the whole of time.

Man, at bottom, is not entirely guilty, since he did not begin history, nor entirely innocent, since he continues it.

Notebooks IV (1942–51)

If Christianity is pessimistic as to man, it is optimistic as to human destiny. Marxism, pessimistic as to destiny, pessimistic as to human nature, is optimistic as to the progress of history.

He who despairs of events is a coward, but he who hopes for the human lot is a fool.

An achievement is a bondage. It obliges one to a higher achievement.

The Plague (1948)

Can one be a saint without God: this is the only concrete problem I know today.

Since the order of the world is shaped by death, mustn't it be better for God if we refuse to believe in Him, and struggle with all our might against death, without raising our eyes towards heaven where He sits in silence.

The Rebel (1954)

Revolt and revolution both wind up at the same crossroads: the police, or folly.

Nobel Prize Speech (1957)

In all circumstances of his life, the writer can recapture the feelings of a living community that will justify him. But only if he accepts as completely as possible the two trusts that constitute the nobility of his calling: the service of truth and the service of freedom.

True artists scorn nothing.

CANON LAW

Concerning players, we have thought it fit to excommunicate them so long as they continue to act.
First Council of Arles, Decree (314)

Let bishops, priests, and deacons, and in general all the clergy who are employed in the service of the altar, abstain from conjugal intercourse with their wives and the begetting of children; let those who persist be degraded from the ranks of the clergy.
Council of Elvira (c. 300)

Under coercion a man may sin except with respect to idolatry, incest and murder.
Council of Lydda, Decree (132)

We believe . . . in one Lord Jesus Christ, the Son of God, born of the Father . . . of the substance of the Father, God from God . . . born, not made, consubstantial with the Father.
"The Nicene Creed," Council of Nicaea (325)

The Church abhors bloodshed.
Council of Tours, Decree (1163)*

---

*In obedience to this decree the Spanish Inquisition introduced the *auto da fé*—heretics were burned alive in the public squares without any blood being shed.

If any one saith that the sacraments of the new law were not all instituted by Jesus Christ, our Lord, or that they are more or less than seven, to wit, baptism, confirmation, the eucharist, penance, extreme unction, orders, and matrimony; or even that any one of these seven is not truly and properly a sacrament; let him be anathema.
Council of Trent, Decree (1545)

If anyone asserts that the sin of Adam injured himself alone, and not his posterity . . . let him be anathema.
Decree, Session 5 (June 17, 1546)

If any one saith that since Adam's sin the freewill of man is lost and extinguished; . . . let him be anathema.
Session 6, Canon 5 (January 15, 1547)

If any one saith that the marriage state is to be placed above the state of virginity or of celibacy and that it is no better or more blessed to remain in virginity or in celibacy than to be united in matrimony, let him be anathema.
Session 24, Canon 10 (November 11, 1563)

If anyone says that the Church is in error when she decides that for many reasons husband and wife may separate from bed and board and for cohabitation for a definite period of time or even indefinitely; let him be anathema.
Council 8 (November 1563)

If any shall say that in the holy sacrament of the eucharist there remains the substance of the bread and wine, and shall deny the wonderful and singular conversion of the whole substance of the bread into the body of our Lord Jesus Christ and of the wine into His blood, the species only of the bread and wine remaining, let him be anathema.
Decree xiii (1563)

Whereas the power of conferring indulgences was granted by Christ to the Church. . . . the Sacred Holy synod teaches and enjoins the use of indulgences is to be retained in the church; it condemns with anathema those who either assert that they are useless, or who deny that there is in the Church the power of granting them.
Decree, Session 25 (December 4, 1563)

God does not ask the impossible.
Decree vi (1564)

CANUTE "THE GREAT"
(995–1035)
King of England and Denmark

I want no money raised by injustice.
"Letter of State," 1027; after pilgrimage to Rome.

AL CAPONE
(1899–1947)
American gangster

Bolshevism is knocking at our gates, we can't afford to let it in. . . . We must keep America whole and safe and unspoiled. We must keep the worker away from red literature and red ruses; we must see that his mind remains healthy.
Contribution, *Liberty* Magazine

CARLO CARAFFA
(fl. 16th century)
Cardinal, nephew of Giovanni Pietro Caraffa, who was Pope Paul IV

Populus vult decipi, decipiatur.
The people want to be deceived, let them be deceived.
Attributed (spoken to Pope Paul IV)

GIOSUÈ CARDUCCI
(1836–1907)
Italian poet

When Caesar shakes hands with Peter,
Human blood flows;
When the Church and the Empire embrace,
The star of a martyr is lit in the heavens.

THOMAS CARLYLE
(1795–1881)
Scottish historian, sociological writer

Chartism (1839)

Democracy is, by the nature of it, a self-cancelling business: and gives in the long run a net result of zero.

Critical and Miscellaneous Essays

. . . the three great elements of modern civilization, Gunpowder, Printing, and the Protestant Religion.

Literary men are . . . a perpetual priesthood.
"State of German Literature," *Edinburgh Review,*
No. XCII, 1827

Man seldom, or rather never for a length of time and deliberately, rebels against anything that does not deserve rebelling against.

Everywhere the human soul stands between a hemisphere of light and another of darkness; on the confines of the two everlasting empires, necessity and free will.

Love is ever the beginning of Knowledge as fire is of light.
"Goethe," *Foreign Review,* No. 111, 1828

Silence is deep as Eternity; speech is shallow as Time.
"Memoirs of the Life of Scott," *London and
Westminster Review,* Nos. XII and LV, 1838

All reform except a moral one will prove unavailing.
"Burns," *Edinburgh Review,* No. XCVI, 1828

The great law of culture is, Let each become all that he was created capable of being; expand, if possible, to his full growth; resisting all impediments, casting off all foreign, especially all noxious adhesions, and show himself at length in his own shape and stature, be these what they may.
"John Paul Friedrich Richter," *Edinburgh Review,*
No. XCI, 1827

As long as our civilization is essentially one of property, of fences, of exclusiveness, it will be mocked by delusions.
"Napoleon"

Perpetual modernness is the measure of merit in every work of art.

No power of genius has ever yet had the smallest success in explaining existence.
"Plato"

What is all knowledge too but recorded experience, and a product of history; of which, therefore, reasoning and belief, no less than action and passion, are essential materials.
"On History," *Fraser's Magazine,* Vol. II, no. X,
1830

Life of Frederick the Great (1860)

Genius (which means transcendent capacity of taking trouble, first of all).
Bk. IV, Ch. 3

Happy the people whose annals are blank in history books!
Bk. XVI, Ch. 1

The French Revolution (1837)

Aristocracy of Feudal Parchment has passed away with a mighty rushing; and now, by a natural course, we arrive at the Aristocracy of the Moneybag . . . the basest yet known.

Free? Understand that well, it is the deep commandment, dimmer or clearer, of our whole being, to be *free.* Freedom is the one purport, wisely aimed at, or unwisely, of all man's struggles, toiling, and sufferings on this earth.

"Heroes and Hero-Worship," lectures, London (May 5, 8 and 19, 1840)

The first duty of man is that of subduing fear. We must get rid of fear; we cannot act at all till then. A man's acts are slavish, not true but specious; his very thoughts are false, he thinks too as a slave and coward, till he has got fear under his feet.

In books lies the *soul* of the whole past time; the articulate, audible voice of the past, when the body and material substance of it has altogether vanished like a dream.

Society is founded on hero worship.

No great man lives in vain. The history of the world is but the biography of great men.

Past and Present (1843)

All work is noble; work is alone noble.

The latest Gospel in this world is, Know thy work and do it. "Know Thyself": long enough has that poor "self" of thine tormented thee; thou will never get to "know" it, I believe! Think it not thy business, this of knowing thyself; thou are an unknowable individual; know what thou canst work at; and work at it, like a Hercules! That will be thy better plan.

Blessed is he who has found his work; let him ask no other blessedness, he has a work, a life-purpose; he has found it and will follow it.
Bk III, Ch. 4

Sartor Resartus (1831)

We do everything by custom, even believe in it; . . . What is philosophy but a continual battle against custom; an ever-renewed effort to transcend the sphere of blind custom, and so become transcendental?

That there should one Man die ignorant who had capacity for Knowledge, this I call tragedy.

The fearful Unbelief is unbelief in yourself.

Be not a slave of words.

The man who cannot laugh is not only fit for treasons, strategems, and spoils, but his whole life is already a treason and a strategem.

Shall I tell you what is the most intolerable sort of slavery, the slavery over which the very gods weep? It is the slavery of the strong to the weak; of the great and nobleminded to the small and mean.

Journal

The difference between Socrates and Jesus Christ? The great Conscious; the immeasurably great Unconscious.
October 28, 1833

Letters

I grow daily to honor facts more and more, and theory less and less. A fact, it seems to me, is a great thing—a sentence printed, if not by God, then at least by the Devil.
To R. W. Emerson, April 29, 1836

The world is a republic of mediocrities, and always was.
To R. W. Emerson, May 13, 1853

It is now almost my sole rule of life to clear myself of cant and formulas, as poisonous Nessus shirts.
To wife, 1835

If Jesus Christ were to come today, people would not even crucify him. They would ask him to dinner, and hear what he had to say, and make fun of it.
Quoted in D. A. Wilson, *Carlyle at his Zenith*

STOKELY CARMICHAEL
(1942–   )
Jamaica-born American Black leader

Black Power
Slogan for SBCC (Student Benevolent Coordinating Committee), May 1966

Black Power . . . is a call for black people in this country to unite, to recognize their heritage, to build a sense of community. It is a call to reject the racist institutions and values of this society.
"Black Power," 1967; with Chas. V. Hamilton

There is a higher law than the law of government. I hat's the law of conscience.
UPI dispatch, October 28, 1966

CARNEADES
(c. 214–129 B.C.)
Greek philosopher (b. Cyrene)

The Fallacy of the Criterion of Truth

There is absolutely no criterion for truth. For reason, senses, ideas, or whatever else may exist are all deceptive.

ANDREW CARNEGIE
(1835–1919)
American steel manufacturer, philanthropist

The Gospel of Wealth (1900)

The Gospel of Wealth advocates leaving free the operation of the laws of accumulation.

Private Property, the Law of Accumulation of Wealth, and the Law of Competition . . . these are the highest results of human experience, the soil in which society so far has produced the best fruit.

This, then, is held to be the duty of the man of wealth: First, to set an example of modest, unostentatious living; . . . to provide moderately for the immediate wants of those dependent upon him; and after doing so to consider all surplus revenues which come to him simply as trust funds, which he is called upon to administer . . . in the manner which, in his judgment, is best calculated to produce the most beneficial results for the community—

the man of wealth thus becoming the mere agent and trustee for the poorer brethren. . . .

The amassing of wealth is one of the worst species of idolatry, no idol more debasing.
> Note found among his papers, dated 1868

EDWARD CARPENTER
(1844–1929)
English poet, essayist

Love's Coming of Age (1911)

The commercial prostitution of love is the last outcome of our whole social system, and its most clear condemnation. It flaunts in our streets, it hides in the garment of respectability under the name of matrimony. . . .

Let every woman whose heart bleeds for the sufferings of her sex, hasten to declare herself and to constitute herself, as far as she possibly can, a free woman. Let her accept the term with all the odium that belongs to it; let her insist on her right to speak, dress, think, act, and above all to use her sex, as she deems best; let her face the scorn and ridicule; let her "lose her own life," if she likes; assured that only so can come deliverance, and that only when the free woman is honored will the prostitute cease to exist.

JIMMY CARTER (James Earl Carter)
(1924–   )
39th President of the United States

To cling to the principles of the Judeo-Christian ethic—honesty, integrity, compassion, love, ideas of hope, charity, humility—is an integral part of any person's life no matter what his position in life may be. . . . the Ten Commandments hold. . . . My prayer is that my life be meaningful in the enhancement of His Kingdom on earth, enhancement of the lives of my fellow human beings; that I may help translate the natural love that exists in this world and do simple justice through government.
> Interview with religious leaders, Indianapolis, *The Churchman*, December 1976

We are now free from that inordinate fear of Communism which once led us to embrace any dictator who joined us in our fear.
> Address, Notre Dame University, May 23, 1977

Human rights is the soul of our foreign policy, because human rights is the very soul of our sense of nationhood.
> Address, White House: as reported in *The New York Times*, December 7, 1978

History teaches perhaps few clear lessons. But surely one such lesson learned by the world at great cost is that aggression unopposed becomes a contagious disease.
> Address to the nation, January 4, 1980

Each generation must renew its foundations. . . . For this generation life is nuclear survival; liberty is human rights; the pursuit of happiness is a planet whose resources are devoted to the physical and spiritual nourishment of its inhabitants. . . .
> Farewell Address, January 14, 1981; written with aid of speechwriter Henrik Hertzberg and Pat Caddell

LEWIS CARROLL (Charles Dodgson)
(1832–1898)
British mathematician

Alice in Wonderland (1865)

"I'll be judge, I'll be jury," said cunning old Fury;
"I'll try the whole cause, and condemn you to death."
> Chapter 3

Through the Looking Glass (1871)

"Now, *here*, you see, it takes all the running *you* can do, to keep in the same place. If you want to get somewhere else, you must run at least twice as fast as that."
> Chapter 2

"The time has come," the Walrus said,
    "To talk of many things:
Of shoes—and ships—and sealing-wax—
    Of cabbages—and kings—
And why the sea is boiling hot—
    And whether pigs have wings."
> Chapter 4, "The Walrus and the Carpenter"

GIACOMO GIROLAMO CASANOVA DE SEINGALT
(1725–1798)
Italian adventurer

Mémoires (Paris, pub. post. 1826–1838)

Man is free, but not if he doesn't believe it.

When you fool a fool you strike a blow for intelligence.

Whether it is happy or unhappy, a man's life is the only treasure he can ever possess. Those who do not love life do not deserve it.

Yes, death is the last line of the book. . . . A man should affirm no more than he positively knows. Doubt begins only at the last frontiers of what is possible. . . .

If there were no happiness on earth, the creation would be a monstrosity, and Voltaire would have been right when he called our planet the latrines of the universe.

SIR ROGER CASEMENT
(1864–hanged 1916)
Irish rebel

If there be no right of rebellion against a state of things that no savage tribes would endure without resistance, then I am sure that it is better for men to fight and die without than to live in such a state of right as this.

Ireland has outlived the failure of all its hopes.
Prisoner's speech, June 29, 1916

PABLO CASALS
(1876–1973)
Spanish cellist

To retire is to begin to die.
Contribution, *Philadelphia Bulletin*, reprinted October 28, 1973

MAGNUS AURELIUS CASSIDORUS
(c. 487–583)
Roman historian

Variae (550)

Poverty is the mother of crime.
Bk. ix, Sect. 13

FIDEL CASTRO
(1926–   )
Liberator of Cuba

History will absolve me.
Declaration at his trial, July uprising, 1953

To betray the poor is to betray Christ.
Slogan on Havana billboards

Men do not shape destiny. Destiny produces the man for the hour.
Taped interview for Ruth Lloyd, *This Week*, May 24, 1959

To sow schools is to reap men.
Quotation on placards, 1960

Politics divides us, but humanity unites us.
Interview with Barbara Walters, May 23, 1977, ABC–TV

VICTOR CATHREIN
(1845–1931)
Jesuit moralist, modernist

If the principle that "the end justifies the means" is to be interpreted as covering the use of means (actions) which are morally wrong and sinful, then it is to be absolutely repudiated. . . . The Jesuits merely hold, as do all reasonable persons, with St. Paul (I Cor., x. 31) that morally indifferent or good actions may and should be justified by good intentions.
Quoted in Réne Fülop-Miller, *The Power and Secret of the Jesuits,* tr. F. S. Flint and D. F. Tait, 1930

MARCUS PORCIUS CATO (The Elder)
(234–149 B.C.)
Roman statesman

"Aulus Gellius"

If thou findest thy wife in adultery, thou art free to kill her without trial, and canst not be punished. If, on the other hand, thou committest adultery, she durst not, and she has no right to, so much as lay a finger on thee.
x, 6

Carmen de moribus

Human life nearly resembles iron. When you use it, it wears out. When you don't, rust consumes it.
xi, 3

Those who steal from private individuals spend their lives in stocks and chains; those who steal from the public treasure go dressed in gold and purple.
xi, 18

The worst ruler is one who cannot rule himself.
Quoted in Plato, "Moralia"

Cato's Defense of the Lex Oppia (tr. Robert Briffault)

Luxury and avarice—these pests have been the ruin of every state.

Suffer women once to arrive at an equality with you, and they will from that moment become your superiors.
>   Quoted in Briffault, *The Mothers* (1927)

He is nearest to the gods who knows how to be silent.
>   Attributed to Cato

Some have said that it is not the business of private men to meddle with government—a bold and dishonest saying, which is fit to come from no mouth but that of a tyrant or slave.

To say that private men have nothing to do with government is to say that private men have nothing to do with their own happiness or misery; that people ought not to concern themselves whether they be naked or clothed, fed or starved, deceived or instructed, protected or destroyed.
>   Attributed

CAIUS VALERIUS CATULLUS
(87–54 B.C.)
Roman poet

Carmina

Let us live and love, my Lesbia, and value at a penny all the talk of crabbed old men. Suns may set and rise again: for us, when our brief light has set, there's the sleep of one everlasting night. Give me a thousand kisses.
>   v, 1

What a woman says to her ardent lover should be written in wind and running water.
>   lxx

I hate and love. You may ask why I do so. I do not know, but I feel it and am in torment.
>   lxxxv, 1

Atque in perpetuum, frater, ave atque vale.
And forever, my brother, hail and farewell.
>   ci, 10

COUNT CAMILLO DI CAVOUR
(1810–1861)
Italian statesman

Speech (March 27, 1861)

A free church in a free state.
>   (Later, a popular slogan)

I can imagine no greater misfortune for a cultured people than to see in the hands of its rulers not only the civil, but also the religious power.
>   Quoted in William de la Rive, *Reminiscences of Life and Character of Count Cavour,* 1912

You can do anything with bayonets except sit on them.
>   Attributed to Cavour (and others)

LOUIS FERDINAND CÉLINE (né Destouches)
(1894–1961)
French novelist, Nazi collaborator

D'un Château à l'autre

To tell the truth, a continent without war is bored . . . as soon as the bugles start up, it's a holiday . . . total vacation. And the bloodlust.

Voyage au bout de la nuit (1932)

Those who talk about the future are scoundrels. It is the present that matters.

CELSUS
(c. 178)
Opponent of Christianity

A True Discourse

Christianity is the bastard progeny of Judaism. It is the basest of all national religions.

Why should we not worship demons? They are the customers of God, and the worshipper of God is right to serve who have His authority.

MIGUEL DE CERVANTES SAAVEDRA
(1547–1616)
Spanish novelist, playwright, poet

Don Quixote (1605–1615)

Works of charity negligently performed are of no worth.*

Those two fatal words, Mine and Thine.
>   Pt. I, ch. 3

Behind the cross is the devil.
>   Pt. I, ch. 6

---

*For this one sentence the book was placed on the Index by the Inquisition, Madrid, in 1640.

Experience, the universal mother of Sciences.

> Pt. I, ch. 7

. . . for historians ought to be precise, faithful, and unprejudiced, and neither interest nor fear, hatred nor affection, should make them swerve from the way of truth, whose mother is history, the rival of time, the depository of great actions, the witness of the past, example of the present, and monitor of the future.

> Pt. I, ch. 9

Anque la traicon aplace, el traidor se aborrece.
Although the treason pleases, the traitor is detested.

> Pt. I, ch. 39

History is in a manner a sacred thing, so far as it contains truth, for where truth is, the supreme Father of it may also be said to be, at least, in as much as concerns truth.

> Pt. II, ch. 3, tr. Peter Anthony Motteux

Everyone is as God made him, and oftentimes a great deal worse.

> Pt. II, ch. 4

The best sauce in the world is hunger.

> Pt. II, ch. 5

We cannot all be friars, and many are the ways by which God bears his chosen to heaven.

> Pt. II, ch. 8

Art may improve, but cannot surpass nature.

> Pt. II, ch. 16

Forewarned, forearmed; to be prepared is half the victory.

> Pt. II, ch. 17

There are two families in the world, as one of my grandmothers used to say, the Haves and the Have-nots.

> Pt. II, ch. 20

The beginning of wisdom is fear of God.

> Pt. II, ch. 20 (cf. I Proverbs 1:7)

Speak the truth and shame the devil.

> Pt. II, ch. 31

Liberty . . . is one of the choicest gifts that heaven hath bestowed upon man, and exceeds in value all the treasures which the earth contains within its bosom, or the sea covers. Liberty, as well as honor, man ought to preserve at the hazard of his life, for without it life is insupportable.

> Pt. II, ch. 58, tr. Jarvis

Blessings light on him who first invented sleep!—it covers a man all over, body and mind, like a cloak; it is meat to the hungry, drink to the thirsty, heat to the cold, and cold to the hot; it is the coin that can purchase all things; the balance that makes the shepherd equal with the king, the fool with the wise man. It has only one fault . . . which is, that it looks like death; for between the sleeper and corpse there is but little to choose.

> Pt. II, ch. 68

"Do not forget, Sancho," replied Don Quixote, "that there are two kinds of beauty, one being of the soul and the other of the body. That of the soul is revealed through intelligence, modesty, right conduct, generosity, and good breeding, all of which qualities may exist in an ugly man; and when one's gaze is fixed upon beauty of this sort and not upon that of the body, love is usually born suddenly and violently."

> Pt. II, ch. LXII, tr. Samuel Putnam

———

Love in young men: for the most part is not love but sexual desire, and its accomplishment is the end.

Delay always breeds danger.

Every man for himself, and God for us all.

Truth may be stretched but cannot be broken, and always gets above falsehood, as oil does above water.

> Attributed

AIMÉ CÉSAIRE
(1913–   )
West Indian poet, exponent of *négritude*

To New York

> New York! I say to you New York!
>   let black blood flow into your blood
> That it may rub the rust from your steel
>   joints,
>   like an oil of life.

SÉBASTIEN ROCH NICOLAS
CHAMFORT
(1741–1794)
French man of letters, Jacobin

Maximes et Pensées (1796)

A little philosophy tends to despise learning; much philosophy leads men to esteem it.

Men of reason have endured; men of passion have lived.

Philosophy, like medicine, has many drugs, very few good remedies, and almost no specifics.

Life is a disease from which sleep gives us relief every sixteen hours. Sleep is a palliative, death is a remedy.

Ch. 2

Almost all men are slaves for the same reason as the Spartans gave for the servitude of the Persians, the inability to pronounce the syllable No. To be able to pronounce this word and to know how to live alone, are the sole means for conserving one's freedom and character.

The poor are the Negroes of Europe.

Ch. 8

Maximes, London edition (1893)

The Scriptures say that the beginning of wisdom is the fear of God, but I declare it is the fear of man.

All is true and all is false in love; love is the only thing about which it is impossible to say anything absurd.

Every man who at forty years is not a misanthrope, has not loved mankind.

Contribution, *Journal de Paris* (1780)

WILLIAM ELLERY CHANNING
(1780–1842)
American Unitarian minister

Complete Works (1879)

Immortality is the glorious discovery of Christianity.

"Immortality"

Unitarian Christianity (1819)

We do, then, with all earnestness, though without reproaching our brethren, protest against the irrational and unscriptural doctrine of the Trinity. . . . With Jesus, we worship the Father, as the only living and true God.

Address, "Self-Culture," Boston, September 1838

Books are the true levellers.

Letters to Jonathan Phillips, 1839

The world is governed much more by opinion than by laws. It is not the judgment of the courts, but the moral judgment of individuals and masses of men, which is the chief wall of defense around property and life.

One anecdote of a man is worth a volume of biography.

Attributed

EDWIN HUBBEL CHAPIN
(1814–1880)
American clergyman

Neutral men are the devil's allies.

Attributed

RALPH CHAPLIN
(1887–1961)
I.W.W. poet

"Solidarity Forever" (song, January 9, 1915)

Mourn not the dead that in the cool earth
    lie— . . .
But rather mourn the apathetic throng—
The cowed and the meek—
Who see the world's great anguish and its
    wrong
And dare not speak.

CHARLES I
(1600–1649)
King of Britain and Ireland

The Twelve Good Rules (attributed to the King)

1. Urge no healths. 2. Profane no divine ordinances. 3. Touch no state matters. 4. Reveal no secrets. 5. Pick no quarrels. 6. Make no comparisons. 7. Maintain no ill opinions. 8. Keep no bad company. 9. Encourage no vice. 10. Make no long meals. 11. Repeat no grievances. 12. Lay no wagers.

CHARLES V
(1500–1558)
Roman Emperor, King of Spain

Memoirs

I appeared, I fought, God conquered.

(a reference to victory at Mühlberg, 1547)

CHARTIST MOVEMENT*
(Founded late 18th century; fl. 1838–1848)
Movement for political and social reform in
England

They that perish by the sword are better
than they that perish by hunger.
> Inscription, Chartist banner

Political power our means, social happiness
our end.
> Chartist slogan; quoted in Wilson, *To the Finland
> Station*, p. 138

That, as the object to be obtained is mutual
benefit, so ought the enactment of laws to be
by mutual consent.

That the universal political right of every
human being is superior and stands apart from
all customs, forms, or ancient usage; a fundamental right not in the power of a man to con-
fer; or justly to deprive him of.
> Petition of the London Workingmen's Association,
> Crown and Anchor Tavern, February 28, 1837

STUART CHASE
(1888–   )
American writer

Guides to Straight Thinking (1956)

Semantics teaches us to watch our prejudices . . . Semantics is the propagandist's
worst friend.

GEOFFREY CHAUCER
(1340?–1400)
The Father of English Poetry

Canterbury Tales (c. 1387–1400)

And gladly wolde he lerne
And gladly teche.
> Prologue

This world hys but a thurghfare ful of wo,
And we been pilgrymes, passing to and fro.
Deeth is an end of every worldly soore.
> "The Knight's Tale"

Foul lust of lechery, behold thy due.
Not only dost thou darken a man's mind,
But bringest destruction on his body
  too. . . .
> "The Man of Law's Tale"

Womman is for mannes help y-wroght.
> "The Marchantes Tale"

Ful wys is he that kan hymselven knowe!
> "The Monkes Tale"

Therefore bihoveth hire a ful long spoon
That shal ete with a feend.
> "The Squire's Tale"

Al things obeyen to moneye.
> "The Tale of Melibeus"

Mordre wol out, that see we day by day.

  *In principio
Mulier est hominis confusio;*
Madame, the sentence of this Latin is—
Womman is mannes joye and al his blis.*
> "The Nun's Priest's Tale"

Now to speak of the first desire, that is, concupiscence, according to the law for our sexual
parts, which were lawfully made and by rightful word of God; I say, for as much as man is
not obedient to God, Who is his Lord, therefore is the flesh disobedient to Him, through
concupiscence, which is also called the nourishing of and the reason for sin.

Therefore all the while that a man has
within him the penalty of concupiscence, it is
impossible but that he will be sometimes
tempted and moved in his flesh to do sin. And
this shall not fail so long as he lives.

This is the Devil's other hand, with the five
fingers to catch the people into his slavery.
The first finger is the foolish interchange of
glances between the foolish woman and the
foolish man. . . . The second finger is vile
touching in wicked manner. . . . The third is
vile words, which are like fire, which immediately burns the heart. . . . The fourth finger is
kissing; and truly he were a great fool who
would kiss the mouth of a burning oven or of a
furnace. And the more fools they are who kiss
in vileness; for that mouth is in the mouth of
Hell; and I speak specifically of those old dot-
ard whoremongers, who will yet kiss though

---

*"In some respects the first labor party in modern
times."—*Socialist Thought,* Albert Fried and Ronald Sanders

*The cock, Chauntecleer, intentionally mistrans-
lates the Latin, which says "In the beginning,
woman is man's undoing," or, "Woman is man's
damnation."

they cannot do anything. . . . and as for the opinion of many that a man cannot sin for any lechery he does with his wife, certainly that opinion is wrong. . . . The fifth finger of the Devil's hand is the stinking act of lechery. . . .
"The Parson's Tale," (tr. J. U. Nicolson)

Whoso would build his whole house out of
    sallows,
And spur his blind horse to run over fallows
And let his wife alone go seeking hallows
Is worthy to be hanged upon the gallows.

By God, if women had but written stories,
As have these clerks within their oratories,
They would have written of men more
    wickedness
Than all the race of Adam could redress.

Or can you say that you have ever heard
That God has ever by his express word
Marriage forbidden? Pray you, now, tell me;
Or where commanded He virginity?

For had Lord God commanded maiden-
    hood,
He'd have condemned all marriage as not
    good;
And certainly, if there were no seed sown,
Virginity—where then should it be grown?

—Virginity is great perfection known,
And continence e'en with devotion shown.

Tell me also, to what purpose or end
The genitals were made, that I defend,
And for what benefit was man first
    wrought?
Trust you right well, they were not made for
    naught. . . .

Why should men otherwise in their books
    set
That man shall pay unto his wife his debt?
Now wherewith should he ever make pay-
    ment,
Except he used his blessed instruments?

Christ was a maid, and yet shaped like a
    man, . . .

I'll not delay, a husband I will get
Who shall be both my debtor and my thrall
And have his tribulations therewithal
Upon his flesh, and while I am his wife
I have the power during all my life

Over his own good body, and not he.
For thus the apostle told it unto me;
And bade our husbands that they love us
    well.
And all this pleases me whereof I tell.
"Prologue to Wife of Bath's Tale"
(tr. J. U. Nicholson)

Truth, Balade de Bon Conseyl

Flee from the press, and dwell with sothfast-
    nesse.

Know thy contree, look up, thank God of
    all;
Hold the heye wey, and lat thy gost thee
    lede;
And trowthe thee shal delivere, it is no
    drede.

Troilus and Creseide

Of harmes two, the lesse is for to chese; . . .
Bk. ii

For of fortunes sharpe adversitee
The worst kynde of infortune is this,
A man to han ben in prosperitee,
And it remembren, whan it passed is.
Bk. iii

JOHN CHEEVER
(1903–1982)
American writer

Damn the bright lights by which no one reads, damn the continuous music that no one hears, damn the grand pianos that no one can play, damn the white houses mortgaged up to their rain gutters, damn them for plundering the ocean for fish to feed the mink whose skins they wear, and damn their shelves on which there rests a single book—a copy of the telephone directory bound in brocade.
Contribution, *The New Yorker,* November 25,
1967

ANTON CHEKHOV
(1860–1904)
Russian writer

The Sea Gull (1896)

Medvedenko: "Why do you wear black all the time?"
Masha: "I am mourning for my life, I'm un-happy."
Act 1

Uncle Vanya (1897)

Everything ought to be beautiful in a human being: face, and dress, and soul, and ideas.

Act 2

Notebooks (1896)

Love, friendship, respect, do not unite people as much as a common hatred of something.

Man is what he believes.

The Personal Papers of Anton Chekhov (tr. Lear, 1950)

To a chemist nothing on earth is unclean. A writer must be as objective as a chemist; he must abandon the subjective line; he must know that dung-heaps play a very respectable part in a landscape, and that evil passions are as inherent in life as good ones.

Letters

Reason and justice tell me that in the electricity and heat of love for man there is something greater than chastity and abstinence from meat.

(tr. Constance Garnett, 1955)

My sense of fair play tells me that there is more love for humanity in electricity and steam than in chastity and abstention from meat.

(tr. David Magarshack, 1955)

Philip Dormer Stanhope, 4th EARL OF CHESTERFIELD
(1694–1773)
English statesman, diplomat

Against Licensing the Stage (speech written for delivery, House of Lords, 1737)

One of the greatest Blessings we enjoy, one of the greatest Blessings a People, my Lords, can enjoy, is Liberty; but every Good in this Life has its alloy of Evil: Licentiousness is the Alloy of Liberty; it is an Ebullition, an Excrescence;—it is a Speck upon the Eye of the Political Body, which I can never touch but with a gentle,—with a trembling Hand lest I destroy the Body, lest I injure the Eye upon which it is apt to appear.

There is such a Connection between Licentiousness and Liberty, that it is not easy to correct the one, without dangerously wounding the other.

Let us consider, my Lords, that arbitrary Power has seldome or never been introduced into any Country at once. It must be introduced by slow degrees, and as it were step by step, lest the people should perceive its approach.

The Stage, my Lords, and the Press, are two of our Out-sentries; if we remove them,—if we hood-wink them,—if we throw them in Fetters; the Enemy may surprize us.

Letters to His Son

Measures not men.

March 6, 1742

The heart . . . commonly triumphs in every struggle with the understanding

March 9, 1748

Women, especially, are to be talked to, as below men, and above children.

September 20, 1748

Women are much more like each other than men; they have, in truth, but two passions, vanity and love; these are their universal characteristics.

December 19, 1749

Depend upon this truth, that every man is the worse looked upon, and the less trusted, for being thought to have no religion; in spite of all the pompous and specious epethets he may assume, of *Esprit fort,* Free-thinker, or Moral Philosopher; and a wise Atheist (if such a thing there is) would, for his own interest, and character in this world, pretend to some religion.

January 8, 1750

History is only a confused heap of facts.

February 5, 1750

People hate those who make them feel their own inferiority.

April 30, 1750

Every numerous assembly is *mob,* let the individuals who compose it be what they will.

March 18, 1751

G(ilbert) K(eith) CHESTERTON
(1874–1936)
British essayist, novelist

Orthodoxy (1909)

Materialists and madmen never have doubts.

Heretics (1905)

Every man has hated mankind when he was less than a man.

Carlyle said that men were mostly fools. Christianity, with its surer and more reverent realism, says that they are all fools. This doctrine is sometimes called the doctrine of original sin. It may also be described as the doctrine of the equality of man.

To say that a man is an idealist is merely to say that he is a man.

G. F. Watts

The thing from which the world suffers just now more than from any other evil is not the assertion of falsehood, but the endless and irrepressible repetition of half-truths.

The Unfinished Temple

The Christian ideal has not been tried and found wanting. It has been found difficult, and left untried.
"What's Wrong With the World" (1910), i.5

CHOU EN-LAI
(1898–   )
Chinese Communist leader

All diplomacy is a continuation of war by other means.
Interview with Edgar Snow, *Saturday Evening Post,* March 27, 1954 (cf. Clausewitz)

CHRYSOSTOM: *see* Dio Chrysostom

ST. JOANNES CHRYSOSTOMUS (St. John Chrysostom)
(345?–407)
Patriarch of Constantinople

Adhortatio ad Theodorum Lapsum

For to sin, indeed is human; but to persevere in sin is not human but altogether satanic.

De Virginitas (c. 390)

Virginity stands as far above marriage as the heavens stand above the earth.

ix

Homilies (c. 388)

Riches are not forbidden, but the price of them is.

The drunken man is a living corpse.

The fornicator is not worthy of compassion, but deserves to be derided and made a mockery of, since he is more irrational than a woman, and a harlot besides.

Although it be with truth thou speakest evil, that also is a crime.

Sorrow is given us on purpose to cure us of sin.

Spending time in the theatres produces fornication, intemperance, and every kind of impurity.

Laughter does not seem to be a sin, but it leads to sin.

———

The rich man is a thief.

Woman—a foe of friendship, an inescapable punishment, a necessary evil.
Attributed

CHAUANG-TZU
(4th–3rd century B.C.)
Chinese mystic

The Preservation of Life (tr. Lin Yutang)

Human life is limited, but knowledge is limitless. To drive the limited in pursuit of the limitless is fatal; and to presume that one really knows is fatal indeed!

In doing good avoid fame. In doing bad, avoid disgrace. Pursue a middle course as your principle. Thus you will guard your body from harm, preserve your life, fulfill your duties to your parents, and live your allotted span of life.

Philosophy

Morality: walking like others upon the path.
Ch. 10

WINSTON SPENCER CHURCHILL
(1874–1965)
British statesman, writer

Speeches and Addresses

The Conservative Party is not a party but a conspiracy.

. . . the seed of imperial ruin and national decay—the unnatural gap between the rich and poor. . . . the exploitation of boy labor,

the physical degeneration which seems to follow so swiftly on civilized poverty. . . . the horrid havoc of the liquor traffic, the constant insecurity in the means of subsistence and employment. . . . the swift increase of vulgar, jobless luxury—are the enemies of Britain.
> Nottingham, January 30, 1908

The maxim of the British people is "Business as usual."
> Guildhall, November 9, 1914

I have nothing to offer but blood, toil, tears and sweat.
> House of Commons, May 13, 1940*

A shadow has fallen upon the scenes so lately lighted by the Allied victory. From Stettin in the Baltic to Trieste in the Adriatic an iron curtain has descended across the continent.
> Fulton, Missouri, March 5, 1946**

The action of Russia . . . is a riddle wrapped in a mystery inside an enigma.
> Radio Broadcast, London, October 1, 1939

We have to combat the wolf of Socialism, and we shall be able to do it far more effectively as a pack of hounds than as a flock of sheep.
> Seconding nomination of Chamberlain as Prime Minister, 1937

Great Contemporaries (1935)

One may dislike Hitler's system and yet admire his patriotic achievement. If our country were defeated I hope we should find a champion as admirable to restore our courage and lead us back to our place among the nations.

---

*Cicero, Livy and Garibaldi used the same expression, with the exception of the word "tears." Browning's *Ixion,* 1883, contains these lines: "Tears, sweat, blood—each spasm, ghastly once, glorified now."

**The phrase "iron curtain" was first used before the war by George W. Crile in *A Mechanistic View of War,* p. 69: "France . . . a nation of 40,000,000 with a deep-rooted grievance and an iron curtain at its frontier." Dr. Goebbels in *Das Reich,* February 23, 1945, mentioned an iron curtain, and Senator Vandenburg used it in a speech, November 15, 1945. *Reynolds News,* London, August 11, 1946, reported: "We are grateful to a correspondent of *The Times* for providing chapter and verse to prove that the phrase 'Iron Curtain' was coined not as had been generally supposed by Mr. Churchill but by Von Krosyg, Hitler's Minister of Finance."

While England Slept (1936)

Dictators ride to and fro upon tigers which they dare not dismount. And the tigers are getting hungry.

In war, Resolution; in defeat, Defiance; in victory, Magnanimity.
> Epigram after the Great War; quoted in Sir Edwin Marsh, *A Number of People,* 1939, p. 15

The inherent vice of Capitalism is the unequal sharing of blessings; the inherent vice of Socialism is the equal sharing of miseries.
> Attributed

COUNT GALEAZZO CIANO (1903–1944)
Italian fascist politician

Ciano Diaries (1939–43)

As always, victory finds a hundred fathers but defeat is an orphan.
> September 9, 1942

JOHN CIARDI (1916–   )
American poet, editor

Contributions, *Saturday Review*

To respect a sick age is to be in contempt of eternity.

A savage is a man who has not had enough news from the human race.

Be selfish. Nothing else makes the human race predictable.
> April 14, 1962

Poetry lies its way to the truth.
> April 28, 1962

Nothing, I will declare, goes further toward a man's liberation than the act of surviving his need for character.
> August 4, 1962

MARCUS TULLIUS CICERO (106–43 B.C.)
Roman orator, poet, statesman

De Amicitia (44 B.C.)

Now friendship may be thus defined: *a complete accord on all subjects human and divine, joined with mutual good will and affection.* And with the exception of wisdom, I am inclined to think nothing better than this has been given to man by the immortal gods.

. . . the real friend . . . is, as it were, another self.

xxii

Epistola ad Atticum

An unjust peace is better than a just war.

Ad Familiares

When you are no longer what you were, there is no reason left for being alive.

vii

De Finibus

Virtue is its own reward.

Ignorance of good and evil is the most upsetting fact of human life.

Bk. I, Ch. 13, sec. 43

Carnal pleasure hinders deliberation, is at war with reason, blindfolds the eyes of the mind, so to speak, and has no fellowship with virtue.

De Lege Agraria

Our character (mores) is not so much the product of race and heredity, as of circumstances by which nature forms habits, by which we are nourished and live.

ii, 95

De Legibus (52 B.C.)

The good of the people is the highest law.

Law is the highest Reason implanted in Nature, which commands what ought to be done, and forbids the opposite.

Because law ought to reform vice and promote virtues, the guiding principles of life can be inferred from it. Wisdom is the mother of all good things, and philosophy has taken its name from the Greek expression that means "love of wisdom." Of all the gifts of the gods to the human race, philosophy is the richest, the most beautiful, the most exalted. Besides all its other wisdoms, Philosophy has informed us that the most difficult thing in the world is to know ourselves. This adage is so decisive for us that credit is given for it not to one person, but to the god at Delphi.*

III

Pro Milone

Laws are silent amidst the clash of arms.

Thought is free.

IV

Pro Murena

Nothing is more unreliable than the people [or populace, or masses], nothing more obscure than human intentions, nothing more deceptive than the whole system of elections.

De Natura Deorum (44 B.C.)*

By some fortuitous concourse of atoms . . .

De Officiis (44 B.C.)

The more laws, the less justice.

De Oratore (55 B.C.)

History, the evidence of time, the light of truth, the life of memory, the directress of life, the herald of antiquity, committed to immortality.

ii, 36

Men decide many more problems by hate, love, lust, rage, sorrow, joy, hope, fear, illusion, or some similar emotion, than by reason (*veritate*) or authority or any legal standards, or legal precedents, or law.

ii, 178

De Re Publica (54–51 B.C.)

In a republic this rule ought to be observed: that the majority should not have the predominant power.

De Senectute (44 B.C.)

The most noble and excellent gift of heaven to man is reason; and of all the enemies that reason has to engage with, pleasure is the chief. . . . Pleasure has no fellowship with virtue.

Avarice of the old . . . absurd to increase one's baggage as one nears his journey's end.

For clearly death is negligible, if it utterly annihilates the soul, or even desirable, if it conducts the soul to some place where it is to live for ever. Surely no other alternative can be found. What, then, shall I fear, if after death I am destined to be either not unhappy or happy?

Gnothi seauton, "Know Thyself," inscribed on the temple of Apollo, frequently credited to Thales, one of the Seven Wise Men of Greece.

---

*"A blind fortuitous concourse of atoms, . . ." Locke, *An Essay Concerning Human Understanding* (1690).

Nor do I regret that I have lived, since I have so lived that I think I was not born in vain, and I quit life as if it were an inn, not a home.

Tusculanes Disputationes (47–44 B.C.)

To live is to think.

Philosophy is the best medicine for the mind.

Nature has planted in our minds an insatiable longing to see the truth.

In fact, the whole passion ordinarily termed love (and heaven help me if I can think of any other term to apply to it) is of such exceeding triviality that I see nothing that I think comparable to it.

The whole life of the philosopher is a preparation for death.

B. M. CIORAN
(1911–   )
Romanian-born, Parisian philosopher

The Temptation to Exist

May some god grant us the power to resign from everything, to betray everything, the audacity of an unspeakable cowardice.

The only free mind is the one that, pure of all intimacy with beings or objects, plies its own vacuity.

It is by undermining the idea of reason, of order, of harmony, that we gain consciousness of ourselves.

I was, I am, I will be, is a question of grammar and not of existence.

Great persecutors are recruited among martyrs whose heads haven't been cut off.

It is from self-hatred that consciousness emerges. I hate myself: I am absolutely a man.

CLAUDIAN (Claudius Claudianus)
(c. 375–408)
Greek-born, Latin poet

In Rufinum

But when I saw the impenetrable mist which surrounds human affairs, the wicked happy and long prosperous and the good discomforted, then in turn my belief in God was weakened and failed.

In Eutropium

Nothing is so cruel as a man raised from lowly station to prosperity.

181

Carmina minora

Hunger I can endure; love I cannot.

xv

De Raptu Proserpinae

Omnia mors aequat.
Death levels all.

Bk. 2

KARL VON CLAUSEWITZ
(1780–1831)
Prussian general

Vom Kriege [*On War*]

Der Krieg ist nichts anderes als die Fortsetzung der Politik mit anderen Mitteln.
War is nothing else than the continuation of state policy with other means.

prefatory note*

It is waste—and worse than waste—of effort to ignore the element of brutality because of the repugnance it excites.

We see, therefore, that war is not merely a political act but a real political instrument, a continuation of political intercourse, a carrying out of the same by other means.

Arming The Nations

There is only one decisive victory: the last.

CASSIUS MARCELLUS CLAY
(Muhammad Ali)
(1942–   )
American boxing champion, Muslim preacher

Damn the money. Damn the heavyweight championship. Damn the white people. Damn everything. I will die before I sell out my people for the white man's money.

Interview, *Esquire,* April 1968

---

*Frequently translated as "continuation of diplomacy with other means." "This was always the viewpoint of Marx and Engels, who regarded *every* war as the *continuation* of politics of the given interested powers."—Lenin, *Selected Works,* vol. v (cf. Chou En-lai).

I

HENRY CLAY
(1777–1852)
American statesman

Speeches, House of Representatives

An oppressed people are authorized whenever they can to rise and break their fetters.
March 4, 1818

All religions united with government are more or less inimical to liberty. All separated from government are compatible with liberty.
March 24, 1818

I had rather be right than be President.
Reply to Senator Preston of South Carolina, 1839*

ELDRIDGE CLEAVER
(1935–   )
American Black leader

We shall have our manhood. We shall have it or the earth will be leveled by our attempt to get it.
Public speech

GEORGES CLEMENCEAU ("The Tiger")
(1841–1929)
French statesman

War! It is too serious a matter to leave to the military.
Quoted in G. Suarez, *Clemenceau* (1886)**

I am sorry for anyone who has not been an anarchist at twenty.
Quoted in James Joll, *The Anarchists*

Cordon sanitaire.
Quarantine line.
Phrase coined by Marcel Proust, Sr., recommended by Clemenceau as a military maneuver to keep the "plague of Bolshevism" from spreading outside Russia.

---

*"The gentleman need not worry. He will never be either."—Speaker Reed. Clay was defeated for the presidency, 1824, 1832, and 1844.
**Talleyrand is credited with a similar remark. Briand repeated it to Lloyd George. The *New York Times,* July 14,1944, substituted "generals" for "the military," and "grave" for "serious."

SAMUEL LANGHORNE CLEMENS
("Mark Twain")
(1835–1910)
American writer*

"The Revised Catechism"

What is the chief end of man?—to get rich. In what way?—dishonestly if he can; honestly if he must.

There are times when one would like to hang the whole human race, and finish the farce.
Contribution, *New York Tribune,* September 27, 1871

A Connecticut Yankee in King Arthur's Court (1889)

A new deal.**

Pudd'nhead Wilson's Calendar (1893)

Adam, the first great benefactor of our race, He brought death into the world.
Ch. 3

The War Prayer (dictated c. 1904)

O Lord our Father, our young patriots, idols of our hearts, go forth to battle—be thou near them! . . . O Lord our God, help us to tear their soldiers to bloody shreds with our shells; help us to cover their smiling fields with the pale forms of their patriot dead: help us to drown the thunder of the guns with the shrieks of their wounded, writhing in pain; help us to lay waste their humble homes with a hurricane of fire; help us to wring the hearts of their unoffending widows with unavailing grief. . . . For our sakes who adore Thee, Lord, blast their hopes, blight their lives, protract their bitter pilgrimage, make heavy their steps, water their way with their tears, stain the white snow with the blood of their wounded feet! We ask it in the spirit of love, of Him

---

*At the suggestion of Cyril Clemens, editor of *The Mark Twain Journal,* the listing is under Clemens and not Mark or Twain. Mr. Clemens has edited the quotes included here.
**"F.D.R. told me that he took his famous phrase from M.T.'s *Connecticut Yankee* when I presented him our Mark Twain Gold Medal, 3rd December 1933."—Letter from Cyril Clemens to G.S. Samuel Clemens also wrote, "We must have a new deal" in a letter dated October 12, 1876.

who is the Source of Love, and who is the ever-faithful refuge and friend of all who are sore beset and seek His aid with humble and contrite hearts. Amen.

Published posthumously in *Harper's Magazine,*
November 1916

"Concerning the Jews"

I am quite sure that (bar one) I have no race prejudices, and I think I have no color prejudices or caste prejudices nor creed prejudices. Indeed I know it. I can stand any society. All that I care to know is that a man is a human being—that is enough for me; he can't be any worse.

Contribution, *Harper's Magazine,* September 1899

Letters From the Earth (1905–09)

Indecency, vulgarity, obscenity—these are strictly confined to man; he invented them. Among the higher animals there is no trace of them. They hide nothing. They are not ashamed.

The first time the Diety came down to earth, he brought life and death; when he came the second time, he brought hell.

The human being, like the immortals, naturally places sexual intercourse far and away above all other joys—yet he has left it out of his heaven.

It [the Bible] is full of interest. It has noble poetry in it; and some clever fables; and some blood-drenched history; and some good morals; and a wealth of obscenity; and upwards of a thousand lies.

There has never been an intelligent person of the age of sixty who would consent to live his life over again. His or anyone else's.

Man is without any doubt the most interesting fool there is. Also the most eccentric. He hasn't a single written law, in his Bible or out of it, which has any but one purpose and intention—to *limit or defeat a law of God.*

Huckleberry Finn (1884)

The pitifulest thing out is a mob; that's what an army is—a mob; they don't fight with courage that's born in them, but with courage that's borrowed from their mass, and from their officers. But a mob without any *man* at the head of it, is *beneath* pitifulness.

Ch. xxii*

The Damned Human Race

Of all the animals, man is the only that is cruel. He is the only one that inflicts pain for the pleasure of doing it. It is a trait that is not known to the higher animals.

The higher animals engage in individual fights, but never in organized masses. Man is the only animal that deals in that atrocity of atrocities, War.

Man is a Religious Animal. He is the only Religious Animal. He is the only animal that has the True Religion—several of them. He is the only animal that loves his neighbor as himself and cuts his throat if his theology isn't straight.

What is Man (published posthumously, 1917)**

Man the machine—man the impersonal engine. Whatsoever a man is, is due to his *make,* and to the *influence* brought to bear upon it by his heredities, his habitat, his associations. He is moved, corrected, COM-MANDED, by exterior influences—solely. He *originates* nothing, not even a thought.

What do you call Love, Hate, Charity, Revenge, Humanity, Magnanimity, Forgiveness?
Different results of the one Master Impulse: the necessity of securing one's self-approval.

The fact that man knows right from wrong proves his *intellectual* superiority to the other

---

*"All modern American literature comes from one book by Mark Twain called *Huckleberry Finn.* American writing comes from that. There was nothing before. There has been nothing as good since."—Ernest Hemingway, *The Green Hills of Africa,* Ch. 1.
**Mencken, *The Smart Set,* October, 1929, wrote that notes, sketches of books, and whole books written by Mark Twain were not published during his lifetime; and that he wrote in a preface to "What is Man?" that it spoke "the truth. Every thought in them has been thought and accepted by unassailable truth by millions upon millions of men—and concealed, kept private. . . . Why have I not been published. . . . I can find no offer." Mencken adds: "It took 25 years to get it published, and the executors suppressed the preface."

creatures; but the fact that he can *do* wrong proves his *moral* inferiority to any creature that *cannot*.

Advice to Youth (published 1923)

The history of the race, and each individual's experience, are thick with evidence that a truth is not hard to kill and that a lie told well is immortal.

Notebook (published 1935)

Of the demonstrably wise there are but two: those who commit suicide, and those who keep their reasoning faculties atrophied with drink.

One of the proofs of the immortality of the soul is that myriads have believed in it. They have also believed the world was flat.

Loyalty to petrified opinion never yet broke a chain or freed a human soul.

Mark Twain in Eruption (published 1949)

The human race is a race of cowards.

God was left out of the Constitution but was furnished a front seat on the coins of the country.

The motto ("In God We Trust") stated a lie. If this nation ever trusted in God, that time has gone by; for nearly half a century its entire trust has been in the Republican Party and the dollar—mainly the dollar.

Say the report is exaggerated. *

I am a revolutionist by birth, reading and principle. I am always on the side of the revolutionists because there never was a revolution unless there were some oppressive and intolerable conditions against which to revolute.
Interview, April 15, 1906, *New York Sun, Tribune, World,* in defense of Maxim Gorki

CLEMENT OF ALEXANDRIA
(150?–220?)
Church father

Paidagogos

We should not be ashamed to name what God has not been ashamed to create.
Bk. II (cf. Charles A. Dana)

---

*To *Evening Sun* correspondent, London, April 3, 1906; re: report of his death.

Stromateis

A movement of the soul contrary to nature in the sense of disobedience to reason, that is what passions are.

Fornication is a lapse from one marriage into another.

Private property is the fruit of iniquity.

I know that God has given us the use of goods, but only as far as is necessary; and he has determined that the use shall be common.

The use of all things that are found in this world ought to be common to all men. Only the most manifest iniquity makes one say to another, "This belongs to me, that to you." Hence the origin of contention among men.

(Stephen) GROVER CLEVELAND
(1837–1908)
22nd and 24th President of the United States

Party honesty is party expediency.
Quoted in New York Commercial Advertiser,
September 19, 1889

Though the people support the government, the government should not support the people.
Veto, Texas Seed Bill, February 16, 1887

Communism is a hateful thing and a menace to peace and organized government; but the communism of combined wealth and capital, the outgrowth of overweening cupidity and selfishness, which insidiously undermines the justice and integrity of free institutions, is no less dangerous than the communism of oppressed poverty and toil, which, exasperated by injustice and discontent, attacks with wild disorder the citadel of misrule.
Annual Message to Congress, 1888

He mocks the people who proposes that the Government shall protect the rich and they in turn will care for the laboring poor.
Message to Congress, March 1, 1886

No man has ever yet been hanged for breaking the spirit of a law.
Quoted in Hibben's Peerless Leader

VOLTARINE DE CLEYRE
(1866–1912)
American radical poet, essayist

Make no laws whatever concerning speech, and speech will be free; so soon as you make a declaration on paper that speech shall be free, you will have a hundred lawyers proving that "freedom does not mean abuse, nor liberty license"; and they will define and define freedom out of existence.

Quoted in Sinclair, *The Cry for Justice* (1920)

FRANK I. COBB
(1869–1923)
Editor, *New York World*

The Bill of Rights is a born rebel. It reeks with sedition. In every clause it shakes its fist in the face of constituted authority . . . it is the one guarantee of human freedom to the American people.

Contribution, *La Follette's Magazine,* January 1920

ARTHUR HUGH CLOUGH
(1819–1861)
English poet

The Last Decalogue (1861)

Thou shalt have one God only; who
Would be at the expense of two?

Thou shalt not kill; but need'st not strive
Officiously to keep alive.

Thou shalt not steal; an empty feat,
When it's so lucrative to cheat.

Thou shalt not covet; but tradition
Approves all forms of competition.

Dipsychus

And almost every one when age,
    Disease, or sorrows strike him,
Inclines to think there is a God,
    Or something very like Him.

WILLIAM COBETT
(1762–1835)
English political writer, reformer

Advice to Young Men

To be poor and independent is very nearly an impossibility.

2, "To a Youth"

SIR ALEXANDER COCKBURN
(1802–1880)
Lord Chief Justice of England

I think the test of obscenity is this: whether the tendency of the matter charged as obscenity is to deprave and corrupt those whose minds are open to such immoral influences, and into whose hands a publication of this sort may fall.

Regina *v.* Hicklin (1868), 3 Q.B. 360, 371;
known as the Hicklin Rule

JEAN COCTEAU
(1891–1963)
French poet, novelist, dramatist

The spirit of creation is simply the spirit of contradiction.

Contribution, *Atlantic,* June 1958

The Hand of a Stranger

To write is to kill something to death.

Le Rappel à l'ordre [*The Call to Order*] (1926)

If it has to choose who is to be crucified, the crowd will always save Barrabas.

COGITO, ERGO SUM
(Variations on a theme by Descartes)

I feel, therefore I exist.

Jefferson, letter to Adams, August 15, 1820

Descartes' *Cogito, ergo sum,* applies no longer.

Haeckel, *The Riddle of the Universe*

Man is timid and apologetic; he is no longer upright; he dares not say "I think," "I am," but he quotes some saint or sage.

Emerson, "Self-Reliance" (1841)

I think that I think; therefore, I think that I am. *Cogito cogito, ergo cogito sum.*

Bierce, *The Devil's Dictionary,* "Cartesian" (1906)

I rebel, therefore I am.

Camus, quoted in *New York Times,*
October 29, 1967

I ought, therefore I can.

Kant

I want, therefore I am.

Tolstoy, quoted by Troyat

Sometimes I think: and sometimes I am.

Paul Valéry

Dubito, ergo credo. (I doubt, therefore I believe.)

Marshall Fishwick

. . . *cogito, ergo sum* . . . can only mean, "I think therefore I am a thinker." The truth is, *sum ergo cogito.*

The real and concrete truth, not the methodical and ideal, is: *homo sum, ergo cogito.*

Unamuno, *The Tragic Sense of Life*

The leading principle of Descartes' philosophy was *Cogito, ergo sum*—"I think, therefore I exist"; and having laid this foundation-stone, he built an enormous building, the ruins of which lie scattered up and down among the sciences in disordered glory and venerable confusion.

Sydney Smith, "Lecture on the Conduct of Understanding," 1806

Only the first word of the Cartesian philosophy is true: it was not possible for Descartes to say *cogito, ergo sum,* but only *cogito.*

Moses Hess

We are, because God is.

Swedenborg

Thinking is identical with being.

Parmenides, quoted by Clement of Alexandria

Descartes' *Cogito, ergo sum* has the meaning "One lives only when one thinks."

. . . the saying should be *labore, ergo sum;* I labor, therefore I am a man.

Stirner, *The Ego and Its Own*

Don Juan: I said, with the foolish philosopher, "I think; therefore I am." It was woman who taught me to say "I am; therefore I think."

Bernard Shaw, *Man and Superman* (1903), Act III

Cogito cogitationes, ergo sum, and *cogito me cogitare, ergo sum* are the correct forms of the famous formula.

Hannah Arendt, quoted in *The New Yorker,* November 21, 1977

There is, of course, the *cogito ergo sum* principle—perhaps the most famous of all philosophical theories . . . which incidentally, is fallacious.

Barrows Dunham, *Man Against Myth* (1947)

THEODORE AND HIPPOLYTE COGINARD
French dramatists

Je suis français, je suis Chauvin.
I am French, I am Chauvin.

La Cocarde tricolor, 1831*

MORRIS R(aphael) COHEN
(1880–1947)
American professor of philosophy

The Faith of a Liberal (1946)

Cruel persecutions and intolerance are not accidents, but grow out of the very essence of religion, namely, its absolute claims.

If religion cannot restrain evil, it cannot claim effective power for good.

SIR EDWARD COKE
(1552–1634)
English judge, writer in law

The Institutes (1628)

Common law is above Parliament and the King.

And the law, that is the perfection of reason, cannot suffer any thing that is inconvenient . . . for reason is the life of the law, nay the common law itself is nothing else but reason.

"A Commentary upon Littleton," First Institute

A man's house is his castle and fortress.

Third Institute

No restraint, be it ever so little, but is imprisonment.

They (corporations) cannot commit treason, nor be outlawed, nor excommunicated, for they have no souls.

"Sutton's Hospital Case," 10 Rep. 32

SAMUEL TAYLOR COLERIDGE
(1772–1834)
British poet, critic, philosopher

Moral and Religious Aphorisms

He who begins by loving Christianity better than the truth, will proceed by loving his own

---

*Origin of the word "chauvinism." Nicholas Chauvin was a worshipper of the Emperor Napoleon.

sect or Church better than Christianity, and end by loving himself better than all.

"Aids to Reflection," 25

Letters

Not one man in a thousand has the strength of mind or the goodness of heart to be an atheist.

To Thomas Allsop, c. 1820

All truth is a species of revelation.

To Thomas Poole, March 28, 1801

Table Talk (23 July 1827)

The man's desire is for the woman; but the woman's desire is rarely other than for the desire of the man.

I believe Plato and Socrates. I believe in Jesus Christ.

Marriage has, as you say, no natural relation to love. Marriage belongs to society; it is a social contract.

Either we have an immortal soul, or we have not. If we have not, we are beasts; the first and wisest of beasts it may be; but still beasts.

Facts are not truths; they are not conclusions; they are not even premises. The truth depends on, and is only arrived at, by a legitimate deduction from all the facts which are truly material.

The happiness of mankind is the end of virtue, and truth is the knowledge of the means.

On the Principals of Political Knowledge (1809)

. . . the folly of men is the wisdom of God.

On Poesy and Art (1818)

Now Art, used collectively, for painting, sculpture, architecture and music, is the mediatress between, and reconciler of, nature and man. It is, therefore, the power of humanizing nature, of infusing the thoughts and passions of man into everything which is the object of his contemplation: color, form, motion, and soul, are the elements which it combines, and it stamps them into unity in the mould of a moral idea.

The primary art is writing.

Lectures and Notes on Shakespeare and Other Dramatists (published 1853)

As it must not, so genius can not be lawless; for it is even this that constitutes its genius—

the power of acting creatively under laws of its own origination.

Biographia Literaria (1817)

. . . the sense of musical delight, with the power of producing it, is a gift of imagination; and this together with the power of reducing multitude into unity of effect, and modifying a series of thoughts by some one predominant thought or feeling, may be cultivated and improved, but can never be learned. It is in these that poeta nascitur do not fit.

The imagination then, I consider either as primary, or secondary. The primary imagination I hold to be the living Power and prime Agent of all human Perception, and as a repetition in the finite mind of the eternal act of creation in the Infinite I AM. The secondary Imagination I consider as an echo of the former, co-existing with the conscious will, yet still as identical with the primary in the kind of its agency, and differing only in degree, and in the mode of its operation. It dissolves, diffuses, dissipates, in order to recreate; or where this process is rendered impossible, yet still at all events it struggles to idealize and to unify. It is essentially vital, even as all objects (as objects) are essentially fixed and dead.

Ch. XIII

The poet, described in ideal perfection, brings the whole soul of a man into activity, with the subordination of its faculties to each other, according to their relative worth and dignity. He diffuses a tone and spirit of unity, that blends, and (as it were) fuses, each into each, by that synthetic and magical power, to which we have exclusively apropriated the name of imagination. This power, first put in action by the will and understanding, and retained under their irremissive, though gentle and unnoticed, control (laxis effertur habenis) reveals itself in the balance or reconciliation of opposite or discordant qualities: of sameness, with difference; of the general, with the concrete; the idea, with the image; the individual, with the representative; the sense of novelty and freshness, with old and familiar objects; a more than usual state of emotion, with more than usual order; judgment ever awake and steady self-possession, with enthusiasm and feeling profound or vehement; and while it blends and harmonizes the natural and the artificial, still subordinates art to nature; the manner to the matter, and our admiration for the poet to our sympathy with the poetry.

Ch. XIV

"The man that hath no music in his soul"
can indeed never be a genuine poet.

Ch. XV

Kubla Khan (1798)

Ancestral voices prophesying war!

The Ancient Mariner (1798)

He prayeth well, who loveth well
    Both man and bird and beast.
He prayeth best who loveth best
    All things both great and small;
For the dear God who loveth us,
    He made and loveth all.

Pt. VII, St. 22

Whenever philosophy has taken into its plan
religion, it has ended in skepticism; and whenever religion excludes philosophy, or the spirit
of free inquiry, it leads to wilful blindness and
superstition.

Quoted in *Allsop's Letters, Conversations, and
Reflections* (1836)

I should have been a Christian had Christ
never lived.

Quoted in Noyes, *Views of Religion*

CHARLES CALEB COLTON
(1780–1832)
English poet, essayist

The Lacon (1829)

Man is an embodied paradox, a bundle of
contradictions; and some set off against the
marvellous things that he has done, we might
fairly adduce the monstrous thing that he has
believed.

The whole family of pride and ignorance
are incestuous, and mutually beget each other.

The greatest friend of truth is Time, her
greatest enemy is Prejudice, and her constant
companion is Humility.

Men will wrangle for religion; write for it;
fight for it; die for it; anything but—live for it.

He that dies a martyr proves that he was not
a knave, but by no means that he was not a
fool.

Ambition is in fact the avarice of power.

Bigotry murders religion to frighten fools
with her ghost.

Tyrants have not yet discovered any chains
that can fetter the mind.

He that is good will infallibly become better, and he that is bad will as certainly become
worse, for vice, virtue, and time are three
things that never stand still.

Power, like the diamond, dazzles the be-
holder, and also the wearer; it dignifies meanness; it magnifies littleness; to what is
contemptible, it gives authority; to what is low,
exaltation.

Despotism can no more exist in a nation
until the liberty of the press be destroyed than
night can happen before the sun is set.

Liberty will not descend to a people; a people must raise themselves to liberty; it is a
blessing that must be earned before it can be
enjoyed.

Religion has treated knowledge sometimes
as an enemy, sometimes as a hostage; often as
a captive and more often as a child; but knowledge has become of age and religion must
either renounce her acquaintance, or introduce her as a companion and respect her as a
friend.

Suicide sometimes proceeds from cowardice, but not always; for cowardice sometimes
prevents it; since as many live because they are
afraid to die, as die because they are afraid to
live.

He that studies books alone will know how
things ought to be; and he who studies men
will know how they are.

It is almost as difficult to make a man unlearn his errors as his knowledge. Malinforma-
tion is more hopeless than noninformation; for
error is always more busy than ignorance. Ignorance is a blank sheet, on which we may
write; but error is a scribbled one, from which
we must first erase. Ignorance is content to
stand still, with her back to the truth; but error
is more presumptuous, and proceeds in the
wrong direction. Ignorance has no light, but
error follows a false one.

Of governments, that of the mob is the most
sanguinary, that of soldiers the most expensive, and that of civilians the most vexatious.

Friendship often ends in love; but love in
friendship never.

HENRY STEELE COMMAGER
(1902–)
American educator

Address, National Conference on Adult Education (1954)

A free society cherishes non-conformity. It knows that from a non-conformist, from the eccentric, have come many of the great ideas of freedom. Free society must fertilize the soil in which non-conformity and dissent and individualism can grow.

Freedom, Loyalty, Dissent (1959)

Loyalty . . . is a realization that America was born of revolt, flourished in dissent, became great through experimentation.

Our tradition is one of protest and revolt, and it is stultifying to celebrate the rebels of the past . . . while we silence the rebels of the present.

"Who is Loyal to America?"

Who would be cleared by their (Un-American) Committees? Not Washington, who was a rebel. Not Jefferson, who wrote that all men are created equal and whose motto was "rebellion to tyrants is obedience to God." Not Garrison, who publicly burned the Constitution. Not Lincoln, who admonished us to have malice toward none, charity for all. . . . or Justice Holmes, who said that our Constitution is an experiment and that while that experiment is being made "we should be eternally vigilant against attempts to check the expression of opinions that we loathe and believe to be fraught with death."

Contribution, *Harper's,* September 1947

AUGUSTE COMTE
(1798–1857)
French founder positivist philosophy

Cours de philosophie positive (1840–42) [*The Positive Philosophy*] (tr. Harriet Martineau, 1853)

From the study of the development of human intelligence, in all directions, and through all times, the discovery arises of a great fundamental law, to which it is necessarily subject, and which has a solid foundation of proof, both in the facts of our organization and in our historical experience. The law is this: that each of our leading conceptions, each branch of our knowledge passes successively through three different theoretical conditons: the Theologica, or fictitious; the Metaphysical, or abstract; and the Scientific, or positive. In other words, the human mind, by its nature, employs in its progress three methods of philosophizing, the character of which is essentially different, and even radically opposed: viz., the theological method, the metaphysical, and the positive. Hence arise three philosophies, or general systems of conceptions on the aggregate of phenomena, each of which excludes the others.

In the theological state, the human mind, seeking the essential nature of beings, the first and final causes (the origin and purpose) of all effects, in short, Absolute knowledge, supposes all phenomena to be produced by the immediate action of supernatural beings.

In the metaphysical state, which is only a modification of the first, the mind supposes, instead of supernatural beings, abstract forces, veritable entities (that is, personified abstractions) inherent in all beings, and capable of producing all phenomena. . . .

In the final, the positive state, the mind has given over the vain search after Absolute notions, the origin and destination of the universe, and the causes of phenomena, and applies itself to the study of their laws, that is, their invariable relations of succession and resemblance. Reasoning and observation, duly combined, are the means of this knowledge.

The point of departure of the individual and of the race being the same, the phases of the mind of a man correspond to the epochs of the mind of the race. Now, each of us is aware, if he looks back upon his own history, that he was a theologian in his childhood, a metaphysician in his youth, and a natural philosopher in his manhood. All men who are up to their age can verify this for themselves.

All good intellects have repeated since Bacon's time, that there can be no real knowledge but that which is based on observed facts.

The positive philosophy has hitherto intervened to examine both [the theological and metaphysical philosophies], and both are abundantly discredited by the process. It is time now to be doing something more effective, without wasting our forces in needless controversy. It is time to complete the vast intellectual operation begun by Bacon, Descartes, and Galileo, by constructing the system of general ideas which must henceforth prevail among the human race. This is the way to put an end to the revolutionary crisis which is tormenting the civilized nations of the world.

Vol. I, Ch. 1

Catechisme Positiviste (1852)

The dead govern the living.

———

Sociology.

Word coined in 1837

The universe displays no proof of an all-directing mind.

Religion is an illusion of childhood, outgrown under proper education.

Quoted in Noyes, *Views of Religion*

JAMES BRYANT CONANT
(1893–   )
American educator

Slogans are both exciting and comforting but they are also powerful opiates for the conscience.

Baccalaureate Address, Harvard, June 17, 1934

Marie Jean Nicolas Antoine de Caritat,
MARQUIS DE CONDORCET
(1743–1794)
French philosopher, Girondin

Sketch for a Historical Picture of the Progress of the Human Spirit (1794)

There has been developing a new doctrine, which must give the final trust to the tottering edifice of prejudices. It is the doctrine of the indefinite perfectibility of the human race.

Men will preserve the errors of their childhood, of their country, and of their age long after having recognized all the truths needed to destroy them.

All the errors of politics and in morals are founded upon philosophical mistakes, which, themselves, are connected with physical errors. There does not exist any religious system, or supernatural extravance, which is not founded on an ignorance of the laws of nature.

Our hopes for the future condition of the human race can be subsumed under three important heads: the abolition of inequality between nations, the progress of equality within each nation, and the true perfection of mankind.

Among those causes of human improvement that are of most importance to the general welfare, must be included, the total annihilation of the prejudices which have established between the sexes an inequality of rights, fatal even to the part which it favors. . . .

CONFEDERATE STATES OF AMERICA

The Confederate Constitution

The citizens of each State shall be entitled to all the privileges and immunities of citizens of the several States, and shall have the right of transit and sojourn in any State of the Confederacy, with their slaves and other property; and the right of property in said slaves shall not be thereby impaired.

Art. vi, March 11, 1861

CONFUCIUS
(551–479 B.C.)
Chinese sage, philosopher*

Confucian *Analects* (tr. James Legge)

The Master said, . . . 'Have no friends not equal to yourself.'

Bk. I, 8

The Master said, 'The superior man thinks of virtue; the small man thinks of comfort. . . .'

Bk. II

———

*Kung Fu Tse, or K'ung tsze, according to the *Britannica*. He "left no writings in which he detailed the principles of his moral and social system." The *Analects* (Lun-yu) were compiled by disciples. His grandson, Tze-sze, compiled his thoughts in *The Doctrine of the Mean.* Tsang Sin, a disciple, did likewise in *The Great Learning.* The *Britannica* considers the attributions by Mencius apocryphal.
"I admire Confucius. He was the first man who did *not* receive a divine inspiration."—Voltaire.
"Confucianism may be a civilization but it is not a religion."—G. K. Chesterton.

The Master said, 'It is only the (*truly*) virtuous man, who can love, or who can hate, others.'

Bk. IV, 3

The Master said, 'They who know *the truth* are not equal to those who love it, and they who love it are not equal to those who delight in it.'

Bk. VI, 18

The Master said, 'The man of virtue makes the difficult *to be overcome* his first business, and success only a subsequent consideration;—this may be called perfect virtue.'

Bk. VI, 20

The Master said, 'The superior man has neither anxiety nor fear.'

Bk. XII, 4

The Master said, . . . 'If names are not correct, language is not in accordance with the truth of things. If language is not in accordance with the truth of things, affairs cannot be carried on to success. . . . Therefore a superior man considers it necessary that the names he uses may be spoken appropriately. . . . What the superior man requires, is just that in his words there may be nothing incorrect.'

Bk. XIII, 3*

The Master said, 'To lead an uninstructed people to war, is to throw them away.'

Bk. XIII, 30

Tsze-kung asked, saying, 'Is there one word which may serve as a rule of practice for all one's life?' The Master said, 'Is not *Reciprocity* such a word? What you do not want done to yourself, do not do to others.'

Bk. XV, 23

The Master said, . . . 'Without knowing the *force* of words, it is impossible to know men.'

Bk. XX, 3

Analects (tr. Arthur Waley)

The Master said, At fifteen I set my heart upon learning. At thirty, I planted my feet firm upon the ground. At forty, I no longer suffered from perplexities. At fifty, I knew what were the biddings of Heaven. At sixty, I heard them with docile ear. At seventy, I

*Popularly, Confucius is credited with saying: "The beginning of wisdom is to call things by their proper names."

could follow the dictates of my own heart; for what I desired no longer overstepped the boundaries of right.

Bk. II, 4*

Tzu-kung asked about the true gentleman. The Master said, He does not preach what he practices till he has practiced what he preaches.

Bk. II, 13**

The Master said, He who learns but does not think, is lost! He who thinks but does not learn is in great danger!

Bk. II, 15

The Master said, Yu, shall I teach you what knowledge is? When you know a thing, to recognize that you know it, and when you do not know a thing, to recognize that you do not know it. That is knowledge

Bk. II, 17

. . . to see what is right and not to do it is cowardice.

Bk. II, 24

The Master said, One who is by nature daring and is suffering from poverty will not long be lawful. Indeed, any man, save those that are truly Good, if their sufferings are very great, will be likely to rebel.

Bk. VIII, 10

There were four things that the Master wholly eschewed: he took nothing for granted, he was never over positive, never obstinate, never egotistic.

Bk. IX, 4†

The Master said, In vain have I looked for one whose desire to build up his moral power was as strong as sexual desire.

Bk. XV, 12

Master K'ung said, There are three sorts of friend that are profitable, and three sorts that are harmful. Friendship with the upright, with the true-to-death and with those who have

*Another translation concludes: "At sixty, my ear was an obedient organ for the reception of Truth. . . ."
**Waley uses the term "gentleman" or "true gentleman"; Legge and others prefer "the superior man."
†"There were four things from which the master was entirely free. He had no foregone conclusions, no arbitrary pre-determinations, no obstinacy, and no egotism."—another translation. "Take nothing for granted," was Karl Marx's motto.

heard much is profitable. Friendship with the obsequious, friendship with those who are good at accommodating their principles, friendship with those who are clever at talk is harmful.

Bk. XVI, 4

Master K'ung said, There are three things against which a gentleman is on his guard. In his youth, before his blood and vital humours have settled down, he is on his guard against lust. Having reached his prime, when the blood and vital humours have finally hardened, he is on his guard against strife. Having reached old age, when the blood and vital humours are already decaying, he is on his guard against avarice.

Bk. XVI, 7

The Master said, It is only the wisest and the very stupidest who cannot change.

Bk. XVII, 3

The Master said, Women and people of low birth are very hard to deal with. If you are friendly with them, they get out of hand, and if you keep your distance, they resent it.

Bk. XVII, 25

Analects (tr. Ezra Pound*)

He said: Only the complete man can love others, or hate them.

Bk. IV, 3

He said: The proper man understands equity, the small man profits.

Bk. IV, 6

He said: Honest men govern a country a hundred years, they could vanquish the malevolent and get rid of the death penalty.

Bk. XIII, 11

Aphorisms (tr. Lin Yutang)

Confucius said, "We don't know yet about life, how can we know about death?"

Analects (various translations)

She who is born beautiful is born with sorrow for many a man.

Silence is a friend who will never betray.

There are four words of which the Master barred the use; he would have no "shall's," no "musts," no "certainly's," no "I's."

*"... the study of the Confucian philosophy is of greater profit than that of Greek . . ."—Ezra Pound.

Men's natures are alike; it is their habits that carry them apart.

Bk. XVII, Ch. 2

The Doctrine of Mean (tr. Legge)

'The duties of universal obligation are five, and the virtues wherewith they are practised are three. The duties are those between sovereign and minister, betweeen father and son, between husband and wife, between elder brother and younger, and those belonging to the intercourse of friends. Those five are the duties of universal obligation. Knowledge, magnanimity, and energy, these three, are the virtues universally binding. And the means by which they carry *the duties* into practice—is singleness.'

Ch. XX, 8

The Master said, 'To be fond of learning is to be near to knowledge. To practice with vigor is to be near to magnanimity. To possess the feeling of shame is to be near to energy.

'He who knows these three things, knows how to cultivate his own character. Knowing how to cultivate his own character, he knows how to govern other men. Knowing how to govern other men, he knows how to govern the kingdom with all its states and families.'

Ch. XX, 10, 11

'Sincerity is the way of Heaven. The attainment of sincerity is the way of men. He who possesses sincerity, is he who, without an effort, hit what is right, and apprehends, without the exercise of thought; he is the sage who naturally and easily embodies the *right* way. He who attains to sincerity, is he who chooses what is good, and firmly holds it fast.'

Ch. XX, 18

Wisdom, compassion and courage—these are the three universally recognized moral qualities of men.

There is only one way for a man to be true to himself. If he does not know what is good, a man cannot be true to himself.

Being true to oneself is the law of God. To try to be true to oneself is the law of man.

Thus absolute truth is indestructible. Being indestructible, it is eternal. Being eternal, it is self-existent. Being self-existent, it is infinite. Being infinite, it is vast and deep. Being vast and deep, it is transcendental and intelligent.

Ch. XXIII

JOSEPH CONRAD (né Korzeniowski)
(1857–1924)
Polish-born British writer

A Personal Record (1912)

All ambitions are lawful except those that climb upward on the miseries or credulities of mankind.

Victory (1915)

Every age is fed on illusions, lest man should renounce life early and the human race come to an end.

Nostromo (1904)

God is for men and religion for women.
Ch. 4

Under Western Eyes (1911)

Remember, Razumov, that women, children and revolutionists hate irony, which is the negation of all saving instincts, of all faith, of all devotion, or all action.

The Nigger of the "Narcissus" (1897)*

A work that aspires, however humbly, to the condition of art should carry its justification in every line.

The artist appeals to the part of our being which is not dependent on wisdom; to that in us which is a gift and not an acquisition—and therefore, more permanently enduring. He speaks to our capacity for delight and wonder, to the sense of mystery surrounding our lives; to our sense of pity, and beauty and pain. . . .

. . . art itself may be defined as a single-minded attempt to render the highest kind of justice to the visible universe, by bringing to light the truth, manifold and one, underlying its every aspect.

. . . All art therefore, appeals primarily to the senses, and the artistic aim when expressing itself in written words must also make its appeal through the senses, if its high desire is to reach the secret spring of responsive emotions. It must strenuously aspire to the plasticity of sculpture, to the colour of paintng, and to the magic suggestiveness of music—which is the art of arts.
Preface

*The first printings in the United States changed the title to *Children of the Sea*.

BENJAMIN CONSTANT
(1767–1834)
Swiss writer, statesman

With newspapers, there is sometimes disorder; without them there is always slavery.
Quoted in editorial, *San Francisco Chronicle*

CALVIN COOLIDGE
(1872–1933)
30th President of the United States

The right of the police of Boston to affiliate, which has always been questioned, never granted, is now prohibited. There is no right to strike against the public safety by anybody, anywhere, anytime.
Telegram to AFL President Gompers, September 14, 1919; widely publicized in 1920 presidential campaign

Civilization and profits go hand in hand.
Speech, New York, November 27, 1920

The business of America is business. . . . The chief ideal of the American people is idealism.
Address, Society of American Newspaper Editors, January 17, 1925

If the spirit of liberty should vanish in other parts of the union and support of our institutions should languish, it could all be replenished from the generous store held by the people of this brave little state of Vermont.
Speech, Bennington, Vermont, September 21, 1928

JAMES FENIMORE COOPER
(1789–1851)
American novelist

The American Democrat (1838)

The tendencies of democracies are, in all things, to mediocrity, since the tastes, knowledge, and principles of the majority form the tribunal of appeal.

It is the besetting vice of democracies to substitute public opinion for law. This is the usual form in which the masses of men exhibit their tyranny.

In America the taint of sectarianism lies broad upon the land. The nation is sectarian, rather than Christian.

They who have reasoned ignorantly, or who have aimed at effecting their personal ends by flattering the popular feeling, have boldly affirmed that "one man is as good as another"; a maxim that is true in neither nature, revealed morals, nor political theory.

Individuality is the aim of political liberty.

Jack Tier

Ignorance and superstition ever bear a close and mathematical relation to each other.

NICHOLAS COPERNICUS
(1473–1543)
Polish physician, founder of modern astronomy*

Commentarioulus

After I had addressed myself to this very difficult and almost insoluble problem, the suggestion at length came to me how it could be solved . . . if some assumptions (which are called axioms) were granted me. They follow in this order:
  1. There is no one center of all the celestial circles or spheres.
  2. The center of the earth is not the center of the universe, but only of gravity and of the lunar sphere.
  3. All the spheres revolve about the sun as their midpoint, and therefore the sun is the center of the universe. . . .

De revolutionibus orbium coelestium (1530; pub. 1543)

Finally we shall place the sun itself at the center of the Universe. All this is suggested by the systematic procession of events and the harmony of the whole Universe, if only we face the facts, as they say, "with both eyes open."

PIERRE CORNEILLE
(1606–1684)
French dramatist

Horace (1640)

Do your duty and leave the rest to the gods.

---

*Born in Thorn, Prussia. Alternative name "Koppernigk" according to the *Britannica;* the U.S. Post Office named him "Nikolaj Kopernik." His works were banned by the Index from 1616 to 1835.

We hold in our hands the power to end our sorrows and he who is willing to die can brave any calamity.

Act II

Cinna (1640)

The worst of all states is the people's state.

Act II

The successful man can never be guilty; whatever he may have done or will do, he is inviolable.

Act V

JOHN COTTON
(1584–1652)
Puritan minister, American colonizer

The Bloody Tenant Washed and Made White in the Blood of the Lamb

Democracy, I do not conceive that ever God did ordain it as a fit government either for church or commonwealth. If the people be governors, who will be governed? As for monarchy, and aristocracy, they are both of them clearly approved, and directed in Scripture, yet so as referreth the sovereignty to Himself, and setteth theocracy in both, as the best form of government in the commonwealth, as well as in the church.

EMILE COUÉ
(1857–1926)
French psychotherapist

Tous les jours, à tous les points de vue, je vais de mieux en mieux.
Every day, in every way, I am getting better and better.

Inscription, sanitarium at Nancy, 1910. Patients were required to repeat the statement 20 times each day.

CHARLES E. COUGHLIN
(1891–1979)
Canadian-born American priest

16 Principles of Social Justice

  1. Liberty of conscience and education. . . . 3. Nationalization of important public resources. . . . 6. Abolition of Federal

Reserve Banking System and Establishment of a Government-owned Central Bank. . . .
15. Conscription of wealth as well as men in event of war. 16. Security of human rights preferred to sanctity of property with Government's chief concern for the poor.

Published on editorial page of *Social Justice* every issue

COUNCILS OF THE ROMAN CATHOLIC CHURCH, *see* Canon Law

VICTOR COUSIN
(1792–1867)
French philosopher

Du Vrai, du Beau, et du Bien (Sorbonne Lecture, 1818; published, 1836)

There should be religion for religion's sake, morality for morality's sake, and art for art's sake.

NORMAN COUSINS
(1912–   )
American editor, writer

Who Speaks for Man? (1953)

War is an invention of the human mind. The human mind can invent peace.

ABRAHAM COWLEY
(1618–1667)
English poet, essayist

Anacreontiques (1656)

Gold alone does passion move!
Gold monopolizes love!
A curse on her and on the man
Who this traffic first began.
A curse on him who found the one,
A curse on him who digged the stone.
A curse on him who did refine it.
A curse on him who first did coin it.
A curse, all curses else above,
On him who used it first in love!
No. 7, "Gold"

Several Discourses by Way of Essays in Verse and Prose; Of Liberty (1668)

Who then is free? This wise man, and the man who is able to govern himself. Not Oeno-mans, who commits himself wholly to a charioteer that may break his neck, but the man,

Who governs his own course with steady hand,
Who does himself with sovereign power command;
Whom neither death, nor poverty does fright,
Who stands not awkwardly in his own light
Against the truth;. . .
This, I confess is a freeman. . . .
(cf. Horace, *Satires*)

"Ode Upon Liberty" (1663)

And steal one day out of thy life to live.

Pindaric Odes (1656)

Let nature and let Art do what they please,
When all's done, life's an incurable disease.
"To Dr. Scarborough"

WILLAM COWPER
(1731–1800)
English poet

"The Progress of Error" (c. 1782)

How shall I speak of thee or thy power address,
Thou God of our idolatry, the Press?
By thee, religion, liberty and laws
Exert their influence and advance their cause;
By thee worse plagues than Pharaoh's land befell,
Diffused, make earth the vestibule of Hell;
Thou fountain, at which drink the good and wise;
Thou ever-bubbling spring of endless lies;
Like Eden's dead probationary tree,
Knowledge of good and evil is from thee!

"Expostulation" (1782)

While thousands, careless of the damning sin,
Kiss the Book's outside who ne'er look within.
Lines 386–387

The rich are too indolent, the poor too weak, to bear the insupportable fatigue of thinking.
Attributed

STEPHEN CRANE
(1871–1900)
American writer, war correspondent

The Blue Hotel (1899)

Every sin is the result of a collaboration.

The Red Badge of Courage (1896)

He wishes that he, too, had a wound, a red badge of courage.

Ch. 9

PROSPER JAYLOT, SIEUR DE CRÉBILLON
(1674–1762)
French dramatist

Xerxes (1714)

Fear created the gods, boldness created kings.

Act 1

MANDELL CREIGHTON
(1843–1901)
English historian, Bishop of London

All true knowledge contradicts common sense.

Quoted in *M. Creighton: Life and Letters* (1904)

CRESCAS, HASDAI BEN ABRAHAM
(1340–1410)
Spanish Jewish philosopher

The Light of the Lord (*Or Adonai*) (c. 1400)

God Himself cannot alter the laws of *a priore* truth.

MICHEL-GUILLAUME JEAN DE CRÈVECOEUR
(1735–1813)
French-born American explorer, writer

Letters from an American Farmer (1782)

Where there is bread there is my country, is the motto of all emigrants.

He is an American, who, leaving behind him all his ancient prejudices and manners receives new ones from the new mode of life he has embraced, the new government he obeys, and the new rank he holds. . . . Here individuals of all nations are melted into a new race of men, whose labors and posterity will one day cause great changes in the world.

The American is a new man who acts upon new principles; he must therefore entertain new ideas, and form new opinions. From involuntary idleness, servile dependency, penury, and useless labor, he has passed to toils of a very different nature, rewarded by ample subsistence—This is an American.

BENEDETTO CROCE
(1866–1952)
Italian philosopher

History as the Story of Liberty (1941)

Historical judgment is not a variety of knowledge, it is knowledge itself; it is the form which completely fills and exhausts the field of knowing, leaving no room for anything else.

Aesthetic

Philosophy removes from religion all reason for existing.

CROESUS
(?–546 B.C.)
Last king of Lydia

In peace sons bury their fathers, but in war fathers bury their sons.

Attributed by Herodotus

OLIVER CROMWELL
(1599–1658)
English general, statesman

I am persuaded that diverse of you, who lead the people, have labored to build yourselves in these things; wherein you have censured others, and established yourselves "upon the Word of God." Is it therefore infallibly agreeable to the Word of God, all that *you* say? I beseech you, in the bowels of Christ, think it possible you may be mistaken.

To the General Assembly of the Kirk of Scotland; or, in the case of their not sitting, To the Commissioners of the Kirk of Scotland (before the Battle of Dunbar), August 3, 1650*

---

*"I should like to have that written over the portals of every church, every school, and every courthouse, and, may I say, of every legislative body in the United States."—Judge Learned Hand, *Morals in Public Life*, 1951.

R(ichard) H(oward) S(tafford) CROSSMAN
(1907–1974)
British writer, Socialist, editor *New Statesman*

It is not power itself, but the legitimation of the lust for power, which corrupts absolutely.
The New Statesman April 21, 1951

Racialism is a universal, anti-Semitism an exclusively Christian disease.
November 19, 1960

Towards a Philosophy of Socialism, New Fabian Essays (1952)

Every economic system, whether Capitalist or Socialist, degenerates into a system of privilege and exploitation unless it is policed by a social morality, which can only reside in a minority of citizens. . . . Every Church becomes a vested interest without its heretics. . . . Freedom is always in danger, and the majority of mankind will always acquiesce in its loss, unless a minority is willing to challenge the privileges of its few and the apathy of the masses.

e(dward) e(stlin) cummings
(1894–1963)
American poet

One Times One (1944)

A politician is an arse upon
which everyone has sat except a man.
Line 10

(pity this busy monster, manunkind,
not.) Progress is a comfortable disease.
Line 14

next to of course god america i (1926)

next to of course god america i
love you land of the pilgrims' and so forth
oh

"Voices to Voices, lip to lip"

While you and I have lips and voices which
are for kissing and to sing with
Who cares if some one-eyed son of a bitch
invents an instrument to measure Spring
with?

Selected Letters (eds. F. W. Dupee and George Stade)

To destroy is always the first step in any creation.

To be nobody-but-myself—in a world which is doing its best, night and day, to make you everybody else—means to fight the hardest battle which any human being can fight, and never stop fighting.
Letter to a high school editor, 1955

JOHN PHILPOT CURRAN
(1750–1817)
Irish statesman

Defense of Rebels (Irish uprising, 1798)

Assassinate me you may; intimidate me you cannot.

Speech "Upon the Right of Election of Lord Mayor of Dublin" (July 10, 1790)

The condition upon which God hath given liberty to man is eternal vigilance; which condition if he break, servitude is at once the consequence of his crime, and the punishment of his guilt.

CHARLES P. CURTIS
(1891–   )
American lawyer, writer, educator

A Commonplace Book (1957)

If the works of God are intelligible to man, if good and evil are what we think they are, a god who is both omnipotent and benevolent is a contradiction. Humanly speaking good and evil are antithetical.

There appear to be three alternatives. God may not be wholly benevolent. If He is not, He is not worthy of our worship. . . . Or God may not be omniscient. But if He is not, how can we be sure He is wiser than some of our wise men?
The third alternative is Plato's final conviction, that God was not coercive, but only persuasive. And is this not Christianity?
(cf. Epicurus)

GEORGE WILLIAM CURTIS
(1824–1892)
American essayist, editor

The test of civilization is the estimate of woman. Among savages she is a slave. In the dark ages of Christianity she is a toy and a sentimental goddess. With increasing moral light, and greater liberty, and more universal justice, she begins to develop as an equal human being.

Contribution, *Harper's,* September 1886

Essays

My advice to a young man seeking deathless fame would be to espouse an unpopular cause and devote his life to it.

"Wendell Phillips"

NICHOLAS DE CUSA (né Krebs)
(1401–1464)
French cardinal, theologian

The Vision of God

The place wherein Thou [God] art found unveiled is girt around with coincidence of contradictories, and this is the wall of Paradise wherein Thou dost abide. The door thereof is guarded by the most proud spirit of Reason, and unless he is vanquished, the way will not lie open.

ADAM PHILIPPE, COMTE DE CUSTINE
(1740–1793)
French general, diplomat

The Russian government is an absolute monarchy tempered by assassination.

Spoken to Ernst F. H. Münster, Hanoverian envoy, and usually credited to him

ST. CYPRIAN
(200–beheaded 258)
Bishop of Carthage

The World and Its Vanities

He is bound fast by his wealth . . . his money owns him rather than he owns it.

On the Unity of the Catholic Church

Whoever is separated from the Church is yoked with an adulteress. . . . Who has not the Church for mother can no longer have God for father.

vi, Sec, 21·19

Letter to Demetrianus, proconsul of Africa

An ever-burning gehenna will burn up the condemned, and a punishment devouring

with living flames; nor will there be any source whence at any time they may have either respite or end to their torments.

Epistulae

Held to be a crime when committed by individuals, homicide is called a virtue when committed by the state.

1, 6

CYRANO DE BERGERAC
(1620–1655)
French dramatist

La Mort d'Agrippine (1653)

Perish the universe, so long I have my revenge.

Act 4

CYRUS
(c. 529 B.C.)
Founder, Persian Empire

No man has any right to rule who is not better than the people over whom he rules.

Attributed by Plutarch, *Moralis: Sayings of Kings*

SALVADOR DALI
(1904–   )
Spanish surrealist artist

Moi, je suis contre la liberté, je suis pour la sainte Inquisition. La liberté, c'est la merde, et c'est pour ça que tous les pays sombrent à cause de l'excès de liberté.

As for me, I am against freedom, I am for the blessed Inquisition. Freedom is shit, and that's why all these countries founder, from an excess of liberty.

L'Express, June 12, 1975

CHARLES A. DANA
(1819–1897)
American editor

. . . whatever the divine Providence permitted to occur, I was not too proud to report.
Editorial, reprinted in last issue, *New York Sun**

GABRIELE D'ANNUNZIO
(1863–1938)
Italian poet, novelist

My aim is the re-establishment of the worship of man.
Attributed

DANTE (or Durante) ALIGHIERI
(1265–1321)
Italian poet

The Divine Comedy (c. 1307–1320): *The Inferno* (tr. Ciardi)

Midway in our life's journey. . . .
Canto I

Know then, O waiting and compassionate
soul,
that is to fear which has the power to
harm,
and nothing else is fearful even in Hell.
Canto II

LASCIATE OGNI ESPERANZA, VOI
CH'ENTRATE.
ABANDON ALL HOPE YE WHO EN-
TER HERE.

And he to me: "These are the nearly soul-
less
whose lives concluded neither blame nor
praise."

They are mixed here with that despicable
corps
of Angels who were neither for God nor
Satan,
but only for themselves. . . .

"Master, what gnaws at them so hideously,
their lamentations stun the very air?"
"They have no hope of death," he answered me. . . .
Canto III

---

*Usually misquoted as "What the good Lord lets happen, I am not ashamed to print," or, ". . . not afraid to print."

But since fraud
is the vice of which man alone is capable,
God loathes it most. Therefore, the
fraudulent
are placed below, and their torment is
more painful.

Fraud, which is a canker to every conscience,
may be practiced by a man on those who
trust him,
and on those who have reposed no confidence.

therefore within the second circle lie
simoniacs, sycophants, and hypocrites,
falsifiers, thieves, and sorcerers,
grafters, pimps, and all such filthy cheats
Canto XI

And he: "Follow your star, for if in all
of the sweet life I saw one truth shine
clearly,
you cannot miss your glorious arrival."
Canto XV

For where the instrument of intelligence
is added to brute power and evil will,
mankind is powerless in its own defense.
Canto XXXI

Purgatorio

Vien dietro a me, e lascia dir le genti.
Come follow me and let the world
babble. *
Canto V

Monarchy (1309)

Mankind is at its best when it is most free.
This will be clear if we grasp the principle of
liberty. We must recall that the basic principle
is freedom of choice, which saying many have
on their lips but few in their mind.

Nature is the Art of God.
Book I

Letters

For what is liberty but the unhampered
translation of will into act.
6, 1311

---

*Karl Marx in the preface to *Das Kapital* quotes this line as "*Sequi il tuo corso, e lascir dir la gente,*" which he translates as "Pursue thy course, and let people talk."

GEORGES JACQUES DANTON
(1759–guillotined 1794)
French revolutionary leader

De l'audace, et encore de l'audace, et toujours de l'audace, et la France est sauvée.
Boldness, more boldness, and always boldness, and France is saved. ·
Address, Legislative Committee of General Defense,
September 2, 1792

What care I that I am called a "drinker of blood?" Well, let us drink the blood of the enemies of humanity.
Address, National Assembly, 1793

CLARENCE (S.) DARROW
(1857–1938)
American lawyer

You can only protect your liberties in this world by protecting the other man's freedom. You can only be free if I am free.
Address to jury, Communist trial, Chicago, 1920

To think is to differ.
Scopes trial, July 1925

The litigants and their lawyers are supposed to want justice, but, in reality, there is no such thing as justice, either in or out of court. In fact, the word cannot be defined.
Interview, *New York Times,* April 19, 1936; also in
Esquire, May 1936

Every man is a potential murderer.
Newspaper interview, Chicago, April 18, 1937

CHARLES (ROBERT) DARWIN
(1809–1882)
English biologist*

The Voyage of the Beagle (1859)

At last gleams of light have come, and I am almost convinced that species are not (it is like confessing a murder) immutable.

The Origin of Species (1859)**

The expression often used by Mr. Herbert Spencer of the Survival of the Fittest is more accurate, . . .

I have called this principle, by which each slight variation, if useful, is preserved, by the term of Natural Selection.

In the survival of favoured individuals and races, during the constantly-recurring Struggle for Existence, we see a powerful and ever-acting form of Selection. . . . Thus, from the war of nature, from famine and death, the most exalted object which we are capable of conceiving, namely the production of the higher animals, directly follows.

There is no exception to the rule that every organic being naturally increases at so high a rate, that, if not destroyed, the earth would soon be covered by the progeny of a single pair. Even slow-breeding man has doubled in 25 years, and at this rate, in less than a thousand years, there would literally be no standing room for his progeny.
Ch. 3

The Descent of Man (1871)

I fully subscribe to the judgment of those writers who maintain that of all the differences between man and the lower animals, the moral sense of conscience is by far the most important. . . . It is the most noble of all the attributes of man.
Ch. 4

With savages the weak in body or mind are soon eliminated. We civilized men, on the other hand, do our utmost to check the process of elimination. . . . There is reason to believe that vaccination has preserved thousands, who from a weak constitution would formerly have succumbed to smallpox. Thus the weak members of civilized society propagate their kind. No one who has attended to the breeding of domestic animals will doubt that this must be highly injurious to the race of men.

---

*"Darwin never proposed that humankind is descended from monkeys . . . human beings and monkeys have a common ancestor." Nor does "survival of the fittest" mean of the strongest. "That organism survives, in Darwin's terms," writes Burnham in *The Dictionary of Misinformation,* "which is best suited to its environs. . . ." Darwin never claimed the theory of evolution original, "nor did Darwin ever try to prove that men are descended

from apes." Aristotle, according to Darwin, "shadowed forth" natural selection.
"The *Origin of Species* introduces a mode of thinking that in the end was bound to transform the logic of knowledge, and hence the treatment of morals, politics, and religion."—John Dewey, *The Influence of Darwin on Philosophy,* 1910.
**The original full title was *On the Origin of Species by Means of Natural Selection, or the Preservation of Favoured Races in the Struggle of Life.*

To do good in return for evil, to love your enemy, is a height of morality to which it may be doubted whether the social instincts would, by themselves, have ever led us. It is necessary that these instincts, together with sympathy, should have been highly cultivated and extended by the aid of reason, and instruction, and the love or fear of God, before any such golden rule would ever be thought of and obeyed.

The idea of a universal and beneficent Creator does not seem to arise in the mind of man, until he has been elevated by long-continued culture.
Ch. 5

The Simiadae then branched off into two great stems, the New World and Old World monkeys; and from the latter at a remote period, Man, the wonder and the glory of the universe, proceeded.
Ch. 6

Man is more courageous, pugnacious and energetic than woman, and has a more inventive genius. His brain is absolutely larger, but whether or not proportionately to his larger body, has not, I believe, been fully ascertained.
Ch. 8

Of all the causes which have led to the differences in external appearance between the races of man and to a certain extent between man and the lower animals, sexual selection has been the most efficient.
Ch. 21

Life and Letters of Charles Darwin (1887)

Without *speculation* there is no good and original observation.
To Alfred Russell Wallace, 1857

Believing as I do that man in the distant future will be a far more perfect creature than he now is, it is an intolerable thought that he and all other sentient beings are doomed to complete annihilation after such long-continued slow progress. To those who fully admit the immortality of the human soul, the destruction of our world will not appear so dreadful.

I feel compelled to look for a first Cause . . . and I deserve to be called a Deist.

I have never been an atheist in the sense of denying the existence of a God. . . . an agnostic would be the more correct description of my state of mind.
To Rev. J. Fordyce, July 7, 1879

A man who dares to waste one hour of time has not discovered the value of life.
Attributed

ERASMUS DARWIN
(1731–1802)
English poet, naturalist

The Botanic Garden (1789)

He who allows oppression shares the crime.

DA VINCI, *see* Leonardo Da Vinci

DAVID DAVIS
(1815–1886)
U.S. Supreme Court justice

The Constitution of the United States is a law for rulers and people, equally in war and peace, and covers with the shield of its protection all classes of men, at all times, and under all circumstances. No doctrine involving more pernicious consequences was ever invented by the wit of man than that any of its provisions can be suspended during any of the great exigencies of government. Such a doctrine leads directly to anarchy or despotism. . . .
Ex-Parte Milligan, 4 Wallace 2 (1866)*

EUGENE V(ictor) DEBS
(1855–1926)
American Socialist leader, convict #9653, Atlanta penitentiary

The Crimson Standard, Appeal to Reason (1905)

The red flag, since time immemorial, has symbolized the discontent of the downtrodden, the revolt of the rabble. That is its sinister significance to the tyrant . . . the pure red that symbolizes the common blood of the human race, is repulsive and abhorrent to him because it is at once an impeachment of his title, a denial of his superiority, and a menace to his power.

---

*In 1864, Lamdin F. Milligan, a civilian, was tried by a military commission and sentenced to death. The Davis decision, "although much criticized by one school of thought, is an outstanding declaration of the rights of man."—Justice Douglas, *An Almanac of Liberty*.

Walls and Bars (1907)

Capitalism needs and must have the prison to protect itself from the criminals it has created.

Speeches

The world's workers have always been and still are the world's slaves. They have borne all the burdens of the race and built all the monuments along the tracks of civilization; they have produced all the world's wealth and supported all the world's governments. They have conquered all things but their own freedom. They are still the subject class in every nation on earth and the chief function of every government is to keep them at the mercy of their masters.
> Acceptance speech, Socialist Party Convention, Indianapolis, May 1912*

I am opposed to every war but one . . . and that is the worldwide war of social revolution.
> Socialist convention, June 16, 1918

Years ago I began to recognize my kinship with all living beings . . . I said then, and I say now, that while there is a lower class I am in it, while there is a criminal element, I am of it; while there is a soul in prison, I am not free.

The martyred Christ of the working class; the inspired evangel of the downtrodden masses, the world's supreme revolutionary leader. . . .
> Speech, quoted in Sinclair, *The Cry for Justice* (1920)

STEPHEN DECATUR
(1779–1820)
American patriot

Our Country! In her intercourse with foreign nations, may she always be in the right; but our country, right or wrong!**
> Toast, Norfolk, Virginia, April 1816. Quoted in A.S. Mackenzie's *Life of Decatur,* Ch. xiv

---

*Debs got almost 1,000,000 votes for President, in 1912.
**"And say not thou 'My country right or wrong'/Nor shed thy blood for an unhallowed cause."—John Quincy Adams, in *Congress, Slavery and an Unjust War,* c. 1847.
" 'My country right or wrong' is like saying, 'My mother, drunk or sober.' "—G.K. Chesterton, *The Defendant,* 1901.

DANIEL DEFOE
(1660?–1731)
English writer

An Essay Upon Projects, "An Academy for Women" (1697)

I have often thought of it as one of the most barbarous customs in the world, considering us as a civilized and Christian country, that we deny the advantages of learning to women.

The capacities of women are supposed to be greater, and their senses quicker than those of men; and what they may be capable of being bred to, is plain from some instances of female wit, which this age is not without, which upbraids us with injustice, and looks as if we denied women the advantage of education, for fear they should vie with the men in their improvements.

And without partiality, a woman of sense and manners is the finest and most delicate part of God's creation, the glory of her Maker, and the great instance of his singular regard to man, his darling creature, to whom he gave the best gift either God could bestow or man receive.

A woman well bred and well taught, furnished with the additional accomplishments of knowledge and behavior, is a creature without comparison.

The True-Born Englishman (1701)

> Wherever God erects a house of prayer,
> The Devil always builds a chapel there;
> And 'twill be found, upon examination,
> The latter has the largest congregation.
> Pt. I

An Essay on the Regulation of the Press (January 7, 1704)

Whatever Party of Men obtain the Reins of Management, and have power to name the Person who shall License the Press, that Party of Men have the whole power of keeping the World in Ignorance, in all matters relating to Religion or Policy, since the Writers of that Party shall have full liberty to impose their Notions upon the World.

I know no Nation in the World, whose Government is not perfectly Despotick, that ever makes preventive Laws.

EDGAR DEGAS
(1834–1917)
French artist

Art is vice. One does not wed it, one rapes it.
> Quoted in *Saturday Review,* May 28, 1966

CHARLES (André Josef Marie) DE GAULLE
(1890–1970)
French general, president

Le fil de l'épée [The Edge of the Sword] (1934)

The perfection preached in the Gospels never yet built up an empire.

The Words of the General (1962)

The worst calamity after a stupid general is an intelligent general.

Greatness is a road leading towards the unknown.
> Quoted in *Esquire,* December 1971

THOMAS DEKKER
(1572–1632)
English playwright

The Honest Whore (in collaboration with Thomas Middleton, 1604)

Oh, what a heaven is love! Oh, what a hell!
> Pt. 1

We are ne'er like angels till our passion dies.
> Pt. 2

Were there no women, men might live like gods.
> Pt. 3

DANIEL DELEON
(1852–1914)
American Socialist leader*

The Vatican in Politics (1891)

The moment religion organizes into a specific creed it becomes a political force. From Moses down to Brigham Young, every creed-founder has been a State-builder.

---

*In an interview, November 18, 1922, Lenin told G.S. that Russian Bolshevism was based on DeLeon's interpretation of Marx.

Reform or Revolution

REVOLUTION, accordingly, stands on its own bottom, hence it cannot be overthrown; REFORM leans upon others, hence its downfall is certain.

Weekly People (July 2, 1910)

It is as workingman, not as Negro, that the Negro is kept down in the South. It is the labor question, not the race questions, that keeps the South in turmoil.

What is Socialism? (Socialist Labor Party publication, 1956)

Socialism has no business to tinker with "reforms." "Reforms" only tend to sweet scent the capitalist rule. For Socialism in the United States to bother with reforms is like washing the garbage before dumping it into the can. Away with the garbage of capitalism.

DE LISLE, *see* Rouget de Lisle

JOSEF DE MAISTRE
(1753–1821)
French diplomat

Considérations sur la France (1796)

Christianity was preached by ignorant men and believed by servants, and that is why it resembles nothing ever known.

Man's destructive hand spares nothing that lives; he kills to feed himself, he kills to clothe himself, he kills to adorn himself, he kills to attack, he kills to defend himself, he kills to instruct himself, he kills to amuse himself, he kills for the sake of killing.

Lettres et opuscules inédits (August 27, 1811)

Every nation has the government it deserves.

DEMOCRITUS
(460 B.C.?–370 B.C.?)
Greek philosopher

The first principles of the universe are atoms and empty space; everything else is merely thought to exist.

Further, the atoms are unlimited in size and number, and they are borne along in the whole universe in a vortex, and thereby generate all composite things—fire, water, air, earth; for even these are conglomerations of given atoms.

Whatever is, is right.
Quoted in Diogenes Laërtius, "Democritus"

DEMONAX
(c. 150 A.D.)
Roman cynic philosopher

Probably all laws are useless; for good men do not want laws at all, and bad men are made no better by them.
Quoted in Lucian, *Demonax*, Section 59

DEMOSTHENES
(384?–322? B.C.)
Athenian orator, statesman

Third Olynthiac (349 B.C.)

Nothing is so easy as to deceive one's self; for what we wish, we readily believe.
Sec. 19

Philippic 2 (344 B.C.)

There is nothing, absolutely nothing, which needs to be more carefully guarded against than that one man should be allowed to become more powerful than the people.
Sec. 24

De Falsa Legatione, 81 (344 B.C.)

The facts speak for themselves.

We have hetairai for our delight, concubines for the daily needs of our bodies, wives in order that we may beget legitimate children; and have faithful housekeepers.
Quoted in Briffault, *The Mothers* (1927)

The three most intractable beasts, the owl, the serpent, and the people.
Quoted in *Plutarch's Lives: Demosthenes* (c. 106 A.D.)

THOMAS DE QUINCEY
(1785–1859)
English essayist

Confessions of an English Opium Eater (1856)

Thou hast the keys of Paradise, O just, subtle, and mighty Opium!
Pt. ii

Essay: Murder Considered as One of the Fine Arts (1827)

As the inventor of murder, and the father of art, Cain must have been a man of first-rate genius.

RENÉ DESCARTES
(1596–1650)
French philosopher

Rules for the Direction of the Mind (1628–29)

. . . of all the sciences known as yet, Arithmetic and Geometry alone are free from any taint of falsity or uncertainty.

A Discourse on Method (1637)

To be possessed of a vigorous mind is not enough; the prime requisite is rightly to apply it.

The greatest minds, as they are capable of the highest excellencies, are open likewise to the greatest aberrations.
Part I

No opinion, however absurd and incredible, can be imagined, which has not been maintained by some one of the philosophers.
Part II

Except our own thoughts, there is nothing absolutely in our power.
Part III

I observed that, whilst I thus wished to think that all was false, it was absolutely necessary that I, who thus thought, should be somewhat; and as I observed that this truth, *I think, hence I am** was so certain and of such evidence, that no ground of doubt, however extravagant, could be alleged by the sceptics capable of shaking it, I concluded that I might, without scruple, accept it as the first principle of the philosophy of which I was in search.
Part IV

Meditationes de prima philosophia (1629–1639)

What is there, then, that can be esteemed true? Perhaps this only, that there is absolutely nothing certain.

But what is man? Shall I say a rational animal? Assuredly not. . . .

**Cogito, ergo sum*—usually translated, "I think, therefore I am." *Cogito cogitationes, ergo sum,* and *Cogito me cogitare, ergo sum,* are the correct forms of the famous formula.—Hannah Arendt, quoted in *The New Yorker,* November 21, 1977.

But what, then am I? A thinking being, it has been said. But what is a thinking thing? It is a thing that doubts, understands (conceives), affirms, denies, wills, refuses, that imagines also, and perceives. Assuredly it is not little, if all these properties belong to my nature.

Principles of Philosophy (1644)

If you would be a real seeker after truth, it is necessary that at least once in your life you doubt, as far as possible, all things.

The chief cause of human error is to be found in prejudices picked up in childhood.

Les passions de l'âme [*The Passions of the Soul*] (1644)

The principal effect of the passions is that they incite and persuade the mind to will the events for which they prepared the body.

CAMILLE DESMOULINS
(1760–1794)
French revolutionist

Burning is no answer.
Reply to Robespierre, January 7, 1794, on burning his newspaper, *Vieux Cordelier.*

MADAME DE STAËL, *see* Staël

DE TOCQUEVILLE, *see* Tocqueville

KARL W. DEUTSCH
(1912–   )
Professor of International Peace, Harvard

The Churchman (April, 1977)

The single greatest power in the world today is the power to change. . . . The most recklessly irresponsible thing we could do in the future would be to go on exactly as we have in the past ten or twenty years. I can imagine no more dangerous policy than the conservatism that exists today.

PETER DE VRIES
(1910–   )
American novelist

The Mackerel Plaza (1958)

It is the final proof of God's omnipotence that he need not exist in order to save us.

JOHN DEWEY
(1859–1952)
American philosopher, educator

My Pedagogic Creed (1897)

I believe that
—the school is primarily a social institution.
—education, therefore, is a process of living and not a preparation for future living.
—education is the fundamental method of social progress and reform.
—all education proceeds by the participation of the individual in the social consciousness of the race. . . .
—education is a regulation of the process of coming to share in the social conscious ness. . . .

The Influence of Darwin on Philosophy (1910)

Intellectually, religious emotions are not *creative* but *conservative.* They attach themselves readily to the current view of the world and consecrate it. They steep and dye intellectual fabrics in the seething vat of emotions; they do not form their warp and woof. There is not, I think, an instance of any large idea about the world being independently generated by religion.

When he [Darwin] said of species what Galileo had said of the earth, *e pur se muove,* he emancipated once for all, genetic and experimental ideas as an organon of asking questions and looking for explanations.

Human Nature and Conduct (1922)

Religion has lost itself in cults, dogmas, and myths. Consequently the office of religion as a sense of community and one's place in it has been lost.

Characters and Events (1929)

While in general, the opposite of the progressive attitude is not so much conservatism as it is disbelief in the possibility of constructive social engineering, the conservative mind is a large factor in propagating this disbelief.

Every thinker puts some portion of an apparently stable world in peril.

Primitive Christianity was devastating in its claims. It was a religion of renunciation and denunciation of the "world"; it demanded a change of heart that entailed a revolutionary change in human relationship. . . . A religion that began as a demand for a revolutionary change and that has become a sanction of established economic, political and international institutions.

Contribution, *Living Philosophies,* 1931

Encyclopedia of Unified Science (c. 1938)

It is demonstrable that many of the obstacles for change which have been attributed to human nature are in fact due to the inertia of institutions and to the voluntary desire of powerful classes to maintain the existing status.

Experience and Education (1938)

The only freedom that is of enduring importance is freedom of intelligence, that is to say, freedom of observation and of judgment exercised in behalf of purposes that are intrinsically worth while.

CHARLES DICKENS
(1812–1870)
British novelist

Hard Times (1854)

Now what I want is, Facts . . . Facts alone are wanted in life.

Mr. Gradgrind, Bk. i, Ch. I

Martin Chuzzlewit (1843-44)

Here's the rule for bargains: "Do other men, for they would do you." That's the true business precept.

Jonas Chuzzlewit, Ch. II

A Tale of Two Cities (1859)

It is a far, far better thing that I do, than I have ever done; it is a far, far better rest that I go to, than I have ever known.

Sidney Carton, Bk. iii, Ch. 15

EMILY DICKINSON
(1830–1886)
American poet

There's a certain Slant of light
Winter Afternoons—
That oppresses, like the Heft
Of Cathedral Tunes—

No. 258 (c. 1861)

The Soul selects her own Society—
Then—shuts the Door—
To her divine Majority—
Present no more—

No. 303 (c. 1862)

After great pain, a formal feeling comes—
The Nerves sit ceremonious, like Tombs—
The stiff Heart questions was it He, that bore,
And Yesterday, or Centuries before?

The Feet, mechanical, go round—
of Ground, or Air, or Ought—
A Wooden way
Regardless grown,
A Quartz contentment, like a stone—

This is the Hour of Lead—
Remembered, if outlived,
As Freezing persons, recollect the Snow—
First—Chill—then Stupor—then the letting go—

No. 341 (c. 1862)

I died for Beauty—but was scarce
Adjusted in the Tomb
When One who died for Truth, was lain
In an adjoining Room—

He questioned softly "Why I failed"?
"For Beauty", I replied—
"And I—for Truth—themselves are One—
We Brethren, are", He said—

No. 449 (c. 1862)

I heard a Fly buzz—when I died—
The Stillness in the Room
Was like the Stillness in the Air—
Between the Heaves of Storm—

No. 465 (c. 1862)

Afraid! of whom am I afraid?
Not Death—for who is He?
The Porter of my Father's Lodge
As much abasheth me!

No. 608 (c. 1862)

Because I could not stop for Death—
He kindly stopped for me—
The carriage held but just Ourselves—
And Immortality.

No. 712 (c. 1863)

I never spoke with God
Nor visited in Heaven—
Yet certain am I of the spot
As if the Checks were given—

No. 1052 (c. 1865)

Who has not found the Heaven—below—
Will fail of it above—
For Angels rent the House next ours,
Wherever we remove—

No. 1544 (c. 1883)

I took one Draught of Life—
I'll tell you what I paid—
Precisely an existence—
The market price, they said.

                              No. 1725 (n.d.)

Love can do all but raise the Dead. . . .
                              No. 1731 (n.d.)

My life closed twice before its close—
It yet remains to see
If immortality unveil
A third event to me

So huge, so hopeless to conceive
As these that twice befell.
Parting is all we know of heaven,
And all we need of hell.

                              No. 1732 (n.d.)

G(oldsworthy) LOWES DICKINSON
(1862–1932)
English writer

The Greek View of Life (1896)

That sunny and frank intelligence . . . that
unique and perfect balance of body and soul,
passion and intellect, represent, against the
brilliant setting of Athenian life, the highest
achievement of the civilization of Greece.

With the Greek civilization, beauty perished from the world.

A Modern Symposium

Anarchy is not the absence of power, it is
the absence of force; it is the free outflowing of
the spirit into the forms in which it delights;
and in such forms alone, as they grow and
change, can it find expression which is not
also a bondage.

DENIS DIDEROT
(1713–1784)
French philosopher, atheist

Essai sur le mérite de la vertu (1745)

There is only one step from fanaticism to
barbarism.

Pensées philosophiques (1746)

Only the passions, only great passions, can
elevate the mind to great things.

                              Bk. I

Of some men we should not say that they
fear God, but that they are *afraid* of Him.

                              Bk. VIII

A thing is not proved because no one has
ever questioned it. . . . Skepticism is the first
step toward truth.

To prove the Gospels by a miracle is to
prove an absurdity by something contrary to
nature.

                              Bk. XXI

A Philosophical Conversation (1777)

The point is to get into heaven by hook or
by crook.

Supposing a man-hater had desired to render the human race as unhappy as possible,
what could he have invented for the purpose
better than belief in an incomprehensible
being about whom men could never be able to
agree?

Fools have been and always will be the majority of mankind.

When God, from whom I have my reason,
demands of me to sacrifice it, he becomes a
mere juggler that snatches from me what he
pretended to give.

If *reason* be a gift of Heaven, and we can say
as much of *faith,* Heaven has certainly made
us two gifts not only incompatible, but in direct contradiction to each other. In order to
solve the difficulty, we are compelled to say
either that faith is a chimera or that reason is
useless.

Footnote to d'Holbach's *The System of Nature*
(1770)

The Judaical and Christian theology show
us a partial god who chooses or rejects, who
loves or hates, according to his caprice; in
short, a tyrant who plays with his creatures;
who punishes in the world the whole human
species for the crimes of a single man; who
predestinates the greater number of mortals to
be his enemies, to the end that he may punish
them to all eternity, for having received from
him the liberty of declaring against him.

Many people have looked upon Jesus as a
true theist, whose religion has been by degrees
corrupted. Indeed in the books which contain
the law which is attributed to him, there is no
mention either of worship, or of priests, or of
sacrifices, or of sufferings, or of the greater part
of the doctrines of actual Christianity, which

has become the most prejudicial of all the superstitions of the earth.

"On Man" (a refutation of Helvetius' work, 1774)

Descartes said: "I think, therefore I am." Helvetius wants to say: "I feel, therefore I want to feel pleasantly." I prefer Hobbes who claims that in order to draw a conclusion which takes us somewhere, we must say, "I feel, I think, I judge; therefore, a part of organized matter like me is capable of feeling, thinking, and judging."

Dithyrambe sur la fête des Rois (c. 1780)

And with the guts of the last priest
Let us strangle the last king!

Last conversation (1784)

The first step toward philosophy is doubt.

DIO CHRYSOSTOM
(c. 40–120 A.D.)
Greek sophist, rhetorician

A comprehended God is no God.
Quoted in Mencken, *Treatise on the Gods,* Ch. 5

DIOGENES "the Cynic"*
(c. 400–c. 325 B.C.)
Greek philosopher

The most beautiful thing in the world is freedom of speech.

Love of money is the mother of all evils.

Demagogues are the mobs' lackeys.

It is the privilege of the Gods to want nothing, and of godlike men to want little.

I am looking for an honest man.
Quoted in Diogenes Laërtius, "Diogenes"

DIOGENES LAËRTIUS
(fl. 200 A.D.)
Biographer of Greek philosophers

Lives and Opinions of Eminent Philosophers

There is a written and an unwritten law. The one by which we regulate our constitutions in our cities is the written law; that which arises from custom is the unwritten law.
"Plato"

---

*"The stories which are told of him are probably true."—*Britannica,* 11th ed., Vol. viii, pp. 281–2.

The question was once put to him, how we ought to behave to our friends; and the answer he gave was, "As we should wish our friends to behave to us."

On one occasion Aristotle was asked how much educated men were superior to those uneducated. "As much," said he, "as the living are to the dead."
"Aristotle"

Solon used to say . . . that laws were like cobwebs—for if any trifling or powerless thing fell into them, they held it fast; while if it were something weightier, it broke through them and was off.
"Solon"

The only good is knowledge, and the only evil is ignorance.
"Socrates"

One of his sayings was, "Even the gods cannot strive against necessity."
"Pittacus"

I know not how to conceive the good, apart from the pleasures of taste, sexual pleasure, the pleasures of sound, and the pleasures of beautiful forms.
"Epicurus"

DIONYSIUS OF HALICARNASSUS
(c. 20 B.C.)
Greek historian

Antiquities of Rome

A generous and noble spirit cannot be expected to dwell in the breasts of men who are struggling for their daily bread.

Governments are not overthrown by the poor, who have no power, but by the rich—when they are insulted by their inferiors, and cannot obtain justice.

De Arte Rhetorica

History is philosophy teaching by example.
(paraphrasing Thucydides) xi, 2

DIONYSIUS THE AREOPAGITE
First "bishop" of Athens*

"Divine Names"

Evil does not exist at all. . . . Evil in its nature is neither a thing nor does it bring any-

---

*Dionysius the Areopagite is quoted in Acts XVII, 34, but little else is known about him.—*Britannica,* 11th ed., Vol. viii, p. 284.

thing forth. . . . All things which are, by the very fact that they are, are good and come from good; but insofar as they are deprived of good, they are neither good nor do they exist.

BENJAMIN DISRAELI (Earl of Beaconsfield)
(1804–1881)
English statesman, novelist

Speeches, House of Commons

A Conservative Government is an organized hypocrisy.
March 17, 1845

A precedent embalms a principle.
February 22, 1848

The difference of race is one of the reasons why I fear that war will always exist: because race implies differences, difference implies superiority, and superiority leads to predominance.
February 11, 1849

Finality is not the language of politics.
February 28, 1859

Assassination has never changed the history of the world.
May 1, 1865; a reference to Lincoln

It has been discovered that the best way to insure implicit obedience is to commence tyranny in the nursery.
June 15, 1874

Address to the SIESL of the Oxford Diocese (November 25, 1864)

The question is this: Is man an ape or an angel? I, my lord, I am on the side of the angels. I repudiate with abhorrence these new-fangled theories.

Speech, Manchester (April 3, 1872)

Increased means and increased leisure are the two civilizers of man.

Coningsby (1844)

Youth is a blunder; Manhood a struggle; Old Age a regret.

No government can be long secure without a formidable Opposition.
Book iii, Ch. 1

Man is only truly great when he acts from the passions.
Book iv, Ch. 13

The Infernal Marriage (1834)

The world is weary of statesmen whom democracy has degraded into politicians.

Religion should be the rule of life, not a casual incident in it.

Lothair (1870)

You know who the critics are? The men who have failed in literature and art.

Every woman should marry, and no man.

Popanilla

In politics experiments mean revolutions.

Sybil (1845)

I was told that the Privileged and the People formed Two Nations, governed by different laws, influenced by different manners, with no thoughts or sympathies in common.

Contarini Fleming (1832)

When men are pure, laws are useless; when men are corrupt laws are broken.

Endymion (1880)

There is no education like adversity.

Tancred (1847)

A Majority is always the best repartee.
Ch. 14

Vivian Grey (1826)

The [armed] services in war time are fit only for desperadoes, but in peace are fit only for fools.

The man who anticipates his century is always persecuted when living, and is always pilfered when dead.

Nature has her own laws, and this is one—a fair day's wage for a fair day's work.

Yes, I am a Jew, and when the ancestors of the right honourable gentlemen were brutal savages in an unknown island, mine were priests in the temple of Solomon.
Reply, 1835, to a racial slur by Daniel O'Connell

Never complain and never explain.
Quoted in Robert Blake, *Disraeli* (1967)

There are three kinds of lies: lies, damned lies, and statistics.
Quoted in Mark Twain, *Autobiography*, I:246

. . . a society which has mistaken comfort for civilization.
> Quoted in Dean Inge, *Outspoken Essays*

From the people and for the people all springs and must exist.
> Quoted in magazine pages by Container Corporation

Christianity is completed Judaism, or it is nothing.
> Attributed

MILOVAN DJILAS
(1911–   )
Former Yugoslav Vice-President

The New Class

It is necessary for the revolution not only to devour its own children, but—one might say—devour itself.

HENRY AUSTIN DOBSON
(1840–1921)
British poet

Ars Victrix

All passes. Art alone
  Enduring stays to us;
The bust outlasts the throne—
  The Coin, Tiberius.
> St. 8

JOHN DONNE
(1573–1631)
English poet, cleric

Devotions (1623)

All mankinde is of one Author, and is one volume; when one Man dies, one Chapter is not torne out of the book, but translated into a better language; and every chapter must be so translated; God emploies several translators; some peeces are translated by age, some by sicknesse, some by warre, some by justice; but God's hand is in every translation; and his hand shall binde up all our scattered leaves againe, for that Librarie where every booke shall lie open to one another.

No man is an Iland intire of itselfe; every man is a peece of the Continent, a part of the maine; if a clod bee washed away by the Sea, Europe is the lesse, as well as if a promontorie were, as well as if a mannor of thy friends or of thine owne were; any man's death diminishes me, because I am involved in Mankinde; and therefore never send to know for whom the bell tolls; it tolls for thee.
> XVII

Meditations

It is too little to call Man a little World; Except God, man is a *diminutive* to nothing.
> Meditation IV

Solitude is a torment which is not threatened in hell itself.
> Meditation V

Sermons (1619)

Chastity is not chastity in an old man, but a disability to be unchaste.

Doth not a man die even in his birth? The breaking of prison is death, and what is our birth, but a breaking of prison?
> No. XV

And when a whirl-winde hath blowne the dust of the Churchyard into the Church, and man sweeps out the dust of the Church into the Church-yard, who will undertake to sift those dusts again, and to pronounce, This is the Patrician, this is the noble flower, and this the yeomanly, this the Plebian bran.

Great sins are great possessions; but levities and vanities possess us too; and men had rather part with Christ than with any possession.
> No. XVII, folio of 1640

God affords no man the comfort, the false comfort of Atheism: He will not allow a pretending Atheist the power to flatter himself, so far, as to seriously think there is no God.
> No. XXII

Paradoxes and Problems

I call not that Virginity a virtue, which resideth onely in the Bodies integrity; much lesse if it be with a purpose of perpetually keeping it: for then it is a most inhumane vice—But I call that Virginity a virtue which is willing and desirous to yeeld it selfe upon honest and lawfull terms, when just reason requireth; and until then, is kept with a modest chastity of Body and Mind.
> X

"To the Countess of Bedford" (c. 1607–8)

Reason is our Soules left hand, Faith her right,
  By these wee reach divinity. . . .

"The Martyrs"

> . . . for Oh, to some
> Not to be Martyres, is a martyrdome.

"Change, An Elegy" (c. 1593–98)

> . . . Change is the nursery
> Of musicke, joy, life, and eternity.

"To His Mistress Going to Bed," Elegy XIX
(c. 1593–98)

> Full nakedness! All joyes are due to thee,
> As souls unbodied, bodies uncloth'd must
> be,. . . .

"Song" (c. 1593–1601)

> Goe and catche a falling starre,
> Get with child a mandrake root,
> Tell me, where all past yeares are,
> Or who cleft the Divel's foot.
> Teach me to hear Mermaides' singing,
> Or to keep off envies stinging,
> And finde
> What winde
> Serves to advance an honest minde.
> St. 1

"The Extasie" (c. 1593–1601)

> This Extasie doth unperplex
> (We said) and tell us what we love,
> Wee see by this, it was not sexe,
> Wee see, we saw not what did move:
> But as all severall soules contain
> Mixture of things, they know not what,
> Love, these mixt souls, doth mixe againe.

> Loves mysteries in soules doe grow,
> But yet the body is his booke.

"Hymne to God My God, in My Sicknesse" (1631
or ?1623)

> We think that *Paradise* and *Calvarie,*
> *Christs* Crosse, and *Adams* tree, stood in
> one place;
> Looke, Lord, and finde both *Adams* met in
> me;
> As the first *Adams* sweat surrounds my
> face,
> May the last *Adams* blood my soule em-
> brace.

Holy Sonnets (before 1615)

> At the round earths imagin'd corners, blow
> Your trumpets, Angells, and arise, arise
> From death, you numberlesse infinities
> Of soules, and to your scatt'red bodies goe,
> All whom the flood did, and fire shall o'er-
> throw;

> All whom warre, dearth, age, agues, tyran-
> nies,
> Despaire, law, chance, hath slaine, and you
> whose eyes,
> Shall behold God, and never tast deaths
> woe.
> . . .

> Teach mee how to repent; for that's as good
> As if Thou'hadst seal'd my pardon, with thy
> blood.
> VII

> If poysonous mineralls, and if that tree
> Whose fruit threw death on else immortall
> us,
> If lecherous goats, if serpents envious
> Cannot be damn'd; Alas; why should I bee?
> IX

> Death be not proud, though some have
> called thee
> Mighty and dreadful, for thou art not so,
> For those whom thou think'st thou dost
> overthrow,
> Die not, poor death, nor yet canst thou kill
> me.
> . . .

> One short sleep past, we wake eternally,
> And death shall be no more; death, thou
> shalt die.

FYODOR DOSTOYEVSKI
(1821–1881)
Russian novelist

The Brothers Karamazov (1880)

> . . . God sets us nothing but riddles.
> Pt. I, bk. III, ch. 3

> The awful thing is that beauty is mysterious
> as well as terrible. God and the devil are fight-
> ing there, and the battlefield is the heart of
> man.

> And man has actually invented God . . .
> the marvel is that such an idea, the idea of the
> necessity of God, could enter the head of such
> a savage, vicious beast as man.
> Bk. V, ch. 3.

> They think to order all things wisely; but
> having rejected Christ they will end by
> drenching the world with blood.

> If the devil doesn't exist, but man created
> him, he has created him in his own image.

> The absurd is only too necessary on earth.
> The world stands on absurdities.

. . . for nothing has ever been more insurmountable for a man and a human society than freedom.

Didst thou forget that man prefers peace, and even death, to freedom of choice in the knowledge of good and evil?

Bk. V, ch. 5

Everyone is really responsible to all men for all men and for everything.

Pt. II, bk. VI

Until you have become really, in actual fact, as brother to everyone, brotherhood will not come to pass.

Bk. VI, ch. 2

If you were to destroy in mankind the belief in immorality, not only love but every living force maintaining the life of the world would at once be dried up. Moreover, nothing then would be immoral, everything would be permissible, even cannibalism.

Even those who have renounced Christianity and attack it, in their inmost being still follow the Christian ideal, for hitherto neither their subtlety nor the ardour of their hearts has been able to create a higher ideal of man and of virtue than the ideal given by Christ.

Remember particularly that you cannot be a judge of anyone. For no one can judge a criminal, until he recognizes that he is just such a criminal as the man standing before him, and that he perhaps is more than all men to blame for the crime. When he understands that, he will be able to be a judge.
Love a man even in his sin for that love is a likeness of the divine love, and is the summit of love on earth.

Mankind will reject and kill their prophets, but men love their martyrs and honour those whom they have done to death.

Bk. VI, Ch. 3

Crime and Punishment (1866)

It would be interesting to know what it is men are most afraid of. Taking a new step, uttering a new word.

The Possessed (1871)

Whoever wants supreme freedom must kill himself. He who cares enough to take his own life is God.

The Idiot (1868)

To kill someone for committing murder is a punishment incomparably worse than the crime itself. Murder by legal sentence is immeasurably more terrible than murder by brigands.

Notes from the Underground (1864)

But there are other things which a man is afraid to tell even to himself, and every decent man has a number of such things stored away in his mind . . . A man's true autobiography is almost an impossibility . . . man is bound to lie about himself.

The Diary of a Writer (1873)

All the Utopias will come to pass only when we grow wings and all people are converted into angels.

Beauty will save the world.
Quoted by Solzhenitsyn, Nobel Prize acceptance speech, 1970

**(George) NORMAN DOUGLAS
(1868–1952)
English writer**

South Wind (1917)

The historian who fails in his duty deceives the reader and wrongs the dead.

The heroes, the saints and sages—they are those who face the world alone. A married man is half a man.

You can tell the ideals of a nation by its advertisements.

As to the majority, the crowd, the herd—they do not exist neither here nor anywhere else. They leave a purely physiological mark upon posterity; they propagate the species and protect their offspring. So do foxes.

Temperance . . . I call it the exercise of our faculties and organs in such a manner as to combine the maximum of pleasure with the minimum of pain.

What is all wisdom save a collection of platitudes. Take fifty of our current proverbial sayings—they are so trite, so threadbare. . . . None the less they embody the concentrated experience of the race, and the man who orders his life according to their teachings cannot go far wrong. . . . Has any man ever attained to inner harmony by pondering the experience of others? Not since the world began! He must pass through the fire.

STEPHEN A(rnold) DOUGLAS
(1813–1861)
American statesman

Now, I do not believe the Almighty ever intended the negro to be the equal of the white man. If He did, He has been a long time demonstrating the fact.

Debate with Lincoln, Ottawa, Ill., August 21, 1858

WILLIAM O. DOUGLAS
(1898–1980)
U.S. Supreme Court Justice

Decisions

We are a religious people whose institutions presuppose a Supreme Being.

Zorach v. Clauson, 343 U.S. 306 (1952)

The right to work, I had assumed, was the most precious liberty that man possessed. Man has indeed as much right to work as he has to live, to be free, to own property.

Dissent, Barsky v. Regents (April 26, 1954)

Thus, if the First Amendment means anything in this field, it must allow protests even against the moral code that the standard of the day sets for the community. In other words, literature should not be suppressed merely because it offends the moral code of the censor.

Dissent, Roth v. U.S., 354 U.S. 476 (1957)

The function of the press is to explore and investigate events, inform the people what is going on, and to expose the harmful as well as the good influences at work. There is no higher function performed under our constitutional regime. . . . A reporter is no better than his source of information. Unless he has a privilege to withhold the identity of his source, he will be the victim of governmental intrigue or aggression. If he can be summoned to testify in secret before a grand jury, his sources will dry up and the attempted exposure, the effort to enlighten the public will be ended. . . .

The intrusion of government into this domain is symptomatic of the disease of this society. As the years pass, the power of government becomes more and more pervasive. It is power to suffocate both people and causes. Those in power, whatever their politics, want only to perpetuate it. Now that the fences of the law and the tradition that has protected the press are broken down, the people are the victims. The First Amendment, as

I read it, was designed precisely to prevent that tragedy.

Dissent, Earl Caldwell case (1972)

An Almanac of Liberty (1954)

The dissenting opinion has continued (since 1792) as a great American tradition. It is as true to the character of our democracy as of speech itself.

Acceptance by government of a dissident press is a measure of the maturity of a nation.

Ideas are indeed the most dangerous weapons in the world. Our ideas of freedom are the most powerful political weapons man has ever forged. If we remember that, we will never have much to fear from Communism.

The right to revolt has sources deep in our history.*

The Fifth Amendment is an old friend and a good friend. It is one of the great landmarks in man's struggle to be free of tyranny, to be decent and civilized.

Points of Rebellion

Today's Establishment is the new George III. Whether it will continue to adhere to his tactics, we do not know. If it does, the redress honored by tradition, is also revolution.

Restriction of free thought and free speech is the most dangerous of all subversions. It is the one un-American act that could most easily defeat us.

Address, Author's Guild, December 3, 1952

The American Government is premised on the theory that if the mind of man is to be free, his ideas, his beliefs, his ideology, his philosophy must be placed beyond the reach of government.

Interview, New York Times, October 29, 1973

A people who extend civil liberties only to preferred groups start down the path either to a dictatorship of the right or the left.

Quoted in New York Times obituary,
January 20, 1980

The struggle is always between the individual and his sacred right to express himself . . . and . . . the power structure that seeks conformity, suppression and obedience.

Quoted in Newsday

---

*Justice Douglas quoted Jefferson, Hamilton and Lincoln's Inaugural.

FREDERICK DOUGLASS
(1817?–1895)
American author, abolitionist

If there is no struggle there is no progress.

The limits of tyrants are prescribed by the endurance of those whom they suppress.

I know of no rights of race superior to the rights of man.
Letter to Gerrit Smith, March 30, 1849

Fellow citizens, I will not enlarge further on your national inconsistencies. The existence of slavery in this country brands your republicanism as a sham, your humanity as a base pretense, and your Christianity as a lie. It destroys your moral power abroad, it corrupts your politicians at home. It saps the foundations of religion; it makes your name a hissing and a byeword to a mocking earth. It is the antagonistic force in your government, the only thing that seriously disturbs and endangers your Union. It fetters your progress, it is the enemy of improvement; the deadly foe of education; it fosters pride; it breeds indolence; it promotes vice; it shelters crime; it is a curse of the earth that supports it; and yet you cling to it as if it were the sheet anchor of all your hopes.
Address, "The Meaning of July 4th for the
American Negro," Rochester, New York,
July 5, 1852

EDWARD DOWLING, S.J.
American priest, editor

The two greatest obstacles to democracy in the United States are, first, the widespread delusion among the poor that we have a democracy, and second, the chronic terror among the rich, lest we get it.
Quoted in Chicago Daily News, August 28, 1941

ERNEST DOWSON
(1867–1900)
English poet

"Vita Summa brevis spem nos vetat incohare longam"

They are not long, the weeping and the
    laughter,
  Love and desire and hate:
I think they have no portion in us after
  We pass the gate.

"Non sum qualis eram bonae sub regno Cynarae"

I have been faithful to thee, Cynara! in my
  fashion.

THEODORE DREISER
(1871–1945)
American writer

The Titan (1914)

Nothing is proved, all is permitted.

Sister Carrie (1900)

Our civilization is still in a middle stage, scarcely beast, in that it is no longer wholly guided by instinct, scarcely human, in that it is not yet wholly guided by reason.

I acknowledge the Furies,
I believe in them, I have heard the disastrous beating of their wings.
Letter to Grant Richards, 1911

Think of the dull functioning of dogma, age after age. How many millions have been led shunted along dogmatic runways from the dark into the dark again . . . endless billions, and at the gates, dogma, ignorance, vice, cruelty, seize them and clamp this or that band upon their brains.

Art is the stored honey of the human soul, gathered on wings of misery and travail.

The government has ceased to function . . . the corporations are the government.
Quoted in Dorothy Dudley, Forgotten Frontiers
(1932)

The American press, with a very few exceptions, is a kept press. Kept by the big corporations the way a whore is kept by a rich man.
Contribution to In fact, 1942, proposing annual
Kept Press Week

WILLIAM DRUMMOND OF HAWTHORNDEN
(1585–1649)
Scottish poet

Academical Questions

He who will not reason, is a bigot; he who cannot is a fool; and he who dares not is a slave.

JOHN DRYDEN
(1631–1700)
English poet, critic

"The Hind and the Panther" (1687)

For truth has such a face and such a mien,
As to be lov'd needs only to be seen.
                                    Pt. I, 1.33

Of all the tyrannies on human kind
The worst is that which persecutes the
   mind.
                                  Pt. I, 1.239

War seldom enters but where wealth al-
   lures.
                                  Pt. II, 1.706

By education most have been misled,
So they believe, because they were so bred.
The priest continues what the nurse began,
And thus the child imposes on the man.
                                 Pt. III, 1.389

"Cleomenes" (1692)

Virtue in distress, and vice in triumph
Make atheists of mankind.

"The Conquest of Granada" (1669–70)

I am as free as nature first made man,
Ere the base laws of servitude began,
When wild in woods and noble savage ran.
                             Pt. 1, Act 1, Sec. 1

"Translation (or imitation) of Horace" (1685)

Happy the Man, and happy he alone,
He who can call today his own;
He who, secure within, can say,
Tomorrow, do thy worst, for I have liv'd
   today.
                           Book III, Ode 29, 1.65

"Amphitryon" (1690)

That very name of wife and marriage
Is poison to the dearest sweets of love.

"Absalom and Achitophel" (1680)

Desire for greatness is a god-like sin.

Great wits are sure to madness near allied,
And thin partitions do their bounds divide.
                                          1.150

Resolv'd to ruin or to rule the State.
                                          1.173

GUILLAUME DUBOIS
(1656–1723)
French cardinal, statesman

To become a great man it is necessary to be
a great rascal.
                                       Attributed

W.E.B. (William Edward Burghardt) DU BOIS
(1868–1963)
American writer, editor

Darkwater (1920)

The white world's vermin and filth:
   All the dirt of London,
   All the scum of New York;
   Valiant spoilers of women
   And conquerors of unarmed men;
   Shameless breeders of bastards,
   Drunk with the greed of gold,
   Baiting their blood-stained hooks
   With cant for the souls of the simple;
   Bearing the white man's burden
   Of liquor and lust and lies!
                                            II

Color line is a great problem of this century. . . . Back of the problem of race and
color lies a greater problem which both ob-
scures and implements it; and that is the fact
that so many civilized persons are willing to
live in comfort even if the price of this is poverty, ignorance and disease of the majority of
their fellowmen; that to maintain this privilege
men have waged war until today war tends to
become universal and continuous, and the excuse for this war continues largely to be color
and race.
                 Quoted in *The Independent*, May 1964

JEAN DUBUFFET
(1901–   )
French painter

For me insanity is super-sanity. The normal
is psychotic—a collective psychosis. Normal
means lack of imagination, lack of creativity.
                 Interview, *The New Yorker*, June 16, 1973

DOROTHY DUDLEY
(1905–   )
American writer

Forgotten Frontiers (biography of Dreiser, 1932)

The strongest desire known to human life is to continue living. The next strongest is to use the instruments by which life is generated for its own rewards, not for the sake of generation. The third potent desire is to excel and be acknowledged.

ALEXANDRE DUMAS, "The Elder"
(1803–1870)
French writer

Les Mohicans de Paris (1854–1855)

Cherchez la femme.
Look for the woman.
                              Vol. III, Ch. 10, 11

The Count of Monte Cristo (1844)

All human wisdom is summed up in two words: wait and hope.

———

My father was a Creole, his father a Negro, and his father a monkey; my family, it seems begins where yours left off.
              Attributed reply to question,
              "Who was your father?"

WILLIAM DUNBAR
(1465?–1530)
Scottish poet

"Lament of the Makaris" (c. 1508)

Since for the death remeid is none,
Best is that we for death dispone.
After our death that life may be:—
Timor Mortis conturbat me.
                              Refrain

ISADORA DUNCAN
(1878–1927)
American dancer

Most human beings today waste some twenty-five to thirty years of their lives before they break through the actual and conventional lies which surround them.

Art is not necessary at all. All that is necessary to make this world a better place to live in is to love—to love as Christ loved, as Buddha loved.
          From first chapter of memoirs, dictated in Berlin,
              December 20, 1924; contracted for *Chicago
              Tribune* by G.S.; never completed

BARROWS DUNHAM
(1905–   )
Professor of philosophy

Man Against Myth (1947)

. . . illusions multiply, and among them there is, I suppose none more ubiquitous than the idea that "you can't change human nature." This ancient platitude might long ago have been relegated to a home for superannuated ideas, were it not so constantly useful.
                              p. 33

Besides concealing the misdeeds of rulers, the doctrine that you can't change human nature has a larger purpose: defense of the existing social arrangements. Since these arrangements are, throughout most of the world, capitalist in character, the doctrine undertakes to show that, human nature being what it is, capitalism is the inevitable form of society.
                              p. 51

The evil is not that you cannot change human nature. The evil is that human nature cannot change you.
                              p. 56

FINLEY PETER DUNNE ("Mr. Dooley")
(1867–1936)
American satirist

Mr. Dooley's Opinions (1900)

A man can be right an' prisident, but he can't be both at th' same time.

No matter whether th' constitution follows th' flag or not, th' supreme coort follows th' iliction returns.

———

Histhry always vidicates th' Dimmycrats, but niver in their lifetime. They see th' thruth first, but th' trouble is that nawthin' is iver officially thrue till a Raypublican sees it.
              Quoted in *New York Times Magazine*,
              December 9, 1962

WILL DURANT
(1885–1981)
and ARIEL DURANT
(1898–1981)
American historians

Caesar and Christ (1944)

Moral reform is the most difficult and delicate branch of statesmanship; few rulers have dared to attempt it; most have left it to hypocrites and saints.

p. 221

Protestantism was the triumph of Paul over Peter, Fundamentalism is the triumph of Paul over Christ.

p. 502

A great civilization is not conquered from without until it has destroyed itself from within. The essential cause of Rome's decline lay in her people, her morals, her class struggle, her failing trade, her bureaucratic despotism, her stifling taxes, her consuming wars . . . Rome was not destroyed by Christianity, any more than by barbarian invasion; it was an empty shell when Christianity arose to influence and invasion came.

p. 665

The Age of Reason Begins (1961)

Religions are born and may die, but superstition is immortal.

Only the fortunate can take life without mythology.

The Lessons of History (1968)

Democracy is the most difficult of all forms of government, since it requires the widest spread of intelligence . . .

SIR EDWARD DYER
(c. 1540–1607)
English courtier, poet

"My Mind to Me a Kingdom Is" (1586)

Some have too much, yet still do crave;
I little have and seek no more.
They are but poor, though much they have,
And I am rich with little store:
    They poor, I rich; they beg, I give;
    They lack, I leave; they pine, I live.

My wealth is health and perfect ease;
My conscience clear my chief defence;
I never seek by bribes to please,
Nor by deceit to breed offence:
    Thus do I live; thus will I die;
    Would all did so well as I.

BOB DYLAN
(1941–   )
American popular musician

"My Back Pages" (1964)

Equality
I spoke the word
As if a wedding vow
Ah, but I was so much older then
I'm younger than that now.

JOHANNES ECKHARD (Meister Eckhard)
(c. 1260–1327)
German monk, mystic

I say, no creature is so vile but it can boast of being; in proportion to its being is its power of being God, for whatever is being, is God.

God can no more do without us than we can do without him.

What is truth? Truth is something so noble that if God could turn aside from it, I would keep to the truth and let God go.

If it is true that God became man, it is also true that man became God.

To get into the core of God at his greatest, one must first get into the core of himself at his least, for no one can know God who has not first known himself.

Quoted in Franz Pfieffer, *Meister Eckhard* (1857)

MARY BAKER EDDY
(1821–1910)
Founder of Christian Science

Science and Health With Key to the Scriptures
(1875)

The basis of all health, sinlessness, and immortality is the first great fact that God is the only Mind; and this Mind must be not merely believed, but it must be understood.

God is mind, and God is infinite; hence all is Mind.

Health is not a condition of matter, but of Mind, nor can the material senses bear reliable testimony on the subject of health.

Sin brought death, and death will disappear with the disappearance of sin.

THOMAS ALVA EDISON
(1847–1931)
American inventor

Do We Live Again?

My mind is incapable of conceiving such a thing as a soul. I may be in error, and man may have a soul; but I simply do not believe it.

I have never seen the slightest scientific proof of the religious theories of heaven and hell, of future life for individuals, or of a personal God.
        Quoted in Matthew Josephson, *Edison, A Biography*

Religion is all bunk.
        Conversation with Burroughs, Firestone, and Edward Marshall, on annual vacation.

EDWARD III
(1312–1377)
King of England

Honi soit qui mal y pense.
Shamed be the one who thinks evil of it.
Attributed in 1349; motto of his Order of the Garter

JONATHAN EDWARDS
(1703–1758)
Colonial American Calvinist, theologian, president of Princeton University

The Eternity of Hell-Torments (1739)

The sight of hell-torments will exalt the happiness of the saints for ever.

Sermon to Children (1740)

All children are by nature children of wrath, and are in danger of eternal damnation in hell.

Discourses on Various Important Subjects (1738)

Can the believing husband in Heaven be happy with his unbelieving wife in Hell? Can the believing father in Heaven be happy with his unbelieving children in Hell? Can the loving wife in Heaven be happy with her unbelieving husband in Hell?
I tell you, yea! Such will be their sense of justice that it will increase rather than diminish their bliss.

"Sinners in the Hands of an Angry God," sermon (1741)

The God that holds you over the pit of hell, much as one holds a spider, or some loathsome insect over the fire, abhors you, and is dreadfully provoked; his wrath towards you burns like fire; . . . he is of purer eyes than to bear to have you in his sight; you are ten thousand times more abominable in his eyes, than the most hateful venemous serpent is in ours. You have offended him infinitely more than ever a stubborn rebel did his prince; and yet it is nothing but his hand that holds you from falling into the fire every moment.

Hell is paved with the skulls of unbaptized children. . . . [Damned infants are] young vipers and [to God] infinitely more hateful than vipers.
        Quoted in *The American Treasury*, ed. Clifton Fadiman, 1955

Men are naturally God's enemies.
Indirect quotation, Santayana, *Winds of Doctrine*

ALBERT EINSTEIN
(1879–1955
German-born, Swiss-American scientist*

Annalen der Physik (1904)**

$$E = mc^2$$

The World as I See It (1934)

Everything that the human race has done and thought is concerned with the satisfaction of deeply felt needs and the assuagement of pain. One has to keep this constantly in mind if one wishes to understand spiritual movements and their development. Feeling and desire are the motive forces behind all human endeavor and human creation, in however exalted a guise the latter may present itself to us.

The religious geniuses of all ages have been distinguished by this kind of (cosmic) religious feeling, which knows no dogma and no God conceived in man's image; . . . Hence it is precisely among the heretics of every age that we find men who are filled with the highest kind of religious feeling and were in many cases regarded by their contemporaries as Atheists, sometimes also as Saints.

A man's ethical behavior should be based effectually on sympathy, education, and social ties; no religious basis is necessary. Man would indeed be in a poor way if he had to be re-strained by fear of punishment and hope of reward after death.

Science without religion is lame, religion without science is blind.

To inquire after the meaning or object of one's own existence or of creation generally has always seemed to me absurd from an objective point of view. And yet everybody has certain ideals which determine the direction of his endeavors and his judgments. In this sense I have never looked upon ease and happiness as ends in themselves—such an ethical basis I call more proper for a herd of swine. The ideals which have lighted me on my way and time and time again given me new courage to face life cheerfully, have been Truth, Goodness and Beauty.

Youth (1932)

Only a life lived for others is a life worth while.

My World-Picture (1934)

The true value of a human being is determined by the measure and the sense in which he has attained liberation from the self.

Ideas and Opinions of Albert Einstein (1954)

Whoever is careless with the truth in small matters cannot be trusted with important matters.

Letters

Nationalism is an infantile disease. It is the measles of mankind.

To G. S. Viereck, 1921

This is the problem: Is there any way of delivering mankind from the menace of war? . . .

As one immune from nationalist bias, I personally see a simple way of dealing with the superficial (i.e., administrative) aspect of the problem: the setting up by international consent of a legislative and judicial body to settle every conflict arising between nations. . . .

Thus I am led to my first axiom: the quest of international security involves the unconditional surrender by every nation, in a certain measure, of its liberty of action, its sovereignty that is to say, and it is clear beyond all doubt that no other road can lead to such security.

To Dr. Freud (q.v.), July 30, 1932

---

*All quotations dated up to October 1954 were acknowledged and corrected by Dr. Einstein, who read the Mss. and replied: "Many things which go under my name are badly translated from the German or are invented by other people." Among the paragraphs Dr. Einstein deleted, for example, was his supposed reply, "There is no hitching-post in the universe" to the request for a "one-line definition of the theory of relativity" made by a boat-train reporter the day he arrived in America (December 11, 1930).
**The paper on relativity in *Annalen der Physik*, entitled "Zur Elektrodynamik bewegter Körper" did not include this equation; it appeared later in 1905 in the same journal, entitled, "Ist die Traheit einer Korpers von seinem Energiegehalt Abhängig?"
"The Atomic Age is built on Einstein's equation $E = mc^2$, where m is the mass of the atom, and c is the speed of light (186,000 miles per second). You square that, and out of the atom comes a bit of energy!"—Stuart Chase, *Saturday Review*, January 22, 1955.

. . . it may become possible to set up nuclear chain reactions in a large mass of uranium, by which vast amounts of power and large quantities of new radium-like elements would be generated. . . . A single bomb of this type, carried by boat or exploded in a port, might very well destroy the whole port, together with some of the surrounding territory.
> To President Roosevelt, written in German, predicting "a new and important source of energy," August 2, 1939

"Einstein on the Atomic Bomb"

The release of atomic energy has not created a new problem. It has merely made more urgent the necessity of solving an existing one. . . . I do not believe that civilization will be wiped out in a war fought with the atomic bomb. Perhaps two-thirds of the people of the earth will be killed. . . .
> *Atlantic Monthly,* November 1945

Man is here for the sake of other men.

Possessions, outward success, publicity, luxury—to me these have always been contemptible.

The most beautiful thing we can experience is the mysterious. It is the source of all art and science.

The next World War will be fought with stones.
> Contribution, *Living Philosophies* (1949), Vol. 7

Not one statesman in a position of responsibility has dared to pursue the only course that holds out any promise of peace, the courage of supra-national security, since for a statesman to follow such a course would be tantamount to political suicide.
> Last written words, April 1955; quoted by Otto Nathan and Heinz Norden in "Einstein on Peace."

God does not play dice.
> Einstein's habitually expressed reaction to the quantum theory; quoted in B. Hoffman, *Albert Einstein Creator and Rebel,* Ch. 10

The Lord God is subtle, but malicious he is not.
> Inscription in Fine Hall, Princeton University

I cannot imagine a God who rewards and punishes the objects of his creation, whose purposes are moulded after our own—a God, in short, who is but a reflection of human frailty. Neither do I believe that the individual survives the death of his body, although feeble souls harbor such thoughts through fear of ridiculous egotisms.
> Quoted in *New York Times* obituary, April 19, 1955

Never do anything against conscience even if the state demands it.
> Quoted in *Saturday Review* obituary, April 30, 1955

Whoever undertakes to set himself up as a judge of Truth and Knowledge is shipwrecked by the laughter of the gods.
> Quoted in John Scott, *Political Warfare*

DWIGHT D(avid) EISENHOWER
(1890–1969)
General, 34th President of the United States*

Addresses and Speeches

And we have got to fight it [Communism] with something better.
> Dartmouth, June 14, 1953

One hundred and eighty-one years ago our forefathers started a revolution that still goes on.
> April 19, 1956

We seek victory—not over any nation or people—but over ignorance, poverty, disease, and human degradation wherever they may be found.
> State of the Union Address, January 9, 1959

Every gun that is made, every warship launched, every rocket fired, signifies in the final sense a theft from those who hunger and are not fed, those who are cold and are not clothed. This world in arms is not spending money alone. It is spending the sweat of its laborers, the genius of its scientists, the houses of its children.
This is not a way of life. . . . Under the cloud of war, it is humanity hanging itself on a cross of iron.
> April 16, 1953

*Eisenhower was incapable of speaking English correctly—all the quotations which follow were written by a corps of White House ghosts, notably the eminent Emmet John Hughes.

This conjunction of an immense military establishment and a large arms industry is new in the American experience. . . . In the councils of government, we must guard against the acquisition of unwarranted influence, whether sought or unsought, by the military-industrial complex. The potential for the disastrous rise of misplaced power exists and will persist.
> Farewell address, January 17, 1961*

Opposed to the idea of two hostile, embittered worlds in perpetual conflict, we envisage a single world community as yet unrealized but advancing rapidly.
> Address, United Nations, September 22, 1960

I will not present myself before God with blood on my hands.
> To General De Gaulle; quoted by Malraux

. . . the right of mankind to knowledge and the free use thereof.
> Slogan for 200th Anniversary celebration, Columbia University, 1950

A democracy smugly disdainful of new ideas would be a sick democracy. A democracy chronologically fearful of new ideas would be a dying democracy.
> Letter to R. B. Downs, American Library Association, June 14, 1953

War in our time has become an anachronism. Whatever the case in the past, war in the future can serve no useful purpose. A war which became general, as any limited action might, would only result in the virtual destruction of mankind.
> Quoted in Mike Wallace, *Fund for the Republic* (1959)

Public opinion wins wars.
> Talk to newspaper editors, Reuters dispatch, April 25, 1944

---

*The Nation called "the military-industrial complex" an immortal remark comparable to Washington's advice to "steer clear of permanent alliances." It stated that Dr. Malcolm Moos, President of the University of Minnnesota, wrote the major part of Eisenhower's valedictory, although Bryce N. Harlow, presidential aide, is also credited with the "immortal" phrase.
The *Milwaukee Journal,* February 27, 1970, accused the Pentagon of suppressing the famous paragraph in its display of an Eisenhower memorial.

GEORGE ELIOT (née Marian Evans Cross) (1819–1880)
English novelist, essayist, poet

Romola (1863)

Marriage must be a relation either of sympathy or of conquest.
> Ch. 48

The Mill on the Floss (1860)

The happiest women, like the happiest nations, have no history.

Daniel Deronda (1876)

The Jews are among the aristocracy of every land; if a literature is called rich in possession of a few classic tragedies, what shall we say of a national tragedy lasting for fifteen hundred years, in which the poets and actors were also the heroes.

T(homas) S(tearns) ELIOT (1888–1965)
American-born English poet

Choruses from "The Rock"

Has the Church failed mankind, or has
> mankind failed the Church?
When the Church is no longer regarded, not
> even opposed,
> and men have forgotten
All gods except Usury, Lust and Power.

Where is the Life we have lost in living?
Where is the wisdom we have lost in knowl-
> edge?
Where is the knowledge we have lost in in-
> formation?
The world turns and the world changes,
But one thing does not change.
In all of my years, one thing does not
> change . . .
The perpetual struggle of Good and Evil.

"The Love Song of J. Alfred Prufrock" (1917)

To wonder, "Do I dare?" and "Do I dare?"
. . .

Do I dare
Disturb the universe?

I have measured out my life with coffee spoons.

"The Hippopotamus" (1920)

> The hippo's feeble steps may err
> In compassing material ends,
> While the True Church need never stir
> To gather in its dividends.

"The Hollow Men" (1925)

> We are the hollow men
> We are the stuffed men
> Leaning together.
>
> Between the idea
> And the reality
> Between the motion
> And the act
> Falls the Shadow.
>
> Between the desire
> And the spasm
> Between the Potency
> And the existence
> Between the essence
> And the descent
> Falls the Shadow.
>
> *This is the way the world ends*
> *Not with a bang but a whimper.*

The Four Quartets (1936–42)

> At the still point of the turning world. Nei-
> ther flesh nor fleshless;
> Neither from nor towards; at the still point,
> there the dance is,
> But neither arrest nor movement. And do
> not call it fixity,
> Where past and future are gathered. Neither
> movement from nor towards,
> Neither ascent nor decline. Except for the
> point, the still point,
> There would be no dance, and there is only
> the dance.
> I can only say, *there* we have been: but I
> cannot say where.
> And I cannot say, how long, for that is to
> place it in time.
>
> Human kind
> Cannot bear very much reality.
> Time past and time future
> What might have been and what has been
> Point to one end, which is always present.
> Yet the enchainment of past and future
> Woven in the weakness of the changing
> body,
> Protects mankind from heaven and damna-
> tion
> Which flesh cannot endure.
> > "Burnt Norton" (1936)

> Do not let me hear
> Of the wisdom of old men, but rather of
> their folly,
> Their fear of fear and frenzy, their fear of
> possession,
> Of belonging to another, or to others, or to
> God.
> > "East Coker" (1940)

> . . . For most of us, this is the aim
> Never here to be realised;
> Who are only undefeated
> Because we have gone on trying. . . .
> > "The Dry Salvages" (1941)

> We shall not cease from exploration
> And the end of all our exploring
> Will be to arrive where we started
> And know the place for the first time.
> > "Little Gidding" (1942)

The Waste Land (1922)

> April is the cruellest month, breeding
> Lilacs out of the dead land, mixing
> Memory and desire, stirring
> Dull roots with spring rain.
> Winter kept us warm, covering
> Earth in forgetful snow, feeding
> A little life with dried tubers.

The Cocktail Party (1950)

> Hell is oneself,
> Hell is alone, the other figures in it
> Merely projections. There is nothing to es-
> cape from
> And nothing to escape to. One is always
> alone.
> > Act I, Sc. III

Sweeney Agonistes (unfinished, pub. 1932)

> Birth, and copulation, and death.
> That's all the facts when you come to brass
> tacks:

Murder in the Cathedral (1935)

> The last temptation is the greatest treason:
> To do the right deed for the wrong reason.

Tradition and the Individual Talent (1917)

> . . . but we should remind ourselves that
> criticism is as inevitable as breathing, and that
> we should be none the worse for articulating
> what passes in our minds when we read a book
> and feel an emotion about it, for criticizing
> our own minds in their work of criticism.
>
> . . . and the historical sense involves a per-
> ception, not only of the pastness of the past,

but of its presence; the historical sense compels a man to write not merely with his own generation in his bones, but with the feeling that the whole of the literature of Europe from Homer and within it the whole of the literature of his own country has a simultaneous existence and composes a simultaneous order.

The progress of an artist is a continual self-sacrifice, a continual extinction of personality.

Poetry is not a turning loose of emotion, but an escape from emotion; it is not the expression of personality but an escape from personality. But, of course, only those who have personality and emotions know what it means to want to escape from these things.

The emotion of art is impersonal. And the poet cannot reach this impersonality without surrendering himself wholly to the work to be done, unless he lives in what is not merely the present, but the present moment of the past, unless he is conscious, not of what is dead, but of what is already living.

So far as we are human, what we do must be either evil or good; so far as we do evil or good, we are human; and it is better, in a paradoxical way, to do evil than to do nothing; at least we exist.
Introduction, Baudelaire's *Intimate Journal* (1930)

The majority of mankind is lazy-minded, incurious, absorbed in vanities, and tepid in emotion, and is therefore incapable of either much doubt or much faith.
Introduction to Pascal's *Pensées* (tr. 1931)

ELIZABETH I
(1533–1603)
Queen of England

Monarchs ought to put to death the authors and instigators of war, as their sworn enemies and as dangers to their states.
Letter

I know I have the body of a weak and feeble woman; but I have the heart and stomach of a king, and of a King of England, too.
Speech, Tillbury, awaiting the Armada, 1588

I grieve, and dare not show my discontent;
I love, and yet am forced to seem to hate;
I do not dare to say I never meant,

I seem stark mute, but inwardly I prate,
I am, and am not, I freeze and yet am burn'd,
Since from myself my other self I turned.
Finis, *Eliza Regina*, Ashmolean Museum Mss.

For me it will be enough that a marble stone should declare that a queen having reigned such a time, lived and died a virgin.
Quoted in Hume, *History of England*

ELIZABETH
(1876–1965)
Queen of Belgium

Between them [the Germans] and me there is now a bloody iron curtain which has descended forever!
Address, 1914; first use of the expression (cf. Bernard M. Baruch)

EBENEZER ELLIOTT
(1781–1849)
English Chartist poet

Poetical Works (1846)

What is a communist? One who has yearnings
For equal division of unequal earnings.
Idler or bungler, or both, he is willing
To fork out his copper and pocket a shilling.
"Epigram"

DR. ALBERT ELLIS
(1913–   )
American psychotherapist

The more sinful and guilty a person tends to feel, the less chance there is that he will be a happy, healthy or law-abiding citizen. . . . He will become a compulsive wrongdoer.
Quoted in *Time*, September 14, 1959

(Henry) HAVELOCK ELLIS
(1859–1939)
British psychologist, writer

Studies in the Psychology of Sex (1897–1928)*

I regard sex as the central problem of life. And now that the problem of religion has practically been settled, and that the problem of labor has at least been placed on a practical

---

*All Volume, part, and page numbers given are for the Random House edition (1936).

foundation, the question of sex—with the racial questions that rest on it—stands before the coming generations as the chief problem for solution. Sex lies at the root of life, and we can never learn to reverence life until we know how to understand sex. [p. xxx]

Vol. I, pt. 1, Preface (1897)

That modesty—like all the closely-allied emotions—is based on fear, one of the most primitive of the emotions, seems to be fairly evident. [p. 36]

Vol. I, pt. I, "The Evolution of Modesty" (1910)

Auto-erotism [coined word, p. 161]

Among auto-erotic phenomena, or on the borderland, we must further include those religious sexual manifestations for an ideal object, of which we may find evidence in the lives of saints and ecstatics. [p. 162]

Vol. I, pt. 1, "Auto-Erotism: A Study of the Spontaneous Manifestations of the Sexual Impulse" (1900)

Love and religion are the two most volcanic emotions to which the human organism is liable, and it is not surprising that, when there is a disturbance in one of these spheres, the vibrations should readily extend to the other. . . . Even when there is absolute physical suppression on the sexual side, it seems probable that thereby a greater intensity of spiritual fervor is caused. Many eminent thinkers seem to have been without sexual desire [p. 310].

Vol. I, pt. 1, Appendix C, "The Auto-Erotic Factor in Religion" (1910)

The ancient saying, *Omne animal post coitum triste,* is of limited application at the best, but certainly has little reference to women. [p. 247]

Vol. I, Pt. 2, "The Sexual Impulse in Women" (1903)

There is no doubt about this: the promise of mutual exclusive and everlasting love is a promise that cannot be kept and should not be made. It cannot form a permanent basis of marriage . . . Yet, there has been a general conspiracy not merely to preserve that fiction but to put it at the front as the primary condition of marriage. [p. 516]

Vol. III, pt. 2, "The History of Marriage" (1928)

A man's destiny stands not in the future but in the past. That, rightly considered, is the most vital of all vital facts. Every child thus has a right to choose his own ancestors. [p. 1]

Nature records the male but a secondary and comparatively humble place in the home, the breeding-place of the race; he may compensate himself if he will, by seeking adventure or renown in the world outside. The mother is the child's supreme parent. . . . [p. 3]

Vol. IV, pt. 1, "The Mother and Her Child" (1910)

But the person who feels that the sexual impulse is bad, or even low and vulgar, is an absurdity in the universe, an anomaly. He is like those persons in our insane asylums, who feel that the instinct of nutrition is evil and so proceed to starve themselves. They are alike spiritual outcasts in the universe whose children they are . . . to pour contempt on the sexual life, to throw the veil of "impurity" over it, is, as Nietzsche declared, the unpardonable sin against the Holy Ghost of Life. [pp. 131–132]

Love, in the sexual sense, is, summarily considered, a synthesis of lust (in the primitive and uncolored sense of sexual emotion) and friendship. . . . There can be no sexual love without lust; but, on the other hand, until the currents of lust in the organism have been irradiated as to effect other parts of the psychic organism—at the least the affections and the social feelings—it is not yet sexual love. Lust, the specific sexual impulse, is indeed the primary and essential element in this synthesis, for it alone is adequate to the end of reproduction, not only in animals but in men. But it is not until lust is expanded and irradiated that it develops into the exquisite and enthralling flower of love. [p. 133]

Vol. IV, pt. 1, "The Valuation of Sexual Love" (1910)

Impressions and Comments

In the degree in which I have been privileged to know the intimate secrets of hearts, I ever more realize how great a part is played in the lives of men and women by some little concealed germ of abnormality. For the most part they are occupied in the task of stifling and crushing those germs, treating them like weeds in their gardens. There is another and better way, even though more difficult and more perilous. Instead of trying to suppress the weeds that can never be killed, they may be cultivated into useful or beautiful flowers. For it is impossible to conceive any impulse in a human heart which cannot be transformed into Truth or into Beauty or into Love.

Without an element of the obscene there can be no true or deep aesthetic or moral conception of life.

A religion can no more afford to degrade its Devil than to degrade its God.

Sexual pleasure, wisely used and not abused, may prove the stimulus and liberation of our finest and most exalted activities.

For until it is generally possible to acquire erotic personality and to master the art of loving, the development of the individual man or woman is marred, the acquirement of human happiness and harmony remains impossible.

The Dance of Life (1923)

On the threshold of the moral world we meet the idea of Freedom, "one of the weightiest conceptions man has ever formed." Once a dogma, in course of time an hypothesis, now in the eyes of many a fiction; yet we cannot do without it, even although we may be firmly convinced that our acts are determined by the laws that cannot be broken. Many other great conceptions have tended to follow the same course. God, the Soul, Immortality, the Moral World-Order. . . . For these things are Ideals, and all Ideals are logically speaking, fictions. As Science leads to the Imaginary, so Life leads to the Impossible; without them we cannot reach the heights we are born to scale.

The place where optimism most flourishes is the lunatic asylum.

Ch. III

The act of intercourse is only an incident, and not an essential of love.
    Quoted in Walter Lippman, *A Preface to Morals*
(1929)

SIR THOMAS ELYOT
(1490–1546)
English lexicographer, scholar, poet

Democracy.

Coined word, derived from the Greek. Used, according to the O.E.D., in 1531, in *Gov.* I.ii

RALPH WALDO EMERSON
(1803–1882)
American poet, Unitarian minister, philosopher

Nature (1836)

A man is a god in ruins.

Essays: First Series (1841)

Beware when the great God lets loose a thinker on this planet. Then all things are at risk . . . The very hope of man, the thoughts of his heart, the religion of nations, the manners and morals of mankind are all at the mercy of a new generalization.

The virtues of society are vices of the saint.

No facts are to me sacred; none are profane; I simply experiment, an endless seeker with no Past at my back.

No truth so sublime but it may be trivial tomorrow in the light of new thoughts. People wish to be settled; only as far as they are unsettled is there any hope for them.

Nothing great was ever achieved without enthusiasm.

"Circles"

But men are better than their theology. Their daily life gives it the lie.

The dice of God are always loaded.

There is a crack in everything God has made.

What will you have? quoth God; pay for it and take it.

If you put a chain around the neck of a slave, the other end fastens itself around your own.

A man cannot speak but he judges himself. . . . no man thoroughly understands a truth until he has contended against it.

Every evil to which we do not succumb is a benefactor.

The history of persecution is a history of endeavors to cheat nature, to make water run up hill, to twist a rope of sand . . . A mob is a society of bodies voluntarily bereaving themselves of reason . . . The martyr cannot be dishonored . . . every burned book or house enlightens the world; every suppressed or expunged word reverberates through the earth from side to side.

"Compensation"

Every man alone is sincere. At the entrance of a second person, hypocrisy begins.

"Friendship"

Life is a festival only to the wise.

Every man is a divinity in disguise, a god playing the fool.

"Heroism"

God offers to every mind a choice between truth and repose. Take which you please—you can never have both.

What is the hardest task in the world? To think.

"Intellect"

The faith that stands on authority is not faith.

The simplest person, who in his integrity worships God, becomes God.

Our faith comes in moments; our vice is habitual.

"The Over-Soul"

Whoso would be a man, must be a nonconformist. He who would gather immortal palms must not be hindered by the name of goodness, but must explore if it be goodness. Nothing is at last sacred but the integrity of your own mind. . . . A man is to carry himself in the presence of all opposition as if every thing were titular and ephemeral but he. I am ashamed to think how easily we capitulate to badges and names, to large societies and dead institutions.

What I must do is all that concerns me, not what the people think. This rule, equally arduous in actual and in intellectual life, may serve for the whole distinction between greatness and meanness. . . . It is easy in the world to live after the world's opinion; it is easy in solitude to live after our own; but the great man is he who in the midst of the crowd keeps with perfect sweetness the independence of solitude.

Imitation is suicide.

A foolish consistency is the hobgoblin of little minds, adored by little statesmen and philosophers and divines. With consistency a great soul has simply nothing to do. He may as well concern himself with his shadow on the wall. Speak what you think now in hard words and tomorrow speak what tomorrow thinks in hard words again, though it contradict every thing you said to-day.—"Ah, so you shall be sure to be misunderstood."—Is it so bad then to be misunderstood? Pythagoras was misunderstood, and Socrates, and Jesus, and Luther, and Copernicus, and Galileo, and Newton, and every pure and wise spirit that ever took flesh. To be great is to be misunderstood.

An institution is the lengthened shadow of one man; as, . . . the Reformation, of Luther; Quakerism, of Fox; Methodism, of Wesley; Abolition, of Clarkson . . . and all history resolves itself very easily into the biography of a few stout and earnest persons.

We are afraid of truth, afraid of fortune, afraid of death, and afraid of each other. Our age yields no great and perfect persons. . . . Our housekeeping is mendicant, our arts, our occupations, our marriages, our religion we have not chosen, but society has chosen for us. We are parlor soldiers. We shun the rugged battle of fate, where strength is born.

Prayer that craves a particular commodity, anything less than all good, is vicious . . . prayer as a means to effect a private end is meanness and theft. . . . As soon as the man is at one with God, he will not beg.

As men's prayers are a disease of the will, so are their creeds a disease of the intellect.

Society never advances . . . It undergoes continual changes; it is barbarous, it is civilized, it is christianized, it is rich, it is scientific; but this change is not amelioration. For every thing that is given something is taken.

. . . and it may be a question whether machinery does not encumber, whether we have not lost by refinement some energy, by a Christianity, entrenched in establishments and forms, some vigor of wild virtue. For every Stoic was a Stoic; but in Christendom where is the Christian?

And so the reliance on Property, including the reliance on governments which protect it, is the want of self-reliance. Men have looked away from themselves and at things so long that they have come to esteem the religious, learned and civil institutions as guards of property, and they deprecate assaults on these, because they feel them to be assaults on property. They measure their esteem of each other by what each has, and not by what each is. But a cultivated man becomes ashamed of his property . . .

"Self-Reliance"

O my brothers, God exists. There is a soul at the center of nature and over the will of every man, so that none of us can wrong the universe.

Besides, why should we be cowed by the name of Action? 'Tis a trick of the senses,—no more. We know that the ancestor of every action is a thought. . . . To think is to act.

"Spiritual Laws"

Essays: Second Series (1844)

A chief event of life is the day in which we have encountered a mind that startled us.

Truth is the summit of being; justice is the application of it to affairs.

No change of circumstances can repair a defect of character. We boast our emancipation from many superstitions; but if we have broken any idols, it is through a transfer of the idolatry. What have I gained, that I no longer immolate a bull to Jove or to Neptune, or a mouse to Hecate; that I do not tremble before the Eumenides, or the Catholic Purgatory, or the Calvanistic Judgment-day—if I quake at opinion, the public opinion . . .

Character is that which can do without success.

"Character"

The multitude of false churches accredits the true religion. Literature, poetry, science are the homage of man to his unfathomed secret, concerning which no sane man can affect an indifference or incuriousity. Nature is loved by what is best in us. It is loved as the city of God, although, or rather because there is no citizen.

Whenever a true theory appears, it will be its own evidence. Its test is that it will explain all phenomena. Now many are thought not only unexplained but unexplainable: as language, sleep, madness, dreams, beasts, sex.

"Nature" (1844)

For the Universe has three children, born at one time, which reappear under different names in every system of thought, whether they are called cause, operation and effect; or, more poetically, Jove, Pluto, Neptune; or, theologically, the Father, the Spirit and the Son; but which we will call here the Knower, the Doer and the Sayer. These stand respectively for the love of truth, for the love of good, and for the love of beauty. These three are equal.

The poets are thus liberating gods. . . . They are free, and they make free.

"The Poet"

The power of Love, as the basis of a State, has never been tried . . . There will always be a government of force where men are selfish . . .

Good men must not obey the laws too well . . . Hence the less government we have the better—the fewer laws and the less confided power. . . . To educate the wise man the State exists, and with the appearance of the wise man the State expires. The appearance of character makes the State unnecessary. The wise man is the State.

"Politics"

Conduct of Life (1860)

Intellect annuls fate. So far as a man thinks he is free.

Leave this hypocritical prating about the masses. Masses are rude, lame, unmade, pernicious in their demands and influences, and need not to be flattered but to be schooled. I wish not to concede anything to them, but to tame, drill, divide, and break them up, and draw individuals out of them. The worst of charity is that the lives you are asked to preserve are not worth preserving. Masses! The calamity is the masses. I do not wish any mass at all, but honest men only, lovely, sweet, accomplished women only, and no shovel-handed, narrow-brained, gin-drinking million stockingers or lazzeroni at all. If government knew how, I should like to see it check, not multiply the population. When it reaches its true law of action, every man that is born will be hailed as essential.

All great men come out of the middle classes.

"Considerations by the Way"

Great men, great nations, have not been boasters and buffoons, but perceivers of the terror of life. . . .

And one may say boldly that no man has a right perception of any truth who has not been reacted on by it so as to be ready to be its martyr.

"Fate"

The glory of the farmer is that, in the division of labors, it is his part to create. . . . The first farmer was the first man, and all historic nobility rests on the possession and use of land.

"Farming"

Tobacco, coffee, alcohol, hashish, prussic acid, strychnine, are weak dilutions; the surest poison is time.

"Old Age"

Life is a search after power.

"Power"

If a man owns land, the land owns him.

"Wealth"

Society and Solitude (1870)

The education of the will is the object of our existence.

But the people are to be taken in very small doses.

Solitude is impractible, and society fatal.

Knowledge is the antidote to fear.
  Vol. III, *Society and Solitude*, "Courage" (1870)

The greatest man in history was the poorest.
  "Domestic Life"

What is civilization? I answer the power of good women.
  "Woman"

Addresses and Lectures

If a man is at heart just, then in so far is he God; the safety of God, the immortality of God, the majesty of God do enter into that man with justice.
  Vol. I, "An Address" (1838)

And now, my brothers, you will ask, What in these depending days can be done by us?. . . . Wherever a man comes, there comes revolution. The old is for slaves. When a man comes, all books are legible, all things transparent, all religions are forms . . .

Yourself a newborn bard of the Holy Ghost, cast behind you all conformity, and acquaint men at first hand with Deity. . . . but live with the privilege of the immeasurable mind.

The hour of that choice is the crisis of your history. . . . Be content with a little light, so it be your own. Explore, and explore. . . . Make yourself necessary to the world, and mankind will give you bread.
  "Literary Ethics" (1838)

Conservatism stands on man's confessed limitations; reform on his indisputable infinitude.

We are reformers in spring and summer, in autumn and winter we stand by the old; reformers in the morning, conservers at night. Reform is affirmative, conservatism negative; conservatism goes for comfort, reform for truth.

The two parties which divide the state, the party of Conservatism and that of Innovation, are very old, and have disputed possession of the world ever since it was made. This quarrel is the subject of civil history. The conservative party established the reverend hierarchies and monarchies of the most ancient world. The battle of patrician and plebeian, of parent state and colony, of old usage and accommodation to new facts, of the rich and the poor, reappear in all countries and times. The war rages not only in battlefields, in national councils and ecclesiastical synods, but agitates every man's bosom with opposing advantages every hour.*
  "The Conservative" (1841)

The philosopher and lover of man have much harm to say of trade; but the historian will see that trade was the principle of Liberty; that trade planted America and destroyed Feudalism; that it makes peace and keeps peace, and it will abolish slavery.
  "The Young American" (1844)

Complete Works of Ralph Waldo Emerson (Concord Edition)

If a man has good corn, or wood, or boards, or pigs to sell, or can make a better chain or knives, crucibles, or church-organs, than anybody else, you will find a broad, hard-beaten road to his house, though it be in the woods.**

The truth, the hope of any time, must always be sought in minorities.
  Vol. VIII

Representative Men (1850)

Great geniuses have the shortest biographies.

Every man is a quotation from all his ancestors.
  "Plato; or, The Philosopher"

The democrat is a young conservative; the conservative an old democrat. The aristocrat is the democrat ripe and gone to seed.
  "Napoleon; or, The Man of the World"

---

*"Six years before Marx and Engels startled Europe with their famous announcement that history is the story of class struggles."—Beards, *Rise of American Civilization*, I, p. 780.
**Emerson did not write or deliver a lecture containing the words about "a better mouse-trap" which a lecture-listener attributed to him. Elbert Hubbard claimed it. See Wittenberg: *The Laws of Literary Property*.

Journals

A nation never fails but by suicide.

Democracy becomes a government of bullies, tempered by editors.

We are always getting ready to live but never living.

"Give All to Love" (1847)

When half-gods go,
The gods arrive.

"Ode," inscribed to Channing (1867)

Things are in the saddle
And ride mankind.

"Brahma" (1857)

They reckon ill who leave me out;
When me they fly, I am the wings;
I am the doubter and the doubt,
And I the hymn the Brahmin sings.

ROBERT EMMET
(1778–hanged 1803)
Irish rebel

Let there be no inscription upon my tomb. Let no man write my epitaph. No man can write my epitaph. I am here ready to die.
  Speech, after trial and conviction, September 1803

FRIEDRICH ENGELS
(1820–1895)
German Socialist, associate of Marx*

Anti-Dühring (1878)

Anyone therefore who sets out on this field to hunt down final and ultimate truths, truths which are pure or absolutely immutable, will bring home but little, apart from platitudes and commonplaces of the sorriest kind. . . .

If we have not made much progress with truth and error, we can make even less with good and bad. This antithesis belongs exclusively to the domain of morals, that is, a domain drawn from the history of mankind, and it is precisely in this field that final and ultimate truths are most sparsely sown. The conception of good and bad have varied so much from nation to nation and from age to age that

they have often been in direct contradiction to each other.

We maintain on the contrary that all former moral theories are the product, in the last analysis, of the economic state which society had reached at that particular epoch. And as society has hitherto moved in class antagonisms, morality was always a class morality; it has either justified the domination and interests of the ruling class, or, as soon as the oppressed class has become powerful enough, it has represented the revolt against this domination and the future interests of the oppressed.
                                                        Pt. I

The perfecting of machinery is making human labor superfluous. . . . Thus it comes about, to quote Marx, that machinery becomes the most powerful weapon in the war of capital against the working class; that the instruments of labor constantly tear the means of subsistence out of the hands of the laborer; that the very product of the worker is turned into an instrument for his subjugation.

Force, however, plays another role (other than that of a diabolical power) in history, a revolutionary role; that, in the words of Marx, it is the midwife of every old society which is pregnant with the new.
                                                       Pt. II

The proletariat seizes the political power of the State and transforms the means of production into State property. But in doing this it abolishes itself as the proletariat, it ends all class distinctions and class antagonisms, it abolishes also the State as a State. . . .

The first act by which the State really becomes representative of society as a whole—the taking possession of the means of production in the name of society—is at the same time its last independent act as a State. The interference of the State in social relations becomes superfluous in one domain after another, and then dies out of itself. . . . The State is not "abolished," *it withers away.**

Tradition is a great retarding force, the *vis inertiae* of history.

By it [historical materialism] History for the first time was placed on its real foundation; the obvious fact, hitherto totally neglected, that first of all men must eat, drink and have shelter and clothing and therefore work, before

---

*For works written in collaboration, see Marx.

*Also translated: "It dies out." Lenin discusses withering away in *The State and Revolution,* 1918, q.v.

they can struggle for supremacy or devote themselves to politics, religion, philosophy, etc., this fact at last found historical recognition.

. . . All religion, however, is nothing but the fantastic reflection in men's minds of those external forces which control their daily life, a reflection in which the terrestrial forces assume the form of supernatural forces.

What, indeed, is agnosticism, but, to use an expressive term, "shamefaced" materialism.

Everything must justify its existence before the judgment seat of Reason, or give up existence.

Pt. III

The Communist Manifesto

The basic thought underlying the [Communist) Manifesto is as follows: The method of production and the organization of social life inevitably arising therefrom constitute in every historical epoch the foundation upon which is built the political and intellectual history of that epoch.

Preface, German edition of 1883

The Origin of the Family (1894)

Accordingly we have three forms of marriage, which in the main correspond to the three principal stages of human development. For the period of savagery, the group marriage; for barbarism, the pairing marriage; for civilization, monogamy supplemented by adultery and prostitution. Between the pairing marriage and monogamy there intervened, at the highest stage of barbarism, the right of men to female slaves, and polygamy.

Prostitution degrades, among women, only the unfortunate ones to whose lot it falls, and even these not at all to the extent that is commonly believed. On the other hand, it degrades the character of the whole world of men.

Woman can be emancipated only when she can take part on a large social scale in production and is engaged in a domestic work only to an insignificant degree, and this has become possible only in the big industry of modern times. . . .

What the proletarian needs, he can obtain only from the bourgeoisie, which is protected in its monopoly by the power of the State. . . .

The proletarian is, therefore, in law and in fact, the slave of the bourgeoisie, which can decree his life or death.

From the first day to this, sheer greed was the driving spirit of civilization.

The proletariat uses the State not in the interests of freedom but in order to hold down its adversaries, and as soon as it becomes possible to speak of freedom the State as such ceases to exist.

Letter to Bebel, August 18, 1875; quoted by Lenin

EPICTETUS*
(c. 50–120 A.D.)
Greek Stoic philosopher living in Rome

The Manual of Epictetus (The Encheiridion)

1. Of all existing things some are in our power, and others are not in our power. In our power are thought, impulse, will to get and will to avoid. . . Things not in our power include the body, property, reputation, office, and, in a word, everything which is not our own doing.

5. To accuse others for one's own misfortunes is a sign of want of education; to accuse oneself shows that one's education has begun; to accuse neither oneself nor others shows that one's education is complete.

12. . . . For it is better to die of hunger, so that you be free from pain and from fear, than to live in plenty and be troubled in mind.

14. . . . Let him then who wishes to be free not wish for anything or avoid anything that depends on others; or else he is bound to be a slave.

21. Keep before your eyes from day to day death and exile and all things that seem terrible, but death most of all, and then you will never set your thoughts on what is low and will never desire anything beyond measure.

29. . . . You must be one man, good or bad; you must develop either your Governing Principle, or your outward endowments; you must study either your inner man, or outward things—in a word, you must choose between the position of a philosopher and that of a mere outsider.

40. Women from fourteen years upwards are called 'madam' by men. Wherefore, when

---

*All quotes here from *The Stoic and Epicurean Philosophers,* ed. Whitney J. Oates, tr. P. E. Matheson (Epictetus).

they see that the only advantage they have got is to be marriageable, they begin to adorn themselves and to set all their hopes on this.

41. It is a sign of a dull mind to dwell upon the cares of the body, to prolong exercise, eating, drinking, and other bodily functions. These things are to be done by the way; all your attention must be given to the mind.

Discourses

Appearances to the mind are of four kinds. Things either are what they appear to be; or they neither are, nor appear to be; or they are, and do not appear to be; or they are not, and yet appear to be. Rightly to aim in all these cases is the wise man's task.

Bk. I

Only the educated are free.

No man who is in fear, or sorrow, or turmoil, is free, but whoever is rid of sorrows and fears and turmoils, that man is by the selfsame course rid also of slavery.

Here is the beginning of philosophy:
a recognition of the conflicts between men,
a search for their cause,
a condemnation of mere opinion. . .
and the discovery of a standard of judgment.

Bk. II

All philosophy lies in two words: sustain and abstain.

Wherever anyone is against his will that is to him a prison.

Bk. IV

EPICURUS
(341–270 B.C.)
Greek philosopher*

Aphorisms

The gods can either take away evil from the world and will not, or, being willing to do so cannot; or they neither can nor will, or lastly, they are able and willing.

If they have the will to remove evil and cannot, then they are not omnipotent. If they can but will not, then they are not benevolent. If they are neither able nor willing, they are neither omnipotent nor benevolent.

Lastly, if they are both able and willing to annihilate evil, why does it exist?

Principal Doctrines

Death is nothing to us: for that which is dissolved is without sensation; and that which lacks sensation is nothing to us.

II

Thus that which is the most awful of evils, death, is nothing to us, since when we exist there is no death, and when there is death we do not exist.

Another translation of the above.

Fragments

9. Necessity is an evil, but there is no necessity to live under the control of necessity.

14. We are born once and cannot be born twice, but for all time must be no more. But you, who are not master of tomorrow, postpone your happiness: life is wasted in procrastination and each of us dies without allowing himself leisure.

25. Poverty, when measured by the natural purpose of life, is great wealth, but unlimited wealth is great poverty.

47. I have anticipated thee, Fortune, and entrenched myself against all thy secret attacks. . . . but when it is time for us to go, spitting contempt on life and on those who here vainly cling to it, we will leave life crying aloud in a glorious triumph-song that we have lived well.

51. You tell me that the stimulus of the flesh makes you too prone to the pleasures of love. Provided that you do not break the laws or good customs and do not distress any of your neighbours or do harm to your body or squander your pittance, you may indulge your inclinations as you please. Yet it is impossible not to come up against one or another of these barriers: for the pleasures of love never profited a man and he is lucky if they do him no harm.

58. We must release ourselves from the prison of affairs and politics.

67. A free life cannot acquire many possessions, because this is not easy to do without servility to mobs or monarchs. . . .

70. Let nothing be done in your life, which will cause you fear if it becomes known to your neighbor.

---

*"I am an Epicurean. I consider the genuine (not the imputed) doctrines of Epicurus as containing everything rational in moral philosophy which Greek and Roman leave to us."—Thomas Jefferson, letter to Wm. Short, 1819.

77. The greatest fruit of self-sufficiency is freedom.

199. If you would enjoy real freedom, you must be the slave of philosophy.

494. The fool, with all his other faults, has this also, he is always getting ready to live.*

522. The knowledge of sin is the beginning of salvation.

Quoted by Seneca

Fragments (from uncertain sources)

If God listened to the prayers of men, all men would quickly have perished: for they are forever praying for evil against one another.

Physics 58

Live unknown.

Ethics 86

Letter to Menoeceus

Live like a god among men.

Steer clear of all culture.

Let us have no myths of divine action.

Letter to Herodotus

The atoms are in continual motion through all eternity.

Moreover, there is an infinite number of worlds, some like this world, others unlike it. For the atoms being infinite in number, as has just been proved, are borne ever further in their course. . . . Hence there will be nothing to hinder an infinity of worlds.

Quoted by Diogenes Laërtius

DESIDERIUS ERASMUS
(1465–1536)
Dutch scholar, theologian

Adagia (1500)

All things obey money.

Fire and sea and woman, three evils.

It is impossible to live with them [women], or without them.

Lewdness lacketh but occasion.

In the kingdom of the blind the one-eyed man is king.

Of two evils the least is to be chosen.

Every definition is dangerous.

Emerson, Journals, Vol. 3: "We are always getting ready to live, but never living."

'Tis an easier matter to raise the devil than to lay him.

Colloquies

Who feed on Hope, hang on but do not live.

A good portion of speaking will consist in knowing how to lie.

Where there is hatred in judgment, judgment is blind.

Luther was guilty of two great crimes—he struck the Pope in his crown, and the monks in their belly.

Procus et Puella

The wedlock of minds will be greater than that of bodies.

Moriae Encomium

The chief happiness [for a man] is to be what he is.

To know nothing is the happiest life.

JOHN SCOTUS ERIGENA
(810–877)
Irish-born philosopher

Patrologia Latina (tr. G. B. Burch)

Metaphysics begins and ends with God.

We do not know what God is . . . because He is infinite and therefore objectively unknowable. God Himself does not know what He is because He is not anything. Therefore, nothing can be predicated of God literally or affirmatively. Literally God *is not,* because He transcends being.

Although we do not know *what* God is, we infer from the existence of the world *that* He is, not that He is any intelligible essence, but merely that He exists as the cause of all things. His inference is threefold. We observe that things are, and infer that their cause is. We observe that order of the universe, and infer that their cause is wise. We observe that things are in constant motion, being alive, and infer that their cause is life. Thus God, considered not in Himself but as the cause of all things, has three aspects: He is, He is wise, and He lives. His being is called the Father, His wisdom is called the Son, His life is called the

Holy Ghost, words which denote not the three aspects themselves, but their relation to each other.

It would suffice for me to answer you briefly when you ask why God should have created man, whom he proposed to make in his own image, in the genus of animals. He wished so to fashion him, that there would be a certain animal in which he manifested his own express image. But whoever asks why He wished that, asks the cause of the divine will; to ask that is too presumptious and arrogant. . . .

ERIK H. ERIKSON
(1902   )
American educator

Personality, too, is destiny.

We live at all times in (at least) a somatic order, a social order and a personal order, and if anything, it is the perpetual conflict of those three orders which makes for human destiny.
Interview, *Newsweek,* December 21, 1970

Life cycle—Identity crisis—Inner space—psychohistory.
Coined words, quoted in *New York Times Book Review,* March 30, 1975

THOMAS ERSKINE
(1750–1823)
Baron, Lord Chancellor of England

Defense of Thomas Paine (December 20, 1792)

Other liberties are held *under* governments, but liberty of opinion keeps governments themselves in due subjection to their duties.

The Press, my Lords, is one of our great out-sentries; if we remove it, if we hoodwink it, if we throw it in fetters, the enemy may surprise us.

Thus I have maintained by English history that in proportion as the Press has been free, English government has been free.

When men can freely communicate their thoughts and their sufferings, real or imaginary, their passions spend themselves in air, like gunpowder scattered upon the surface— but pent up by terrors, they work unseen, burst forth in a moment, and destroy everything in their course. Let reason be opposed to reason, and argument to argument, and every good government will be safe.

EUGENIUS IV
(c. 1383–1447)
Pope from 1431

Decree (1442)

We decree and order that from now on, and for all time, Christians shall not eat or drink with Jews, nor admit them to feasts, nor cohabit with them, nor bathe with them.

Christians shall not allow Jews to hold civil honors over Christians, or to exercise public offices in the state.

EURIPIDES
(485–406 B.C.)
Greek tragic dramatist

Andromache (c. 427 B.C.)

The gods have sent medicines for the venom of serpents, but there is no medicine for a bad woman. She is more noxious than the viper, or any fire itself.

Friends, and I mean real friends—reserve nothing;
The property of one belongs to the other.

The Cyclops (424–23 B.C.)

I sacrifice to no god save myself—
And to my belly, greatest of deities.

The Trojan Women (415 B.C.)

Account no man happy till he dies.

Electra (415 B.C.)

Poverty has this defect: it prompts a man to evil deeds.

The wife should yield in all things to her lord.

Hecuba (c. 425 B.C.)

No man is wholly free. He is a slave to wealth, or to fortune, or the laws, or the people restrain him from acting according to his will alone.

Slavery . . .
That thing of evil, by its nature evil,
Forcing submission from a man to what
No man can yield to.*

Hippolytus (429 B.C.)

I hate a clever woman—God forbid that I
should ever have a wife at home with more
than woman's wits.

Iphigenia in Aulis (c. 405 B.C.)**

If there are none, [i.e., gods]
All our toil is without meaning.

Iphigenia in Tauris (c. 413 B.C.)

To the lowly, the powerful and rich are as
gods.

Medea (431 B.C.)

Speak not so hastily: the gods themselves
By gifts are swayed, as fame relates, and
gold
Hath a far greater influence o'er the souls
Of mortals than the most persuasive words.

Oedipus

Man's greatest tyrants are his wife and children.

Fragment 5

Orestes (408 B.C.)

We must obey the gods, whatever those
gods are.
I say that kings,
Kill, rob, break oaths, lay cities waste by
fraud,

And doing thus are happier than those
Who live calm pious lives day after day.
How many little states that serve the gods
Are subject to the godless but more strong,
Made slaves by might of a superior army!

The Phoenissae (411 B.C.)

Men set most store by wealth, and of all
things
In the wide world it hath the greatest power.

Plain and unvarnished are the words of
truth.

The Suppliants (c. 420 B.C.)

There are three classes of citizens. The first
are the rich, who are indolent and yet always
crave more. The second are the poor, who
have nothing, are full of envy, hate the rich,
and are easily led by demagogues. Between the
two extremes lie those who make the state secure and uphold the laws.

The demagogue, putting up the people with
words, sways them to his interest. When calamity follows he escapes from justice.

Life is a struggle.
Hope is not to be trusted.

Hope is man's curse: many states has it
Involved in strife, by leading them to exces-
sive rage.
For, if the city votes on the question of war,
No man ever takes his own death into ac-
count,
But shifts his misfortune to his neighbor.

Fragments

Man's best possession is a sympathetic wife.
164

A woman should be good for everything at
home, but abroad good for nothing.
525

The facts speak for themselves.
840

Whoso neglects learning in his youth, loses
the past and is dead for the future.
927

———

What man who dreads not death can be a
slave?
Quoted in Plutarch's Moralia

If gods do evil then they are not gods.
Quoted in Edith Hamilton, The Greek Way of Life

Whom the gods would destroy, they first
make mad.
Quoted in Boswell's Life of Johnson

Who dares not speak his free thoughts is a
slave.
Quoted in Noyes, Views of Religion

The god of war hates him who hesitates.
Quoted by E.A. Mowrer

———

*"To Euripides the glory belongs for being the first
to condemn it."—Edith Hamilton, The Greek Way
of Life
**This play was completed after Euripides' death by
his son.

F

WILLIAM FAULKNER
(1897–1962)
American writer, Nobel Prize 1950

The Bear (1932)

They [the Negroes] will endure. They are better than we are. Stronger than we are. Their vices are vices aped from white men or that white men and bondage have taught them. . . . And their virtues . . . endurance . . . and pity and tolerance and forebearance and fidelity and love of children.
Pt. IV

Nobel Prize Speech, Stockholm (1950)

I decline to accept the end of man.

I believe that man will not merely endure; he will prevail. He is immortal, not because he alone among creatures has an inexhaustible voice, but because he has a soul, a spirit capable of compassion and sacrifice and endurance.*

The artist's only responsibility is to his art. He will be completely ruthless if he is a good one. . . . Everything goes by the board: honor, pride, decency, security, happiness, all, to get the book written.

If a writer has to rob his mother, he will not hesitate; the "Ode to a Grecian Urn" is worth any number of old ladies.

The aim of every artist is to arrest motion, which is life, by artificial means.
"An Interview with Faulkner," by Jean Stein (*Writers at Work, The Paris Review Interviews,* 1959)

---

*To his wife, Estelle, he added: "The human race stinks," according to Paul Gray, reviewing Blotner biography, *Time,* March 25, 1974.

FEDERAL COUNCIL OF CHURCHES

The Social Gospel (quadrennial report, 1923)

In economic terms, the Christian ideal demands a basic standard of living for the masses of people, adequate to assure security and freedom for the development of spiritual values.

The Christian ideal calls for hearty support of a planned economic system. . . . It assumes that the personalities of human beings are of more value than their labor power and deserve prior consideration. . . . Industrial democracy is a goal comparable to that of political democracy.

FRANÇOIS DE SALIGNAC DE LA MOTHE-FÉNELON
(1651–1715)
French writer, Archbishop of Cambray

Sermon (1685)

All wars are civil wars, because all men are brothers. . . . Each one owes infinitely more to the human race than to the particular country in which he was born.

FERDINAND I
(1503–1564)
Spanish-born, Holy Roman Emperor

Let justice be done, though the world perish.
Quoted in M. Manlius, *Loci Communes* (1563)
II, 290

FERDINAND VII
(1784–1833)
King of Spain

Far be it from us, the danger of thinking.
Quoted by Gerald Brenan

FRANCISCO FERRER
(1859–executed 1909)
Spanish freethinker

The Modern School

We must destroy all which in the present school answers to the organization of constraint, the artificial surroundings by which children are separated from nature and life, the intellectual and moral discipline made use of to impose ready-made ideas upon them, beliefs which deprave and annihilate natural bent.

All the value of education rests in respect for the physical, intellectual and moral will of the child.

Let no more gods or exploiters be served. Let us learn rather to love one another.
> Will, written on cell wall in Barcelona

LUDWIG FEUERBACH
(1804–1872)
German philosopher

The Essence of Christianity (1841)

Wherever morality is based on theology, wherever right is made dependent on divine authority, the most immoral, unjust, infamous things can be justified and established.

Theology is anthropology.

The first and highest law must be the love of man to man. *Homo homini Deus est*—this is the supreme practical maxim, this the turning point of the world's History.

In religion, man denies his reason.

Consciousness of God is self-consciousness. Knowledge of God is self-knowledge.

What yesterday was still religion is no longer such today; and what today is atheism tomorrow will be religion.

To think is to be God.

The belief in God is nothing but the belief in human dignity, the belief in the absolute reality and significance of the human nature.

Miracle owes its origin to the negation of thought.

The decline of culture was identical with the victory of Christianity . . . religious man feels no need of culture.

The Essence of Religion (1845)

A man thinks differently in a palace and in a hut.

In practice all men are atheists; they deny their faith by their actions.
> Attributed

JOHANN GOTTLIEB FICHTE
(1762–1814)
German philosopher

Über den Grund unseres Glaubens [*On the Foundations of Faith*] (1798)

It is a mistake to say that it is doubtful whether there is a God or not. It is not in the least doubtful, but the most certain thing in the world, nay, the foundation of all other certainty—the only solid absolute objectivity— that there is a moral government of the world.

Bestimmung des Menschen [*Vocation of Man*] (1800)

I cannot think of the present state of humanity as that in which it is destined to remain. . . . Only in so far as I can regard this state as the means toward a better, as the transition-point into a higher and more perfect state, has it any value in my eyes.

HENRY FIELDING
(1707–1754)
English writer

Tom Jones (1749)

There is perhaps no surer mark of folly, than to attempt to correct natural infirmities of those we love.
> Bk II, ch. 7

There are a set of religions, or rather moral writings, which teach that virtue is the certain road to happiness, and vice to misery, in this world. A very wholesome and comfortable doctrine, and to which we have but one objection, namely, that it is not true.

. . . composed that monstrous animal, a husband and wife.
> Bk. XV, ch. 9

Jonathan Wild (1743)

A man may go to Heaven with half the pains which it costs him to purchase Hell.

MILLARD FILLMORE
(1800–1874)
13th President of the United States

Peace at Any Price; Peace and Union.
> Slogan for his Native American Party (1856)

H(erbert) A(lbert) L(aurens) FISHER
(1865–1940)
British writer

A History of Europe (1934)

Purity of race does not exist. Europe is a continent of energetic mongrels.

Ch. 1

MARSHALL W. FISHWICK
American writer

The uncommitted life isn't worth living.

We need tough-minded thinkers, gadflies, doubters. Doubt is an angel, not a devil; it assumes an order of truth. Only through the agony of doubt can we have the courage to be; to supplement the motto of Descartes' day (*cogito, ergo sum*) with one suitable for our day—*dubito, ergo credo*.
Contribution, *Saturday Review,* December 21, 1963

EDWARD FITZGERALD
(1809–1883)
British writer*

The Rubáiyát of Omar Khayyám (anonymously published 1859, revised and expanded, 1868)

A Book of Verses underneath the Bough,
A Jug of Wine, a loaf of bread—and Thou
    Beside me singing in the Wilderness—
Oh, Wilderness were Paradise enow!

XII

Ah, my Beloved, fill the Cup that clears
To-Day of past Regret and future Fears:
    To-morrow!—Why, To-morrow I may be
Myself with Yesterday's Sev'n thousand
    Years.

XXI

Strange, is it not? that of the myriads who
Before us pass'd the door of Darkness
    through,
    Not one returns to tell us of the Road,
Which to discover we must travel too.

LXIV

*Authorities have always given Fitzgerald credit for many of *The Rubáiyát*'s best stanzas; Robert Graves credits all to him and has published a new translation of *Omar Khayyam* (q.v.)

I sent my Soul through the Invisible,
Some letter of that After-life to spell:
    And by and by my soul return'd to me,
And answer'd "I myself am Heav'n and
    Hell."

LXVI

The Moving Finger writes; and, having
    writ,
Moves on: nor all your Piety nor Wit
    Shall lure it back to cancel half a Line,
Nor all your Tears wash out a Word of it.

LXXI

F(rancis) SCOTT (Key) FITZGERALD
(1896–1940)
American writer

The Crackup (1936)

You can take your choice between God and Sex. If you choose both you're a hypocrite; if neither, you get nothing.

Show me a hero and I will write you a tragedy.

GUSTAVE FLAUBERT
(1821–1880)
French novelist

The Temptation of St. Antony (1848)

My kingdom is as wide as the universe and my wants have no limits. I go forward always, freeing spirits and weighing worlds, without fear, without compassion, without love, without God. I am called Science.

Ch. V

Letters

In art there is nothing without form.
    To Mlle. Louise Colet, August 12, 1846

A thinker (and what is an artist if not a triple thinker?) should have neither religion nor fatherland nor even any social convictions.
    To Mlle. Louise Colet, 1853

Nothing great is ever done without fanaticism. Fanaticism is religion: and the 18th century *philosophes* who decried the former actually overthrew the latter. Fanaticism is faith, the essence of faith, burning faith, the faith that works miracles. Religion is a relative conception, a thing invented by man—an idea, in sum; the other is feeling. . . .

In Art too the creative impulse is essentially fanatical.
>   To Mlle. Louise Colet, March 31, 1853

One's existence should be in two parts: one should live like a bourgeois and think like a demi-god. . . .
If you seek happiness and beauty simultaneously, you will attain neither one or the other, for the price of beauty is self-denial. Art, like the Jewish God, wallows in sacrifices.
>   To Mlle. Louise Colet, August 21–22, 1853

Concern with morality makes every work of the imagination false and stupid.
>   To Mlle. Louise Colet, January 2, 1864

Axiom: Hatred of the Bourgeois is the beginning of virtue. But for me the term "bourgeois" includes the bourgeois in overalls as well as the bourgeois who wears a frock coat. It is we, and we alone—that is, the educated—who are the People, or, more accurately, the tradition of Humanity.
>   To George Sand, May 10, 1867

Neo-Catholicism on the one hand and Socialism on the other have brought France to stupidity. Between the Immaculate Conception and free lunches for workingmen, everything marches toward ruin.
>   To George Sand, September 1868

The whole dream of democracy is to elevate the proletarian to the level of the imbecility of the bourgeois.
>   Letter, 1871

Earth has its boundaries but human stupidity is limitless.

That which is beautiful is moral, that is all, nothing more.
>   To Maupassant, October 26, 1871

The artist ought no more to appear in his work than God in nature.
>   Quoted in Wilson, *The Triple Thinkers*

Art is a quest for the useless.
>   Quoted in Blekhanov, *Art and Society*

PAUL FLEMIN
(1609–1640)
German physician, poet

"Der beste Rath" ["The Best Advice"]

*Wer Weibern traut, pflügt die Winde
Und saet aus die Wüste See,
Misst des verborgenen Meeres Gründe,*

*Schreibt sein Gedächtniss in den Schnee,
Schöpft, wie die Schwestern ohne Liebe,
Das Wasser mit dem hohlen Siebe.*

He who trusts women ploughs the wind, sows the barren sea, finds not the bottom of the barren ocean, writes his recollections in the snow, draws water like the Danaides, with pitchers full of holes.

JOHN FLETCHER
(1579–1625)
English dramatist

Wit Without Money (1614)

Speak boldly, and speak truly,
Shame the devil.
>   Act 4

Upon an Honest Man's Fortune (1613)

Man is his own Star; and that Soul that can
Be honest, is the only perfect man.

Sir John Van Olden (1619)

Read but o'er the stories
Of men most fam'd for courage or for counsel,
And you shall find that the desire of glory
(That last infirmity of noble minds)
Was the last frailty wise men e'er put off.
>   Act 1*

ABRAHAM FLEXNER
(1866–1959)
American educator

Universities (1930)

Probably no nation is rich enough to pay for both war and education.

The Common School Is The Greatest Discovery Ever Made By Man.
>   Inscription on his bust, Hall of Fame

WILHELM FLIESS
(1858–1928)
German psychoanalyst

Sublimation.
>   Coined word, attributed by Ernest Jones, *The Life and Work of Sigmund Freud*

---

*"That last infirmity of noble minds" appears in Milton, Ruskin, and other writings.

JOHN (Giovanni) FLORIO
(1553?–1625)
English writer, lexicographer

First Frutes (1578)

Time is the father of truth, and experience is the mother of all things.

Luste is lorde of al: it hath overcome Lordes, Learned Men, Wise and eloquent: it hath vanquished the gretest Knights that have ben.

Second Frutes (1591)

There is no virtue that poverty destroyeth not.

A man of straw is worth more than a woman of gold.

England is the paradise of women, the purgatory of men, and the hell of horses.

FERDINAND FOCH
(1851–1929)
French marshal

Victory is a thing of the will.
Message to Marshal Joffre, 1914

My center is giving way, my right is in retreat; situation excellent. I shall attack!
Quoted in Major-General Sir G. Aston,
Marshal Foch (1929)

The military mind always imagines that the next war will be on the same lines as the last. That has never been the case and never will be. One of the great factors in the next war will be aircraft obviously. The potentialities of aircraft attack on a large scale are almost incalculable.
Attributed in 1920s

FONTAINE, see La FONTAINE

LOUIS MARQUIS DE FONTANES
(1757–1821)
French poet, politician

Sire, the desire of perfection is the worst disease that ever afflicted the human mind.
To Napoleon, Senate, 1804; attributed by Emerson

FORD MADOX FORD (né Hueffer)
(1873–1939)
British novelist

A Man Could Stand Up.
Book title, 1926*

Eighty per cent of mankind is stuff to fill graves with.
Quoted in *Esquire,* August 1966

GERALD R(udolph) FORD
(1913–   )
38th President of the United States

A government big enough to give you everything you want is a government big enough to take from you everything you have.
Quoted in *Time,* November 8, 1976

HENRY FORD
(1863–1947)
American auto-maker

I don't know much about history, and I wouldn't give a nickel for all the history in the world. History is more or less bunk. It is tradition. We want to live in the present, and the only history that is worth a tinker's damn is the history we make today.*
Quoted in Jonathan Newton Leonard, *The Tragedy of Henry Ford* (1932)

Anyone who stops learning is old, whether at twenty or eighty. Anyone who keeps learning stays young. The greatest thing in life is to keep your mind young.

Capital punishment is as fundamentally wrong as a cure for crime as charity is wrong as a cure for poverty.
Attributed

JOHN FORD
(1586–1639?)
English dramatist

'Tis Pity She's a Whore
Play title, 1633

---

*Called a "stroke of genius" by Joseph Conrad; a reference to the armistice following four years of trench warfare.
**Henry Ford never said "History is bunk." *The Chicago Tribune* lawyers tried to attribute this misquotation to him in his original libel suit against it in 1919. Historian Nevins in *Expansion and* Challenge quotes Ford saying, "I did not say it was bunk. It was bunk to me."

JOSEPH FOUCHÉ, DUKE OF OTRANTE (1765–1820)
French statesman, Napoleon's minister of police

Mémoires (1824)

C'est plus qu'un crime, c'est une faute.
It is more than a crime, it is a blunder. *

FRANCE
(Official and semi-official)

"Decree," August 11, 1789

The National Assembly completely abolishes the feudal regime.

Art. 1

Declarations of the Rights of Man and Citizen, National Assembly (1789)

Men are born and remain free and equal in rights. Social distinctions can be based only upon public utility.

Art. 1

The aim of every political association is the preservation of the natural and imprescriptible rights of man. These rights are liberty, property, security, and resistance to oppression.

Art. 2

Liberty consists in the power to do anything that does not injure others; accordingly, the exercise of the rights of man has no limits except those that secure to the other members of society the enjoyment of these same rights. These limits may be determined only by law.

Art. 4

Every man being presumed innocent until he is pronounced guilty . . .

Art. 9

The free communication of ideas and opinions is one of the most precious of the rights of man. Every citizen then can freely speak, write, and print, subject to responsibility for the abuse of this freedom in the cases determined by law.

Art. 11

---

*In his memoirs Fouché records this criticism of Napoleon's execution of the Duc d' Enghien, March 21, 1804, because the remark had been attributed to others. It is attributed to Talleyrand, Boulay de la Meurthe, and by Emerson, wrongly, to Napoleon himself.

Property being a sacred and inviolable right . . .

Art. 17

Constitution (1791)

The law no longer recognizes religious vows, nor any other obligation which may be contrary to natural rights or to the Constitution.

Preamble

Liberty to every man to speak, write, print, and publish his opinions without having his writings subject to any censorship or inspection before their publication, and to worship as he pleases.

Code Napoléon (1804)

Property is the right to enjoy and dispose of things in the most absolute manner.

Art. 544

Declaration of the Rights and Duties of Man and Citizen (1795, tr. J. H. Stewart)

The rights of man in society are liberty, equality, security, and property.

Art. 1

Liberty consists of being able to do whatever is not injurious to the rights of others.

Art. 2

ANATOLE FRANCE (né Jacques Anatole François Thibault) (1844–1924)
French writer

Le Lys rouge (1894)

The law, in its majestic equality, forbids the rich as well as the poor to sleep under bridges, to beg in the streets, and to steal bread.

Ch. 7

Le Jardin d'épicure (1894)

Chance is perhaps the pseudonym of God when he did not wish to sign.

La Vie littéraire (1888)

The good critic is one who recounts the adventures of his soul among masterpieces.

Preface

Hunger and love are the pivots on which the world turns. Mankind is entirely determined by love and hunger.

La Révolte des anges (1914)

To die for an idea is to place a pretty high price upon conjectures.

Ch. 8

Crainquebille (1916)

Nature, in her indifference, makes no distinction between good and evil.

Epigrams

What is called the triumph of Christianity is more accurately the triumph of Judaism, and to Israel fell the singular privilege of giving a god to the world.

Religion has done love a great service by making it a sin.

You believe you are dying for the fatherland—you die for some industrialists.
Quoted in Van Paasson, *Days of Our Years*

Make love now, by night and by day, in winter and in summer . . . You are in the world for that and the rest of life is nothing but vanity, illusion, waste. There is only one science, love; only one riches, love; only one policy, love. To make love is all the law, and the prophets.
Quoted in J. J. Brousson, *Anatole France en pantoufles*

ST. FRANÇOIS DE SALES
(1567–1622)
Bishop of Geneva

Letters to Persons in the World

We must not fear fear.

4, 12

Fear is a greater evil than the evil itself.

6, 12

FRANCISCO FRANCO
(1892–1975)
Caudillo of Spain, Fascist dictator

Speeches

Strikes are a crime . . . the law of jungles and primitive societies. *
1961, quoted in *Time,* May 21, 1961

---

*A Franco law, passed by the Cortos, prescribed the death penalty for organizing unions or calling strikes.

We abhor political parties. We are against political parties, and we have none.
Pamplona, 1953, reported by Richard Mowrer, *Christian Science Monitor*

Liberal democracy easily ends in Communism.
Burges, 1964

Our regime is based on bayonets and blood, not on hypocritical elections.
Quoted in H. L. Matthews, *Half of Spain Died*

LEONARD ROY FRANK
20th century American epigrammist

Democracy + Private Ownership – Capitalism.
Democracy + Public Ownership = Socialism.
Dictatorship + Private Ownership = Fascism.
Dictatorship + Public Ownership = Communism.
From a privately published booklet

FELIX FRANKFURTER
(1882–1965)
U.S. Supreme Court Justice

Freedom of expression is the well-spring of our civilization. . . . The history of civilization is in considerable measure the displacement of error which once held sway as official truth by beliefs which in turn have yielded to other truths. Therefore the liberty of man to search for truth ought not to be fettered, no matter what orthodoxies he may challenge. Liberty of thought soon shrivels without freedom of expression. Nor can truth be pursued in an atmosphere hostile to the endeavor or under dangers which are hazarded only by heroes.
Concurring Opinion, Dennis *et al. v.* U.S. (1951)

Freedom of the press is not an end in itself but a means to the end of a free society.
Concurring Opinion, Pennekamp *v.* Florida

Dissent is essential to an effective judiciary in a democratic society.
Quoted in *Time,* February 15, 1971

BENJAMIN FRANKLIN
(1706–1790)
American scientist, diplomat, publisher

A Modest Inquiry Into the Nature and Necessity of a Paper Currency (April 3, 1729)

By labor may the value of silver be measured as well as other things. . . . Trade in general being nothing else but the exchange of labor for labor, the value of all things is, as I have said before, most justly measured by labor.*

Rules for his own conduct (c. 1730)

Rarely use venery but for health or offspring, never to dullness, weakness, or the injury of your own or another's peace or reputation.

Apology for Printers (1731)

Printers are educated in the belief, that when men differ in opinion, both sides ought equally to have the advantage of being heard by the public; and that when truth and error have fair play, the former is always an overmatch for the latter.

Articles of Belief and Acts of Religion (November 20, 1728)

I cannot conceive otherwise than that He, the Infinite Father, expects or requires no worship or praise from us, but that He is even infinitely above it.

*Poor Richard's Almanac***

After three days men grow weary of a wench, a guest, and rainy weather.

1733

Where there's marriage without love, there will be love without marriage.

He who shall introduce into public affairs the principles of primitive Christianity, will revolutionize the world.

Sin is not hurtful because it is forbidden, but it is forbidden because it is hurtful.

. . . a good conscience is a continual Christmas.

1734

---

*Quoted in Karl Marx, *Critique of Political Economy.*
**The Almanac was published from 1732 to 1758 under the name of Richard Saunders. The maxims are from the prefaces.

Opportunity is the great bawd.

1735

Sell not virtue to purchase wealth, nor liberty to purchase power.

Laws gentle are seldom obeyed; too severe seldom executed.

1738

Dost thou love Life? Then do not squander Time; for that's the stuff Life is made of.

1746

When knaves fall out, honest men get their goods; when priests dispute, we come to the truth.

1758

Letters

There never was a good war or a bad peace.
To Josiah Quincy, September 11, 1783

Our Constitution is in actual operation; everything appears to promise that it will last; but nothing in this world is certain but death and taxes.
To M. Leroy of the French Academy of Sciences, 1789

As to Jesus of Nazareth, my opinion of whom you particularly desire, I think the system of morals and his religion, as he left them to us, the best the world ever saw or is likely to see; but I apprehend it has received various corrupting changes, and I have, with most of the present dissenters in England, some doubts of his divinity.
To Ezra Styles (of Yale), March 9, 1790

Advice to a Young Tradesman (1748)

Remember that time is money.

"Positions to be Examined Concerning National Wealth" (April 4, 1769)

There seem to be but three ways for a nation to acquire wealth: the first is by war, as the Romans did, in plundering their conquered neighbors—this is robbery; the second by commerce, which is generally cheating; the third by agriculture, the only honest way, wherein man received a real increase of the seed thrown into the ground, in a kind of continual miracle, wrought by the hand of God in his favor, as a reward for his innocent life and his virtuous industry.

On signing the Declaration of Independence, in Continental Congress (July 4, 1776)

We must indeed all hang together, or, most assuredly, we shall all hang separately.

Historical Review of Pennsylvania (1759)

They that can give up essential liberty to obtain a little temporary safety deserve neither liberty nor safety.

Liberté, égalité, fraternité.
Attributed, suggested to French leaders as a slogan

SIR JAMES (George) FRAZER
(1854–1941)
Scottish anthropologist

The Golden Bough (1890–1915)

Men make the gods; women worship them.

FREDERICK (II) THE GREAT
(1712–1784)
King of Prussia

Letters to Voltaire

Religion is the idol of the mob; it adores everything it does not understand.
July 7, 1737

The mob does not deserve to be enlightened.
August 7, 1766

An Essay on Forms of Government (1777)

Let it be carefully remembered that the preservation of the laws was the sole reason which induced men to allow of, and to elect a superior; because that is the true origin of sovereign power.

With respect to the true monarchial government, it is the best or the worst of all others, accordingly as it is administered.

No government can exist without taxation. . . . This money must necessarily be levied on the people; and the grand art consists of levying so as not to oppress.

. . . among Christian nations, the majority are Anthromorphites; that, among the Catholics, most of the people are idolators. . . . Therefore there are a number of heretics in all Christian sects. What is more, each man believes that which appears to him to be the truth.

Posthumous Works

An author who wishes to write without passion, and without prejudice, ought, it is said, to have neither religion nor country; and this is nearly the case with Voltaire.

All religions must be tolerated . . . for in this way must every one be saved in his own way.*
Cabinet order, June 22, 1740

Rascals, would you live forever?
To the hesitating Guards, Battle of Köln, June 18, 1757

PHILIP M. FRENEAU
(1752–1832)
American journalist, rebel

"Tobacco" (1790)

Tobacco surely was designed
To poison and destroy mankind.

SIGMUND FREUD
(1856–1939)
Austrian originator of psychoanalysis**

Wit and Its Relation to the Unconscious (1905)

No matter how much restriction civilization imposes on the individual, he nevertheless finds some way to circumvent it. Wit is the best safety valve modern man has evolved; the

---

*Also translated, "Every man must get to heaven in his own way."
**The Freud quotations were submitted to Dr. Ernest L. Freud in London, who submitted them to James Strachey. Corrections were made. But Mr. Strachey protested that some quotations were out of context. All quotations are.
"Freud stands supreme among the men of the earth along with Galileo, Columbus, Darwin, Leonardo, and Newton."—Dr. Karl A. Meninger, *The Human Mind*
"Freud, even more than Lincoln, might well be called The Great Emancipator."—Walter Kaufman, *The Faith of a Heretic*
"The misconceptions and distortions, the falsifications and misrepresentations to which psychoanalysis was subjected in its popularizations, threaten to transform the magnificent house that Freud built into a stable similar to that of King Augeus."—Theodore Reik, preface, *Freud: Dictionary of Psychoanalysis,* 1950
"The Freudian theory is one of the most important foundation stones for an edifice to be built by future generations, the dwelling of a freer and wiser humanity." —*New York Times,* June 21, 1939

more civilization, the more repression, the more need there is for wit.

Beyond the Pleasure Principle (1920)

No neurotic harbors thoughts of suicide which are not murderous impulses against others redirected upon himself.

If we may assume as an experience admitting of no exception that everything living dies from causes within itself, and returns to the inorganic, we can only say, "The goal of all life is death," and, casting back, "The inanimate was there before the animate."

Civilization and Its Discontents (1930)

The impression forces itself upon one that men measure by false standards, that everyone seeks power, success, riches for himself and admires others who attain them, while undervaluing the truly precious things in life.

Opening lines

The derivation of a need for religion from the child's feeling of helplessness and the longing it evokes for a father seems to me incontrovertible, especially since this feeling is not simply carried on from childhood days but is kept alive perpetually by the fear of what the superior power of fate will bring.

p. 21

Life as we find it is too hard for us; it entails too much pain, too many disappointments, impossible tasks. We cannot do without palliative remedies. . . . There are perhaps three of these means: powerful diversions of interest, which lead us to care little about our misery; substitute gratifications, which lessen it; and intoxicating substances, which make us insensitive to it. Something of this kind is indispensable.

p. 25

The question, "What is the purpose of human life?" has been asked times without number; it has never received a satisfactory answer; perhaps it does not admit of such an answer.

. . . So again, only religion is able to answer the question of the purpose of life. One can hardly go wrong in concluding that the idea of a purpose in life stands and falls with the religious system.

p. 26

Voluntary loneliness, isolation from others, is the readiest safeguard against the unhappiness that may arise out of human relations.

p. 29

The goal towards which the pleasure-principle impels us—of becoming happy—is not attainable; yet we may not—nay, cannot—give up the effort to come nearer to realization of it by some means or other.

p. 39

Sublimation of instinct is an especially conspicuous feature of cultural evolution; this it is that makes it possible for the higher mental operations, scientific, artistic, ideological activities, to play such an important part in civilized life. . . . It is impossible to ignore the extent to which civilization is built up on renunciation of instinctual gratifications, the degree to which the existence of civilization presupposes the non-gratification (suppression, repression or something else?) of powerful instinctual urgencies. This "cultural privation" dominates the whole field of social relations between human beings; we know already that it is the cause of the antagonism against which all civilization has to fight.

p. 63

Women represent the interests of the family and sexual life; the work of civilization has become more and more men's business; it confronts them with ever harder tasks, compels them to sublimations of instinct which women are not easily able to achieve.

p. 73

Man, too, is an animal with an unmistakably bisexual disposition. . . . Sex is a biological fact which is hard to evaluate psychologically, although it is of extraordinary importance in mental life. We are accustomed to say that every human being displays both male and female instinctual impulses, needs and attributes, but the characteristics of what is male and female can only be demonstrated in anatomy, and not in psychology.

p. 77

Once the apostle Paul had laid down universal love between all men as the foundation of his Christian community, the inevitable consequence in Christianity was the utmost intolerance towards all who remained outside of it.

p. 91

Those who love fairy-tales do not like it when people speak of the innate tendencies in mankind toward aggression, destruction, and, in addition, cruelty. God has made them in his own image, with his own perfections; no one wants to be reminded how hard it is to reconcile the undeniable existence—in spite of all the protestations of Christian Science—of evil with His omnipotence and supreme goodness.

pp. 99–100

The meaning of the evolution of culture is no longer a riddle to us. It must present to us the struggle between Eros and Death, between the instincts of life and the instincts of destruction, as it works itself out in the human species.

p. 103

The symptoms of neurosis, as we have learnt, are essentially substitute gratifications for unfulfilled sexual wishes.

p. 132

To command to love our neighbors as ourselves . . . is impossible to fulfill; such an enormous inflation of love can only lower its value and not remedy the evil. Civilization pays no heed to all this.

pp. 139–140

The fateful question of the human species seems to me to be whether and to what extent the cultural process developed in it will succeed in mastering the derangements of communal life caused by the human instinct of aggression and self-destruction. . . . Men have brought their powers of subduing the forces of nature to such a pitch that by using them they could now very easily exterminate one another to the last man. . . . And now it may be expected that the other of the two "heavenly forces," eternal Eros, will put forth his strength so as to maintain himself alongside to his equally immortal adversary.

pp. 143–144

(From the same work, other editions)

It seems to be my faith to discover only the obvious: that children have sexual feelings, which every nursemaid knows; and that night dreams are just as much a wish fulfillment as day dreams.

The sexual life of civilized man is seriously disabled, whatever we may say; it sometimes makes an impression of being a function in process of becoming atrophied, just as organs like our teeth and our hair seem to be.

The Ego and the Id (1923)

We have to distinguish two classes of instincts, one of which, Eros or the sexual instinct, is by far the most conspicuous and accessible to study. It comprises not merely the uninhibited sexual instinct proper and the impulses of a sublimated or aim-inhibited nature derived from it, but also the self-perservative instinct.

The second class of instincts was not so easy to define; in the end we came to recognize sadism as its representative. As a result of theoretical considerations, supported by biology, we assumed the existence of a death-instinct, the mask of which is to lead organic matter back into the inorganic state.

Let us consider the polarity of love and hate. . . . Now, clinical observation shows not only that love is with unexpected regularity accompanied by hate (ambivalence), and not only that in human relationships hate is frequently a forerunner of love, but also that in many circumstances hate changes into love and love into hate.

The Future of an Illusion (1927)

We may insist as often as we like that man's intellect is powerless in comparison with his instinctual life and we may be right in this.

Religion is comparable to a childhood neurosis.

It is only by the influence of individuals who can set an example, whom the masses recognize as their leaders, that they can be induced to submit to the labours and renunciations on which the existence of culture [civilization] depends.

p. 7

Religious ideas have sprung from the same need as all the other achievements of culture: from the necessity for defending itself against the crushing supremacy of nature.

p. 34

Just as no one can be forced into belief, so no one can be forced into unbelief.

p. 55

The more the fruits of knowledge become accessible to men, the more widespread is the decline of religious belief.

p. 69

It [religion], like the child's, originated in the Oedipus complex, the relation to the father. According to this conception one might prophesy that the abandoning of religion must take place with the fateful inexorability of the process of growth, and that we are just now in the middle of this phase of development.

p. 78

In the long run nothing can withstand reason and experience, and the contradiction religion offers to both is only too palpable.

p. 98

A General Introduction to Psychoanalysis (twenty-eight lectures) (1916–1917)

The educability of a young person as a rule comes to an end when sexual desire breaks out in its final strength. . . . The little human being is frequently a finished product in his fourth or fifth year, and only gradually reveals in later years what lies buried in him.

In psychoanalytic treatment nothing happens but an exchange of words between the patient and the physician. . . . Words and magic were in the beginning one and the same thing, and even today words contain much of their magical power. By words one can give to another the greatest happiness or bring about utter despair. . . . Words call forth emotion and are universally the means by which we influence our fellow creatures. Therefore let us not despise the use of words in psycho-therapy.

Do you not know how uncontrolled and unreliable the average human being is in all that concerns sexual life?

And now look away from individuals to the great war still devastating Europe: think of the colossal brutality, cruelty and mendacity which is now allowed to spread itself over the civilized world. Do you really believe that a handful of unprincipled place-hunters and corrupters of men would have succeeded in letting loose all this latent evil, if the millions of their followers were not also guilty?

Humanity has in the course of time had to endure from the hands of science two great outrages upon its self-love. The first was when it realized that our earth was not the center of the universe. . . . The second was when biological research robbed man of his peculiar privilege of having been specially created, and relegated him to descent from the animal world, implying an irradicable animal nature in him. . . . But man's craving for grandiosity is now suffering the third and most bitter blow from present day psychological research, which is endeavoring to prove to the *ego* in each one of us that he is not even master in his own house, but that he must remain content with the veriest scraps of information about what is going on unconsciously in his own mind.

From the time of puberty onward the individual must devote himself to the great task of *freeing himself from the parents;* and only after this detachment is accomplished can he cease to be a child and become a member of the social community. For a son the task consists in releasing the libidinal desires from his mother, in order to employ them in the quest for an external love-object in reality; and in reconciling himself with his father from the domination if in the reaction to the infantile revolt he has lapsed into subservience to him. These tasks are laid down for every man; it is noteworthy how seldom they are carried through ideally, that is, how seldom they are solved in a manner psychologically as well as socially satisfactory. In neurotics, however, this detachment from the parents is not accomplished at all; the son remains all his life in subjection to the father, and incapable of transferring his libido to a new sexual object. In the reversed relationship the daughter's fate may be the same. In this sense the Oedipus Complex is justifiably regarded as the kernel of the neuroses.

We have to conclude that all the feelings of sympathy, friendship, trust and so forth which are expended in life are genetically connected with sexuality and have developed out of purely sexual desires by an enfeebling of their sexual aim, however pure and nonsexual they may appear in the forms they take on to our conscious self-perception.

Group Psychology and the Analysis of the Ego (1921)

A group* is extraordinarily credulous and open to influence, it has no critical faculty, and the improbable does not exist for it. It thinks in images.

---

*Freud's word is *Masse,* Le Bon's *foule,* both translatable as "crowd" and "mass."

Since a group is in no doubt as to what constitutes truth or error, and is conscious moreover, of its own great strength, it is as intolerant as it is obedient to authority. It respects force and can only be slightly influenced by kindness, which it regards as a form of weakness. What it demands of its heroes is strength, or even violence. It wants to be ruled and oppressed and to fear its masters. Fundamentally it is entirely conservative, and it has a deep aversion from all innovations and advances and an unbounded respect for tradition.

In order to make a correct judgment upon the morals of crowds, one must take into consideration the fact that when individuals come together in a group all their individual inhibitions fall away and all the cruel, brutal, and destructive instincts, which lie dormant in individuals as relics of a primitive epoch, are stirred up to fine free gratification.

The evidence of psychoanalysis shows that almost every intimate emotional relation between two people which lasts for some time—marriage, friendship, the relations between parents and children—leaves a sediment of feelings of aversion and hostility, which have first to be eliminated by repression.

Love for oneself knows only one barrier—love for others, love for objects.

And in the development of mankind as a whole, just as in individuals, love alone acts as the civilizing factor in the sense that it brings a change from egoism to altruism.

Even those who do not regret the disappearance of religious illusions from the civilized world of today will admit that so long as they were in force they offered those who were bound by them the most powerful protection against the danger of neurosis.

Postscript

The Interpretation of Dreams* (1900)

As regards intellectual work, it remains a fact, indeed, that great decisions in the realms of thought and momentous discoveries and solutions of problems are only possible to an individual, working in solitude.

The majority of the dreams of adults deal with sexual material and express erotic wishes.

No one believes in his own death, or, to put the same thing in another way, that in the unconscious every man of us is convinced of his own immortality.

Every dream reveals as a psychological structure, full of significance. . . . The dream is not meaningless, not absurd. . . . it is a perfectly valid phenomenon, actually a wish-fulfillment.

Dream-distortion, then, proves in reality to be an act of the censorship.

The dream is a disguised fulfillment of a suppressed (repressed) wish *

Dreams of nakedness are exhibition dreams

It has been my experience—and to this I have found no exception—that every dream treats of oneself. Dreams are absolutely egoistic.

Dreams of falling are most frequently characterized by anxiety. Their interpretation when they occur in women offers no difficulty, because they nearly always accept the symbolic meaning of falling which is a circumlocution for giving way to an erotic temptation.

Nothing can be brought to an end in the unconscious; nothing is past or forgotten.

Leonardo da Vinci (1909)

In all our male homosexuals there was very intense erotic attachment to a feminine person, as a rule to the mother, which was manifest in the very first period of childhood and later entirely forgotten by the individual. This attachment was produced or favored by too much love from the mother herself, but was also furthered by the retirement or absence of the father during the childhood period. . . . Following this primary stage, a transformation takes place whose mechanism we know but whose motive forces we have not yet grasped. The love of the mother cannot continue to develop consciously so that it merges into repression. The boy represses the love for the mother by putting himself in her place, by identifying himself with her, and by taking his own person

---

*Dr. Max Schur, in his book *Freud: Living and Dying,* says this masterpiece was "killed by silence," reviewed with "malicious distortion and derision." Strachey said 351 copies were sold in the first six years after publication.

---

*"Dreams are true interpreters of our inclinations; but there is art required to sort and understand them."—Montaigne, *Essays.*

as a model through the similarity of which he is guided in the selection of his love-object. He thus becomes homosexual; as a matter of fact he returns to the stage of auto-eroticism, for the boys whom the growing adult now loves are only substitute persons or revivals of his own childish person, whom he loves in the same way as his mother loved him. We say that he finds his love-object on the road to narcissism.

. . . the psychic development of the individual is a short repetition of the course of the development of the race.

Moses and Monotheism (1939)

Neurosis seems to be a human privilege.

The pre-eminence given to intellectual labors throughout two thousand years in the life of the Jewish people has, of course, had its effect. It has helped to check the brutality and the tendency to violence which are apt to appear where the development of muscular strength is the popular ideal.

The Christian religion did not keep to the lofty heights of spirituality to which the Jewish religion had soared. The former was no longer monotheistic; it took over from the surrounding peoples numerous symbolic rites, re-established the great mother goddess, and found room for many deities of polytheism in an easily recognizable disguise, though in subordinate positions.

The Superego is the successor and representative of the parents (and ancestors) who superintended the actions of the individual in his first years of life; it perpetuates their function almost without a change.

New Introductory Lectures in Psychoanalysis (1933)

In popular language we may say that the ego stands for reason and sanity, in contrast to the id which stands for untamed passions.

The God-Creator is openly called Father. Psychoanalysis concluded that he really is the father, clothed in the grandeur in which he first appeared to the small child. The religious man's picture of the creation of the universe is the same as his picture of his own creation. . . . He therefore looks back on the memory-image of the overrated father of his childhood, exalts it into a Deity, and brings it into the present and into reality. The emo-

tional strength of this memory-image and the lasting nature of his need for protection are the two supports of his belief in God.

. . . artistic talent . . . is still a psychological riddle.

The claims of our civilization make life too hard for the greater part of humanity, and so further aversion to reality and the origin of neurosis.

Theoretical Marxism, as realized in Russian Bolshevism, has acquired the energy and the self-contained exclusive character of a *Weltanschauung,* but at the same time an uncanny likeness to what it is fighting against. . . . Though originally . . . built . . . upon science and technology, it has created a prohibition of thought which is just as ruthless as was that of religion in the past. Any critical examination of Marxist theory is forbidden, doubts of its correctness are punished in the same way as heresy was once punished in the Catholic Church. The writings of Marx have taken the place of the Bible . . . , though they would seem to be no more free from contradictions . . . than those older sacred books.

The whole of psychoanalytic theory is in fact built upon the perception of the resistance exerted by the patient when we try to make him conscious of the unconscious.

The sense of inferiority and the sense of guilt are exceedingly difficult to distinguish.

The first love object of a boy is his mother, and she remains in the formation of his Oedipus-complex, and, ultimately throughout his whole life. For the little girl, too, her mother must be her first object. . . . In the Oedipus situation, however, from that, in the normal course of development, she should find her way to her ultimate object-choice. The girl has, then, in the course of time to change both her erotogenic zone and her object, while the boy keeps both of them unchanged.

Modesty, which is regarded as a feminine characteristic *par excellence,* but is far more a matter of convention than one would think, was, in our opinion, originally designed to hide a deficiency in her genitals.

We must not overlook one particular constant relation between femininity and instinctual life. The repression of their aggressiveness which is imposed upon women by their constitution and by society, favors the development of strong masochistic impulses, which have the effect of binding erotically the destructive tendencies which have been turned inward. Masochism is then, as it were, truly feminine.

The only thing that brings a mother undiluted satisfaction is her relation to a son. It is quite the almost complete relationship between human beings, and the one that is the most free from ambivalence.

Even a marriage is not firmly assured until the woman has succeeded in making her husband into her child and in acting the part of a mother toward him.

Throughout the ages, the problem of woman has puzzled people of every kind.

An Outline of Psychoanalysis (pub. posthumously 1940)

There are some neurotics in whom, to judge by all their reactions, the instinct of self-preservation has actually been reversed. They seem to have nothing in view but self-injury and self-destruction. It is possible that people who in the end in fact commit suicide belong to this group.

The principal characteristics of the ego are these. In consequence of the relation which was already established between sensory perceptions and muscular action, the ego is in control of voluntary movement. It has the task of self-preservation. . . . The ego pursues pleasure and seeks to avoid displeasure.

To the oldest of the mental provinces or agencies we give the name of *id.* It contains everything that is inherited, that is present at birth, that is fixed in the constitution—above all, therefore, the instincts, which originate in the somatic organizations and which find their first mental expression in the id in the forms unknown to us.

Ch. 1

After long doubts and vacillations we have decided to assume the existence of only two basic instincts, *Eros and the destructive instinct.*

We may suppose that the final aim of the destructive instinct is to reduce living things to an inorganic state. For this reason also we call it the *death instinct.*

The holding back of aggressiveness is in general unhealthy and leads to illness.

Ch. 2

There are people whose desires behave in every way like sexual ones, but who at the same time entirely disregard the sexual organs or their normal use; people of this kind are known as "perverts."

Ch. 3

A male child commonly suffers from anxiety lest his father rob him of his male member; and so castration anxiety is one of the strongest influences on the development of his character, and decisive for his sexual tendencies later.

Ch. 4

We shall be justified in assuming that there arises at birth an instinct to return to the intrauterine life that has been abandoned—an instinct to sleep. Sleep is a return of this kind to the womb.

The Super-Ego is the vehicle for the phenomenon we call "conscience."

They [neurotics] complain of their illness, but they make the most of it, and when it comes to taking it away from them they will defend it like a lioness her young; there is no use in reproaching them with their contradictions.

Ch. 5

The primeval custom of circumcision, another symbolic substitute for castration, is only intelligible if it is an expression of subjugation to the father's will. (Compare the puberty rites of primitive peoples.)

We must not forget, therefore, to include the influence of civilization among the determinants of neuroses. It is easy, as we can see, for a barbarian to be healthy; for a civilized man the task is a hard one.

The symptoms of neuroses are exclusively, it might be said, either a substitute satisfaction of a sexual impulse or measures to prevent such satisfaction, and are as a rule a compromise between the two, of the kind that arise according to the laws operative between contraries in the unconscious.

Most of the impulses of sensual life are not of a purely erotic nature but arise from alloys of the erotic instinct with components of the destructive instinct.

Much of our most highly valued cultured heritage has been acquired at the cost of our sexuality.

Ch. 7

Neuroses could be avoided if the child's sexual life were allowed free play, as happens among many primitive races.

Ch. 8

Thoughts for the Times on War and Death (1915)

To endure life remains, when all is said, the first duty of all living beings. . . . If you would endure life, be prepared for death.

Three Essays on the Theory of Sexuality (1901)

The roots of active algolagnia, sadism, can be readily demonstrated in the normal individual. The sexuality of most men shows an admixture of aggression, or a desire to subdue, the biological significance of which lies in the necessity for overcoming the resistance of the sexual object by actions other than mere *courting.* Sadism would then correspond to an aggressive component part of the sexual instinct which has become independent and exaggerated and has been brought to the foreground by displacement.

I

Totem and Taboo (1912–1913)

Love cannot be much stronger than the lust to kill.

To touch is the beginning of every act of possession, of every attempt to make use of a person or thing.

"Some Neurotic Mechanisms in Jealousy, Paranoia and Homosexuality" (1922)

The theory of repression became the foundation alone of our understanding of the neuroses. . . . It is possible to take repression as the center and to bring all the elements of psychoanalytical theory into relation with it.

Jealousy is one of those affective states, like grief, that may be ascribed as normal. . . .

Contributions to the Psychology of Love: "The Taboo of Virginity" (1917)

We may say that the act of defloration has not merely the socially useful result of binding the woman closely to the man; it also liberates an archaic reaction of enmity towards the man, which may assume pathological forms, and often enough expresses itself by inhibitions in the erotic life of the pair, and to which one may ascribe the fact that second marriages so often turn out better than first.

"Female Sexuality" (1931)

There can be no doubt that the bisexual disposition which we maintain to be characteristic of human beings manifests itself much more in the female than in the male.

"Instincts and Their Vicissitudes" (1915)

The ego abhors, and pursues with intent to destroy all objects which are for it a source of painful feeling, without taking into account whether they mean for it frustration of sexual satisfaction or of gratification of the needs of self-preservation. Indeed it may be asserted that the true prototypes of the hate relation are derived not from sexual life, but from the struggle of the ego for self-preservation and self-maintenance.

The Problem of Anxiety

. . . the female sex is certainly more disposed to neurosis. . . . It is precisely in the female that object loss seems to remain the most effective situation of danger. . . . Since it is certainly true that hysteria has a greater affinity with femininity, just as compulsion has with masculinity, the idea suggests itself that, as a determinant of anxiety, loss of love plays a role in hysteria similar to that of the threat of castration in the phobias and of dread of the superego in compulsion neurosis.

Psychoanalytical Notes Upon an Autobiographical Account of Paranoia (1911)

On the basis of . . . clinical evidence we can suppose that paranoics are endowed with a *fixation at the stage of narcissism,* and we can assert that the amount of *regression* characteristic of paranoia is indicated by the length of *the step from sublimated homosexuality to narcissism.*

The Psychopathology of Everyday Life (1901)

. . . the analogy to paranoia must here come to our aid. We venture to explain in this way the myths of paradise and the fall of man, of God, of good and evil, of immortality and the like—that is, to transform metaphysics into meta-psychology. The gap between the paranoic's displacement and that of superstition is narrower than appears at first sight.

"The Sexual Enlightenment of Children" (1907)

What is the aim of withholding from children, or let us say from young people, the information about the sexual life of human beings? Is it fear of arousing interest in such matters prematurely before it spontaneously stirs in them? Is it hope of retarding by concealment of this kind the development of the sexual instinct in general. . . . Or is it genuinely and seriously intended that later on they should consider everything connected with sex as something despicable and abhorrent from which their parents and teachers wish to keep them apart as long as possible?

I am really at a loss to say which of these can be the motive for the customary concealment from children of everything connected with sex. I only know that these arguments are one and all really foolish and that I find it difficult to pay them the compliment of serious refutation.

"Reply to Criticisms of My Paper on the Anxiety Neurosis" (1895)

. . . *phobias do not occur at all when the vita sexualis is normal.*

Three Contributions to the Theory of Sex (1910)

In human beings there is no such thing as pure masculinity or femininity, either in the psychological or the biological sense.

"The Uncanny" (1919)

Religions continue to dispute the importance of the undeniable fact of individual death and to postulate a life after death. . . . Since almost all of us still think as savages do on this topic, it is no matter of surprise that the primitive fear of the dead is still so strong within us and always ready to come to the surface on any provocation.

"Why War?" (with Einstein, 1932)

Anything that encourages the growth of emotional ties between men must operate against war.

Letters

That men are divided into leaders and the led is but another manifestation of their inborn and irremediable inequality. Men should be at greater pains than heretofore to form a superior class of thinkers, unamenable to intimidation and fervent in the quest of truth, whose function it would be to guide the masses dependent on their lead.

There is but one sure way of ending war and that is the establishment, by common consent, of a central control which shall have the last word in any conflict of interests. For this two things are needed: first, the creation of such a supreme court of Judicature; secondly, its investment with adequate executive force. Unless the second requirement is fulfilled, the first is unavailing.
> To Einstein, September 1932, published, *Free World*, 1933

The moment a man questions the meaning and value of life, he is sick, since objectively neither has any existence; by asking this question one is merely admitting to a store of unsatisfied libido to which something else must have happened, a kind of fermentation leading to sadness and depression.
> To Marie Bonaparte, April 27, 1926

Whoever undertakes to write a biography binds himself to lying, to concealment, to flummery, and even to hiding his own lack of understanding, since biographical material is not to be had, and if it were it could not be used. Truth is not accessible; mankind does not deserve it.
> To Dr. Fliess, undated

A man should not try to eliminate his complexes but to get into accord with them; they are legitimately what directs his conduct in the world.
> To Ferenczi, November 17, 1911

Anyone who promises to mankind liberation from the hardships of sex will be hailed as a hero, let him talk whatever nonsense he chooses.
> To Dr. Ernest Jones, 1913, referring to Jung

The beginnings of religion, ethics, society and art meet in the Oedipus Complex.
> To Max Eastman, quoted in *Great Companions*

Love cannot be anything but egotistical.
> To Martha Bernays, 1882

Jesus could have been an ordinary deluded creature.
> To Oskar Pfister

The task of subduing so powerful an instinct as the sexual impulse, otherwise than by giving it satisfaction, is one which may employ the whole strength of a man. Subjugation through sublimation, by guiding the sexual forces into higher civilizational paths, may succeed with a minority, and even with these only for a time, least easily during years of ardent youthful energy. Most others become neurotic or other-

wise come to grief. Experience shows that the majority of people constituting your society are constitutionally unequal to the task of abstinence. . . . But in by far the majority of cases the struggle with sensuality uses up the available energy of character, and this at the very time when the young man needs all his strength in order to win his place in the world.
Contribution, *Sexual Problems,* March 1908

The great question that has never been answered, and which I have not been able to answer, despite my thirty years of research into the feminine soul, is: What does a woman want?*
From a conversation with Marie Bonaparte, quoted in Jones's biography of Freud

The goal of all life is death.

A neurosis is the result of a conflict between the ego and the id; the person is at war with himself. A psychosis is the outcome of a similar disturbance in the relation between the ego and the outside world.**
Quoted in *N.Y. Times Magazine,* May 6, 1956

We hate the criminal, and deal with him severely, because we view in his deed, as in a distorting mirror, our own criminal instincts.
Quoted in Wittels, *Freud and His Time*

. . . the first man to use abusive language instead of his fists was the founder of civilization.
Quoted by Anna Freud, 27th International Psychoanalytic Association Meeting, Vienna, 1971

Natural homosexuality is something pathological, it is an arrested development.
Quoted in Dr. Joseph Wortis, *Fragments of an Analysis with Freud,* 1954

Psychoanalysis is for hysterical pathological cases, not for silly rich American women who should be learning to darn socks.
Quoted by Dorothy Thompson, after an interview, 1925

---

*Walter Kaufmann, in *The Faith of a Heretic,* p. 352, accuses Erich Fromm of missing the point that it was a "mildly humorous remark."
**Regarding the terms, Id, Ego and Super-Ego, David Severn writes (*Time,* May 7, 1956): "Freud used understandable terms: es, Ich and Über-Ich—literally translatable as the it, the I and the beyond-I."

ERICH FROMM
(1900–1980)
American psychologist

The Sane Society (1955)

Man today is confronted with the most fundamental choice: not that between Capitalism and Communism, but that between *robotism* (of both the capitalist and communist variety), or Humanistic Communitarian Socialism.

Marx's Concept of Man (1961)

Socialism is the abolition of human self-alienation, the return of man as a real human being.

"Creators and Destroyers"

Good is all that serves life, evil is all that serves death. Good is reverence for life . . . and all that enhances life. Evil is all that stifles life, narrows it down, cuts it to pieces.
Saturday Review, January 4, 1964

Psychoanalysis and Religion (1950)

Human history begins with man's act of disobedience which is at the very same time the beginning of his freedom and development of his reason.

Escape from Freedom (1968)

Destructiveness is the outcome of an unlived life.

Theologians and philosophers have been saying for a century that God is dead, but what we confront is the possibility that man is dead, transformed into a thing, a producer, a consumer, an idolator, or other things.
Address, American Orthopsychiatric Association, San Francisco, April 16, 1966

So many people are in love with death. They want war.

Dostoevsky said, "If there is no God, then *anything* is possible." I would say that if there is no love, *nothing* is possible. Man absolutely cannot live by himself.

Religion: What at one time was a dynamic structure, mediating between man and his destiny and interpersonal responsibilities, has become mere mechanical ritual that dwarfs men rather than strengthens them.
Contribution, *Look,* May 5, 1964

Uniformity and freedom are incompatible. Uniformity and mental health are incompatible.
> Quoted in Huxley, *Brave New World Revisited* (1956)

ROBERT FROST
(1874–1963)
American poet

"Not All There" (1936)

> I turned to speak to God
> About the world's despair;
> But to make bad matters worse
> I found God wasn't there.

"The Lesson for Today" (1942)

> I had a lover's quarrel with the world

"To The Clearing" (1962)

> Forgive, O Lord, my little joke on Thee
> And I'll forgive Thy great big one on me.

"The Road Not Taken" (1916)

> Two roads diverged in a wood, and I—
> I took the one less traveled by,
> And that has made all the difference.

"Ten Mills," I. "Precaution" (1936)

> I never dared to be radical when young
> For fear it would make me conservative
>   when old.

"Mending Wall" (1914)

> Something there is that doesn't love a wall,
> He only says, "Good fences make good
>   neighbors."

A civilized society is one which tolerates eccentricity to the point of doubtful sanity.
> Contribution, *New Republic,* October 25, 1958

I hold it to be the inalienable right of anybody to go to hell in his own way.
> Address, Berkeley, California, 1935

Poetry is a way of taking life by the throat.
> A comment

JAMES A(nthony) FROUDE
(1818–1894)
English historian

Address, "Calvinism," St. Andrew's, March 17, 1871

To deny the freedom of the will is to make morality impossible.

Lecture, London, February 5, 1864; also, "The Science of History" (1864)

For every false word or unrighteous deed, for cruelty and oppression, for lust or vanity, the price has to be paid at last, not always by the chief offenders, but paid by some one.

Oceana (1886)

Wild animals never kill for sport. Man is the only one to whom the torture and death of his fellow-creatures is amusing in itself.
> *Oceana,* 1886

J. WILLIAM FULBRIGHT
(1905–   )
American senator

Government by the people is possible, but highly improbable.
> Fund for the Republic pamphlet, 1963

The Arrogance of Power (1966)

In a democracy dissent is an act of faith.

To criticize one's country is to do it a service. . . . Criticism, in short, is more than a right; it is an act of patriotism—a higher form of patriotism, I believe, than the familiar rituals and national adulation.

My question is whether America can overcome the fatal arrogance of power.

R(ichard) BUCKMINSTER FULLER
(1895–1983)
American architect, writer

"No More Secondhand God"

> Don't oppose forces; use them.
> God is a verb,
> Not a noun.

Either war is obsolete or men are.
> Quoted by Calvin Tomkins, *The New Yorker,* January 8, 1966

(Sarah) MARGARET FULLER, Marchioness Ossoli
(1810–1850)
American feminist leader

Woman in the Nineteenth Century (1845)

. . . . when not one man, in the million, shall I say? no, not in the hundred million, can rise above the belief that Woman was made *for Man,*—when such traits as these are daily forced upon the attention, can we feel that Man will always do justice to the interests of Woman? . . . The lover, the poet, the artist, are likely to view her nobly. The father and the philosopher have some chance of liberality; the man of the world, the legislator for expedience, none.

We would have every arbitrary barrier thrown down. We would have every path laid open to Woman as freely as to Man.

I accept the Universe.*
Quoted in Bell Gale Chevigny, *The Woman and the Myth* (1976)

THOMAS FULLER
(1608–1661)
English clergyman

The Holy State and the Profane State (1642)

A little skill in antiquity, inclines a man to Popery; but depth in that study brings him about again to our religion.
Bk. II, ch. vi, "The True Church Antiquary"

Anger is one of the sinews of the Soul; he that wants it hath a maimed mind.
Bk. III, ch. viii, "Of Anger"

Men have a touchstone whereby to trie gold, but gold is the touch-stone whereby to trie man.
Ch. v, "The Good Judge"

Security is the mother of danger and the grandmother of destruction.

The Church History of Britain (1655)

Miracles are the swaddling clothes of infant churches.

THOMAS FULLER
(1654–1734)
English cleric

Gnomologia (1732)

A good Life is the only Religion.
No. 158

Cruelty is a tyrant, that is always attended with Fear.
No. 1213

---

*"By God, she'd better!"—Carlyle.

Idle men are dead all their Life long.
No. 3055

One Year of Joy, another of Comfort, the rest of Contentment, make the married Life happy.
No. 3806

Religion without Piety hath done more Mischief in the World, than all other Things put together.
No. 4012

Serving one's own Passions is the greatest Slavery.
No. 4103

The Mob has many Heads, but no Brains.
No. 4653

The Pleasures of the Rich are bought with the Tears of the Poor.
No. 4707

No Vice
Like Avarice.
No. 6171

They that worship God merely for Fear
Would worship the Devil too, if he appear.
No. 6419

JOHN KENNETH GALBRAITH
(1908–   )
Canadian-born American economist

The Affluent Society (1958)

Wealth is the relentless enemy of understanding.
Ch. 1

The Age of Uncertainty (1977)

Money . . . ranks with love as man's greatest joy. And it ranks with death as his greatest source of anxiety.

People of privilege will always risk their complete destruction rather than surrender any material part of their advantage.

———
. . . those with a vested interest in error.
Contribution, *The New Republic*,
November 2, 1974

CLAUDIUS GALEN (Galenus)
(c. 130–200 A.D.)
Physician born at Pergamus

Every animal is sad after coitus except the human female and the rooster.
Quoted by Dr. Kinsey; requoted in *Time*,
January 24, 1964

GALILEO GALILEI
(1564–1642)
Italian astronomer

The Authority of Scripture in Philosophical Controversies *

The doctrine of the movements of the earth and the fixity of the sun is condemned on the ground that the Scriptures speak in many places of the sun moving and the earth standing still. . . .
It is piously spoken that the Scriptures cannot lie. But none will deny that they are frequently abstruse and their true meaning difficult to discover, and more than the bare words signify.

I think that in the discussion of natural problems we ought to begin not with the Scriptures, but with experiments and demonstrations.

Recantation (June 22, 1633)

Having been admonished by the Holy Office entirely to abandon the false opinion that the Sun was the center of the universe and immovable, and that the Earth was not the center of the same and that it moved . . . I have been . . . suspected of heresy, that is, of having held and believed that the Sun is the center of the universe and immovable, and that the Earth is not the center of the same, and that it does move . . . I abjure with a sincere heart and unfeigned faith, I curse and detest the same errors and heresies, and generally all

———
*Condemned by the Inquisition. Its decision read: "The doctrine that the earth is neither the center of the universe nor immovable, but moves even with a daily rotation, is absurd, and both philosophically and theologically false, and at the least an error of faith."

and every error and sect contrary to the Holy Catholic Church.

———
E pur si muove!

But it does move!
Attributed to Galileo, in reference to the earth, after
his recantation.

MOHANDES KARAMCHAND GANDHI
(1869–assassinated 1948)
Hindu national leader*

Young India (a weekly journal)

Life and death are but phases of the same thing, the reverse and obverse of the same coin. . . . I want you all to treasure death and suffering more than life and to appreciate their cleansing and purifying character.
Death which is an Eternal verity is revolution, as birth and after is slow and steady evolution. Death is as necessary for man's growth as life itself.
March 12, 1920

Political power means capacity to regulate national life through national representatives. If national life becomes so perfect as to become self-regulated, no representation becomes necessary. There is then a state of enlightened anarchy. In such a state every one is his own ruler. He rules himself in such a manner that he is never a hindrance to his neighbor. In the ideal State, therefore, there is no political power because there is no State.
November 17, 1921

Satyagraha . . . means "holding on to Truth," hence "Truth-force." I have also called it "Love-force" or "Soul-force." I discovered in the earliest stages that pursuit of Truth did not admit of violence being inflicted on one's opponent, but that he must be weaned from error by patience and sympathy. For what appears to be Truth to one, may appear to be error to the other.
September 6, 1922

Ahimsa [infinite love] is a weapon of matchless potency. It is the *summum bonum* of life. It is an attribute of the brave, in fact it is their all. It does not come within the reach of the coward. It is no wooden or lifeless dogma but a

———
*Usually called "Mahatma" Gandhi; in India, "Gandhiji."

living and lifegiving force. It is the special attribute of the soul.

May 29, 1924

Let us study our Eastern institutions . . . we shall evolve a truer Socialism and a truer Communism than the world has yet dreamed of. It is surely wrong to presume that Western Socialism or Communism is the last word on the question of mass poverty.

January 7, 1926

To call women the weaker sex is a libel: it is man's injustice to woman. If by strength is meant brute strength, then indeed, is woman less brute than man. If by strength is meant moral power, then woman is immeasurably man's superior. Has she not greater intuition, is she not more self-sacrificing, has she not greater powers of endurance, has she not greater courage? Without her, man would not be. If non-violence is the law of our being, the future is with women.

April 10, 1930

Harijan (a weekly)

I believe in the fundamental Truth of all the great religions of the world. I believe that they are all God-given . . .
I came to the conclusion long ago . . . that all religions were true, and also that all had some error in them.

February 16, 1934

Woman is the companion of man gifted with equal mental capacities. She has the right to participate in the minutest detail of the activities of man, and she has the same right of freedom and liberty as he. She is entitled to a supreme place in her own sphere of activity as man is in his. This ought to be the natural condition of things.

February 22, 1940

To say that God permits evil in this world may not be pleasing to the ear. But if He is held responsible for the good, it follows that He has to be responsible for the evil too . . .
I cannot account for the existence of evil by any rational method. To want to do so is to be co-equal with God . . . I know that He has no evil in Him, and yet if there is evil, He is the author of it and yet untouched by it.

March 3, 1946

Letters From Bapu

All fear is a sign of want of faith.

No. 8

The Story of My Experiments with Truth (1929)

I can say without the slightest hesitation, and yet in all humility, that those who say that religion has nothing to do with politics do not know what religion means.

I believe in the doctrine of non-violence as a weapon of the weak. I believe in the doctrine of non-violence as a weapon of the strongest. I believe that a man is the strongest soldier for daring to die unarmed.

Address, Madras, August 12, 1920

To a man with an empty stomach food is God.

To Edgar Snow, 1938

Hate the sin and love the sinner.

Attributed

JAMES A(bram) GARFIELD
(1831–1881)
20th President of the United States

In the long, fierce struggle for freedom of opinion, the Press, like the church, counted its martyrs by the thousands.

Address, July 11, 1878

Give me a log hut, with only a simple bench, Mark Hopkins on one end and I on the other, and you may have all the buildings, apparatus and libraries without him.

Address to Williams College alumni, N.Y., December 28, 1871

GIUSEPPE GARIBALDI
(1807–1882)
Italian patriot

I offer neither pay, nor quarters, nor provisions; I offer hunger, thirst, forced marches, battles, and death. Let him who loves his country in his heart and not with his lips only, follow me.

Quoted in G. M. Trevelyan, *Garibaldi's Defense of the Roman Republic* (1907–1911)

Man has created God, not God man. The priest is the personification of falsehood.

Quoted in Noyes, *Views of Religion*

The Vatican is a dagger in the heart of Italy.

Quoted by Mussolini, 1929

DAVID GARRICK
(1717–1779)
English actor

Corrupted freemen are the worst of slaves.
Prologue, *The Gamesters*

WILLIAM LLOYD GARRISON
(1805–1879)
American editor, abolitionist

The Liberator

I will be as harsh as truth and as uncompromising as justice. On this subject I do not wish to think, or speak, or write, with moderation.
January 1, 1831 (first issue)

If the State cannot survive the anti-slavery agitation, then let the State perish. If the Church must be cast down by the strugglings of Humanity to be free, then let the Church fall, and its fragments to be scattered to the four winds of heaven, never more to curse the earth.
December 15, 1837

Written for the Massachusetts Anti-Slavery Society; adopted January 27, 1843

RESOLVED: That the compact which exists between the North and the South is a covenant with death and an agreement with hell, involving both parties in atrocious criminality, and should be immediately annulled.

PAUL GAUGUIN
(1848–1903)
French painter

Art is either a revolutionist or a plagiarist.
Attributed

THÉOPHILE GAUTIER
(1811–1872)
French writer

Mademoiselle de Maupin (1855)

Virginity, mysticism, melancholy! Three unknown words, three new maladies brought by Christ.

JOHN GAY
(1688–1732)
English playwright

The Captives (1724)

She who has never lov'd, has never liv'd.
Act 2

The Beggar's Opera (1728)

Man may escape from rope and gun;
Nay, some have outliv'd the doctor's pill;
Who takes a woman must be undone,
That basilisk is sure to kill.
Act 2, sc. 8

GELASIUS I
(?–496)
Pope from 492

The toleration of heretics is more injurious than the devastation of the provinces by the barbarians.

There are two powers by which chiefly this world is ruled: the sacred authority of the priesthood and the authority of kings. And of these, the authority of the priests is so much the weightier, as they must render before the tribunal of God an account even for the kings of men.
Letter to Byzantine Emperor Anastasius I, 494

AULUS GELLIUS
(130–175 A.D.)
Latin author, grammarian

Noctis Atticae

Truth is the daughter of time.
Bk. 12, ch. 11

GENGHIS KAHN, *see* Jenghis Kahn

(David) LLOYD GEORGE
(né David George)
(1863–1945)
British Prime Minister

A young man who isn't a Socialist hasn't got heart; an old man who is a Socialist hasn't got a head.
Quoted in *The Businessman's Encyclopedia*

A new deal for everyone.
Election slogan, 1919

I think I did as well as might be expected—
seated between Jesus Christ [President Wilson]
and Napoleon Bonaparte [Clemenceau].
Quoted in *Time,* June 23, 1961

HENRY GEORGE
(1839–1897)
American economist, single tax proponent

Progress and Poverty (1879)*

This association of poverty with progress is
the great enigma of our times. It is the central
fact from which spring industrial, social, and
political difficulties that perplex the world, and
with which statesmanship and philanthropy
and education grapple in vain . . . It is the
riddle which the Sphinx of Fate puts to our
civilization, and which not to answer is to be
destroyed.

So long as all the increased wealth which
modern progress brings goes but to build up
great fortunes, to increase luxury and make
sharper the contrast between the House of
Have and the House of Want, progress is not
real and cannot be permanent.
Introductory: The Problem

The ideal of Socialism is grand and noble;
and it is, I am convinced, possible of realization, but such a state of society cannot be
manufactured—it must grow. Society is an organism, not a machine.
Bk. VI, ch. I

This, then, is the remedy for the unjust and
unequal distribution of wealth apparent in
modern civilization, and for all the evils which
flow from it:
We must make land common property.
Bk. VI, ch. II

To put political power in the hands of men
embittered and degraded by poverty is to tie
firebrands to foxes and turn them loose amid
the standing corn.
Bk. VI, ch. X

---

*"Few other American books and certainly no other
economic treatise exercised a comparable influence
in the world at large."—Henry Steele Commager,
Living Ideas in America, p. 153.

Social Problems (1884)

There is danger in reckless change; but
greater danger in blind conservatism.

Let no man imagine that he has no influence. Whoever he may be, and wherever he
may be placed, *the man who thinks* becomes a
light and a power.

There are three ways by which an individual
can get wealthy—by work, by gift, and by
theft. And, clearly, the reason why the workers
get so little is that the beggars and thieves get
so much.

Great wealth always supports the party in
power, no matter how corrupt it may be. It
never exerts itself for reform for it instinctively
fears change.

How can a man be said to have a country
when he has no right to a square inch of it?

Protection or Free Trade (1886)

Property in land is as indefensible as property in man.
XXIX

GERMANICUS CAESAR
(15 B.C.–19 A.D.)
Roman general

Spaniards can be impressed by the courtesy
of the conqueror, French by his riches, Greeks
by his respect for the arts, Jews by his moral
integrity, Africans by his calm and authorita-
tive bearing, but Germans are impressed by
none of these things. They must be struck into
the dust, struck down again as they rise. Struck
again while they lie groaning, while their
wounds still pain them; they will respect the
hand that dealt them.
Attributed

GESTA ROMANORUM ("Deeds of the
Romans")
Latin collection
(13th or 14th century A.D.)

*Tempora mutantur et homines deterioran-
tur.*

Times change and men deteriorate.

Si finis bonus est, totum bonum erit.

If the end be good, all will be good.

J(ean) PAUL GETTY
(1892–1976)
American businessman

No one can possibly achieve any real and lasting success or "get rich" in business by being a conformist.

Interview, Paris *Herald Tribune,* January 10, 1961

ARNOLD GEULINEX
(1624–1669)
Belgian philosopher

Ethics

Some of these philosophers tried to extinguish all of their passions, as did the Cynics and Stoics. That is evidently madness, for we cannot extinguish passion without destroying our whole body.

MUHAMMAD IBN MUHAMMAD ABŪ HĀMID AL-GHAZĀLI
(1058–1111)
Arabian philosopher, theologian

The Main Problems of Abu Nasr Al-Paraba

Man's nature is made up of four elements, which produce in him four attributes, namely, the beastly, the brutal, the satanic, and the divine. In man there is something of the pig, the dog, the devil, and the saint.

EDWARD GIBBON
(1737–1794)
English historian

The Decline and Fall of the Roman Empire (1776–1788)

After a diligent inquiry, I can discern four principal causes for the ruin of Rome, which continued to operate in a period of more than a thousand years. I. The injuries of time and nature. II. The hostile attacks of the barbarians and Christians. III. The use and abuse of the materials. And IV. The domestic quarrels of the Romans.

As the happiness of a *future* life is the great object of religion, we may hear without surprise or scandal that the introduction, or at least the abuse, of Christianity had some influence on the decline and fall of the Roman empire. The clergy successfully preached the doctrines of patience and pusillanimity; the active virtues of society were discouraged; and the last remains of military spirit were buried in the cloister. A large portion of public and private wealth was consecrated to the specious demands of charity and devotion, and the soldiers' pay was lavished on the useless multitudes of both sexes who could only plead the merits of abstinence and chastity. Faith, zeal, curiosity, and more earthly passions of malice and ambition kindled the flame of theological factions, whose conflicts were sometimes bloody and always implacable; the attention of the emperors was diverted from camps to synods; the Roman world was oppressed by a new species of tyranny, and the persecuted sects became the secret enemies of the country.

When Caesar subdued the Gauls, that great nation was already divided into three orders of men: the clergy, the nobility, and the common people. The first governed by superstition, the second by arms, but the third and last was not of any weight or account in their public councils.

Personal interest is often the standard of our belief, as well as of our practice.

History . . . is, indeed, little more than a register of the crimes, follies, and misfortunes of mankind.

All that is human must retrograde if it does not advance.

The various modes of worship which prevailed in the Roman world were all considered by the people as equally true; by the philosopher as equally false; and by the magistrate as equally useful.

The Church of Rome defended by violence the empire which she had acquired by fraud.

I have recorded the triumphs of barbarism and religion.

———

The evidence of the heavenly witnesses— the Father, the Word, and the Holy Ghost— would now be rejected in any court of Justice.

Quoted in Noyes, *Views of Religion*

JAMES GIBBONS
(1834–1921)
American cardinal

The Faith of Our Fathers (1876)

The Church is not susceptible to being re-formed in her doctrines. The Church is the work of an incarnate God. Like all God's works, it is perfect. It is, therefore, incapable of reform.

vii

Marriage is the most inviolable and irrevoc-able of all contracts that were ever formed. Every human compact may be lawfully dis-solved but this.

xxxi

KAHLIL GIBRAN
(1883–1931)
Lebanese mystic

Sand and Foam (1926)

We shall never understand one another un-til we reduce the language to seven words.

The lust for comfort; that stealthy thing that enters the house a guest, and then becomes a host, and then a master.

The Prophet (1923)

He who wears his morality but as his best garment were better naked.

"On Religion"

ANDRÉ GIDE
(1869–1951)
French novelist, essayist

Journal (1947)

Wisdom begins where the fear of God ends.
January 15, 1929

No progress of humanity is possible unless it shakes off the yoke of authority and tradition.
March 17, 1931

Les Nouvelles nourritures (1936)

Families! I hate you! Shut-in homes, closed doors, jealous possessors of happiness.

It is much more difficult than one thinks not to believe in God.

Thésée (1946)

A man's first and greatest victory must be won against the gods.

So Be It, or The Chips Are Down (1960)

There is more light in Christ's words than in any other human words. This is not enough, it seems, to be Christian: in addition, one must believe.

Letter to François Le Grix (not sent)

I say that without sensuality, sexuality, and price no work of art could exist.

ALLEN GINSBERG
(1926–   )
American poet

Whoever controls the language, the images, controls the race.
Contribution, *The New Yorker*, August 24, 1968

ARTURO GIOVANNITTI
(1884–1959)
Italian-born American poet

*The Walker**

For infinite are the nine steps of a prison
cell, and endless is the march of him who
walks between the yellow brick wall and
the red iron gate, thinking things that
cannot be chained and cannot be locked,
but that wander far away in the sunlit
world, each in a wild pilgrimage after a
destined goal.

Wonderful is the supreme wisdom of the
jail that makes all think the same
thought. Marvellous is the providence of
the law that equalizes all, even in mind
and sentiment.

I, who have never killed, think like the
murderer!
I, who have never stolen, reason like the
thief!
I think, reason, wish, hope, doubt, wait like
the hired assassin, the embezzler, the
forger, the counterfeiter, the incestuous,

---

*"One of the greatest poems ever produced in the English language. It challenges comparison with 'The Ballad of Reading Gaol.' "—Joyce Kornbluh, *Rebel Voices*.

the raper, the drunkard, the prostitute, the pimp, I, I who used to think of love and life and flowers and song and beauty and the ideal.

GEORGE (Robert) GISSING
(1857–1903)
British novelist

The Private Papers of Henry Ryecroft (1903)

Time is money—says the vulgarest saw known to any age or people. Turn it round about, and you get a precious truth—Money is time.

It is because nations tend to stupidity and baseness that mankind moves so slowly; it is because individuals have a capacity for better things that it moves at all.

"Winter"

JOSIAH WiLLIAM GITT
(1884–1973)
American editor

Humanity's most valuable assets have been the non-conformists. Were it not for the non-conformists, he who refuses to be satisfied to go along with the continuance of things as they are, and insists upon attempting to find new ways of bettering things, the world would have known little progress indeed.

Editorial, *Gazette & Daily,* York, Pennsylvania, February 2, 1957

WILLIAM EWART GLADSTONE
(1809–1898)
British statesman

You cannot fight against the future. Time is on our side.

Speech on the Reform Bill, House of Commons, April 27, 1866

All the world over, I will back the masses against the classes.

Speech, Liverpool, June 28, 1886

The American Revolution . . . was a conservative revolution.

Contribution, *North American Review,* September, 1878

No more cunning plot was ever devised against the intelligence, the freedom, the happiness, and the virtue of mankind, than Catholicism.

Quoted in Noyes, *Views of Religion*

ELLEN GLASGOW
(1874–1945)
American writer

I Believe

The mob that would die for a belief seldom hesitates to inflict death upon any opposing heretical group.

JOSEPH ARTHUR COUNT DE
GOBINEAU
(1816–1882)
French diplomat, racist writer

The Inequality of Human Races (1853–1855)

The word *degenerate,* when applied to a people, means (as it ought to mean) that the people has no longer the same intrinsic value as it had before, because it has no longer the same blood in its veins, continual adulterations having gradually affected the quality of that blood.

WILLIAM GODWIN
(1756–1836)
English minister, reformer, philosopher

An Inquiry Concerning Political Justice, and Its Influence on General Virtue and Happiness* (1793)

The most desirable condition of the human species, is a state of society.

The injustice and violence of man in a state of society, produced the demand for government.

---

*"Although this work is little known and less read now, it marks a phase in English thought. . . . *Political Justice* takes its place with Milton's *Aeropagitica,* with Locke's 'Essay on Education,' and with Rosseau's *Emile.*"—*Encyclopedia Brittanica,* 11th edition, Vol. XII, p. 177. (The Summary is printed at the beginning. The pagination given here is from the Third Edition facsimile, University of Toronto Press.)

Government, as it was forced upon mankind by their vices, so has it commonly been the creature of their ignorance and mistakes.

By concentrating the force of the community, it gives occasion to wild projects of calamity, to oppression, despotism, war and conquest.

By perpetuating and aggravating the inequality of property, it fosters many injurious passions, and excites men in the practice of robbery and fraud.

Government was intended to suppress injustice, but its effect has been to embody and perpetuate it.

Vol. 1, Summary, p. xxiv

The immediate object of government, is security.
The means employed by government, is restriction, an abridgement of individual independence. . . .
Consequently, the most desirable state of mankind, is that which maintains general security, with the smallest encroachment upon individual independence.

pp. xxiv–xxv

Soundness of understanding is connected with freedom of enquiry; consequently, opinion should, as far as public security will admit, be exempted from restraint.

p. xxvii

Martyrs are suicides by the very definition of the term.

Bk. II, ch. 2

Incessant change, everlasting innovation, seem to be dictated by the true interests of mankind. But government is the perpetual enemy of change.

Bk. III, ch. 7

Make men wise, and by that very operation you make them free. Civil liberty follows as a consequence of this; no usurped power can stand against the artillery of opinion.

The wise man is satisfied with nothing.

. . . a grand revolution includes in it the sacrifice of one generation.

Bk. IV, ch. 1

Above all, we should not forget, that government is, abstractly speaking, an evil, an usurpation upon the private judgment and individual conscious of mankind; and that, however we may be obliged to admit it as a necessary evil for the present, it behooves us, as the friends of reason and the human species, to admit as little of it as possible, and carefully to observe, whether in consequence of the gradual illumination of the human mind, that little may not hereafter be diminished.

Vol. 2, Bk. V, ch. 1

Opinion is the castle, or rather the temple of human nature; and, if it be polluted, there is no longer any thing sacred or venerable in sublunary existence.

Bk. VI, ch. 1

The first duty of men is, to take none of the principles of conduct upon trust; to do nothing without a clear and individual conviction that it is right to be done.

Ch. 3

Law tends, no less than creeds, catechisms and tests, to fix the human mind in a flagrant condition, and to substitute a principle of permanence, in the room of that unceasing progress which is the only salubrious element of mind. . . .
From all these considerations we can scarcely hesitate to conclude universally, that law is an institution of the most pernicious tendency.

And here with grief it must be confessed, that, however great and extensive are the evils that are produced by monarchies and courts, by the imposture of priests and the iniquity of criminal laws, all these are imbecile and impotent, compared with the evils that arise out of the established administration of property.

Bk. VIII, ch. 2

The pretense of collective wisdom is the most palpable of all impostures.

Ch. 3

Sketches of History (1784)

God Himself has no right to be a tyrant.

PAUL JOSEPH GOEBBELS
(1897–1945)
German Nazi propaganda minister

Michael (a novel, 1921)

Intellectual activity is a danger to the building of character . . . The intellect has poisoned our people. How much elementary strength in that fellow compared with sickly intellectuals.

It is the absolute right of the State to supervise the formation of public opinion.

Speech, 1923

The past is lying in flames. The future will arise from the flames within our hearts. These flames . . . light up a new era . . . Spirits are awakening, and oh, Century, it is a joy to live!

Spoken to a crowd at Nazi book-burning, May 10, 1933

Christ cannot possibly have been a Jew. I don't have to prove that scientifically. It is a fact.

Quoted by John Gunther, *The Nation*, February 6, 1935

The National Socialist movement is in its nature a masculine movement . . . The outstanding and highest calling of women is always that of wife and mother.

Quoted in Clifford Kirkpatrick, *Nazi Germany: Its Women and Family Life* (1938)

Our critics are morbid, degenerate, democratic individuals. Some even say the Jew is a human being.

Press report, *New York Post*, November 16, 1938

JOHANN WOLFGANG VON GOETHE (1749–1832)
German poet, dramatist, philosopher

Faust (1806, tr. Bayard Taylor)

Two souls, alas! reside within my breast,
And each withdraws from, and repels, its
  brother;[*]
One with tenacious organs holds in love
And clinging lust the world in its embraces;
The other strongly sweeps, this dust above,
Into the high ancestral spaces.

Sc. II

The Church alone beyond all question
Has for ill-gotten goods the right digestion.

Sc. IX

---

[*]These lines are regarded as the key to the drama and also as indicating "the Faustian character of German nature."

(From another translation)

Live dangerously and you live right.

To bear all-naked truths
And to envisage circumstances all calm,
That is the top of sovereignty.
The Deed is everything, the Glory nought.
Yes! To this thought I cling with firm per-
  sistence;
The last result of wisdom stamps it true:
He only earns his freedom and existence
  Who daily conquers them anew.

I am the spirit that always dissents.

In the beginning was the Deed.

Ay, what is knowledge among men? Who dares call the child by its true name? The few, who have known somewhat of these things, who foolishly did not keep a guard over their full hearts, who revealed their feelings and thoughts to the people, these, from time immemorial, have been crucified and burned.

I hear the message, but my faith is weak: miracle is faith's dearest child.

We are accustomed to see men deride what they do not understand, and snarl at the good and beautiful because it lies beyond their sympathies.

All that is transient
Is but a symbol;
Here imperfection
Becomes actuality;
The indescribable
Here is fulfilled;
The eternal feminine
Draws us on high.

—Last lines[*]

Wilhelm Meisters Lehrjahre (1796)

Who never ate his bread in sorrow, who never sat through the sorrowful nights weeping on his bed, he knows you not, you heavenly Powers.

II, 13

One ought, every day at least, to hear a little song, read a good poem, see a fine picture, and, if it were possible, to speak a few reasonable words.

---

[*]Bayard Taylor's translation is "The Woman Soul leadeth us upward and on." He wrote that he could find no English equivalent for *Ewigweibliche*. Dyson Carter objects to "eternal feminine," saying Goethe meant "Only the woman of man's desire can lift him heavenward."

Men are so inclined to content themselves with what is commonplace; the spirit and the senses so easily grow dead. It is only because they are not used to taste of what is excellent that the generality of people take delight in silly and insipid things, provided they are new.

V, I

Art is long, life short; judgment difficult, opportunity fleeting.

VII, 5

Herman und Dorothea (1797)

He who moves not forward, goes backward.

The soul-stirring image of death is no bugbear to the sage, and is looked on without despair by the pious. It teaches the former to live, and it strengthens the hopes of the latter in salvation in the midst of distress. Death is new life to both.

Vanitas! Vanitatum Vanitas!

I have set my affairs on nothing.

First line

Torquato Tasso (1790)

Talents are best nurtured in solitude; character is best formed in the stormy billows of the world.

i.2

Egmont (1775–1787)

Freedom! A fine word when rightly understood. What freedom would you have? What is the freedom of the most free? To act rightly!

Götz von Berlichingen (1773)

. . . he alone is great and happy who requires neither to command nor to obey in order to secure his being of some importance in the world.

Iphigenie auf Tauris (1787)

An unused life is an early death.

Act 1, sc. 1

Die Geheimnisse (1776)

From the forces that all creatures bind, who overcomes himself his freedom finds.

Conversations with Eckerman (1822–1832)

The classical I call healthy and the romantic sick.

National hatred is something peculiar. You will always find it strongest and most violent where there is the lowest degree of culture.

Architecture is frozen music.

Maxims

Truth is a torch, but a terrific one; therefore we all try to grasp it with closed eyes, fearing to be blinded.

With wisdom grows doubt.

Sprüche in Prosa

The fool and the wise man are equally harmless; it is the half-wise and the half-foolish who are most to be feared.

We are never betrayed, we betray ourselves.

The world wants to be betrayed.

Wisdom is found only in truth.

Italienische Reise (1816)

In art the best is good enough.

Taschenbuch für Damen

The commonplace masters us all.

———

There are nine requisites for contented living: Health enough to make work a pleasure; Wealth enough to support your needs; Strength enough to battle with difficulties and forsake them; Grace enough to confess your sins and overcome them; Patience enough to toil until some good is accomplished; Charity enough to see some good in your neighbor; Love enough to make you useful and helpful to others; Faith enough to make real the things of God; Hope enough to remove all anxious fears concerning the future.

Quoted in "Words to Live By," *This Week,*
February 10, 1963

EMMA GOLDMAN
(1869–1940)
Russian-born American feminist, writer, revolutionary*

Definition of Anarchism

The philosophy of a new social order based on liberty unrestricted by man-made law; the

———

*"She is about eight thousand years ahead of her age. Her vision is the vision of every truly great-souled man or woman who has ever lived."—William Marion Reedy, *St. Louis Mirror,* November 5, 1908.

theory that all forms of government rest on violence, and are therefore wrong and harmful as well as unnecessary.
*Lusk Committee Report,** vol. 1, p. 840.

Anarchism (Mother Earth edition, 1910)

Anarchy stands for the liberation of the human mind from the dominion of religion, the liberation of the human body from the dominion of property; liberation from the shackles and restraints of government.

Anarchism (1917 edition)

Anarchism is the only philosophy which brings to man the consciousness of himself; which maintains that God, the State, and Society are non-existent, that their promises are null and void, since they can be fulfilled only through man's subordination.

No real social change has ever been brought about without a revolution. . . . Revolution is but thought carried into action.

Conceit, arrogance, and egotism are the essentials of patriotism.

My Further Disillusion (1924)**

No revolution ever succeeds as a factor of liberation unless the Means used to further it be identified in spirit and tendency with the Purpose to be achieved.

The ultimate end of all revolutionary social change is to establish the sanctity of human life, the dignity of man, the right of every human being to liberty and well-being.

"The Place of the Individual in Society" (pamphlet, undated)

The individual is the true reality of life. A cosmos in himself, he does not exist for the State, nor for that abstraction called "society," or the "nation," which is only a collection of individuals.

All progress has been essentially the unmasking of "divinity" and "mystery," or alleged sacred eternal "truth."

The State, every government whatever its form, character or color—be it absolute or constitutional, monarchy or republic, Fascist, Nazi or bolshevik—is by its very nature conservative, static, intolerant of change and opposed to it.

The strongest bulwark of authority is uniformity.

———

The institution of marriage makes a parasite of woman, an absolute dependent. It incapacitates her for life's struggle, annihilates her social consciousness, paralyzes her imagination, and then imposes its gracious protection, which is in reality a snare, a travesty on human character.

Love, the strongest and deepest element in all lives, the harbinger of hope, of joy, of ecstasy; love, the defier of all laws, of all conventions; love, the freest, the most powerful moulder of human destiny; how can such an all-compelling force be synonymous with that poor little State and Church-begotten weed, marriage?
Quoted in *Feminism: The Essential Historical Writings* (ed. Miriam Schneir; reprinted *N.Y. Times,* July 8, 1972)

Art is part of a rebellion against the realities of its unfilled desire.
Contribution, *Montreal Star,* February 25, 1935

OLIVER GOLDSMITH
(1728–1774)
Irish-born English poet, dramatist, novelist

"The Deserted Village" (1770)

Ill fares the land, to hastening ills a prey,
Where wealth accumulates, and men decay;
Princes and lords may flourish, or may fade;
A breath can make them, as a breath has
  made;
But a bold peasantry, their country's pride,
When once destroyed, can never be
  supplied.

O luxury! thou curst by Heaven's decree.

"The Traveller" (1764)

Where wealth and freedom reign contentment fails,
And honor sinks where commerce long pre-
  vails.
Line 91

---

*The Lusk Committee was the forerunner of the Dies and the McCarthy Committees.
**Deported to Soviet Russia in 1920, Miss Goldman returned to Canada and wrote books and articles on her disillusionment.

Laws grind the poor, and rich men rule the law.

Line 386

BARRY GOLDWATER
(1909–   )
American politician

I would remind you that extremism in the defense of liberty is no vice! And let me remind you also that moderation in the pursuit of justice is no virtue!

Speech accepting presidential nomination,
July 16, 1964; written by Karl Hess*

SAMUEL GOMPERS
(1850–1924)
London-born American labor leader

*"More! More! More!" Speech**

What does labor want? We want more schoolhouses and less jails; more books and less arsenals; more learning and less vice; more leisure and less greed; more justice and less revenge; in fact, more of the opportunities to cultivate our better natures, to make manhood more noble, womanhood more beautiful, and childhood more happy and bright.

As one voice labor must speak—to reward its friends and punish its enemies.

Quoted in *Labor* (Railroad Brotherhoods' weekly),
August 4, 1956

Seventy Years of Life and Labor (1925)

The labor of a human being is not a commodity or article of commerce. You can't weigh the soul of a man with a bar of pig-iron.

Vol. II, ch. 36

Show me the country in which there are no strikes and I'll show you that country in which there is no liberty.

Quoted in Charles Madison, *American Labor Leaders*

---

*Thomas Paine wrote. "Moderation in temper is always a virtue; moderation in principle is always a vice."—*Rights of Man,* 1791, pt. 11, ch. 5.
**Gompers repeated this speech in every town; I actually heard him once.—G.S.

MAKSIM GORKI (né Aleksei Maksimovich Peshkov)
(1868–1936)
Russian novelist, playwright

The Lower Depths (1903)

Lies—there you have the religion of slaves and taskmasters. Truth is the god of the free man.

Enemies (1906)

All vile acts are done to satisfy hunger.

Fragment, written in 1928

I bow to man because beyond the incarnations of man's reason and imagination, I feel and see nothing in our world. God has been one of man's inventions, just like photography, with the difference that the latter fixes that which really exists, whereas God is a photograph of an idea which man invents, of a being one wishes—and is able—to be omniscient, omnipotent and perfectly just.

And if it is thought necessary to speak of sacred things, then the one sacred thing is the dissatisfaction of man with himself and his striving to be better than he is; sacred is his hatred of all the trivial rubbish he himself has created; sacred is his desire to do away with greed, envy, crime, disease, war, and all enmity between man on earth; and sacred is his labor.

To American Intellectuals (1922)

The function of the intellectual has always been confined, in the main, to embellishing the bored existence of the bourgeoisie, to consoling the rich in the trivial troubles of their life. The intelligentsia was the nurse of the capitalist class. It was kept busy embroidering white stitches on the philosophical and ecclesiastical vestments of the bourgeoisie—that old and filthy fabric, besmeared so thickly with the blood of the toiling masses.

JOHN BARTHOLOMEW GOUGH
(1817–1886)
British-born American temperance orator

Sunlight and Shadow (1880)

What is a minority? The chosen heroes of this earth have been a minority. There is not a social, political, or religious privilege that you enjoy today that was not brought for you by the blood and tears and patient suffering of the minority.

It is the minority that have . . . achieved all that is noble in the history of the world.

RÉMY DE GOURMONT
(1858–1915)
French symbolist writer

Promenades philosophiques (1904–1913)

Chastity is the most unnatural of the sexual perversions.

(cf. Aldous Huxley)

BALTASAR GRACIÁN
(1601–1658)
Spanish Jesuit writer

The Art of Worldly Wisdom (1648)

It is as hard to tell the truth as to hide it.

. . . and common sense has availed many a man more than the seven arts, however liberal they may be.

One lie will destroy a whole reputation for integrity.

Never contend with a man who has nothing to lose.

The passions are the gates of the soul.

Gracian's Manuals (1653)

Trust in today's friends as if they might be tomorrow's enemies; use human means as if there were no divine ones, and divine means as if there were no human ones.

Always act as if you were seen.

Without telling lies, do not yet tell all the truth; do not live by fixed principles, live by opportunity and circumstances.

MADISON GRANT
(1865–1937)
American racist writer

The Passing of the Great White Race (1916)

The cross between a white man and an Indian is an Indian; the cross between a white man and a Negro is a Negro; the cross between a white man and a Hindu is a Hindu; and the cross between any races and a Jew is a Jew.

When it becomes thoroughly understood that the children of mixed marriages between contrasted races belong to the lower types . . . to bring half-breeds into the world will be regarded as a social and racial crime of the first magnitude.

(Hiram) ULYSSES S(impson) GRANT
(1822–1885)
18th President of the United States

Personal Memoirs (1885)

To this day [I] regard the [Mexican] war as one of the most unjust ever waged by a stronger against a weaker nation.

The right of revolution is an inherent one. When people are oppressed by their government, it is a natural right they enjoy to relieve themselves of the oppression, if they are strong enough, whether by withdrawal from it, or by overthrowing it and substituting a government more acceptable.

Vol. I

Addresses and occasional statements

. . . that cause [slavery] was, I believe, one of the worst for which a people ever fought.

On Lee's surrender

I know of no method to secure the repeal of bad or obnoxious laws so effective as their stringent execution.

Inaugural Address, March 4, 1869

I believe that our Great Maker is preparing the world, in His own good time, to become one nation, speaking one language . . . When armies and navies will no longer be required.

Second Inaugural, March 4, 1873

GÜNTHER GRASS
(1927–   )
German writer

I don't know about God . . . The only things I know are what I see, hear, feel and smell.

Quoted in Paris *Herald Tribune,* March 23, 1970

GRATIAN (Flavius Gratianus Augustus)
(350–assassinated 383)
Roman Christian emperor

All heresies are forbidden by both divine
and imperial laws and shall forever cease.

Decree

ROBERT GRAVES
(1895–   )
British novelist, classical scholar

Yet no scientist, however specialized his
field, can factually accept even the Book of
Genesis; and what the scientist thinks today,
everyone else will be thinking on the day after
tomorrow.

Lecture, M.I.T., 1963

THOMAS GRAY
(1716–1771)
British poet

"Elegy Written in a Country Churchyard" (1750)

Let not ambition mock their useful toil,
Their homely joys, and destiny obscure;
Nor grandeur hear with a disdainful smile
The short and simple annals of the poor.

St. 8

The boast of heraldry, the pomp of pow'r,
And all that beauty, all that wealth e'er
    gave,
Awaits alike the inevitable hour:
The paths of glory lead but to the grave.

St. 9

The Epitaph

Here rests his head upon the lap of Earth,
A youth to fortune, and to fame unknown.
Fair Science frown'd not on his humble
    birth,
And Melancholy mark'd him for her own.

St. 1

EL GRECO (né Domenico Theotocopuli)
(1541–1614)
Greek-born Spanish artist

Nada me complace.
Nothing pleases me.

Written across unpainted canvas

THE GREEK ANTHOLOGY
(490 B.C.–1000 A.D.)*

In the end then the choice is of one of these
two, either not to be born, or, as soon as born,
to die.

Attributed to Posidippus (cf. Homer)

The choice is not then one of the two,
either never to be born or to die; for all things
are good in life.

Attributed to Metrodorus

Moderation is best.

Sayings of the Sages, attributed to Cleobulus

Master anger.

Attributed to Periander of Corinth

Look at the end of life.

Attributed to Solon of Athens

Most men are bad.

Attributed to Bias of Priene

Shun security.

Attributed to Thales of Miletus

HORACE GREELEY
(1811–1872)
American publisher, educator

Better incur the trouble of testing and ex-
ploding a thousand fallacies than by rejecting
stifle a single beneficient Truth.

Editorial, New York *Tribune*, 1845

But the world does move, and its motive
power under God is the fearless thought and
speech of those who dare to be in advance of
their time—who are sneered at and shunned
through their days of struggle as lunatics,
dreamers, impracticables and visionaries; men
of crochets, vagaries and isms.

Editorial, New York *Tribune*

GREGORY I (the Great)
(540–604)
Pope from 590 and saint

Dialogues (c. 593)

Ad Majoram Dei Gloriam.
To the greater glory of God.

Sec. i (adopted motto of the Society of Jesus)

---

*"The most valuable relic of antique literature
which we possess."—John Aldington Symonds.

Homilies on the Gospels

If the work of God would be comprehended by reason, it would be no longer wonderful, and faith would have no merit if reason provided proof.

26, i

GREGORY VII (Hildebrand)
(1020?–1085)
Pope from 1073

"Dictatus Papae" (c. 1075, document found among his letters)

1. The Roman Church alone has been founded by Christ.

9. The Pope is the only one whose feet are kissed by princes.

18. His [the Pope's] judgment may not be revised by anyone, and he alone may revise the judgment of others.

22. The Roman Church has never erred, and, according to the scripture, never shall err.

The Holy See has absolute power over all spiritual things: why should it not also rule temporal affairs? God reigns in the heavens; His vicar should reign over all the earth.

Attributed

SIR THOMAS GRESHAM
(1519–1579)
Founder of the Royal Exchange, London, and Gresham's College

When depreciated, mutilated, or debased coinage (or currency) is in concurrent circulation with money of high value in terms of precious metals, the good money automatically disappears.

Columbia Encyclopedia*

SIR EDWARD GREY
(1862–1933)
British liberal statesman

Twenty-five Years: 1892–1916 (1925)

The moral is obvious: it is that great armaments lead inevitably to war.

---

*For "Gresham's Law," *see* MacLeod.

The increase of armaments that is intended in each nation to produce consciousness of strength, and a sense of security, does not produce these effects. On the contrary, it produces a consciousness of the strength of other nations and a sense of fear. Fear begets suspicion and distrust and evil imaginings of all sorts.

Vol. 1

The lights are going out all over Europe; we shall not see them lit again in our lifetime.

Comment, Foreign Office, August 3, 1914

ALFRED WHITNEY GRISWOLD
(1906–1963)
President of Yale

Essays on Education

Books won't stay banned. They won't burn. Ideas won't go to jail.

In the long run of history, the censor and the inquisitor have always lost. The only sure weapon against bad ideas is better ideas. The source of better ideas is wisdom. The surest path to wisdom is a liberal education.

ERWIN N. GRISWOLD
(1904–   )
Dean, Harvard Law School

The right to be let alone is the underlying principle of the Constitution's Bill of Rights.

Address, Northwestern University Law School, June 11, 1960

HUGO GROTIUS (Huig van Groot)
(1583–1645)
Dutch jurist, theologian, historian, philosopher, poet and diplomat

De Jure Belli ac Pacis Libris [*Rights of War and Peace*] (1625)

. . . with good fortune equity is where strength is, and that the commonwealth cannot be administered without doing some wrong.

For the mother of natural law is human nature itself.

The law of nature is so unalterable that it cannot be changed by God Himself.

There was never any government, so purely popular, as not to require the exclusion of the poor, of strangers, women, and minors from the public councils.

———

Even God cannot make two times two not make four.
Quoted by Hannah Arendt, "Reflections," *The New Yorker*

STEFANO GUAZZO
(1530–1593)
Italian writer

Civil Conversations (1574)

The ignorant in comparison of the learned, are worse than dead.
Bk. 2

PHILIP GUEDALLA
(1889–1944)
British writer

Supers and Supermen (1920)

Any stigma will do to beat a dogma.

FRANCESCO GUICCIARDINI
(1483–1540)
Italian statesman

Storia d'Italia (1561)

He who speaks of the people, speaks of a madman; for the people is a monster full of confusion and mistakes; and the opinions of the people are as far removed from the truth as, according to Ptolemy, the Indies are from Spain.

FRANÇOIS GUIZOT
(1787–1874)
French Premier, historian

L'État de la poésie en France avant Corneille

Men who make revolutions are always despised by those who profit from them.

RAMON GUTHRIE
(1896–1973)
World War I U.S. aviator, Dartmouth College professor, poet

Graffiti (1959)

A man dies as he dies. Only the saint chooses his death as he has chosen his life; is master of his coming and his going.

MARC R. GUTWIRTH
(1919–1969)
Dutch-born American college professor

The Essence is to Question

Anti-intellectualism is the same as self-destruction.

Intellect shows the unity of mankind; pride and contempt, lust and hatred, zeal and indifference are what divide them.

HADRIAN (Publius Aelius Hadrianus)
(76–138 A.D.)
Roman Emperor

Ad Animam Suam [*Dying Address to his Soul*]

Little soul, wandering, gentle guest and companion of the body, into what places will you now go, pale, stiff, and naked, no longer sporting as you did!

ERNST HEINRICH HAECKEL
(1834–1919)
German biologist

Die Weltträtsel [*The Riddle of the Universe*] (1899)

The *anthropomorphic* dogma is likewise connected with the creation myth of the three aforesaid religions (Mosaic, Christian, and Mohammedan), and of many others. . . . God, as creator, sustainer, and ruler of the world, is thus represented after a purely human fashion in his thought and work. Hence it follows, in turn, that man is godlike.

This boundless presumption of conceited man has misled him into making himself "the image of God," claiming an "eternal life" for his ephemeral personality, and imagining that he possesses unlimited "freedom of will."

By reason only can we attain to a correct knowledge of the world and a solution of its great problems. Reason is man's highest gift, the only prerogative that essentially distinguishes him from the lower animals.

Ch. I

The belief in the immortality of the human soul is a dogma which is in hopeless contradiction with the most solid empirical truths of modern science.

Ch. XI

The Christians of the early centuries were generally pure Communists, sometimes "Social Democrats," who, according to the prevailing theory in Germany today, ought to have been exterminated with fire and sword.

Ch. XVII

Under the influence of our new monistic views, we do reverence to the real trinity of the nineteenth century—the trinity of "the true, the good, and the beautiful."

Ch. XVIII

Nothing great and elevated has ever taken place without egoism, and without the passion that urges us to great sacrifices.

Sexual love, the first foundation of the family union, seems to have been regarded by Jesus as a necessary evil. His most enthusiastic apostle, Paul, went still farther in the same direction, declaring it to be better not to marry than to marry. "It is good for a man not to touch a woman." . . . As Christ never knew the love of woman, he had no personal acquaintance with that refining of man's true nature that comes only with the intimate life of man and woman. The intimate sexual union, on which the preservation of the human race depends, is just as important on that account as the spiritual penetration of the two sexes, or the mutual complement which they bring to each other in the practical wants of daily life as well as in the highest ideal function of the soul.

Ch. XIX

Der Kampf um den Entwicklungsgedanken [*The War Over the Evolution Theory*] (1900)

The belief in the freedom of the will is inconsistent with the truth of evolution. Modern philosophy shows clearly that the will is never really free in man or animal, but determined by the organization of the brain; and that in turn acquires its individual character by the laws of heredity and the influence of environment.

The Wonders of Life (1905)

. . . experience and thought—or empirical knowledge and speculation . . . these two methods supplemented each other, and they alone, under the direction of reason, lead to the attainment of truth.

The soul of man is—objectively considered—essentially similar to that of all other vertebrates; it is the physiological action or function of the brain.

Ch. I

The myth of the conception and birth of Jesus Christ is mere fiction, and is at the same stage of superstition as a hundred other myths of other religions.

Ch. III

Nothing is constant but change! All existence is a perpetual flux of "being and becoming"! That is the broad lesson of the evolution of the world.

The real cause of personal existence is not the favor of the Almighty, but the sexual love of one's earthly parents.

The voluntary death by which a man puts an end to intolerable suffering is really an act of redemption.

Ch. V

J(ohn) B(urdon) S(anderson) HALDANE (1892–1964)
British scientist

Living Philosophies (1931)

I believe that the scientist is trying to express absolute truth and the artist absolute beauty, so that I find in science and art, and in an attempt to lead a good life, all the religion that I want.

GEORGE SAVILE, MARQUESS OF HALIFAX (1633–1695)
English statesman

Political, Moral and Miscellaneous Reflections

If none were to have Liberty but those who understand what it is, there would not be many freed Men in the world.

Mis-spending a man's time is a kind of self-homicide.

When people contend for their Liberty, they seldom get anything for their Victory but new Masters.

Complete Works (published 1912)

Liberty can neither be got nor kept, but by so much Care that Mankind are generally unwilling to give the Price of it.

Ignorance maketh most Men go into a Party, and Shame keepeth them from getting out of it.

Men are not hanged for stealing horses, but that horses may not be stolen.

A Man that would call everything by its right Name would hardly pass in the Streets without being knocked down as a common enemy.

E. BEATRICE HALL, *see* **Tallentyre**

HENRY HALLAM
(1777–1859)
English historian

The View of the State of Europe During the Middle Ages (1818)

As we find in the history of all usurping governments, time changes anamony into system, and injury into right; examples become custom, and custom ripens into law; and the doubtful precedent of one generation becomes the fundamental maxim of another.

HENRY WAGER HALLECK
(1815–1872)
American Union general, Civil War

Elements of Military Art and Science (1859)

The Bible nowhere prohibits war. In the Old Testament we find war and even conquest positively commanded, and although war was raging in the world in the time of Christ and His Apostles, still they said not a word of its unlawfulness and immorality.

ALEXANDER HAMILTON
(1757–killed in duel 1804)
American statesman

Your people is a great beast.
Attributed in Beards, *Basic History of the United States**

---

*Justice Douglas, *An Almanac of Liberty,* quotes Hamilton: "The people is a great beast." Clinton Rossiter, *Alexander Hamilton and the Constitution,* calls the remark, "Your people, Sir, is a great beast," apocryphal.

Addresses

The voice of the people has been said to be the voice of God; and, however generally the maxim has been studied and believed, it is not true to fact. The people are turbulent and changing; they seldom judge to determine right.
Federal Convention, June 18, 1787

Take mankind in general; they are vicious, their passions may be operated upon.
Federal Convention, June 22, 1787

Against the mischiefs of foreign influence all the jealousy of a free people ought to be constantly asserted.

Permanent alliance, intimate connection with any part of the foreign world is to be avoided.
Original draft by Hamilton for Washington's Farewell, May 10, 1796

The Federalist (1787–1788)

Why was government instituted at all? Because the passions of men will not conform to the dictates of reason and justice without restraint.
#15

Justice is the end of government. It is the end of civil society. It ever has been and ever will be pursued until it is obtained or until liberty be lost in the pursuit.
#51

I trust the friends of the proposed Constitution will never concur with its enemies in questioning that fundamental principle of republican government which admits the right of the people to alter or abolish the established Constitution whenever they find it inconsistent with their happiness.
#78

History teaches that among the men who have overturned the liberties of republics, the greatest number have begun their career by paying obsequious court to the people; commencing demagogues and ending tyrants.
#79

A national debt, if it is not excessive, will be to us a national blessing.

The interest of the State is in intimate connection with those of the rich individuals belonging to it.

If government is in the hands of a few they will tyrannize the many; if in the hands of the many, they will tyrannize the few. It ought to be in the hands of both, and they should be separated. This separation must be permanent. Representation alone will not do; demagogues will generally prevail; and, if separated, they will need a mutual check. This check is a monarch.

Letter to Robert Morris, April 30, 1781

ANDREW HAMILTON
(1676?–1741)
American colonial lawyer

It is the best Cause; the Cause of Liberty; and I make no Doubt but that your upright Conduct, this Day, will not only entitle you to the Love and Esteem of your Fellow Citizens: but every Man who prefers Freedom to a Life of Slavery will bless and honour You, as Men who have baffled the attempts of Tyranny: and by an impartial and uncorrupted Verdict, have laid a Noble Foundation for securing for ourselves, our Posterity, and our Neighbors, That to which Nature and the Laws of our Country have given us a Right,—the Liberty—both of exposing and opposing arbitrary Power . . . by speaking and writing—Truth.

Defense of John Peter Zenger, publisher of New York Weekly Journal, against charges of seditious libel, 1735

EDITH HAMILTON
(1867–1963)
American scholar, writer

The Greek Way (1930)

Not the mind but the spirit is its own place, and can make a Hell of Heaven, a Heaven of Hell. When the mind withdraws into itself and dispenses with facts it makes only chaos.

Ch. II

Civilization, a much abused word, stands for a high matter quite apart from telephones and electric lights. It is a matter of imponderables, of delight in the things of the mind, of love of beauty, of honor, grace, courtesy, delicate feeling. Where imponderables are the things of first importance, there is the height of civilization, and if, at the same time, the power of art exists unimpaired, human life has reached a level seldom attained and very seldom surpassed.

Ch. VI

The dignity and the significance of human life—of these, and of these alone, tragedy will never let go. Without them there is no tragedy. To answer the question, what makes a tragedy, is to answer the question wherein lies the essential significance of life, what the dignity of humanity depends upon in the last analysis. . . . It is by our power to suffer, above all, that we are of more value than the sparrows. . . . What do outside trappings matter, Zenith or Elsinore? Tragedy's preoccupation is with suffering.

Ch. XI

The innocent suffer—how can that be and God be just? That is not only the central problem of tragedy, it is the great problem everywhere when men begin to think, and everywhere at the same stage of thought they devise the same explanation, the curse, which caused by sin in the first instance, works on of itself through the generations and lifts from God the awful burden of injustice.

Ch. XII

Only individuals can suffer and only individuals have a place in tragedy.

Ch. XVI

DAG HAMMARSKJÖLD
(1905–1961)
Secretary General, United Nations

Markings (1961)

Do not seek death. Death will find you. But seek the road which makes death a fulfillment.

HAMMURABI
(2067–2025 B.C.)
Babylonian king

Code of Hammurabi (written on a stone column, now in the Louvre)

If a noble has destroyed the eye of an aristocrat, his eye shall be destroyed.

If he has destroyed the eye of a commoner or broken the bone of a commoner, he shall pay one mina of silver.

If he has destroyed the eye of a noble's slave or broken the bone of a noble's slave, he shall pay one half his value.

If a son has struck his father, they shall cut off his hand.

If a noble charge another noble with murder but fails to prove it, the accuser shall be put to death.

If a married woman shall be caught lying with another man, both shall be bound and thrown into the river.

LEARNED HAND
(1872–1961)
American jurist

The Spirit of Liberty (1944)

Liberty lies in the hearts of men and women; when it dies there, no constitution, no law, no court can save it.

Addresses and Lectures

Right knows no boundaries and justice no frontiers; the brotherhood of man is not a domestic institution.

> May 20, 1961

Heretics have been hated from the beginning of recorded time; they have been ostracized, exiled, tortured, maimed and butchered; but it has generally proved impossible to smother them; and when it has not, the society that has succeeded has always declined.
> "A Fanfare for Prometheus," January 29, 1955

In the end it is worse to suppress dissent than to run the risk of heresy.
> O. W. Holmes Lecture, Harvard, 1958

HANNIBAL
(247–183 B.C.)
Carthaginian general

We will either find a way or make one.
> Attributed

WARREN G(amaliel) HARDING
(1865–1923)
29th President of the United States

Government after all is a very simple thing.*

America's present need is not heroics but healing; not nostrums but normalcy; not revolution but restoration; not surgery but serenity; not the dramatic but the dispassionate; not experiment but equipoise; not submergence in

---

*Quoted by Justice Frankfurter, who added: "There was never a more pathetic misapprehension of responsibility than Harding's touching statement."

internationality but sustainment in triumphant nationality.
> Speech, Boston, May 27, 1920 (probably ghost-written by Sen. Vandenberg—*The New Yorker*, May 24, 1962)

THOMAS HARDY
(1840–1928)
English novelist, poet

Life's Little Ironies.
> Short story title (1894)

The Dynasts (1903)

A local cult, called Christianity.
> Part 1

Tess of the D'Urbervilles (1891)

The new Testament was less a Christiad than a Pauliad.
> Ch. 25

"Justice" was done, and the President of the Immortals (in the Aeschylean phrase) had ended his sport with Tess.
> Ch. 59, conclusion

"Heredity" (1916)

I am the family face;
Flesh perishes, I live on,
Projecting trait and trace
Through time to times anon,
And leaping from place to place
Over oblivion.

"The Darkling Thrush" (1900)

So little cause for carolings
Of such ecstatic sound
Was written on terrestrial things
Afar or nigh around,
That I could think there trembled through
His happy good-night air
Some blessed hope, whereof he knew
And I was unaware.
> Stanza 4

"Neutral Tones" (1867)

We stood by a pond that winter day,
And the sun was white, as though chidden
of God,
And a few leaves lay on the starving sod;
—They had fallen from an ash, and were
gray.

Your eyes on me were as eyes that rove
Over tedious riddles of years ago;

And some words played between us to and
fro
On which lost the more by our love.

The smile on your mouth was the deadest
thing
Alive enough to have strength to die;
And a grin of bitterness swept thereby
Like an ominous bird a-wing . . .

Since then, keen lessons that love deceives,
And wrings with wrong, have shaped to me
Your face, and the God-curst sun, and a
tree,
And a pond edged with grayish leaves.

JOHN MARSHALL HARLAN
(1833–1911)
U.S. Supreme Court Justice

Our Constitution is color-blind and neither
knows nor tolerates classes among citizens.
Sole dissent, Plessy v. Ferguson, 165 U.S. 537
(1896)

ALAN HARRINGTON
(1919–   )
American novelist

The Immoralist (1969)

The primary source of our fears, and of all
evil and meanness afflicting the human spirit,
has been acknowledged and publicly identified. It was death all the time, and nothing
else.

Death is an imposition on the human race
and no longer acceptable.

The time has come for men to turn into
gods or perish.

SIR JOHN HARRINGTON
(1561–1612)
English courtier, wit, satirical writer

Epigrams

Treason doth never prosper: what's the rea-
son?
For if it prosper, none dare call it Treason.
Bk. IV, Ep. 259

The Oceana

Every man, either to his terror or consolation, has some sense of religion.

FRANK (né James Thomas) HARRIS
(1854–1931)
Welsh-born writer and editor

My Life and Loves (1923)

The Christian churches were offered two
things: the spirit of Jesus and the idiotic morality of Paul, and they all rejected the higher inspiration. . . . Following Paul, we have
turned the goddess of love into a fiend and degraded the crowning impulse of our being into
a capital sin.

Sex is the gateway of life.
Quoted in Enid Bagnold's *Autobiography* (1970)

All the faults of the age come from Christianity and Journalism.
Quoted in Margot Asquith's *Autobiography*, vol. 1,
ch. 10

WILLIAM HENRY HARRISON
(1773–1841)
9th President of the United States

. . . all the measures of the Government are
directed to the purpose of making the rich
richer and the poor poorer.
Speech, October 1, 1840

WILLIAM HARVEY
(1578–1657)
English physician

Where Are We and Whither Tending

Civilization is simply a series of victories over
nature.
Lecture 1

On the Motion of the Heart and Blood (1628)

The heart, consequently, is the beginning of
life; the sun of the microcosm, even as the sun
in its turn might well be designated the heart
of the world; for it is the heart by whose virtue
and pulse the blood is moved, perfected, made
apt to nourish, and is preserved from corruption and coagulation; it is the household divinity which, discharging its function, nourishes,
cherishes, quickens the whole body, and is indeed the foundation of life, the source of all
action.
Addressed to the Royal College of Physicians

Animal Generation (1651)

. . . there is no perfect knowledge which can be entitled ours, that is innate; none but what has been obtained from experience, or derived in some way from our senses; all knowledge, at all events, is examined by these, approved by them, and finally presents itself to us firmly grounded upon some pre-existing knowledge which we possessed; because without memory there is no experience, which is nothing else than reiterated memory; in like manner memory cannot exist without endurance of the things perceived, and the thing perceived cannot remain where it has never been.

Introduction

HASDAI IBN SHAPRUT
(fl. 10th century A.D.)
Jewish scholar, physician to Abd-ar-Rahman

Your son at five is your master, at ten your slave, at fifteen your double, and after that, your friend or your foe, depending on his bringing up.

Quoted in *Ban HaMelek VeHaNazir*, ch. 7

ERIC HASS
(1905–1980)
American Socialist writer, editor

A spectre is haunting mankind. It is the spectre of annihilation in a thermonuclear war.

CBS-TV interview, October 25, 1958

NATHANIEL HAWTHORNE
(1804–1864)
American novelist

Passages from the American Notebooks (1868)

Labor is the curse of the world, and nobody can meddle with it without becoming proportionately brutified.

The House of Seven Gables (1851)

What we call real estate—the solid ground to build a house on—is the broad foundation on which nearly all the guilt of the world rests.

The world owes all its onward impulses to men ill at ease. The happy man inevitably confines himself within ancient limits.

WILLIAM ("Big Bill") HAYWOOD
(1869–1928)
American labor leader

We are here to confederate the workers of this country into a working-class movement. The aims and objects of this organization shall be to put the working-class in possession of economic power, the means of life, in control of the machinery of production and distribution without regard to capitalist matters.

Address to delegates forming the Industrial Workers of the World (I.W.W.), January 2, 1905

WILLIAM HAZLITT
(1778–1830)
English essayist, critic

Table Talk (1821–1822)

All uneducated persons are hypocrites.

Great acts grow out of great occasions, and great occasions spring from great principles, working changes in society, and tearing it up by the roots.

No young man ever thinks he shall die.

Words are the only things that last forever.

Great thoughts reduced to practice become great acts.

Selected Essays

The heaviest charge we can bring against the general texture of society is that it is commonplace.

The Plain Speaker (1826)

If mankind had wished for what is right, they might have had it long ago.

Pure good soon grows insipid, wants variety and spirit. Pain is bitter-sweet, which never surfeits. Love turns, with a little indulgence, to indifference or disgust; hatred alone is immortal.

"The Pleasure of Hating"

Characteristics (1823)

The only vice that cannot be forgiven is hypocrisy. The repentance of a hypocrite is itself hypocrisy.

Want of principle is power.

CXVII

"The Spirit of Controversy" (January 31, 1830)

When a thing ceases to be a subject of controversy, it ceases to be a subject of interest.

LAFCADIO HEARN
(1850–1904)
American writer of Irish-Greek ancestry

I think the proverb above quoted—(*in medio tutissimus ibis;* thou will go most safely by taking the middle course)—is one of the most mischievous, one of the most pernicious, one of the most foolish that ever was invented in the world. I believe very strongly in extremes; and I am quite sure that all progress in the world, whether literary, or scientific, or religious, or political, or social, has been obtained only with the assistance of extremes.
Lecture, University of Tokyo

WILLIAM RANDOLPH HEARST
(1863–1951)
American press lord

We hold that the greatest right in the world is the right to be wrong, that in the exercise thereof people have an inviolable right to express their unbridled thoughts on all topics and personalities, being liable only for the use of that right.
Platform, Independence League, *New York Journal*, February 1, 1924

You furnish the pictures and I'll furnish the war.
Cable to Frederick Remington, artist, Cuba, March 1898*

Please realize that the first duty of newspaper men is to get the news and PRINT THE NEWS.
Requoted, *Editor and Publisher*, August 12, 1944

JACQUES RENÉ HÉBERT
(1755–guillotined 1794)
French journalist

Le Père Duchesne (1793)

Everywhere and at all times men of commerce have had neither heart nor soul; their

---

*Hearst, and other editors, were later accused of fomenting the war with Spain over Cuba.

cash-box is their God. . . . They traffic in all things, even human flesh. . . . Their country? *Foutre!* Business men have no country.

BEN HECHT
(1894–1964)
American journalist, author

A Guide for the Bedevilled (1947)

Prejudice is a raft onto which the shipwrecked mind clambers and paddles to safety.

GEORG WILHELM FRIEDRICH HEGEL
(1770–1831)
German philosopher*

The Philosophy of Right (1821)

Freedom is nothing but the recognition and adoption of such universal objects as right and law, and the production of a reality that is accordant with the State.

The basis of the State is the power of Reason actualizing itself as Will.

In considering the idea of the State, we must not have our eyes on particular states or on particular institutions. Instead, we must consider the Idea, this actual God.

It is a dangerous and false prejudice, that the People *alone* have reason and insight, and know what justice is; for each popular faction may represent itself as the people, and the question as to what constitutes the State is one of advanced science, and not popular decisions.

Thus to be independent of public opinion is the first formal condition of achieving anything great or rational whether in life or in science.

To define freedom of the press as freedom to say and write whatever we please, is parallel to the assertion that freedom as such means free-

---

*Probably the best-known statement credited to Hegel is: "The State is the march of God through the world," from the *The Philosophy of Right,* written in 1821. Walter Kaufmann states that "much damage has been done" by this attribution, which appears in the Scribner edition of *Hegel Selections.* It is not only a mistranslation, says Dr. Kaufmann, but in the original German appears as a *Zusatz,* meaning an addition, by Eduard Ganz.

dom to do as we please. Talk of this kind is due to wholly uneducated, crude, and superficial ideas.

Marriage results from the free surrender by both sexes of their personality—a personality in every possible way unique in each of the parties.

It must be noticed in connection with sex-relations that a girl in surrendering her body loses her honour. With a man, however, the case is otherwise, because he has a field of ethical activity outside the family. A girl is destined in essence for the marriage tie, and for that only; it is therefore demanded of her that her love shall take the form of marriage and that the different moments in love shall attain their true rational relation to each other.

The middle class, to which civil servants belong, is politically conscious and the one in which education is most prominent. For this reason it is also the pillar of the State so far as honesty and intelligence are concerned. A State without a middle class must therefore remain on a low level.

The Philosophy of History (1832)

This is the seal of the absolute and sublime destiny of man—that he knows what is good and what is evil; that his destiny *is* his very ability to will either good or evil.

Introduction

The idea of God constitutes the general foundation of a people. Whatever is the form of religion, the same is the form of a state and its constitution; it springs from religion.

The History of the World is none other than the progress of the consciousness of Freedom.

Only that which obeys law is free; for it obeys itself—it is independent and so free.

The State is Mind, *per se.*

For Truth is the Unity of the universal and subjective Will; and the Universal is to be found in the State, its laws, its universal and rational arrangements. The State is the Divine Idea as it exists on Earth.

It was Anaxagoras who first said that *nous,* Reason, governs the world; now for the first time man arrives at recognizing that Thought ought to govern spiritual reality.

We may affirm absolutely that nothing great in the World has been accomplished without passion. . . . Passion is regarded as a thing of sinister aspect, as more or less immoral. Man is required to have no passions. Passion, it is true, is not quite the suitable word for what I wish to express. I mean here nothing more than the human activity as resulting from private interests—special, or if you will, self-seeking designs—with this qualification, that the whole energy of will and character is devoted to their attainment; that other interests . . . or rather all things else, are sacrificed to them.

But to *explain* History is to depict the passions of mankind, the genius, the active powers, that play their part on the great stage.

The highest point in the development of a people is this,—to have gained a conception of life and condition,—to have reduced its laws, its ideas of justice and morality to a science.

The people is that part of the State that does not know what it wants.

———

The sentiment underlying religion in the modern age . . . the sentiment God is dead.

Quoted by Hannah Arendt*

HEINRICH HEINE
(1797–1856)
German lyric poet, critic

The Town of Lucca (1830)

When an individual endeavors to lift himself above his fellows, he is dragged down by the mass, either by means of ridicule or of calumny.

Preface to "Don Quixote"

Wit, Wisdom, and Pathos

To be wholly loved with the whole heart, one must be suffering. Pity is the last consecration of love, or is, perhaps love itself.

Morphine

Sleep is good, death is better; however, it would be best never to have been born.

Baths of Lucca (1828)

O woman! woman! What a benefactor to his race is that man who frees us from your chains!

Ch. 10

———

*"It was not Nietzsche but Hegel who first declared . . . 'God is dead.' " Hannah Arendt, *The New Yorker,* November 21, 1977.

Salon (1834)

Whether a revolution succeeds or miscarries, men of great hearts will always be the victims.
Vol. II

Germany to Luther (1834)

Since the Exodus, Freedom has always spoken with a Hebrew accent.

Lutetia (June 20, 1842)

Communism, though it be at present but little discussed, and now yearns away its life in forgotten garrets on wretched straw pallets, is still the gloomy hero to whom a great if transitory role is assigned in the modern tragedy and which only awaits its cue to enter the stage.

This Communism, so threatening to my peace of mind, so opposed to my interests, casts a spell over me. I cannot struggle against its logic. . . . Let the old social order be destroyed. . . . Let right be done, though the world perish.

Geständnisse [*Confessions*] (tr. W. Kaufmann)

I see now that the Greeks were only beautiful youths; the Jews, however, were always men . . . martyrs who gave the world a god and a morality and fought and suffered on all the battlefields of thought.

Gedanken und Einfalle (tr. Minna Curtis)

In dark ages people are best guided by religion, as in a pitch-black night a blind man is the best guide; he knows the roads and paths better than a man who can see. When daylight comes, however, it is foolish to use blind, old men as guides.

No Jew can ever believe in the divinity of another Jew.
Vol. 10

"Für die Mouche" (last poem)

Ever will Truth struggle against the Beautiful.

Miscellaneous Papers

People who have no heart are stupid, because thoughts come not from the head, but from the heart.

Atheism is the last word of theism.

If you wish to strive for peace of soul and pleasure, then believe; if you wish to be a devotee of truth, then enquire.
Letter to his sister, 1817

Christianity has occasionally calmed the brutal German lust for battle, but it cannot destroy that savage ecstasy. . . . When once that restraining talisman, the Cross, is broken . . . the old stone gods will leap to life among forgotten ruins, and Thor will crash down his mighty hammer on the Gothic cathedrals.
Quoted in Carr, *The Paths of Dictatorship* (1959)

Where books are burned, human beings will be burned too.
Quoted in *Times Literary Supplement,* London, March 17, 1961

Dieu me pardonnera; c'est son métier.
God will pardon me, that's his job.
Spoken February 17, 1856, one day before his death

LILLIAN HELLMAN
(1906–1984)
American writer

I cannot and will not cut my conscience to fit this year's fashions.
Letter to the House Un-American Activities Committee, May 19, 1952

CLAUD-ADRIAN HELVÉTIUS
(1715–1771)
French philosopher, man of letters

De l'Homme

Pleasure and pain are the only springs of action in man, and always will be.

The cause of the different opinions of men.
That this difference is the effect of the uncertain signification of words; such as
Good,
Interests, and
Virtue.
That if words were precisely defined, and their definitions ranged in a dictionary, all the propositions of morality, politics, and metaphysics would become as susceptible of demonstration as the truths of geometry.

De l'Esprit (1758)

Men love themselves; they all desire to be happy, and think their happiness would be complete, if they were invested with a degree of power sufficient to procure them every sort of pleasure.

Almost all philosophers agree, that the most sublime truths once reduced to their plainest terms, may be converted into facts, and in that case present nothing more to the mind than this proposition, *white is white, and black is black.*

To limit the press is to insult the nation; to prohibit reading of certain books is to declare the inhabitants to be either fools or slaves.

By annihilating the desires, you annihilate the mind. Every man without passions has within him no principle of action, nor motive to act.

Truth is a torch that gleams through the fog without dispelling it.

ERNEST HEMINGWAY
(1898–suicide 1961)
American writer, Nobel Prize 1954

For Fascism is a lie told by bullies. A writer who will not lie cannot live or work under Fascism.
Because Fascism is a lie, it is condemned to literary sterility. And when it is past, it will have no history, except the bloody history of murder.

It is very dangerous to write the truth in war, and the truth is also very dangerous to come by.
> Address, American Writers Congress, NYC, June 4, 1937

"On the American Dead in Spain"

For our dead are a part of the earth of Spain now and the earth of Spain can never die.
Just as the earth will never die, neither will those who have been free return to slavery.
As long as all our dead live in the Spanish earth, and they will live as long as the earth lives, no system of tyranny ever will prevail in Spain.
> Quoted in *New Masses*, February 14, 1939 (a tribute to the fallen of the Abraham Lincoln Brigade)

Notes on the Next War

They wrote in the old days that it is sweet and fitting to die for one's country. But in modern war there is nothing sweet or fitting in your dying. You will die like a dog for no good reason.

A Farewell to Arms (1929)

. . . that is the great fallacy; the wisdom of old men. They do not grow wise. They grow careful.

Death in the Afternoon (1932)

Killing cleanly and in a way which gives you esthetic pride and pleasure has always been one of the greatest enjoyments of a part of the human race.

"The Three-Day Blow" (1927)

"Once a man's married he's absolutely bitched."

"A Clean Well-Lighted Place" (1933)

Our nada who art in nada, nada be thy name. Thy kingdom nada, thy will be nada as it is in nada. Give us this nada our daily nada and nada us our nada as we nada our nadas and nada us into nada but deliver us from nada; pues nada. Hail nothing full of nothing, nothing is with thee.
> ["Nada" is Spanish for "nothing"]*

[Courage is] Grace under pressure.
> Quoted in *N.Y. Times*, November 24, 1963**

Fear of death increases in exact proportion to increase in wealth.
> Hemingway's Law of the Dynamics of Dying

Man can be destroyed but not defeated.

Man can be defeated but not destroyed.
> Quoted in A. E. Hotchner, *Papa Hemingway* (1955)

WILLIAM ERNEST HENLEY
(1849–1903)
English poet

Echoes

Out of the night that covers me,
Black as the pit from pole to pole,
I thank whatever gods may be
For my unconquerable soul.

It matters not how strait the gate,
How charged with punishments the scroll,
I am the master of my fate;
I am the captain of my soul.
> #IV ("Invictus")

---

*Nietzsche in "Human, All Too Human," wrote: "The most serious parody I ever heard was this: 'In the beginning was nonsense,' etc."
**The *Times* Book Review of April 24, 1977, repeating the phrase, said it is "perhaps his most famous coinage."

HENRY IV
(1553–1610)
King of France from 1589

Hang yourself, brave Crillon, we have conquered at Arques, and you were not there.
> Letter, 1597, from *Collection des document inédits de l'histoire de France,* vol. IV (1847)

I want there to be no peasant so poor in all my realm that he will not have a chicken in his pot every Sunday.
> Quoted in Hardovin de Perefixe, *Histoire de Henri le Grande* (1681)*

Paris vaut bien une messe.
Paris is well worth a Mass
> Attributed to Henry IV on his conversion to Catholicism, 1593

O. HENRY (William Sydney Porter)
(1862–1910)
American writer

"Heart of the West" (1904)

Love and business and family and religion and art and patriotism are nothing but shadows of words when a man's starving.

PATRICK HENRY
(1736–1799)
American Revolutionary War statesman

Is life so dear, or peace so sweet, as to be purchased at the price of chains and slavery? Forbid it, Almighty God! I know not what course others may take; but as for me, give me liberty or give me death!
> Speech in Virginia Convention, March 23, 1775

HERACLITUS
(c. 540–c. 470 B.C.)
Greek Philosopher

On the Universe

A man's character is his fate.
> Line 21

The people must fight for its laws as for its walls.
> Line 100

---

*President Hoover (q.v.) denied he ever said anything about two chickens in every pot.

Fragments

Religion is a disease, but it is a noble disease.

Strife is the source and master of all things.
> 53

War is the father and king of all: some he has made gods, and some men; some slaves, and some free.
> 83

There is always a majority of fools.
> Attributed

All is flux, nothing is stationary.

There is nothing permanent except change.
> Quoted in Diogenes Laertius, *Lives of Eminent Philosophers,* Bk. IX, Sec. 8

AUBERON HERBERT
(1838–1906)
British journalist, politician

"A Voluntarist's Creed"

There never yet has been a great system sustained by force under which all the best faculties of men have not slowly withered.

Deny human rights, and however little you may wish to do so, you will find yourself abjectly kneeling at the feet of that old-world god, Force—that grimmest and ugliest of gods that men have ever erected for themselves out of the lusts of their hearts. You will find yourself hating and dreading all other men who differ from you; you will find yourself obliged by the law of conflict into which you have plunged, to use every means in your power to crush them before they are able to crush you; you will find yourself day by day growing more unscrupulous and intolerant, more and more compelled by the fear of those opposed to you, to commit harsh and violent actions.
> Contribution, Westminster *Gazette,* November 22, 1893

GEORGE HERBERT
(1593–1633)
English metaphysical poet

"Jacula Prudentum" (pub. 1640)

The devil divides the world between atheism and superstition.

Nothing lasts but the Church.

The love of money and the love of learning rarely meet.

Prosperity destroys the fools and endangers the wise.

Follow not truth too near the heels, lest it dash out thy teeth.

Words are women, deeds are men.

A man is known to be mortal by two things; sleep and lust.

"Outlandish Proverbs" (pub. 1640)

He begins to die, that quits his desires.

#2

He that feares death lives not.

#781

"The Church Porch" (1633)

Dare to be true: Nothing can need a lie;
A fault, which needs it most, grows two
    thereby.

xiii

JOHANN GOTTFRIED VON HERDER
(1744–1803)
German preacher, writer

Philosophy of History (1774)

Everyone loves his own country, customs, language, wife, children, not because they are the best in the world, but because they are his established property, and he loves in them himself, and the labor he has bestowed on them.

The working of revolutions, therefore, misleads me no more; it is as necessary to our race as its waves to the stream, that it may not be a stagnant marsh. Ever renewed in its forms, the genius of humanity blossoms.

JOSEPH HERGESHEIMER
(1880–1954)
American writer

"The Three Black Pennys" (1917)*

No one can walk backward into the future.

---

*"Conservatives walk backward, pretending it is the future."—G.S.

HERODOTUS
(485–425 B.C.)
Greek historian, "father of history"*

Histories

No one is fool enough to choose war instead of peace. For in peace sons bury fathers, but war violates the order of nature, and fathers bury sons.

Call no man happy till you know the nature of his death. Till then, at most, he can only be counted fortunate.

I, "Clio"

Darius: whether men lie, or say true, it is with one and the same object. Men lie because they think to gain by deceiving others; and speak the truth, because they expect to get something by their true speaking, and to be thrust afterwards into more important matters. Thus, though their conduct is so opposite, the end of both is alike.

For there is nothing so void of understanding, nothing so full of wantonness, as the unwieldy rabble. It were folly not to be borne, for men, while seeking to escape the wantonness of a tyrant, to give themselves up to the wantonness of a rude unbridled mob.

III, "Thalia"

Men are dependent on circumstances, not circumstances on men.

VII, "Polyhymnia"

GEORGE D. HERON
(1862–1925)
American clergyman, Socialist

The New Redemption (1893)

Labor is not a commodity any more than human souls are a commodity; labor is life.

Either the people will become atheistic, or the wealth which is in Christian hands must obey the social laws of the Sermon on the Mount.

---

*Herodotus was also the first muckraker; he exposed the Delphic oracle in the Temple of Apollo for accepting bribes from military leaders to predict favorable outcome of battles.—G.S.

ROBERT HERRICK
(1591–1674)
English poet

"Temptations" (1648)

Satan o'ercomes none, but by willingnesse.

"The Eye" (1648)

A wanton and lascivious eye
Betrayes the Heart's adulterie.

"Corinna's Going a-Maying" (1648)

Come, let us goe, while we are in our
prime,
And take the harmlesse follie of the time!
We shall grow old apace, and die
Before we know our liberty.

ALEXANDER IVANOVICH HERTZEN
(1812–1870)
Russian writer

The Development of Revolutionary Ideas in Russia
(1851)

Communism is a Russian autocracy turned
upside down.

THEODORE HERZL
(1860–1904)
Viennese journalist, founder of the Zionist
movement

The Jewish State (1896)

A nation is a historical group of men of recognizable cohesion, held together by a common enemy.

HESIOD
(fl. 8th century B.C.)
Father of Greek Didactic poetry

Theogony (tr. Evelyn-White)

Zeus who thunders on high made woman to
be an evil to mortal men, with a nature to do
evil. And he gave them a second evil to be the
price for the good they had; whoever avoids
marriage and the sorrows that women cause,
and will not wed, reaches deadly old age without anyone to tend his years, . . . when he is
dead, his kinsfolk divide his possessions among
them.

600

Works and Days

We men have made our gods in our own
image.
I think that horses, lions, oxen too,
Had they but hands would make their gods
like them.
Horse-gods for horses, oxen-gods for oxen.

Before the gates of Excellence the high gods
have placed sweat.

JOHN LOFT HESS
(1917–   )
American foreign correspondent

To withhold news is to play God.
Contribution, Nieman Reports, Summer issue,
1976

MOSES HESS
(1812–1875)
Pre-Marxist German Socialist

The Philosophy of the Act (1843)

The first words through which the God of
reflection made himself known to man was
that curse that the Bible loyally handed down
. . . "in the sweat of thy face shalt thou eat
bread." The first words through which the free
spirit made itself known to man . . . was the
famous dictum of Spinoza's Ethics: "What activity furthers and the love of life extols, is
good." The work "by the sweat of thy face" has
reduced man to slavery and misery; the "activity out of love" will make him free and happy.

Without revolution no new history can begin. . . . History has already broken through
the closed circle of slavery. The revolution is
the break from captivity, from the condition of
bigotry and oppression in which the spirit
found itself before it became self-conscious.

HERMANN HESSE
(1877–1962)
German writer, Nobel prize 1946

Demian (1949)

Nothing in the world is so distasteful to man
as to go the way which leads him to himself!
"Two Worlds"

Der Steppenwolf (1927)

[The bourgeois] prefers comfort to pleasure, convenience to liberty, and a pleasant temperature to that deathly inner consuming fire.

HENRY HETHERINGTON
(1792–1849)
English printer, libertarian

The Poor Man's Guardian

We shall begin by protesting and upholding this grand bulwark and defense of all our rights—this key to all our liberties—THE FREEDOM OF THE PRESS—the Press, too of the IGNORANT AND THE POOR!

Editorial, first issue, 1831

It is property which has made tyrants and not tyrants property. . . . Down then with property; the Kings, Lords, and Priests will go down by themselves.

THOMAS HEYWOOD
(c.1574–c. 1641)
English dramatist

Golden Age (1611)

. . . then I go the way of all flesh.

Act III

Hierarchie of the Blessed Angels (1635)

Seven cities warred for Homer being dead,
Who living had no roof to shroud his head.

JOE HILL (Joseph Hillstrom)
(1879–executed 1915)
American union organizer, poet*

You will eat bye and bye
In the glorious land above the sky;
Work and pray,
Live on hay,
You'll get pie in the sky,
When you die.

Chorus, "The Preacher and the Slave," adopted I.W.W. song, Chicago, 1916

---

*Born in Sweden, Joel Hägglund or Haaglund changed his name to Joe Hillstrom in America, 1902, and to Joe Hill on joining I.W.W., 1910.

Onward Christian soldiers, rip and tear and smite!
Let the gentle Jesus bless your dynamite.

I.W.W. Songbook

Goodbye, Bill. I die like a true-blue rebel. Don't waste any time in mourning. Organize.

Telegram to Bill Haywood; quoted in Barry Stavis, *The Man Who Never Died*

HILLEL
(fl. 30 B.C.–9 A.D.)
Jewish rabbi, teacher

Babylonian Talmud

He who wishes to make a name for himself loses his name; he who does not increase it [his knowledge] decreases it; he who does not learn is worthy of death; he who works for the sake of a crown is lost.

Avoth, i, 13

What is hateful to thyself do not do to another. This is the whole Law, the rest is Commentary.

i, 42

The Living Talmud (ed. Judah Holdin)

Do not withdraw from the community.

Put no trust in thyself until the day of thy death.

He used to say:
The more flesh the more worms.
The more possessions, the more worry.
The more wives, the more witchcraft.
The more maidservants, the more unchastity.
The more slaves, the more robbery.

GERTRUDE HIMMELFARB
(1922–   )
American writer

On Liberty and Liberalism (1974)

Liberals have learned at a fearful cost, the lesson that absolute power corrupts absolutely. They have yet to learn that absolute liberality corrupts absolutely.

The generality of the male sex cannot yet tolerate the idea of living with an equal.

HIPPOCRATES
(c. 460–c. 400 B.C.)
Greek father of medicine

Physician's Oath

I swear by Apollo Physician, by Asclepiades, by Health, by Panacea, and all the gods and goddesses, making them my witnesses, that according to my ability and judgment I will carry out this oath. . . .
To hold my teacher in this art equal to my own parents; to make him partner in my livelihood; when he is in need of money to share mine with him; to consider his family as my own brothers, and to teach them this art, if they want to learn it, without fee or indenture. . . .
I will give no deadly medicine to anyone if asked, nor suggest any such counsel. . . . I will use treatment to help the sick according to my ability and judgment but never with a view of injury or wrong doing. . . . I will keep pure and holy both my life and my art. . . .
Into whatever houses I enter I will go into them for the benefit of the sick, and will abstain from every voluntary act of mischief or corruption, further, from the seduction of females and males, of freemen and slaves. . . .
Whatever, in connection with my professional practice, or not in connection with it, I see or hear, in the life of men, which ought not to be spoken of abroad, I will not divulge, as believing that all such should be kept secret. . . .

Attributed*

The Law

Whoever is to acquire a competent knowledge of medicine, ought to be possessed of the following advantages: a natural disposition; instruction; a favorable position for the study; early tuition; love of labor; leisure. First of all, a natural talent is required; for, when Nature opposes, everything else is vain.

---

*The Britannica, 11th ed., vol. XIII, p. 518, says skeptically, "Perhaps also the Oath may be accepted as genuine." Hippocrates, it also states, "was the first to dissociate medicine from priesthood." In several translations there is also included the line: "I will not give to any woman the instrument to procure abortion."

Aphorisms

Life is short, art long,* opportunity fugitive, experimenting dangerous, reasoning difficult; it is necessary to do oneself what is right, but also to be seconded by the patient, by those who attend him, by external circumstances.

To do nothing is sometimes a good remedy.

Extreme remedies are very appropriate for extreme diseases.

Everything in excess is opposed to nature.

ADOLF HITLER
(1889–suicide 1945)
Austrian-born German chancellor, leader
Nazi party

Mein Kampf (1925–1926)**

The German people have no idea of the extent to which they have to be gulled in order to be led.

Epigraph†

Any alliance whose purpose is not the intention to wage war is senseless and useless.

The size of the lie is a definite factor in causing it to be believed, for the vast masses of the nation are in the depths of their hearts more easily deceived than they are consciously and intentionally bad. The primitive simplicity of their minds renders them a more easy prey to a big lie than a small one, for they themselves often tell little lies but would be ashamed to tell a big one.

All propaganda must be so popular and on such an intellectual level, that even the most stupid of those towards whom it is directed will understand it. Therefore, the intellectual level of the propaganda must be lower the larger the number of people who are to be influenced by it.

Through clever and constant application of propaganda, people can be made to see para-

---

*Usually given in Latin as Ars longa, vita brevis.
**Rudolf Hess, Hitler's cellmate, to whom the book was dictated, is generally credited with being its chief author. Robert Payne wrote that Ilse Hess claimed she and Rudolf spent countless hours on the manuscript galleys, but Payne believed Mein Kampf to be largely Hitler's.
†Omitted after 1932 edition, according to Sebastian Haffner, The Meaning of Hitler, 1979.

dise as hell, and also the other way round, to consider the most wretched sort of life as paradise.

Either the world will be ruled according to the ideas of our modern democracy, or the world will be dominated according to the natural law of force; in the latter case the people of brute force will be victorious.

We all of us foresee that in a distant future mankind will be faced with the problems for whose solution only a supreme race as the master nation, supported by the means of possibilities of the whole globe, will be called.

Today Germany is ours, and tomorrow the whole world.

One should guard against believing the great masses to be more stupid than they actually are.

All advertising, whether it lies in the field of business or of politics, will carry success by continuity and regular uniformity of application.

Success is the sole earthly judge of right or wrong.

The whole purpose of education . . . an instinctive and comprehensive sense of race.

[Democracy], the deceitful theory that the Jew would insinuate—namely, that theory that all men are created equal.

We stand for the maintenance of private property. . . . We shall protect private enterprise as the most expedient, or rather the sole possible, economic order.

Statement, 1926; quoted in Heiden, *Der Führer,*
ch. XII

I believe today that I am acting in the sense of the Almighty Creator. By warding off the Jews I am fighting for the Lord's work.

Speech, Reichstag, 1936

There is a road to freedom. Its milestones are Obedience, Endeavor, Honesty, Order, Cleanliness, Sobriety, Truthfulness, Sacrifice, and love of the Fatherland.

Message, signed Hitler, painted on walls of
concentration camps; *Life,* August 21, 1939

I shall give a propagandist cause for starting the war. Never mind whether it is plausible or not. The victor will not be asked, later on,

whether he told the truth or not. In starting and waging a war, it is not Right that matters but Victory. Have no pity. Adopt a brutal attitude. . . . Right is on the side of the strongest.

Speech, August 22, 1939, to high officers

Universal education is the most corroding and disintegrating poison that liberalism has ever invented for its own destruction.

If I can send the flower of the German nation into the hell of war without the smallest pity for the spilling of precious German blood, then surely I have the right to remove millions of an inferior race that breeds like vermin.

Anti-Semitism is a useful revolutionary expedient. My Jews are a valuable hostage given to me by democracy.

We do not intend to abolish the inequality of man. . . . There will be a Herrenclass. . . . There will be a great hierarchy of party members. They will be the new middle class. And there will be the great mass of the anonymous, the serving collective, the eternally disenfranchised.

Beneath them there will still be the class of subject alien races—we need not hesitate to call them the northern slave class.

Quoted in Hermann Rauschning, *The Voice of
Destruction: Hitler Speaks*

A violently active, dominating, intrepid, brutal youth—that is what I am after. . . . I will have no intellectual training. Knowledge is ruin to my young men.

Quoted by John Gunther, *The Nation*

Woman's world is her husband, her family, her children and her home. We do not find it right when she presses into the world of men.

Quoted in Lucy Komisar, *The New Feminism*

THE HITOPADESA
Collection of Hindu writings (c. 500)

Fables and Proverbs

Amongst all things, knowledge is truly the best thing: from its not being liable ever to be stolen, from its not being purchasable, and from its being imperishable.

The mind is lowered, O son, through association with inferiors. With equals it attains equality; and with superiors, superiority.

The age, the actions, the wealth, the knowledge, and even the death of everyone is determined in his mother's womb.

Six faults ought to be avoided by a man seeking prosperity in this world: sleep, sloth, fear, anger, laziness, prolixity.

There is not a man in the world who doth not look at another's wife, if beautiful and young, with a degree of desire.

Idleness, women, disorder, a foolish partiality for one's own native place, discontent and timidity are six obstructions to greatness.

Learning is superior to beauty; learning is better than hidden treasure; learning is a companion on a journey to a strange country; learning is strength inexhaustible.

A man in this world without learning is as a beast of the field.

HO CHI MINH*
(1890?–1969)
North Vietnamese leader

It is better to sniff the French's dung [*merde*] for a while than eat China's all our lives.
> Quoted in Jean Lacouture, *Ho Chi Minh: A Political Biography* (1968)

You will kill ten of our men, and we will kill one of yours, and in the end it will be you who tire of it.
> Quoted in UPI obituary, September 4, 1969

Innocent, I have now endured a whole year
    in prison,
    Using my tears for ink, I turn my
      thoughts into verses.
> Written in prison, 1942; quoted in UPI obituary

THOMAS HOBBES
(1588–1679)
English philosopher

Leviathan (1651)

For the laws of nature (as justice, equity, modesty, mercy, and, in sum, *doing to others*

---

*Ho Chi Minh means "He who enlightens"; he was born Nguyen Tat Thanh, and later changed his name to Nguyen Ai Quoc, "Nguyen the Patriot," according to Jean Lacouture.

as we would be done to) of themselves, without the terror of some power, to cause them to be observed, are contrary to our natural passions, that carry us to partiality, pride, revenge and the like.

Another doctrine repugnant to civil society, is that *whatsoever a man does against his conscience, is sin;* and it dependeth on the presumption of making himself judge of good and evil. For a man's conscience and his judgment are the same thing, and as the judgment, so also the conscience may be erroneous.

Leisure is the mother of philosophy.
> Pt. I, ch. 1

Words are wise men's counters, they do but reckon by them; but they are the money of fools, that value them by the authority of an Aristotle, a Cicero, or a Thomas, or any other doctor whatsoever, if but a man.
> Ch. 4

. . . in the first place, I put for a general inclination of all mankind, a perpetual and restless desire of power after power, that ceaseth only in death.

Man gives indifferent names to one and the same thing from the difference of their own passions; as they that approve a private opinion call it opinion; but they that mislike it, heresy: and yet heresy signifies no more than private opinion.
> Ch. 11

In these four things, opinion of ghosts, ignorance of second causes, devotion towards what men fear, and taking of things casual for prognostics, consisteth the natural seed of religion; which by reason of the different fancies, judgments, and passions of several men, hath grown up into ceremonies so different, that those which are used by one man, are for the most part ridiculous to another.
> Ch. 12

During the time men live without a common power to keep them all in awe, they are in that condition which is called war; and such a war, as is of every man, against every man.

To this war of every man against every man, this also is consequent; that nothing can be unjust. The notions of right and wrong, justice and injustice have there no place. Where there is no common power, there is no law, where no law, no injustice. Force, and fraud, are in war the cardinal virtues.

No arts; no letters; no society; and which is worst of all, continual fear, and danger of violent death; And the life of man, solitary, poor, nasty, brutish, and short.

Ch. 13

Moral philosophy is nothing else but the science of what is good, and evil, in the conversation, and society of mankind. *Good,* and *evil,* are names that signify our appetites, and aversions; which in different tempers, customs, and doctrines of men, are different.

Ch. 15

The source of every crime, is some defect of the understanding; or some error in reasoning; or some sudden force of the passions.

Pt. II, ch. 27

Corporations are many lesser commonwealths in the bowels of a greater, like worms in the entrails of a natural man.

Ch. 29

Intemperance is naturally punished with diseases; rashness, with mischance; injustice, with violence of enemies; pride, with ruin; cowardice, with oppression; and rebellion, with slaughter.

ch. 31

I am about to take my last voyage, a great leap in the dark.

Attributed last words

ERIC HOFFER
(1902–   )
San Francisco longshoreman, writer

The True Believer (1951)

It is doubtful if the oppressed ever fight for freedom. They fight for pride and for power—power to oppress others. The oppressed want above all to imitate their oppressors; they want to retaliate.

The Ordeal of Courage (1963)

Power corrupts the few, while weakness corrupts the many. Hatred, malice, rudeness, intolerance and suspicion are the fruits of weakness.

"Aphorisms"

No one has a right to happiness.

The New Yorker, January 7, 1967

It is easier to love humanity than to love your neighbor.

Interview, Eric Severeid, CBS, November 14, 1967

QUINTIN HOGG
(1845–1903)
English merchant, founder of the Royal Polytechnic Institute

Do not confuse biology and religion—one is a science to be proved or disproved, the other is a life to be lived.

Letter to his son, Sir Douglas McG. Hogg

Whatever else may be shaken, there are some facts established beyond warring; for virtue is better than vice, truth is better than falsehood, kindness than brutality. These, like love, never fail.

Address, quoting his father

PAUL HENRI THIRY, BARON D'HOLBACH
(1723–guillotined 1789)
French Materialist philosopher

The System of Nature* (1770)

If God has spoken, why is not the universe convinced?

If we go back to the beginning we shall find that ignorance and fear created the gods, that fancy, enthusiasm, or deceit adorned or disfigured them; that weakness worships them; that credulity preserves them and that custom, respect, and tyranny support them in order to make the blindness of man serve its own interests.

The source of man's unhappiness is his ignorance of nature.

Man . . . is born without his own consent; his organization does in no wise depend on himself; his ideas come to him involuntarily; his habits are in the power of those who cause him to contract them; he is unceasingly modified by causes, whether visible or concealed, over which he has no control; which necessarily regulate his mode of existence, give the hue to his way of thinking, and determine his manner of acting. He is good or bad, happy or miserable, wise or foolish, reasonable or irrational, without his will being for any thing in

---

*Called "the Bible of freethinkers." Footnotes by Diderot, q.v.

their various states. Nevertheless . . . it is pretended he is a free agent, or . . . determines his own will, and regulates his own condition.

The moralist preaches reason, because he believes it necessary to man; the philosopher writes, because he believes truth must sooner or later prevail over falsehood; theologians and tyrants necessarily hate truth and despise reason, because they believe them prejudicial to their interests.

Reason, the fruit of experience, is only the art of choosing those passions, to which, for his own peculiar happiness, he ought to listen. . . . Legislation is the art of restraining dangerous passions, and of exciting those which may be conducive to the public welfare.

If no evil had existed in this world, man would never have dreamt of divinity.
Vol. I

The Jehovah of the Jews is a suspicious tyrant, who breathes nothing but blood, murder, and carnage, and who demands that they should nourish him with the vapours of animals. The Jupiter of the Pagans is a lascivious monster. The Moloch of the Phoenicians is a cannibal; the pure mind of the Christians resolved, in order to appease his fury, to crucify his own son; the savage god of the Mexicans cannot be satisfied without thousands of mortals which are immolated to his sanguinary appetite.

All Religious notions are uniformly founded on authority; all the religions of the world forbid examination, and are not disposed that men should reason upon them.
Vol. II

Bon sens [*Good Sense*] (1772) (tr. Mendum)

The sectaries of a religion, which preaches, in appearance, nothing but charity, concord, and peace, have proved themselves more ferocious than cannibals or savages, whenever their divines excited them to destroy their brethren. There is no crime which men have not committed under the idea of pleasing the Divinity or appeasing his wrath.

The less men reason, the more wicked they are. Savages, princes, nobles, and the dregs of the people, are commonly the worst of men, because they reason least.

JOHN JAYNES HOLMES
(1879–1964)
American clergyman

Sensible Man's View of Religion (1933)

If Christians were Christians, there would be no anti-Semitism.

Jesus was a Jew. There is nothing that the ordinary Christian so dislikes to remember as this awkward historical fact.

Such is the debt which Christianity owes to Judaism! Not Jesus merely, nor the Bible, the Church and the Sunday, but the whole substance of Christian teaching!

We find here an explanation at least, and a very important one, of why the Christians dislike and persecute the Jews. They hate them and would get rid of them because they are heavily indebted to them. This is a very simple law of psychology.
Sermon, Community Church, New York City,
January 17, 1943

OLIVER WENDELL HOLMES
(1809–1894)
American poet, novelist, physician

The Autocrat of the Breakfast Table (1858)

All generous minds have a horror of what we commonly call 'facts.' They are the brute beasts of the intellectual domain. . . . (The above remark must be conditioned and qualified for the vulgar mind. . . .)

Sin has many tools, but a lie is the handle that fits them all.

The Professor at the Breakfast Table (1860)

Rough work, iconoclasm, but the only way to get at truth.

The Poet at the Breakfast Table (1872)

We are all tattooed in our cradles with the beliefs of our tribe; the record may seem superficial, but it is indelible. You cannot educate a man wholly out of the superstitious fears which were implanted in his imagination, no matter how utterly his reason may reject them.

Don't be "consistent" but be simply true.

The Pope put his foot on the neck of kings, but Calvin and his cohorts crushed the whole human race under their heels in the name of the Lord of Hosts.

Over the Teacups (1890)

We are all sentenced to capital punishment for the crime of living.

The history of most countries has been that of majorities—mounted majorities, clad in iron, armed with death, treading down the tenfold more numerous minorities.

If the whole *materia medica* as now used, could be sunk to the bottom of the sea, it would be all the better for mankind—and all the worse for the fishes.
Address, Massachusetts Medical Society, May 30, 1860

OLIVER WENDELL HOLMES
(1841–1935)
U.S. Supreme Court Justice

Decisions and Dissents

Great cases like hard cases make bad law.
Northern Securities Co. *v.* U.S., 193 U.S. 197, 400 (1904)

General propositions do not decide concrete cases.

Every opinion tends to become a law.

The Fourteenth Amendment does not enact Mr. Herbert Spencer's 'Social Statics.' A Constitution is not intended to embody a particular economic theory.
Lochner *v.* N.Y., 198 U.S. 45, 78 (1905)

The character of every act depends on the circumstances in which it is done. . . . The most stringent protection of free speech would not protect a man in falsely shouting fire in a theatre and causing a panic.
Schenck *v.* U.S., 249 U.S. 47 (1919)

When men have realized that time has upset many fighting faiths, they may come to believe even more than they believe the very foundations of their own conduct, that the ultimate good desired is better reached by free trade in ideas—that the best test of truth is the power of the thought to get itself accepted in the competition of the market, and that truth is the only ground upon which their wishes safely can be carried out. That at any rate is the theory of our Constitution. It is an experiment as all life is an experiment.
Abrams *v.* U.S., 250 U.S. 616, 630 (1919)

Every idea is an incitement. . . . Eloquence may set fire to reason.

If in the long run the beliefs expressed in proletarian dictatorships are destined to be accepted by the dominant forces of the community, the only meaning of free speech is that they should be given their chance to have their say.
Gitlow *v.* N.Y., 268 U.S. 652 (1925)

It is better for all the world, if instead of waiting to execute degenerate offspring for crime, or let them starve for their imbecility, society can prevent those who are manifestly unfit from continuing their kind. The principle that sustains compulsory vaccination is broad enough to cover cutting the Fallopian tubes. . . . Three generations of imbeciles are enough.
Buck *v.* Bell, 274 U.S. 200 (1927)

If there is any principle of the Constitution that more imperatively calls for attachment than any other it is the principle of free thought—not free thought for those who agree with us but freedom for the thought that we hate.
Dissent, U.S. *v.* Schwimmer (1928)

It is our duty to declare lynch law as little valid when practiced by a regularly drawn jury as when administered by a mob intent on death.
Dissent, Leo Frank case

On the whole, I am on the side of the unregenerate who affirm the worth of life as an end in itself, as against the saints who deny it.
Letter to Lady Pollock, 1906

The great act of faith is when a man decides that he is not God.
Letter to William James, 1907

To have doubted one's own first principles is the mark of a civilized man.

To rest upon a formula is a slumber that prolonged, means death.
"Ideals and Doubts" (1920)

The life of the law has not been logic; it has been experience.
"The Common Law," lecture 1, 1881

Certainty, generally, is illusion, and repose is not the destiny of man.
Address, "The Path of the Law," 1897

A man's mind stretched by a new idea can never go back to its original dimensions.
Quoted by Robert M. Hutchins

No generalization is wholly true, not even this one.
Attributed

HOMER
(c. 700 B.C.)
Greek poet

The Odyssey

Put me on earth again, and I would rather be a serf in the house of some landless man . . . than king of all these dead men that have done with life.

. . . for no man can know who was his father.

No trust is to be placed in women.
Bk. XI

We love too much, hate in the same extreme.
Bk. XIV

The Iliad

Enlighten me, O Muses, tenants of Olympian homes,
For you are goddesses, inside on everything, know everything,
But we mortals hear only the news and know nothing at all.

Sleep . . . the twin of death.

The worst of tyrants, an usurping crowd.

Who dares think one thing and another tell.
My heart detests him as the gates of hell.

Men grow tired of sleep, love, singing and dancing sooner than war.

For men on earth 'tis better never to be born at all; or being born, to pass through the gates of Hades with all speed.
Quoted by Theogenis, "Elegies," 1, 425 (cf. Greek Anthology)

HERBERT CLARK HOOVER
(1874–1964)
31st President of the United States

Hunger is the mother of anarchy.
Statement to reporters, January 1, 1919, re German food blockade

In America, today, we are nearer a final triumph over poverty than in any land.

The American system of rugged individualism.
Campaign Speech, N.Y., October 22, 1928

We are in danger of developing a cult of the Common Man, which means a cult of mediocrity.
Speech

GERARD MANLEY HOPKINS
(1844–1889)
English poet

"Thou art indeed just, Lord" (pub. 1889)

Thou art indeed just, Lord, if I contend
With thee; but, sir, so what I plead is just.
Why do sinners' ways prosper? and why must
Disappointment all my endeavor end?

Birds build—but not I build; no, but strain,
Time's eunuch . . .

Mine, O thou lord of life, send my roots rain.

"No worst, there is none" (pub. 1889)

Life death all does end and each day dies with sleep.

"God's Grandeur" (pub. 1889)

The world is charged with the grandeur of God.

"The Leaden Echo and the Golden Echo" (pub. 1889)

Give beauty back, beauty, beauty, beauty, back to God,
beauty's self and beauty's giver.

HORACE (Quintus Horatius Flaccus)
(65–8 B.C.)
Roman poet

Odes

Bk. 1 (35 B.C.)

Pale Death knocks with impartial foot at poor men's hovels and kings' palaces.

iv

*Carpe diem, quam minimus credula pos-
tero.*
Seize today, and put as little trust as you can in tomorrow.

xi

The man of upright life, unstained by guilt.

xxii

Bk. 2 (30 B.C.)

Whoever cultivates the golden mean avoids the poverty of a hovel and the envy of a palace.

x

Alas, the years glide swiftly away.

xiv

Bk. 3 (23 B.C.)

Dulce et decorum est pro patria mori.
It is sweet and beautiful to die for your country. *

ii

Force without mind falls by its own weight.

iv

It is not the possessor of many things whom you will rightly call happy. The name of the happy man is claimed more justly by him who has learnt the art whereby to use what the gods give, and who can endure the hardships of poverty, who dreads disgrace as something worse than death. He will not fear to die for the friend he loves, or for his country.

ix (Ben Johnson tr.)

Epistles

Bk. I.I (13 B.C.)
To flee vice is the beginning of virtue, and the beginning of wisdom is to have got rid of folly.

Line 41

---

*"It was a Roman who said it was sweet to die for one's country. The Greeks never said it was sweet to die for anything. They had no vital lies."—Edith Hamilton, *The Greek Way*.

By right means if you can, but by any means make money.

Line 66

Thou [the Roman multitude] art a many-headed beast.

Line 76

Nothing is better than a celibate life.

Line 90

Bk. I.II

He who has begun his task has half done it. Have the courage to be wise; Begin!*

Line 43

. . . *omnem credi diem tibi dilexisse supre-
mum. . . .*
Hold for yourself the belief that each day that dawns is your last.

. . . a wife and dower, credit and friends, even birth and beauty, are all the gifts of Queen Money.

Bk. II

Who lives in fear will never be a free man.

Who then is free? The wise man, who is lord over himself, whom neither poverty, or death, nor bonds affright, who bravely defies his passions, and scorns ambition, who in himself is a whole, smoothed and rounded, so that nothing outside can rest on the polished surface, and against whom Fortune in her onset is ever defeated.

Ars Poetica [*The Art of Poetry*]

Sound sense is the first principle and source of writing.

KAREN HORNEY
(1885–1952)
American psychoanalyst

A perfectly normal person is rare in our civilization.

Quoted in obituary, *Time,* 1952

A(lfred) E(dward) HOUSMAN
(1859–1936)
English poet and scholar

"If here today the cloud of thunder lours"

The troubles of our proud and angry dust
Are from eternity, and shall not fail.

---

* *Sapere aude: incipe!*—also translated: "Dare to be wise; begin to live!"

Bear them we can, and if we can we must.
Shoulder the sky, my lad, and drink your
   ale.

"The laws of God, the laws of man"

The laws of God, the laws of man,
He may keep that will and can;
Not I: let God and man decree
Laws for themselves but not for me.

I, a stranger and afraid
In a world I never made.

IRVING HOWE
(1920–   )
American writer

Essential Works of Socialism (1971)

Socialism must then be redefined—or better, thought through once again, as a society
in which the means of production, to an extent that need not be determined rigidly in advance, are collectively owned and in which
they are democratically controlled; a society
requiring as its absolute prerequisite the preservation and extension of democracy. Without
socialism, democracy tends to wither . . . but
without democracy, socialism is impossible.
                                   Introduction

WILLIAM DEAN HOWELLS
(1837–1920)
American writer*

Mark Twain—Howells Letters

If ever the public was betrayed by its press,
it's ours.

They [our Money-Bags] mostly inspire the
people's voice, the press; the press is dumb.

Inequality is as dear to the American heart
as liberty itself.
              Quoted in *Time,* December 19, 1960

HU SHIH
(1891–1962)
Chinese philosopher

The sun exactly at noon is exactly [begin-
ning to] go down. And a creature exactly when
he is born is exactly [beginning to] die.
              Chinese Philosophy (Everyman edition)

---

*"Howells was the first distinguished American man
of letters to espouse Socialism."—Parrington's *Main
Currents in American Thought,* vol. III, p. 245.

ELBERT HUBBARD
(1856–1915)
American writer, publisher

Formal religion was organized for slaves; it
offered them consolation which earth did not
provide.
              Contribution, *The Philistine*

Dictionary of Epigrams (1910)

An idea that is not dangerous is unworthy to
be called an idea at all.

The Note Book (1927)

God is good, there is no devil but fear.

CHARLES EVANS HUGHES
(1862–1948)
Chief Justice, U.S. Supreme Court

Where there is muck to be raked, it must be
raked, and the public must know of it, that it
may mete out justice. . . .
   Publicity is a great purifier because it sets in
action the forces of public opinion, and in this
country public opinion controls the course of
the nation.
      Address, Manufacturers' Association, May 1908; a
            criticism of Theodore Roosevelt, who had
            encouraged, then attacked, muckrakers.

The greater the importance to safeguarding
the community from incitements to the overthrow of our institutions by force and violence,
the more imperative is the need to preserve the
constitutional rights of free speech, free press
and free assembly in order to maintain the opportunity for free political discussion, to the
end that government may be responsive to the
will of the people and that changes, if desired,
may be obtained be peaceful means. Therein
lies the security of the Republic, the very
foundation of constitutional government.
      DeJonge v. Oregon, 299 U.S. 353, 365 (1937)

A dissent in a court of last resort is an appeal
to the brooding spirit of the law, to the intelligence of a later day, when a later decision may
possibly correct the error into which the dissenting judge himself believes the court to
have been betrayed.
      Quoted in Alan Barth, *Prophets with Honor,* 1974

LANGSTON HUGHES
(1902–1967)
American poet

"Let America Be America Again" (1938)

> I am the poor white, fooled and pushed
>   apart,
> I am the Negro, bearing slavery's scar,
> I am the Red man driven from the land,
> I am the immigrant clutching the hope I
>   seek—
> And finding only the same old stupid plan
> Of dog eat dog, or might crush the weak.
>
> O, yes,
> I say it plain,
> America never was America to me
> And yet I swear this oath—
> America will be!

HUGO OF ST. VICTOR
(c. 1078–1111)
Saxon mystic philosopher

The best is to consider that we have a home somewhere, and only then does one really love the world.

Attributed

VICTOR HUGO
(1802–1885)
French poet, novelist, dramatist

The Future of Man

Nothing else in the world . . . not all the armies . . . is so powerful as an idea whose time has come.*

Les Misérables (1862)

I am for religion against religions.

The sewer is the conscience of the city.

_____

*Frequently misquoted, as: "There is one thing stronger than all the armies of the world: and that is an idea whose time has come," or, "Nothing in this world is so powerful as an idea whose time has come." Mussolini used this quotation daily in his *Popolo d'Italia*.

Who stops revolution half way? The bourgeoisie.

The three problems of the age: the degradation of man by poverty, the ruin of women by starvation, and the dwarfing of childhood by physical and spiritual night.

Les Châtiments (1853)

Savoir, penser, rêver. Tout est là.
To know, to think, to dream. That is everything.

People who are slaves [Art] makes free;
People who are free [Art] makes great.

Ruy Blas (1838)

God made himself man: granted. The Devil made himself woman.

Histoire d'un crime (1877)

An invasion of armies can be resisted; an invasion of ideas cannot be resisted.

"La Chute," X

Quatre-vingt-treize [*Ninety-three*] (1879)

A fixed idea ends in madness or heroism.

Pt. 2

Préfaces philosophiques

Religion is nothing but the shadow cast by the universe on human intelligence.

Toute la lyre (1888)

And now, Lord God, let us explain ourselves to each other.

_____

He [Voltaire] was more than a man; he was an age.
Jesus wept; Voltaire smiled. Of that divine tear and of that human smile the sweetness of the present civilization is composed.

Centenary oration, May 30, 1878

I represent a party which does not yet exist: the party of revolution, civilization. This party will make the 20th Century. There will come from it, first, the United States of Europe, then the United States of the World.

Written on wall of his death chamber, Place des
Vosges, Paris

We are all under sentence of death, but with a sort of indefinite reprieve.

Quoted in Walter Pater, *The Renaissance*

ALEXANDER VON HUMBOLT
(1769–1859)
German scientist

There are no inferior races; all are destined to attain freedom.
Quoted in Helmuth de Terra, *Humbolt*

All religion rests on a mental want: we hope, we fear, because we wish.
Quoted in Noyes, *Views of Religion*

DAVID HUME
(1711–1776)
Scottish philosopher

An Enquiry Concerning Human Understanding (1748)

The same motives always produce the same actions; The same events follow from the same causes.

Ambition, avarice, self-love, vanity, friendship, generosity, public spirit: these passions, mixed in various degrees, and distributed through society, have been, from the beginning of the world, and still are, the source of all the actions and enterprises, which have ever been observed among mankind.

There is no method of reasoning more common, and yet none more blamable, than, in philosophical disputes, to endeavor the refutation of any hypothesis, by a pretense of its dangerous consequences to religion and morality.

When any opinion leads to absurdities, it is certainly false; but it is not certain that an opinion is false, because it is of dangerous consequences.

All laws being founded on rewards and punishments . . .

The many instances of forged miracles, and prophecies, and supernatural events, which, in all ages, have either been detected by contrary evidence, or which detect themselves by their absurdity, prove sufficiently the strong propensity of mankind to the extraordinary and marvellous, and ought reasonably to beget a suspicion against all relations of this kind.

A wise man, therefore, proportions his belief to the evidence.

Be a philosopher; but amidst all your philosophy, be still a man.

A Treatise of Human Nature (1739–1740)

There is implanted in the human mind a perception of pain and pleasure as the chief spring and moving principle of all actions.

In general, it may be affirmed that there is no such passion in human minds, as the love of mankind, merely as such, independent of personal qualities, or services, or of relation to ourselves.

We speak not strictly and philosophically when we talk of the combat of passion and of reason. Reason is, and ought only to be, the slave of the passions, and can never pretend to any other office than to serve and obey them.

The Essays, Moral, Political and Literary of David Hume (1741–1742)

The spirit of the people must frequently be roused, in order to curb the ambition of the court; and the dread of rousing the spirit must be employed to prevent that ambition. Nothing so effectual to this purpose as the liberty of the press; by which all the learning, wit, and genius of the nation, may be employed on the side of freedom, and every one be animated to its defense.
"Of Liberty of the Press"

That *the corruption of the best of things produces the worst,* is grown into a maxim, and is commonly proved, among other instances, by the pernicious effects of *superstition* and *enthusiasm,* the corruptions of true religion.

Weakness, fear, melancholy, together with ignorance, are, therefore, the true sources of Superstition.
"Of Superstition and Enthusiasm"

Avarice, the spur of industry . . .

. . . a government of Laws, not of Man.
"Of Civil Liberty"

If we can depend upon any principle which we learn from philosophy, this, I think, may be considered as certain and undoubted, that there is nothing, in itself, valuable or despicable, desirable or hateful, beautiful or deformed; but that these attributes arise from the particular constitution and fabric of human sentiment and affection.
"The Skeptic"

On the other hand, it may be urged with better reason, that this sovereignty of the male is a real usurpation, and destroys that nearness of rank, not to say equality, which nature has established between the sexes. We are, by nature, their lovers, their friends, their patrons: would we willingly exchange such endearing appellations for the barbarous title of master and tyrant?

. . . nothing can be more cruel than to preserve, by violence, an union which, at first, was made by mutual love, and is now, in effect, dissolved by mutual hatred.

But the liberty of divorces is not only a cure to hatred and domestic quarrels; it is also an admirable preservative against them, and the only secret for keeping alive that love which first united the married couple.
"Of Polygamy and Divorces"

Suicide is supposed a crime, it is only cowardice can impel us to it. If it be no crime, both prudence and courage should engage us to rid ourselves at once of existence when it becomes a burden.

I believe that no man ever threw away life while it was worth keeping.
"Of Suicide"

JAMES GIBBONS HUNEKER
(1860–1921)
American writer

Painted Veils (1920)

Sex is the salt of life.

Pathos of Distance (pub. 1925)

Great art is an instant arrested in eternity.

JOHN HUS (or Huss)
(c. 1373–burned at the stake 1415)
Bohemian reformer, Czech hero

Seek the truth
Listen to the truth
Teach the truth
Love the truth
Abide by the truth
And defend the truth
Unto death.
Written prayer

Love the Truth. Let others have their truth, and the truth will prevail.
Inscription on Hus statue, Prague

Sancta simplicitatis!
Holy simplicity!
Last words, when a peasant added a faggot to the pyre

FRANCIS HUTCHESON
(1649–1746)
Scottish professor of moral philosophy

Inquiry Concerning Moral Good and Evil (1720)

That action is best which procures the greatest happiness for the greatest numbers.
Sec. 3

ROBERT M(aynard) HUTCHINS
(1899–1977)
American educator

Education can be dangerous. It is very difficult to make it not dangerous. In fact, it is almost impossible.
Q and A, Modern Forum, Los Angeles, 1963

The Political Animal (published by the Center for the Study of Democratic Institutions, July 1962)

There is no true university in the United States today. . . . There is no true medium of mass communication in the United States today. . . . The United States is aligned with the status quo everywhere in the world.

The principal enemy of freedom is illusion . . . the illusion of the importance of the size or quantity . . . the illusion of our technical superiority. There is the illusion that we don't dare to think. And there is the illusion which is related to all these illusions—the illusion of progress.

A liberal education . . . frees a man from the prison-house of his class, race, time, place, background, family, and even his nation.

ALDOUS HUXLEY
(1894–1963)
British writer

Collected Essays (1959)

That men do not learn very much from the lessons of history is the most important of all the lessons of history.

Chrome Yellow (1922)

The proper study of mankind is books.

Brave New World Revisited (1958)

Divisive forces are more powerful than those which make for union. Vested interests in language, philosophies of life, table manners, sexual habits, political, ecclesiastical and economic organizations are sufficiently powerful to block all attempts, by rational methods, to unite mankind for its own good. And there is nationalism. With the 57 varieties of tribal gods, nationalism is the religion of the 20th Century. We may be Christians, Jews, Moslems, Hindus, Buddhists, Confucians or Atheists; but the fact remains that there is only one faith for which large masses of us are prepared to die and kill, and that faith is nationalism.

Hunger and self government are incompatible.

The Marxian formula, "Religion is the opium of the people," is reversible, and one can say, with even more truth, that "opium is the religion of the people."

The older dictators fell because they never could supply their subjects with enough bread, enough circuses, enough miracles and mysteries. Nor did they possess a really effective system of mind-manipulation.

Under a scientific dictator, education will really work—with the result that most men and women will grow up to love their servitude and will never dream of revolution. There seems to be no good reason why a thoroughly scientific dictatorship should ever be overthrown.

The effectiveness of political and religious propaganda depends upon the methods employed, not on the doctrine taught. These doctrines may be true or false, wholesome or pernicious—it makes little or no difference. . . . Under favorable conditions, practically everybody can be converted to practically anything.

An unexciting truth may be eclipsed by a thrilling lie.

The Perennial Philosophy (1946)

Except by saints the problem of power is finally insoluble.

Eyeless in Gaza (1938)

Chastity—the most unnatural of the sexual perversions.

(cf. de Gourmont)

Time Must Have a Stop (1944)

If we must play the theological game, let us never forget it is a game. Religion, it seems to me, can survive only as a consciously accepted system of make-believe.

JULIAN HUXLEY
(1877–1975)
British biologist, writer

The Humanist Frame (1961)

Man's destiny is to be the sole agent for future evolution of this planet. He is the highest dominant type to be produced over two and a half billion years of the slow biological movement effected by the blind opportunistic workings of natural selection; if he does not destroy himself, he has at least an equal stretch of evolutionary time before him to exercise his agency.

I use the word "Humanist" to mean someone who believes that man is just as much a natural phenomenon as an animal or a plant; that his body, mind or soul were not supernaturally created but are products of evolution, and that he is not under the control or guidance of any supernatural being, but has to rely on himself and his own powers.

Essays of a Humanist (1964)

Gods and God in any meaningful sense seem destined to disappear.

The implications of evolutionary humanism are clear. If the full development of human possibilities are the overriding aims of our evolution, then any overpopulation which brings malnutrition and misery, or which erodes the world's material resources or its resources of beauty or intellectual satisfaction are evil.

Though undoubtedly man's genetic nature changed a great deal during the long proto-human stage, there is no evidence that it has in any important way improved since the time of the Aurignanian cave man. . . . Indeed, during this period it is probable that man's nature has degenerated and is still doing so.

In general, the most elaborate social life is, the more it tends to shield individuals from the action of natural selection; and when this occurs . . . harmful mutations accumulate instead of being weeded out. . . . There is also the fact that modern industrial civilization fa-

vors the differential decrease of the genes concerned with civilization.
Quoted in *N.Y. Times* obituary, February 15, 1975

T(homas) H(enry) HUXLEY
(1825–1895)
British biologist, writer*

Life and Letters of Thomas Henry Huxley, ed.
Leonard Huxley (1900)

True science and true religion are twin-sisters, and the separation of either from the other is sure to prove the death of both. Science prospers exactly in proportion as it is religious; and religion flourishes in exact proportion to the scientific depth and firmness of its bases.

Letter, 1859

Truth is better than much profit. I have searched over the grounds of my belief, and if wife and child and name and fame were all lost to me one after the other as the penalty, still I will not lie.

Sit down before a fact as a little child, be prepared to give up every preconceived notion. Follow humbly wherever and to whatever abysses nature leads, or you shall learn nothing.
Letter to Charles Kingsley, September 23, 1860

A Liberal Education (1868)

The only medicine for suffering, crime, and all other woes of mankind, is wisdom. Teach a man to read and write, and you have put into his hands the great keys of the wisdom box. But it is quite another thing to open the box.

Lay Sermons (1870–1875)

That man, I think, has had a liberal education who has been so trained in his youth that his body is the ready servant of his will, and does with ease and pleasure all the work that, as a mechanism, it is capable of; whose intellect is a clear, cold, logic engine, with all its parts of equal strength, and in smooth working order; ready, like a steam engine, to be turned to any kind of work, and spin the gossamers as well as forge the anchors of the mind; whose mind is stored with a knowledge of the great and fundamental truths of Nature and of the laws of her operations; one who, no stunted as-

---

*For assistance, additions and corrections, I am indebted to Albert Ashforth of the *New York Times,* a devoted Huxley student.—G.S.

cetic, is full of life and fire, but knows passions are trained to come to heel by a vigorous will, the servant of a tender conscience; who has learned to love all beauty, whether of Nature or of art, to hate all vileness, and to respect others as himself.

Every great advance in natural knowledge has involved the absolute rejection of authority.

Science and Culture (1880)

The great end of life is not knowledge but action.

Science and Christian Tradition (1893)

Throughout the history of the western world, the Scriptures, Jewish and Christian, have been the great instigators of the revolt against the worst forms of clerical and political despotism. The Bible has been the *Magna Carta* of the poor and of the oppressed; down to modern times, no State has had a constitution, in which the interests of the people are so largely taken into account, in which the duties, so much more so than the privileges, of rulers are insisted upon, as that drawn up for Israel in Deuteronomy and in Leviticus; nowhere is the fundamental truth that the welfare of the State, in the long run, depends on the uprightness of the citizens so strongly laid down.

Prologue

Agnosticism, in fact, is not a creed, but a method, the essence of which lies in the rigorous application of a single principle. That principle is of great antiquity; it is as old as Socrates, as old as the writer who said, "Try all things, hold fast by that which is good"; it is the foundation of the Reformation, which simply illustrated the axiom that every man should be able to give a reason for the faith that is in him; it is the great principle of Descartes; it is the fundamental axiom of modern science. Positively the principle may be expressed: In matters of the intellect, follow your reason as far as it will take you, without regard to any other consideration. And negatively: In matters of the intellect, do not pretend that conclusions are certain which are not demonstrated or demonstrable. That I take to be the agnostic faith, which if a man keep whole and undefiled, he shall not be ashamed to look the universe in the face, whatever the future may have in store for him.

Ch. VII

The Coming of Age of the Origin of Species (1880)

It is the customary fate of new truths to begin as heresies and to end as superstitions.

Science and Morals (1886)

The foundation of morality is to have done, once and for all, with lying.

Evolution and Ethics, Rights and Political Rights (1893)

Much can be done to change the nature of man himself. The intelligence which has converted the brother of the wolf into the faithful guardian of the flock ought to be able to do something toward curbing the instincts of savagery in civilized man.

Emancipation–Black and White (1865)

With few exceptions girls have been educated to be drudges, or toys, beneath men; or a sort of angel above him . . . The possibility that the ideal of womanhood lies neither in the fair saint nor in the fair sinner; that the female type of character is neither better nor worse than the male, but only weaker; that women are meant neither to be men's guardians nor their playthings, but their comrades, their fellows and their equals, so far as Nature puts no bar to the equality, does not seem to have entered into the minds of those who have had the conduct of the education of girls.

Joseph Priestley (1874)*

Becky Sharp's acute remark that it is not difficult to be virtuous on £10,000 a year has its application to nations: and it is futile to expect a hungry and squalid population to be anything but violent and gross.

Evolution excludes creation and all other kinds of supernatural intervention.
Quoted in Noyes, *Views of Religion*

"Learn what is true in order to do what is right" is the summing up of the whole duty of man.

Attributed

---

*Mr. Huxley's £10,000 is exaggerated. Becky Sharp, in Thackeray's *Vanity Fair,* felt that it would be easy to be virtuous on £5,000 a year (Ch. xx).

I CHING
or Book of Changes*
(c. 12th Century B.C.)

Fellowship With Man

But when two people are at one in their inmost hearts,
They shatter even the strength of iron or of bronze.
And when two people understand each other in their inmost hearts,
Their words are sweet and strong, like the fragrance of orchids.

VICENTE BLASCO IBANEZ
(1867–1928)
Spanish novelist

Sangre y Arena [*Blood and Sand*] (1908)

It was the roar of the real, the only beast in the Plaza de Toros, the crowd.

DOLORES IBARRURI (La Pasionara)
(1895–1983)
Spanish Republican leader

Mas vale morir a pie que vivir en rodillas.
Better to die on one's feet than to live on one's knees.**
Rallying cry of Spanish Republic during war

It is better to be the widow of a hero than the wife of a coward.
Speech, Valencia, 1936, Paris, 1937

---

*See *Britannica,* 11th ed., vol. VI, pp. 227b and 911b; "held by some to be the oldest Chinese work and which forms part of the Confucian Canon."
**Leigh White in *The Long Balkan Night,* p. 390, says Emiliano Zapata used a similar expression in the Mexican Revolution, 1920; President F. D. Roosevelt at Cambridge, Mass., June 1941, said: "We . . . would rather die on our feet than live on our knees."

HENRIK IBSEN
(1828–1906)
Norwegian dramatist, lyric poet

An Enemy of the People (1882)

The majority never had right on its side. Never, I say. Intelligent men must wage war. Who is it that constitutes the majority of the population of the country? Is it the wise folk or the fools? . . . The stupid people are an overwhelming majority all over the world. The majority has *might* on its side—unfortunately; but *right* it has *not*. . . . The minority is always in the right.

IV

The strongest man in the world is he who stands most alone.

V

Notes for *A Doll's House* (Rome, October 10, 1878)

There are two kinds of moral law, two kinds of consciences, in men and women, and they are altogether different. The two sexes do not understand each other. But in practical life, the woman is judged by man's law, as if she were a man, not a woman.

Brand (1866)

The man whom God wills to stay in the struggle of life, He first individualizes.

The Wild Duck (1884)

Rob the average man of his life-illusion and you rob him of his happiness.

V

Peer Gynt (1867)

What's a man's first duty? The answer is brief: to be himself.

Letters to George Brandes

Friends are a costly luxury, and when one invests one's capital in a mission in life, one cannot afford to have friends.

. . . the only thing about liberty that I love is the fight for it; I care nothing about the possession of it.

The State is the curse of the individual. . . . And on the other hand, take the Jewish people, the aristocracy of the human race—how is it they have kept their place apart, their poetical halo, amid surroundings of coarse cruelty? By having no State to burden them. Had they remained in Palestine, they would long ago have lost their individuality in the process of their State's construction, like all other nations.

One of the qualities of liberty is that, as long as it is being striven after, it goes on expanding. Therefore, the man who stands in the midst of the struggle and says, "I have it," merely shows by doing so that he has just lost it.

February 17, 1871

I hold that man is in the right who is most closely in league with the future.

January 3, 1882*

ST. IGNATIUS OF LOYOLA, *see* Loyola

WILLIAM R(alph) INGE
(1860–1954)
English clergyman, theologian, Dean of St. Paul's Cathedral

Sermon, Modern Church Union, Cambridge, 1950

It was either under Persian influence or by a parallel development of thought that the later Judaism came to believe in a future life, a resurrection, a last judgment, heaven and hell, a cosmic duel between right and darkness, and a divine Saviour. A cynic might even say that we owe more to Zarathustra than to Moses.

December 25th is the birthday, not of Christ, but of Mithras the Invincible Sun. Isis of many names has acquired a new one as the Madonna.

At the Reformation the composite elements flew apart. . . . The Catholic became two-thirds a pagan; the Protestant, at least in England, two-thirds a Jew.

ROBERT G(reen) INGERSOLL
(1833–1899)
American lawyer, orator, freethinker

The Liberty of Man, Woman and Child (1877)

As long as woman regards the Bible as the charter of her rights, she will be the slave of man. The Bible was not written by a woman. Within its leaves there is nothing but humiliation and shame for her.

*Quoted verbatim, without credit, by Eisenhower, 1956 acceptance speech.

There is no slavery but ignorance.

The Gods (1876)

An honest God is the noblest work of man.

"Has Freethought a Constructive Side?"
The object of the Freethinker is to ascertain the truth—the conditions of well-being—to the end that his life will be made of value.
Contribution, *The Truth Seeker,* 1890

Some Mistakes of Moses (1879)

A fact never went into partnership with a miracle. Truth scorns the assistance of wonders. A fact will fit every other fact in the universe, and that is how you can tell whether it is or is not a fact. A lie will not fit anything except another lie.

Give the Church a place in the Constitution, let her touch once more the sword of power, and the priceless fruit of all the ages will turn to ashes.
Letter to the *Houston Post,* August 17, 1866

The most significant thing in the world today is, that in nearly every village under the American flag, the schoolhouse is larger than the church.
Address, December 13, 1886

Our hope of immortality does not come from any religion, but clearly all religions come from that hope.
Speech, quoted in *Chicago Times,* November 14, 1879

The hope of science is the perfection of the human race. The hope of theology is the salvation of a few, and the damnation of almost everybody.
Quoted in *The Age of Reason,* March/April, 1967

Banish me from Eden when you will, but first let me eat of the tree of Knowledge.
Quoted in Noyes, *Views of Religion*

INNOCENT III*
(c. 1160–1216)
Pope 1198–1216

Yea, so much must I live for others, that almost I am a stranger to myself.

———
*Quotations from *Britannica,* 11th ed., vol. XIV.

The Lord left to Peter the governance not of the Church only but of the whole world.
Letter to Patriarch of Constantinople

Jews, like the fratricide Cain, are doomed to wander about the earth as fugitives and vagabonds, and their faces must be covered with shame. They are . . . to be condemned to serfdom.
Letter to Count Nevers, 1208

EUGENE IONESCO
(1912–   )
Rumanian-born French writer

Découvertes (1969)

It is not the answer that enlightens, but the question.

A creative work of art is, by its very novelty, aggressive; spontaneously aggressive, it strikes out at the public, against the majority; it arouses indignation by its non-conformity, which is, in itself, a form of vindication.
Quoted in *Writers in Revolt* (1963)

Despite his atheism, Marx cannot be understood without the Bible. His myth of a perfect society, surmounting history, beyond history, is in fact the Biblical myth of Paradise on Earth. . . . What is Marxism if not Messianism?
Remarks, Jerusalem Book Fair, reported in *N.Y. Times,* June 6, 1973

WASHINGTON IRVING
(1783–1859)
American writer

Almighty dollar.
Coined phrase, "The Crayon Papers" (1837) and "Wolforth's Roost, The Creole Village" (1836)

ST. ISIDORE OF SEVILLE
(c. 560–636)
Archbishop of Seville

Sentences

Because of the sin of the first man the punishment of slavery was divinely imposed on the human race, so that He might inflict slavery more mercifully on those who He perceived are not suited to liberty. Although original sin was remitted for all the faithful by the grace of baptism, yet God in His justice has so ordered the lives of men, establishing some as slaves, others as masters, that the power of slaves to do evil is restrained by the power of those who rule them. For if all were without any fear, who could restrain anyone from evil?

3, 47

ISOCRATES
(436–338 B.C.)
Athenian orator, rhetorician*

Advice to Nicocles * *

Do not do to others what angers you if done to you by others.

xiii, 61

Ad Demonicum

Of all our possessions wisdom alone is immortal.

iv, 19

If you truly wished to find out what is best for the country you would listen more to those who oppose you than to those who try to please you.

[True democracy] is the renunciation of the struggle for power.
Quoted in Edith Hamilton, *The Echo of Greece*

ANDREW JACKSON
(1768–1845)
7th President of the United States

I am one of those who do not believe that a national debt is a national blessing, but rather

---

*"But the fact that he was the first to declare (under Thucydides' guidance) that power tends to corrupt and absolute power corrupts absolutely, and the first to urge giving up war as a policy and substituting good will for armed forces, sets him so far in advance of his age that on that score alone he could not be forgotten."—Edith Hamilton, *The Echo of Greece*.
* *Nicocles was the young king of Cyprian Salamis.

a curse to a republic; inasmuch as it is calculated to raise around the administration a moneyed aristocracy dangerous to the liberties of the country.
Letter to L.H. Coleman, April 26, 1824

Every monopoly and all exclusive privileges are granted at the expense of the public, which ought to receive a fair equivalent.

Mere precedent is a dangerous source of authority.
Veto, Bank Renewal Bill, July 10, 1832 (largely written by Justice Taney)

The mischief springs from the power which the moneyed interest derives from a paper currency which they are able to control, from the multitude of corporations with exclusive privileges which they have succeeded in obtaining . . . and unless you become more watchful in your States and check this spirit of monopoly and thirst for exclusive privileges you will in the end find that the most important powers of Government have been given or bartered away, and the control of your dearest interests have been passed into the hands of these corporations.
Farewell Address, March 4, 1837

ROBERT H(oughwout) JACKSON
(1892–1954)
U.S. Supreme Court Justice

If there is any fixed star in our constitutional constellation, it is that no official, high or petty, can prescribe what shall be orthodox in politics, nationalism, religion, or other matters of opinion, or force citizens to confess by word or act their faith therein.

Those who begin coercive elimination of dissent soon find themselves exterminating dissenters. Compulsory unification of opinion achieves only a unanimity of the graveyard.
Minersville School District *v.* Grobitis, 319 U.S. 624, 642, 1940

MAX JACOB
(1876–1944)
French Jewish poet, Catholic convert

Art poétique (1922)

When you get to the point where you cheat for the sake of beauty, you are an artist.

JAMES I
(1566–1625)
King of England

Kings are justly called Gods, for they exercise a manner of resemblance of Divine power upon earth; For if you consider the Attributes of God, you shall see how they agree in the person of a King.
> Address to Parliament, 1609

A custom loathsome to the eye, hateful to the nose, harmful to the brain, dangerous to the lungs, and in the black stinking fume thereof, nearest resembling the horrible Stygian smoke of the pit that is bottomless.
> *A Counterblaste to Tobacco* (1604)*

The intention makes the lye, not the words.
> Quoted in Overbury's *Crumbs Fall'n from King James's Table*

HENRY JAMES (Sr.)
(1811–1882)
American theologian

The natural inheritance of everyone who is capable of spiritual life is an unsubdued forest where the wolf howls and the obscene bird of night chatters.
> Letter to William James and Henry James, Jr.

HENRY JAMES (Jr.)
(1843–1916)
American novelist

The Spoils of Poynton (1897)

Life being all inclusion and confusion, and art being all discrimination and selection . . . life has no direct sense whatever for the subject and is capable, luckily for us, of nothing but splendid waste. Hence the opportunity for the sublime economy of art, which rescues, and saves, and hoards, and "banks," investing and reinvesting these fruits of toil in wondrous useful "works" and thus making up for us, desperate spendthrifts that we all naturally are, the most princely incomes.

---

*King James's allegation that smoking was harmful to the lungs was confirmed by the Johns Hopkins Medical School report, 1938, a seminal study in establishing our current views of smoking.

The fatal futility of Fact.
> Preface to the New York Edition (1908)

The Madonna of the Future (1879)

Cats and monkeys, monkeys and cats—all human life is there.

The American (1877)

The deep well of unconscious cerebration.
> Preface to the New York Edition (1908)

It is art that *makes* life, makes interest, makes importance . . . and I know of no substitute whatever for the force and beauty of its process.
> Letter to H. G. Wells, July 10, 1915

WILLIAM JAMES
(1842–1910)
American psychologist, philosopher

The Principles of Psychology (1890)

Habit is . . . the enormous flywheel of society, its most precious conservative agent.

The hell to be endured hereafter, of which theology tells, is no worse than the hell we make for ourselves in this world by habitually fashioning our characters in the wrong way.
> Ch. 4

In the practical use of our intellect, forgetting is as important as remembering.
> Ch. 16

The sin of "Science" is to attain conceptions so adequate and exact that we shall never need to change them. There is an everlasting struggle in every mind between the tendency to keep unchanged, and the tendency to renovate its ideas. Our education is a ceaseless compromise between the conservative and the progressive factors.

Genius . . . means little more than the faculty of perceiving in an unhabitual way.
> Ch. 19

The hunting and the fighting instinct continue in many manifestations. They both support the emotion of anger; they combine in the fascination which stories of atrocities have for most minds . . . the pleasure of disinterested cruelty has been thought a paradox and writers have sought to show that it is no primitive attribute of our nature, but rather a resultant of the subtile or other less malignant elements of mind. This is a hopeless task. If evolution and the survival of the fittest be true at all, the destruction of prey and of human rivals must have been among the most important. . . . It is just because human bloodthirstiness is such a primitive part of us that it is so hard to eradicate, especially when a fight or a hunt is promised as part of the fun.

Ch. 24

The Will to Believe (1897)

Our belief in truth itself; for instance, that there is a truth, and that our minds and it are made for each other,—what is it but a passionate affirmation of desire, in which our social system backs us up?

As a rule we disbelieve all facts and theories for which we have no use.

The Varieties of Religious Experience (1902)

Religion, in short, is a monumental chapter in the history of human egotism.

Lecture 2

The opposition between the men who *have* and the men who *are* is immemorial.

Lectures 11, 12, and 13

Yet the fact remains that war is a school of strenuous life and heroism; and, being in the line of aboriginal instinct, is the only school that as yet is universally available. . . . What we now need to discover in the social realm is the moral equivalent of war; something heroic that will speak to men as universally as war does, and yet will be as compatible with their spiritual selves as war has proved itself to be incompatible.

The praise of poverty need once to be boldly sung. We have grown literally afraid to be poor. We despise anyone who elects to be poor in order to simplify and save his inner life. . . . We have lost the power even of imagining what the ancient idealization of poverty could have meant: the liberation from material attachments, the unbribed soul, the manlier indifference, the paying our way by what we are or do and not by what we have, the right to fling away our life at any moment irresponsibly,—the more athletic trim, in short, the moral fighting shape.

The arguments for God's existence have stood for hundreds of years with the waves of unbelieving criticism breaking against them, never totally discrediting them in the ears of the faithful, but on the whole slowly and surely washing out the mortar from between

their joints. . . . The "argument *ex consensus gentium*" is that the belief in God is so widespread as to be grounded in the rational nature of man, and should therefore carry authority with it.

There is no worse lie than a truth misunderstood by those who hear it.

Lectures 14 and 15

Pragmatism* (1907)

Philosophy is at once the most sublime and the most trivial of human pursuits. . . . It "bakes no bread," as has been said, but it can inspire our souls with courage; and repugnant as its manners, its doubting and challenging, its quibblings and dialectics, often are to common people, no one of us can get along without the far-flashing beams of light it sends over the world's perspectives.

Lecture 1

The prince of darkness may be a gentleman, as we are told he is, but whatever the God of earth and heaven is, he can surely be no gentleman. His menial services are needed in the dust of our human trials, even more than his dignity is needed in the empyrean.

(Pragmatism is) the attitude of looking away from first things, principles, "categories," supposed necessities; and of looking towards last things, fruits, consequences, facts.

Pragmatism is uncomfortable away from facts. Rationalism is comfortable only in the presence of abstractions. . . . Objective truth must be something non-utilitarian, haughty, refined, remote, august, exalted. . . . Down with psychology, up with logic, in all this question.

Lecture 2

The true is the name of whatever proves itself to be good in the way of belief, and good too, for definite, assignable reasons.

'The true,' to put it briefly, is only the expedient in the way of our thinking, just as 'the right' is only the expedient in the way of our behaving.

Lecture 6

The Meaning of Truth (1909)

How will the truth be realized? What, in short, is the truth's cash-value in experimental terms? The moment pragmatism asks this

*Charles Peirce is called the father of Pragmatism, James the expounder.

question, it sees the answer: *True ideas* are those that we can assimilate, validate, corroborate, and verify. False ideas are those that we *cannot*. That is the practical difference it makes to us to have true ideas; that therefore is the meaning of truth, for it is all that truth is known as.

Memoirs and Studies (1911)

Without any exception known to me, militarist authors take a highly mystical view of their subject, and regard war as a biological or sociological necessity, uncontrolled by ordinary psychological checks and motives. When the time of development is ripe the war must come, reason or no reason, for the justifications pleaded are invariably fictitious. War is, in short, a permanent human *obligation*. . . .

I devoutly believe in the reign of peace and in the gradual advent of some sort of socialistic equilibrium. The fatalistic view of the war-function is to me nonsense. . . . And when whole nations are the armies, and the science of destruction vies in intellectual refinement with the sciences of production, I see that war becomes absurd and impossible from its own monstrosity.

"The Moral Equivalent of War"

Man, biologically considered, is the most formidable of all beasts of prey, and, indeed, the only one that preys systematically on his own species.

"Remarks at the Peace Banquet"

Thought and Character (c. 1900)

Faith branches off from the highroad before reason begins.

Letters

The difference between a good man and a bad one is the choice of the cause.

To E.L. Godkin, Christmas Eve, 1895

We "intellectuals" in America must all work to keep our precious birthright of individualism, and freedom from these institutions [church, army, aristocracy, royalty]. *Every* great institution is perforce a means of corruption.

To William M. Salter, September 11, 1899

The moral flabbiness born of the exclusive worship of the bitch-goddess SUCCESS. That—with the squalid cash interpretation put on the word "success"—is our national disease.

To H.G. Wells, September 11, 1906

The world . . . is only beginning to see that the wealth of a nation consists more than in anything else in the number of superior men that it harbors.

Quoted in Mach, *Civilization in the United States*

A great many people think they are thinking when they are rearranging their prejudices.

Quoted by Clifton Fadiman

My first act of free will shall be to believe in free will.

Quoted in G.W. Allen, *William James* (1967)

(Auguste Marie Joseph) JEAN (-LEON) JAURES
(1859–assassinated 1914)
French Socialist Leader

"The Rights of Man to Socialism" (*Oeuvres*, 1931–39, vol. 2)

Every individual has a right to demand of humanity everything that will aid his effort; he has the right to work, to produce, to create; and no category of men may draw usury from his work or put it under its yoke.

Life does not abolish the past; it subdues it. The Revolution is not a break, it is a conquest.

Socialism is not an arbitrary and Utopian conception. . . . To the aridity of bourgeois arrogance and egotism, shrunken by monopolist and elitist exploitation, it has opposed a revolutionary bitterness, an avenging and provoking irony, a deadly analysis that dissolves lies.

SIR JAMES (Hopwood) JEANS
(1877–1946)
British scientist, Astronomer Royal

Physics and Philosophy (1942)

The plain fact is that there are no conclusions.

The Wider Aspects of Cosmogony (1928)

Taking a very gloomy view of the future of the human race, let us suppose that it can only expect to survive for two thousand million years longer, a period about equal to the past age of the earth.

The Mysterious Universe (1930)

From the intrinsic evidence of his creation, the Great Architect of the Universe now begins to appear as a *pure mathematician*.

THOMAS JEFFERSON
(1743–1826)
3rd President of the United States

The original draft of the Declaration of Independence (to which notable persons, including Thomas Paine, contributed)

We hold these truths to be sacred and undeniable: that all men are created equal and independent, that from that equal creation they derive rights inherent and inalienable, among which are the preservation of life and liberty, and the pursuit of happiness.

He [King George III] has waged cruel war against human nature itself, violating its most sacred rights of life and liberty in the persons of a distant people who never offended him, captivating and carrying them into slavery in another hemisphere . . . determined to keep open a market where MEN should be bought and sold . . . he is now exciting those very people to rise in arms amongst us, and to purchase that liberty of which *he* has deprived them, by murdering the people upon whom *he* also obtruded them; . . . thus paying off former crimes committed against the *liberties* of one people, with crimes which he urges them to commit against the *lives* of another. *

"A Bill for Establishing Religious Freedom," known as "The Virginia Statute for Religious Freedom" (1779)**

That Almighty God hath created the mind free;—that all attempts to influence it by tem-

---

*This, the most important excision, relating to the slave trade, was according to Jefferson himself, "struck out in complaisance to S. Carolina and Georgia, who had never attempted to restrain importation of slaves and who on the contrary still wish to continue it. Our northern brethren also, I believe, felt a little tender under these censures, for tho' their people have very few slaves themselves, yet they have been pretty considerable carriers of them to others."
**"Probably the most famous single document in the history of religious freedom in America."— Henry Steele Commager. In his "Autobiography" Jefferson wrote that "an amendment was proposed by inserting the words, 'Jesus Christ . . . the holy author of our religion,' " which was rejected "by a great majority, in proof that they meant to comprehend, within the mantle of its protection, the Jew and the Gentile, the Christian and the Mohammedan, the Hindoo and the Infidel of every denomination."

poral punishments, or burthens, or by civil incapacitations, tend only to beget habits of hypocrisy and meanness . . . that the impious presumption of legislators and rulers, civil as well as ecclesiastical, who, being themselves but fallible and uninspired men, have assumed dominion over the faith of others, setting up their own opinions and modes of thinking as the only true and infallible. . . . hath established and maintained false religions over the greatest part of the world, and through all time: . . . that our civil rights have no dependence on our religious opinions, any more than our opinions in physics and geometry . . . that to suffer the civil magistrate to intrude his powers into the field of opinion and to restrain the profession or propagation of principles on supposition of their ill tendency is a dangerous fallacy, which at once destroys all religious liberty, . . . and finally, that truth is great and will prevail if left to herself; that she is the proper and sufficient antagonist to error, and has nothing to fear from the conflict unless by human interposition disarmed of her natural weapons, free argument and debate, errors ceasing to be dangerous when it is permitted freely to contradict them.

"Notes on the State of Virginia" (1781–1785)

The legitimate powers of government extend to such acts only as are injurious to others. But it does me no injury for my neighbor to say there are twenty gods, or no God. It neither picks my pocket nor breaks my leg.

Reason and free inquiry are the only effectual agents against error. Give a loose to them, they will support the true religion by bringing every false one to their tribunal, to the test of their investigation. They are the natural enemies of error, and of error only. Had not the Roman government permitted free inquiry, Christianity could never have been introduced. Had not free inquiry been indulged at the era of the Reformation, the corruptions of Christianity could not have been purged away.

17

The whole commerce between master and slave is a perpetual exercise of the most boisterous passions, the most unremitting despotism on the one part, and degrading submission on the other. . . .

Indeed, I tremble for my country when I re-

flect that God is just; that his justice cannot
sleep forever.*

18

Those who labor in the earth are the chosen
people of God, if ever he had a chosen people.

Every government degenerates when trusted
to the rulers of the people alone. The people
themselves are its only safe depositories.

19

Virginia and Kentucky Resolutions (1799)

To the press alone, checquered as it is with
abuses, the world is indebted for all the
triumphs which have been gained by reason
and humanity over error and oppression.

First Inaugural Address, March 4, 1801

All, too, will bear in mind this sacred principle, that though the will of the majority is in
all cases to prevail, that will, to be rightful,
must be reasonable; that the minority possess
their equal rights, which equal laws must protect, and to violate which would be oppression.

If there be any among us who would wish to
dissolve this union or to change its republican
form, let them stand undisturbed as monuments of the safety with which error of opinion
may be tolerated where reason is left free to
combat it.

Force (is) the vital principle and immediate
parent of despotism.

"Bill for the More General Diffusion of Knowledge"
(1778)

Experience hath shewn, that even under the
best forms [of government] those entrusted
with power have, in time, and by slow operations, perverted it into tyranny.

Works (published 1904–1905)

The whole of government consists in the art
of being honest.

Vol. VI

Say nothing of my religion. It is known to
God and myself alone. Its evidence before the
world is to be sought in my life: if it has been
honest and dutiful to society the religion
which has regulated it cannot be a bad one.

Vol. VII

Writings of Thomas Jefferson

The merchant has no country.

Vol. XIV

I have ever deemed it fundamental for the
United States never to take an active part in
the quarrels of Europe. Their political interests
are entirely distinct from ours. . . . They are
nations of eternal war.

Vol. XV

I hope it is practical, by improving the mind
and morals of society, to lessen the disposition
to war; but of its abolition I despair.

Vol. XVIII

———

May it [the Declaration of Independence] be
to the world what I believe will be (to some
parts sooner, to others later, but finally to all),
the signal of arousing man to burst the chains
under which monkish ignorance and superstition has persuaded them to bind themselves,
and to assume the blessings of security and
self-government.

Last known writing, ten days before his death

It is still in our power to direct the process of
emancipation and deportation of [Negro
slaves] peaceably, and in such slow degree that
the evil will wear off insensibly; and their
places be *pari passu,* filled up by free white laborers. If, on the contrary, it is left to force itself on, human nature must shudder at the
prospect held up.

Quoted by Lincoln, Cooper Union, February 27,
1860

Letters: On Religion

Shake off all the fears of servile prejudices,
under which weak minds are servilely
crouched. Fix reason firmly in her seat, and
call on her tribunal for every fact, every opinion. Question with boldness even the existence
of a God, because, if there be one, he must
more approve of the homage of reason than
that of blind faith.

To Peter Carr, his nephew, August 10, 1785

———

*"While Mr. Jefferson was the owner of slaves, as
undoubtedly he was, in speaking upon this very subject he used the strong language that 'he trembled
for his country when he remembered that God was
just.' "—Abraham Lincoln, Galesburg, Ill., October 7, 1858.

They [the clergy] believe that any portion of power confided to me, will be exerted in opposition to their schemes. And they believe rightly: for I have sworn upon the altar of god eternal hostility against every form of tyranny over the mind of man.

To Dr. Benjamin Rush, September 23, 1800*

We should all then, like the Quakers, live without an order of priests, moralize for ourselves, follow the oracle of conscience, and say nothing about what no man can understand, nor therefore believe.

To John Adams, 1803

If the obstacles of bigotry and priestcraft can be surmounted, we may hope that common sense will suffice to do everything else.

To Kosciuszko, 1811

Of all the systems of morality, ancient or modern, which have come under my observation, none appears to me so pure as that of Jesus.

To W. Canby, September 18, 1813

In every country and in every age, the priest has been hostile to liberty. He is always in alliance with the despot. . . . they have perverted the purest religion ever preached to man into mystery and jargon, unintelligible to all mankind, and therefore the safer engine for their purpose.

To Horatio Spafford, March 17, 1814

Paul was the great Coryphaeus, and first corrupter of the doctrines of Jesus.

To W. Short, April 13, 1820

The metaphysical insanities of Athanasius, of Loyola, and of Calvin, are, to my understanding, mere lapses into polytheism, differing from paganism only by being more unintelligible.

To Jared Sparks, 1820

Had the doctrines of Jesus been preached always as pure as they came from his lips, the whole civilized world would now have been Christian.

To Benjamin Waterhouse, June 26, 1822

And the day will come, when the mystical generation of Jesus, by the Supreme Being as

His Father, in the womb of a virgin, will be classed with the fable of the generation of Minerva, in the brain of Jupiter.

To John Adams, April 11, 1823

Letters: On Freedom of the Press

Our liberty depends on the freedom of the press, and that cannot be limited without being lost.

To Dr. J. Currie, 1786

The basis of our government being the opinion of the people, the very first object should be to keep that right; and were it left to me to decide whether we should have a government without newspapers, or newspapers without a government, I should not hesitate for a moment to prefer the latter. But I should mean that every man should receive those papers, and be capable of reading them.

To Colonel Edward Carrington, January 16, 1787

Nothing can now be believed which is seen in a newspaper. Truth itself becomes suspicious by being put into that polluted vehicle.

To John Norvell, June 11, 1807

The man who never looks into a newspaper is better informed than he who reads them: inasmuch as he who knows nothing is nearer to truth than he whose mind is filled with falsehood and errors.

To Thos. Seymour, and other citizens of Hartford, February 11, 1807

Perhaps an editor might begin a reformation in some such way as this. Divide his paper into four chapters, heading the 1st, Truths. 2d, Probabilities. 3d, Possibilities. 4th, Lies. The first chapter would be very short.

To John Norvell, June 11, 1807

Letters: Miscellaneous

The art of life is the avoiding of pain.

To Mrs. Cosway, 1786

The tax which will be paid for the purpose of education is not more than the thousandth part of what will be paid to kings, priests and nobles who will rise up among us if we leave the people to ignorance.

To George Wythe, 1786

The spirit of resistance to government is so valuable on certain occasions that I wish it to be always kept alive. It will often be exercised when wrong, but better so than not to be exercised at all.

To Abigail Adams, 1787

---

*John H. Latta of Oklahoma City obtained from the Library of Congress a positive photostat of the original, recipient's copy. The word "god" has a small 'g,' there is no comma after, and no words are italicized. The retained copy of this letter may differ. —G.S.

God forbid we should ever be twenty years without such a rebellion.

What country before, ever existed a century and a half without a rebellion? And what country can preserve its liberties, if its rulers are not warned from time to time, that his people preserve the spirit of resistance. Let them take arms. The remedy is to set them right as to facts, pardon and pacify them. What signify a few lives lost in a century or two.

The tree of liberty must be refreshed from time to time, with the blood of patriots and tyrants. It is their natural manure.*
To Col. William S. Smith, 1787 (referring to Shay rebellion)

I hold it, that a little rebellion, now and then, is a good thing, and as necessary in the political world as storms in the physical.
Letter to James Madison, January 30, 1787

A subject comes into my head. . . . The question whether one generation of men has a right to bind another. . . . I set out on this ground which I suppose to be self evident: *"that the earth belongs in usufruct to the living: that the dead have neither powers or rights over it."*
To James Madison, ambassador to France, September 6, 1789**

The republican is the only form of government which is not eternally at open or secret war with the rights of mankind.
To William Hunter, March 11, 1790

Nature has given to our black brethren talents equal to those of the other colours of men.
To Benjamin Benneker, slave-born inventor, 1792

---

*"The tree of liberty will grow only when watered with the blood of tyrants."—Barère, 1792.
**Brought home by Jefferson, posted January 9, 1790, with a covering note: ". . . I find no occasion to alter my mind." The idea appears also in Tom Paine's 1796 pamphlet on banking, which Jefferson read later. In publishing the Philadelphia edition of *The Rights of Man,* May 1791, Paine uses an endorsement from Jefferson without permission, taken from a letter. In a Monticello revision Jefferson wrote within quotation marks, "The earth belongs usufruct to the living." In the second rephrased statement on this subject Jefferson wrote, "The earth belongs always to the living generation." See Alexander Laing's contribution, *The Nation,* July 3, 1976.

No man can bring out of the Presidency the reputation which carries him into it.
To Rutledge, 1795

I sincerely believe that banking establishments are more dangerous than standing armies and that the principle of spending money to be paid by posterity, under the name of funding, is but swindling on a large scale.
To Eldridge Gerry, January 26, 1799

The appointment of a woman to office is an innovation for which the public is not prepared, nor am I.
To Albert Gallatin, 1807

That government is the strongest of which every man feels himself a part.
To H.D. Tiffin, 1807

All eyes are opened or opening to the rights of man. The general spread of the light of science has already laid open to every view the palpable truth that the mass of mankind has not been born with saddles on their backs, nor a favored few booted and spurred ready to ride them legitimately by the grace of God.
To Roger G. Weightman, June 24, 1826 (anniversary of the Declaration of Independence)

There is no truth existing which I fear, or would wish unknown to the whole world.
To Henry Lee, 1826

Experience declares that man is the only animal which devours his own kind; for I can apply no milder term to the governments of Europe, and to the general prey of the rich on the poor.
To Col. Edw. Carrington, January 16, 1787

When a man assumes a public trust, he should consider himself public property.
To Baron von Humboldt, the scientist, in conversation, 1804

Resistance to tyrants is obedience to God.
Motto, found among his papers

JENGHIZ KHAN
(1162–1227)
Mongol emperor

Every man who does not go to war must work for the emperor, without reward, for a certain time.
Law (c. 1200)

A man's greatest work is to break his enemies, to drive them before him, to take from
them all the things that have been theirs, to
hear the weeping of those who cherished
them, to take their horses between his knees
and to press in his arms the most desirable of
their women.

Attributed

SAINT JEROME (Eusebius Hieronymus) (c. 340–420)
Dalmatian-born Roman theologian, chief preparer of the Vulgate

Sermon 354

Holy virginity is a better thing than conjugal
chastity. . . . A mother will hold a lesser place
in the kingdom of heaven, because she has
been married, than the daughter, seeing that
she is a virgin. . . . But if thy mother has been
humble and not proud, she will have some
sort of place, but not thou.

9, 9

Epistles

Adultery, without two persons to commit it,
is not possible.

1

Though God can do all things, he cannot
raise a virgin after she has fallen.

22*

Avarice, the root of all evil.

125

"The Virgin's Confession" (c. 420)

Virginity can be lost even by a thought.

Virginity is natural and marriage came after
the Fall.

Amor ordinem nescit.
Love knows no rule.

Letter to Chromatius

All riches come from iniquity, and unless
one has lost another cannot gain.

Opulence is always the result of theft. If not
committed by the actual possessor, then by his
predecessor.

---

*A translation of St. Augustine's quotation read: "He
cannot bring it about that a woman who was seduced was not seduced."

Matrimony is always a vice, all that can be
done is to excuse and to sanctify it; therefore it
was a religious sacrament.

Quoted in *Labor,* American Catholic Trade Union
Weekly

JOAN OF ARC
(1412–burned at the stake, 1431)
French national heroine, Catholic martyr

Yes, my voices were of God; my voices have
not deceived me.

Last words, attributed, Rouen, May 30

JOHN XXIII
(1881–1963)
Pope from 1958

Ad Petri Cathedram (July 2, 1959)

The source and root of all the evils which
affect individuals, people and nations with a
kind of poison, and confuse the minds of
many is this: ignorance of the truth and not
only ignorance, but at times a contempt for,
and a deliberate turning away from it.

It is therefore necessary to confront evil and
erroneous writing with what is right and
sound: against broadcasts, motion pictures,
and television shows which incite to error or
the attractions of vice, must be projected those
which uphold truth and strive to preserve
wholesome morality.

Pacem in Terris (April, 11, 1963)

If civil authorities legislate for or allow anything that is contrary to that order and therefore contrary to the will of God, neither the
laws made or the authorizations granted can
be binding on the consciences of the citizens,
since God has more right to be obeyed than
man.

. . . it cannot be lawful for the press, under
the pretext that it is free, to make daily and systematic attempts on the religious and moral
health of mankind.

Quoted in *N.Y. Times,* Paris, December 9, 1959

The world is interested only in making
money, enjoying life and getting ahead at all
costs, even unfortunately insolence.

Letter to a brother, quoted in *N.Y. Times,*
June 8, 1963

JOHN PAUL II (Karol Wojtyle)
(1920–)
Pope from 1978

The Easter Vigil (1966) (tr. Jerzy Peterkiewiecz)*

The human body in history dies more often
   and earlier than the tree.
Man endures beyond the doors of death in
   catacombs and crypts,
Man who departs endures in those who follow.
Man who follows endures in those departed.
Man endures beyond all coming and going
   in himself and in you.
                    "A Conversation with God Begins"

Speeches and Addresses

Christ will never approve that man be considered or may consider himself merely as a
means of production.
                                          June 1979

The exclusion of Christ from the history of
man is an act against man.

The chief rights are the rights of existence
and self-determination.
           Warsaw (quoted in *Time,* June 18, 1979)

When the institution of marriage is abandoned to human selfishness or reduced to a
temporary conditional arrangement that can
be terminated, we will stand up and affirm the
indissolubility of the marriage bond.

When the sacredness of life before birth is
attacked, we will stand up and proclaim that
no one ever has the authority to destroy unborn life.
          To American bishops (quoted in *Boston Globe,*
                               September 17, 1979)

Adultery in the heart is committed not only
because a man looks in a certain way at a
woman who is not his wife, but precisely because he is looking at a woman that way. Even
if he were to look that way at the woman who
is his wife, he would be committing the same
adultery in the heart.
   To his weekly audience, Rome, October 8, 1980,
               (quoted in *N.Y. Times,* October 12)

Husband and wife are also equal. The differences should be respected but not used to
justify the domination of one by the other. In

---

*This poem, and many others, were signed "A.J."
for "Andrzej Jawien," the future Pope's pen name.

collaboration with society, the Church must
collectively affirm and defend the rights of
women.

By virtue of their baptism they [divorced
couples who remarry] can and ought to participate in the life of the Church . . . live in complete continence; that is, by abstinence of acts
in which only married couples can engage.
       To Synod of Bishops, Rome, October 25, 1980
                     (quoted in *N.Y. Times,* October 26)

ANDREW JOHNSON
(1808–1875)
17th President of the United States

Speeches and Addresses

Tyranny and despotism can be exercised by
many, more rigorously, more vigorously, and
more severely, than by one.
                          To serenaders, April 8, 1866

Humble as I am, plebian as I may be
deemed, permit me in the presence of this
brilliant assemblage to enunciate the truth,
that courts and cabinets, the President and his
advisers, derive their power and their greatness
from the people.
        Senate, March 4, 1865, on being sworn in

LYNDON BAINES JOHNSON
(1908–1973)
36th President of the United States

I am a free man, an American, a United
States Senator, and a Democrat, in that order.
   Quoted by Adlai Stevenson, introduction, *Johnson,
                          A Time for Action* (1964)

I am a compromiser and manoeuverer. I try
to get *something*. That's the way our system
works.
         Quoted in *N.Y. Times,* December 8, 1963

The Great Society rests on abundance and
liberty for all. It demands an end to poverty
and racial injustice; to which we are totally
committed in our time.
     Address, University of Michigan, May 22, 1964*

---

*The Great Society was first proposed by Mo-Ti (d.
396 B.C.), then by Tzu Szu (d. 288 B.C.), grandson
of Confucius. It was discussed by Adam Smith, and
made current by the British Socialist writer Graham
Wallace, who wrote *The Great Society* in 1921.

We are trying to build a Great Society that will make your children and your grandchildren and the people three or four generations from today proud of what we are doing.
Talk, Montana Centennial delegation, White House, April 17, 1965

As it was 189 years ago, so today the cause of America is a revolutionary cause.
To students, White House, August 4, 1965

SAMUEL JOHNSON
(1709–1784)
English lexicographer, essayist, poet

Quoted in Boswell's *Life of Johnson*, 1791

A newswriter is a man without virtue, who lies at home for his own profit.*
November 11, 1758

Letters to the Earl of Chesterfield**

Is not a patron, my lord, one who looks with unconcern on a man struggling for life in the water, and, when he has reached ground, encumbers him with help? The notice which you have been pleased to take of my labors, had it been early, had been kind; but it has been delayed till I am indifferent, and cannot enjoy it; till I am solitary, and cannot impart it; till I am known, and do not want it.
February 7, 1754

Sir, a woman's preaching is like a dog's walking on his hind legs. It is not done well; but you are surprised to find it done at all.
July 31, 1763

The general rule is, that Truth should never be violated, because it is of the utmost importance to the comfort of life, that we should have a full security by mutual faith; and occasional inconvenience should be suffered that we may preserve it. There must however, be some exceptions.
June 13, 1764

I do not know, Sir, if the fellow be an infidel; but if he be an infidel, he is an infidel as a dog is an infidel, that is to say, he has never thought upon the subject.
October 19, 1769

A man who is converted from Protestantism to Popery parts with nothing; he is only superadding to what he already had. But a convert from Popery to Protestantism, gives up so much of what he has held as sacred as anything that he retains.
October 26, 1769

Every society has a right to preserve publick peace and order, and therefore has a good right to prohibit the propagation of opinions which have a dangerous tendency. . . . Every man has a right to liberty of conscience, and with that the magistrate cannot interfere. People counfound liberty of thinking with liberty of talking; nay, with liberty of preaching. . . . But, Sir, no member of society has a right to *teach* any doctrine contrary to what the society holds to be true.
Sir, the only method by which religious truth can be established is by martyrdom. . . . I am afraid there is no other way of ascertaining the truth, but by persecution on the one hand and enduring it on the other.
May 7, 1773

They [Americans] are a race of convicts, and ought to be thankful for anything we allow them short of hanging.*
March 27, 1775

Patriotism is the last refuge of a scoundrel.**
April 7, 1775

No man but a blockhead ever wrote except for money.

In all countries there has been fornication, as in all countries there has been theft; but there may be more or less of the one, as well as of the other, in proportion to the force of law. All men will naturally commit fornication, as all men will naturally steal. And, Sir, it is very absurd to argue, as has been often done, that prostitutes are necessary to prevent violent effects of appetite from violating the decent order of life; nay, should be permitted in order to preserve the chastity of our wives and daughters. Depend upon it, severe laws,

---

*Dr. Johnson's addition to Wotton's famous Latin pun: "An ambassador is an honest man, sent to lie abroad for the good of his country."
**In 1754 Johnson said to Boswell: "They [Chesterfield's Letters] teach the morals of a whore, and the manners of a dancing master."

---

*Many who bear the proudest names in American history are descended of persons released from debtors' jails in England, who served as indentured servants, i.e., serfs, or slaves, for a number of years. The British called them "convicts." They were merely the poor.
**"But let it be considered, he did not mean a real and generous love of our country, but that pretended patriotism which on so many, is a cloak for self interest."—Boswell.

steadily enforced, would be sufficient against these evils, and would promote marriage.

April 5, 1776

A poor man has no honor.

September 22, 1777

When we talk of pleasure, we mean sensual pleasure. When a man says, he had pleasure with a woman, he does not mean conversation, but something of a very different nature.

April 7, 1778

I am willing to love all mankind, except an *American*.

April 15, 1778

Were it not for imagination, Sir, a man would be as happy in the arms of a chambermaid, as of a duchess.

May 9, 1778

Many falsehoods are passing into uncontradicted history.

October 27, 1779

Every man has a right to utter what he thinks is truth, and every other man has a right to knock him down for it.

The whole of life is but keeping away the thoughts of death.

Nature has given women so much power that the law has very wisely given them little.

A decent provision for the poor is the true test of a civilization.

1780

Rasselas (1759)

Integrity without knowledge is weak and useless, and knowledge without integrity is dangerous and dreadful.

Ch. XI

Marriage has many pains but celibacy no pleasures.

Ch. XXVI

Taxation No Tyranny (1775)

All government is ultimately and essentially absolute.

The Rambler (1750–1752)

As all error is meanness, it is incumbent on every man who consults his own dignity, to retract it as soon as he discovers it, without fearing any censure so much as that of his own mind.

31

Curiousity is one of the permanent and certain characteristics of a vigorous intellect.

103

No man ever yet became great by imitation.

154

What are all the records of history, but narratives of successive villainies, of treasons and usurpations, massacres and wars?

175

The Idler (1758–1760)

Among the calamities of war may be justly numbered the diminution of the love of truth by the falsehoods which interest dictates and credulity encourages.

Promises, large promises, is the soul of advertising. . . . I cannot but propose it as a moral question to these masters of the public ear, whether they do not sometimes play too wantonly with our passions.

The Adventurer (1753–1754)

He has learned to no purpose, that is not able to teach.

He that never compares his notions with those of others, readily acquiesces in his first thoughts, and very seldom discovers the objections which may be raised against his opinions; he, therefore, often thinks himself in possession of truth, when he is only fondling an error long since exploded.

Dictionary (1755)

I am not so lost in lexicography as to forget that words are the daughters of earth, and that things are the sons of heaven.

Every quotation contributes something to the stability or enlargement of the language.

Preface

The Preface to Shakespeare (1765)

The irregular combinations of fanciful invention may delight a while, by that novelty of which the common satiety of life sends us all in quest; but the pleasures of sudden wonder are soon exhausted, and the mind can only repose on the stability of truth.

In the writing of other poets a character is too often an individual, in those of *Shakespeare* it is commonly a species.

Yet his real power is not shewn in the splendour of particular passages, but by the progress of his fable, and the tenour of his dialogue; and he that tries to recommend him by select quotations, will succeed like the pedant in *Hierocles,* who, when he offered his house to sale, carried a brick in his pocket as a specimen.

Shakespeare has no heroes; scenes are occupied only by men, who act and speak as the reader thinks that he should himself have spoken or acted on the same occasion . . . *Shakespeare* approximates the remote, and familiarizes the wonderful.

Shakespeare with his excellencies has likewise faults, and faults sufficient to obscure and overwhelm any other merit.

His first defect is that to which may be imputed most of the evil in books or in men. He sacrifices virtue to convenience, and is so much more careful to please than to instruct, that he seems to write without any moral purpose. . . . He makes no just distribution of good or evil. . . . He carries his persons indifferently through right and wrong. . . . This fault the barbarity of his age cannot extenuate, for it is always a writer's duty to make the world better, and justice is a virtue independent of time or place.

HANNS JOHST
(1890–killed in World War II)
German writer

Schlageter (1933)

When I hear the word "culture" I reach for my revolver. *

DR. ERNEST JONES
(1879–1958)
British psychoanalyst, biographer of Freud

Rationalization.

Coined term

The Psychology of Religion

Psychoanalysis fully confirms the view frequently put forward in a general way that sexuality is one of the most important sources of religious feeling.

Psychoanalysis can show by detailed investigation of the psychology of the various rituals

and other manifestations of the religious feeling that they contain an extensive, concealed, gratification of repressed sexuality, principally of the infantile and therefore of the incestuous kind.

The Life and Work of Sigmund Freud (1953)

Amid the turmoil of conflicting ideas in which we live . . . there seems to be one proposition commanding nearly universal assent: *The control man has secured over nature has far outrun his control over himself.*

Vol. 3

HOWARD MUMFORD JONES
(1892–1980)
American writer

Primer of Intellectual Freedom (1949)

Persecution is the first law of society because it is always easier to suppress criticism than to meet it.

Introduction

BEN JONSON
(c. 1573–1637)
English actor, poet, dramatist

"Explorata"

Naught that delights is sin.

I know of no disease of the soul but ignorance.

Tale of a Tub (1633)

Speak then the truth, and the whole truth, and nothing but the truth.

Every Man Out of his Humour (1599)

Art hath an enemy called Ignorance.

Love no man: trust no man: speak ill of no man to his face, nor well behind his back. . . . Spread yourself upon his bosom publicly, whose heart you would eat in private.

"To the Memory of My Beloved, the Author, Mr. William Shakespeare" (1623)

He was not of an age but for all time.

Cataline (1611)

Ambition, like a torrent, ne'er looks back;
And is a swelling, and the last affliction
A high minde can put off; being both a rebell
Unto the soule, and reason, and enforceth

---

*Other quoters use the word "Browning" in place of "revolver," and frequently attribute the remark to Goebbels, wrongly.

All laws, all conscience, trades upon religion,
And offereth violence to nature's selfe.
Act 3, sc. 2

"Random Thoughts"

Many might go to heaven with half the labour they go to hell if they would venture their industry the right way.

FLAVIUS JOSEPHUS (né Joseph ben Matthias)
(37–?105 A.D.)
Judean general, historian

Against Apion

Fools must be rejected not by arguments, but by facts.
II

JOSEPH JOUBERT
(1754–1824)
French essayist

Pensées (1842)

Enseigner, c'est apprendre deux fois.
To teach is to learn twice.

VICTOR JOSEPH ETIENNE DE JOUY
(1764–1846)
French writer

Without women, the beginning of our life would be helpless; the middle devoid of pleasure; and the end, of consolation.
Quoted in Schopenhauer, *Parerga* (1851)

WILLIAM (Iliya) JOVANOVICH
(1920–   )
American publisher, writer

. . . *Now, Barrabas* (1964)

The greatest vested interest is not property but ignorance.

JAMES JOYCE
(1882–1941)
Irish writer

A Portrait of the Artist as a Young Man (1916)

The artist, like the God of the creation, remains within or behind or beyond or above his handiwork, invisible, refined out of existence, indifferent, paring his fingernails.

Welcome, O life! I go to encounter for the millionth time the reality of experience and to forge in the smithy of my soul the uncreated conscience of my race.

Ulysses (1922)

It is as painful perhaps to be awakened from a vision as to be born.

A father, Stephen said, battling against hopelessness, is a necessary evil.

A man of genius makes no mistakes. His errors are volitional and are the portals of discovery.

History, Stephen said, is a nightmare from which I am trying to awake.

JULIAN (The Apostate)
(332–363 A.D.)
Roman emperor

Vicisti, Gallilaee!
You have conquered, Gallilean!
Dying words, attributed by Theodoret, *Historia Eccles*, 3, 20

JULIUS III (Gianmaria del Monte)
(1487–1555)
Pope from 1550

Learn, my son, with how little wisdom the world is governed.
Quoted in Büchmann, *Geflügelte Worte*

CARL GUSTAV JUNG
(1875–1961)
Swiss psychologist, psychiatrist*

Psyche and Symbol (1958)

Understanding does not cure evil, but it is a definite help, inasmuch as one can cope with a comprehensible darkness.

*President, International Psychoanalytical Society, before rejecting Freud, 1913. "The edifice of C.G. Jung's work is reminiscent of a cathedral . . . Like a cathedral with its altar, its cross and its rose window, this edifice has been erected *ad majorem Dei Gloriam*—to the greater glory of God—as is true of all valid creative efforts, often those which appear to be agnostically motivated."—Violet S. de Lazlo, editor of *Psyche and Symbol*

Instincts are the most conservative determinants of any kind of life.

XV

Communism is an archaic, primitive and therefore highly insidious pattern which characerizes primitive social groups. It implies lawless chieftainship as a vitally necessary compensation, a fact which can only be overlooked by means of a nationalistic one-sidedness, the prerogative of a barbarous mind.

XVI

Aion

The de-Christianization of our world, the Luciferian development of science and technology, and the frightful material and moral destruction left behind by the Second World War have been compared more than once with the *eschatological* events foretold in the New Testament. These, as we know, are concerned with the coming of the Antichrist.

The coming of the Antichrist is not just a prophetic prediction—it is an inexorable psychological law.

The subsequent developments that led to the Enlightenment and the French Revolution have produced a world-wide situation today which can only be called "Antichristian" in a sense that confirms the early Christian anticipation of the "end of time."

Psychology does not know what good and evil are in themselves; it knows them only as judgments about relationships.

Today as never before it is important that human beings should not overlook the danger of the evil lurking within them. It is unfortunately only too real, which is why psychology must insist on the reality of evil and must reject any definition that regards it as insignificant or actually non-existent.

Only with Christ did a devil enter the world as the real counterpart of God, and in early Jewish-Christian circles Satan, as already mentioned, was regarded as Christ's elder brother.

One must be positively blind not to see the colossal role that evil plays in the world. Indeed, it took the intervention of God himself to deliver humanity from the curse of evil, for without his intervention men would have been lost.

The Phenomenology of the Spirit in Fairy Tales (1945/1948)

But we continue to ask: what have all our other cultural achievements led to? The fearful answer is there before our eyes: man has been delivered from no fear, a hideous nightmare lies upon the world. So far reason has failed lamentably. . . . But already we are fascinated by the possibility of atomic fission and promise ourselves a Golden Age—the surest guarantee that the abomination of desolation will grow to limitless dimensions.

The Special Phenomenology of the Child Archetype (1940)

The popular faith in words is a veritable disease of the mind.

As civilization develops, the bisexual "primary being" turns into a symbol of the unity of personality, a symbol of the *self* where the war of opposites finds peace. . . . Just as every individual derives from masculine and feminine genes, and the sex is determined by the predomination of the corresponding genes, so in the psyche it is only the conscious mind, in a man, that has the masculine sign, while the unconscious is by nature feminine. The reverse is true in the case of a woman.

Transformation Symbolism in the Mass (1942/1954)

The realities of faith lie outside the realm of psychology.

Commentary on "The Secret of the Golden Flower" (1929)

The greatest and most important problems of life are all in a certain sense insoluble. . . . They can never be solved but only outgrown.

Let the convinced Christian believe, for that is the duty he has taken upon himself. The non-Christian has forfeited the grace of faith. (Perhaps he was cursed from birth in not being able to believe but only to know.)

Memories, Dreams, Reflections (1961)

The decisive question for man is: Is he related to something infinite or not? That is the telling question of life.

The more a man lays stress on false possessions, and the less sensitivity he has for what is essential, the less satisfying is his life.

The psyche is distinctly more complicated and inaccessible than the body. It is, so to speak, the half of the world which comes into existence only when we become conscious of it. For that reason the psyche is not only a personal but a world problem, and the psychiatrist has to deal with an entire world.

The more the critical reason dominates, the more impoverished life becomes; but the more of the unconscious, and the more of myth we are capable of making conscious, the more of life we integrate. Overvalued reason has this in common with political absolutism: under its dominion the individual is pauperized.

As far as we can discern, the sole purpose of human existence is to kindle a light in the darkness of mere being. It may even be assumed that just as the unconscious affects us, so the increase in our consciousness affects the unconscious.

"What nature leaves imperfect, the art perfects," say the alchemists. Man, I, in an invisible act of creation put the stamp of perfection on the world by giving it objective existence. This act we usually ascribe to the Creator alone, without considering that in so doing we view life as a machine calculated down to the last detail, which, along with the human psyche, runs on senselessly, obeying foreknown and predetermined rules. In such a cheerless clockwork fantasy there is no drama of man, world, and God; there is no "new day" leading to "new shores," but only the dreariness of calculated processes. . . . Human consciousness created objective existence and meaning, and man found his indispensable place in the great process of being.

Modern Man in Search of a Soul (1933) (tr. W.S. Bell and C.F. Payne)

What is essential in the work of art is that it should rise far above the realm of personal life and speak from the spirit and heart of mankind. The personal aspect is a limitation—and even a sin—in the realm of art. When a form of "art" is primarily personal it deserves to be treated as if it were a neurosis.

The artist's life cannot be otherwise than full of conflicts, for two forces are at war within him—on the one hand the common human longing for happiness, satisfaction and security in life, and on the other a ruthless passion for creation which may go so far as to override every personal desire.

The creative force can drain the human impulses to such a degree that the personal ego must develop all sorts of bad qualities—ruthlessness, selfishness and vanity (so-called "auto-eroticism")—and even every kind of vice, in order to maintain the spark of life and to keep itself from being wholly bereft.

The creative process has feminine quality, and the creative work arises from unconscious depths—we might say, from the realm of the mothers. Whenever the creative force predominated, human life is ruled and moulded by the unconscious as against the active will, and the conscious ego is swept along on a subterranean current, being nothing more than a helpless observer of events. The work in process becomes the poet's fate and determines his psychic development. It is not Goethe who creates 'Faust' but 'Faust' which creates Goethe.

A great work of art is like a dream; for all its apparent obviousness it does not explain itself and is never unequivocal.

The secret of artistic creation and of the effectiveness of art is to be found in the return to the state of *participation mystique*—to that level of experience at which it is man who lives and not the individual, and at which the weal or woe of a single human being does not count, but only human existence. This is why every great work of art is objective and impersonal, but none the less profoundly moves us each and all.

There appears to be a conscience in mankind which severely punishes the man who does not somehow and at some time, at whatever cost to his pride, cease to defend and assert himself, and instead confess himself fallible and human. Until he can do this, an impenetrable wall shuts him out from the living experience of feeling himself a man among men. Here we find a key to the great significance of true, unstereotyped confessions—a significance known in all the initiation and mystery cults of the ancient world, as is shown by a saying from the Greek mysteries: "Give up what thou hast, and then thou wilt receive."

Ch. II

However far-fetched it may sound, experience shows that many neuroses are caused by the fact that people blind themselves to their own religious promptings because of a childish passion for rational enlightenment. The psychologist of today ought to realize once and for all that we are no longer dealing with questions of dogma and creed. A religious attitude is an element in psychic life whose importance can hardly be overrated. And it is precisely for the religious outlook that the sense of historical continuity is indispensable.

Ch. III

Aging people should know that their lives are not mounting and unfolding, but that an inexorable inner process forces the contraction of life. For a younger person it is almost a sin—and certainly a danger—to be too much occupied with himself; but for the aging person it is a duty and a necessity to give serious attention to himself. After having lavished its light upon the world, the sun withdraws its rays in order to illumine itself.

In my picture of the world there is a vast outer realm and an equally vast inner realm; between these two stands a man, facing now one and now the other, and, according to his mood or disposition, taking the one for the absolute truth by denying or sacrificing the other.

It is easy enough to drive the spirit out of the door, but when we have done so the salt of life grows flat—it loses its savour.

Ch. VI

Art is a kind of innate drive that seizes a human being and makes him its instrument. The artist is not a person endowed with free will who seeks his own ends, but one who allows art to realize its purpose through him. As a human being he may have moods and a will and personal aims, but as an artist he is "man" in a higher sense—he is "collective man"—one who carries and shapes the unconscious, psychic forms of mankind.

Ch. VIII

When the primitive world disintegrated into spirit and nature, the West rescued nature for itself. It was prone to a belief in nature, and only became the more entangled in it with every painful effort to make itself spiritual. The East, on the contrary, took mind for its own, and by explaining away matter as mere illusion (*maya*), continued to dream in Asiatic filth and misery. But since there is only *one* earth and *one* mankind, East and West cannot rend humanity into two different halves.

Psychic reality exists in its original oneness, and awaits man's advance to a level of consciousness where he no longer believes in the one part and denies the other, but recognizes both as constituent elements of one psyche.

Ch. IX

Collected Works (1954)

The erotic instinct is something questionable, and will always be so. . . . It belongs, on the one hand, to the original animal nature of man, which will exist as long as man has an animal body. On the other hand, it is connected with the highest form of the spirit. . . . Too much of the animal disfigures the civilized human being, too much culture makes a sick animal.

Where love rules, there is no will to power; and where power predominates, there love is lacking. The one is the shadow of the other.

The symbol is not a sign that veils something everybody knows. Such is not its significance; on the contrary, it represents an attempt to elucidate, by means of analogy, something that still belongs entirely to the domain of the unknown or something that is yet to be.

. . . the self is a quantity that is supraordinate to the conscious ego. It embraces not only the conscious but also the unconscious psyche, and is therefore, so to speak, a personality which we *also* are. . . . There is little hope of our ever being able to reach even approximate consciousness of the self, since however much we may make conscious there will always exist an indeterminate and indeterminable amount of unconscious material which belongs to the totality of the self.

Vol. 7

The deeper "layers" of the psyche lose their individual uniqueness as they retreat farther and farther into darkness. "Lower down," that is to say as they approach the autonomous functional systems, they become increasingly collective until they are universalized and extinguished in the body's materiality, i.e., in chemical substances. The body's carbon is simply carbon. Hence "at bottom" the psyche is simply "world."

There are as many archetypes as there are typical situations in life. Endless repetition has engraved these experiences into our psychic constitution, not in the forms of images filled with content, but at first only as forms without content, representing merely the possibility of a certain type of perception and action.

Vol. 9

The concept of the archetype . . . is derived from the repeated observation that, for instance, the myths and fairytales of world literature contain definite motifs which crop up everywhere. We meet these same motifs in the fantasies, dreams, deliria, and delusions of individuals living today. . . . They impress, influence, and fascinate us. They have their origin in the archetype, which in itself is an irrepresentable, unconscious, pre-existent form that seems to be part of the inherited structure of the psyche and can therefore manifest itself spontaneously anywhere, at any time. Because of its instinctual nature, the archetype underlies the feeling-toned complexes and shares their autonomy.

The dream is a little hidden door in the innermost and most secret recesses of the psyche, opening into the cosmic night which was psyche long before there was any ego-consciousness, and which will remain psyche no matter how far our ego-consciousness may extend. . . . All consciousness separates; but in dreams we put on the likeness of that more universal, truer, more eternal man dwelling in the darkness of primordial night. There he is still the whole, and the whole is in him, indistinguishable from nature and bare of all egohood. Out of these all uniting depths arises the dream, be it never so childish, grotesque, and immoral.

Vol. 10

It is only through the psyche that we can establish that God acts upon us, but we are unable to distinguish whether these actions emanate from God or from the unconscious. We cannot tell whether God and the unconscious are two different entities. Both are border-line concepts for transcendental contents. But empirically it can be established, with a sufficient degree of probability, that there is in the unconscious an archetype of wholeness which manifests itself spontaneously in dreams, etc., and a tendency, independent of the conscious will, to relate other archetypes to this center. Consequently, it does not seem improbable that the archetype produces a symbolism which has always characterized and expressed the Deity. . . . The God-image does not coincide with the unconscious as such, but with a special content of it, namely the archetype of the self. It is this archetype from which we can no longer distinguish the God-image empirically.

Vol. 11

The unconscious is not just evil by nature, it is also the source of the highest good: not only dark but also light, not only bestial, semi-human, and demonic but superhuman, spiritual, and in the classical sense of the word, "divine."

Vol. 16, *The Practice of Psychotherapy*

Personality is the supreme realization of the innate idiosyncracy of a living being. It is an act of high courage flung in the face of life, the absolute affirmation of all that constitutes the individual, the most successful adaptation to the universal conditions of existence coupled with the greatest possible freedom for self-determination.

Vol. 17

The Integration of Personality (1939)

All ages before ours believed in gods in some form or other. Only an unparalleled impoverishment in symbolism could enable us to rediscover the gods as psychic factors, which is to say, as archetypes of the unconscious. No doubt this discovery is hardly credible as yet.

For woman is increasingly aware that love alone can give her her full stature, just as the man begins to discern that spirit alone can endow his life with its highest meaning. Fundamentally, therefore, both seek a psychic relation one to the other; because love needs the spirit, and the spirit love, for their fulfillment.

Contribution, *Analytical Psychology*, 1928

Nobody can deny that without the psyche there would be no world at all and still less a human world.

The weal or woe of the future will be decided neither by the attacks of wild animals nor the natural catastrophies nor by the danger of world-wide epidemics, but simply by the psychic changes in man.

Quoted in *Atlantic Monthly*, November 1957

A misunderstood development of the soul will inevitably carry a total psychological destruction. The actual situation is at this time so sinister that it is difficult not to see that the Creator is preparing another deluge to exterminate the human race.

"Questa e una filosofia," Milan, 1960

I know! I have had the experience of being gripped by something stronger than myself, something that people call God.

Attributed reply to question: "Do you believe in God?"

All personal secrets have the effect of sin or guilt.

Quoted in *Time*, August 22, 1969

Death is psychologically as important as birth. . . . Shrinking away from it is something unhealthy and abnormal which robs the second half of life of its purpose.

Quoted in *Time*, obituary, June 16, 1961

Called or Not Called, God is Present.

Carved on stone tablet over Jung's door.

JUNIUS
(c. 1769–1771)
Anonymous English letter writer*

Letters of Junius (1768–1772)

Let it be impressed upon your minds, let it be instilled into your children, that the Liberty of the Press is the Palladium of all the civil, political and religious rights of an Englishman.

Dedication

All despotism is bad; but the worst is that which works with the machinery of freedom.

To attack vices in the abstract, without touching persons, may be safe fighting, but it is fighting with shadows.

ANDOCHE JUNOT
(1771–1813)
French general

Moi, je suis mon ancêtre.
I am my own ancestor.

Attributed reply to questions, after he had been created Duke of Abrantes by Napoleon for a brilliant campaign in Portugal.

---

*The *Letters of Junius* have been attributed to several notable persons, Sir Philip Francis the likeliest.

JUSTINIAN I
(483–565 A.D.)
Byzantine emperor, surnamed "the Great"

The Institutes of Justinian (tr. Moyle)

Justice is the set and constant purpose which gives to every man his due. Jurisprudence is the knowledge of things divine and human, the science of the just and the unjust.

The precepts of the law are these: to live honestly, to injure no one, and to give every man his due.

Title I, bk. 1

In the law of persons, then, the first division is into free men and slaves. Freedom, from which men are called free, is a man's natural power of doing what he pleases, so far as he is not prevented by force or law; slavery is an institution of the law of nations, against nature subjecting one man to the dominion of another.

Title III, bk. 1

JUVENAL (Decimus Iunius Juvenalis)
(c. 60–140 A.D.)
Roman rhetorician, satirical poet

Satires

Probitas laudatur et alget.
Honesty is praised and starves.

Majestic mighty wealth is the holiest of our gods.

No. 1

No one ever became extremely wicked suddenly.

No. 2

Bitter poverty has no sharper pang than that it makes men ridiculous.

No. 3

Vitam inpendere vero.
Stake life upon truth.

Nemo malus felix.
No evil man is happy.

No. 4

Nothing is more intolerable than a wealthy woman.

No. 5

Oh, may the gods save us from a learned wife.

Quis custodiet ipsos custodes?
Who will watch the watchers?

Duas tantum res anxius optat,
Panem et circenses.
The people long eagerly for two things—
Bread and circuses.

Orandum est ut sit mens sana in corpore
sano.
Your prayer must be for a sound mind in a
sound body.

No. 10

Morte magis metuenda benectus.
Old age is more to be feared than death.

No. 11

No guilty man is ever acquitted at the bar of
his own conscience.

Revenge is always the delight of a little weak
and petty mind; of which you may straightway
draw proof from this, that no one so rejoices in
revenge as a woman.

No. 13

Crescit amor nummi quantum ipsa pecunia
crescit.
The love of money grows as the money itelf
grows.

No. 14

KABĪR
(1400–1499)
Hindu philosopher, reformer

Men have always looked before and after,
and rebelled against the existing order. But for
their divine discontent men would not have
been men, and there would have been no
progress in human affairs.
Quoted in *The American Scholar,* 1957

FRANZ KAFKA
(1883–1924)
Prague-born Austrian writer

Parables and Paradoxes: Paradise

We are sinful not merely because we have
eaten of the Tree of Knowledge, but also because we have not yet eaten of the Tree of
Life.

Letter to His Father

"And there is the fighting of vermin, which
not only sting but at the same time suck the
blood too, to sustain their own life. That is,
after all, what the professional soldier really is,
and that is what you are. You are unfit for
life . . ."
(Kafka puts these words in his father's mouth)

Aphorisms (tr. Willa and Edwin Muir)

You can hold back from the suffering of the
world, you have free permission to do so and it
is in accordance with your nature, but perhaps
this very holding back is the one suffering that
you could have avoided.

No. 99

Kafka Diaries

Parents who expect gratitude from their
children (there are even some who insist on it)
are like usurers who gladly risk their capital if
only they receive interest.

But what is it to be a writer? Writing is a
sweet, wonderful reward, but its price? During
the night the answer was transparently clear to
me: it is the reward for service to the devil.
This descent to the dark powers . . . of which
one no longer knows anything above
ground. . . . And what is devilish in it seems
to me quite clear. It is the vanity and the craving for enjoyment, which is forever whirring
around oneself or even around someone else
. . . and enjoying it.
Letter to Max Brod, July 5, 1922

The dream reveals the reality which conception lags behind. That is the horror of
life—the terror of art.
Quoted in Janouch, *Conversations with Kafka*
(1968)

Our world is merely a practical joke of God.
Quoted in *A Treasury of Jewish Quotations*

Youth is happy because it has the capacity to see Beauty. Anyone who keeps the ability to see Beauty never grows old.
Quoted in *Saturday Review,* October 2, 1976

I think we ought to read only the kind of books that wound and stab us.
Quoted in *N.Y. Times* Book Review

Only our concept of time makes it possible for us to speak of the Day of Judgment by that name; in reality it is a summary court in perpetual session.
Quoted in letter department, *Time*

IMMANUEL KANT
(1724–1804)
German philosopher*

Critique of Practical Reason (1788)

So act as to treat humanity, whether in thine own person or in that of any other, in every case as an end withal, never as a means only.

Critique of Pure Reason (1781)

Two things fill my mind with ever-increasing wonder and awe: The starry heavens above me and the moral law within me.

The only objects of practical reason are therefore those of *good* and *evil.* For by the former is meant an object necessarily desired according to a principle of reason; by the latter one necessarily shunned, also according to a principle of reason.

Our age is the age of criticism, to which everything must be subjected. The sacredness of religion, and the authority of legislation, are by many regarded as grounds for exemption from the examination by this tribunal. But, if they are exempted, they become the subjects of just suspicion, and cannot lay claim to sincere respect, which reason accords only to that which has stood the test of a free and public examination.

Supreme Being is, therefore, for the speculative reason, a mere ideal, though a faultless one, . . . the objective reality of which can neither be proved or disproved by pure reason.

*Descendant of Scottish family, Cant—*Brittanica,* 11th ed., vol. xv

All our knowledge begins with the senses, proceeds then to the understanding, and ends with reason. There is nothing higher than reason.

As the moral precept is at the same time my maxim, reason commanding that it should be so, I shall inevitably believe in the existence of God, and in a future life, and I feel certain that nothing can shake this belief, because all moral principles would be overthrown at the same time, and I cannot surrender them without becoming hateful in my own eyes.

All knowledge, if it refers to an object of pure reason, can be communicated.

Critique of Teleological Judgment (1790)

The value of life for us, measured simply by what we enjoy (by the natural end of the sum of all our inclinations, that is, by happiness), is easy to decide. It is less than nothing. For who would enter life afresh under the same conditions?
83, fn. 1

Doctrine of Virtue

By a lie a man throws away and, as it were, annihilates his dignity as a man.

Elements of Ethics

War itself, provided it is conducted with order and a sacred respect for the rights of civilians, has something sublime about it. . . . On the other hand, a prolonged peace favors the predominance of a more commercial spirit, and with it a debasing self-interest, cowardice, and effeminancy and tends to degrade the character of the nation.

The Metaphysics of Morals (1797)

A free will and a will subject to moral laws are one and the same.

Nothing in the whole world, or even outside of the world, can possibly be regarded as good without limitation, except a *good will.* No doubt it is a good and desirable thing to have intelligence, sagacity, judgment, and other intellectual gifts, by whatever name they may be called; it is also good and desirable in many respects to possess by nature such qualities as courage, resolution, and perseverance; but all these gifts of nature may be in the highest degree pernicious and hurtful if the will which directs them, or what is called the 'character' is not itself good.

It is therefore not inconsistent with the wisdom of nature that the cultivation of reason which is essential to the furtherance of its first and unconditional object, the production of good will, should, in this life at least, in many ways limit, or even make impossible, the attainment of happiness, which is its second and conditioned object.

Ch. I

There is . . . only a single categorical imperative and it is this: *Act only on that maxim through which you can at the same time will that it should become a universal law!*

Perhaps a fall of personal despotism, or avariciousness, or tyrannical oppression may be accomplished by revolution, but never a true reform in ways of thinking. Rather, new prejudices will serve as well as old ones to harness the great unthinking masses.

Ch. II

Perpetual Peace (1795)

With men, the state of nature is not a state of peace, but war.

Prolegomena to Any Future Metaphysics (1783) (ed. Lewis W. Beck)

There are only four transcendant ideas. . . . In accordance with these cosmological Ideas, there are only four kinds of dialectical assertions of pure reason, which, being dialectical, prove that to each of them, on equally specious principles of pure reason a contradictory assertion stands opposed: . . .
  1. *Thesis:* The world has, as to time and space a beginning (limit).
     Antithesis: The world is, as to time and space, infinite.
  2. *Thesis:* Everything in the world consists of [elements that are] simple.
     Antithesis: There is nothing simple, but everything is composite.
  3. *Thesis:* There are in the world causes through freedom.
     Antithesis: There is no freedom, but all is nature.
  4. *Thesis:* In the series of the world-causes there is some necessary being.
     Antithesis: There is nothing necessary in the world, but in this series all is contingent.

*"There is no categorical imperative but only the operation of instincts and interests more or less subject to discipline and mutual adjustment."—Santayana, *Egotism in German Philosophy*.

This Is My Own

Art to my thoughts, art for myself, has always been as though of inner necessity a by-product of living, or a co-product with living—and all the interests and activities that living is—of that essential self of which they both are expression.

Lectures

In law a man is guilty when he violates the rights of others. In ethics he is guilty if he only thinks of doing so.

Suicide is not abominable because God prohibits it; God prohibits it because it is abominable.

The desire of a man for a woman is not directed at her because she is a human being, but because she is a woman. That she is a human being is of no concern to him.

Konigsberg, 1775

Prudence reproaches; conscience accuses.
On Ethics

The death of dogma is the birth of reality.

God, freedom, and immortality are untenable in the light of pure reason.

Quoted in Noyes, *Views of Religion*

WALTER KAUFMANN
(1921–1980)
American philosopher

The Faith of a Heretic (1961)

Faith means intense, usually confident, belief that is not based on evidence sufficient to command assent from every reasonable person.

Prologue

Faith in immortality, like belief in God, leaves unanswered the ancient question: is God unable to prevent suffering, and thus not omnipotent? or is he able and not willing it and thus not merciful? And is he just?

Hope is as great an enemy of courage as is fear.

Ch. XII, 98

Nietzsche (1950)

Paul substituted faith in Christ for the Christlike life.

Ch. 12, II

NIKOS KAZANTZAKIS
(1883–1957)
Greek writer

The Saviors of God (1923)

Die every day. Be born again every day. Deny everything you have every day. The superior virtue is not to be free but to fight for freedom.

It is not God who will save us, it is we who will save God—by battling, by creating, and by transmuting matter into spirit.

Report to Greco (1957)

God is not man's ancestor, but his descendant.

———

I hope for nothing.
I fear nothing.
I am free.

Inscribed on tomb at Heraklion

ALFRED KAZIN
(1915–   )
American writer

Telling Lives

To write is in some way to cut the seemingly automatic pattern of violence, destructiveness, and death wish. To write is to put the seeming insignificance of human existence into a different perspective. It is the need, the wish, and, please God, the ability, to reorder our physical faith.

JOHN KEATS
(1795–1821)
English poet

Letters

I am certain of nothing but the holiness of the Heart's affections, the truth of Imagination. What the Imagination seizes as Beauty must be truth—whether it existed before or not,—for I have the same idea of all our passions as of Love: they are all, in their sublime, creative of essential Beauty.

To Benjamin Bailey, November 22, 1817

I have not the slightest feeling of humility towards the Public—or to anything in existence,—but the eternal Being, the Principle of Beauty,—and the Memory of great Men.

To J. H. Reynolds, April 9, 1818

The only means of strengthening one's intelligence is to make up one's mind about nothing—to let the mind be a thoroughfare for all thoughts.

To George and Georgiana Keats,
September 21, 1819

"Ode on a Grecian Urn" (1819)

Thou still unravish'd bride of quietness,
Thou foster-child of silence and slow time,
Sylvan historian, who canst thus express
A flowery tale more sweetly than our rhyme:
What leaf-fring'd legend haunts about thy
    shape
Of deities or mortals, or of both,
In Tempe or the dales of Arcady?

St. 1

Heard melodies are sweet, but those un-
    heard
Are sweeter; therefore, ye soft pipes, play
on.

St. 2

When old age shall this generation waste,
Thou shalt remain, in midst of other woe
Than ours, a friend to man, to whom thou
    say'st,
"Beauty is truth, truth beauty,—that is all
Ye know on earth, and all ye need to
    know."*

St. 5

"Lamia" (1820)

Love in a hut, with water and a crust,
Is—Love, forgive us!—cinders, ashes, dust;
Love in a palace is perhaps at last
More grievous torment than a hermit's
    fast:—

Lines 1–4

Do not all charms fly
At the mere touch of cold Philosophy?

Line 230

Philosophy will clip an Angel's wings.

Line 234

———

*"There is no greater poem in English than the 'Ode on a Grecian Urn.' "—J. Donald Adams, *N.Y. Times,* March 8, 1964. Mr. Adams restored the original, 1820, placement of the quotation marks in the two last lines.

"Ode to a Nightingale" (1820)

> Darkling I listen; and for many a time
>   I have been half in love with easeful
>   Death.
>   St. VI

> Perhaps the self-same song that found a path
>   Through the sad heart of Ruth, when,
> sick for home,
> She stood in tears amid the alien corn;
>   The same that oft-times hath
> Charm'd magic casements, opening on the
>   foam
> Of perilous seas, in faery lands forlorn.
>   St. VII

"On First Looking Into Chapman's Homer" (1817)

> Then felt I like some watcher of the skies
>   When a new planet swims into his ken;
> Or like stout Cortez, when with eagle eyes
>   He star'd at the Pacific—and all his men
> Look'd at each other with a wild surmise—
>   Silent, upon a peak in Darien.

This grave contains all that was mortal of a young English poet, who, on his deathbed, in the bitterness of his heart at the malicious power of his enemies, desired these words to be graven on his tombstone, "Here lies one whose name was writ in water."
>   Epitaph (on his tombstone, Rome)

HELEN KELLER
(1880–1968)
American writer, Socialist, member IWW

The Story of My Life (1902)

There is no king who has not had a slave among his ancestors, and no slave who has not had a king among his.*

Let Us Have Faith (1940)

No nation is wise enough to rule another.

The Open Door (1957)

Security is mostly a superstition. It does not exist in nature. . . . Life is either a daring adventure or nothing.

The country is governed for the richest, for the corporations, the bankers, the land speculators, and for the exploiters.
>   Letter, 1911

---

*"Every king springs from a race of slaves, and every slave has had kings among his ancestors."—Plato.

KEMPIS, *see* Thomas à Kempis

KENKŌ HOSHI
(fl. 14th century A.D.)
Japanese Buddhist

The Harvest of Leisure (c. 1330)

If life were eternal all interest and anticipation would vanish. It is uncertainty which lends it satisfaction.

So long as people, being ill-governed, suffer from hunger, criminals will never disappear. It is extremely unkind to punish those who, being sufferers from hunger, are compelled to violate laws.
>   Quoted in Sinclair, *The Cry for Justice*

JOHN F(itzgerald) KENNEDY*
(1917–assassinated 1963)
35th President of the United States

Profiles in Courage (1956)

Compromise does not mean cowardice.

Speeches and Addresses

I believe in an America where the separation of Church and State is absolute.
>   Houston Ministerial Association,
>   September 12, 1960

We stand today on the edge of a new frontier. . . .
>   Nomination Acceptance Speech, 1960

The world is very different now. For man holds in his mortal hands the power to abolish all forms of human poverty and all forms of human life.

Let every nation know, whether it wishes us well or ill, that we shall pay any price, bear any burden, meet any hardship, support any friend, oppose any foe to assure the survival and the success of liberty.

Let us never negotiate out of fear; but let us never fear to negotiate.

---

*Following Wilson, most Presidents have employed ghost writers; three of Kennedy's were Theodore Sorenson, Arthur Schlesinger, Jr., and John K. Galbraith, who wrote the best-known lines of the inaugural.

And so, my fellow Americans: ask not what your country can do for you—ask what you can do for your country.*
Inaugural address, January 10, 1961

Mankind must put an end to war or war will put an end to mankind.
Address to the United Nations, September 25, 1961

Those who make peaceful revolutions impossible will make violent revolutions inevitable.
To Latin-American diplomats, March 12, 1962

The great enemy of truth is very often not the lie—deliberate, contrived, and dishonest—but the myth—persistent, persuasive and realistic. Too often we hold fast to the clichés of our forebears.
Commencement, Yale, 1962

I see little of more importance to the future of our country and our civilization than full recognition of the place of the artist. If art is to nourish the roots of our culture, society must set the artist free to follow his vision wherever it takes him.

Where power corrupts, poetry cleanses.
Amherst College, honoring Robert Frost, October 26, 1963

Free people do not accept the claim of historical inevitability for the communist revolution. . . . The great revolution in the history of man, past, present and future, is the revolution of those determined to be free.
Note to Khrushchov, 1961

ELLEN KEY
(1849–1926)
Swedish feminist, writer

Love has been in perpetual strife with monogamy.

Instead of defending "free love," which is a much-abused term capable of many interpretations, we ought to strive for the freedom of love; for while the former has come to imply freedom for any sort of love, the latter must only mean freedom for a feeling which is worthy of the name love.

A great poet has seldom sung of lawfully wedded happiness, but often of free and secret love; and in this respect, too, the time is coming when there will no longer be one standard of morality for poetry, and another for life.
Quoted in Sprading, *Liberty and the Great Libertarians* (1913)

FRANCIS SCOTT KEY
(1729–1843)
American poet

"The Star-Spangled Banner" (1814)*

The land of the free and the home of the brave.

Then conquer we must, when our cause it is just,
And this be our motto: "In God is our trust."

JOHN MAYNARD KEYNES
(1883–1946)
British economist

The End of Laissez-Faire (1925)

Marxian Socialism must always remain a portent to the historians of opinion—how a doctrine so illogical and so dull can have exercised so powerful and enduring an influence on the minds of men, and, through them, the events of history.
Ch. 3

Essays in Persuasion (1931)

When the accumulation of wealth is no longer of high social importance, there will be great changes in the code of morals. We shall be able to rid ourselves of many of the pseudo-moral principles which have hag-ridden us for two hundred years, by which we have exalted some of the most distasteful of human qualities into the position of highest virtues.
Pt. V

The General Theory of Employment, Interest, and Money (1936)

It is ideas, not vested interests, which are dangerous for good or evil.

---

*Justice Holmes in his Memorial Day address, Keene, New Hampshire, said in 1884: "We pause . . . to recall what our country has done for each of us, and to ask ourselves what we can do for our country in return." Browning in "Home Thoughts From Abroad" wrote: "Here and here did England help me: how can I help England?—say?"

*Originally called "Defense of Fort M'Henry"; declared national anthem, 1931.

Capitalism . . . is not intelligent, it is not beautiful, it is not just, it is not virtuous—and it doesn't deliver the goods.
> Statement, 1933, quoted in *N.Y. Times,*
> April 27, 1975

HAJJI KHALIFAH
(? –1658)
Turkish writer

As to its [tobacco's] harmful effects there is no doubt. . . . Tobacco is medically noxious in that it makes morbid the aerial essence. . . . For the men of dry temperament . . . it is in no wise permissible. It will increase his dryness and will constantly dessicate the moisture of his lungs.
> Quoted in *An Anthology of Islamic Literature*
> (1964)

RUHOLLAH KHOMEINI
(1901–   )
Ayatollah, Iranian leader

Islam is justice. Dictatorship is the greatest sin in the religion of Islam. Fascism and Islamism are absolutely incompatible.

Islam prohibits alcoholic drinks. . . . drinking makes people lose their heads and impedes clear thinking. Even music dulls the mind.
> Interview with Oriana Fallaci, *N.Y. Times*
> *Magazine,* October 7, 1979

There is no room for play in Islam. . . . It is deadly serious about everything.

All western governments are just thieves. Nothing but evil comes from them.
> Speech at Qum, reported in *Time,* January 7, 1980

NIKITA S(ergeyevich) KHRUSHCHOV
(1894–1971)
Soviet Russian ruler*

Creative work in literature and art must be permeated with the spirit of a struggle for

Communism. . . . Particular attention must be devoted to enhancing further the part played by the press in all aspects of ideological, political and organizational work.
> Report to Central Committee, 1956

We are convinced that sooner or later capitalism will perish, just as feudalism perished earlier. . . . All the world will come to Communism. History does not ask whether you want it or not.
> Interview, Asahi Shimbum, Osaka, June 18, 1957

Get rid of the devil and the priest will have nothing to do.
> Quoted by Richard Nixon, *N.Y. Times,*
> July 18, 1959

Whether you like it or not, history is on our side. We will bury you.
> Address to ambassadors, Kremlin; quoted in *Look,*
> September 15, 1959*

President Roosevelt proved that a President could serve for life. Truman proved that anyone could be elected. Eisenhower proved that your country can be run without a President.
> To Joe Curran, president National Maritime Union;
> quoted by Pearson, August 19, 1960

Peaceful coexistence of the Socialist and capitalist countries is an objective necessity for the development of human society.
> Draft Program for Soviet Communist Party
> Congress, July 30, 1961

Capitalism isn't just an unjust economic system. It's a way of life that leads to a corruption of important values. Television is only one example.
> Interview, Norman Cousins, *Saturday Review,*
> November 7, 1964

Liberation wars will continue to exist as long as imperialism exists.
> 1961; repeated in *N.Y. Times,* July 11, 1965

*A misquotation or misinterpretation of this statement caused considerable international mischief. On September 20th Khrushchov told the N.Y. *Herald Tribune:* "The expression I used was distorted because what was meant was not the physical burial of any people, but the question of the historical force of development. . . . Socialism, Communism, will take the place of Capitalism and Capitalism therefore will be, so to speak, buried."

"Khrushchov Remembers"

We Communists believe that capitalism is a hell in which laboring people are condemned to slavery.

Quoted in *Life, N.Y. Times,* 1970*

SÖREN KIERKEGAARD
(1813–1855)
Danish theologian

Preparations for a Christian Life

Let us worship God again in simplicity, instead of making a fool of him in splendid edifices.

The intention of Christianity was to change everything.

"The Splendid Moment"

But all desire is egotistic. Now, to be sure, the lover's desire is not egotistic in respect to the one he loves, but the desire of both in conjunction is absolutely egotistic insofar as they in their union and love represent a new ego. And yet they are deceived; for in the same moment the race triumphs over the individual, the race is victorious, and the individuals are debased to its bidding.

"The Stages of Life's Road"

Ah, wicked thoughtlessness which thus interprets Sacred History like profane history, which makes Christ a man! But can one, then, learn anything from history about Jesus? No, nothing. Jesus Christ is the object of faith—one either believes in him or is offended by him, for "to know" means precisely that such knowledge does not pertain to him. History can, therefore, to be sure, give one knowledge in abundance; for "knowledge" annihilates Jesus Christ.

Christendom has done away with Christianity, without being aware of it. Therefore, if anything is to be done about it, the attempt must be made to reintroduce Christianity.

The process of becoming a Christian (that is, being changed into the likeness of God) is, in a human sense, a greater torment and wretchedness and pain than the greatest conceivable human suffering, and moreover a crime in the eyes of one's contemporaries. And thus will it always be; that is, if becoming

---

*Khrushchov denied the authenticity of his memoirs.

a Christian in reality means becoming contemporaneous with Christ. And if becoming a Christian does not have that meaning, then all your chatter about becoming a Christian is a vanity, a delusion, and a snare, and likewise a blasphemy and a sin against the Holy Ghost.

Diary (ed. Peter P. Rohde)

They have changed Christianity (into) too much of a *consolation,* and forgotten that it is a *demand* upon men.

Not until a man has become so utterly unhappy, or has grasped the woefulness of life so deeply that he is moved to say, and mean it: Life for me has no value—not until then is he able to make a bid for Christianity.

Philosophical Fragments (1844)

For if the God does not exist it would of course be impossible to prove it; and if he does exist it would be folly to attempt it.

. . . the paradox is the source of the thinker's passion, and the thinker without a paradox is like a lover without feeling; a paltry mediocrity.

3

Works of Love

The truth must essentially be regarded as in conflict with this world; the world has never been so good, and will never become so good that the majority will desire the truth.

Edifying Discourses

The fact of being able to occupy himself with the future is then an indication of man's nobility; the conflict with it is most enobling. He who strives with the present strives with a single thing against which he can use his entire strength. He who fights with the future has a more dangerous enemy, he can never remain ignorant about himself; for he fights with himself. The future is not; it borrows its strength from the man himself, and when it has tricked him out of this, then it appears outside of him as the enemy he must meet. Let a man then be as strong as he will, no man is stronger than himself.

The Last Years: Journals 1853–55 (1966)

The daily press is the evil principle of the modern world. . . . The capacity of the newspaper for degeneration is sophistically without limit, since it can always sink lower and lower in its choice of readers. At last it will stir up all those dregs of humanity which no state or government can control.

Oh Luther, Luther; your responsibility is great indeed, for the closer I look the more clearly do I see that you overthrew the Pope—and set the public on the throne.

Luther nailed up 95 theses on the church door; that was a fight about doctrine. Nowadays one might publish one single thesis in the papers: "Christianity does not exist."

To be a Christian is the most terrible of all torments, it is—and must be—to have one's hell on earth . . . One shudders to read what an animal must suffer which is used for vivisection; yet this is only a fugitive image of the suffering involved in being a Christian—in being kept alive in a state of death.

It is a fearful thing to fall into the hands of the living God.
> Quoted by John Updike, *The New Yorker,* 1982

(Alfred) JOYCE KILMER
(1886–1918)
American poet

"The Peacemaker"
> What matters Death, if Freedom be not dead?
> No flags are fair, if Freedom's flag be furled.
> Who fights for Freedom, goes with joyful tread
> To meet the fires of Hell against him hurled.

MARTIN LUTHER KING, JR.
(1929–assassinated 1968)
American Black leader, Nobel Prize 1964

Strength and Love (1963)

Nothing in the world is more dangerous than a sincere ignorance and conscientious stupidity.

Speeches

If man hasn't discovered something that he will die for, he isn't fit to live.
> June 23, 1963

I have a dream that some day every valley shall be exalted, every hill and mountain shall be made low, the rough places will be made plains, and the crooked places will be made straight, and the glory of the Lord shall be revealed, and all flesh shall see it together.

I have a dream that my four little children will one day live in a nation when they will not be judged by the color of their skin, but by the content of their character.
> Civil Rights March on Washington, D.C., August 28, 1963

The question is not whether we will be extremists, but what kind of extremists we will be. . . . The nation and the world are in dire need of creative extremists.
> 1963 (published 1968)

The choice today is not between violence and non-violence. It is either non-violence or non-existence.
> Nobel Prize acceptance speech, December 11, 1964

The Negro needs the white man to free him from his fears. The white man needs the Negro to free him from his guilt.
> Quoted in *N.Y. Times* obituary, April 7, 1968

Segregation is the offspring of an illicit intercourse between injustice and immorality.
> Attributed

REV. CHARLES KINGSLEY
(1819–1875)
English founder of Christian Socialism, clergyman, poet, novelist

---

Health and Education (1874)

To be discontented with the divine discontent, and to be ashamed with the noble shame, is the very germ and first upgrowth of all virtue.
> "The Science of Health"

Truth, for its own sake, has never been a virtue with the Romish clergy. Father Newman informs us that it need not, and on the whole, ought not to be; that cunning is the weapon which heaven has given to the saints wherewith to withstand the brute male force of the wicked world which marries and is given in marriage.
> Review of Froude's *History of England*

ALFRED CHARLES KINSEY
(1894–1956)
American physician, author

Sexual Behavior of the Human Male (1953)

Males do not represent two discrete populations, heterosexual and homosexual. Not all things are black nor all things white. The living world is a continuum in each and every one of its aspects. The sooner we learn this concerning human sexual behavior the sooner we shall reach a sound understanding of the realities of sex.

RUDYARD KIPLING
(1865–1936)
British poet, Nobel Prize 1907

"The White Man's Burden"
Title of poem, 1899

"Epitaphs of the War"

If any question why we died,
Tell them because our fathers lied.

"Tomlinson"

The sin ye do by two and two
ye must pay for one by one!
Line 60

"The Betrothed"

And a woman is only a woman, but a good
    cigar is a smoke.
St. 25

"Gentlemen Rankers"

Damned from here to Eternity.
Refrain

"The Song of the Dead" (1896)

If blood be the price of admiralty,
Lord God, we ha' paid in full!

"The Ballad of East and West"

Oh, East is East, and West is West, and
    never the twain shall meet,
Till Earth and Sky stand presently at God's
    great Judgment Seat;
But there is neither East nor West, Border,
    nor Breed, nor Birth,
When two strong men stand face to face,
    though they come from the ends of the
    earth!

"Recessional" (1897)

The tumult and the shouting dies;
    The Captains and the Kings depart:
Still stands Thine ancient sacrifice
    An humble and a contrite heart.

Lord God of Hosts, be with us yet,
Lest we forget—lest we forget!
St. 2

"The Press"

King over all the children of pride
Is the Press—the Press—the Press!

Words are, of course, the most powerful
drug used by mankind.
Speech, February 14, 1923

HENRY KISSINGER
(1923–   )
U.S. Secretary of State

Intelligence is not all that important in the
exercise of power, and is often, in point of
fact, useless.
Interview with Oriana Fallaci, Esquire, June 1975

(Horatio Herbert) LORD KITCHENER
(1850–1916)
British field-marshal

Don't talk to me about atrocities; all war is
an atrocity.
To Lloyd George; quoted in Soldier from the War
Returning

RUDOLF KJELLEN
(1864–1922)
Swedish geographer

Lebensraum.
Living space.
Originated word, appropriated by Karl Haushofer

FRIEDRICH MAXIMILLIAN VON KLINGER
(1752–1831)
German dramatist

Sturm und Drang
Storm and Stress
Play title, 1776

KNIGHTS OF LABOR
(Founded 1869)
Workingmen's organization formed to defend the interests of labor

The alarming development and aggressiveness of great capitalists and corporations, unless checked, will inevitably lead to the
pauperization and hopeless degradation of the
working masses. It is imperative if he desire to
enjoy the full blessings of life, that a check be
placed upon unjust accumulation and the
power of evil of aggregate wealth.
(First) Constitution, 1869

To secure for both sexes equal pay for equal work.

Constitution, 1878

Eight hours of work, eight hours of rest, eight hours for what we will.

Slogan, first Labor Day parade, September 1882

JOHN KNOX
(1505–1572)
Scottish reformer, historian

The First Blast of the Trumpet Against the Monstrous Regiment of Women (1558)

The nobility both of England and Scotland are inferior to brute beasts, for they do that to women which no male among the common sort of beasts can be proved to do to their females: that is, they reverence them, and quake at their presence; they obey their commandments, and that is against God.

One man with God is always in the majority.

Inscription, Reformation Monument, Geneva

HANS KOHN
(1891–1971)
Professor of History, Smith College

Revolution and Dictatorship

In our days, on a shrinking earth, with a growing interdependence of all people, a dynamic self-centered nationalism becomes the gravest menace to peace (which it despises) and to the progress of civilization (which it denies). . . . The new nationalism threatens chaos at a moment when all efforts should be bent on building up of universal order. . . . Seen in this light, Fascism becomes, and prides itself in being, the counter-revolution against, and the denial of, history and humanity.

ANDREW (David) KOPKIND
(1935–   )
American writer

Revolution is what societies do instead of committing suicide, when the alternatives are exhausted and all the connections that bind men's lives to familiar patterns are cut.

To be a revolutionary is to love your life enough to change it, to choose struggle instead of exile, to risk everything with only the glimmering hope of a world to win.

Quoted in *N.Y. Times Magazine,*
November 10, 1968

BARON RICHARD VON KRAFFT-EBING
(1840–1902)
German neurologist, professor of psychiatry, Vienna

Psychopathia Sexualis (1866)

The propagation of the human race is not left to mere accident or the caprices of the individual, but is guaranteed by the hidden laws of nature which are enforced by a mighty, irresistible impulse.

Man puts himself at once on the level of the beast if he seeks to gratify lust alone, but he elevates his superior position when, by curbing the animal desire, he combines with the sexual functions ideas of morality, of the sublime, and of the beautiful.

If man were deprived of sexual fulfillment and the nobler enjoyments arising therefrom, all poetry, and probably all moral tendency, would be eliminated from his life.

Love unbridled is a volcano that burns down and lays waste all ground around it; it is an abyss that devours all—honour, substance and health.

It is of great psychological interest to follow up the gradual development of civilization and the influence exerted by sexual life upon habits and morality. The gratification of the sexual instinct seems to be the primary motive in man as well as in beast.

The episodes of moral decay always coincide with the progression of effeminancy, lewdness and luxuriance of the nations.

We find that the sexual instinct, when disappointed and unappeased, frequently seeks and finds a substitute in religion.

Purely sensual love is never true or lasting, for which reason first love is, as a rule, but a passing infatuation, a fleeting passion.

True love is rooted in the recognition of the moral and mental qualities of the beloved person.

Woman loves with her whole soul. To woman love is life, to man it is the joy of life.

But where the body of the beloved person is made the sole object of love, or if sexual pleasure *only* is sought without regard to the communion of a soul and mind, true love does not exist. Neither is it found among the disciples of Plato, who love the soul *only* and despise sexual enjoyment. In the one case the body is the fetish, in the other the soul, and love is fetishism.

Pt. 1

IVAR KREUGER
(1880–suicide 1932)
Swedish industrialist

But what certainty is there about money, which, after all, holds all the world together? It depends on the good will of a few capitalists to keep to the agreement that one metal is worth more than another.

Quoted in *The New Yorker,* October 13, 1959

PRINCE PETER (Alekseyevich) KROPOTKIN
(1842–1921)
Russian geographer, philosophical Anarchist

"Anarchism"

Anarchism (is) the name given to a principle or theory of life and conduct under which society is conceived without government—harmony in such a society being obtained, not by submission to law, or by obedience to any authority, but by free agreements concluded between the various groups, territorial and professional, freely constituted for the sake of production and consumption, as also for the satisfaction of the infinite variety of needs and aspirations of a civilized being.

The Anarchists consider the wage-system and capitalist production altogether as an obstacle to progress. . . . The state was, and continues to be, the chief instrument for permitting the few to monopolize the land, and the capitalists to appropriate for themselves a quite disproportionate share of the yearly accumulated surplus of production.

When men are reasonable enough to follow their natural instincts, they will unite across the frontiers and constitute the Cosmos. They will have no need of law-courts or police, will have no temples and no public worship, and use no money—free gifts taking the place of exchanges.

Freedom of the press, freedom of association, the inviolability of domicile, and all the rest of the rights of man are respected so long as no one tries to use them against the privileged class. On the day they are launched against the privileged they are thrown overboard.

Contribution, *Britannica,* 11th ed., vol. 1

Paroles d'un révolté (1884)

The word *state* is identical with the word *war.*

The Great French Revolution

Revolutions, we must remember, are always made by minorities.

The ultimate aim of society is the reduction of the function of government to *nil*—that is, to a society without government, to an-archy.

Quoted in *Revolutionary Pamphlets,* ed. Roger Baldwin, 1927

KU KLUX KLAN
(Founded 1915*)
Racist secret society

This is an institution of Chivalry, Humanity, Mercy, and Patriotism; embodying in its genius and its principles all that is chivalric in conduct, noble in sentiment, generous in manhood, and patriotic in purpose.

"Principles of the Ku Klux Klan," quoted in Lester and Wilson, *The Ku Klux Klan*

---

*This Ku Klux Klan, which is still active in the American South, was patterned after a similar organization, also called the Ku Klux Klan, which aimed to suppress the newly-acquired rights of black people for several years after the Civil War.

JEAN DE LA BRUYÈRE
(1645–1696)
French essayist, moralist

Les Charactères (1688)

Tout notre mal vient de ne pouvoir être seule.

All our evils come from not being able to be alone.*

A wise man neither suffers himself to be governed, nor attempts to govern others.

Women run to extremes; they are either better or worse than men.

Children are overwhelming, supercilious, passionate, envious, inquisitive, egotistical, idle, fickle, timid, intemperate, liars and dissemblers; they laugh and weep easily, are excessive in their joys and sorrows, and that about the most trifling subjects; they bear no pain, but like to inflict it on others; already they are men.

Time, which strengthens friendship, weakens love.

There is nothing of which we are so fond, and withal so careless, as life.

There are only two ways by which to rise in this world, either by one's own industry or by the stupidity of others.

If poverty is the mother of crime, lack of sense is the father.

There are but three great events in a man's life: birth, life, and death. Of birth he is insensible, he suffers when he dies, and he forgets to live.

Most men employ the first half of their lives in making the other half miserable.

---

*"All men's misfortunes spring from their hatred of being alone: gambling, luxury, wine, women, ignorance, suspicion, envy, forgetfulness of ourselves and of God."—British edition, 1713.

It [philosophy] consoles us for the small achievements in life, and the decline of strength and beauty; it arms us against poverty, old age, sickness and death, against fools and evil sneerers; it enables us to live without a wife, and makes us able to endure her with whom we live.

The impossibility for me to prove that there is no God proves to me His existence. . . . I feel that there is a God, and I do not feel that there is none; that satisfies me, all the reasoning in the world is useless; I conclude there is a God.

LACTANIUS FIRMIANUS
(c. 260–c. 340)
The African-born "Christian Cicero"

Divinae institutiones
Everyone should remember that the union of the two sexes is meant only for the purpose of procreation. . . . The mind is guilty of adultery even if it merely pictures to itself a vision of carnal pleasure.

Bk. vi, ch. 23

PAUL LAFARGUE
(1842–1911)
French socialist (Marx's son-in-law)

The Right to Be Lazy

A strange delusion possesses the working classes of the nations where capitalist civilization holds its sway. This delusion drags in its train the individual and social woes which for two centuries have tortured humanity. This delusion is the love of work.

In capitalist society, work is the cause of all intellectual degeneracy, of all organic deformity. . . . Look at the noble savage whom the missionaries of trade and the traders of religion have not yet corrupted with Christianity, syphilis, and the dogma of work, and then look at our miserable slaves of the machines.

Jesus in his Sermon on the Mount preaches idleness: "Consider the lilies of the field. . . ." Jehovah, the bearded and angry god, gave his worshippers the supreme example of ideal laziness: after six days of work he rested for all eternity.

If, uprooting from its heart the vice which dominates and degrades its nature, the working class were to rise in its terrible strength, not to demand the Rights of Man . . . not to demand the Right to work . . . but to forge a brazen law forbidding any man to work more than three hours a day, the earth, the old earth, trembling with joy, would feel a new universe leaping within her.

MARQUIS DE LAFAYETTE
(1757–1834)
French statesman, general

When the government violates the people's rights, insurrection is, for the people and for each portion of the people, the most sacred of the rights and the most indispensable of duties.
> To Constituent Assembly, February 20, 1790

For a nation to love liberty, it is sufficient that she knows it; to be free, it is sufficient that she wills it.
> Quoted in Paine, *The Rights of Man*

If the liberties of the American people are ever destroyed, they will fall by the hands of the clergy.
> Attributed

ROBERT M(arion) LAFOLLETTE, SR.
(1855–1925)
American political and reform leader

The cure for the evils of democracy is more democracy.
> Progressive Party campaign slogan

Let no man think that we can deny civil liberty to others and retain it for ourselves. . . . When zealous agents of the Government arrest suspected "radicals" without warrant, hold them without prompt trial, deny them access to counsel and admission of bail . . . we have shorn the Bill of Rights of its sanctity as a shield to every American citizen.
> Quoted in *The Progressive*, March, 1920

JEAN DE LA FONTAINE
(1621–1695)
French writer

Fables (1668)

> *C'est double plaisir de tromper le trompeur.*
> It is double pleasure to deceive the deceiver.

Man is ice to truth and fire to falsehood.

Anyone entrusted with power will abuse it if not also animated with the love of truth and virtue, no matter whether he be a prince, or one of the people.

The strongest passion is fear.

Nothing is as dangerous as an ignorant friend; a wise enemy is to be preferred.

ALPHONSE DE LAMARTINE
(1790–1869)
French writer

Méditations poétiques (1820)

> *La paix à tout prix.*
> Peace at any price

Man is a fallen god who remembers the heavens.
> Sermon 2

Nouvelles harmonies poétiques et réligeuses (1830)

> God is but a word invoked to explain the world.

Voyage en Orient (1835)

> . . . museums, the cemeteries of the arts.

Marseillaise de la Paix (1841)

> I am a fellow citizen of all men who think. Truth; that is my country.

———

> The revolution had mysteries, but no enigmas.
> Indirect quotation, Lord Acton, *Lectures on the French Revolution*

CHARLES LAMB
(1775–1834)
English writer

O money, money, how blindly thou hast been worshipped, and how stupidly abused! Thou art health, and liberty, and strength; and he that has thee may rattle his pockets at the foul fiend.
> Letter to Coleridge, June 7, 1809

"A Farewell to Tobacco"

> For thy sake, Tobacco, I
> Would do anything but die.

John Woodvil (1799)

> Men die but once, and the opportunity
> Of a noble death is not an everyday fortune:
> It is a gift noble spirits pray for.
> Act 2

ROBERT HUGHES FÉLICITÉ DE LAMENNAIS
(1782–1854)
French priest, metaphysician, sociologist

Words of a Believer (1834)

He who asks himself how much justice is worth, profaneth justice in his heart; and he who stops to calculate what liberty will cost hath renounced liberty in his heart. Liberty and justice will weigh you in the balance in which you have weighed them.

Justice is the harvest of nations.
Justice is the bread of nations.

Liberty is the wealth of nations.
Liberty is the repose of nations.
Liberty is the glory of nations.

JULIEN OFFRAY DE LA METTRIE
(1709–1751)
French physician, philosopher

Atheism is the only means of ensuring the happiness of the world, which has been rendered impossible by the wars brought about by theologians.

The soul is only the thinking part of the body, and with the body it passes away. When death comes, the farce is over, therefore let us take our pleasure while we can.
Indirect quotation, *Britannica*, 11th ed., from "L'Art de jouir" and other works

CORLISS LAMONT
(1902–   )
American philosopher

The wise man looks at death with honesty, dignity and calm, recognizing that the tragedy it brings is inherent in the great gift of life.
Contribution, *Journal of Philosophy*, January, 1965

EDWIN H(erbert) LAND
(1909–   )
American scientist, inventor

We work by exorcising incessant superstition that there are mysterious tribal gods against you. Nature has neither rewards nor punishments, only consequences. You can use science to make it work for you. There's only nothingness and chaos out there until the human mind recognizes it.
Attributed

WALTER SAVAGE LANDOR
(1775–1864)
English writer

Imaginary Conversations (1824–1829)

Every great writer is a great reformer.

If there were no falsehoods in the world, there would be no doubt; if there were no doubt, there would be no inquiry; if no inquiry, no wisdom, no knowledge, no genius.

Pericles and Aspasia (1836)

Study is the bane of boyhood, the oil of youth, the indulgence of manhood, and restorative of old age.

"Dying Speech of an Old Philosopher"

I strove with none; for none was worth my
    strife;
Nature I loved, and, next to Nature, Art;
I warmed both hands before the fire of life;
It sinks, and I am ready to depart.
written on his 75th birthday

SUSANNE K(nauth) LANGER
(1895–   )
American writer

Tradition and the Individual Talent

Art is the objectivication of feeling, and the subjectification of nature.

WILLIAM LANGLAND
(c. 1330–c. 1400)
English poet

Piers Plowman (1362–1390)

For ignorantia non excusat, as ich have heard. Ignorance does not excuse . . .

Chastity without charity lies chained in
    hell,
It is but an unlighted lamp.

LÂO - TZU (né Li Urh)
(c. 565 B.C.)
Chinese philosopher, founder of Taoism*

Tâo Teh King

To yield is to be preserved whole.
To be bent is to become straight.

---

*Britannica calls him Lâo-Tsze, his work the *Tâo Teh King;* Waley calls it *Tâo Teh Ching;* it is variably translated The Way, or The Way of Life.

To be hollow is to be filled.
To be tattered is to be renewed.
To be in want is to possess.
To have plenty is to be confused.

One who would guide a leader of men in
the uses of life
Will warn him against the use of arms for
conquest.

Even the finest arms are an instrument of
evil;
An army's harvest is a waste of thorns.

In time of war men, civilized in peace,
Turn from their higher to their lower
nature.
But triumph is not beautiful.
He who thinks a triumph beautiful
Is one with a will to kill.
The death of a multitude is cause for
mourning.
Conduct your triumph as a funeral.

A sound leader's aim
Is to open people's hearts,
Fill their stomachs,
Calm their wills,
Brace their bones,
And so to clarify their thoughts and cleanse
their needs
That no cunning meddler could touch
them:
Without being forced, without strain or
constraint,
Good government comes of itself.

To be constantly without desire is the way to
have a vision of the mystery (of heaven and
earth):
For constantly to have desire is the means
by which their limitations are seen.

It is better to say nothing and to hold fast to
the mean (between too much and too little
confidence in heaven and earth).

The truth is that some creatures go before
and others follow behind,
Some breathe one way, and others breathe
another,
Some feel strong, and others feel weak,
Some like constructing and others like destroying.
This is why the sage has nothing to do with
the excessive,
the extravagant, or with being exalted.

To know men is to be wise:
To know one's self is to be illumined.

To conquer men is to have strength:
To conquer one's self is to be stronger still,
And to know when you have enough is to be
rich.

To die and not be lost, is the
real blessing of a long life.

To rejoice in conquest is to rejoice in
murder.

It is the way of Tao not to act from any personal motive, to conduct affairs without feeling the trouble of them, to taste without being
aware of flavour, to account the great as small
and the small as great, to recompense injury
with kindness.

Do away with learning and grief will not be
known.
Do away with sageness and eject wisdom,
and the people will be more benefited a
hundred times. . . .
Do away with artifice and eject gains, and
there will be no robbers and thieves.

Without even going out of the door
One can know the whole world.

There is no greater curse than the lack of
contentment.
No greater sin than the desire for possession.
Therefore he who is contented with contentment shall always be content.

To produce without possessing; to work
without expecting; to enlarge without
usurping: this is the supreme virtue.

He who follows the path of virtue becomes
as a little child.

He who knows the Eternal Law is tolerant;
Being tolerant, he is impartial;
Being impartial, he is kingly;
Being kingly, he is in accord with Nature;
Being in accord with Nature, he is in accord
with Tâo;
Being in accord with Tâo, he is eternal.
And his whole life is preserved from harm.

Of the best rulers
The people (only) know they exist;
The next best they love and praise;
The next they fear;
And the next they revile.

LA ROCHEFOUCAULD, *see* **Rochefoucauld.**

HAROLD J(oseph) LASKI
(1893–1950)
British political scientist

Plan or Perish (1945)

Free enterprise and the market economy mean war; socialism and planned economy mean peace. We must plan our civilization or we must perish.

It is not by accident that our schools and colleges, our universities and foundations, even the churches, are the instruments of big business. It is no accident that the press is now a branch of big business too. It would be madness to let the purposes or the methods of private enterprise set the habits of the age of atomic energy.

BISHOP HUGH LATIMER
(c. 1485–burned at the stake for heresy, 1555)
Bishop of Worcester

Who is the most diligent bishop and prelate in all England? . . . It is the devil . . . he is never out of his diocese.

You rich men . . . remember that thy riches be not thy own, but thou art but a steward over them.
                          Sermon on the Plowers, 1548

Say the truth, and shame the devil.
                          Sermon, 1552

Play the man, Master Ridley; we shall this day light such a candle, by God's grace, in England, as I trust shall never be put out.
                          To Nicholas Ridley, at the stake

WILLIAM L(eonard) LAURENCE
(1888–1977)
Science writer

The Atomic Age began at exactly 5:30 Mountain War Time on the morning of July 15, 1945, on a stretch of semi-desert land about 50 airline miles from Alamogordo, New Mexico.

And just at that instance there rose from the bowels of the earth a light not of this world, the light of many suns in one.
                          N. Y. Times, September 26, 1945

JOHANN KASPAR LAVATER
(1741–1801)
Swiss-born German physiognomist

Aphorisms on Man (c. 1788)

He knows not how to speak who cannot be silent. . . . Loudness is impotence.

Who will sacrifice nothing, and enjoys all, is a fool.

Let none turn over books or scan the stars in quest of God who sees Him not in man.

The public seldom forgives twice.

He who has not forgiven an enemy has never yet tasted one of the most sublime enjoyments of life.

D(avid) H(erbert) LAWRENCE
(1885–1930)
British writer

"Pornography and Obscenity"

What is pornography to one man is the laughter of genius to another.

If a woman hasn't got a tiny streak of harlot in her, she's a dry stick as a rule.

Every man has a mob self and an individual self, in varying proportions.

And there are, of course, many people who are genuinely repelled by the simplest and most natural stirrings of sexual feeling. But these people are perverts who have fallen into hatred of their fellow man: thwarted, disappointed, unfulfilled people, of whom, alas, our civilization contains so many.

Pornography is the attempt to insult sex, to do dirt on it. This is unpardonable.
                          Contribution to *This Quarter* (Paris, 1929)

Studies in Classic American Literature (1922, written 1916)

Men are freest when they are most unconscious of freedom.

The world fears a new experience more than it fears anything. Because a new experience displaces so many old experiences. . . . The world doesn't fear a new idea. It can pigeon-hole any idea. It can't pigeon-hole a new experience.

Away with eternal truth. Truth lives from day to day, and the marvellous Plato of yesterday is chiefly bosh today.

Sin is a queer thing. It isn't the breaking of divine commandments. It is the breaking of one's own integrity.

The Defence of Lady Chatterly

Marriage is only an illusion, if it is not lastingly and radically phallic, if it is not bound to the sun and the earth, to the moon, to the stars and the planets, to the rhythm of the seasons, the years, the lustra, and the centuries. Marriage is nothing if it is not based on a correspondence of blood. For blood is the substance of the soul.

The Letters of D.H. Lawrence (ed. Aldous Huxley, 1932)

My great religion is a belief in the blood, the flesh, as being wiser than the intellect.

_____

I worship Christ, I worship Jehovah, I worship Pan, I worship Aphrodite. But I do not worship hands nailed and running with blood, upon a cross, nor licentiousness, nor lust. I want them all, all the gods. They are all God.
Quoted by Kenneth Rexroth, preface, *Selected Poems by D.H. Lawrence*

The great mass of humanity should never learn to read or write.
Quoted in *N.Y. Times,* December 20, 1956

Man is willing to accept woman as an equal, as a man in skirts, as an angel, a devil, a baby-face, a machine, an instrument, a bosom, a womb, a pair of legs, a servant, an encyclopedia, an ideal or an obscenity; the one thing he won't accept her as, is a human being of the female sex.
Quoted in *N.Y. Times,* May 15, 1966

HALLDÓR LAXNESS
(1902–   )
Icelandic author, Nobel Prize 1955

It is hard to say whether man was one of nature's mistakes from the outstart, or whether he has by degrees developed into being the only known beast that enjoys killing his own kin.

. . . man is also unique as a moral beast. Paradoxically, the killing of one man by his fellow men, whether in the case of a common murder, or collectively, as in war, is never practiced without a moral justification on the killer's side. It is not far from the point to say that morality is the prerogative of mankilling.
Contribution, *N.Y. Times,* February 9, 1973

EMMA LAZARUS
(1849–1887)
American poet

"The New Colossus" (1883)

Give me your tired, your poor,
Your huddled masses yearning to breathe free,
The wretched refuse of your teeming shore,
Send these, the homeless, tempest-tossed, to me;
I lift my lamp beside the golden door!
(inscribed on the Statue of Liberty)

GUSTAVE LEBON
(1841–1931)
French physician, psychologist

Psychologie des foules (1895)

All the civilizations we know have been created and directed by small intellectual aristocracies, never by people in the mass. The power of crowds is only to destroy.

The populace is sovereign, and the tide of barbarism mounts. The divine right of the masses is about to replace the divine right of kings.

WILLIAM E(dward) H(artpole) LECKY
(1838–1903)
Irish essayist, historian

History of the Rise and Influence of the Spirit of Nationalism in Europe (1871)

There is no wild beast so ferocious as Christians who differ concerning their faith.

In one age the persecutor burned the heretic; in another, he crushed him with penal laws; in a third, he withheld from him places

of emolument and dignity; in a fourth, he subjected him to excommunication of society.
Each stage of advancing toleration marks a
stage in the decline of dogmatism and of the
increase of the spirit of truth.

History of European Morals (1872)

Herself the supreme type of vice, she [the
prostitute] is ultimately the most efficient
guardian of virtue. But for her, the unchal-
lenged purity of countless happy homes would
be polluted, and not a few who, in the pride of
their untempted chastity, think of her with an
indignant shudder, would have known the agony of remorse and despair. On that one degraded and ignoble form are concentrated the
passions that might have filled the world with
shame. She remains, while creeds and civilizations rise and fall, the eternal priestess of humanity, blasted for the sins of the people.

Vol. 2, ch. 5

LE CORBUSIER
(pseudonym of Charles Edouard Jeanneret)
(1887–1965)
French architect

Vers une architecture (1923)

Une maison est une machine-à-habiter.
A house is a machine to live in.

ROBERT E(dward) LEE
(1807–1870)
Confederate general

Letters

In this enlightened age there are few, I believe, but that will acknowledge that slavery as
an institution is a moral and political evil in
any country. . . . I think it, however, a greater
evil to the white man than to the black race,
and while my feelings are strongly on behalf of
the latter, my sympathies are more strong for
the former.

To Mrs. Lee, December 6, 1856

The blacks are immeasurably better off here
than in Africa, morally, socially, and physically. . . . How long their subjugation may be
necessary is known and ordered by a wise Merciful Providence.

To Mrs. Lee, December 27, 1856

It is well that war is so terrible—lest we
should grow too fond of it.

To James Longstreet, December 13, 1862

Madam, don't bring up your sons to detest
the United States Government. Recollect that
we form one country now. Abandon all these
local animosities, and make your sons
Americans.

Advice to a Southern Lady

BARON GOTTFRIED WILHELM
LEIBNITZ
(1646–1716)
German philosopher

The Monadology (1714)

There are two kinds of truths: *those of reasoning* and *those of fact.* The truths of reasoning are necessary and their opposite is
impossible; the truths of fact are contigent and
their opposites are possible.

33

LENIN (Vladimir Ilyich Ulyanov)
(1870–1924)
Russian teacher, revolutionary, Communist
leader*

"What Is To Be Done?" (1902)**

Without a revolutionary theory there can be
no revolutionary movement.

One Step Forward, Two Steps Backward (1904)

The fundamental thesis of dialectics is: there
is no such thing as abstract truth, truth is always concrete.

The Task of the Proletariat (1917)

Democracy is but one form of *state,* and we
Marxists are opposed to *all* and every *kind* of
state.

---

*The name "Lenin" was first used on the pamphlet
"What Is To Be Done?," 1902. His wife, Nadezhda
Krupskaya, whom he called his "comrade," believed
it came from the Lena River, near which the family
lived. Lenin also used the names Talin, Karpov,
Starek, and Petrov.
**This, and the majority of quotations that follow,
were also published in "Soviet World Outlook" by
the U.S. State Department in 1954. There are
scores of forgeries and misquotes still current. In
The Hoaxers (Brandon Press, 1970), Morris Komin-
sky exposes the 19 most notorious Lenin fabrica-
tions—as well as hoaxes and forgeries attributed to
Washington, Lincoln, and others.

Mankind may pass directly from capitalism into Socialism, i.e., into social ownership of the means of production. . . . Socialism is bound sooner or later to ripen into Communism, whose banner bears the motto: "From each according to his ability, to each according to his needs."

State and Revolution (1917; published 1918)

Democracy for an insignificant minority, democracy for the rich—that is the democracy of capitalistic society.

But democracy is by no means a limit one may not overstep; it is only one of the stages in the course of development from feudalism to capitalism, and from capitalism to Communism.

While the state exists there is not freedom. When there is freedom, there will be no state.

Letter to American Workers, August 20, 1918

Even if for every hundred correct things we committed 10,000 mistakes, our revolution would still be—and it will be in the judgment of history—great and invincible; for this is the first time that not a minority, not the rich alone, not the educated alone, but the real masses, the overwhelming majority of the working people are themselves building a new life and are by their own experience solving the most difficult problems of socialist organization.

Proletariat Revolution and Renegade Kautsky (1918)

Dictatorship is power based directly upon force and unrestricted by any laws. The revolutionary dictatorship of the proletariat is power won and maintained by the violence of the proletariat against the bourgeoisie, power that is unrestricted by any laws.

"A Great Beginning" (June 1919)

Notwithstanding all the liberating laws that have been passed, woman continues to be a *domestic slave,* because *petty housework* crushes, strangles, stultifies and degrades her, chains her to the kitchen and to the nursery, and wastes her labor on barbarously unproductive, petty, nerve-wracking, stultifying and crushing drudgery. The real *emancipation of women,* real Communism, will begin only when a mass struggle . . . is started against this petty domestic economy, or rather, when it is

transformed on a mass scale into a large scale Socialist economy.

Selected Works (U.S. State Department publication, 1954)

The periodical and non-periodical press must be (and all publishing enterprises must be) entirely subordinated to the Central Committee of the Party, . . . publishing enterprises must not be permitted to abuse their authority by pursuing a policy that is not entirely the Party policy.

Vol. 10

Religion is the opium of the people. Religion is a kind of spiritual vodka in which the slaves of capitalism drown their human shape and their claim for any decent human life.

"Socialism and Religion" (1905), Vol. 11

Never play with insurrection; but, having begun it, make up your mind to go through with it to the end.

Vol. 17

Collected Works

People always have been the foolish victims of deception and self-deception in politics, and they always will be until they have learnt to seek out the *interests* of some class or other behind all moral, religious, political and social phrases, declarations and promises. . . . Every old institution, however absurd and rotten it may appear, is kept in being by the force of one or the other of the ruling classes.

Vol. 19

Seizure of power is the point of the uprising; its political task will be clarified after the seizure. To delay action is the same as death.
Letter to Central Committee, eve of November Revolution, November 6, 1917

If Socialism can only be realized when the intellectual development of *all* the people permits it, then we shall not *have* Socialism for at least 500 years.

If compromise continues, the revolution disappears.
Speech, November 27, 1917, quoted in John Reed, *Ten Days That Shook the World*

The Jewish bourgeoisie are our enemies, not as Jews but as bourgeoisie. The Jewish worker is our brother.
Speech, Council of People's Commissars, August 9, 1918

Communism is Soviet power plus the electrification of the whole country.
> Report to 8th Congress, December 22, 1920

Every man who occupies himself with the construction of a God, or merely even agrees to it, prostitutes himself in the worst way, for he occupies himself not with activity, but with self-contemplation and self-reflection, and tries thereby to deify his most unclean, most stupid, and most servile features and pettinesses.

From the social and not the personal point of view, all God-creating is nothing but the tender self-contemplation of the dull *petite bourgeoisie,* the feeble Philistine, the dreamy self-reviling, doubting and tired bourgeois.
> Quoted in Fülop-Muller, *The Mind and Face of Bolshevism*

Do not deny the Terror. Don't minimize the evils of a Revolution.
> To Lincoln Steffens; quoted in Justin Kaplan, *Lincoln Steffens, a Biography* (1975)

Give me four years to teach the children and the seed I have sown will never be uprooted.
> Quoted by Duranty, *N.Y. Times Magazine**

The worst enemies of the new radicals are the old liberals.
> Attributed

In the last analysis, the success of our struggle will be determined by the fact that Russia, China and India constitute the overwhelming majority of the population of the globe.
> Deathbed statement, quoted by Chairman Mao to André Malraux in *Anti-Memoirs*

What else could we have done.
> Last words, according to *N.Y. Times,* requoted April 21, 1968

LEO XIII (Gioacchino Pecci)
(1810–1903)
Pope from 1878

Arcanum divinae sapientiae, February 10, 1880**

The husband is the chief of the family and the head of the wife.

Divorce is born of perverted morals, and leads, as experience shows, to vicious habits in public and private life.

Immortale Dei, November 1, 1885

To despise legitimate authority, no matter in whom it is invested, is unlawful, it is rebellion against God's will.

Just as the end at which the Church aims is by far the noblest of all ends, so is its authority the most exalted of all authority, nor can it be looked upon as inferior to the civil power, or in *any manner* dependent upon it.

The liberty of thinking and publishing whatsoever each one likes, without any hindrances, is not in itself an advantage over which society can wisely rejoice. On the contrary, it is the fountainhead and origin of many evils.

To exclude the Church, founded by God Himself, from life, from laws, from the education of youth, from domestic society, is a grave and fatal error. A state from which religion is banished can never be well regulated.

The equal toleration of all religions . . . is the same as atheism.

Quod apostolici muneris, December 28, 1878

The Church . . . enjoins that the right of property and its disposal, which are derived from nature, should in every case remain inviolate.

Rerum novarum, May 15, 1891*

The Church has never neglected to adapt itself to the genius of nations.

Let it be laid down in the first place, that humanity is destined to remain as it is.

It is impossible to reduce human society to one dead level. Socialists may in that intent do their utmost, but all striving against nature is in vain.

Women, again, are not suited for certain occupations; a woman is by nature fitted for home-work, and it is that which is best adopted at once to preserve her modesty and promote the good bringing-up of children and the well-being of the family.

---

*Saint Francis Xavier is quoted as saying, "Give me the children until they are seven, and anyone may have them afterwards."

**The encyclicals are quoted alphabetically.

*The *Britannica,* 11th ed., states that this encyclical was influenced by Cardinal Manning. It has been called an answer to Marx.

The death sentence is a necessary and efficacious means for the Church to attain its ends when rebels against it disturb the ecclesiastical unity, especially obstinate heretics who cannot be restrained by any other penalty from continuing to disturb ecclesiastical order.
> Preface, vol. 2, *Book of Canon Law*, by M. de Luca, S.J., (Rome 1901)

LEONARDO DA VINCI
(1452–1519)
Florentine painter, sculptor, architect, engineer, inventor

Note Books (c. 1500)

Experience never errs; what alone may err is our judgment, which predicts effects that cannot be produced by our experiments.

Nature is full of infinite causes that have never occurred in experience.

Nature never breaks her own laws.

Iron rusts from disuse, stagnant water loses its purity, and in cold weather becomes frozen; even so does inaction sap the vigors of the mind.

Necessity is the mistress and guardian of nature. Necessity is the theme and artificer of nature, the bridle, and eternal law.

II

[Three classes]: Those who see. Those who see when they are shown. Those who do not see.
> Quoted by Madariaga, *Saturday Review,* April 22, 1967

COUNT GIACOMO LEOPARDI
(1798–1837)
Italian poet

"Song of the Wild Cock"

A time will come when this Universe and Nature itself will be extinguished. . . . Of the entire world and of the vicissitudes and calamities of all created things there will remain not a single trace, but a naked silence and a most profound stillness will fill the immensity of space. And so before ever it has uttered or understood, this admirable and fearful secret of universal existence will be obliterated and lost.

IGNACE LEPP
(1909–1966)
French priest, psychotherapist

Death and Its Mysteries (1968)

Love for another which included no love of self would not be human; in fact, it is psychologically impossible.

. . . the more the fear of death is repressed the greater harm it does.

In fact, almost all who commit suicide exhibit schizoid tendencies. All have broken or lost the sense of those vital values which bind men to one another, the world, and history. In this sense we may say the suicide is dead long before he kills himself.

It can be said, without fear of exaggeration, that the whole of Christianity is founded on the mysterious bond that its founder established between death and love. . . . For the authentic Christian, death can never be separated from love.

The awareness of dying for something great and noble strips death of its absurd character, not only for those who die, but those who survive.

MAX LERNER
(1902–   )
American educator, writer

Life is a protracted struggle against the Adversary, who is man himself.
> Contribution, *Saturday Review,* December 5, 1959

The press is the most class-conscious segment of big business, since its stock in trade consists of the legends and folklore of capitalism.
> Contribution, *St. Louis Post-Dispatch* symposium, December 1938

GOTTHOLD EPHRAIM LESSING
(1729–1781)
German critic, dramatist

Emilia Galotti (1772)

Nothing under the sun is accidental.
> Act iv

A heretic is a man who sees with his own eyes.
Quoted in Noyes, *Views of Religion*

LEUCIPPUS
(fl. 450 B.C.)
Greek philosopher, founder Atomistic Theory

The sum of things is unlimited, and they all change into one another. The All includes the empty as well as the full. The worlds are formed when atoms fall into the void and are entangled with one another; and from their motion as they increase in bulk, arises the substance of the stars.
Summary of Leucippus' theory by Diogenes Laërtius (tr Hicks)

JOHN L(lewellyn) LEWIS
(1880–1969)
American labor leader

"It Won't Happen Here"

Here in this country the worst Fascists are those who, disowning Fascism, preach enslavement to capitalism under the cloak of liberty and the Constitution. They steal not only wages but honor.
Contribution, *N.Y. Times Magazine*

You can't dig coal with bayonets.
Testimony, Congressional Committee, March 1, 1956

(Harry) SINCLAIR LEWIS
(1885–1951)
American novelist, Nobel Prize 1930

Main Street.
Book title (1920)

Babbitt.
Book title (1922)

It Can't Happen Here.
Book title (1935)*

All prizes, like all titles, are dangerous.

Between the Pulitzer Prize, the American Academy of Arts & Letters, amateur boards of censorship, and the inquisition of earnest liter-

*A reference to Fascism.

ary ladies, every compulsion is put upon writers to become safe, polite, obedient and sterile.
Letter refusing Pulitzer Prize, May 6, 1926

Our American professors like their literature clear and cold and pure and very dead.
Nobel Prize address, December 12, 1930

God damn the society that will permit such poverty! God damn the religions that stand for such a putrid system!
Spoken to Frazier Hunt, quoted in his *One American;* also in Mark Schorer's biography, *Sinclair Lewis: An American Life* (1961.)

KARL LIEBKNECHT
(1871–assassinated 1919)
German Socialist

The enemy is at home.
Speech on outbreak of war, 1914

WILHELM LIEBKNECHT
(1826–1900)
German Socialist

The essence of revolution lies not in the means, but in the ends. Violence has been for thousands of years a reactionary factor.
Quoted frequently in Berlin newspapers

A(bbott) J(oseph) LIEBLING
(1904–1963)
American journalist

Freedom of the press is guaranteed to those who own one.
Contribution, *The New Yorker,* May 14, 1960

ABRAHAM LINCOLN
(1809–assassinated 1865)
16th President of the United States

Speeches, Addresses, etc.

Upon the subject of education, not presuming to dictate any plan or system respecting it, I can only say that I view it as the most important subject which we as a people may be engaged in. That everyone may receive at least a moderate education . . . appears to be an object of vital importance.

For my part, I desire to see the time when education—and by its means, morality, sobriety, enterprise and industry—shall become much more general than at present.

First public address, Sangamo County,
March 9, 1832

These capitalists generally act harmoniously, and in concert, to fleece the people.

Illinois legislature, January 11, 1837

Any people anywhere, being inclined and having the power, have the *right* to rise up, and shake off the existing government, and form a new one that suits them better. This is a most valuable, a most sacred right—a right, which we hope and believe, is to liberate the world. Nor is this right confined to cases in which the whole people of an existing government, may choose to exercise it. Any portion of such people that *can, may* revolutionize, and make their *own,* of so much of the territory as they inhabit. More than this, *a majority* of any portion of such people may revolutionize, putting down *a minority,* intermingled with, or near about them, who may oppose their movement.

House of Representatives, replying to President Polk
on Mexico, January 12, 1848

And, inasmuch [as] most good things are produced by labor, it follows that [all] such things of right belong to those whose labor has produced them. But it has so happened in all the ages of the world, that *some* have labored, and *others* have, without labor, enjoyed a large proportion of the fruits. This is wrong, and should not continue. To [secure] to each laborer the whole product of his labor, or as nearly as possible, is a most worthy object of any good government.

Fragment of a Tariff Discussion, December 1, 1847

Be not deceived. Revolutions do not go backward.

The ballot is stronger than the bullet.

Let us draw a cordon . . . around the slave estates, and that hateful institution, like a reptile poisoning itself, will perish of its own infamy.

Speech, May 19, 1856

Now I protest against the counterfeit logic which concludes that, because I do not want a black woman for a *slave* I must necessarily want her for a *wife.* I need not want her for either. I can just leave her alone.

On Dred Scott decision, Springfield, Ill.,
June 26, 1857

"A house divided against itself cannot stand."

I believe this Government cannot endure, permanently half slave and half free.

I do not expect the Union to be dissolved—I do not expect the house to fall—but I do expect it will cease to be divided. . . . Either the opponents of slavery will arrest the further spread of it, and place it where the public mind shall rest in the belief that it is in the course of ultimate extinction; or its advocates will push it forward till it shall become alike lawful in all the states, old as well as new, North as well as South.

Republican State Convention, June 16, 1858

All I ask for the Negro is that if you do not like him, let him alone. If God gave him but a little, that little let him enjoy.

Republican State Convention, July 17, 1858

What constitutes the bulwark of our own liberty and independence? It is not our frowning battlements, our bristling sea coasts, the guns of our war steamers, or the strength of our gallant and disciplined army. . . . Our reliance is in the *love of liberty* which God has implanted in us. . . . Destroy this spirit, and you have planted the seeds of despotism at your own doors. Familiarize yourselves with the chains of bondage and you prepare your own limbs to wear them. Accustomed to trample on the rights of others, you have lost the genius of your own independence and become the fit subjects of the first cunning tyrant who rises among you.

Edwardsville, Ill., September 11, 1858

This is a world of compensations; and he who would *be* no slave must consent to *have* no slave. Those who deny freedom to others deserve it not for themselves, and, under a just God, cannot long retain it.

To Henry L. Pierce and others, April 6, 1859

Let us have faith that right makes might, and in that faith let us to the end dare to do our duty as we understand it.

Cooper Union, N.Y., February 27, 1860*

---

*"The Cooper Union speech got him the Presidency."—H.L. Mencken.

But if this country cannot be saved without giving up that principle [the Declaration of Independence] I was about to say I would rather be assassinated on this spot than surrender it.

Independence Hall, Philadelphia, February 22, 1861

Why should there not be a patient confidence in the ultimate justice of the people? Is there any better or equal hope in the world?

First Inaugural Address, March 4, 1861

Labor is prior to, and independent of, capital. Capital is only the fruit of labor, and could never have existed if labor had not first existed. Labor is the superior of capital, and deserves much the higher consideration. Capital has its rights, which are as worthy of protection as any other rights. . . . A few men own capital, and that few avoid labor themselves.

No men living are more worthy to be trusted than those who toil up from poverty, none less inclined to take or touch aught which they have not honestly earned. Let them beware of surrendering a political power which they already possess.*

Annual message to Congress, December 3, 1861

Fellow citizens, we cannot escape history. . . . In giving freedom to the slave, we assure freedom to the free—honorable alike in what we give and what we preserve. We shall nobly save or meanly lose the last, best hope of earth.

Annual message to Congress, December 1, 1862

The world will little note nor long remember what we say here, but it can never forget what they did here. It is for us, the living, rather to be dedicated here to the unfinished work which they who fought here have thus far so nobly advanced. It is rather for us to be here dedicated to the great task remaining before us—that from these honored dead we take increased devotion to that cause for which they gave the last full measure of devotion; that we here highly resolve that these dead shall not

have died in vain; that this nation* shall have a new birth of freedom; and that government of the people, by the people, for the people, shall not perish from the earth.

Gettysburg Address, November 19, 1863**

Both read the same Bible and pray to the same God, and each invokes His aid against the other. It may seem strange that any men should dare to ask a just God's assistance is wringing their bread from the sweat of other men's faces.

With malice toward none; with charity for all; with firmness in the right as God gives us to see the right, let us strive on to finish the work we are in, to bind up the nation's wounds, to care for him who shall have borne the battle and for his widow and his orphan, to do all which may achieve and cherish a just and lasting peace among ourselves, and with all nations.

Second Inaugural Address, March 4, 1865

Emancipation Proclamation, January 1, 1863

And by virtue of the power and for the purposes aforesaid, I do order and declare that all persons held as slaves within said designated states and parts of states are, and henceforward shall be, free; and that the executive Government of the United States, including the military and naval authorities thereof, will recognize and maintain the freedom of said persons.

Lincoln–Douglas Debates

I have no purpose to introduce political and social equality between the white and black races. There is a physical difference between the two, which, in my judgment, will probably forever forbid living together upon the footing of perfect equality; and inasmuch as it

---

*"An extraordinary little treatise on what Lincoln considered the basic point of the American economic and political system. . . . This passage is a rough-hewn sketch of American society, placing the farmer and the laborer as the living and controlling elements in a government of the people."—Carl Sandburg

---

*At this point in the Gettysburg Address the words "under God" appear in various books quoting Lincoln. They do not appear in either Lincoln's first draft nor in his "reading copy," now in the Library of Congress. Lincoln later made copies for friends.
**Daniel Webster, January 26, 1830, in his reply to Hayne, referred to "the people's government, made for the people, made by the people, and answerable to the people." Theodore Parker, in his lecture to the New England Anti-Slavery Convention, Boston, said, "Democracy is direct self-government, over all the people, for all the people, by all the people."

becomes a necessity that there must be a difference, I, as well as Judge Douglas, am in favor of the race to which I belong having the superior position.

I am not, nor ever have been, in favor of bringing about in any way the social and political equality of the white and black races—I am not, nor ever have been, in favor of making voters or jurors of Negroes,—nor of qualifying them to hold office, nor to intermarry with white people.
> First Debate, August 21, 1858; widely publicized in the 1960s by White Citizens Councils

This *declared* indifference, but as I must think, covert *real* zeal for the spread of slavery, I can not but hate. I hate it because of the monstrous injustice of slavery itself. I hate it because it deprives our republican example of its just influence in the world—enables the enemies of free institutions, with plausibility, to taunt us as hypocrites—causes the real friends of freedom to doubt our sincerity and especially because it forces so many really good men amongst ourselves into an open war with the very fundamental principles of civil liberty—criticizing the Declaration of Independence, and insisting that there is no right principle of action but *self-interest.*
> Reply to Douglas, Peoria, Ill., October 18, 1854

Letters

Our progress in degeneracy appears to me to be pretty rapid. As a nation, we began by declaring that "all men are created equal." We now practically read it "all men are created equal, except Negroes." When the Know-Nothings get control, it will read "all men are created equal, except Negroes and foreigners and Catholics." When it comes to this, I shall prefer emigrating to some country where they make no pretense of loving liberty—to Russia, for instance, where despotism can be taken pure and without the base alloy of hypocrisy.
> To Joshua F. Speed, August 24, 1855

The strongest bond of human sympathy outside the family relation should be one uniting all working people of all nations and tongues, and kindreds.
> To N.Y. Workingmen's Association, 1864

If slavery is not wrong, nothing is wrong. I cannot remember when I did not so think and feel.
> To A.D. Hodges, April 4, 1864

If I could save the Union without freeing any slave, I would do it; and if I could save it by freeing all the slaves, I would do it; and if I could save it by freeing some and leaving others alone, I would also do that. What I do about slavery and the colored race, I do because I believe it helps to save the Union; and what I forebear, I forebear because I do not believe it would help to save the Union.
> To Horace Greeley, August 22, 1862

Military glory—that attractive rainbow that rises in showers of blood.
> Quoted in Gross, *Lincoln's Own Story*

In grave emergencies, moderation is generally safer than radicalism.
> Quoted in *Lincoln Encyclopedia*

If you once forfeit the confidence of your fellow citizens, you can never regain their respect and esteem. It is true that you may fool all the people some of the time; you can even fool some of the people all of the time; but you can't fool all of the people all of the time.
> Quoted in Alexander McClure, *Lincoln's Yarns and Stories*

To sin by silence when they should protest makes cowards of men.
> Attributed

I am a firm believer in the people. If given the truth, they can be depended upon to meet any national crisis. The great point is to bring them the real facts.
> Attributed

CHARLES A(ugustus) LINDBERGH SR. (1859–1924)
American Congressman

*Why Is Our Country at War?** (1917)

Government is less progressive than the people.

A radical is one who speaks the truth.
> Quoted in *Labor,* June 15, 1957

Under the rule of the "Dollar" human life has fallen to its lowest value.
> Quoted in Kenneth Davis, *The Hero*

---

*Book suppressed, plates destroyed by the Department of Justice.

(Nicholas) VACHEL LINDSAY
(1879–1931)
American poet

"The Unpardonable Sin"

This is the sin against the Holy Ghost:—
To speak of bloody power as right divine,
And call on God to guard each vile chief's
    house,
And for such chiefs, turn men to wolves and
    swine.

CAROLUS LINNAEUS (Carl von Linné)
(1707–1778)
Swedish botanist

What is the difference between man and
ape, based on natural history? Most definitely I
see no difference. I wish some one could show
me even one distinction.
                        Letter to J.G. Gmelin, February 14, 1747

WALTER LIPPMANN
(1889–1974)
American writer, editor

Liberty and the News (1920)

True opinions can prevail only if the facts to
which they refer are known; if they are not
known, false ideas are just as effective as true
ones, if not a little more effective.

A Preface to Morals (1929)

When men can no longer be theists, they
must, if they are civilized, become humanists.

The Good Society (1937)

Private property was the original source of
freedom. It still is its main bulwark.

The unexamined life, said Socrates, is unfit
to be lived by man. This is the virtue of liberty, and the ground on which we may justify
our belief in it, that it tolerates error in order
to serve truth.

In the blood of martyrs to intolerance are
the seeds of unbelief.
                        Atlantic Monthly, August, 1939

Men who are "orthodox" when they are
young are in danger of being middle-aged all
their lives.
                        Harvard Monthly (c. 1910)

A free press is not a privilege but an organic
necessity in a great society. . . Without criticism and reliable and intelligent reporting, the
government cannot govern.
                        Address, International Press Institute, May 27, 1965

LI T'AI-PO
(fl. 8th century A.D.)
Chinese poet

Empty your golden glasses to the dregs,
Life is dark, so is death.
                        Attributed

MAXIM LITVINOV
(1876 1951)
Soviet Russian diplomat

Food is a weapon.
Statement to Hoover's assistant, W. L. Brown, and
                        U.S. journalists, Riga, Autumn, 1922

Peace is indivisible.
Address, League of Nations, Geneva, July 1, 1936

LIVY (Titus Livius)
(59 B.C.–A.D. 17)
Roman historian

History of Rome

Adversity reminds men of religion.

Suicide, the supreme boon that God has bestowed on men among all the penalties of life.

No crime is rational.
                        Bk. II

DAVID LLOYD GEORGE, *see* George

HENRY DEMAREST LLOYD
(1847–1903)
American reformer

Wealth Against Commonwealth (1894)

Liberty produces wealth, and wealth destroys liberty.

Monopoly is business at the end of its journey.

I

JOHN LOCKE
(1632–1704)
English philosopher*

An Essay Concerning Human Understanding
(begun 1670, completed 1687, published 1690)

New opinions are always suspected, and usually opposed, without any other reason but because they are not already common.
Dedicatory epistle

The great question which, in all ages, has disturbed mankind, and brought on them the greatest part of their mischiefs, which has ruined cities, depopulated countries, and disordered the peace of the world, has been, not whether be power in the world, nor whence it came, but who should have it.
Bk. II, ch. XXI

False and doubtful positions, relied upon as unquestionable maxims, keep those who build on them in the dark from truth. Such are usually the prejudices imbibed from education, party, reverence, fashion, interest, et cetera.

A blind, fortuitous concourse of atoms.
Book IV, ch. VII

Reason, therefore, here, as contradistinguished to *Faith,* I take to be the discovery of the certainty or probability of such propositions or truths, which the mind arrives at by deductions made from such *Ideas,* which it has got by the use of its natural faculties: viz., by sensation or reflection.
Faith, on the other side, is the assent to any proposition, not thus made out by the deductions of reason, but upon the credit of the proposer, as coming from GOD, in some extraordinary way of communication. This way of discovering truth to men, we call *Revelation.*

Nothing that is contrary to, and inconsistent with, the clear and self-evident dictates of reason, has a right to be urged or assented to as a matter of faith, wherein reason hath nothing to do.

So that, in effect, religion, which should most distinguish us from the beasts, and ought most particularly to elevate us, as rational creatures, above brutes, is that wherein men often appear most irrational, and more senseless than beasts themselves. *Credo, quia impossible est** (I believe, because it is impossible) might, in a good man, pass as a sally of zeal; but would prove a very ill rule for men to choose their opinions and religions by.
Ch. XVIII

The Second Treatise of Government (1690)

The natural liberty of man is to be free from any superior power on earth, and not to be under the will or legislative authority of man, but to have only the law of nature for his rule. The liberty of man in society is to be under no other legislative power but that established by consent in the commonwealth; nor under the dominion of any will or restraint of any law but what that legislative shall enact according to the trust put in it.

But freedom of men under government is to have a standing rule to live by, common to every one of that society, and made by the legislative power erected in it, a liberty to follow my own will in all things where that rule prescribes not, and not to be subject to the inconstant, uncertain, unknown, arbitrary will of another man; as freedom of nature is to be under no other restraint but the law of nature.

Freedom from absolute, arbitrary power is so necessary to, and closely joined with, a man's preservation, that he cannot part with it but by what forfeits his preservation and life together. For a man, not having the power of his own life, cannot by compact or his own consent enslave himself to any one, nor put himself under the absolute, arbitrary power of another to take away his life when he pleases.
Ch. IV, "Of Slavery"

The reason why men enter into society is the preservation of their property, and putting themselves under government, is the preservation of their property.
Ch. XIX, "Of the Dissolution in Government"

---

*"Locke has a valid claim to be called the philosopher of the American Revolution."—Commager, *Living Ideas in America*
Jefferson, at a dinner for Washington and Hamilton, said concerning his portrayal of Bacon, Newton and Locke: "I told them they were my trinity of the greatest men the world had ever produced."

---

*Locke's Latin quotation is usually attributed to Tertullian—who did say *Certum est, quia impossible est* ("it is certain because it is impossible"). *See* Tertullian, *De Carna Christi.*

A Letter Concerning Toleration (1689)

Lastly, those are not at all to be tolerated who deny the being of a God. Promises, covenants, and oaths, which are the bonds of human society, can have no hold upon an atheist.

Some Thoughts Concerning Education (1693)

Possibly if a true estimate were made of the morality and religions of the world, we would find that the far greater part of mankind received even those opinions and ceremonies they would die for, rather from the fashions of their countries and the constant practice of those about them, than from any conviction of their reason.

Of Reading

Reading furnishes the mind only with materials for knowledge; it is thinking [that] makes what we read ours.

There can be no injury, where there is no property.
> Quoted in Rousseau, *The Social Contract*

CESARE (L.) LOMBROSO
(1836–1909)
Italian alienist, criminologist

The Man of Genius (1891)

Unfortunately, goodness and honor are rather the exception than the rule among exceptional men, not to speak of geniuses.

Genius is one of the many forms of insanity.

JACK (John Griffith) LONDON
(1876–suicide 1916)
American writer

Knowing no God, I have made of man my worship.
> Quoted in *Letters from Jack London* (1966)

No man has a right to scab so long as there is a pool of water to drown his carcass in, or a rope long enough to hang his body with. Judas Iscariot was a gentleman compared with a scab. For betraying his master, he had character enough to hang himself. A scab hasn't.
> "A Scab," quoted in *CIO News,* September 13, 1946

HUEY P. LONG
(1893–assassinated 1935)
Governor of Louisiana

Share the wealth!
> Campaign slogan, title of pamphlet

Every Man a King.
> Campaign slogan and song

Goddamn it, there ain't but one thing that I'm afraid of—and that's the people.
> Quoted in A.M. Schlesinger, Jr., *The Politics of Upheaval*

If Fascism comes to America it would be on a program of Americanism.
> Quoted in U.S. War Department, *Army Talk,* Fact Sheet 64*

HENRY WADSWORTH LONGFELLOW
(1807–1882)
American poet

"Hyperion" (1839)

Art signifies no more than this. Art is power.

Art is the revelation of man; and not merely that, but likewise the revelation of nature, speaking through man.

"A Psalm of Life" (1839)

Trust no future, howe'er pleasant;
Let the dead past bury its dead,
Act—act in the living present,
Heart within, and God O'erhead.

"The Arsenal of Springfield" (1846)

Were half the power that fills the world with terror,
Were half the wealth bestowed on camps and courts,
Given to redeem the human mind from error,
There were no need of arsenals or forts.

"Nuremberg" (1846)

Gathering from the pavement's crevice, as a flowerlet of the soil,
The nobility of labor,—the long pedigree of toil.

---

*"Sure we'll have Fascism, but it will come disguised as Americanism."—another version.

"My Lost Youth" (1858)

> A boy's will is the wind's will.
> (Icelandic saying)

FREDERICO GARCIA LORCA
(1899–murdered by Franco's Fascists 1936)
Spanish poet, playwright

Doña Rosita (1935)

> If I die,
> leave the balcony open.
>
> > Act 2

> And yet, hope pursues me, encircles me,
> bites me; like a dying wolf tightening his grip
> for the last time.
>
> > Act 3

LOUIS XIV
(1638–1717)
King of France

Maximes pour le Dauphin

> In every treaty, insert a clause which can
> easily be violated, so that the entire agreement
> can be broken in the case the interests of the
> State make it expedient to do so.

> *L' Etat, c'est moi.*
> I am the state.
> > Attributed in DeLaure, *History of Paris,* 1853

LOUIS XV
(1710–1774)
King of France

> Sovereignty lies in me alone. The legislative
> power is mine unconditionally and indivisibly.
> > To Parliament, March 3, 1766

JAMES RUSSELL LOWELL
(1819–1891)
American poet, critic, diplomat

"Democracy"

> England, indeed, may be called a monarchy
> with democratic tendencies, the United States
> a democracy with conservative instincts.

> One of the most curious of these frenzies of
> exclusion was that against the emancipation of
> the Jews. All share in the government of the
> world was denied for centuries to perhaps the
> ablest, certainly the most tenacious, race that
> had ever lived in it—the race to whom we

owed our religion and the purest spiritual stimulus and consolation to be found in all literature.

> Communism means barbarism, but Social-
> ism means, or wishes to mean, cooperation
> and community of interests, sympathy, the
> giving to the hands not so large a share as to
> the brains, but a larger share than hitherto in
> the wealth they must continue to produce—
> means, in short, the practical application of
> Christianity to life, and has in it the secret of
> an orderly and benign reconstruction.

> The foolish and the dead alone never
> change their opinion.
> > Address, Birmingham, England, October 6, 1884

Among My Books (1870)

> He who is firmly seated in authority soon
> learns to think security, and not progress, the
> highest lesson of statecraft.

Literary Essays (1880–1890)

> It was in making education not only com-
> mon to all, but in some sense compulsory on
> all, that the destiny of the free republics of
> America was practically settled.

> Puritanism, believing itself quick with the
> seed of religious liberty, laid, without knowing
> it, the egg of democracy.
> > vol. II

The Elections in November 1860

> Whatever be the effect of slavery on the
> States where it exists, there can be no doubt
> that its moral influence upon the North has
> been most disastrous. It has compelled our
> politicians into that first fatal compromise with
> their moral instincts and hereditary principles
> which makes all consequent ones come easy; it
> has accustomed us to makeshifts instead of
> statesmanship, to subterfuge instead of policy,
> to party-platforms for opinions, and to a defi-
> ance of the public sentiment of the civilized
> world of patriotism.

"A Glance Behind the Curtain" (1843)

> New times demand new measures and new
>   men;
> The world advances, and in time outgrows
> The laws which in our fathers' day were
>   best.

"The Present Crisis" (1844)

> Then to side with Truth is noble when we
>   share her wretched crust,

Ere her cause bring fame and profit, and 'tis
  prosperous to be just;
Then it is the brave man chooses, while the
  coward stands aside,
Doubting in his abject spirit, till his Lord is
  crucified.

ROBERT LOWELL
(1917–1977)
American poet

"The Drunken Fisherman" (1946)

Is there no way to cast my hook
Out of this dynamited brook?
The Fisher's sons must cast about
When shallow waters peter out.
I will catch Christ with a greased worm,
And when the Prince of Darkness stalks
My bloodstream to his Stygian term . . .
On water the Man Fisher walks.

ST. IGNATIUS OF LOYOLA
(1491–1556)
Spanish founder of the Society of Jesus

Exercita spiritualia (1541)

We should always be disposed to believe
that that which appears to us to be white is
really black, if the hierarchy of the Church so
decides.

The first point consists in this, that I see
with the eye of imagination those enormous
fires, and the souls as it were in bodies of fire.
The second point consists in this, that I hear
with the ears of imagination the lamentations,
howlings, cries, the blasphemies against Christ
Our Lord and against His saints.
The third point consists in this, that I taste
with the sense of taste of the imagination the
bitter things, the tears, sorrows and the worms
of conscience in hell.

LUCAN (Marcus Annaeus Lucanus)
(39–65 A.D.)
Spanish-born Roman poet

De Bello Civili

Poverty, the mother of manhood.
                                                    Bk. 1

Death itself has often fled from a man.
                                                    Bk. 2

HENRY ROBINSON LUCE
(1898–1967)
Co-founder of *Time* newsweekly

America's great achievement has been business.

The business of business is to take part in
the creation of the Great Society.

The only basic principle of authority in the
American nation is God.
            Quoted in obituary, *Time*, March 10, 1967

LUCIAN
(120–200 A.D.)
Greek satirist

How History Should Be Written (c. 170)

The historian should be fearless and incorruptible; a man of independence, loving frank-
ness and truth; one who, as the poet says, calls
a fig a fig and a spade a spade. He should yield
to neither hatred nor affection, but should be
unsparing and unpitying. He should be neither shy nor deprecating, but an impartial
judge, giving each side all it deserves but no
more. He should know in his writings no
country and no city; he should bow to no authority and acknowledge no king. He should
never consider what this or that man will
think, but should state the facts as they really
occurred.

Hermotimus

Deus ex machina
The God from the machine.
                                                    86

Mortuorum Dialogi (c. 175)

We have given so many hostages to fortune.
                                                    cf. Bacon

LUCRETIUS (Titus Lucretius Carus)
(c. 99–55 B.C.)
Roman poet

On the Nature of Things

Nil posse creare de nilo.
Nothing from nothing ever yet was born.

Men from the sea
Might rise.

Nothing exists per se except atoms and the
  void.
                                                    Bk. I

Hence too it comes that Nature all dissolves
Into their primal bodies again, and naught
Perishes ever to annihilation.

Bk. II

Therefore death to us
Is nothing, nor concerns us in the least,
Since nature of mind is mortal evermore.

Nothing arises in the body of order that we
may use it, but what arises brings forth its own
use. . . . It was no design of the atoms that led
them to arrange themselves in order with keen
intelligence . . . but because many atoms in
infinite time have moved and met in all manner of ways, trying all combinations. . . .
Whence arose the beginnings of things . . .
and the generation of living creatures.

The nature of the universe has by no means
been made through divine power, seeing how
great are the faults that mar it.

Often for fear of death men are seized by a
hatred of life, forgetting that this fear is the
fountain of all care.

Bk. III

. . . but no pleasure is comparable to the
standing upon the vantage ground of truth.

No single thing abides; but all things flow.

Globed from the atoms falling slow or swift
I see the suns, I see the systems live
    Their forms; and even the systems and
        the suns
Shall go back slowly to the eternal drift.

Even if there lurk behind some veil of sky
The fabled Maker, the Immortal Spy,
    Ready to torture each poor life he made,
Thou canst do more than God can—thou
    canst die.

For I, if still you are haunted by the fear
Of Hell, have one more secret for your ear.
    Hell is indeed no fable; but, my friends,
Hell and its torments are not there, but
    here.

The greatest wealth is to live content with
little, for there is never want where the mind is
satisfied.

Bk. V

Fear of death was the first thing on earth to
make the gods.

I give instruction concerning mighty things
and proceed to free the mind from the closely-
confining shackles of religion.

ERICH VON LUDENDORFF
(1865–1937)
German general, World War I

Belief in a German God

I decline Christianity because it is Jewish,
because it is international, and because in
cowardly fashion, it preaches peace on Earth.

RAMON LULLY
(1235–1313)
Majorcan, Christian martyr

The Book of the Lover and the Beloved

Between Hope and Fear, Love makes her
home. She lives on thought, and then she is
forgotten, dies. So unlike the pleasure of this
world are their foundations.

MARTIN LUTHER
(1483–1546)
Father of the Reformation*

*Disputation on the Power and Efficacy of Indul-
gences* (commonly called The Ninety-Five Theses)
(1517)

27. There is no divine authority for preaching that the soul flies out of purgatory immediately as the money clinks in the till.

Theses for the Heidelberg Disputation (April 1518)

3. The works of man may always be attractive and seemingly good. It appears nevertheless that they are mortal sins.
13. "Free Will" after the Fall is nothing but
a word.
18. It is certain that a man must completely
despair of himself in order to become fit to obtain the grace of Christ.
    Quoted in *Martin Luther,* ed. John Dillenberger

Proclamation, Diet of Worms, April 18, 1521

Hier steh' ich. Ich kann nicht anders.
    Here I stand, I cannot do otherwise. God
help me. Amen.

---

*"Yet the 31st of October in the year 1517, the day
on which Martin Luther nailed his 95 theses on the
wooden door of Wittenburg Cathedral, must be regarded as the commencement of a new epoch; for
on that day was forced the iron door of the prison in
which the papal church had detained fettered reason
for 1200 years."—Ernst Haeckel, *The Riddle of the
Universe.*

Preface to the New Testament

The gospel demands no works to make us holy and to redeem us. Indeed, it condemns such works, and demands only faith in Christ, because He has overcome sin, death and hell for us.

An Open Letter to Pope Leo X, September 6, 1520

The Roman church, once the holiest of all, has become the most licentious den of thieves, the most shameless of all brothels, the kingdom of sin, death, and hell. It is so bad that even Antichrist himself, if he should come, could think of nothing to add to its wickedness.

Furthermore, I acknowledge no fixed rules for the interpretation of the Word of God.

Against the Robbing and Murdering Hordes of Peasants (1525)*

Besides, any man against whom it can be proved that he is a maker of sedition is outside the law of God and Empire, so that the first that can slay him is doing right and well. For if a man is an open rebel every man is his judge and executioner.

Preface to Latin Writings (1545)

The pope is not the head of the church by divine right. . . . The pope must be of the devil. For what is not of God must of necessity be of the devil.

The Babylonian Captivity of the Church (1520)

I, for one, will take my understanding prisoner and bring it into obedience to God.

I have such hatred of divorce that I prefer bigamy to divorce.

The Bondage of the Will (1525)

But inasmuch as He is the one true God, wholly incomprehensible and inaccessible to man's understanding, it is reasonable, indeed inevitable, that His justice also should be incomprehensible.

Proverbs, and experience the parent of proverbs, bear record that the more abandoned men are, the more successful they are . . . Is it not, pray, universally held to be most unjust that bad men should prosper, and good men be afflicted? Yet that is the way of the world.

---

*The nobility and landowners had butchered 100,000 rebellious peasants.

Hereupon some of the greatest minds have fallen into denying the existence of God.

And a summary explanation of this whole inexplicable problem is found in a single little word: *There is a life after this life: and all that is not punished and repaid here will be punished and repaid there.*

Table Talk (1569) (tr. Hazlitt)

Superstition, idolatry, and hypocrisy, have ample wages, but truth goes a-begging.

LIII

For where God built a church, there the devil would also build a chapel.

LXVII

God will not have that we should attain a higher knowledge of things

CLX

Where great wealth is, there are also all manner of sins; for through wealth comes pride, through pride, dissension, through dissension, wars, through wars, poverty, through poverty, great distress and misery. Therefore, they that are rich, must yield a strict and great account; for to whom much is given, of him much will be required.

CLXV

The papists took the invocation of saints from the heathen, who divided God into numberless images and idols, and ordained to each his particular office and worth.

CLXXVIII

The Jews crucified Christ with words, but the Gentiles have crucified him with works and deeds.

CCIV

For, first, free-will led us into original sin, and brought death upon us afterwards; upon sin followed not only death, but all manner of mischiefs, as we daily find in the world, murder, lying, deceiving, stealing, and other evils.

This is my absolute opinion: he that will maintain that man's free-will is able to do or work anything in spiritual cases, be they never so small, denies Christ.

I confess that mankind has a free-will, but it is to milk kine, to build houses, &c., and no further. . . . Faith is far another thing than free-will; nay, free-will is nothing at all, but faith is all in all.

CCLXII

Reason is the greatest enemy that faith has; it never comes to the aid of spiritual things, but—more frequently than not—struggles against the divine Word, treating with contempt all than emanates from God.

CCCLIII

Had one ravished the Virgin Mary, or crucified Christ anew, the pope would, for money, have pardoned him.

CCCCLI

The state of celibacy is great hypocrisy and wickedness. Christ with one sentence confutes all their arguments: God created them male and female.

CCCCXCI

Men have broad and large chests, and small narrow hips, and more understanding than women, who have but small and narrow breasts, and broad hips, to the end they should remain at home, sit still, keep house, and bear and bring up children.

DCCXXV

Marrying cannot be without women, nor can the world subsist without them. To marry is physic against incontinence. Thereunto are they chiefly created, to bear children, and be the pleasure, joy, and solace of their husbands.

DCCXXVI

God created Adam master and lord of living creatures, but Eve spoilt all, when she persuaded him to set himself above God's will. 'Tis you women, with your tricks and artifices, that lead men into error.

DCCXXVII

The fear of death is merely death itself; he who abolishes that fear from his heart, neither tastes nor feels death.

DCCLXXXV

The Jews are the most miserable people on earth. They are plagued everywhere, and scattered about all countries, having no certain resting place. They sit as on a wheelbarrow, without a country, people or government . . . but they are rightly served, for seeing they refused to have Christ and his gospel, instead of freedom they must have servitude.

DCCCLII

Either God must be unjust, or you, Jews, wicked and ungodly. You have been, about fifteen hundred years, a race rejected of God.

DCCCLXI

The ministry was intended to train a church, with pastors living among the people and keeping house as other people do. Such men should be granted permission to marry, in order to avoid temptation and sin.

DCCCCIII

Secular Authority (1523) (tr. J.J. Schindel, 1930)

We must firmly establish secular law and the sword, that no one may doubt that it is in the world by God's will and ordinance.

Bk. I

And if all the world were composed of real Christians, that is, true believers, no prince, king, lord, sword, or law would be needed.

You ask, Why then did God give to all men so many commandments, . . . Since, however, no one is by nature Christian or pious, but every one sinful and evil, God places the restraints of the law upon them all, so that they may not dare give rein to their desires and commit outward, wicked deeds.

Bk. III

All who are not Christians belong to the kingdom of the world and are under the law. Since few believe and still fewer live a Christian life, do not resist the evil, and themselves do no evil, God has provided for non-Christians a different government outside the Christian estate and God's kingdom, and has subjected them to the sword.

It is indeed true that Christians, so far as they themselves are concerned, are subject to neither law nor sword and need neither; but first take heed and fill the world with real Christians before ruling it in a Christian and evangelical manner. This you will never accomplish; for the world and the masses are and always will be unchristian, although they are all baptized and are nominally Christian.

Bk. IV

Because the sword is a very great benefit and necessary to the whole world, to preserve peace, to punish sin, and to prevent evil.

You ask, Why did not Christ and the apostles bear the sword? Tell me, Why did He not also take a wife, or become a cobbler or a tailor? If an occupation or office is not good because Christ Himself did not occupy it, what would become of all occupations and offices, with the exception of the ministry which alone

He exercised? Christ fulfilled His own office and vocation, but thereby did not reject any other. It was not meet that he bear the sword.

Therefore, even though Christ did not bear the sword nor prescribe it, it is sufficient that he did not forbid or abolish it, but rather endorsed it; just as it is sufficient that He did not abolish the state of matrimony, but endorsed it, though He Himself took no wife and gave no commandment concerning it.

Bk. V

Sämtliche Schriften (Collected Writings)

Whoever wants to be a Christian should tear the eyes out of his Reason.

V

What shall we Christians do now with this depraved and damned people of the Jews? . . . I will give my faithful advice: First, that one should set fire to their synagogues. . . . Then that one should also break down and destroy their houses. . . . That one should drive them out of the country.

XX

God does not work salvation for fictitious sinners. Be a sinner and sin vigorously (*Esto peccator et pecca fortiter*); but even more vigorously believe and delight in Christ, who is victor over sin, death, and the world.
Letter to Melanchton, August 1, 1521

Gedanken sind zoll-frei.
Thoughts are duty-free.

Motto

Die verfluchte Huhre, Vernunft.
The damned whore, Reason.
Quoted in Briffanlt, *Rational Evolution*

God uses lust to impel men to marriage, ambition to office, avarice to earning, and fear to faith.
Quoted in *Time*, March 24, 1967

Since we punish thieves with the halter, murderers with the sword, and heretics with fire, why do we not turn on all those evil teachers of perdition, those popes, cardinals, and bishops, and the entire swarm of the Roman Sodom with arms in hand, and wash our hands in their blood.
Quoted in Engels, *The Peasant War in Germany*, 1850

ALBERT (John) LUTHULI
(1898–1967)
Zulu leader, Noble Peace Prize 1960

This is Africa's age.

The laws of the land [South Africa] virtually criticize God for having created men of color.
Nobel acceptance speech, December 11, 1961

HENRY LUTTRELL
(c. 1765–1881)
English wit, writer

"An Aspiration"

O that there might in England be
A duty on Hypocrisy,
A tax on humbug, an excise
On solemn plausibilities.

LU WANG
(1139–1192)
Chinese metaphysician

Human nature is originally good. Any evil in it results from any changes made upon it by [external] things.

Where there is good there must be evil.

Common men and vulgarians are submerged by poverty or wealth, or by high or low positions, or by benefit or injury, or by profit or loss, or by sounds and colors, or by sensuality and desire. They [thus] destroy their "virtuous Mind," and have no regard for Righteousness and Law.
American Oriental Series, vol. 27

ROSA LUXEMBURG
(1870–assassinated 1919)
German Socialist leader

There is nothing more subject to rapid change than human psychology. The psyche of the masses embraces a whole world, a world of almost limitless possibilities: breathless calm and raging storm; base treachery and supreme heroism.

"Disappointment" in the masses is always a compromising sign for political (i.e., Socialist) leaders. A real leader, a leader of real moment, will make his tactics dependent, not on the temporary spirit of the masses, but on the inexorable laws of historical development. He will steer his course by these laws in defiance of all disappointments and he will rely on history to bring about the gradual maturing of his actions.

Credo, in letter from prison to Matilde Wurm, Berlin, February 16, 1917

The Problem of Dictatorship (1919)

But with the repression of political life in the land as a whole, life in the Soviets must also become more and more crippled. Without general elections, without unrestricted freedom of the press and assembly, without a free struggle of opinion, life dies out in every public institution, becomes a mere semblance of life, in which only the bureaucracy remains as the active element.

JOHN LYLY
(1553–1606)
English writer

Euphues: The Anatomy of Wit (1579)

Love knoweth no law.

Though all men be made of one metal, yet they be not cast in one mold.

You see what love is, begun with griefe, continued with sorrow, ended with death. A paine full of pleasure, a joye replenished with misery, a Heaven, a Hell, a God, a Divell, and what not, that either hath in it solace or sorrowe?

The sun shineth upon the dunghill, and is not corrupted.

How rare a thing it is to match virginity with beauty.

EDWARD GEORGE BULWER-LYTTON
(Lord Lytton)
(1803–1873)
British literary patron, writer

Last of the Barons (1843)

"It is destiny,"—phrase of the weak human heart! "It is destiny!"—dark apology for every error! The strong and the virtuous admit *no* destiny.

Bk. X, ch. 6

Caxtonia

Character is money; and according as the man earns or spends the money, money in turn becomes character. As money is the most evident power in the world's uses, so the use that he makes of money is often all that the world knows about a man.

Essay VII

The Disowned (1828)

The easiest person to deceive is one's self.

Ch. 42

The Bones of Raphael

For something in the envy of the small
Still loves the vast Democracy of Death.

Money (1840)

Time is money.

Act 3

Richelieu (1839)

Laws die, books never.

Act 1

Beneath the rule of men entirely great
The pen is mightier than the sword.

Act 2

Ernest Maltravers

When the people have no tyrant, their own public opinion becomes one.

DOUGLAS MacARTHUR
(1880–1964)
American general

A warlike spirit, which alone can create and civilize a state, is absolutely essential to national defense and to national perpetuity. . . . The more warlike the spirit of the people, the less need for a large standing army. . . . Every male brought into existence should be taught from infancy that the military service of the Republic carries with it honor and distinction, and his very life should be permeated with the

ideal that even death itself may become a boon when a man dies that a nation may live and fulfill its destiny.
Contribution, *Infantry Journal,* March 1927

I know war as few other men now living know it, and nothing to me is more revolting. I have long advocated its complete abolition, as its very destructiveness on both friend and foe has rendered it useless as a method of settling international disputes.

Appeasement but begets new and bloodier wars.

In war there is no substitute for victory.

"Old soldiers never die; they just fade away."
Address, Congress, April 19, 1951

Global war has become a Frankenstein's monster, threatening to destroy both sides . . . It contains now only the germs of a double suicide.
Address, July 5, 1961

Wars are caused by undefended wealth.
Quoted in *N. Y. Daily News,* November 18, 1945

THOMAS BABINGTON MACAULAY
(1800–1859)
English historian, essayist, statesman

No war ought ever to be undertaken but under circumstances which render all interchange of courtesy between the combatants impossible. It is a bad thing that men should hate each other; but it is far worse that they should contract the habit of cutting one another's throats without hatred.
Review of *Mitford's History of Greece,* November 1824

The gallery in which the reporters sit has become the Fourth Estate of the realm.
Review of *Hallam's Constitutional History,* September 1828*

If it be admitted that on the institution of property the well-being of society depends, it

---
*Carlyle, fifth lecture, "Heroes and Hero Worship," 1840, credited Burke with saying: "There are Three Estates in Parliament; but in the Reporters' Gallery yonder sits a *Fourth Estate* more important by far than they all." There is no such reference in Burke, according to *Editor & Publisher,* November 15, 1952.

follows surely that it would be madness to give supreme power in the state to a class which would not be likely to respect that institution.
Speech on The People's Charter, May 3, 1842

She [the Roman Catholic Church] saw the commencement of all the governments and of all the ecclesiastical institutions that now exist in the world; and we feel no assurance that she is not destined to see the end of them all. She was great and respected before the Saxon had set foot in Britain, before the Frank had crossed the Rhine, when Grecian eloquence still flourished in Antioch, when idols were still worshipped in the temples of Mecca. And she may still exist in undiminished vigor when some traveler from New Zealand shall, in the midst of a vast solitude, take his stand on a broken arch of London Bridge to sketch the ruins of St. Paul's.
"On Ranke's History of the Popes," 1840

What are laws but the expressions of the opinion of some class which has power over the rest of the community? By what was the world ever governed but by the opinion of some person or persons? By what else can it ever be governed?
Review of *Southey's Colloquies,* 1830

History of England (1849–1861)

For political and intellectual freedom, and for all the blessing which political and intellectual freedom have brought in their train, she [England] is chiefly indebted to the great rebellion of the laity against the priesthood.

We deplore the outrages which accompany revolutions. But the more violent the outrage, the more assured we feel that a revolution was necessary. The violence of these outrages will always be proportioned to the ferocity and ignorance of the people; and the ferocity and ignorance of the people will be proportioned by the oppression and degradation under which they have been accustomed to live.

In every age the vilest specimens of human nature are to be found among demagogues.
Vol. I, ch. 1

The emancipation of the press produced a great and salutary change. . . . Some weak men had imagined that religion and morality stood in need of protection of the licenser. The event signally proved that they were in error. . . . From the day on which emancipation of our literature was accomplished, the purification of our literature began.

The puritan hated bear-baiting, not because it gave pain to the bear, but because it gave pleasure to the spectators.

Vol. I, ch. 2

On Moore's Life of Lord Byron (1831)

We know no spectacle so ridiculous as the British public in one of its periodical fits of morality.

NICCOLÓ MACHIAVELLI
(1469–1527)
Italian statesman*

The Prince (1513)

The fact is that a man who wants to act virtuously in every way necessarily comes to grief among so many who are not virtuous.

Ch. v

Hence it comes about that all armed Prophets have been victorious, and all unarmed Prophets have been destroyed.

Ch. vi

He who usurps the government of any state should execute all the cruelties which he thinks material all at once, that he may have no occasion to renew them often.

Ch. viii

A prince, then, should have no other thought or object so much at heart, and make no other thing so much his special study, as the art of war, and the organization and discipline of his army; for this is the only art that is expected of him who commands.

War should be the only study of a prince. He should consider peace only as a breathing-time, which gives him leisure to contrive, and furnishes ability to execute.

Ch. xiv

It may be said of men in general that they are ungrateful and fickle, dissemblers, avoiders of danger, and greedy of gain. So long as you shower benefits upon them, they are all yours; they offer you their blood, their substance, their lives and their children, provided the ne-

cessity for it is far off; but when near at hand, then they revolt.

. . . it is much more safe to be feared than to be loved, when you have to choose between the two.

And, above all things, abstain from taking people's property, for men will sooner forget the death of their fathers than the loss of their patrimony.

A state which has freshly achieved liberty makes enemies and no friends.

Nevertheless a prince ought to inspire fear in such a way that, if he does not win love, he avoids hatred; because he can endure very well being feared while he is not hated, which will always be as long as he abstain from the property of his citizens and subjects and from their women.

Ch. xvii

A sagacious prince then cannot and should not fulfill his pledges when their observance is contrary to his interest, and when the causes which induced him to pledge his faith no longer exist. If men were all good, then indeed this precept would be bad; but as men are naturally bad, and will not observe their faith toward you, you must, in some way, not observe yours to them; and no prince ever yet lacked legitimate reasons with which to color his want of good faith.

It is necessary that the prince should know how to color his nature well, and how to be a hypocrite and dissembler. For men are so simple, and yield so much to immediate necessity, that the deceiver will never lack dupes.

You must know, then, that there are two methods of fighting, the one by law, the other by force: the first method is that of men, the second of beasts; but as the first method is often insufficient, one must have recourse to the second. It is therefore necessary for a prince to know well how to use both the beast and the man.

Thus it is well to seem merciful, faithful, humane, sincere, religious, and also to be so; but you must have the mind so disposed that when it is needful to be otherwise you may be able to change to the opposite qualities.

Ch. xviii

Hatred is acquired as much by good works as by bad ones.

Ch. xix

---

*"Discoverer of political science."—Count Sforza. "I affirm that the doctrine of Machiavelli is more alive today than it was four thousand years ago."—Mussolini, 1924.

I judge necessity to be better than caution; for Fortune is a woman, and if you wish to master her, you must strike and beat her, and you will see that she allows herself to be more easily vanquished by the rash and the violent than those who proceed more slowly and coldly. And, therefore, as a woman, she ever favors youth more than age, for youth is less cautious and more energetic, and commands Fortuna with greater audacity.

Ch. xxv

Discourses on the First Ten Books of Titus Livius (1513–1517)

For where the fear of God is wanting, destruction is sure to follow.

Bk. I, Ch. 11

The Church has ever kept and keeps our country divided.

Politics has no relations to morals.

Those Princes or Republics that would save themselves from growing corrupt should above all else keep uncorrupted the ceremonies of religion, holding them always in veneration. For there can be no surer sign of decay in a country than to see the rites of religion held in contempt.

Bk. I, Ch. 12

. . . for the people resemble a wild beast, which, naturally fierce and accustomed to live in woods, has been brought up, as it were, in a prison and in servitude, and having by accident got its liberty . . . easily becomes the prey of the first who seeks to incarcerate it again.

Bk. I, Ch. 16

For the great majority of mankind are satisfied with appearances, as though they were realities and are often more influenced by the things that *seem* than by those that *are*.

Bk. I, Ch. 25

But men generally decide upon a middle course, which is most hazardous, for they know neither how to be entirely good nor entirely bad.

Bk. I, Ch. 26

Men ever praise the olden time, and find fault with the present, though often without reason. . . . Having grown old, they also laud all they remember to have seen in their youth. Their opinion is generally erroneous. . . . We never know the whole truth about the past.

Men's hatreds generally spring from fear or envy.

Bk. II, Introduction

Our religion, moreover, places the supreme happiness in humility, lowliness, and a contempt for worldly objects. . . . If our religion claims of us fortitude of soul, it is more to enable us to suffer than to achieve great deeds.

These principles seem to me to have made men feeble, . . . an easy prey to evil-minded men, who can control them more securely, seeing that the great body of men, for the sake of gaining Paradise, are more disposed to endure injuries than to avenge them.

Bk. II, Ch. 2

Every one may begin a war at his pleasure, but cannot so finish it. . . . And money alone, so far from being a means of defense, will only render a prince the more liable to being plundered. There cannot, therefore, be a more erroneous opinion than that money is the sinews of war.

I maintain, then, contrary to the general opinion, that the sinews of war are not gold, but good soldiers; for gold alone will not procure good soldiers, but good soldiers will always procure gold. By making their wars with iron, they never suffered for the want of gold.

Bk. II, Ch. 10

I believe it to be most true that it seldom happens that men rise from low condition to high rank without employing either force or fraud, unless that rank should be attained either by gift or inheritance.

Bk. II, Ch. 13

He who takes upon himself a tyranny and does not slay Brutus, and he who employing either force or fraud makes a free state, and does not slay the son of Brutus, maintains his work only for a short time.

Bk. III, Ch. 3

For when men are well governed, they neither seek nor desire any other liberty.

Bk. III, Ch. 5

Although fraud in all other actions be odious, yet in matters of war it is laudable and glorious, and he who overcomes his enemies by strategem is as much to be praised as he who overcomes them by force.

Bk. III, Ch. 40

A neutral is bound to be hated by those who lose and despised by those who win.

To Francesco Vettor, December 22, 1514

How perilous it is to free a people who prefer slavery.

For *our* country, wrong is right.

You do not know the unfathomable cowardice of humanity . . . servile in the face of
force, pitiless in the face of weakness, implacable before blunders, indulgent before crimes
. . . and patient to the point of martyrdom before all the violence of bold despotism.

Attributed

ARCHIBALD MacLEISH
(1892–1982)
American poet, essayist

The weakness of political programs—Five
Year Plans and the like—is that they can be
achieved. But human freedom can never be
achieved because human freedom is a continuously evolving condition.

Contribution, *N.Y. Times*, May 30, 1960

The remedy in the United States is not less
liberty but real liberty—and end to the brutal
intolerance of churchly hooligans and flag-
waving corporations and all the rest of the
small but bloody despots who have made the
word Americanism a synonym for coercion
and legal crime.

The dissenter is every human being at those
moments of his life when he resigns momen-
tarily from the herd and thinks for himself.

Contribution, *The Nation,* December 4, 1937

"The Black Day"

God help that country where informers
thrive!
Where slander flourishes and lies contrive
To kill by whispers! Where men lie to live!

God help that country by informers fed
Where fear corrupts and where suspicion's
spread
By look and gesture, even to the dead.

"Ars Poetica" (1926)

A poem should not mean
But be.

"America Was Promises" (1939)

The Aristocracy of Wealth and Talents
Turned its talents into wealth and lost them.
Turned enlightened selfishness to wealth.
Turned self-interest into bank books: bal-
anced them.
Bred out: bred to fools. . . .

Tom Paine Knew.
Tom Paine knew the People.
The promises were spoken to the People.
History was voyages toward the People.
Americas were landfalls of the People.
Stars and expectations were the signals of the
People.

Poems are speaking voices. And a poem that
is hard to get rid of is a voice that is hard to get
rid of. And a voice that is hard to get rid of is a
man.

Essay on Robert Frost, quoted in *N.Y. Times*
obit-editorial, April 22, 1982

HENRY DUNNING MACLEOD
(1821–1902)
Scottish economist

The worst form of currency in circulation
regulates the value of the whole currency and
drives all other forms of currency out of circulation.

Quoted in *Britannica*, 11th ed., vol. 12*

HAROLD MACMILLAN
(1894–   )
Prime Minister of Great Britain

Tradition does not mean that the living are
dead; it means that the dead are living.

Quoted in *Manchester Guardian,*
December 18, 1958

MACROBIUS
(fl. 400 A.D.)
African-born Latin writer

Saturnalia

These men whom you call your chattel
slaves have the same origin as you, enjoy the
same sky, live and die as you do. Slaves? No.
Fellow slaves, when you consider that fortune
has equal sway over them and you.

I, ii, 7

Love and fear exclude each other.

13

---

*"Gresham's Law," that bad money drives out good,
was mistakenly credited by MacLeod to Sir Thomas
Gresham (1519–1570), founder of the Royal Exchange. Oresme and Copernicus stated the principle
in similar language.

SALVADOR DE MADARIAGA
(1886–1978)
Spanish writer

Americans Are Boys

Woman governs America because America is a land of boys who refuse to grow up.

Anarchy or Hierarchy (1937)

Inequality is the inevitable consequence of liberty.

No one has ever succeeded in keeping nations at war except by lies.

Yet one can be an atheist in a Protestant and Catholic way: the first argues God out of court, the second fights against him for dear life.

Liberty is the bread of man's spirit.

Liberty evokes a need. Fraternity, a hankering for an ideal. But Equality makes a claim, utters a protest, forecasts a rebellion. It is at the root of the class war and of the struggle for a classless society.
Contribution, *Saturday Review,* April 4, 1967

The trouble today is that the Communist world understands unity but not liberty, while the free world understands liberty but not unity. Eventually the victory may be won by the first of the two sides to achieve the synthesis of both liberty and unity.
Quoted by E.B. White, *The New Yorker,* June 18, 1960

JAMES MADISON
(1751–1836)
4th President of the United States

A Memorial and Remonstrance* (1784)

1. . . . The religion then of every man must be left to the conviction and conscience of every man; it is the right of every man to exercise it as these may dictate.

---

*Considered by scholars to rank with the Declaration of Independence and the Gettysburg Address. This protest was made against the bill introduced by Patrick Henry, December 1784, "establishing a provision for Teachers of Religion." According to Dr. Eva Brann, Washington and Marshall supported Henry, Jefferson supported Madison.

3. It is proper to take alarm at the first experiment on our liberties. . . . Who does not see that the same authority which can establish Christianity, in exclusion of all other Religions, may establish with the same ease any particular sect of Christians, in exclusion of all other Sects?

4. While we assert for ourselves a freedom to embrace, to profess and to observe the Religion which we believe to be of divine origin, we cannot deny an equal freedom to those whose minds have not yet yielded to the evidence which has convinced us.

7. Experience witnesseth that ecclesiastical establishments, instead of maintaining the purity and efficacy of Religion, have had a contrary operation. During almost fifteen centuries has the legal establishment of Christianity been on trial. What have been its fruits? More or less in all places, pride and indolence in the Clergy, ignorance and servility in the laity, in both, superstition, bigotry and persecution. . . .

8. . . . What influence in fact, have ecclesiastical establishments had on Civil Society? In some instances they have been seen erecting a spiritual tyranny on the ruins of Civil authority; in many instances they have been seen upholding the thrones of political tyranny; in no instance have they been seen the guardians of the liberties of the people. Rulers who wished to subvert the public liberty, may have found an established Clergy convenient auxiliaries. A just Government instituted to secure & perpetuate it needs them not. Such a government will be best supported by protecting every Citizen in the enjoyment of his Religion with the same equal hand which protects his person and his property; by neither invading the equal rights of any Sect, nor suffering any Sect to invade those of others.

9. . . . What a melancholy mark is the Bill of sudden degeneracy! Instead of holding forth an Asylum to the persecuted, it is itself a signal of persecution. . . . Distant as it may be in its present form from the Inquisition, it differs from it only in degree. The one is the first step, the other, the last in the career of intolerance. . . .

Letters

Those who contend for a simple Democracy, or a pure republic, actuated by the sense

of majority and operating within narrow limits, assume or suppose a case which is altogether fictitious.
To Jefferson, October 24, 1787

To secure the public good and private rights against the danger of the propertyless or proletarians and at the same time preserve the spirit and form of popular government was then the great object to which the Convention inquiries were directed.

Divide et impera, the reprobated axiom of tyranny is, under certain qualifications, the only policy by which a Republic can be administered on just principles.
To Jefferson, *Works,* I

The Federalist (1788)

Liberty is to faction what air is to fire, an aliment without which it instantly expires. But it could not be less folly to abolish liberty, which is essential in political life, because it nourishes faction, than it would be to wish the annihilation of air, which is essential to animal life, because it imparts to fire its destructive agency.
No. 10, signed Publius

It is of great importance in a republic not only to guard the society against the oppression of its rulers, but to guard one part of the society against the injustice of the other part.
If men were angels, no government would be necessary.
No. 51

To the press alone, checquered as it is with abuses, the world is indebted for all the triumphs which have been gained by reason and humanity over error and oppression.
Quoted in Justice William O. Douglas, *An Almanac of Liberty* (1954)

A popular government without popular information or the means of acquiring it, is but a prologue to a farce, or a tragedy, or perhaps both.
Quoted by Sen. Hatfield, *Saturday Review,* July 1, 1967

If there be a principle that ought not to be questioned within the United States, it is that every man has a right to abolish an old government and establish a new one. This principle is not only recorded in every public archive,

written in every American heart, and sealed with the blood of a host of American martyrs, but is the only lawful tenure by which the United States hold their existence as a nation.
Quoted by Commager, *N. Y. Times,* July 2, 1961

MAURICE MAETERLINCK
(1862–1949)
Belgian dramatist

Pelléas et Mélisande (1892)

Si j'étais Dieu, j'aurais pitié du coeur des hommes.
If I were God, I would have mercy on men.

The end of life would be much less frightening if it were not called death any more. The fear of death is the source of all religions.
Quoted in *N. Y. Times,* May 8, 1960

MAGNA CARTA*
(written 1215)

XXXIX. No freeman shall be taken, or imprisoned, or outlawed, or exiled, or in any way harmed, nor will we go upon him, nor will we send upon him, except by the legal judgment of his peers, or by the law of the land.

XL. To none will we sell, to none deny or delay, right or justice.

THE MAHABHARATA
(c. 350 B.C.)
Hindu epic poem

This is the sum of all true righteousness: deal with others as thou wouldst thyself be dealt by. Do nothing to thy neighbor which thou wouldst not have him do to thee hereafter.

---

*"Magna Carta, or the Great Charter, the name of the famous charter of liberties granted at Runnimede in June 1215 by King John to the English people. . . . Many regard Magna Carta as giving equal rights to all Englishmen. . . . [T]his . . . is true only with large limitations. The villeins, who formed the majority of the population, got very little from it . . . . [They were] property—the property of their lords—and therefore valuable. They got neither political nor civil rights. . . ."—*Britannica,* 11th ed., vol xvii.

A falsehood uttered for the sake of a righteous end ceaseth to be a falsehood.

To you, I declare the holy mystery;
There is nothing nobler than humanity.

Whenever a woman commits adultery with a man of a caste inferior to her husband's she shall be torn to pieces by dogs, and in some public place.

ALFRED THAYER MAHAN
(1840–1914)
American admiral, historian

The Interest of America in Sea Power (1897)

Neither the sanctions of international law nor the justice of a cause can be depended upon for a fair settlement of differences, when they come into conflict with a strong political necessity on the one side opposed to comparative weakness on the other.

If the latter [our own navy] be superior to the force that can thus be sent against it . . . we can maintain our right; not merely the rights which international law concedes, and, which the moral sense of nations supports, but also those equally clear rights which, though not supported by law, depend upon a clear preponderance of interest, upon obviously necessary policy, upon self-preservation, either total or partial.

The Freedom of Asia (1900)

Habit has familarized men's minds with the idea of national power spreading beyond the bounds of the continent.

"Armaments and Arbitration"

Of the Christian religion the great constituent is power; which in another shape, easily assumed, becomes force. Force is power in action. . . .

[I]f force is necessary, force must be used for the benefit of the community, of the commonwealth of the World. This fundamental proposition is not impaired by the fact that force is best exercised through law, when adequate law exists. Except as the expression of right, law is an incubus.

To such a view aggression, in its primary sense of onward movement, is inevitable. Those who will not move must be swept aside.
Harper's, 1912

NORMAN MAILER
(1932–   )
American writer

The Naked and the Dead (1946)

The natural role of twentieth-century man is anxiety.

Try to keep the rebel artist alive in you, no matter how attractive or exhausting the temptation.

"Advertisement for Myself on the Way Out" (1959)*

America is a cruel soil for talent. It stunts it, blights it, uproots it, or overheats it with cheap fertilizer. And our literary gardeners, our publishers, editors, reviewers and general flunkeys, are drunks, cowards, respectables, prose couturiers, fashion-mongers, old maids, time servers and part-time pimps on the Avenue of President Madison. The audiences are not much better—they seem to consist in nine parts of the tense, tasteless victims of a mass-media culture, incapable of confronting a book unless it is successful.

Christians and Cannibals (1966)

What characterizes the Cannibals is that most of them are born Christians, think of Jesus as Love, and get an erection from the thought of whippings, blood, burning crosses, burning bodies, and screams in mass graves. Whereas their counterpart, the Christians— the ones who are not Christian but whom we choose to call Christians—are utterly opposed to the destruction of human life and succeed within themselves in starting all the wars of our own time.
Part I, 1

Obscenity is where God and Devil meet, and so is another of the avatars in which art ferments and man distills.
Quoted in *Esquire*, December 1967

MAIMONIDES (Moses ben Maimon)
(1135–1204)
Spanish-born Jewish philosopher

Guide to the Perplexed (1190)

Anticipate charity by preventing poverty.

*Reply to Lyle Stuart's request for advice to young writers.

Preservation of Youth

Generally, it may be stated that what people consider to be good is really bad, and most of the things that are considered bad are really good.

Letter to Marseilles (1195)

Astrology is a disease, not a science. . . . It is a tree under the shadow of which all sorts of superstitions thrive. . . . Only fools and charlatans lend value to it.

"Responsa," ii, 25b

HAROUN AL MAKHZOUMI
(13th century A.D.)
Arab scholar, physician

The Fountain of Pleasure

Woman has no need nor does she have compassion for a weak man, and will look with loathing and contempt on such a man because in his weakness she sees a reflection of her own weakness.

The sweetest woman can be turned into a shrew by a man if he excites her but does not fulfill her. To tame her and bring her back to sweetness he must make love to her and bring forth her pleasures, and she will change immediately as night changes to day. . . . [S]he will become a good wife, a good companion, a good mother, and a good human being.

BERNARD MALAMUD
(1914–   )
American writer, novelist

Dubin's Lives (1979)

All biography is ultimately fiction.

MALCOLM X
(1925–1965)
American Black leader

Power never takes a back step—only in the face of more power.

Power recognizes only power, and all of them who realize this have made gains.

Speech, delivered at various times and places

BRONISLAW MALINOWSKI
(1884–1942)
Polish-born anthropologist

Magic, Science and Religion (1925)

The physiological phases of human life, and above all, its crises, such as conception, pregnancy, birth, puberty, marriage, and death, form the nuclei of numerous rites and beliefs.

In primitive conditions tradition is of supreme value for the community and nothing matters as much as uniformity and conservativism of its members.

Sex has been, from some older writers up to the psychoanalytic school, frequently regarded as the main source of religion. In fact, however, it plays an astonishingly insignificant part in religion, considering its force and insidious-ness in human life in general.

The belief in immortality is the result of a deep emotional revelation, standardized by religion, rather than a primitive philosophic doctrine.

Speaking in terms of evolution, we find that war is not a permanent institution of mankind. . . . The chaotic brawls, the internecine fighting of the lowest savages have nothing in common with the institution of war.

Address, Harvard, September 17, 1936

SIR THOMAS MALORY
(c. 1408–1471)
Author of *Le Morte d'Arthur**

Le Morte d'Arthur (c. 1469)

I shall curse you with book and bell and candle.

Bk. XXI, ch. 1

Ever will a coward show no mercy.

Ch. 9

---

*Malory lived during the reign of King Edward IV of England; his identity was established by Prof. G.L. Kittredge, *Harvard Studies and Notes,* vol. V, 1896. See *Britannica,* 11th ed., vol. xvii.

ANDRÉ MALRAUX
(1901–1976)
French writer, aviator

La Condition humaine [Man's Fate] (1933)

The great mystery is not that we should have been thrown down here at random between the profusion of matter and that of the stars; it is that from our very prison we should draw, from our own selves, images powerful enough to deny our nothingness.

Voices of Silence (1951)

A man becomes truly Man only when in quest of what is most exalted in him. True arts and cultures relate Man to duration, something other than the most favored denizen of a universe founded on absurdity.

The Metamorphoses of the Gods (1956)

For Greece, we know, the truth of the world is in man, as for Egypt, the truth of man was in the eternal.

Greece invented a goddess, Reason, with a triangle for a head.

Greek art bequeathed what is called culture, a world risen from the confusion of life, as the Victory (of Samothrace) rose from the melee of battle.

Man's Hope (1938)

There is no place in communism for anyone who first of all wants to be himself, in short, to exist separately from the rest.

Liberty does not always have clean hands.

Be careful,—with quotations you can damn anything.
> Anti-censorship address, Assembly,
> November 12, 1966

Our time recognizes that art is one of the fundamental defenses against our fate.
> Contribution, *Anchor Review,* No. 1

Communism destroys democracy. Democracy can also destroy Communism.
> C.L. Sulzberger interview, *New York Times,*
> June 25, 1958

The road from political idealism to political realism is strewn with the corpses of our dead selves.
> Quoted in *Saturday Review,* December 9, 1961

Comedy is so important that it alone has unified the capitalist world, doing what the will to revolution did for the Communist world.

But, comedy aside, what remains is the essential, what I have called the external—to put it clearly, the realm of sex and the realm of blood.
> Quoted in *The New Yorker,* April 18, 1964

If our civilization is not the first to deny the immortality of the soul, it is certainly the first for which the soul has no importance.
> Reply to De Gaulle quoted in *The New Yorker,*
> April 24, 1971

THOMAS ROBERT MALTHUS
(1766–1834)
English minister, economist, historian*

Essay on the Principle of Population (1798)

Population, when unchecked, increases in a geometrical ratio. Subsistence increases only in an arithmetical rate. A slight acquaintance with numbers will show the immensity of the first power in comparison to the second.

Other circumstances being the same, it may be affirmed that countries are populous according to the quantity of food which they produce or can acquire, and happy according to the liberality with which this food is divided, or the quantity which a day's labor will purchase.

Famine seems to be the last, the most dreadful resource of nature. The power of population is so superior to the power of the earth to provide subsistence . . . that premature death must in some shape or other visit the human race.

It would be hard indeed if the gratification of so delightful a passion as virtuous love did not sometimes more than counterbalance all its attendant evils.

If those stimulants to exertion which arise from the wants of the body, were removed from the mass of mankind, we have much rea-

---

*Darwin credits Malthus's *Essay on the Principle of Population* and the term "struggle for existence" with providing him "a theory by which to work."

son to think that they would be sunk to the level of brutes from a deficiency of excitements, than that they would be raised to the level of philosophers by the possession of leisure.

It is probable, therefore, that improved reason will always tend to prevent the abuse of sensual pleasures, though it by no means follows that it will extinguish them.

A laborer who marries without being able to support a family may in some respects be considered as an enemy of all his fellow-laborers.
Bk. I

BERNARD DE MANDEVILLE
(1670?–1733)
English philosopher

The Fable of the Bees (5th ed., 1728)

It would be easier, where property is well secured, to live without money than without poor; for who would do the work? . . . As they [the poor] ought to be kept from starving, so they should receive nothing worth saving. . . . Those who get their living by their daily labor . . . have nothing to stir them up to be serviceable but their wants which it is a prudence to relieve, but folly to cure.

JEHAN DE MANDEVILLE (Sir John Mandeville)
(1300?–1372)
English traveler, adventurer, writer*

The Travels of Sir John Mandeville (c. 1371)

And this Star, that is toward the North, that we clepe the Lode Star, appeareth not to them. For which cause, men may well perceive, that the Land and the Sea be of round shape and form. . . . And if I had had Company and Shipping, for to go more beyond, I trow well, in certain, that we should have seen all roundness of the Firmament all about.**
Ch. 20

---

*First prose writer in the annals of English literature."—Halliwell, 1839 ed. of Mandeville, from 300-year-old manuscript. The *Britannica*, 11th ed., vol. xvii, characterizes the claim that Mandeville was the father of English prose as spurious.
**" . . . written nearly 150 years before the discovery of America, it proves beyond a doubt, that Mandeville had a distinct idea of the rotundity of the earth."—Chas. D. Cleveland.

HORACE MANN
(1796–1859)
American educator

The common school is the greatest discovery ever made by man.
Inscribed on Mann's bust, Hall of Fame

Be ashamed to die until you have won some victory for humanity.
Commencement oration, Antioch College, 1859

Now surely nothing but universal education can counterwork the tendency to the domination of capital and the servility of labor. If one class possesses all the wealth and the education, while the residue of society is ignorant and poor, it matters not by what name the relation between them may be called: the latter in fact and in truth, will be the servants, dependents and subjects of the former. But, if education be equally diffused, it will draw property after it be the strongest of all attractions; for such a thing never did happen, as that an intelligent and practical body of men should be permanently poor . . .

Education, then, beyond all other devices of human origin, is a great equalizer of conditions of men,—the balance wheel of the social machinery. . . . It does better than to disarm the poor of their hostility toward the rich: it prevents being poor. Agrarianism is the revenge of poverty against wealth.
Twelfth Annual Report to the President of Antioch, 1848

THOMAS MANN
(1875–1955)
German novelist

Reflections of a Non-Political Man (1917)

The German soul is opposed to the pacifist ideal of civilization, for is not peace an element of civil corruption?

The Magic Mountain (1924)

The invention of printing and the Reformation are and remain the two outstanding services of central Europe to the cause of humanity.
Ch. 6

Diary: "Treasury of the Free World" (1946)

It was left to the Germans to bring about a revolution of a character never seen before: a revolution without ideas, opposed to ideas, to everything higher, better, decent; opposed to liberty, truth and justice. Nothing like it has ever occurred in history.

Must conservatism always be in the hands of cave men, or brutal enemies of the spirit?
Letter to *Der neue Merkur,* 1921

MARYA MANNES
(1904–   )
American writer

People minus Space equals Poverty.

We come inevitably to the fundamental question: What are people for? What is living for? If the answer is a life of dignity, decency and opportunity, then every increase in population means a decrease in all three. The crowd is a threat to every single being.
Contribution, *Life,* June 12, 1964

HENRY EDWARD MANNING
(1808–1892)
English Cardinal

Every man has a right to work or to bread.
Letter, quoted in *Britannica,* 11th ed.

Politicals are a part of morals.

The future of Catholicism is in America.
Sermon, Pro-Cathedral, Kensington

The Church: Its Own Witness *

Next to the sun at noonday, there is nothing in the world more manifest than the one visible Universal Church. Both the faith and the infidelity of the world bear witness to it. It is loved and hated, trusted and feared, served and assaulted, honored and blasphemed: it is Christ or Antichrist, the Kingdom of God or the imposture of Satan. It pervades the civilized world. No man and no nation can ignore it, none can be indifferent to it.

William Murray, 1st **EARL OF MANSFIELD**
(1704–1793)
Lord Chief Justice of England

When we apply the maxim that every man's house is his castle we mean not to persuade

*Written before 1851, when Manning was still an Anglican.

the inhabitor of a poor hut that it is provided with drawbridges and portcullises, but only than it is under such sufficient protection as may provide for his security in a more pleasant, or perhaps, a better way—that it is fortified by the law.
Judgment, Lee v. Gansell, 1774

The air of England has long been too pure for a slave, and every man is free who breathes it. Every man who comes to England is entitled to the protection of English law, whatever oppression he may heretofore have suffered, and whatever may be the color of his skin.
Case of James Somersett, May 1772

I will not do that which my conscience tells me is wrong to gain the huzzahs of thousands, or the daily praise of all the papers which come from the press; I will not avoid doing what I think is right, though it should draw on me the whole artillery that falsehood and malice can invent, or the credulity a deluded population can swallow.
Credo for Judges

Iustitia fiat, ruat coelum.
Let justice be done, though the sky falls.
Rex v. Wilkes, June 8, 1768

The greater the truth the greater the libel.
Attributed

MANU*

Code of Manu (c. 400 B.C.–200 A.D.)

In childhood a woman must be subjected to her father; in youth to her husband; when her husband is dead, to her sons. A woman must never be free of subjugation.

A wife must worship her husband as if he were a god, though he may be without virtue or other good qualities, and seek pleasure with other women.

Not a single act here [below] appears ever to be done by a man free from desire; whatever [man] does, it is [the result of] the impulse of desire.

*In Hindu mythology, a progenitor of the human race. Manu (Sanscrit for "man"), "the first man, ancestor of the world."—*Britannica,* 11th ed. vol. xvii.

A barren wife may be superseded in the eighth year, she whose children [all] die in the tenth, she who bears only daughters in the eleventh, but she who is quarrelsome, without delay.

MAO ZEDONG
(1893–1976)
Founder of Chinese Communist State

Several hundred million peasants will rise like a mighty storm, a force so swift and violent, that no power, however great, will be able to hold it back.
> Speech, 1927 ("The Great Leap Forward")

The enemy advances: we retreat
The enemy halts: we harass
The enemy tires: we attack
The enemy retreats: we pursue.
> Party Report, 1928

The deepest source of military strength lies in the masses of people. Armaments constitute an important factor in war, but not the deciding factor. The deciding factor is man, not material.

War cannot be divorced from politics for a single moment.
> Lectures, 1938

Selected Works of Mao Tse-tung

Liberalism is extremely harmful. It is a corrosive which disrupts unity. . . . It deprives the revolutionary ranks of compact organization and discipline.
> "Combat Liberalism," September 7, 1937

Every Communist must grasp the truth; "Political power grows out of the barrel of a gun." Our principle is that the Party commands the gun and the gun will never be allowed to command the Party.
> "Problems of War and Strategy"

Letting a hundred flowers bloom and a hundred schools of thought contend is the policy.*
> "On the Correct Handling of Contradiction Among the People," February 27, 1957

---

*George Paloczi-Horvath, in *Mao Tse-tung: Emperor of the Blue Ants,* says this slogan is a combination of two old Chinese sayings, and the word "hundred" should be translated "numerous."

Was not Hitler a paper tiger? . . . The tzar of Russia, the emperor of China and Japanese imperialism were all paper tigers. U.S. imperialism has not yet been overthrown and it has the atom bomb. I believe it also will be overthrown. It, too, is a paper tiger.
> Address, Moscow, November 11, 1957

*Quotations from Chairman Mao***

Revisionism is the opium of the people.

A revolution is not a dinner party, or writing an essay, or painting a picture, or doing embroidery; it cannot be so refined, so leisurely and gentle, so temperate, kind, courteous, restrained and magnanimous. A revolution is an insurrection, an act of violence by which one class overthrows another.

We should support whatever the enemy opposes and oppose whatever the enemy supports.

War is the highest form of struggle for resolving contradictions when they have developed to a certain state, between classes, nations, states, or political groups, and it has existed ever since the emergence of private property and of classes.

We are advocates of the abolition of war; we do not want war, but war can only be abolished through war, and in order to get rid of the gun it is necessary to take up the gun. . . . [W]hen classes and states are eliminated there will be no more wars.

In the last analysis, all the truths of Marxism can be summed up in the sentence: To rebel is justified.
> Quoted in *Sunday Times,* London, March 5, 1967

A wave of liberalism followed the publication. Criticism flourished. There was a student uprising. Mao, alarmed, revised his slogan. Paloczi-Horvath states: "The signal that *real blooming* was a crime, punishable by death, came on June 18 when the amended text of Mao's original 'contradiction speech' was finally published." The *Observer* and *Sunday Times* of London reported tens of thousands executed for participation in revolts, uprisings, and violent demonstrations "during the hundred flowers disturbances."
**These, and several following quotations, are from the English edition of the book, Peking, 1956, plastic-bound, marked "First Edition" although it has a preface "to the second edition." Sold in the U.S. for 40 cents.

The world rolls on,
Time presses.
Ten thousand years are too long!
Seize the day! Seize the hour!
                Quoted in *Time*, July 12, 1971*

Dogma is less useful than cow dung.

Uninterrupted revolution.
Quoted in Malraux, *Anti-Memoirs;* cf. Trotsky, *The
                          Permanent Revolution*

Politics is war carried out without bloodshed, and war is politics carried out with
bloodshed.
Quoted by H.C. Lodge, NBC, November 15, 1964

We are always revolutionists and never reformers.
        To Edgar Snow, quoted in *The Battle for Asia*
                                      (1941)

Communism is not love, communism is a
hammer which we use to crush the enemy.
            Quoted in *Time*, December 18, 1950

. . . But the changing of man himself has
not yet been completed. Men have to be
changed.
            Quoted in *People's Daily*, Peking,
                          September 18, 1957

MARCUS AURELIUS ANTONIUS
(121–180 A.D.)
Roman Emperor, Stoic philosopher*

Meditations

I have comprehended the nature of Good,
that it is beautiful, and the nature of Evil that
it is ugly, and the nature of the wrongdoer
himself, that it is akin to me, not as a partaker
of the same blood and seed, but of intelligence
and a morsel of the divine.

Say to yourself at daybreak: I shall come
across the busybody, the thankless, the over-
bearing, the treacherous, the envious, the un-

---

*Repeated by President Nixon at Peking banquet,
February 1972.
*Original name Marcus Annius Verus. His father,
born in Spain, named him Annius Verus. "Their
[the two Antonines] united reigns are possibly the
only period of history in which the happiness of a
great people was the sole object of government."—
Gibbon, *Decline and Fall of the Roman Empire*.

neighborly. All this has befallen them because
they know not good from evil.
                                      II, 1

And thou wilt give thyself relief, if thou
doest every act of thy life as if it were the last,
laying aside all carelessness and passionate
aversion from the commands of reason, and
all hypocrisy, and self-love, and discontent
with all the portion which has been given to
thee.
                                      II, 5

Life is a warfare and a stranger's sojourn,
and after-fame is oblivion.

Nothing is evil which is according to nature.
                                      II, 17

Never value anything as profitable to thyself
which shall compel thee to break thy promise,
to lose thy self-respect, to hate any man, to
suspect, to curse, to act the hypocrite, to desire
anything which needs walls and curtains: for
he who has prefered to everything else his own
intelligence and daemon and the worship of its
excellence, acts no tragic part, does not groan,
will not need either solitude or much company; and, what is chief of all, he will live
without either pursuing or flying from death.
                                      III, 7

Men seek out retreats for themselves in the
country, by the seaside, on the mountains. . . . But all this is unphilosophical to
the last degree . . . when thou canst at a moment's notice retire into thyself.

Let thy chief fort and place of defense be, a
mind free from passions. A stronger place and
better fortified than this, hath no man.

The universe is change.

Our life is what our thoughts make it.
                                      IV, 3

Death hangs over thee. While thou still
live, while thou may, do good.
                                      IV, 17

How much trouble he avoids who does not
look to see what his neighbor says or does or
thinks.
                                      IV, 18

Occupy thyself with few things, says the
philosopher, if thou wouldst be tranquil.
                                      IV, 24

Live with the gods.
                                      V, 27

Death is the cessation of the impressions through the senses, of the tyranny of the passions, the errors of the mind, and the servitude of the body.

VI, 28

On Pain: what we cannot bear removes us from life; what lasts can be borne.

VII, 33

Remember this, that very little is needed to make a happy life.

VII, 67

Whatever action of thine that, either immediately or afar off, hath not reference to the common good, that is an exorbitant action; yea, it is seditious.

IX, 23

Either there is a God and all is well. Or, if all things go by chance and fortune, yet mayest thou use thine own providence in those things that concern thee properly, and then art thou well.

XII, 14

There is nothing truly good and beneficial unto man, but that which makes him just, temperate, courageous, liberal; and there is nothing truly evil and hurtful unto man, but that which causes contrary effects.

Poverty is the mother of crime.

Attributed

HERBERT MARCUSE
(1898–1979)
American philosopher

Many people are afraid of freedom. They are conditioned to be afraid of it.

The liberation of man depends neither on God nor on the nonexistence of God. It is not the idea of God which has been an obstacle to human liberation, but the use that has been made of the idea of God.

There is no free society without silence . . .

Law and order are always and everywhere the law and order which protect the established hierarchy.

Interview, *L'Express,* Paris; reprinted in *N.Y. Times,* October 27, 1968

PIERRE SYLVAIN MARECHAL
(1750–1803)
French poet, revolutionist

Manifesto of the Equals* (April 1796)

From time immemorial it has been repeated, with hypocrisy, that *men are equal;* and from time immemorial the most degrading and the most monstrous inequality ceaselessly weigh on the human race.

Let the revolting distinction of rich and poor disappear, once and for all, the distinction of great and small, of masters and valets, of governors and governed. Let there be no difference between human beings other than those of age and sex. Since all have the same needs and the same faculties, let there be one education for all, one food for all.

(Filippo) TOMMASO MARINETTI
(1876–1944)
Italian writer

"Futurist Manifesto" (1909)

A roaring motor-car, which looks as though running on shrapnel, is more beautiful than the Victory of Samothrace.

We wish to glorify war—the only health-giver of the world—militarism, patriotism, the destructive arm of the Anarchist, the beautiful Ideas that kill the contempt for woman.

Figaro, Paris, February 20, 1909

JACQUES MARITAIN
(1882–1963)
French writer

Introduction to Philosophy

The sole philosophy open to those who doubt the possibility of truth is absolute silence—even mental.

II. IV

I Believe

Christianity taught men that love is worth more than intelligence.

*The Manifesto was appropriated by Babeuf and his followers.

GAIUS MARIUS
(c. 155–86 B.C.)
Roman consul, soldier

The Law speaks too softly to be heard amid the din of arms.
> Reply to censure in the Forum, c. 92 B.C.

CHRISTOPHER MARLOWE
(1564–1593)
English dramatist

"Tamburlaine the Great" (c. 1587)

Accurst be he that first invented war.
> Pt. I, line 664

"The Jew of Malta" (c. 1589)

To undo a Jew is charity, and not sin.

I count religion but a childish toy,
And hold there is no sin but ignorance.
> Prologue

Friar Bernardine: Thou hast committed—
Barabas: Fornication—but that was in another country:
And besides, the wench is dead.
> IV.i, 40

The Tragical History of Dr. Faustus (published 1604)

The reward of sin is death: that's hard.

If we say that we have no sin, we deceive ourselves, and
there's no truth in us. Why, then, belike we must sin,
and so consequently die:
Ay, we must die an everlasting death,
What doctrine call you this, *Che sera sera.*
What will be, shall be? Divinity, adieu!

Mephistopheles: Hell hath no limits, nor is circumscribed
In one self place, where we are is Hell,
And where Hell is, there must we ever be,
And to be short, when all the world dissolves,
And every creature shall be purified,
All places shall be hell that are not heaven.
> II.i, 120

Was this the face that launched a thousand ships,
And burnt the topless towers of Ilium?

Sweet Helen, make me immortal with a kiss!
Her lips suck forth my soul: see, where it flies!
Come Helen, come give me my soul again.
Here will I dwell, for heaven be in these lips,
And all is dross that is not Helena.
> V.i, 97

"Hero and Leander" (published 1598)
Who ever loved, that loved not at first sight?

JOHN MARSHALL
(1755–1835)
Chief Justice, U.S. Supreme Court

The government of the United States has been emphatically termed a government of laws, and not of men.

That the people have an original right to establish for their future government, such principles as, in their opinion, shall most conduce to their own happiness, is the basis, on which the whole American fabric has been erected.
> Marbury v. Madison, 1 Church 137 (1803)

That the power to tax involves the power to destroy; that the power to destroy may defeat and render useless the power to create; that there is plain repugnance, in conferring on one government a power to control the constitutional measures of another, which other, with respect to those very measures is declared to be supreme over that which exerts the control, are propostions not to be denied.
> McCulloch v. Maryland, 4 Wheaton 316 (1819)

A corporation is an artificial thing, invisible, intangible, and existing only in the contemplation of the law.
> Darmouth College v. Woodward, 4 Wheaton 518 (1819)

JOSÉ MARTÍ (y Perez)
(1853–1895)
Cuban patriot, national hero

"Granos de Oro" (pub. posthumously 1942)

Habit creates the appearance of justice; progress has no greater enemy than habit.

MARTIAL (Marcus Valerius Martialis)
(c. 40–c. 104 A.D.)
Iberia-born Roman poet

Epigramata

Sera nimis vita crastine; vive hodie.
Too late is tomorrow's life; live for today.
I, 15

Property given away (to friends) is the only
kind that will forever be yours.
V, 42

ANDREW MARVELL
(1621–1678)
English poet, Milton's Latin secretary

"Doleful Evils"

For the press hath owed him a shame a long
time, and is but now beginning to pay off the
debt,—the press (that *villaneous* engine), invented about the same time with the Reformation, that hath done more mischief to the
discipline of our church than all the doctrine
can make amends for.
O Printing! how hath thou disturbed the
peace of mankind! That lead, when moulded
into bullets, is not so mortal as when founded
into letters.

"To His Coy Mistress" (1650–1652)

But at my back I always hear
Time's wingéd chariot hurrying near;

The grave's a fine and private place,
But none, I think, do there embrace.

(Heinrich) KARL MARX
(1818–1893)
German journalist, founder of Communism*

Dynamic principle.
Title of dissertation for Ph.D. (1841)

The free press is the omnipresent eye of the
spirit of the people, the embodied confidence
of a people in itself, the articulate bond that
ties the individual to the state and the world,
the incorporated culture which transfigures
material struggles into intellectual struggles. It
is the ruthless confession of a people to itself,
and it is well known that the power of confession is redeeming.

Freedom of the press is the intellectual mirror in which a people sees itself, and self-view-
ing is the first condition of wisdom.
Discussion before Rhenish Diet, 1841; quoted in
Saul K. Padover, *Karl Marx: On the Freedom
of the Press*

The essence of the free press is the reliable,
reasonable and moral nature of freedom. The
character of the censored press is the nondes-
cript confusion of tyranny.
Contribution, *Neue Rheinische Zeitung,*
May 13, 1842

"Critique of the Hegelian Philosophy of Right"
(*Deutsche-franzöische Yahrbücher,* 1844)

The foundation of irreligious criticism is
this: man makes religion; religion does not
make man. Religion is, in fact, the self-consciousness and self-esteem of a man who has
either not yet gained himself or has lost himself again.

Religion is the general theory of the world,
its encyclopedic compendium, its logic in
popular form, its spiritualistic *point d'hon-
neur,* its enthusiasm, its moral sanction, its
solemn complement, its universal basis of
consolation and justification.

The wretchedness of religion is at once an
expression and a protest against real wretchedness. Religion is the sigh of the oppressed creature, the feeling of a heartless world, just as it
is the spirit of unspiritual conditions. It is the
opium of the people. **

---

*From 1842 to 1847 Marx "considered himself to be
primarily a crusading journalist."—Saul K. Padover,
Karl Marx: On the Freedom of the Press.
Henry Adams in a letter to Brooks Adams: "The
Marxian theory of hisory I take to be the foundation
of yours. . . . The assertion of the law of economy
as the law of history is the only contribution that the
Socialists have made to my library of ideas."
"Marx was the best hated and calumniated man of
his time."—Friedrich Engels, funeral oration,
March 17, 1883.

Marx was a Christian in his childhood and youth,
his parents having converted from Judaism when he
was six.
**"Marx's position is widely misunderstood. . . .
When the essay in question was written opium was
used in Europe almost exclusively for relieving
pain. . . . Marx was using the word 'opium' in *this*
sense and *not* in the sense that religion is a stupefier
deliberately administered to the people by the agents
of the ruling class."—*Weekly People,* official organ,
Socialist Labor Party, U.S.A., January 31, 1959.

The criticism of religion is therefore in embryo the criticism of the vale of woe, the halo of which is religion.

The task of history, therefore, once the world beyond the truth has disappeared, is to establish the truth of the world.

Introduction

On the Jewish Question (1844)*

The emancipation of the Jews in the last significance is the emancipation of mankind from Judaism.

Statement, 1844

To be radical is to grasp the matter by its roots. Now, the root for mankind is man.

The German Ideology (1846, written with Friedrich Engels)

Men's ideas are the most direct emanation of their material state. This is true in politics, law, morality, religion, metaphysics, etcetera.

Deutsch-Baseler-Zeitung (1847)

The social principles of Christianity justified the slavery of antiquity; glorified the serfdom of the Middle Ages; and equally know, when necessary, how to defend the oppression of the proletariat, although they make a pitiful face over it.

The social principles of Christianity preach cowardice, self-contempt, abasement, submission, humility, in a word all the qualities of the *canaille;* and the proletariat, not wishing to be treated as *canaille,* needs its courage, its self-esteem, its pride, and its sense of independence more than its bread.

The Communist Manifesto (written with Engels in 1848)

A spectre is haunting Europe—the spectre of Communism. All the powers of old Europe have entered into a holy alliance to exorcise this spectre: Pope and Czar, Meternich and Guizot, French Radicals and German police spies.

Opening lines

The history of all hitherto existing society is the history of class struggles.

---

*By Judaism Marx meant commercialism, according to Eduard Bernstein, *Britannica,* 11th ed.

Lumpenproletariat.

Law, morality, religion are to him [the proletarian] so many bourgeois prejudices, behind which lurk in ambush just as many bourgeois interests.

Sec. 1

The theory of the Communists may be summed up in the single sentence: Abolition of private property.

Our bourgeoisie, not content with having the wives and daughters of their proletarians at their disposal, not to speak of common prostitutes, take the greatest pleasure in seducing each others' wives.

Abolition of the family! Even the most radical flare up at this infamous proposal of the Communists.

The bourgeois family will vanish as a matter of course when its complement vanishes, and both will vanish with the vanishing of capital.

1. Abolition of property in land and application of all rents to public purposes.
2. A heavy progressive income tax.
3. Abolition of all right of inheritance.
4. Confiscation of the property of emigrants and rebels.
5. Centralization of credit in the hands of the State.
6. Centralization of the means of communication and transport . . .
7. Extension of factories and instruments of production owned by the State . . .
8. Equal liability of all to labor. Establishment of industrial armies, especially for agriculture.
9. Combination of agriculture with manufacturing industries; gradual abolition of the distinction between town and country . . .
10. Free education for all children in public schools. Abolition of child factory labor . . .

Sec. 2

The bourgeois clap-trap about the family and education, about the hallowed co-relation of parent and child, become all the more disgusting, the more, by the action of Modern Industry, all family ties among the proletariat are torn asunder, and their children transformed into simple articles of commerce and instruments of labor.

In proportion as the antagonism between classes within the nation vanishes, the hostility of one nation to another will come to an end.

Christian Socialism is but the Holy Water with which the priest consecrates the heart-burnings of the aristocrat.

The Communists disdain to conceal their views and aims. They openly declare that their ends can be attained only by the forcible overthrow of all existing social conditions. Let the ruling classes tremble at a Communist revolution. The proletarians have nothing to lose but their chains. They have a world to win.

Workingmen of all countries, unite!

Sec. 3

"The Eighteenth Brumaire of Louis Napoleon" (1856)

Hegel remarks somewhere that all great, historical facts and personages occur as it were, twice. He forgets to add: the first time as tragedy, the second as farce.

Das Kapital, Vol. I* (1867)

Capital is dead labor, that, vampire-like, only lives by sucking [blood] from living labor.

. . . money . . . like the radical leveller that it is, does away with all distinctions. . . . Modern society . . . greets gold as its Holy Grail, as the glittering incarnation of the very principle of its own life.

Books are, in one sense, the basis of all social progress.

Ch. 5

Capitalistic production is not merely the production of commodities; it is essentially the production of surplus value.

Ch. 6

All surplus value, whatever particular (profits, interest, or rent) it may subsequently crystallize into, is in substance the materialization of unpaid labor.

Accumulation of wealth at one pole is . . . at the same time accumulation of misery, agony of toil, slavery, ignorance, brutality, men-

tal degradation, at the other pole, i.e., on the side of the class that produces its own product in the form of capital.

Ch. 7

Labor in a white skin cannot be free as long as labor in a black skin is branded.

Ch. 10

Critique of the Gotha Program (1875)

When labor has become not only a means of living, but itself the first necessity of life . . . it will be possible . . . for society to inscribe on its banners: From each according to his abilities; to each according to his needs. *

"Theses on Feuerbach" (1888)

The philosophers have only *interpreted* the world in various ways; the point is to *change* it.

xi* *

Philosophy makes no secret of the fact. Her creed is the creed of Prometheus—"In a word, I detest all the gods." This is the device against all deities of heaven or earth who do not recognize as the highest divinity the human self-consciousness itself.

Philosophy stands in the relation to the study of the actual world, as onanism is to sexual life.

I hope the bourgeoisie as long as they live will have cause to remember my carbuncles.

Letter to Engels

Their battle-cry must be The Permanent Revolution.

Address, Communist League, March 1850

What was new on my part was to prove the following:

1. that the existence of classes is connected only with certain historical struggles which arise out of the development of production;
2. that class struggle necessarily leads to the dictatorship of the proletariat;
3. that this dictatorship itself is only a transition to the *abolition of all classes* and to a *classless society*.

Letter to Joseph Wedemeyer, March 5, 1852

---

*Volumes II and III were completed by Engels from Marx's unfinished manuscript writings. In his preface to Vol. I, second edition, Marx wrote (Jan. 24, 1873): "The learned and unlearned spokesmen of the German Bourgeoisie tried at first to kill *Das Kapital* by silence, as they had managed to do with my earlier writings." Marx was maligned, libeled, attacked, and unpublished. His one sympathetic outlet was the New York *Tribune,* which paid him about $5 per contribution.

---

*Jeder nach seinen Fähigkeiten, jedem nach seinen Bedürfnissen. In 1848, Louis Blanc, French Socialist, wrote: "From each according to his abilities, to each according to his needs."
**Inscribed on Marx's tomb, London.

History is the judge—its executioner the proletarian.
Address, anniversary of the English Chartists, 1856

Instead of the *conservative* motto: "A fair day's wages for a fair day's work!" they ought to inscribe on their banner the *revolutionary* watchword: "Abolition of the wages system."
"Value, Price and Profit," address, General Council of the First Internationale, June 27, 1865

From the commencement of the titanic American strife [the Civil War] the working-men of Europe felt instinctively that the star-spangled banner carried the destiny of their class.

The workingmen of Europe feel sure that as the American War of Independence initiated a new era of ascendency for the middle class, so the American anti-slavery War will do for the working classes. They consider it an earnest of the epoch to come, that it fell to the lot of Abraham Lincoln, the single-minded son of the working class, to lead his country through the matchless struggle for the rescue of the en-chained race and the reconstruction of a social world.
Letter to President Lincoln, January 7, 1865

The policy of Russia is changeless. . . . Its methods, its tactics, its maneuvers may change, but the polar star of its policy—world domination—is a fixed star.
Written, published, in 1867

The imaginary flowers of religion adorn man's chains. Man must throw away the flow-ers and also the chains.
Quoted in Simon Emler, *The Wisdom of Karl Marx*

Force is the midwife of every old society pregnant with a new one.
Quoted in Engels, "Anti-Dühring"; also by J. Edgar Hoover

Once an uprising has begun, one must act with the greatest decisiveness, one must take the offensive, absolutely, and under all cir-cumstances. "Defense is the death of an armed uprising."
Quoted by Lenin, letter, October 21 [old style], 1917

Dialectical materialism.
Attributed to Marx in Engels' "Ludwig Feuerbach"

The rich will do everything for the poor ex-cept get off their backs.

Never play at uprising, but once it is begun, remember firmly that you have to go to the very end.

Uprising, like war, is an art.
Attributed

TOMAS G. MASARYK
(1850–1937)
Liberator of Czechoslovakia

Dictators always look good until the last minutes.
Attributed

JOHN MASEFIELD
(1878–1967)
Britain's poet laureate from 1930

"To His Mother, C.L.M."

In the dark womb where I began
My mother's life made me a man.
Through all the months of human birth
Her beauty fed my common earth.
I cannot see, nor breathe, nor stir.
But through the death of some of her.

"Truth"

Man with the burning soul
Has but an hour of breath.
To build a ship of Truth
In which his soul may sail,
Sail on the sea of death,
For death takes toll
Of beauty, courage, youth,
Of all but Truth.

"On Growing Old"

Be with me, Beauty, for the fire is
dying, ...

Beauty, have pity, for the strong have
power,
The rich their wealth, the beautiful their
grace,
Summer of man its sunlight and its flower,
Spring-time of man all April in a face.
Let me have wisdom, Beauty, wisdom and
passion,
Bread to the soul, rain where the summers
parch.
Give me these, and though the darkness
close
Even the night will blossom as the rose.

"A Consecration"

> Theirs be the music, the color, the glory,
>   and gold;
> Mine be a handful of ashes, a mouthful of
>   mould.
> Of the maimed, of the halt and the blind in
>   the rain and the cold,
> Of these shall my songs be fashioned, my
>   tale be told. AMEN.

The Tragedy of Nan (1908)

Commonplace people dislike tragedy because they dare not suffer and cannot exult.

The truth and rapture of man are holy things, not lightly to be scorned. A carelessness of life and beauty mark the glutton, the idler, and the fool in their deadly path across history.

Preface

GEORGE MASON
(1725–1792)
American Revolutionary leader, Founding Father

Virginia Declaration of Rights, June 12, 1776

That all power is vested in, and consequently derived from, the People; that magistrates are their trustees and servants, and at all times amenable to them.

Article 2

That Government is, or ought to be, instituted for the common benefit, (protection) and security of the people, nation or community; . . . and that whenever any government shall be found inadequate or contrary to these purposes, a majority of the community hath an indubitable, unalienable, indefeasible right, to reform, alter, or abolish it, in such manner as shall be judged most conducive to the public Weal.

Article 3

MASSACHUSETTS COLONY

Body of Liberties (1641)

94. Capital Laws.
1. If any man after legall conviction shall have or worship any other god, but the lord god, he shall be put to death.
2. If any man or woman be a witch, (that is hath consulteth with a familiar spirit,) They shall be put to death.

3. If any person shall Blaspheme the name of god, the father, Sonne or Holie ghost, with direct, expresse, presumptuous or high handed blasphemie, or shall curse God in the like manner, he shall be put to death.

EDGAR LEE MASTERS
(1868–1950)
American poet

"The Village Atheist" (1915)

> Listen to me, ye who live in the senses
> And think through the senses only:
> Immortality is not a gift,
> Immortality is an achievement;
> And only those who strive mightily
> Shall possess it.

The Great Valley (1916)

> He is sent to school
> Little or much, where he imbibes the rule
> Of safety first and comfort; in his youth
> He joins the church and ends the quest of
>   truth.

"The Typical American?"

> He stripped off the armor of institutional
>   friendships
> To dedicate his soul
> To the terrible deities of Truth and Beauty.

"Poem for R.G. Ingersoll"

COTTON MATHER
(1663–1728)
American Congregational minister

"The Wonders of the Invisible World" (1693)

That there is a Devil is a thing doubted by none but such as are under the influence of the Devil. For any to deny the being of a Devil must be from ignorance or profaneness worse than diabolical.

HENRI MATISSE
(1869–1954)
French painter

"Notes of a Painter" (1908)

Rules have no existence outside of individuals.

W(illiam) SOMERSET MAUGHAM
(1874–1965)
British writer

Christmas Holiday (1939)

A proverb distills the wisdom of the ages and only a fool is scornful of the commonplace.

One should only have acquaintances and never make friends.

Pity is the flattery the failure craves so that he may preserve his self-esteem.

What does democracy come down to? The persuasive power of slogans invented by wily self-seeking politicians.

Through the history of the world there have always been exploiters and exploited. There always will be . . . because the great mass of men are made by nature to be slaves, they are unfit to control themselves, and for their own good need masters.

A dictator . . . must fool all the people all the time and there's only one way to do that, he must also fool himself.
"Stranger in Paris"

The Summing Up (1938)

No one can tell the whole truth about himself. It is not only vanity that has prevented those who have tried to reveal themselves to the world from telling the whole truth; it is direction of interest; their disappointment with themselves, their surprise that they can do things that seem to them abnormal, make them place too great an emphasis on occurrences that are more common than they suppose.

The artist can within limits make what he likes of his life. . . . It is only the artist, and maybe the criminal, who can make his own.

I learned that . . . love was the only dirty trick that nature played on us to achieve the continuation of the species.

I cannot believe in a God that has neither honor nor common sense.

Now the answer . . . is plain, but it is so unpalatable that most men will not face it. There is no reason for life and life has no meaning.

The great tragedy of life is not that men perish, but that they cease to love.

The Bread Winners

The Tasmanians, who never committed adultery, are now extinct.

———

Suffering does not enoble, it degrades.

The value of money is that with it you can tell anyone to go to the devil.
Attributed*

GUY DE MAUPASSANT
(1850–1893)
French writer

. . . the experience of centuries . . . has proved that woman is, without doubt, incapable of any artistic or scientific work.
Quoted in Prévost, *Manon Lescault,* introduction, 1885

ANDRÉ MAUROIS (né Emile Herzog)
(1885–1967)
French writer

The Art of Writing (1960)

The need to express one's self in writing springs from a maladjustment of life, or from an inner conflict which the adolescent (or the grown man) cannot resolve in action.

MAXIMILIAN I
(1459–1519)
Roman Emperor

Since Christendom comprehends only a small part of the globe, should not everyone who believes in God be saved by his own religion?
Letter to Abbot Tritemius, 1508

The King of France is called the Most Christian King, but this does him an injustice, for he never did a Christian thing. . . . The Pope is called His Holiness but he is the biggest scoundrel on earth.
Letter to Henry VIII of England, according to Luther, *Table Talk* (1542)

———

*In 1959 Mr. Maugham confirmed all quotations with no source given in a letter to George Seldes.

ROLLO MAY
(1909–   )
Existential therapist, humanist

Love and Will (1969)

I conceive—I can—I will—I am.

Human will begins in a "no." The "no" is a protest against a world we never made, and it is also the assertion of one's self in the endeavor to remold and reform the world.

Power and Innocence (1972)

I need my enemy in my community. He keeps me alert, vital. . . . But beyond what we specifically learn from our enemies, we need them emotionally; our psychic economy cannot get along well without them. . . . [O]ur enemy is as necessary for us as is our friend. Both together are part of authentic community.

Deeds of violence in our society are performed largely by those trying to establish their self-esteem, to defend their self-image, and to demonstrate that they, too, are significant. . . . Violence arises not out of superfluity of power but out of powerlessness.

VLADIMIR MAYAKOVSKY
(1894–1930)
Leading poet, first Soviet epoch

"Left March!" (1918)

Beat on the street the march of rebellion,
Sweeping over the heads of the proud;
We, the flood of a second deluge,
Shall wash the world like a bursting cloud.

JOHN McCAFFREY
(1806–1881)
American Catholic educator

A Catechism of Doctrine for General Use (1866)

Presuming on God's mercy, despair, resisting the known truth, envy of another's spiritual good, obstinancy in sin, and final impenitence, are the six sins against the Holy Ghost.

Pride, covetousness, lust, anger, gluttony, envy and sloth are the seven capital sins.

Humility, liberality, chastity, meekness, temperance, brotherly love, and diligence, are the virtues contrary to the seven capital sins.

Prudence, justice, fortitude and temperance are the four Cardinal Virtues.

MARY McCARTHY
(1912–   )
American writer

Bureaucracy, the rule of no one, has become the modern form of despotism.
Contribution, *The New Yorker,* October 18, 1958

CARL McGEE
Editor, Albuquerque *Tribune*

Give Light and the People Will Find Their Own Way.
Slogan for all Scripps-Howard newspapers

GEORGE McGOVERN
(1922–   )
American Senator

For two centuries we have asserted the propositions of human equality, the sanctity of life, the blessings of liberty and the pursuit of happiness. These liberating ideals not only fueled a revolution; they raised standards of national measurement so high that they are not likely to be fully realized. Thus, we live with a continuing, unfinished revolution that challenges each succeeding generation.
Contribution, *The Nation,* July 19, 1975

CLAUDE McKAY
(1891–1948)
Jamaica-born American poet

"America" (1921)

Although she feeds me bread of bitterness,
And sinks into my throat her tiger's tooth,
Stealing my breath of life, I will confess
I love this cultured hell that tests my youth.

FLOYD BIXLER McKISSICK
(1922–   )
American Black leader

Forget about civil rights. I'm talking about Black Power.
Quoted in *N.Y. Times,* October 1, 1967

HARRY KIRBY MCLINTOCK
(1883–1957)
Radio hillbilly, hobo, member I.W.W.

And *The Day* shall come, with a red, red
  dawn;
And you in your gilded halls,
Shall taste the wrath and vengeance of the
  men in overalls.
  "Hymn of Hate," *Solidarity*, January 1, 1916

MARSHALL McLUHAN
(1911–1980)
**Canadian, director of Center of Culture and
Technology, University of Toronto**

The Medium is the Message.
  Lecture remark, 1959
  Book title, 1967

Understanding Media: The Extensions of Man
(1964)

"The medium is the message" because it is
the medium that shapes and controls the scale
and form of human association and action.
  Pt. I, Ch. 1

The name of a man is a numbing blow from
which he never recovers.
  Pt. I, Ch. 2

Language has always been held to be man's
richest art form, that which distinguishes him
from the animal creation.
  Pt. II, Ch. 8

Like any other extension of man, typogra-
phy had psychic and social consequences that
suddenly shifted previous boundaries and patterns of culture. In bringing the ancient and
medieval worlds into fusion—or, as some
would say, confusion—the printed book created a third world, the modern world, which
now encounters new electric technology or a
new extension of man.
  Pt. II, Ch. 18

All media exist to invest our lives with artificial perceptions and arbitrary values.
  Pt. II, Ch. 20

Real news is bad news.
  Pt. II, Ch. 21

The car is a superb piece of uniform, standardized mechanism that is of a piece with the
Gutenberg technology and literacy which created the first classless society in the world.
  Pt. II, Ch. 22

The historians and archeologists will one
day discover that the ads of our times are the
richest and most faithful daily reflection that
any society ever made of its entire range of activities.
  Pt. II, Ch. 23

War and Peace in the Global Village (with Quentin
Flore, 1968)

Life. Consider the alternative.

From Cliché to Archetype (with Wilfred Watson,
1970)

New means create new ends as new services
create new discomforts.

Class in society is determined by voice.

America is the only country ever founded
on the printed word.
  Address, Harvard, reprinted in *Harvard Today*,
  Spring, 1976

CAREY McWILLIAMS
(1905–1980)
American writer, editor of *The Nation*

A Mask for Privilege (1948)

Anti-Semitism is a social disease. . . . Anti-
Semitism is an excellent diagnostic device to
use in studying the health and wellbeing of society. For it is a harbinger of war, the fear of
inadequacy that, in moments of crisis, breeds
havoc and social panic.

MARGARET MEAD
(1901–1978)
American anthropologist

Love is the invention of a few high cultures,
independent, in a sense, of marriage—although society can make it a requisite for marriage, as we periodically attempt to do. But in
terms of a personal, highly intense choice, it is
a cultural artifact.

To make love the requirement of a lifelong
marriage is exceedingly difficult, and only a
very few people can achieve it. I don't believe
in setting up universal standards that a large
proportion of people can't reach.
  Quoted in *N.Y. Times Magazine*, April 26, 1970

HERMAN MELVILLE
(1819–1891)
American novelist

But it is better to fail in originality than to succeed in imitation.

He who has never failed somewhere, that man can not be great.

Try to get a living by the Truth—and go to the Soup Societies. Heavens! Let any clergyman try to preach the Truth from its very stronghold, the pulpit, and they would ride him out of the church on his own pulpit bannister.

The reason the mass of men fear God, and *at bottom dislike Him,* is because they rather distrust His Heart, and fancy Him all brain like a watch.

> Contribution, "The Literary World,"
> August 17/24, 1850

Moby Dick (1851)

Better sleep with a sober cannibal than a drunken Christian.

> Ch. III

He [the white whale] tasks me; he heaps me; I see in him outrageous strength, with an inscrutable malice sinewing it. That inscrutable thing is chiefly what I hate; and be the white whale agent, or be the white whale principal, I will wreak that hate upon him. Talk not to me of blasphemy, man; I'd strike the sun if it insulted me. For, could the sun do that, I then could do the other; since there is ever a sort of fair play herein, jealousy presiding over all creations. But not my master, man, is even that fair play. Who's over me? Truth hath no confines.

> Ch. XXXVI

But not yet have we solved the incantation of this whiteness, and learned why it appeals with such power to the soul; and more strange and far more portentous—why, as we have seen, it is at once the most meaning symbol of spiritual things, nay, the very veil of the Christian's Deity; and yet should be as it is, the intensifying agent in things the most appalling to mankind.
Is it that by its indefiniteness it shadows forth the heartless voids and immensity of the universe, and thus stabs us from behind with the thought of annihilation, when beholding the white depths of the milky way?

> Ch. XLII

There are certain queer times and occasions in this strange mixed affair we call life when a man takes his whole universe for a vast practical joke.

Give me a condor's quill! Give me Vesuvius's crater for an inkstand. . . . To produce a mighty book you must choose a mighty theme. No great and enduring volume can ever be written on a flea, though many there be that have tried it.

An utterly fearless man is a far more dangerous comrade than a coward.

Doubt all things earthly, and intuitions of some things heavenly; this combination makes neither believer nor infidel, but makes a man who regards them both with equal eye.

Man's insanity is heaven's sense; and wandering from all mortal thought, which, to reason is absurd and frantic; and weal or woe, feels then uncompromised, indifferent to his God.

> Ch. XCIII

We talk of the Turks and abhor the cannibals; but may not some of them go to heaven before some of us? We may have civilized bodies and yet barbarous souls. We are blind to the real sights of this world; deaf to its voice; and dead to its death.

. . . and take high abstracted man alone, and he seems a wonder, a grandeur, and a woe. But from the same point take mankind in mass, and for the most part they seem a mob of unnecessary duplicates, both contemporary and hereditary.

> Ch. CVI

Hawthorne and His Mosses (1850)

Genius all over the world stands hand in hand, and one shock of recognition runs the whole circle round.

Pierre (1852)

There is no faith, and no stoicism, and no philosophy, that a mortal man can possibly evoke, which will stand the final test in a real impassioned onset of Life and Passion upon him. Faith and philosophy are air, but events are brass.

"The March into Virginia"

All wars are boyish, and are fought by boys,
The champions and enthusiasts of the state.

MENANDER
(c. 342–c. 291 B.C.)
Greek comic dramatist

Greek Anthology

Opportunity is a god.

Nothing is worse than a woman, even a good one.

For the crowd, the incredible has sometimes more power and is more credible than Truth
Fragment 622

Marriage, if one will face the truth, is an evil, but a necessary evil.
Fragment 651

More love a mother than a father shows:
He *thinks* this is his son; she only *knows*.
Fragment 657

"Thrasyleon"

"Know Thyself" is a good saying, but not in all situations. In many it is better to say, "Know Others."

"Monosticha"

Art is man's refuge from adversity.
309

Gold opens every gate; e'en that of hell.
538

"The Woman Possessed with a Divinity"

A god from the machine.
227

The chief beginning of evil is goodness in excess.
Quoted in Philo, De Abrahamo

MENCIUS (Meng-tse)
(372?–289? B.C.)
Chinese philosopher

Works (tr. Legge)

He who wishes to be benevolent will not be rich.
Bk. III, pt. I

The great man is he who does not lose his child's heart.
Bk. IV, pt. II

The Living Thoughts of Confucius (ed. Arthur Doeblin)

Let a prince seek by his excellence to nourish men, and he will be able to subdue the whole kingdom. It is impossible that anyone should become ruler of the people to whom they have not yielded the subjection of the heart.

What belongs by nature to the superior man are benevolence, righteousness, propriety, and knowledge.

The men of old wanting to clarify and diffuse throughout the empire that light which comes from looking straight into the heart and then acting, first set up good government in their own states; wanting good government in their own states, they first established order in their families; wanting good order in their families, they first rectified their hearts.

Book of History

A man must [first] despise himself, and then others will despise him. A family must [first] overthrow itself, and then others will overthrow it. A State must [first] smite itself, and then others will smite it.
Bk. IV, pt. I

The people are the most important element [in a country]; the Spirits of the land and grain are the next; the ruler is the least important.
Bk. VII, pt. II

Discourses, 3

Those who labor with their minds govern others; those who labor with their strength are governed by others.

Portable World Bible (Viking)

The great man does not think beforehand of his words that they may be sincere, nor of his actions that they may be resolute,—he simply speaks and does what is right.

The tendency of man's nature to good is like the tendency of water to flow downward. There are nought but have this tendency to good, just as all water flows downward.

Those who follow that part of themselves which is great are great men; those who follow that part which is little are little men.

He who has exhausted all his mental constitution knows his nature. Knowing his nature, he knows heaven. To preserve one's mental constitution, and nourish one's nature, is the way to serve heaven.

H(enry) L(ouis) MENCKEN
(1880–1956)
American editor, critic, lexicographer*

Damn! A Book of Calumny (1918)

The most satisfying and ecstatic faith is almost purely agnostic. It trusts absolutely without professing to know at all.

All great religions in order to escape absurdity, have to admit a dilution of agnosticism. It is only the savage, whether of the African bush or the American gospel tent, who pretends to know the will and intent of God exactly and completely.

Prejudices (1919, first series**)

The basic fact about human existence is not that it is a tragedy, but that it is a bore.

To die for an idea; it is unquestionably noble. But how much nobler it would be if men died for ideas that were true!

Prejudices (1920, second series)

A great literature is chiefly the product of inquiring minds in revolt against the immovable certainties of the nation.

The worshipper is the father of the gods.

Prejudices (1922, third series)

No man ever quite believes in any other man.

Nine times out of ten, in the arts as in life, there is actually nothing to be discovered; there is only error to be exposed.

Faith may be defined briefly as an illogical belief in the occurrence of the improbable.

The anthropomorphic theory of the world is made absurd by modern biology. . . . All the errors and incompetencies of the Creator reach their climax in man. As a piece of mechanism he is the worst of them all. . . .

If we assume that man actually resembles God, then we are forced into the impossible theory that God is a coward, an idiot, and a blunderer. . . .

The only practical effect of having a soul is that it fills man with anthropomorphic and anthropocentric vanities. . . . He struts and plumes himself because he has a soul—and overlooks the fact that it doesn't work. Thus he is the supreme clown of creation, the *reductio ad absurdum* of animated nature.

Prejudices (1924, fourth series)

I know of no existing nation that deserves to live, and I know of very few individuals.

Notes on Democracy (1926)

The fact is that liberty, in any true sense, is a concept that lies quite beyond the reach of the inferior man's mind. He can imagine and even esteem, in his way, certain false forms of liberty—for example, the right to choose between two political mountebanks, and to yell for the more obviously dishonest—but the reality is incomprehensible to him. And no wonder, for genuine liberty demands of its votaries a quality he lacks completely, and that is courage. The man who loves it must be willing to fight for it; blood, said Jefferson, is its natural manure. More, he must be able to endure it—an even more arduous business.
Pt. 1, Ch. 7

Treatise on the Gods (1930)

The whole Christian system, like every other similar system, goes to pieces upon the problem of evil. Its most adept theologians, attempting to reconcile the Heavenly Father of their theory with the dreadful agonies of man in His world, men can only retreat behind Chrysostom's despairing maxim, that "a comprehended God is no God."
Pt. I

Certainly religion must be granted to be one of the greatest inventions ever made on earth.

The clergy repay this friendly recognition of their place in society by an almost unfailing devotion to the constituted authorities. When they take part in rebellions, it is almost always against subversive usurpers, not legitimate rulers. At all times and always they have been the bulwark of orthodoxy in politics. . . . Their prayers always go up for kings, not for rebels and reformers.

---

*"The Voltaire of his time."—Fanny Butcher, Chicago *Tribune* Book Review.
**The first volume was published in 1919, succeeding volumes throughout the 1920s.

The Old Testament, as everyone who has looked into it is aware, drips with blood; there is, indeed, no more bloody chronicle in all the literature of the world.

Pt. III

But any man who afflicts the human race with *ideas* must be prepared to see them misunderstood, and that is what happened to Jesus.

Pt. IV

The truth is that every priest who really understands the nature of his business is well aware that science is its natural and implacable enemy. . . .
The truth is that Christian theology like every other theology, is not only opposed to the scientific spirit, it is also opposed to all attempts at rational thinking. . . .

Pt. V

A Mencken Chrestomathy (1949)

The most costly of all follies is to believe passionately in the palpably not true. It is the chief occupation of mankind.

Every man is his own hell.

In every unbeliever's heart there is an uneasy feeling that, after all, he *may* awake after death and find himself immortal. This is his punishment for his unbelief. This is the agnostic's Hell.

A Galileo could no more be elected President of the United States than he could be elected Pope of Rome. Both posts are reserved for men favored by God with an extraordinary genius for swathing the bitter facts of life in bandages of self-illusion.

The Philosophy of Friedrich Nietzsche

It is only doubt that creates. It is only the minority that counts.

Government, in its very essence, is opposed to all increase in knowledge. Its tendency is always toward permanence and against change . . . . [T]he progress of humanity, far from being the result of government, has been made entirely without its aid and in the face of its constant and bitter opposition.

___

I believe that religion, generally speaking, has been a curse to mankind.
Contribution, *N.Y. Times Magazine,* September 11, 1955

The Booboisie.
Invented word, *American Mercury;* frequently used

His [De Witt Wallace's] magazine [*Reader's Digest*] is so bad it may go over. There's no underestimating the intelligence of the American public.
Remark to Charles Angoff, associate editor*

For men become civilized, not in proportion to their willingness to believe, but in proportion to their readiness to doubt.

I believe that religion, generally speaking, has been a curse to mankind—that its modest and greatly overestimated services on the ethical side have been more than overcome by the damage it has done to clear and honest thinking.
I believe that no discovery of fact, however trivial, can be wholly useless to the race, and that no trumpeting of falsehood, however virtuous in intent, can be anything but vicious.
I believe that all government is evil, in that all government must necessarily make war upon liberty. . . .
I believe that the evidence for immortality is no better than the evidence of witches, and deserves no more respect.
I believe in the complete freedom of thought and speech. . . .
I believe in the capacity of man to conquer his world, and to find out what it is made of, and how it is run.
I believe in the reality of progress.
I—
But the whole thing, after all, may be put very simply. I believe that it is better to tell the truth than to lie. I believe that it is better to be free than to be a slave. And I believe that it is better to know than to be ignorant.
Contribution, *Living Philosophies,* 1931

"Patriotism," said the late Dr. Johnson, glowering at Boswell, "is the last refuge of scoundrels." But there is something worse: it is the first, last and middle refuge of fools.
Contribution, *N.Y. World,* November 7, 1926

All of them [sex hygiene books] are devoted to promoting the absurd and immoral idea that

___

*This is the correct version. There are a dozen (wrong) variations; e.g.: "Nobody ever went broke underestimating the intelligence of the American public."—*Time,* February 16, 1970. "No one ever went broke by underestimating the taste of the American public."—*Newsweek,* March 5, 1973. Angoff wrote me: "Mencken did make that remark . . . he repeated the essence of it in conversations with me many times."—G.S.

the sexual instinct is somewhat degrading and against God. . . .

Life without sex might be safer but it would be unbearably dull. It is the sex instinct which makes women seem beautiful, which they are once in a blue moon, and men seem wise and brave, which they never are at all. Throttle it, denaturalize it, take it away, and human existence would be reduced to the prosaic, laborious, boresome, imbecile level of life in an anthill.

Contribution, *N.Y. World,* September 12, 1926

DR. KARL MENNINGER
(1893–   )
American psychiatrist

The Crime of Punishment (1968)

Society secretly *wants* crime, *needs* crime, and gains definite satisfactions from the present mishandling of it! We condemn crime; we punish offenders for it; but we need it. The crime and punishment ritual is part of our lives.

The great sin by which we all are tempted is the wish to hurt others.

Is it hard for the reader to believe that suicides are sometimes committed to forestall the committing of murder? There is no doubt of it. Nor is there any doubt that murder is sometimes committed to avert suicide.

GEORGE MEREDITH
(1828–1909)
English writer

The Ordeal of Richard Feverel (1859)

"I expect that Woman will be the last thing civilized by Man."

Ch. 1

Diana of the Crossways (1885)

"It [politics] is the first business of men, the school to mediocrity, to the covetously ambitious a sty, to the dullard an ampitheatre, arms of Titans to the desperately enterprising, Olympus to the genius."

Ch. 1

RAPHAEL MERRY DEL VAL
(1865–1930)
English-born Spanish Cardinal

Index Librorum Prohibotorum (1929 ed.)

Hell is now stirring against the Church a more terrible battle than those of earlier centu-ries. . . . For the evil press (*la stampa cattiva*) is a more perilous weapon than the sword.

Preface

JEAN MESLIER
(1678–1733)
Curé d'Etrepigny, France

Je voudrais que le dernier rois fut étranglé avec les boyaux du dernier prêtre.
I would that the last king were strangled with the guts of the last priest.

Attributed by La Harpe, *Cours de littérature ancienne et moderne,* 1, iv, ch. 3; from his will, published by Voltaire*

Superstition of all Ages

It is absurd to call him a God of justice and goodness, who inflicts evil indiscriminately on the good and the wicked, upon the innocent and the guilty. It is idle to demand that the unfortunate should console themselves for their misfortunes in the very arms of the one who alone is the author of them.

heading, ch. LXXVIII

ELIE (né Ilya) METCHNIKOFF
(1845–1916)
Russian-French scientist

The Prolongation of Life

A man is as old as his arteries.

(cf. Bogomoletz)

PRINCE METTERNICH
(1773–1859)
Austrian statesman

Memoirs (ed. Prince Richard Metternich, 1881)

The world desires to be governed by facts and according to justice, not by phrases and theories; the first need of society is to be maintained by strong authority (no authority without real strength deserves the name) and not to govern itself.

Italy is a geographical expression.

Letter, November 19, 1849

---

*Also attributed to Diderot. "Humanity will not be happy until the last capitalist is hanged with the guts of the last bureaucrat."—graffiti, Paris, during riots, 1968.

MICHELANGELO (Michelangelo Buonarroti)
(1475–1564)
Florentine artist

Ancora imparo.
I am still learning.
Motto

Beauty is the purgation of superfluities.
Quoted in Emerson, *The Conduct of Life* (1860),
"Beauty"

JULES MICHELET
(1798–1874)
French historian

Histoire de France (1833–1867)

The historian's first duties are sacrilege and the mocking of false gods. They are his indispensable instruments for establishing the truth.
vol. I

Universal History

With the world began a war which will end only with the world: the war of men against nature, of spirit against matter, of Liberty against fatality.
Introduction

History of the French Revolution (1798–1874)

He who knows how to be poor knows everything.

Man is his own Prometheus. There is no need for any faith but in humanity.
Quoted in Cardiff, *What Great Men Think of Religion*

MIDRASH
Early Jewish Bibilical commentary

He who lives by usury in this world shall not live in the world to come.

Who hath not worked shall not eat.
"Rabbah"

EARL SCHENCK MIERS
(1910–1972)
Editor, Lincoln Sesquicentennial Commission

All Presidents grow in office.
Contribution, *Saturday Review*, August 29, 1959

MIHAJLO MIHAJLOV
(1934–   )
Yugoslav dissident writer

Art is a direct challenge [to communist totalitarianism]. One true artist is more dangerous to a totalitarian regime than any political adversary. . . .
The collision of art with a social system is always a collision of freedom against repression, a combat of truth and lies, the struggle of life against decadent mechanism.
Contribution, *New York Times*, October 24, 1970

COUNT JEAN BAPTISTE MILHAUD
(1766–1833)
French general, revolutionist

If death did not exist today it would be necessary to invent it.
In voting for execution of Louis XVI, 1793
(cf. Voltaire)

JAMES MILL
(1773–1836)
Scottish Utilitarian philosopher

"An Essay on Government"*

. . . the lot of every human being is determined by his pains and pleasures, and that his happiness corresponds with the degree in which his pleasures are great and his pains are small.

Of the laws of nature on which the condition of man depends, that which is attended with the greatest number of consequences is the necessity of labor for obtaining the means of subsistence as well as the means of the greatest parts of our pleasures. This is no doubt the primary cause of government; for if nature had produced spontaneously all the objects which we desire, and in sufficient abundance for the desires of all, there would have been no source of dispute or of injury among men, nor would any man have possessed the means of ever acquiring authority over another.

When it is considered that most of the objects of desire and even the means of subsistence are the product of labor, it is evident that

---

*First published as a supplement to the *Encyclopedia Britannica,* 5th ed.

the means of insuring labor must be provided for as the foundation of all. The means for the insuring of labor are of two sorts: the one made out of the matter of evil, the other made out of the matter of good. The first sort is commonly dominated "force," and under its application the laborers are slaves.

The other mode of obtaining labor is by allurement, or the advantages which it brings. To obtain all the objects of desire in the greatest possible quantity, and to obtain labor in the greatest possible quantity, we must raise to the greatest possible height the advantage attached to labor. Why so? Because if you give more to one man than the produce of his labor, you can do so only by taking it away from the produce of some other man's labor. The greatest possible happiness of society is, therefore, attained by insuring to every man the greatest possible quantity of the produce of his labor.

How is this to be accomplished? . . . One mode is sufficiently obvious, and it does not appear that there is any other: the union of a certain number of men to protect one another.

All the difficult questions of government relate to the means of restraining those in whose hands are lodged the powers necessary for the protection of all from making bad use of it.

. . . the smaller the number of hands into which the powers of government are permitted to pass, the happier it will be for the community.

That one human being will desire to render the person and property of another subservient to his pleasures, notwithstanding the pain or loss of pleasure which it may cause to that other individual, is the foundation of government. . . .

Power is a means to an end. The end is everything, without exception, which the human being calls pleasure and the removal of pain.

The positions which we have already established with regard to human nature, and which we assume as foundations, are these: that the actions of men are governed by their wills, and their wills by their desires; that their desires are directed to pleasure and relief from pain as *ends,* and that wealth and power as the principal means; that to the desire of these means there is no limit; and that the actions which flow from this unlimited desire are the constituents whereof bad government is made.

It is indisputable that the acts of men follow their will, that their will follows their desires, and that their desires are generated by their apprehension of good or evil, in other words, by their interests.

The power bestowed upon the people of judging for themselves has been productive of good effects, to a degree which has totally altered the condition of human nature and exalted man to what may be called a different stage of existence.

It is to be observed that the class which is universally described as both the most wise and the most virtuous part of the community, the middle rank, are wholly in that part of the community which is not the aristocratical.

There can be no doubt that the middle rank, which gives to science, to art, and to legislation itself their most distinguished ornaments, and is the chief source of all that has exalted and refined human nature, . . .

He who desires obedience to a high degree of exactness cannot be satisfied with the power of giving pleasure, he must have the power of inflicting pain.

Terror is the grand instrument. Terror can work only through assurance that evil will follow any want of conformity between the will and the action willed.

. . . to whomsoever the community entrusts this power of government, whether one or a few, they have an interest in misusing them.

JOHN STUART MILL
(1806–1873)
English political economist, philosopher

On Liberty (1859)*

In political speculations "the tyranny of the majority" is now generally included among the evils against which society requires to be on its guard.

Society . . . practices a social tyranny more formidable than many kinds of political

---

*"He published, with a touching dedication to his wife [Mrs. Taylor—Harriet Hardy—whom he married in 1851] the treatise on *Liberty,* which they wrought out together."—*Britannica,* 11th ed., vol. xviii.

oppression, . . . penetrating much more deeply into the details of life, and enslaving the soul itself. Protection, therefore, against the tyranny of the magistrate is not enough: there needs protection also against the tyranny of the prevailing opinion and feeling; against the tendency of society to impose, by other means than civil penalties, its own ideas and practices as rules of conduct on those who dissent from them.

The great writers to whom the world owes what religious liberty it possesses, have mostly asserted freedom of conscience as an indefeasible right, and denied absolutely that a human being is accountable to others for his religious belief. Yet so natural to mankind is intolerance in whatever they really care about, that religious freedom has hardly anywhere been practically realized.

The object of this Essay is to assert one very simple principle, . . . that the sole end for which mankind are warranted, individually or collectively, in interfering with the liberty of action of any of their number, is self-protection. That the only purpose for which power can be rightly exercised over any member of a civilized community, against his will, is to prevent harm to others.

The only part of the conduct of any one, for which he is amenable to society, is that which concerns others. In the part which merely concerns himself, his independence is, of right, absolute. Over himself, over his own body and mind, the individual is sovereign.

The only freedom which deserves the name, is that of pursuing our own good in our own way, so long as we do not attempt to deprive others of theirs, or impede their efforts to obtain it.

Ch. 1

If all mankind minus one were of one opinion, and only one person were of the contrary opinion, mankind would be no more justified in silencing that one person, than he, if he had the power, would be justified in silencing mankind.

But the peculiar evil of silencing the expression of an opinion is, that it is robbing the human race; posterity as well as the existing generation; those who dissent from the opinion, still more than those who hold it. If the opinion is right, they are deprived of the opportunity of exchanging error for truth; if

wrong, they lose, what is always as great a benefit, the clearer perception and livelier impression of truth, produced by its collision with error.

It is a piece of idle sentimentality that truth, merely as truth, has any inherent power denied to error or prevailing against the dungeon and the stake. Men are not more zealous for truth than they often are for error . . . The real advantage which truth has consists in this, that when an opinion is true, it may be extinguished once, twice, or many times, but in the course of ages there will generally be found persons to rediscover it.

Men might as well be imprisoned, as excluded from the means of earning their bread.

There is never any fair and thorough discussion of heretical opinions. . . . The greatest harm done is to those who are not heretics, and whose whole mental development is cramped and their reason cowed, by the fear of heresy.

No one can be a great thinker who does not recognize, that as a thinker it is his first duty to follow his intellect to whatever conclusions it may lead.

Culture without freedom never made a large and liberal mind.

Truth, in the great practical concerns of life, is so much a question of the reconciling and combining of opposites, that very few have minds sufficiently capacious and impartial to make the adjustment with an approach to correctness.

Christian morality (so-called) has all the characters of a reaction; . . . Its ideal is negative rather than positive; passive rather than active; Innocence rather than Nobleness; Abstinence from Evil, rather than energetic Pursuit of Good. . . . It holds out the hope of heaven and the threat of hell, as the appointed and appropriate motives to a virtuous life: in this falling far below the best of the ancients, and doing what lies in it to give to human morality an essentially selfish character. . . . It is essentially the doctrine of passive obedience; it inculcates submission to all authorities found established.

It can do truth no service to blink the fact, known to all who have the most ordinary acquaintance with literary history, that a large portion of the noblest and most valuable moral teachings has been the work, not only of men who did not know, but of men who knew and rejected, the Christian faith.

Ch. 2

Customs are made for customary circumstances and customary characters. . . .

The mind itself is bowed to the yoke: even in what people do for pleasure, conformity is the first thing thought of; they live in crowds: they exercise choice only among things commonly done: peculiarity of taste, eccentricity of conduct, are shunned equally with crimes: until by dint of not following their own nature they have no nature to follow: their human capacities are withered and starved: they become incapable of any strong wishes or native pleasures, and are generally without either opinions or feelings of home growth, or properly their own.

Whatever crushes individuality is despotism.

In this age, the mere example of nonconformity, the mere refusal to bend the knee to custom, is itself a service.

Ch. 3

I am not aware that any community has a right to force another to be civilized.

Ch. 4

The Subjugation of Women (1869)

The love of power and the love of liberty are in eternal antagonism. Where there is least liberty the passion for power is the most ardent and unscrupulous. The desire for power over others can only cease to be a depraving agency among mankind, when each of them individually is able to do without it: which can only be where respect for liberty in the personal concerns of each is an established principle.

All causes, social and natural, combine to make it unlikely that women should be collectively rebellious to the power of men. They are so far in a position different from all other subject classes, that their masters require something more from them than actual service. Men do not want solely the obedience of women, they want their sentiments . . . not a forced slave but a willing one; not a slave merely, but a favorite. They have therefore put everything in practice to enslave their minds. The masters of all other slaves rely, for maintaining obedience, on fear; either fear of themselves, or religious fears. The masters of women wanted more than simple obedience,

and they turned the whole force of education to effect their purpose.

Ch. 1

Whoever has a wife and children has given hostages to Mrs. Grundy.

Ch. 3

The moral regeneration of mankind will only really commence, when the most fundamental of the social relations [marriage] is placed under the rule of equal justice, and when human beings learn to cultivate their strongest sympathy with an equal in rights and in cultivation.

Ch. 4

Essays on Politics and Culture

Mankind are then divided into those who are still what they were, and those who have changed: into the men of the present age, and the men of the past. To the former, the spirit of the age is a subject of exultation; to the latter, of terror.

The grand achievement of the present age is the diffusion of *superficial* knowledge.

A person may be without a single prejudice, and yet utterly unfit for every purpose in nature. To have erroneous convictions is one evil; but to have no strong or deep-rooted convictions at all, is an enormous one.

One single well-established fact, clearly irreconcilable with a doctrine, is sufficient to prove that is is *false*.

Judging by common sense is merely another phrase for judging by first appearance. . . . The men who place implicit faith in their own common sense are, without any exception, the most wrong-headed, and impracticable persons.

The people in general have not, nor ever had, any reason or motive for adhering to the established religion, except that it was the religion of their political superiors.

In highly civilized countries, and particularly among ourselves, the energies of the middle classes are almost confined to money-getting, and those of the higher classes are nearly extinct.

The principle itself of dogmatic religion, dogmatic morality, dogmatic philosophy, is what requires to be rooted out; not any particular manifestation of that principle.

"The Spirit of the Age"

Principles of Political Economy (1848)

After the means of subsistence are assured, the next in strength of the principal wants of human beings is liberty; and (unlike the physical wants, which as civilization advances become more moderate and more amenable to control) it increases instead of diminishing in intensity as the intelligence and moral faculties are more developed.

The question is whether there would be any asylum left for individuality of character; whether public opinion would not be a tyrannical yoke; whether the absolute dependence of each on all, and surveillance of each by all, would not grind down into a tame uniformity of thoughts, feelings and actions. . . . No society in which eccentricity is a matter of reproach, can be in a wholesome state.

If the choice were to be made between Communism with all its chances, and the present state of society, with all the sufferings and injustices . . . if this, or Communism, were the alternatives, all the difficulties great or small of Communism would be as dust in the balance.

Bk. II

Hitherto it is questionable if all the mechanical inventions yet made have lightened the day's toil of any human being. They have enabled a great population to live the same life of drudgery and imprisonment, and an increased number of manufacturers to make fortunes. They have increased the comforts of the middle classes. But they have not begun to effect those great changes in human history, which it is in their nature and in their futurity to accomplish.

Bk. IV

Theism (1869–1870)

The rational attitude of a thinking mind toward the supernatural, whether in natural or revealed religion, is that of scepticism as distinguished from belief on one hand, and from atheism on the other. . . . The notion of a providential government by an omnipotent Being for the good of his creatures must be entirely dismissed. . . . The possibility of life after death rests on the same footing—of a boon which this powerful Being who wishes well to man, may have the power to grant. . . . The whole domain of the supernatural is thus removed from the region of Belief into that of simple Hope; and in that, for anything we can see, it is likely to always remain.

Representative Government (1861)

Whenever it ceases to be true that mankind, as a rule, prefer themselves to others, and those nearest to them to those more remote, from that moment Communism is not only practicable, but the only defensible form of society; and will, when that time arrives, be assuredly carried into effect.

Ch. 3

One person with a belief is a social power equal to ninety-nine who have only interests.

Nobody pretends to think that women would make a bad use of suffrage. The worst that is said is that they would vote as mere dependents, at the bidding of their male relations. If it be so, so let it be. If they think for themselves, great good will be done, and if they do not, no harm. It is a benefit to human beings to take off their fetters, even if they do not desire to walk.

Ch. 8

EDNA ST. VINCENT MILLAY
(1892–1950)
American poet

"A Few Figs from Thistles" (1920)

My candle burns at both ends;
  It will not last the night;
But, ah, my foes, and oh, my friends—
  It gives a lovely light!

First Fig

"Fatal Interview" (1923)

Love is not all; . . .
Love can not fill the thickened lung with
  breath,
Nor clean the blood, nor set the fractured
  bone;
Yet many a man is making friends with
  death
Even as I speak, for lack of love alone.

Sonnet XXX

"Conversation at Midnight" (1937)

There is no God.
But it does not matter.
Man is enough.

"Dirge Without Music" (1928)

Down, down, down into the darkness of the
  grave
Gently they go, the beautiful, the tender,
  the kind;

Quietly they go, the intelligent, the witty, the brave.
I know. But I do not approve. And I am not resigned.

Aria da Capo (1920)

[Pierrot:] I love humanity but I hate people.

ARTHUR MILLER
(1915–   )
American playwright

When any creativity becomes useful, it is sucked into the vortex of commercialism, and when a thing becomes commercial, it becomes the enemy of man.
> Contribution, *The New Yorker,*
> September 16, 1961

I feel that America is essentially against the artist, that the enemy of America is the artist because he stands for individuality and creativeness, and that's *un*American somehow. I think that of all countries—we have to overlook the communist countries of course—America is the most mechanized, robotized, of all.
> Interview with George Wickes, *The Paris Review,*
> No. 28, 1962

When the guns roar, the arts die.
> Telegram to President Johnson protesting the
> Vietnam war, 1965

HENRY MILLER
(1891–1980)
American writer

The Time of the Assassins

Youth ends where manhood begins, it is said. A phrase without meaning, since from the beginning of history man has never enjoyed the full measure of youth or known the limitless possibilities of adulthood. How can one know the splendor and fullness of youth if one's energies are consumed in combating errors and falsities of parents and ancestors?

Ideas have to be wedded to action; if there is no sex, no vitality in them, there is no action. Ideas cannot exist alone in the vacuum of the mind. Ideas are related to living. . . .

Tropic of Cancer (1934)

The monstrous thing is not that men have created roses out of this dung heap, but that,

for some reason or other, they should *want* roses.

For some reason or other man looks for the miracle, and to accomplish it he will wade through blood. He will debauch himself with ideas, he will reduce himself to a shadow if for only one second of his life he can close his eyes to the hideousness of reality. Everything is endured—disgrace, humiliation, poverty, war, crime, *ennui*—in the belief that overnight something will occur, a miracle, which will render life tolerable.

If now and then we encounter pages that explode, pages that wound and sear, that wring groans and tears and curses, know that they come from a man with his back up, a man whose only defenses left are his words and his words are always stronger than the lying, crushing weight of the world, stronger than all the racks and wheels which the cowardly invent to crush out the miracle of personality.

The task which the artist implicity sets himself is to overthrow existing values, to make of the chaos about him an order which is his own, to sow strife and ferment so that by the emotional release those who are dead may be restored to life.

The Colossus of Maroussi (1941)

Warrior, jailer, priest—the eternal trinity which symbolizes our fear of life.

God long ago abandoned us in order that we might realize Godhead through our own efforts.

There are two paths to take: one back toward comfort and security of death, the other forward to nowhere.

The more liberated one feels the less one needs.

The greatest miracle is the discovery that all is miraculous. And the nature of the miraculous is—utter simplicity.

Why change the world? Change *worlds*!
> Quoted in *Esquire,* November 1961

It's silly to go on pretending that under the skin we are all brothers. The truth is more likely that under the skin we are all cannibals, assassins, traitors, liars, hypocrites, poltroons.
> Contribution, Op-Ed page, *N.Y. Times,*
> September 7, 1974

JOAQUIN (Cincinnatus Heine) MILLER
(1841–1913)
American poet

"Walker in Nicaragua"

That man who lives for self alone
Lives for the meanest mortal known.

"To Russia"

Who taught you tender Bible tales
Of honey-lands, of milk and wine? . . .
Who gave the patient Christ? I say
Who gave your Christian creed?
    Yea, yea.
Who gave your very God to you?
Your Jew! Your Jew! Your hated Jew!

If you want immortality, make it.
    Quoted in Cardiff, *What Great Men Think of*
    Religion

ROBERT MILLIKAN
(1868–1953)
American physicist, Nobel Prize 1923

There are three ideas which seem to me to
stand out above all others in the influence they
have exerted and are destined to exert upon
the development of the human race. . . . The
first of these and the most important of the
three, was the gift of religion to the race; the
other two sprang from the womb of science.
They are the following:
    1. The idea of the Golden Rule;
    2. The idea of natural law;
    3. The idea of age-long growth, or evolu-
tion.

There are only two kinds of immoral conduct. The first is due to indifference, thoughtlessness, failure to reflect upon what is for the
common good. The second type of immorality
is represented by "the unpardonable sin" of
which Jesus spoke—deliberate refusal, after reflection, to follow the light when seen.
    Contribution, *Living Philosophies* (1931)

C. WRIGHT MILLS
(1916–1962)
American sociologist

The Power Elite (1956)

The Power Elite.
    Title

In all systems of human relationship, from
the family to the superstate, there is an element of coercion, and this element, whenever
it occurs and in whatever degree it is significant or controlling, we conveniently designate
as "power."

The men of the higher circles are not representative men; their high position is not a result of moral virtue; their fabulous success is
not firmly connected with meritorious ability.
Those who sit in the seats of the high and
mighty are selected and formed by means of
power, their sources of wealth, the mechanics
of celebrity which prevail in our society.

America—a conservative country without
any conservative ideology.

If you do not specify and confront real issues, what you say will surely obscure them. If
you do not alarm anyone morally, you yourself remain morally asleep. If you do not embody controversy, what you say will be an
acceptance of the drift of the coming human
hell.
    Contribution, *The Nation*, April 14, 1962

JOHN MILTON
(1608–1674)
English poet

Areopagitica; A Speech of Mr. John Milton for the
Liberty of Unlicensed Printing, to the Parliament of
England, November 24, 1644*

For books are not absolutely dead things,
but do contain a potency of life in them to be
as active as that soul was whose progeny they
are. . . . And yet, on the other hand, unless
wariness be used, as good almost kill a man as
kill a good book; who kills a man kills a reasonable creature, God's image; but he who destroys a good book, kills reason itself, kills the
image of God, as it were, in the eye.

"To the pure all things are pure;"** not
only meats and drinks, but all kinds of knowledge whether of good or evil; the knowledge
cannot defile, nor consequently the books, if
the will and conscience be not defiled.

He that can apprehend and consider vice
with all her baits and seeming pleasures, and

---

*" . . . the most popular and eloquent, if not the
greatest of all Milton's prose writings."—*Britannica*,
11th ed.
**I Thess., V, 21.

yet abstain, and yet distinguish, and yet prefer that which is truly better, he is the true wayfaring* Christian. I cannot praise a fugitive and cloistered virtue, unexercised and unbreathed, that never sallies out and sees her adversary, but slinks out of the race, where that immortal garland is to be run for, not without dust and heat.

Since therefore, the knowledge and survey of vice is in this world so necessary to the constituting of human virtue, and the scanning of error to the confirmation of truth, how can we more safely and with less danger scout into the regions of sin and falsity than by reading all manner of tractates and hearing all manner of reason?

Truth is compared in scripture to a streaming fountain; if her waters flow not in a perpetual progression, they sicken into a muddy pool of conformity and tradition. A man may be a heretic in the truth; and if he believes things only because his pastor says so, or the Assembly so determines, without knowing other reason, though his belief be true, yet the very truth he holds becomes his heresy.

Give me the liberty to know, to utter, and to argue freely according to my conscience, above all liberties.

And though all the winds of doctrine were let loose to play upon the earth, so Truth be in the field, we do injuriously by licensing and prohibiting to misdoubt her strength. Let her and falsehood grapple; who ever knew Truth put to the worse, in a free and open encounter.

For who knows not that Truth is strong, next to the Almighty. She needs no policies, nor stratagems, nor licensings to make her victorious—those are the shifts and the defenses that error uses against her power. Give her but room, and do not bind her while she sleeps.

I fear yet this iron yoke of outward conformity hath left a slavish print upon our necks; the ghost of a linen decency yet haunts us.

Doctrine and Discipline in Divorce (1643)

The greatest burden in the world is superstition, not only of ceremonies in the church but of imaginary and scarecrow sins at home.
                                            The dedication

---

*In a later copy Milton changed "wayfaring" to "warfaring."

Truth is as impossible to be soiled by any outward touch as the sunbeam.

Truth . . . ne'er comes into the world but like a Bastard, to the ignominy of him that brought her forth.

An Apology of Smectymnuus (1642)

If unchastity in a woman, whom St. Paul terms the glory of man, be such a scandal and dishonor, then certainly in a man, who is both the image and glory of God, it must, though commonly not so thought, be much more deflowering and dishonorable.

The Tenure of Kings and Magistrates (1649)

None can love freedom but good men; the rest love not freedom but license, which never hath more scope than under tyrants.

The Ready and Easy Way to Establish a Free Commonwealth (1860)

And what government comes so nearer to this precept of Christ than a free commonwealth, wherein they who are greatest, are perpetual servants and drudges to the public at their own cost and charges, neglect their own affairs, yet are not elevated above their brethren, live soberly in their families, walk the streets as other men, may be spoken to freely, familiarly, friendly, without adoration?

Certainly then that people must needs be mad or strangely infatuated that build the chief hope of their common happiness or safety on a single person; who, if he happen to be good, can do no more than another man; if to be bad, hath in his hands to do more evil without check than millions of other men.

Paradise Lost (1667)

What in me is dark
Illumine, what is low raise and support;
That to the height of this great Argument
I may assert Eternal Providence,
And justify the ways of God to men.
                                    Bk. I, lines 22–26

What though the field be lost?
All is not lost; the unconquerable Will,
And study of revenge, immortal hate,
And courage never to submit or yield.
                                    Lines 105–108

The mind is its own place, and in itself
Can make a Heav'n of Hell, a Hell of
    Heav'n.
                                    Lines 254–255

To reign is worth ambition, though in Hell.
Better to reign in Hell, than serve in
·Heav'n.
Lines 262–263

Who overcomes
By force, hath overcome but half his foe.
Lines 648–649

For neither Man nor Angel can discern
Hypocrisy, the only evil that walks
Invisible, except to God alone,
By his permissive will, through Heav'n and
Earth.
Bk. III, lines 682–685

And with necessity,
The Tyrant's plea, excused his dev'lish
deeds.
Bk. IV, lines 393–394

O why did God,
Creator wise, that peopl'd highest Heav'n
With Spirits Masculine, create at last
This novelty on Earth, this fair defect
Of Nature, and not fill the World at once
With Men as Angels without Feminine,
Or find some other way to generate
Mankind? this mischief had not befall'n.
Bk. X, lines 888–895

Paradise Regained (1671)

Where no hope is left, is left no fear.
Bk. III, line 206

Lycidas (1637)

Look homeward angel.
Line 163

"Sonnet, To the Lord General Cromwell" (1652)

Peace hath her victories,
No less renowned than war.

"Sonnet, On Fairfax" (pub. 1694)

For what can War, but endless war still
breed.

"Comus" (1634)

'Tis Chastity, my brother, Chastity;
She that has that, is clad in complete steel.

Samson Agonistes (1671)

Just are the ways of God,
And justifiable to men;
Unless there be who think not God at all.

But what more oft in Nations grown corrupt,

And by their vices brought to servitude,
Than to love Bondage more than Liberty,
Bondage with ease than strenuous Liberty?

"On Time" (c. 1637)

When once our heav'nly-guided soul shall
climb,
Then all this Earthly grossness quit,
Attir'd with Stars, we shall for ever sit,
Triumphing over Death, and Chance, and
thee
O Time.

On the Morning of Christ's Nativity (1629)

Yea, Truth and Justice then
Will down return to men,
The 'namel'd *Arras* of the Rainbow wearing,
And Mercy will sit between
Thron'd in Celestial sheen,
With radiant feet the tissued clouds down
steering,
And Heav'n as at some festival,
Will open wide the Gates of her high Palace
Hall.
"The Hymn," st. XV

"On His Blindness" (1652)

When I consider how my light is spent
Ere half my days, in this dark world and
wide,
And that one Talent which is death to hide,
Lodged with me useless, though my Soul
more bent
To serve therewith my Maker, and present
My true account, lest he returning chide;
"Doth God exact day-labour, light denied?"
I fondly ask. . .

"On His Deceased Wife" (c. 1658)

Methought I saw my late espoused Saint
Brought to me like Alcestis from the grave.

————

Our country is wherever we are well off.
Letter

What man in his senses would deny that
there are those whom we have the best
grounds for considering that we ought to deceive—as boys, madmen, the sick, the intoxi-
cated, enemies, men in error, and thieves . . .
Quoted by Cardinal Newman, *Apologia*
Pro Vita Sua

MIMNERMUS
(c. 650–590 B.C.)
Greek elegiac poet

What life is there, what delight, without
golden Aphrodite?

Fragment I

HONORÉ GABRIEL RIQUETTI, COMTE DE MIRABEAU
(1749–1791)
French statesman

The freedom of conscience is a right so sacred that even the name of tolerance involves
a species of tyranny.

Address, National Convention, 1791

OCTAVE MIRBEAU
(1850–1918)
French playwright

Les affaires sont les affaires
Business is business

Play title, April 20, 1903

ISKANDER MIRZA
(1899–1969)
President of Pakistan

Democracy is hypocrisy without limitation.

Proclamation on abolition of parliament (quoted in
Time, October 20, 1958)

MARIA MITCHELL
(1818–1889)
American astronomer

Life, Letters and Journals (compiled by Phoebe
Mitchell Kendall)

Endow the already established with money.
Endow the woman who shows genius with
time.

We cannot take anything for granted, beyond the first mathematical formulae. Question everything else.

Besides learning to see, there is another art
to be learned—*not to see* what is not.

MOLIÈRE (Jean Baptiste Poquelin)
(1622–1673)
French dramatist

Sganarelle, ou Le Cocu imaginaire [*The Imaginary Cuckold*] (1660)

Love is often the fruit of marriage.

Act I, sc. i

Les Femmes savantes (1672)

To grammar even kings bow.

Act II, sc. vi

Don Juan (1665)

Man's greatest weakness is his love for life.

Aristotle and the philosophers notwithstanding, there's nothing to equal tobacco. It's an
honest man's habit and anyone who can live
without it doesn't deserve to live at all.

L'École des maris (1661)

The best of them [women] is at all times full
of mischief: they are a sex for the damnation of
the world. I denounce forever this deceitful
sex, and give with all my heart the whole of
them to the devil.

Act III, sc. x

Amphitryon (1668)

I prefer an accommodating vice to an obstinate virtue.

Act I, sc. iv

L'École des femmes (1662)

The obedience which the soldier, instructed
in his duty, shows to his general, the valet to
his master, a child to his father, the lowest
friar to his superior, does not approach the do-
cility, the obedience, the humility and the
profound respect which a wife should show to
her husband, chief, lord and master.

Act III, sc. iii

HELMUTH VON MOLTKE
(1800–1891)
Prussian field marshal

Eternal peace is a dream, and not even a
beautiful one, and war is a part of God's world
order. In it are developed the noblest virtues of
man, courage and abnegation, dutifulness and
self-sacrifice at the risk of life. Without war the
world would sink to materialism.

Letter to Bluntschli, December 11, 1880

JACQUES MONOD
(1910–1976)
French biologist, Nobel Prize 1965

Le Hasard et la nécessité (1971)

The scientific attitude implies . . . the postulate of objectivity—that is to say, the fundamental postulate that there is no plan; that there is no intention in the universe.

JAMES MONROE
(1758–1831)
5th President of the United States

That the American continents, by the free and independent condition which they have assumed and maintained, are henceforth not to be considered as subjects for future colonization by any European power.

We owe it, therefore, to candor, and to the amicable relations existing between the United States and those powers to declare that we should consider any attempt on their part to extend their system to any portion of this hemisphere as dangerous to our peace and safety.

> Message to Congress, December 2, 1823
> ("The Monroe Doctrine")

ASHLEY MONTAGU
(1905–   )
American anthropologist, biologist

The Humanization of Man

Evil is not inherent in nature, it is learned.

Aggressiveness is taught, as are all forms of violence which human beings exhibit. . . . Aggression is the expression of frustrated expectation of love.

The Natural Superiority of Women (1952)

The evidence indicates that woman is, on the whole, biologically superior to man.

The natural superiority of women is a biological fact, and a socially acknowledged reality.

Because women live creatively, they rarely experience the need to depict or write about that which to them is a primary experience and which men know only at a second remove. Women create naturally—men create artificially.

Nothing can be said in favor of tobacco.

The majority of people believe in incredible things which are absolutely false. The majority of people daily act in a manner prejudicial to their general well-being.

> Contribution, *In fact* (newsletter), 1940

WILLIAM PEPPERELL MONTAGUE
(1873–1953)
American theist

The Way of Things (1940)

The moral idea of Christian love is like a pillar of flaming light extending from earth to heaven, but the supernatural religion of freedom, solace, and joy that should have evolved from it was choked and poisoned. The successors of Christ, from St. Paul down to the censors, obscurantists, and tyrants of today have done their conscientious worst to hide the light from men.

MICHEL EYQUEM DE MONTAIGNE
(1533–1592)
French philosopher, essayist

Essays (1580–1595)

This noble precept is often cited by Plato: "Do thine own work, and know thyself." Each of these two parts generally cover the whole duty of man, and each includes the other. He who will do his own work well, discovers that his first lesson is to know himself, and what is his duty.

> Bk. I, Ch. 3

If falsehood, like truth, had but one face, we would be on more equal terms. For we would consider the contrary of what the liar said to be certain. But the opposite of truth has a hundred thousand faces and an infinite field.

Anyone who does not feel sufficiently strong in memory should not meddle with lying.

In truth lying is an accursed vice. We are men, and held together, only by our word. If we recognize the horror and the gravity of lying, we would persecute it with fire more justly than other crimes.

> Bk. I, Ch. 9

That which I fear most is fear.

Bk. I, Ch. 18

To philosophize is nothing else than to prepare oneself for death.

[Quote from Cicero]

One of the greatest blessings of virtue is the contempt of death. . . . He who has learned how to die has unlearned how to serve. . . . To be ready to die frees us from all bondage, and thralldom.

He who would teach men to die would at the same time teach them to live.

Bk. I, Ch. 20

The woman who goes to bed with a man should take off her modesty with her skirt and put it on again with her petticoat.

Bk. I, Ch. 21

And what all philosophy cannot implant in the head of the wisest men, does not custom by her sole ordinance teach the crudest common herd?

The laws of conscience, which we pretend to be derived from nature, proceed from custom.

The principal effect of the power of custom is to seize and ensnare us in such a way that it is hardly within our power to get ourselves back out of its grip and return unto ourselves to reflect and reason about its ordinances. . . . And the common notions that we find in credit around us and infused into our soul by our fathers' seed, these seem to be the universal and natural ones. Whence it comes to pass that what is off the hinges of custom, people believe to be off the hinges of reason: God knows how unreasonably, most of the time.

Bk. I, Ch. 23

How many things which served us yesterday as articles of faith, are fables for us today.

I have never seen any effect in rods but to make children's minds more base, or more maliciously headstrong.

The laws keep up their credit, not by being just, but because they are laws; 'tis the mystic foundation of their authority; they have no other, and it well answers their purpose. They are often made by fools; still oftener by men who, out of hatred to equality, fail in equity; but always by men, vain and irresolute authors.

After all it is setting a high value upon our opinions to roast men and women alive on account of them.

To understand via the heart is not to understand.

Bk. I, Ch. 26

Each man calls barbarism whatever is not his own practice; for indeed it seems we have no other test of truth and reason than the example and pattern of the opinions and customs of the country we live in.

Bk. I, Ch. 31

It comes to pass that nothing is so firmly believed as that which we know least; nor are there any persons so sure of themselves as those who tell us fables, such as alchemists, prognosticators, seers, chiromanticists, quacks, *id genus omne*. To which I would join, if I dared, a host of persons, interpreters and versifiers-in-ordinary of the designs of God.

Bk. I, Ch. 32

The greatest thing in the world is for a man to know how to be himself.

Miracles arise from our ignorance of nature, not from nature itself.

We must not mock God. Yet the best of us are not so much afraid to offend Him as to offend our neighbors, kinsmen, or rulers.

What kind of truth is this which is true on one side of a mountain and false on the other?

There is nothing men more readily give themselves to than pushing their own beliefs. When ordinary means fail, they add commandment, violence, fire and sword.

Bk. I, Ch. 39

It may be said with some plausibility that there is an abecedarian ignorance that comes before knowledge, and another doctoral ignorance that comes after knowledge: an ignorance that knowledge creates and engenders, just as it undoes and destroys the first.

The lack of wealth is easily repaired but the poverty of the soul is irreplaceable.

Perhaps it is not without reason that we attribute facility in belief and conviction to simplicity and ignorance; for it seems to me I once learned that belief was a sort of impression made on our mind, and that the softer and less resistant the mind, the easier it was to imprint something on it.

O belief! How much you hinder us.

To storm a breach, conduct an embassy, govern a people, those are brilliant actions. To scold, laugh, sell, pay, love, hate, and deal gently and justly with one's family and oneself, not to relax or contradict oneself: that is something rarer, more difficult and less noticed in the world.

The most desirable laws are those that are rarest, simplest, and most general; and I even think that it would be better to have none at all than to have them in such numbers as we have.

Bk. I, Ch. 54

That which cannot be compassed by reason, wisdom and discretion, can never be attained by force.

Belike we must be incontinent that we may be continent; burning is quenched by fire.

Bk. II, Ch. 11

Philosopher c'est doubter.
To philosophize is to doubt.

Our speech has its weaknesses and its defects, like all the rest. Most of the occasions for the troubles of the world are grammatical. Our lawsuits spring only from debate over the interpretation of the laws, and most of our wars from the inability to express clearly the conventions and treaties of agreement of princes.

Que scay-je? [What do I know?] And it is this question, together with a pair of balanced scales, which I use as my emblem.

Is there not some rashness in philosophy to consider that men produce their greatest deeds and those most closely approaching divinity when they are out of their minds and frenzied and mad? We improve by the privation and deadening of our reason. The two natural ways to enter the cabinet of the gods and there foresee the course of destinies are madness and sleep. This is amusing to think about: by the dislocation that the passions bring about in our reason, we become virtuous; by the extirpation of reason that is brought about by madness or the semblance of death, we become prophets and soothsayers.

Reason does nothing but go astray in everything, and especially when it meddles with divine things.

Desires are either natural and necessary, like eating and drinking; or natural and not necessary, like intercourse with females; or neither natural nor necessary.

Bk. II, Ch. 12

He who knows not how to dissimulate, does not know how to rule.

Bk. II, Ch. 17 (also attributed to Tiberius and Frederick Barbarossa)

Cowardice, mother of cruelty.

Bk. II, Ch. 27 (chapter title)

Whoever would withdraw the seeds of these qualities (ambition, jealousy, envy, revenge, superstition, and despair) from the constitution of man, would destroy the fundamental condition of human life. . . . Vices have their place in nature, and are employed to make up the warp of our union, as poisons are useful in the preservation of our health.

I speak truth not so much as I would, but as much as I dare, and I dare a little more as I grow older.

There is no man so good, who, were he to submit all his thoughts to the laws, would not deserve hanging ten times in his life.

Bk. III, Ch. 1

He that in ancient times said that he was beholden to the years because they had rid him of voluptuousness, was not of my opinion. I shall never give impotence thanks for any good it can do me.

We abandon not vices so much as we change them; and in my opinion for the worse.

Malice sucks up the greater part of its own venom, and poisons itself. Vice leaves, like an ulcer in the flesh, repentence in the soul, which is always scratching and bloodying itself; for reason overcomes all other griefs and sorrows, but it begets repentence.

Bk. III, Ch. 2

Why was the act of generation made so natural, so necessary, and so just, seeing we fear to speak of it without shame, and exclude it from our serious and regular discourses; we pronounce boldly to rob, to murder, to betray; and this we dare not put between our teeth.

Love hates people to be attached to each other except by himself, and takes a laggard part in relations that are set up and maintained under another title, as marriage is.

I see no marriage fail sooner or more troubles than such as are concluded for beauty's sake, and huddled up for amorous desire.

A good marriage (if any there be) refuseth the company and conditions of love; it endeavoureth to present those of amity.

Women are not altogether in the wrong when they refuse the rules of life prescribed in the world, forsomuch as men have established them without their consent.

An untempted woman can not boast of her chastity.

One does not marry for oneself, whatever may be said; a man marries as much, or more, for his posterity, for his family; the usage and interest of marriage touch our race beyond ourselves. Thus it is a kind of incest to employ, in this venerable and sacred parentage, the efforts and the extravagance of amorous license.*

Bk. III, Ch. 5

We are born to inquire into truth; it belongs to a greater power to possess it.

Bk. III, Ch. 8

Wonder is the foundation of all philosophy, inquiry its progress, ignorance its end.

Bk. III, Ch. 11

It is a sign of contraction of the mind when it is content, or of weariness.

We are great fools. "He has spent his life in idleness," we say; "I have done nothing today." What, have you not lived?

Have you been able to think out and manage your own life? You have done the greatest task of all.

He who fears he will suffer, already suffers from his fear.

We need very strong ears to hear ourselves judged frankly, and because there are few who can endure frank criticism without being stung by it, those who venture to criticize us perform

a remarkable act of friendship, for to undertake to wound or offend a man for his own good is to have a healthy love for him.

Et au plus élève throne du monde si ne sommes nous assis que sur notre cul.
On the most exalted throne in the world, we are still seated only on our arse.*

Bk. III, Ch. 13

It is perhaps easier to do without the whole sex than to behave rightly in every respect in association with our wives; and a man may live more carefree in poverty than in justly dispensed abundance. Enjoyment conducted according to reason is more arduous than abstinence. Moderation is a virtue that gives more trouble than suffering does.

Bk. III, Ch. 33

CHARLES DE SECONDAT, BARON DE LA BRÈDE ET DE MONTESQUIEU (1669–1755)
French jurist, philosopher

The Spirit of Laws (1748)

Laws, in their most general signification, are the necessary relations arising from the nature of things. In this sense all beings have their laws: the Deity His laws, the material world its laws, the intelligences superior to man their laws, the beasts their laws, man his laws.

Bk. I, Ch. 1

As soon as man enters into a state of society he loses the sense of his weakness; equality ceases, and then commences the state of war.

Law in general is human reason.

Bk. I, Ch. 3

As virtue is necessary in a republic, and in a monarchy honor, so fear is necessary in a despotic government: with regard to virtue, there is no occasion for it, and honor would be extremely dangerous.

Bk. III, Ch. 9

In republican governments, men are all equal; equal they are also in despotic governments: in the former, because they are everything; in the latter, because they are nothing.

Bk. VI, Ch. 2

---

*"This point of view easily commends itself to the early Christians, who, however, deliberately overlooked its reverse side, the establishment of erotic interests outside marriage."—Havelock Ellis, *Studies in the Psychology of Sex,* vol. 3, pt. 2.

*The translation of *cul* has troubled many translators and biographers, who prefer "rear" and "rump."

Luxury is therefore absolutely necessary in monarchies; as it is also in despotic states. In the former, it is the use of liberty, in the latter, it is the abuse of servitude. . . .

Hence arises a very natural reflection. Republics end with luxury; monarchies with poverty.

Bk. VII, Ch. 4

In despotic government women do not introduce, but are themselves an object of, luxury. They must be in a state of the most rigorous servitude.

Bk. VII, Ch. 9

As distant as heaven is from earth, so is the true spirit of equality from that of extreme equality. . . .

In a true state of nature, indeed, all men are born equal, but they cannot continue in this equality. Society makes them lose it, and they recover it only by the protection of the laws.

Bk. VIII, Ch. 3

We must have constantly present in our minds the difference between independence and liberty. Liberty is a right of doing whatever the laws permit.

Bk. XI, Ch. 3

But constant experience shows us that every man invested with power is apt to abuse it, and to carry his authority as far as it will go. Is it not strange, though true, to say that virtue itself has need of limits?

Bk. XI, Ch. 4

Philosophic liberty consists in the free exercise of the will; . . . Political liberty consists in security, or, at least, in the opinion that we enjoy security.

Bk. XII, Ch. 2

Commerce is a cure for the most destructive prejudices.

Bk. XX, Ch. 1

Peace is the natural effect of trade.

Bk. XX, Ch. 2

Men are extremely inclined to the passions of hope and fear; a religion, therefore, that has neither a heaven nor a hell could hardly please them.

Bk. XXV, Ch. 2

Thoughts and Judgments

Disrespect for women has invariably been the surest sign of moral corruption.

MARIA MONTESSORI
(1870–1952)
Italian educator

The Montessori Method (1912)

The pedagogical method of observation has for its base the liberty of the child, and liberty is activity. . . . Discipline must come through liberty.

The first idea that the child must acquire, in order to be actively disciplined, is that of the difference between good and evil, and the task of the educator lies in seeing that the child does not confound good with immobility, and evil with activity.

Ch. V

VISCOUNT MONTGOMERY OF ALAMEIN (Sir Bernard Law)
(1887–1976)
British officer, World War II

The United States has broken the second rule of war. That is, don't go fighting with your land army on the mainland of Asia. Rule # One is, don't march on Moscow. I developed these two rules myself.

"Of American Policy in Vietnam," quoted in Chalfont, *Montgomery of Alamein* (1976)

HENRI DE MONTHERLANT
(1896–1972)
French novelist

Costals and the Hippogriff (1939)

It was because he was unhappy that God created the world.

Young Girls (1936)

The story of humanity, ever since Eve, is the story of the efforts made by woman to diminish man and make him suffer, so that he may become her equal.

Women are too infirmed to bear reality.

GEORGE MOORE
(1852–1933)
Irish novelist, essayist

Confessions of a Young Man (1888)

I don't care how the poor live, my only regret is that they live at all.

Humanity is a pigsty where liars, hypocrites, and the obscene in spirit congregate.

Nature intended woman for the warrior's relaxation, to succeed as actresses, queens, and courtesans—yes, and as saints.

I wonder why murder is considered less immoral than fornication in literature.

The substance of our lives is woman. All other things are irrelevancies, hypocrisies, subterfuges. We sit talking of sports and politics, and all the while our hearts are filled with memories of women and the capture of women.

A male figure rises to the head, and is a symbol of the intelligence; a woman's figure sinks to the inferior parts of the body, and is expressive of generation.

THOMAS MOORE
(1779–1852)
Irish poet

"The Sceptic"

Rebels in Cork are patriots in Madrid.

"Lalla Rookh" (1817)

And from the lips of Truth one mighty
  breath
Shall, like a whirlwind, scatter in its breeze
That whole dark pile of human mocker-
  ies;—
Then shall the reign of mind commence on
  earth,
And starting fresh as from a second birth,
Man, in the sunshine of the world's new
  spring,
Shall walk transparent, like some holy thing!

Faith, fantastic faith, once wedded fast
to some dear falsehood, hugs it to the last.

HANNAH MORE
(1745–1833)
English religious writer

Cheap Repository Tracts (1792)

I do not hesitate for a moment to pronounce the theatre to be one of the broadest avenues that lead to destruction: fascinating, no doubt, it is, but on that account the more delusive and the more dangerous. Vice in every form lives, and moves, and has its being in the pur-lieus of the theatre. Light and darkness are no more opposed to each other than the Bible and the play-book. If the one be good, the other must be evil.

The only way to justify this state, as it is, as it has ever been, and as it is likely to be, is to condemn the Bible—the same individual cannot defend both.

SIR THOMAS MORE
(1478–beheaded 1535)
Lord Chancellor of England, canonized 1915

Utopia (1516)

They have but few laws . . . but they think it against all right and justice that men should be bound to these laws, which either be in number more than be able to read, or else blinder and darker than that any man can well understand them.

Furthermore, they utterly exclude and banish all attorneys, proctors, and sergeants at the laws, which craftily handle matters, and subtely dispute of the laws. For they think it most meet that every man should plead his own matter, and tell the same tale before the judge that he would tell to his man of law. So shall there be less circumstance of words, and the truth shall sooner come to light, whiles the judge with a discreet judgment doth weigh the words of him whom no lawyer hath instruct with deceit.

This is one of the ancientest laws among them, that no man shall be blamed for reasonings in the maintenance of his own religion. For Kyng Utopus . . . made a decree, that it should be lawful for every man to favore and follow what religion he would, and that he might do the best he could to bring other to his opinion, so that he did it peaceably, gently, quietly, and soberly, without hasty and contentious rebuking and inveighing against others.

They detest war as a very brutal thing; and which, to the reproach of human nature is more practiced by men than any sort of beasts; and they, against the custom of almost all other nations, think that there is nothing more inglorious than that glory which is gained by war. They should be both troubled and ashamed of a bloody victory over their enemies; and in no victory do they glory so much, as in that which is gained by dexterity and good conduct without bloodshed.

Man can no more do without iron than without fire and water. But gold and silver have no indispensable qualities. Human folly has made them precious only because of their scarcity.

MORELLY
(fl. 1755)
French utopian philosopher*

Code of Nature (1755)

The only vice that I perceive in the universe is *Avarice;* all the others, whatever name they be known by, are only variations, degrees, of this one.

The sacred and fundamental laws that would tear out the roots of vice and of all the evils of society:
1. Nothing in society will belong to anyone . . . except the things for which the person has immediate use, for either his needs, his pleasures or his daily work.
2. Every citizen will be a public man, sustained by, supported by, and occupied at the public expense.
3. Every citizen will make his particular contribution to the activities of the community according to his capacity, his talent and his age; it is on this basis that his duties will be determined, in conformity with the *distributive* laws.

J(ohn) P(ierpont) MORGAN
(1837–1913)
American financier

Autobiography

Of all forms of tyranny the least attractive and the most vulgar is the tyranny of wealth; the tyranny of plutocracy.

It will fluctuate.
> Reply to a question concerning stock market. Quoted in *Time,* August 19, 1966

Remember, my son, that any man who is a bear on the future of this country will go broke.
> Quoted by his son, Chicago Club, December 10, 1908

*"His first name, the dates of his birth and death, where he was born, and other elementary biographical details are not known."—Albert Pried and Ronald Sanders, *Socialist Thought.*

LEWIS HENRY MORGAN
(1818–1881)
American ethnologist

Centralize property in the hands of a few and the millions are under bondage to property—a bondage as absolute and deplorable as if their limbs were covered with manacles.
> Lecture, "Diffusion against Centralization," 1852

Ancient History

As the monogamian family has improved greatly since the commencement of civilization, and very sensibly in our times, it is at least supposable that it is capable of still further improvement until the equality of the sexes is attained.

JOHN MORLEY
(1838–1923)
British statesman, Viscount of Blackburn

On Compromise (1874)

It has been often said that he who begins life by stifling his convictions is in a fair way to ending it without any convictions to stifle.

As to those who deliberately and knowingly sell their intellectual birthright for a mess of pottage, making a brazen compromise with what they hold despicable, lest they should have to win their bread honorably. Men need to expend no declamatory indignation upon them. They have a hell of their own; words can add no bitterness to it.

The law of things is that they who tamper with veracity, from whatever motive, are tampering with the vital force of human progress.

You have not converted a man, because you have silenced him.

The small reform may become the enemy of the great one.
> Ch. 3

Rousseau (1876)

Those who would treat politics and morality apart will never understand the one or the other.

Oracles on Man and Government (1923)

The most frightful idea that has ever corroded human nature—the idea of eternal punishment.

THE BOOK OF MORMON*
(Written 1827–1830)
Sacred book of the Mormon Church

For it must needs be that there is an opposition in all things. If not so, righteousness could not be brought to pass, neither wickedness, neither holiness nor mystery, neither good nor bad.

And if ye say there is no law, ye shall also say there is no sin. And if ye say there is no sin, ye shall also say there is no righteousness. And if there be no righteousness there be no happiness.

2 Nephi 2: 11, 13

And He denieth none that come unto Him, black or white, bond or free, male or female; and He remembereth the heathen and all are like unto God, Jew and Gentile.

Nephi, 22, 33

Faith is not to have a perfect knowledge of things; therefore if ye have faith ye hope for things which are not seen, which are true.

Alms 32: 21

Whosoever perisheth, perisheth unto himself; and whosoever doeth iniquity, doeth it unto himself; for behold, ye are free, ye are permitted to act for yourselves.

Helaman 14: 30

And he that saith that little children need baptism denieth the mercies of Christ, and setteth at naught the atonement of Him and the power of His redemption.

Moroni 8: 20

GOUVERNEUR MORRIS
(1752–1816)
American statesman

Give the vote to the people who have no property, and they will sell them to the rich, who will be able to buy them.

Speech, August 7, 1787, in favor of "Patricians"

---

*Believed by Mormons to be a record by the prophet Mormon of certain ancient peoples in America, discovered and translated by Joseph Smith. My thanks to Dean John T. Bernhard, College of Social Sciences, Brigham Young University, for the following quotations.—G.S.

WILLIAM MORRIS
(1834–1896)
English writer, artist

The Beauty of Life (1880)

If you want a golden rule that will fit everybody, this is it: Have nothing in your house that you do not know to be useful, or believe to be beautiful.

Art under Plutocracy (1883)

Art is man's expression of his joy in labor.

Justice (1894)

What I mean by Socialism is a condition of society in which there should be neither rich nor poor, neither master nor master's man, neither idle nor overworked, neither brain-sick brain workers nor heart-sick hand workers; in a word, in which all men would be living in equality of condition, and would manage their affairs unwastefully, and with the full consciousness that harm to one would mean harm to all—the realization at last of the meaning of the word *commonwealth*.

It is right and necessary that all men should have work to do; first, Work worth doing; second, Work of itself pleasant to do; third, Work done under conditions as would make it neither over-wearisome nor over anxious.

Lecture, Secular Society of Leicester, 1884

Settle the economic question and you settle all other questions. It is the Aaron's rod which swallows up the rest.

Quoted in *Weekly People,* December 6, 1958

MO-TI
(470–396 B.C.)
Chinese philosopher, general

Any one in the Great Society* who takes any business in hand, cannot dispense with a standard pattern.

Take then the Great Society. There are no large or small states; all are Heaven's townships. Take men. There are no young men or old, no patricians or plebians: all are Heaven's

---

*The first use of the term "Great Society" was either by Tzu Szu, grandson of Confucius, or by Mo-Ti. Cf. Lyndon Baines Johnson.

subjects. . . . Can this be anything else than heaven owning all and giving food to all.
Quoted in *Chinese Philosophy in Classical Times,*
Everyman Library

RICHARD MOWRER
American foreign correspondent

The greatest worry of all our dictators is to be found out by their own people.
Conversation, Madrid, with G.S., 1970

MALCOLM MUGGERIDGE
(1903–   )
British writer

Power is evil; and everything that belongs to power belongs to the devil.
ABC-TV, March 19, 1968

Sex is the ersatz or substitute religion of the 20th Century.
Contribution, *N.Y. Times Magazine,*
March 24, 1968

Copulo, ergo sum.
Contribution, *Esquire,* December 1970

The Most of Malcolm Muggeridge (1966)

The orgasm has replaced the Cross as the focus of longing and the image of fulfillment.

HERBERT J. MULLER
(1905–1967)
American historian

Freedom in the Ancient World (1961)

Religion is always degraded or corrupted by worldly success.

Altogether, both the glory and the tragedy of Israel may be traced to the singular idea cherished by its people—the exalted, conceited, preposterous idea that they alone were God's chosen people.

The essential teachings of Jesus . . . were literally revolutionary, and will always remain so if they are taken seriously.

HERMANN JOSEPH MULLER
(1890–1967)
American scientist, Nobel Prize 1946

The way to eliminate the unfit is to keep them from being born. . . . We should not only check degeneration—negatively—but further evolution, positively, by artificial insemination and work for the production of a nobler and nobler race of beings.

The biologist . . . knows that life as a whole is a ceaseless change, that the accomplishments even of *natural* evolution far surpasses any other type of progress that he could have imagined possible, and that there is no sign of a physical limit yet.
Notes for lecture, 1910

(Fredreich) MAX MÜLLER
(1823–1900)
English philologist, philosopher

Biographies of Words (1888)

To me an ethnologist who speaks of Aryan race, Aryan blood, Aryan eyes and hair, is as great a sinner as a linguist who speaks of a dolichocephalic dictionary or a brachycephalic grammar.

There never was a false God, nor was there ever a really false religion, unless you call a child a false man.
Letter to Rev. M.K. Schermerhorn, 1893

He who knows only one religion knows none.
Quoted in Noyes, *Views of Religion*

LEWIS MUMFORD
(1895–   )
American writer

The Condition of Man (1944)

Man alone has created out of the constant threat of death a will-to-endure, and out of the desire for continuity and immortality in all their conceivable forms, a more meaningful kind of life, in which Man redeems the littleness of individual men.

Variation, experiment, and insurgence are all of them attributes of freedom.

A day spent without the sight or sound of beauty, the contemplation of mystery, or the search for truth and perfection, is a poverty-stricken day; and a succession of such days is fatal to human life.

COUNT ERNST VON MÜNSTER
(1766–1839)
German diplomat

Absolutism tempered by assassination.
A reference to the Russian Tzarist regime; in letter quoting an unidentified person.

HUGO MÜNSTERBERG
(1863–1916)
German-born Harvard psychologist

Only a cheap curiosity could desire personal immortality.
Quoted in Cardiff, *What Great Men Think of Religion*

BENITO MUSSOLINI
(1893–shot and hanged 1945)
Journalist, Fascist dictator of Italy

L'Homme et la Divinité (July 1904)

When we claim that "God does not exist," we mean to deny by this declaration the personal God of theology, the God worshipped in various ways and diverse modes by believers the world over, that God who from nothing created the universe, from chaos matter, that God of absurd attributes who is an affront to human reason.
"Dieu n'existe pas"*

Miscellaneous Writings, Addresses, Etc.

Journalism is not a profession but a mission. Our newspaper is our party, our ideal, our

---

*Young Mussolini, a stone-mason, was greatly influenced by Dr. Angelica Balabanoff, who taught him to be a Socialist. In 1914 he received $50,000 from Jules Guède, a French member of the Cabinet, was expelled from the Socialist party for accepting bribes, and after World War I became the seventh member of the Milan Fascio.

soul, and our banner which will lead us to victory.
Editorial, *Avanti!*, Socialist Party organ, 1912

Italy is the only country in all Europe which in the past hundred years has not had a revolution. Italy has need of a blood bath.
To Bruno Buozzi, labor leader; quoted in *Sawdust Caesar*

We who detest from the depths of our soul all Christianity, from Jesus' to Marx's, look with extraordinary sympathy upon this "resurgence" of modern life in the pagan cult of force and daring.
Speech, Milan, 1919, quoted in Fermi, *Mussolini*, ch. 11

There is a violence that liberates, and a violence that enslaves; there is a violence that is moral, and a violence that is immoral.
Speech, Udine, September 20, 1922

Order, Hierarchy, Discipline.
(Proposed slogan)

Fascism now throws the noxious theories of liberalism upon the rubbish heap. . . . The truth, apparent to everyone whose eyes are not blinded by dogmatism, is that men are perhaps weary of liberty. They have had surfeit of it. Liberty is no longer the virgin, chaste and severe, fought for by the generations of the first half of the past century.

Know then, once for all, that Fascism recognizes no idols, worships no fetishes. It has already passed over the more or less decayed body of the Goddess of Liberty, and is quite prepared, if necessary, to do so once more.
Contribution, *Gerarchia*, 1923, reported in *N.Y. World*

The struggle between the two worlds [Fascism and Democracy] can permit of no compromises. It's either Us or Them!
Address, from Palazzo Venezia balcony, October 27, 1930

War alone brings up to its highest tension all human energy, and puts the stamp of nobility upon the peoples who have the courage to meet it. All other trials are substitutes, which never really put men into the position where they have to make the great decision—the alternatives of life or death.
Contribution, *Encyclopedia Italiana*, 1932

Another weapon I discovered early was the power of the printed word to sway souls to me. The newspaper was soon my gun, my flag—a thing with a soul that could mirror my own.

"Can a dictator ever be loved?" My answer is this: He can—when the masses at the same time fear him. For the crowd will always love strong men; in that respect the mob resembles a woman.

I was the artist, summoned to a mission that was to make me immortal.

The masses have little time to think. And how incredible is the willingness of modern man to believe.

We become strong, I feel, when we have no friends upon whom to lean, or to look to for moral guidance.
> Contributions, *London Sunday Express,* December 8, 1935

The history of the Church informs me that it has never accepted a peace for the principle of peace, a peace at all costs.
> Reply to Pope Pius XII's appeal to prevent World War II, April 2, 1940

No man can be a martyr when he is running for the privy. The call to nature takes precedence over a call to revolutionary action.
> Interview with John Clayton, *Chicago Tribune;* unpublished until November 30, 1969

VLADIMIR NABOKOV
(1899–1977)
Russian-born American writer

Pale Fire (1962)

No free man needs a God.
> Canto I, Line 101

Ada, or Ardor: A Family Chronicle (1969)

You lose your immortality when you lose your memory.

Revelation can be more perilous than Revolution.
> Pt. 5, Ch. 6

"On Chekhov"

. . . perhaps the most admirable among the admirable laws is the survival of the weakest.

Beauty plus pity—that is the closest we can get to a definition of art.
> University lecture on Kafka's *Metamorphosis*

A creative writer must study carefully the works of his rivals, including the Almighty.
> Quoted in *Newsweek,* July 31, 1967

What is a translation? On a platter
A poet's pale and glaring head;
A parrot's screech, a monkey's chatter,
And profanation of the dead.
> Quoted in *Harper's,* September 1981

NAPOLEON BONAPARTE
(1769–1821)
Corsican Emperor of France*

Soldiers, from the summit of yonder pyramids, forty centuries look down at you.
> To Army of Egypt, July 21, 1798**

I am sick of humanity: I need solitude and isolation.
> Letter to Joseph Bonaparte, July 25, 1798

A nation must have a religion, and that religion must be under the control of the government.
> To Count Thibaudeau, June 1801†

If they want peace, nations should avoid the pin-pricks that precede cannon-shots.

War is not at all such a difficult art as people think. . . . In reality it would seem that he is vanquished who is afraid of his adversary and that the whole secret of war is this.
> To Tzar Alexander, Tilsit, 1807

---

*Napoleon was born in Corsica one year after the island was sold to France by the Republic of Genoa.
**Attributed by General Bertrand. The usual quotation, "*Soldats, songez que, de haut de ces pyramides, quarantes siècles vous contemplent,*" does not appear in the reports of the Directorate, the letters of Berthier, or Napoleon's own history, 1799; it was first used in an anonymous *Histoire de Bonaparte,* published in 1803.
†Several biographers quote Napoleon saying "Religion is excellent stuff for keeping common people quiet." No datum is given.

In the few months in which the Bourbons reigned they have shown that they have forgotten nothing and learned nothing.
Proclamation, March 1, 1815

A man may have no religion, and yet be moral.

Soldiers were made on purpose to be killed.

Women are nothing but machines for producing children.
To Gaspard Gourgaud, at St. Helena, 1815

England is a nation of shopkeepers.

The religion of Jesus is a threat; that of Mohammed, a promise.
To Barry O'Meara, at St. Helena, 1815

My system was to have no predominant religion, but to allow perfect liberty of conscience and thought, to make all men equal. . . . I made everything independent of religion.

My great principle was to guard against reaction, and to bury the past in oblivion.

General rule: no social revolution without terror. . . . How, indeed, can we understand that one could say to those who profess fortune and public situations, "be gone and leave us your fortunes and situations!" Without intimidating them and rendering any defense impossible.
Quoted in *Opinions and Reflections of Napoleon,*
ed. L.C. Breed

Men of my stamp do not commit crimes.

If I were to give the liberty of the press, my power could not last three days.

There are two levers for moving men,—interest and fear.

Love is a silly infatuation, depend upon it. Friendship is but a name. I love nobody.

The desire of perfection is the worst disease that ever afflicted the human mind.
Quoted in Emerson, *Representative Men,*
"Napoleon, or the Man of the World"

A revolution is an opinion which has found its bayonets.

The stupid speak of the past, the wise of the present, fools of the future.
Quoted in Guillon, *Napoleon*

GEORGE JEAN NATHAN
(1882–1958)
American writer, critic

A life spent in constant labor is a life wasted, save a man be such a fool as to regard a fulsome obituary notice as an ample reward.

To be thoroughly religious, one must, I believe, be sorely disappointed. One's faith in God increases as one's faith in the world decreases. The happier the man, the farther he is from God.

Patriotism, as I see it, is often an arbitrary veneration of real estate above principles.

Athletic sports, save in the case of young boys, are designed for idiots.
Contribution, *Living Philosophies* (1931)

SCOTT NEARING
(1883–1983)
American sociologist

From Capitalism to Communism (1946)

During the whole period of written history, it is not the workers but the robbers who have been in control of the world.

SERGEI GENADYEVICH NECHAYEV
(1847–1882)
Russian revolutionary writer

Catechism of the Revolution

The revolutionist despises and abhors the existing social ethic in all its manifestations and expressions. For him everything is moral which assists the triumph of revolution. Immoral and criminal is everything which stands in its way. . . . All the tender and effeminate emotions of kinship, friendship, love, gratitude, and every honor must be stifled in him by a cold and single-handed passion for the revolutionary cause. . . . Night and day he must have but one thought, one aim—merciless destruction.
Art. 4

The nature of the true revolutionist excludes all romanticism, all tenderness, all ecstasy, all love.
Quoted in Gunther, *Inside Russia Today* (1958)

JAWAHARLAL NEHRU
(1889–1964)
Indian Prime Minister

The Unity of India (1937)

Long experience has taught us that it is dangerous in the interest of truth to suppress opinions and ideas; it has further taught us that it is foolish to imagine that we can do so. It is far easier to meet an evil in the open and defeat it in fair combat in people's minds, than to drive it underground and have no hold on it or proper approach to it. Evil flourishes far more in the shadows than in the light of day.

Credo

Democracy and Socialism are means to an end, not the end itself.

Communism became too deeply associated with the necessity of violence and thus the idea which it placed before the world became a tainted one. Means distorted ends.
Reprinted *N.Y. Times,* September 7, 1958

I want nothing to do with any religion concerned with keeping the masses satisfied to live in hunger, filth and ignorance. I want nothing to do with any order, religious or otherwise, which does not teach people that they are capable of becoming happier and more civilized, on this earth, capable of becoming true *man,* master of his fate and captain of his soul. To attain this I would put priests to work, also, and turn the temples into schools.
Quoted in Edgar Snow, *Journey to the Beginning* (1958)

HORATIO NELSON
(1758–1805)
English admiral

Nelson confides that every man will do his duty.
Proposed signal, Trafalgar, October 21, 1805*

---

*Capt. Blackwood substituted "England" for "Nelson," Lieut. Pasco substituted "expects" for "confides," according to George Fielding Eliot, contribution, *N.Y. Times,* October 5, 1958.

NEW HAMPSHIRE

New Hampshire Bill of Rights (1784)

Art. 10. Right of Revolution: Government being instituted for the common benefit, protection, and security of the whole community and not for the interests or emoluments of any one man, family, or class of men; therefore, whenever the ends of government are perverted, and public liberty manifestly endangered, and all other means of redress ineffectual, the people may, and of right ought to, reform the old, or establish a new government. The doctrine of non-resistance against arbitrary power and oppression is absurd, slavish and destructive of the good and happiness of mankind.

JOHN HENRY NEWMAN
(1801–1890)
English cardinal, writer

The Development of Christian Doctrine (1834)

To live is to change, and to be perfect is to have changed often.

Apologia pro Vita Sua (1864)

By liberalism I mean false liberty of thought, or the exercise of thought upon matters, in which, from the constitution of the human mind, thought cannot be brought to any successful issue, and therefore is out of place. Among such matters are first principles of any kind; and of these the most sacred and momentous are especially to be reckoned the truths of Revelation.
Footnote, Ch. I

There are but two ways, the way of Rome and the way of atheism.

The Catholic Church claims, not only to judge infallibly on religious questions, but to animadvert on opinions in secular matters which bear upon religion, on matters of philosophy, of science, of literature, of history, and it demands our submission to her claim.
Ch. V

Essay on the Miracles (1843)

Some infidel authors advise us to accept no miracles which would have verdict in their favor in a court of justice; that is, they employ against Scripture a weapon which Protestants would confine to attacks upon the Church; as if moral and religious questions required legal proof, and evidence were the test of truth.

2nd essay

Difficulties of the Anglicans (1833)

Herein is the strength of the Catholic Church; herein she differs from all Protestant mockeries of her. She proposes to be built upon facts, not opinions; on objective truths, not on variable sentiments; on immemorial testimony, not on private judgment; on convictions or perceptions, not on conclusions. None else but she can make this profession.

[The Church] holds that it were better for sun and moon to drop from heaven, for the earth to fall, and for all the many millions who are upon it to die of starvation in the extremest agony, so far as temporal affliction goes, than that one soul . . . should commit one single venial sin, should tell one willful untruth.

Grammar of Assent (1847)

How are we to explain it [evil], the existence of God being taken for granted, except by saying that another will, besides His, has had a part in the disposition of his works, that there is a quarrel without remedy, a chronic alienation, between God and man.

Liberalism in religion is the doctrine that there is no positive truth in religion, but that one God is as good as another.

Biglietto speech, on being made a Cardinal, 1879

Historical Sketches (1872)

I do not see the difference between avowing that there is no God, and implying that nothing definite can for certain be known about Him.

The Idea of a University (1873)

It is almost a definition of a gentleman to say that he is one who never inflicts pain.

SIR ISAAC NEWTON
(1642–1727)
English mathematician, philosopher*

Principia (1687)

Every body continues in its state of rest or of uniform motion in a straight line, except in so far as it is compelled to change that state by forces impressed upon it.

First Law of Motion

Opticks (1704)

The course of nature . . . seems delighted with transmutations.

The Correspondence of Isaac Newton (ed. H.W. Turnbull and J.F. Scott, 1959–1974)

If I have seen farther [than Descartes] it is by standing on the shoulders of giants.

It is the weight, not numbers of experiments that is to be regarded.

I shall not mingle conjectures with certainties.

I do not know what I may appear to the world; but to myself I seem to have been only a boy playing on the sea-shore, and diverting myself in now and then finding a smoother pebble or a prettier shell than ordinary, whilst the great ocean of truth lay all undiscovered before me.

Quoted in Brewster, *Memoirs of Newton,*
Vol. 2, Ch. 27

FRIEDRICH (Wilhelm) NIETZSCHE
(1844–1900)
German philosopher*

The Anti-Christ (1888)

What is good? All that elevates the feeling of power, the will to power, the power itself in man.
What is bad? All that proceeds from weakness.
What is happiness? The feeling that power *increases*—that resistance is being overcome.

I preach not contentedness, but more power; not peace, but war; not virtue, but efficiency. The weak and defective shall perish; and they shall be given assistance: that is the first principle of the dionysian charity.

Aphorism 2

---

*Biographers quote Nietzsche as having said: "I am proud of my Polish descent" and as having at one time become a Swiss citizen. He was a college professor, suffered eye and brain trouble in 1876, was pensioned in 1879, lived 10 years in pain, and was declared insane in 1888.
"Revolt against the whole civilized environment in which he was born is the keynote to Nietzsche's literary career."—Britannica, 11th ed.

3

*". . . the greatest discovery ever made by man, namely, the law of the attraction of gravity, was also attacked by Leibnitz, 'as subversive of natural and inferentially of revealed religion.' "—Darwin, *Recapitulation and Conclusion.*

Christianity has waged a deadly war against the higher type of man. It has put a ban on all his fundamental instincts. It has distilled evil out of these instincts. It makes the strong and efficient man its typical outcast man. It has taken the part of the weak and the low; it has made an ideal out of its antagonism to the very instincts which tend to preserve life and well-being. . . . It has taught men to regard their highest impulses as sinful—as temptations.

Aphorism 5

Where the will to power is wanting, there is decline.

Aphorism 6

Again, sympathy thwarts the law of development, of evolution of the survival of the fittest. It preserves what is ripe for extinction . . . . It is the principal tool for the advancement of decadence.

Aphorism 7

"Faith" means not *wanting* to know what is true.

So long as the priest, that professional negator, slanderer and poisoner of life, is regarded as a superior type of human being, there cannot be any answer to the question: "What is truth?"

Aphorism 8

The preponderance of pain over pleasure is the cause of our fictitious morality and religion.

Aphorism 15

Almost two thousand years, and no new god!

Aphorism 19

The Jews are the most remarkable nation of world history because, faced with the question of being or not being, they preferred, with a perfectly uncanny conviction, being at any price; the price they had to pay was the radical falsification of all nature, all naturalness, all reality, the entire inner world as well as the outer. They defined themselves counter to all those conditions under which a nation was previously able to live, was permitted to live; they made of themselves an antithesis of natural conditions—they inverted religion, religious worship, morality, history, psychology, one after the other, in an irreparable way into the contradiction of their natural values.

Aphorism 24

What is Jewish, what is Christian morality? Chance robbed of its innocence; unhappiness polluted with the idea of "sin"; well-being represented as a danger, as a "temptation"; a physiological disorder produced by the canker worm of conscience.

Aphorism 25

Morality is the best of all devices for leading mankind by the nose.

The Christian, the *ultimo ratio* of lying, is the Jew all over again—he is threefold Jew.

Aphorism 44

God created woman. And boredom did indeed cease from that moment—but many other things ceased as well. Woman was God's second mistake.

Aphorism 48

From a psychological point of view, 'sins' are indispensable in any society organized by priests; they are the actual levers of power, the priest lives on sins, he needs the 'commission of sins.'

Aphorism 49

At every step, one has to wrestle for truth; one has to surrender to it almost everything to which the heart, to which our love, our trust in life clings otherwise. That requires greatness of soul: the service of truth is the hardest service. . . . Faith makes blessed: *consequently,* it lies.

Aphorism 50

The conclusion that all idiots, women and plebeians come to, that there must be something in a cause for which any one goes to his death (or which, under primitive Christianity, set off epidemics of death-seekers)—this conclusion has been an unspeakable drag upon the whole spirit of inquiry and investigation. The martyrs have damaged the truth.

Aphorism 53

The man of belief is necessarily a dependent man. . . . He does not belong to himself, but to the author of the idea he believes.

Aphorism 54

The most common lie is that with which one lies to oneself: lying to others is relatively an exception.

There are questions whose truth or untruth cannot be decided by men; all the supreme questions, all the supreme problems of value are beyond human reason.

Aphorism 55

The order of castes is the dominating law of nature. . . . The first caste comprises those who are obviously superior to the mass intellectually; the second includes those whose existence is chiefly muscular, and the third is made up of the mediocre. The third class, very naturally, is the most numerous, but the first is the most powerful. . . . Whom do I hate most among the men of today? The socialist who undermines the workingman's healthy instincts, who takes from him his feeling of contentedness with his existence, who makes him envious, who teaches him revenge. . . . There is no wrong in unequal rights: it lies in the vain pretension to equal rights.

Aphorism 57

Beyond Good and Evil (1886)

Life is will to power. Self-preservation is only one of the indirect results of that will to power, though it is the most frequent.

13

It is the business of the very few to be independent; it is a privilege of the strong.

29

The Christian faith from the beginning, is sacrifice: the sacrifice of all freedom, all pride, all self-confidence of spirit; it is at the same time subjection, a self-derision, and self-mutilation.

46

Wherever the religious neurosis has appeared on the earth so far, we find it connected with three dangerous prescriptions as to regimen: solitude, fasting, and sexual abstinence.

47

Why Atheism nowadays? "The father" in God is thoroughly refuted; equally so "the judge," "the rewarder." Also his "free will": he does not hear—and even if he did, he would not know how to help.

53

We are most unfair to God: we do not allow him to sin.

65a

The degree and kind of sexuality of a human being reaches up into the ultimate pinnacle of his spirit.

75

It was subtle of God to learn Greek when he wished to become an author and not to learn it better.

121

Even concubinage has been corrupted—by marriage.

123

Man wishes woman to be peaceable, but in fact she is essentially warlike, like the cat.

131

When a woman turns to scholarship [or, learning] there is usually something wrong with her sexually.

144

What is done from love is always beyond good and evil.

153

In individuals insanity is rare, but in groups, parties, nations and epochs it is the rule.

156

The thought of suicide is a great consolation: with the help of it, one has got through many a bad night.

157

Christianity gave Eros poison to drink: he did not die of it but degenerated—into vice.

168

The *universal degeneracy of mankind* to the level of the "man of the future"—as idealized by the socialistic fools and shallow-pates—this degeneracy and dwarfing of men to an absolutely gregarious animal (or as they call it, to a man of "free society"), this brutalizing of man into a pigmy with equal rights and claims, is undoubtedly possible!

203

Blessed are the forgetful; for they get over their stupidities too.

217

Did any woman ever acknowledge profundity in another woman's mind, or justice in another woman's heart?

232

The pathos of distance.

257

There are master-morality and slave-morality.

260

Egoism is the very essence of a noble soul.

265

The Dawn (1861)

All history treats almost exclusively of wicked men who, in the course of time, have come to be looked upon as good men. All progress is the result of successful crime.

Aphorism 20

All religions bear traces of the fact that they arose during the intellectual immaturity of the

human race—before it had learned the obligations to speak the truth. Not one of them
makes it the duty of its god to be truthful and
understandable in his communications.

Aphorism 91

In times of extremity, the people of Israel
less often sought refuge in drink, or suicide,
than any other race of Europe. . . . The Jews
hid their bravery under the cloak of submis-
siveness; their heroism in facing contempt,
surpasses that of saints.

Aphorism 205

Ecce Homo (published 1908)

Revaluation of all values: that is my formula
for an act of ultimate self-examination by
mankind in which he has become flesh and
genius.

Pt. I, 1

Wherever Germany extends her sway, she
ruins culture.

Pt. II, 3

All idealism is falsehood in the face of necessity.

Pt. II, 10

Woman is unspeakably more wicked than
man, also cleverer. Goodness in woman is
really nothing but a form of degeneracy.

Pt. III, 5

All truths are for me soaked in blood.

Pt. IV, i

A Genealogy of Morals (1887)

A herd of blond beasts of prey, a race of
conquerors and masters, with military organization, with the power to organize, unscrupu-
lously placing their fearful paws upon a
population perhaps vastly superior in numbers
. . . this beast founded the State.

Napoleon, the synthesis of brute and Superman.

First Essay, Aphorism 17

In itself, an act of injury, violation, exploitation or annihilation cannot be wrong, for life
operates, essentially and fundamentally, by injuring, violating, exploiting and annihilating
and cannot even be conceived of outside of
this character.

To regard the rights of others as being inherent in them, and not as mere compromises for
the benefit of the mass-unit, would be to
enunciate a principle hostile to life itself.

Second Essay, Aphorism 11

A married philosopher is a figure of comedy.

Third Essay, Aphorism 7

Human, All-too-Human (1878)

There are no eternal facts, as there are no
absolute truths.

The most serious parody I have ever heard
was this: In the beginning was nonsense, and
the nonsense was with God, and the nonsense
was God. *

Hope is the worst of evils, for it prolongs the
torments of Man.

The whole problem of the *Jews* exists only
in nation states, for here their energy and
higher intelligence, their accumulated capital
of spirit and will, gathered from generation to
generation through a long schooling in suffering, must become so preponderant as to arouse
mass envy and hatred. In almost all contemporary nations, therefore—in direct proportion to
the degree to which they act up nationalisti-
cally—the literary obscenity is spreading of
leading Jews to slaughter as scapegoats of every
conceivable public and internal misfortune.
As soon as it is no longer a matter of preserving
nations, but of producing the strongest posible
European mixed race, the Jew is just as useful
and desireable an ingredient as any other national remnant. . . .

One owes to them the noblest man (Christ),
the purest sage (Spinoza), the most powerful
book, and the most effective moral law of the
world. Moreover, in the darkest times of the
Middle Ages, . . . it was Jewish free-thinkers,
scholars, and physicians who clung to the banner of enlightenment and spiritual independence. . . . We owe it to their exertions, not
least of all, . . . that the bond of culture
which now links us with the enlightenment of
Greco-Roman antiquity remained unbroken.

One's belief in truth begins with doubt of all
truths one has believed hitherto.

One will seldom go wrong if one attributes
extreme actions to vanity, average ones to
habit, and petty ones to fear.

The Gay Science (1882)

Live dangerously. Build your cities on the
slopes of Vesuvius.

283

---

* *See* Hemingway: "Our nada who is in nada, nada
be thy name . . ."

Thus Spake Zarathustra (1883–1891)

When Zarathustra was alone, however, he said to his heart: "Could it be possible! This old saint in the forest hath not yet heard of it, that *God is dead!*"

Prologue, 2

I teach you the Superman. Man is something that is to be surpassed.

What is the ape to man? A laughing-stock, a thing of shame. And yet the same shall man be to the Superman: a laughing-stock, a thing of shame.

3

Man is a rope stretched between the animal and the Superman—a rope over an abyss.

What is great in man is that he is a bridge and not a goal: what is lovable in man is that he is an *over-going* and not a *down-going*.

4

I tell you: one must have chaos in one, to give birth to a dancing star. I tell you: ye have still chaos in you.

A little poison at last for a pleasant death.

5

There is no devil and no hell. Thy soul will be dead even sooner than thy body: fear therefore, nothing any more!

6

Of all that is written, I love only what a person hath written with his blood. Write with blood, and thou wilt find that blood is spirit.

I, 7

I should only believe in a God that would know how to dance.

Far too long hath there been a slave and a tyrant concealed in woman. On that account woman is not yet capable of friendship: she knoweth only love.

In woman's love there is injustice and blindness to all she doth not love. And even in woman's conscious love, there is still always surprise and lightning and night, along with the light.

As yet woman is not capable of friendship: women are still cats, and birds. Or at best, cows.

As yet woman is not capable of friendship. But tell me, ye men, who of you are capable of friendship?

14

"Give me, woman, thy little truth!" said I. And thus spake the old woman:

"Thou goest to women? Do not forget thy whip!"

18

Your love to woman, and woman's love to man—ah, would that it were sympathy for suffering and veiled deities! But generally two animals light on one another.

20

Many die too late, and some die too early. Yet strangeness soundeth the precept: "Die at the right time!"

21

There is an old illusion—it is called good and evil.

54

I love the great despisers. Man is something that hath to be surpassed.

67

The Twilight of the Idols (1888)

The spiritualization of sensuality is called love: it is a great triumph over Christianity.
"Morality as Anti-nature," 3

What is it: is man only a blunder of God's, or God only a blunder of man's?
"Maxims and Arrows," 7

Whatever does not destroy me makes me stronger. *

8

Without music life would be a mistake.
"The Skirmishes of an Untimely Man," 10

In certain cases it is indecent to go on living. To continue to vegetate in a state of cowardly dependence upon doctors, once the meaning of life has been lost, ought to be regarded with the greatest contempt of mankind.

36

ROBERT GEORGES NIVELLE
(1856–1924)
French general

Ils ne passeront pas.
They shall not pass.
To Gen. Castlenau, at Verdun, February 1916; mistakenly attributed to Pétain.

*Painted on entrances to Hitler youth camps for leaders, Ordensburg and Vogelsang.

RICHARD M(ilhous) NIXON
(1913–   )
37th President of the United States

. . . if there is another war there will be no victors, only losers.
> New York Times report from Moscow, July 24, 1968

Let us begin by committing ourselves to the truth—to see it as it is, and tell it like it is—to find the truth, to speak the truth, and to live the truth.
> Speech, accepting nomination, 1968

When a president does it then it is not illegal.
> Quoted in CBS television report, May 19, 1977

KWAME NKRUMAH
(1909–1972)
Founder of Ghana

We prefer self-government with danger to servitude with tranquility.
> Inscribed on monument, Accra, 1958

ALFRED (Bernhard) NOBEL
(1833–1896)
Swedish munitions manufacturer,
philanthropist

I intend to leave after my death a large fund for the promotion of the peace idea, but I am skeptical as to its results. The savants will write excellent volumes. There will be laureates. But wars will continue just the same until the force of circumstances renders them impossible.
> Public statement, 1890

Perhaps my dynamite plants will put an end to war sooner than your [peace] congresses. On the day two army corps can annihilate each other in one second all civilized nations will recoil from war in horror.
> To Bertha von Suttner, peace congress, Switzerland, 1892

One part shall be awarded to the person who shall have done the best work for fraternity among the nations, for the abolition or reduction of standing armies and the promotion of peace congresses.
> First will, 1895, creating Nobel Peace Prize; first award in 1901

Second to agriculture, humbug is the biggest industry of our age.
> Quoted in Saturday Review

MAX NORDAU (né Sudfeld)
(1849–1923)
German writer, physician

Morals and the Evolution of Man

Morality will conquer war, even as it has conquered human sacrifices, slavery, feuds, head-hunting and cannibalism.

The Jews are not hated because they have evil qualities; evil qualities are sought for them, because they are hated.
> Quoted in Leo Rosten, *Treasury of Jewish Quotations*

FRANK NORRIS
(1870–1902)
American novelist

The Responsibilities of the Novelist (published 1903)

The People have a right to the Truth as they have a right to life, liberty and the pursuit of happiness.

NOVALIS (Friedrich Leopold, Baron von Hardenburg)
(1772–1801)
German poet, novelist

The service of philosophy, or speculative culture, towards the human spirit, is to arouse, to startle it to a life of constant and eager conservation.
> Quoted in Pater, *The Renaissance* (1873), conclusion

There is but one Temple in the Universe and that is the Body of Man. Nothing is holier than that high form. Bending before men is a reverence done to the Revelation in the Flesh. We touch Heaven as we lay our hand on a human body.
> Quoted in Carlyle, *Heroes and Hero-Worship* (1841), lecture 1

JULIUS NYERERE
(1921–   )
President of Tanganyika

Independence and Work.
Motto and slogan

Small nations are like indecently dressed women. They tempt the evil-minded.
Quoted in *The Reporter,* April 9, 1964

JAMES O'BRIEN (né Bronterre)
(1805–1864)
Irish Chartist leader

The desire of one man to live on the fruits of another's labor is the original sin of the world.
Attributed

SEAN O'CASEY
(1884–1964)
Irish dramatist

Death of Thomas Ashe (1918)

You cannot put a rope around the neck of an idea; you cannot put an idea up against the barrack-square wall and riddle it with bullets; you cannot confine it in the strongest prison cell your slaves could ever build.

God be my judge that I hate fighting. If I be damned for anything, I shall be damned for keeping the two-edged sword of thought tight in the scabbard when it should be searching the bowels of fools and knaves.
In conversation, to Mrs. G. Bernard Shaw

Communism is not to be found in a booklet, but springs to life from within, like the Kingdom of Heaven.
Quoted in D. Krause, *Sean O'Casey: The Man and His Work* (1960)

ADOLPH S(imon) OCHS
(1858–1935)
American newspaper publisher

To give the news impartially, without fear or favor, regardless of any party, sect or interests involved.
Credo, *New York Times,* August 9, 1896

All the news that's fit to print.
Slogan for the *New York Times*

DANIEL O'CONNELL
(1775–1847)
Irish nationalist leader

Bigotry has no head and cannot think; no heart and cannot feel. When she moves it is in wrath; when she pauses it is amid ruin. Her prayers are curses, her god is a demon, her communion is death, her vengeance is eternity, her decalogue written in the blood of her victims, and if she stops for a moment in her infernal flight it is upon a kindred rock to whet her vulture fang for a more sanguinary desolation.
Attributed

LIAM O'FLAHERTY
(1897–   )
Irish novelist

It is impossible for a creative artist to be either a Puritan or a Fascist, because both are a negation of the creative urge. The only things the creative artist can be opposed to are ugliness and injustice.
Interview, *N.Y. Post,* November 27, 1937

OMAR I
(581?–644)
2nd Caliph, captor of Jerusalem

Burn the libraries, for their value is in this one book [the Koran].
At the capture of Alexandria; quoted in Emerson, *Representative Men*

If these writings of the Greeks agree with the word of God [Allah], they are useless and need not be preserved; if they disagree, they are pernicious and ought to be destroyed.
Quoted by Gibbon, but Gibbon denies Omar's guilt in the destruction of the Alexandrian library

OMAR KHAYYAM
(d. 1123 A.D.)
Persian mathematician, astronomer, poet

A gourd of red wine and a sheaf of poems—
A bare subsistence, half a loaf, no more—
Supplies us two alone in the free desert:
What sultan would we envy on his throne.
"The Rubaiyat," st. 12, tr. Robert Graves, aided by
    Omar Ali-Shah, 1967, using a 12th century
              manuscript. (*See* Fitzgerald)

EUGENE O'NEILL
(1888–1953)
American dramatist

The Emperor Jones (1920)

For de little stealin' dey gits you in jail soon
or late. For the big stealin' dey makes you emperor and puts you in de Hall o' Fame when
you croaks.
                            Sc. i

Strange Interlude (1928)

Our lives are merely strange dark interludes
in the electrical display of God the Father!
                   Pt. II, act IX

The playwright of today must dig at the
roots of the sickness of today as he feels it—the
death of the old God and the failure of science
and materialism to give any satisfactory new
one.
            Letter to G.J. Nathan, c. 1925

The tragedy of man is perhaps the only significant thing about him.
        Quoted in *N.Y. Times Magazine,*
                November 12, 1961

J(ulius) ROBERT OPPENHEIMER
(1904–1967)
American physicist

There must be no barriers for freedom in inquiry. There is no place for dogma in science.
The scientist is free, and must be free to ask
any question, to doubt any assertion, to seek
for any evidence, to correct any errors.
        Contribution, *Life,* October 10, 1949

You can certainly destroy enough of humanity so that only the greatest act of faith can
persuade you that what's left will be human.
        To Ed Murrow, CBS, January 4, 1955

ORIGEN
(185–253 A.D.)
Alexandrian theologian

De principiis

This also is clearly defined in the teachings
of the Church, that every rational soul is possessed of free-will and volition; that it has a
struggle to maintain with the devil and his angels, and opposing influences, because they
strive to burden it with sins.
                    Bk. I, Ch. 5

JOSÉ ORTEGA Y GASSET
(1883–1955)
Spanish philosopher

The Revolt of the Masses (1930)

The masses, by definition, neither should
nor can direct their own personal existence,
and still less rule society in general.

To be surprised, to wonder, is to begin to
understand. This is the sport, the luxury, special to the intellectual man.

The most radical division that it is possible
to make of humanity is that which splits it into
two classes of creatures: those who make great
demands on themselves, piling up difficulties
and duties; and those who demand nothing
special of themselves, but for whom to live is
to be every moment what they already are,
without imposing on themselves any effort toward perfection; mere buoys that float on
waves.
                      Ch. I

If anyone in a discussion with us is not concerned with adjusting himself to truth, if he
has no wish to find the truth, he is intellectually a barbarian. That, in fact, is the position
of the mass-man when he speaks, lectures, or
writes.
                Ch. VIII, note

The political doctrine which has represented the loftiest endeavor toward common
life is liberal democracy. . . . Liberalism—it is
well to recall this to-day—is the supreme form
of generosity; it is the right which the majority
concedes to minorities and hence it is the noblest cry that has ever resounded in this planet.
                   Ch. VIII

We have need of history in its entirety, not
to fall back into it, but to escape from it.
                    Ch. X

Marxian Socialism and Bolshevism are two historical phenomena which have hardly a single common denominator.

Ch. XIV, note

The man who discovers a new scientific truth has previously had to smash to atoms almost everything he had learnt, and arrives at the new truth with hands bloodstained from the slaughter of a thousand platitudes.

Ch. XIV

**GEORGE ORWELL (né Eric Blair)
(1903–1950)
India-born British policeman, tramp, dishwasher, Socialist, volunteer in Spanish war, writer**

1984 (1949)

Power is in inflicting pain and humiliation. Power is in tearing human minds to pieces and putting them together again in new shapes of our own choosing.

Big brother is watching you.

Newspeak.

Doublethink.

War is Peace
Freedom is Slavery
Ignorance is Strength.

Who controls the past controls the future, who controls the present controls the past.

Animal Farm (1945)

If liberty means anything at all, it means the right to tell people what they do not want to hear.*

All animals are equal, but some animals are more equal than others.

Down and Out in Paris and London (1933)

The great redeeming feature of poverty: the fact that it annihilates the future.

Ch. 3

Looking Back on the Spanish War (1945)

War is evil, but it is often the lesser evil.

The major problem of our time is the decay of the belief in personal immortality. . . .

---

*This quotation is from the introduction, which was suppressed; published by the *N.Y. Times,* 1972.

How right the working classes are in their "materialism." How right they are to realize that the belly comes before the soul.

Reflections on Gandhi (1949)

Saints should always be judged guilty until they are proven innocent.

Many people genuinely do not wish to be saints, and it is probable that some who achieve or aspire to sainthood have never felt much temptation to be human beings.

One must choose between God and Man, and all "radicals" and "progressives," from the mildest Liberals to the most extreme Anarchists, have in effect chosen Man.

Politics and the English Language (1946)

But if thought corrupts language, language can also corrupt thought.

All issues are political issues, and politics itself is a mass of lies, evasions, folly, hatred and schizophrenia.

Political language—and with variations this is true of all political parties, from Conservatives to Anarchists—is designed to make lies sound truthful and murder respectable, and to give an appearance of solidity to pure wind.

Why I Write (1947)

I think there are four great motives for writing. . . .
(1) Sheer egoism. Desire to seem clever, to be talked about, to be remembered after death, to get your own back on grown-ups who snubbed you in childhood, etc. . . .
(2) Aesthetic enthusiasm . . .
(3) Historical impulse. Desire to see things as they are, to find out true facts and store them up for the use of posterity.
(4) Political purpose—using the word "political" in the widest possible sense. Desire to push the world in a certain direction, to alter other people's idea of the kind of society that they should strive after.

Every book is a failure.

Writing a book is a horrible, exhausting struggle, like a long bout of some painful illness. One would never undertake such a thing if one were not driven on by some demon whom one can neither resist nor understand.

Selected Essays

Patriotism is usually stronger than class-hatred, and always stronger than internationalism.

To accept civilization *as it is* practically means accepting decay.

It is doubtful whether any sense of tragedy is compatible with the belief in God.

In a society in which there is no law, and in theory no compulsion, the only arbiter of behavior is public opinion. But public opinion, because of the tremendous urge to conformity in gregarious animals, is less tolerant than any system of law.

SIR WILLIAM OSLER
(1849–1919)
Canadian-born British physician

My second fixed idea is the uselessness of men above 60 years of age, and the incalculable benefit it would be in commercial, political, and professional life, if, as a matter of course, men stopped work at this age.
Address, Johns Hopkins University, February 22, 1905*

Humanity has but three great enemies: fever, famine and war; . . . by far the most terrible is fever.
Quoted in Cushing, *Life of William Osler,* Vol. I, Ch. 14

A man is sane morally at 30, rich mentally at 40, wise spiritually at 50—or never.
Quoted in *Forbes Magazine,* June 1961

JOHN LOUIS O'SULLIVAN
(1813–1895)
American journalist, diplomat

Our manifest destiny to overspread the continent allotted by Providence for the free development of our yearly multiplying millions.
U.S. Magazine & Diplomatic Review, July-August, 1845

*An international sensation was caused by this address.

JAMES OTIS
(1725–1783)
American patriot, pamphleteer

If life, liberty, and property could be enjoyed in as great perfection in solitude as in society, there would be no need of government.
"The Rights of the British Colonies Asserted and Proved" (1764)

Taxation without representation is tyranny.
Attributed, 1763

OUIDA (Marie Louise de la Ramée)
(1838–1908)
British writer

Wisdom, Wit and Pathos (1870)

Take hope from the heart of man, and you have left a beast of prey.

Christianity has ever made of death a horror which was unknown to the gay calm of the Pagan.

PETER DEMIANOVICH OUSPENSKY
(1878–1947)
Russian philosopher

A New Model of the Universe

Art is the communication of ecstasy.

OVID
(43 B.C.–18 A.D.)
Roman poet

Ars amatoria

It is expedient that there be gods, and as it is expedient, let us so believe.
Bk. I, Line 637

Deceive the deceivers.
Line 645

Pure women are only those who have not been asked; and a man who is angry at his wife's amours is a mere rustic.

Love is a kind of warfare.
Bk. II, Line 233

If art is concealed, it succeeds.
Line 313

If she is chaste when there be no fear of de-
tection, she is truly chaste . . .

Bribes, believe me, buy both gods and men.
Bk. III

Metamorphoses

The criminal love of riches.

All things change, nothing perishes.

I see the right, and I approve it, too.
Condemn the wrong and yet the wrong pursue.

Pia mendacia fraude.
With pious fraud.

Tristia

The deeds of men never deceive the gods.
I.II 99

Heroides

Habits change into character.

Exitus acta probat.
The result justifies the means.

ROBERT OWEN
(1771–1858)
English Socialist, philanthropist

What ideas individuals may attach to the
term Millennium I know not; but I know that
society may be formed so as to exist without
crime, without poverty, with health greatly
improved, with little, if any, misery, and with
intelligence and happiness increased a hun-
dredfold; and no obstacle whatsoever intervenes at this moment, except ignorance, to
prevent such a state of society from becoming
universal.

Had it not been a law of nature, that any
impression, however ridiculous and absurd,
and however contrary to fact, may be given in
infancy, so as to be tenaciously retained
through life, men could not have passed the
previous ages of the world without discovering
the gross errors in which they have been
trained.
"An Address, for Better Working Conditions in
England" (1816)

WILFRED OWEN
(1894–killed in battle 1918)
British poet

"Strange Meeting" (published 1920)

I went hunting wild
After the wildest beauty in the world,
Which lies not calm in eyes, or braided
hair,
But mocks the steady running of the hour.

. . . I mean the truth untold,
The pity of war, the pity war distilled.

Foreheads of men have bled where no
wounds were.
I am the enemy you killed, my friend.

"Anthem for Doomed Youth" (published 1920)

What passing-bells for these who die as cat-
tle?
Only the monstrous anger of the guns.
Only the stuttering rifles' rapid rattle
Can patter out their hasty orisons.

"Dulce et Decorum Est"* (published 1920)

My friend, you would not tell with such
high zest
To children ardent for some desperate glory,
The old Lie: *Dulce et decorum est
Pro patria mori.*

COUNT AXEL GUSTAFSSON
OXENSTIERNA
(1583–1654)
Chancellor of Sweden

Behold, my son, with what little wisdom the
world is ruled.
Letter, 1648

MARCUS PACUVIUS
(c. 220–130 B.C.)
Roman tragic poet

Teucer

Wherever we are content, that is our country.

---

*Horace: "It is sweet and beautiful to die for one's
country."

MOHAMMED REZA PAHLEVI
(1919–1980)
Shah of Iran

What do these feminists want? You may be equal in the eyes of the law but not in ability. You have never even produced a good cook . . . you have produced nothing great, nothing.

From an interview with Oriana Fallaci,
New Republic, December 1, 1973

THOMAS PAINE
(1737–1809)
English staymaker, American patriot, Deist, Quaker*

The original draft of the Declaration of Independence**

When in the course of Human Events it becomes necessary for a People to advance from that Subordination in which they have hitherto remained, and to assume among the Powers of the Earth, the equal and independent Station to which the Laws of Nature and of Nature's God entitle them, a decent respect to the opinions of Mankind requires that they should declare the Causes, which impel them to the Change.

We hold these truths to be Self evident: that all Men are created equal and independent; that from that equal Creation they derive Rights inherent and unalienable; among which are the Preservation of Life, and Liberty, and the Pursuit of Happiness; that to Secure these ends, Governments are instituted

---

*"How many Americans know that Tom Paine inspired the Declaration of Independence? How many know that he actually gave this country its name—the United States of America? Not many."—W.E. Woodward, *Tom Paine, America's Godfather* (1945).

"History will ascribe the (American) Revolution to Thomas Paine. . . . Without the pen of Paine, the sword of Washington would have been wielded in vain."—John Adams.
**Submitted to Jefferson by Paine; largely embodied in Jefferson's "Rough Draft." This and following paragraphs published by Prophylaen Weltgeschichte, ed. Walter Goetz, from facsimile of the original manuscript, Berlin, 1922–23, vol. vi, pp. 464–5; published in America by The Thomas Paine Foundation.

among Men, deriving their just Powers from the consent of the Governed; that whenever, any form of Government, Shall become destructive of these Ends, it is the Right of the People to alter or to abolish it, and to institute new Government. . . .

He [King George III] has waged cruel War against human Nature itself, violating its most Sacred Rights of Life and Liberty in the Persons of distant People who never offended him, captivating and carrying them into Slavery in another hemisphere, or to incur miserable Death in their Transportation thither. This piratical Warfare, the opprobrium of Infidel Powers [the Arab-Muslim slavers], is the Warfare of the *Christian* King of Great Britain.

We therefore the Representatives of the United States of America. . . . do assert and declare these Colonies to be free and independent States. . . . And for the Support of this Declaration, We mutually pledge to each other our Lives, our Fortunes, and our Sacred Honour.

Common Sense (February 14, 1776)*

Time makes more Converts than Reason.

The cause of America is, in a great measure, the cause of all mankind.

When we are planning for posterity, we ought to remember that virtue is not hereditary.

Society is produced by our wants, and government by our wickedness.

Here, then is the origin and rise of government; namely, a mode rendered necessary by the inability of moral virtue to govern the world; here too is the design and end of government, viz., Freedom and security.

As to religion, I hold it to be the indispensable duty of all government to protect the conscientious professors thereof, and I know of no other business which government hath to do therewith.

For myself, I fully and conscientiously believe, that it is the will of the Almighty, that there should be a diversity of religious opinion among us; it affords a larger field for our Christian kindness. . . . I look to the various

---

*The original, published in Philadelphia, was anonymous—"Written by an Englishman."

denominations among us to be like children of the same family, differing only in what is called their Christian names.

Introduction

The American Crisis

These are the times that try men's souls. The summer soldier and the sunshine patriot will, in this crisis, shrink from the service of their country; but he that stands it *now*, deserves the love and thanks of man and woman.

Tyranny, like hell, is not easily conquered.

No. 1, December 23, 1776

Those who expect to reap the blessings of freedom must, like men, undergo the fatigue of supporting it.

No. 4, September 12, 1777

The Age of Reason (1793)

I believe in one God, and no more; and I hope for happiness beyond this life.

When a man has so far corrupted and prostituted the chastity of his mind, as to subscribe his professional belief to things he does not believe, he has prepared himself for the commission of every other crime. . . . Infidelity does not consist in believing or in disbelieving, it consists in professing to believe what (one) does not believe.

I do not believe in the creed professed by the Jewish church, by the Roman church, by the Greek church, by the Turkish church, by the Protestant church, nor by any church that I know of. My own mind is my own church.

The adulterous connection of church and state . . .

As to the Christian system of faith, it appears to me as a species of atheism; a sort of religious denial of God. It professes to believe in a man rather than in God. It is a compound made up chiefly of man-ism with but little deism, and is as near to atheism as twilight is to darkness.

The declaration which says God visits the sins of the fathers upon the children, is contrary to every principle of moral justice.

What is it the new Testament teaches us? To believe that the Almighty committed debauchery with a woman engaged to be married; and the belief of this debauchery is called faith.

The Rights of Man (1792)

Moderation in temper is always a virtue, but moderation in principle is always a vice.

The more perfect civilization is, the less occasion has it for government, because the more does it regulate its own affairs, and govern itself. . . . All the great laws of society are laws of nature.

Agrarian Justice (1797)

It is wrong to say that God made *rich* and *poor*; He made only *male* and *female*; and He gave them the earth for their inheritance. . . . The earth, in its natural uncultivated state was, and ever would have continued to be, *the common property of the human race.*

———

Deism is the only profession of religion that admits of worshipping and reverencing God in purity. . . . God is almost forgotten in the Christian religion. Everything, even the creation, is ascribed to the son of Mary.

Letter to Mr. Moore of New York, commonly called "Bishop Moore," *The Prospect*, 1804

Reconciliation is thought of now by none but knaves, fools, and madmen; and as we cannot offer terms of peace to Great Britain until, as other nations have before us, we agree to call ourselves by some name, I shall rejoice to hear the title of the UNITED STATES OF AMERICA, in order that we may be on a proper footing to negotiate a peace.

Letter, signed "Republicus," *Penna. Evening Post,* January 29, 1776

That government is best which governs least.

Masthead slogan of the *Democratic Review,* to which Thoreau, who wrote, "I accept the motto," contributed.

Franklin: *Ubi libertas, ibi patria.* Where there is liberty, there is my country.
Paine: Where liberty is not, there is mine.

Attributed conversation

WILLIAM PALEY
(1743–1805)
English divine, philosopher

Moral Philosophy (1785)

Who can refute a sneer?

Vol. II, Bk. V, ch. 9

PALLADAS
(fl. 400 A.D.)
Greek epigrammatist

Silence is man's chief learning.

46

The body is an affliction of the soul; it is Hell, Fate, a burden, a necessity, a strong chain, and a tormenting punishment.

88

Naked to earth was I brought—naked to earth I descend.

Why should I labor for naught, seeing how naked the end?

Quoted, in *Greek Anthology*

HENRY JOHN TEMPLE, LORD PALMERSTON
(1784–1865)
English statesman

We have no eternal allies and we have no perpetual enemies. Our interests are eternal and perpetual, and these interests it is our duty to follow.

Speech on the Polish Question in the House of Commons, March 1, 1848

CHRISTABEL PANKHURST
(1880–1958)
British militant suffragist

We are here to claim our right as women, not only to be free, but to fight for freedom . . . which, as we believe, means the regeneration of all humanity.

Speech, March 23, 1911

EMMELINE PANKHURST
(1858–1928)
British militant suffragist

As long as women consent to be unjustly governed, they will be; but directly women say: "We withhold our consent," we will not be governed any longer as long as government is unjust. Not by the forces of civil war can you govern the very weakest woman. You can kill that woman, but she escapes you then; you cannot govern her.

Address, Hartford, Conn., November 13, 1913

Trust in God: She will provide.

Quoted in *Time*, November 21, 1969

PHILIPUS AUREOLUS PARACELSUS
(c. 1493–1541)
German physician

Selected Writings

Thoughts give birth to a creative force that is neither elemental nor sidereal. . . . Thoughts create a new heaven, a new firmament, a new source of energy, from which new arts flow.

When a man undertakes to create something, he establishes a new heaven, as it were, and from it the work that he desires to create flows into him. . . . For such is the immensity of man that he is greater than heaven and earth.

"Man and the Created World"

Archidoxies (c. 1525)

Man is a microcosm, or a little world, because he is an extract from all the stars and planets of the whole firmament, from the earth and the elements; and so he is their quintessence.

Medicine is not merely a science but an art. The character of the physician may act more powerfully upon the patient than the drugs employed.

I

AMBROISE PARÉ
(1517–1590)
French surgeon

I treated him—God cured him.

Inscription on his statue, his favorite saying

DOROTHY PARKER
(1893–1967)
American writer

"Art"

Art is a form of catharsis.

Sunset Gun (1928)

Accursed from birth they be
Who seek to find monogamy,
Pursuing it from bed to bed—
I think they would be better dead.

"Reuben's Children"

JOSEPH PARKER
(1830–1902)
British preacher

Ecce Deus

Only a Christ could have conceived a Christ.

Ch. XI

THEODORE PARKER
(1810–1860)
American preacher, abolitionist

No "respectable" paper is opposed to slavery; no Whig paper, no Democratic paper. You would as soon expect a Catholic newspaper to oppose the Pope and his church, for the slave power is the pope of America, though not exactly a pious pope. The churches show the same thing; they also are in the main pro-slavery, at least not anti-slavery.

Address, Anti-Slavery Convention, May 31, 1848*

There is what I call the American idea . . . a democracy,—that is, a government of *all* the people, by *all* the people, for *all* the people . . ."

Address, "The American Idea," May 29, 1850**

Look at those ancient States, the queenliest queens of earth. There is Rome, the widow of two civilizations—the Pagan and the Catholic . . . the Niobe of Nations.

Sermon, Thanksgiving Day, 1850

FRANCIS PARKMAN
(1823–1893)
American historian

Pioneers of France in the New World (1865)

Faithfulness to the truth of history involves far more than a research, into special facts. . . . The narrator must . . . himself be, as it were, a *sharer* or a spectator of the action he describes.

Introduction

---

*Two churches did oppose slavery: the Society of Friends (Quakers), and the Unitarians.
**In Lincoln's copy of the book of Parker's sermons and speeches, these words were found underlined.

PARMENIDES OF ELEA
(fl. 485 B.C.)
Greek philosopher

Thinking is identical with being.
Quoted by Clement of Alexandria, "Stromata," v

BLAISE PASCAL
(1623–1662)
French mathematician, philosopher

Pensées (1670)

Men have contempt for religion, and fear that it is true.

#12

The present is never our goal: the past and present are our means: the future alone is our goal. Thus, we never live but we hope to live; and always hoping to be happy, it is inevitable that we will never be so.

#47

Truth on this side of the Pyrenees may be heresy on the other!

#60

One must know oneself. If this does not serve to discover truth, it at least serves as a rule of life, and there is nothing better.

#72

Desire and force between them are responsible for all our actions: desire causes our voluntary acts, force our involuntary.

#97

What a chimera, then, is man! What a novelty, what a monster, what a chaos, what a contradiction, what a prodigy! Judge of all things, helpless earthworm, depository of truth, a sink of uncertainty and error. Glory and scum of the universe.

#131

All the miseries of mankind come from one thing, not knowing how to remain alone.

#136

There are only three kinds of persons: those who serve God, having found Him; others who are occupied in seeking Him, not having found Him; while the remainder live without seeking Him, and without having found Him. The first are reasonable and happy, the last are foolish and unhappy; those between are unhappy and unreasonable.

#160

If we submit everything to reason, our religion will have nothing in it mysterious or supernatural. If we violate the principles of reason, our religion will be absurd and ridiculous.

#173

Man is but a reed, the most feeble thing in nature; but he is a thinking reed.

#200

All men naturally hate each other.

#210

The carnal Jews hold a middle place between the Christians and the pagans. The Pagans do not know God, and love only the earth. The Christians know the true God, and do not love the earth.

#289

If man is not made for God, why is he happy only in God? If man is made for God, why is he opposed to God?

#399

He who would fully know human vanity has but to consider the causes and effects of love. The cause is a *je ne sais quoi* (Corneille), and the effects are fearful. This *je ne sais quoi,* so slight a thing it cannot be further identified, moves earth, princes, armies, the whole world.

Cleopatra's nose: if it had been shorter the face of the whole world would have been changed.

#413

If there is a God, He is infinitely incomprehensible, having neither parts nor limits. He has no relation to us. We are therefore incapable of knowing what He is, or whether He is. This being so, who will dare to solve the problem? Not we, who have no relation to Him.

You must wager. . . . Which will you choose? . . . Let us weigh the gain and loss in calling "heads" that God is. Let us weigh the two cases: if you win, you win all; if you lose you lose nothing. Wager then unhesitatingly that He is.

#418

The heart has its reasons which reason does not understand.

#423

It is the heart which experiences God, and not reason. This, then, is faith: God felt by the heart, not reason.

#424

Custom is the tyrant from which nothing frees us. . . . But being compelled to live under its foolish laws, the wise man is never the first to follow nor the last to keep it.

Not to care for philosophy is to be a true philosopher.

#513

It is force, not opinion, that queens it over the world, but it is opinion that looses the force.

#554

There are only two kinds of men: those righteous who believe themselves sinners; the others sinners who believe themselves righteous.

#562

All great amusements are dangerous to the Christian life; but among all those which the world has invented there is none more to be feared than the theatre. It is a representation of the passions so natural and so delicate that it excites them and gives birth to them in our hearts, and, above all, to that of love, principally, when it is represented as very chaste and virtuous. For the more innocent it may appear to innocent souls, the more they are likely to be touched by it.

#764

Reason commands us far more imperiously than a master: when we disobey the latter we are punished; in disobeying the former we are fools.

#768

Men never do evil so completely and cheerfully as when they do it from religious conviction.

#813

What shall we say is good? Celibacy? I say no; for the world would come to an end. Marriage? No, continence is better. Not to kill? No; for disorders would be horrible, and the wicked would kill the good. To kill? No; for that destroys nature. We have neither the true nor the good but in part, and mixed with the false and the evil.

#905

———

. . . the people imagine they are pursuing the Glory of God when actually they are only pursuing their own.

Letter to M. Perier, 1661

BORIS PASTERNAK
(1890–1960)
Russian writer, Nobel Prize 1958

Doctor Zhivago (1958)

Man is born to live and not to prepare to live.

LOUIS PASTEUR
(1822–1895)
French chemist, bacteriologist

Chance favors the trained mind.
Quoted in *The Sciences,* August 1981

The greatest disorder of the mind is to let will direct belief.
Quoted in René Vallery-Radot, *The Life of Pasteur* (1927)

KENNETH PATCHEN
(1911–1972)
American writer

Some Little Sayings and Observations (March 1956)

God must have loved the People in Power, for he made them so much like their own image of Him.

The Journal of Albion Moonlight (1941)

The revolutions of the future must be directed not against the rich but against the poor. The poor have been the slop-pails of capitalism, repositions for all the filth and brutality of a filthy, brutal world. Do not liberate the poor; destroy them.

It has been said that property is theft. I say property is murder.

Capitalism and Fascism are one under the iron mask.
Fascism is the expression of Capitalism's death struggle.
War is the life blood of Capitalism; it is the body and soul of Fascism.
Capitalist economy leads inevitably to War; Fascist economy begins and ends in war.

WALTER (Horatio) PATER
(1839–1894)
English man of letters

Studies in the History of the Renaissance (1873)

She is older than the rocks among which she sits; like the vampire, she has been dead many times, and learned the secrets of the grave; and has been a diver in deep seas, and keeps their fallen day about her; and trafficked for strange webs with Eastern merchants; and as Leda, was the mother of Helen of Troy; and, as Saint Anne, the mother of Mary; and all this has been to her but as the sound of lyres and flutes, and lives only in the delicacy with which it has moulded the changing lineaments and tinged the eyelids and hands.
"Leonardo Da Vinci [Mona Lisa]"

All art constantly aspires towards the condition of music.
"The School of Giorgione"

The service of philosophy, of speculative culture, towards the human spirit, is to rouse, to startle it to a life of constant and eager observation.

Not the fruit of experience, but experience itself, is the end. A counted number of pulses only is given to us of a variegated, dramatic life. How shall we pass most swiftly from point to point, and be present always at the focus where the greatest number of vital forces unite in their purest energy?
To burn always with this hard, gemlike flame, to maintain this ecstasy, is success in life.

What we have to do is to be for ever curiously testing new opinions and courting new impressions, never acquiescing in a facile orthodoxy of Comte, or of Hegel, or of our own. . . . "Philosophy is the microscope of thought."

Well! we are all *condamnés* as Victor Hugo says: we are all under sentence of death, but with a sort of indefinite reprieve.

Great passions may give us this quickened sense of life, ecstasy and sorrow of love, the various forms of enthusiastic activity, disinterested or otherwise, which come naturally to many of us. Only be sure it is passion—that it does yield you this fruit of a quickened, multiplied consciousness. Of such wisdom, the poetic passion, the desire of beauty, the love of art for its own sake, has most. For art comes to you proposing frankly to give nothing but the highest quality to your moments as they pass, and simply for those moments' sake.

Conclusion*

Marius the Epicurean (1895)

The aim of a true philosophy must lie, not in futile efforts towards the complete accommodation of man to circumstances in which he chances to find himself, but in the maintenance of a kind of candid discontent, in the face of the very highest achievement.

GAIUS VELLEIUS PATERCULUS
(20 B.C.–30 A.D.)
Roman praetor, historian

Historiae Romanes

To stand still on the summit of perfection is difficult, and in the natural course of things, what cannot go forward slips back.

I, 17

COVENTRY PATMORE
(1823–1896)
English writer

"The Angel in the House" (1854–56)

Ah, wasteful woman, she who may
On her sweet self set her own price,
Knowing he cannot choose but pay,
How has she cheapen'd paradise.

Bk. I, canto VII

ALAN PATON
(1903–   )
South African writer

Too Late the Phalarope (1953)

For once a charge is made, a charge is made; and once a thing is written down, it will not be unwritten. And a word can be written

---

*Written in 1868, printed in 1873, this conclusion was suppressed by Pater in the second edition, but restored in the third, with a note saying "This brief Conclusion was omitted in the second edition as I conceived it might possibly mislead some of those young men into whose hands it might fall."

down that will destroy a man and his house and his kindred, and there is no power of God or Man or State, nor any Angel, nor anything present or to come, nor any height, nor any depth, nor any other creature that can save him, when once the word is written down.

Ch. XXXIV

GEORGE S(mith) PATTON, JR.
(1885–1945)
American General, World Wars I and II

I love war. . . . Peace will be hell for me.
Letter to his wife, quoted in CBS-TV documentary, July 23, 1963

I want you to remember that no bastard ever won a war by dying for his country. He won it by making the other poor dumb bastard die for his country.
Exhortation to troops, North Africa; quoted in film *Patton*

Americans love to fight. All real Americans love the sting of battle.
Speech, Third Army, England, July 1944

War as I Knew It (1947)

If we take the generally accepted definition of bravery as a quality which knows no fear, I have never seen a brave man. All men are frightened. The more intelligent they are, the more they are frightened.

PAUL VI
(1897–1978)
Pope from 1963

The wealthier classes should recognize the respect of the Church for private property in the essential forms, its constant, vigilant, often stern, but always right and fatherly warnings on the moral and social dangers of selfish wealth.

The social doctrine of the Church has never denied the function of private enterprise, provided this does not damage human dignity and the legitimate aspirations of those who take part in the productive process.
Quoted in *N.Y. Times*, June 22, 1963

You must strive to multiply bread so that it suffices for the tables of mankind, and not

rather favor an artificial control of birth, which would be irrational in order to diminish the number of guests at the banquet of life.
Address, United Nations, October 4, 1965

Increased possession is not the ultimate goal of nations nor of individuals.

Private property does not constitute for anyone an absolute and unconditional right. No one is justified in keeping for his exclusive use what he does not need, when others lack necessities.
"The Development of People," 5th encyclical, March 28, 1967

Chastity is not acquired all at once but results from a laborious conquest and daily affirmation.
"On Priestly Celibacy," 6th encyclical, June 23, 1967

There must be something radically wrong with a system [capitalism] that gives rise to such social injustice.
Remarks to a delegation of Pistoia businessmen

The Christian who wants to live his faith in political action conceived as service cannot, without contradicting himself, adhere to ideological systems that are radically, or in substantial points, opposed to his faith and the concepts of man—neither to the ideology of Marxism, its atheistic materialism, its dialectics of violence and the way it absorbs any transcendental character of man and his personal and collective history; nor to the ideology of liberalism, which tends to exalt individual freedom without any limitation.
Letter to Cardinal Roy, quoted in *N.Y. Times,* May 12, 1971

The Devil is at the origin of the first misfortune of mankind.
So we know that this dark and disturbing spirit really exists, and that he still acts with treacherous cunning; he is the secret enemy that sows errors and misfortunes in human history . . . who finds his way into us by way of the senses, the imagination, lust, utopian logic, or disorderly social contacts in the give and take of life.
Address, November 7, 1972, *Osservatore Romano* and *N.Y. Times* report

We dare to think that the recent solemn reaffirmation of the rejection by the Catholic Church of every form of anti-Semitism . . . may, on the Catholic side, provide the conditions for beneficial development.
Address to Liaison Committee Between Church and World Judaism, January 10, 1975

LINUS PAULING
(1901–   )
American scientist, Nobel Prize for Chemistry 1954, Nobel Peace Prize 1962

No More War! (1958)

Science is the search for truth—it is not a game in which one tries to beat his opponent, to do harm to others.

The power to destroy the world by the use of nuclear weapons is a power that cannot be used—we cannot accept the idea of such monstrous immorality. . . . [T]he time has now come for the nations of the world to submit to the just requisition of their conduct by international law.

Man has reached his present state through the process of evolution. The last great step in evolution was the mutational process that doubled the size of the brain, about one million years ago; this led to the origin of man. It is this change in the brain that permits the inheritance of acquired characteristics of a certain sort—the inheritance of knowledge, of learning, through communication from one human being to another. . . . Man's great power of thinking, remembering, and communicating are responsible for the evolution of civilization.
Contribution, "To Live as Man," *Fund for the Republic,* 1965

IVAN PAVLOV
(1849–1936)
Russian physiologist, Nobel Prize 1904

Facts are the air of science. Without them you never can fly.

Do not become archivists of facts. Try to penetrate to the secret of their occurrence, persistently search for the laws which govern them.

Science demands from a man all his life.
"To the Academic Youth of Russia," February 27, 1936

THOMAS LOVE PEACOCK
(1785–1866)
English writer

Crochet Castle (1831)

Where the Greeks had modesty, we have cant; where they had poetry, we have cant; where they had patriotism, we have cant; where they had anything that exalts, delights, or adorns humanity, we have nothing but cant, cant, cant.

CHARLES PÉGUY
(1873–1914)
French Catholic writer

Basic Verities: Prose and Poetry (1943)

He who does not bellow the truth when he knows the truth makes himself the accomplice of liars and forgers.

A brave man—and so far, there are not many—for the sake of the truth breaks with his friends and his interests. Thus a new party is formed, originally and supposedly the party of justice and truth, which in less than no time becomes absolutely identical with the other parties. A party like the others; like all others; as vulgar, as gross; as unjust; as false. Then for the second time, a super-brave man would have to be found to make a second break: but of these, there are hardly any left.

The man who wishes to remain faithful to justice must make himself continually unfaithful to inexhaustibly triumphant injustice.

Everything begins in mysticism and ends in politics.

CHARLES S(anders) PEIRCE
(1839–1914)
American philosopher; author of Pragmatism*

Selected Writings of Charles S. Peirce

The Reformation was a struggle for humanity to regain its rightful master; in our day the aim is absolute liberty.

---

*There was once a great literary dispute as to who "founded" Pragmatism, William James or Peirce. James was assailed by critics early on for his use of such terms as "Truth is what works," "The true is the expedient," and "The cash-value of true theories"; Peirce later labeled this theory Pragmatism. In 1898 James honored Peirce as the founder of the doctrine that both developed.

The doctrine of a first cause and the very idea of miracles vanish with the notion of causality.

All the progress we have made in philosophy, that is, all that has been made since the Greeks, is the result of that methodical skepticism which is the first element of human freedom.

You will find an ever-increasing irreverence toward rulers, from the days of Hampden to ours, when some of the more advanced spirits look forward to the time when there shall be no government.

The fulcrum has yet to be found that shall enable the lever of love to move the world.
"Science, Materialism and Idealism"

Wildest dreams are the necessary first steps toward scientific investigation.

It is the man of science, eager to have his every opinion regenerated, his every idea rationalized, by drinking at the fountain of fact, and devoting all the energies of his life to the cult of truth, not as he understands it, but as he does not yet understand it, that ought properly to be called a philosopher.
"Lessons on the History of Science"

. . . the objections that have been made to my word "pragmatism" are very trifling. It is the doctrine that truth consists in future serviceableness for our needs.
Letter to Lady Welby, December 1, 1903

WILLIAM PENN
(1644–1718)
English Quaker, founder of Pennsylvania

Some Fruits of Solitude (1693)

The humble, meek, merciful, just, pious and devout souls everywhere are of one religion, and when death has taken off the mask, they will know one another, though the diverse liveries they wore here make them strangers.

Religion is nothing else than love of God and man.

Inquiry is human; blind obedience brutal. Truth never loses by the one but often suffers by the other.

To do evil that good may come of it is for bunglers in politics as well as morals.

Passion is a sort of fever of the mind, which ever leaves us weaker than it found us. It, more than anything, deprives us of the use of our judgment; for it raises a dust very hard to see through. It may unfitly be termed the mob of the man, that commits a riot without reason.

Charter of Liberties (1701)

No people can be truly happy, though under the greatest Enjoyment of Civil Liberties, if abridged of the Freedom of their Consciences.

I do hereby grant and declare, That no Person or Persons, inhabiting in this province or Territories, who shall confess and acknowledge *One* almighty God, the Creator, Upholder and Ruler of the World; and profess him or themselves obliged to live quietly under the Civil Government, shall be in any case molested or prejudiced, in his or their Person or Estate, because of his or their conscientious Persuasion or Practice, nor be compelled to frequent or maintain any religious Worship, Place or Ministry, contrary to his or their Mind, or to do or suffer any other Act or Thing, contrary to their religious persuasions.

Men must choose to be governed by God or they condemn themselves to be ruled by tyrants.

O God, help us not to despise or oppose what we do not understand.

Attributed

PERIANDER
(625–585 B.C.)
Tyrant of Corinth, one of the Seven Sages of Greece

Nothing is impossible to industry.
Inscribed on the Delphic Temple

PERICLES
(495–429 B.C.)
Athenian statesman

No Athenian has ever put on mourning through any action of mine.
Statement to friends surrounding death-bed

JUAN DOMINGO PÉRON
(1895–1975)
Dictator of Argentina

There is no such thing as a bad system of government. Not even Communism. It is the men who execute it who make it good or bad.
Interview with Ed Gress, *Newsweek,* December 1968

We believe that capitalism as well as Communism are systems that have been overtaken by time. We consider capitalism as the exploitation of man by capital and Communism the exploitation of the individual by the state. Both "insectify" a person through different systems.
"Force Is the Right of Beasts," quoted in *N. Y. Times* obituary

PETRARCH (Francesco Petrarca)
(1304–1374)
Italian poet

Rime in Vila e Morte di Madonna Laura (c. 1348)

A good death does honor to a whole life.
Canzone 16

De Remediis (1366)

Five great enemies to peace inhabit within us: viz., avarice, ambition, envy, anger, and pride. If those enemies were to be banished, we should infallibly enjoy perpetual peace.

PETRONIUS (called Arbiter)
(suicide, c.66 A.D.)
Roman writer

The Satyricon

One man will tell you one rule of life, and another'll tell you another. But *I* say, "Buy cheap and sell dear," and so you see I'm bursting with wealth.

Fragments

Fear first in the world created the gods.
Fragment 27

A wife is a burden imposed by law.
Fragment 78

The pleasure of the act of love is gross and brief and brings loathing after it.
Fragment 101

WENDELL PHILLIPS
(1811–1884)
American orator, abolitionist

Revolution is the only thing, the only power, that ever worked out freedom for any people. The powers that have ruled long and learned to love ruling, will never give up that prerogative until they must, till they see the certainty of overthrow and destruction if they do not.

To plant—to revolutionize—these are the twin stars that have ruled our pathway. What have we then to dread in the word Revolution—we, the children of rebels!
                Speech, 1848, commenting on European
                                                revolutions

Government commenced in usurpation and oppression . . . [L]iberty and civilization, at present, are nothing else than the fragments of rights which the scaffold and stake have wrung from the strong hands of the usurpers.

Every step of progress the world has made has been from scaffold to scaffold, and from stake to stake.
                Speech on women's rights, 1851

One, on God's side, is a majority.*

Every man meets his Waterloo at last.

Whether in chains or in laurels, Liberty knows nothing but victories.
                Speech on John Brown, November 1, 1859

Revolutions never go backwards.
                Speech, Boston, February 17, 1861

We affirm, as a fundamental principle, that labor, the creator of wealth, is entitled to all it creates.

Therefore, Resolved, That we declare war with the wages system, which demoralizes the life of the hirer and the hired, cheats both, and enslaves the workingman . . . and turns a republic into an aristocracy of capital. . . .
                Resolution, written by Phillips, Labor-Reform
                convention, Worcester, Mass., 1870

---

*"One, with God, is always a majority, but many a martyr has been burned at the stake while the votes were being counted."—Thomas B. Reed, House of Representatives, 1885.

It is momentous, yes, a fearful truth, that the millions have no literature, no school and almost no pulpit but the press. Not one in ten reads books. . . . But every one of us, except a few helpless poor, poisons himself every day with a newspaper. It is parent, school, college, pulpit, theatre, example, counselor, all in one. Every drop of our blood is colored by it.

Let me make the newspapers and I care not what is preached in the pulpit or what is enacted in Congress.

Write on my gravestone, "Infidel, Traitor"—infidel to every church that compromises with the strong; traitor to every government that oppresses the people.
                Address, "The Press" (pub. 1863)

PHILO (called Philo Judaeus)
(20? B.C.–45? A.D.)
Alexandrian Jewish philosopher

Money, it has been said, is the cause of good things to a good man and of evil things to a bad man.

Every good man is free.
                "Noah's Work as a Planter," Bk. I

The demagogue, mounting the platform, like a slave in the market, is a slave . . . and because of the honors which he seems to receive, is the slave of ten thousand masters.
                "Joseph"

PHILOXENUS
(c. 435–380 B.C.)
Greek dithyrambic poet

We should honor our teachers more than our parents, because while our parents cause us to live, our teachers cause us to live well.
                Quoted by Strobaeus, "Florilegium"

PABLO RUIZ Y PICASSO
(1881–1973)
Spanish painter, sculptor*

We all know that art is not truth. Art is a lie that makes us realize truth—at least, the truth

---

*Picasso's father was named Ruiz; he took his mother's name when he left Spain for France.

that is given us to understand. . . . Nature and art, being two different things, cannot be the same thing. Through art we express our conception of what nature is not. . . . Academic training in beauty is a sham.
> Quoted in *The Arts,* 1923, reprinted in *N. Y. Times,* obituary, 1973

What I want is that my picture should evoke nothing but emotion.

There is no abstract art. One always has to begin with something. One can then remove all appearance of reality; one can run no risk, for the idea of the abstract has left an inneffaceable imprint. It is the thing that aroused the artist, stimulated his ideas, stirred his emotions. Ideas and emotions will ultimately be prisoners of his work; whatever they do, they can't escape from the picture; they form an integral part of it, even when their presence is no longer discernible. Whether he likes it or not, man is the instrument of nature; it imposes its character, its appearance upon him.

There is not, moreover, a figurative and nonfigurative art. Everything appears to us in the form of figures. Even in metaphysics ideas are expressed in figures: thus you can understand how absurd it would be to think of painting without images or figures. A person, an object, a circle, are figures; they act upon us more or less intensely. . . . They must all be accepted, for my spirit has as much need of emotion as my senses.

Everyone wants to understand painting. Why is there no attempt to understand the song of birds?

One ought above all to make a revolution against good sense.
> Quoted in Christian Zervos, *Conversations with Picasso,* 1935

My whole life as an artist has been nothing more than a continuous struggle against Reaction and the death of Art.
> Message to the Committee to Aid Spanish Democracy, 1936 or 1937

What do you think an artist is? An imbecile who has only his eyes if he is a painter, or his ears if he is a musician, or a lyre at every level of his heart if he is a poet, or, if he is merely a boxer, only his muscle?
On the contrary, he is at the same time a political being, constantly alert to the heart-rending, burning, or happy events in the world, moulding himself in their likeness.

How could it be possible to feel no interest in other people and because of an ivory-tower indifference, detach yourself from the life they bring with their open hands?

No, painting, is not made to decorate apartments. It is an instrument of war, for attack and defense against the enemy.
> From a reply to criticism and attacks for joining French Communist Party during War in Spain, quoted in *Les Lettres françaises* (1944)

It takes a very long time to become young.
> Quoted in Cocteau, *The Hand of a Stranger*

Photography has arrived at the point where it is capable of liberating painting from all literature, from the anecdote, and even from the subject.
> Quoted in Dore Ashton, *Picasso on Art*

I don't seek, I find.

[Art] should not be a *trompe l'oeil,* but a *trompe l'esprit.*

Art is always subversive. It's something that should *not* be free. Art and liberty, like the fire of Prometheus, are things that one must steal, to be used against the established order.
> Quoted in Françoise Gilot and Carlton Lake, *Life with Picasso* (1964)

Every artist and every poet is an anti-social being.

Anything new, anything worth doing, can't be recognized. People just don't have that much vision.

A picture used to be the sum of additions. In my case a picture is the sum of destructions.
> Quoted in *Saturday Review,* May 28, 1966

JAMES A(lbert) PIKE
(1913–1969)
American Episcopal Bishop

If This Be Heresy (1967)

There is no way that the "God" whom we could alternately lean on and blame can be made credible again.

The Moslems offer one God and three wives; we offer three Gods and one wife.
> Quoted in *Time,* November 11, 1966

PINDAR
(c. 518–438 B.C.)
Greek lyric poet

Pythian Odes

O my soul, do not aspire to immortal life,
But exhaust the limits of thy possible.
                                    3, line 109

Olympian Odes

Even Time, the father of all, cannot undo
what has been done, whether right or wrong.
                                    2, line 15

Fragments

Custom, Lord of all mortals and immortals.
                                    169

Gold is a child of God; neither moth nor
rust devoureth it; but the mind of man is de-
voured by this supreme possession.
                                    222

Forge thy tongue on an anvil of truth
And what flies up, though it be but a spark,
Shall have weight.
                                    Attributed

PETER PINDAR (né John Wolcot)
(1738–1819)
English poet, satirist

To the Royal Academicians (1782–1785)

What rage for fame attends both great and
    small!
Better be damned than mentioned not at all!

LUIGI PIRANDELLO
(1867–1936)
Italian dramatist

The Rules of the Game (1918)

The facts are to blame, my friend. We are
all imprisoned by facts: I was born, I exist.

WILLIAM PITT, EARL OF CHATHAM
(1708–1778)
English statesman

The poorest man may in his cottage bid defiance to all the forces of the Crown. It may be
frail—its roof may shake—the wind may blow

through it—the storm may enter—the rain
may enter—but the King of England cannot
enter—all his force dares not cross the threshold of the ruined tenement.
                Speech on the Excise Bill, House of Lords;
                quoted in H. Brougham, *Statesmen in the Time
                of George III*

Unlimited power is apt to corrupt the minds
of those who possess it; and this I know, my
lords, that where law ends, tyranny begins.
                Defense of John Wilkes, January 9, 1770

The press is like the air, a chartered libertine.
                Letter to Lord Grenville, 1757

WILLIAM PITT
(1759–1806)
English statesman

Necessity is the plea of every infringement
of human freedom. It is the argument of tyrants; it is the creed of slaves.
                Speech on the India Bill, November 18, 1783

PITTACUS OF LESBOS
(650–570 B.C.)
One of the Seven Sages of Greece

Nothing in excess.

The best state is that in which bad men are
not allowed to hold office, and good men are
not allowed to refuse office.
                Inscribed on the Temple of Apollo at Delphi,
                quoted in Plutarch's *Lives*

Do not that to thy neighbor that thou
wouldst not suffer from him.
                                    Attributed*

PIUS IV (Giovanni Angelo Medici)
(1499–1565)
Pope from 1559

We order that each and every Jew of both
sexes in our temporal domain, and in all the
cities, lands, places and baronies subject to
them, shall depart completely out of the con-

---

*Haeckel, *The Riddle of the Universe,* believes Pittacus was the first to utter the Golden Rule. Confucius proclaimed it c. 500 B.C.

fines thereof within the space of three months and after these letters have been made public.
Decree, issued posthumously, 1565

PIUS IX (Giovanni Maria Mastai-Ferretti) (1792–1878)
Pope from 1846

"Ineffabilis Deus"

We declare, pronounce, and define that the doctrine which holds that the most blessed Virgin Mary, in the first instance of her conception, by a singular grace and privilege granted by Almighty God, in view of the merits of Jesus Christ, the Saviour of the human race, was preserved free from all stain of original sin, is a doctrine revealed by God and therefore to be believed firmly and constantly by all the faithful.
Papal bull, known as the Dogma of the Immaculate Conception, December 8, 1854

"Syllabus of Errors" (1864)

Human reason, without any reference whatsoever to God, is the sole arbiter of truth and falsehood, and of good and evil: it is law to itself, and it suffices by its natural force to secure the welfare of men and of nation.
Condemned proposition 3

The Roman Pontiff can and ought to reconcile himself, and come to terms, with progress, liberalism, and modern civilization. . . .
Condemned proposition 80

The Dogma of Papal Infallibility* (July 18, 1870)

Therefore faithfully adhering to the tradition received from the beginning of the Christian faith, for the glory of God our Saviour, the exaltation of the Catholic religion, and the salvation of the Christian people, the Sacred Council approving, we teach and define that it is a dogma divinely revealed: that the Roman Pontiff, when he speaks *ex cathedra,* that is, when in discharge of the office of the pastor

---

*"The famous encyclical and syllabus which the militant Pope Pius IX sent out into the entire world . . . were a declaration of war on the whole of modern science; they demanded a blind submission of reason to the dogmas of the infallible Pope."
—Haeckel, *The Riddle of the Universe.*

and doctor of all Christians, by virtue of his supreme Apostolic authority, he defines a doctrine regarding faith or morals to be held by the universal Church, by the divine assistance promised to him in blessed Peter, is possessed of that infallibility with which the divine Redeemer willed that his Church should be endowed for defining doctrine regarding faith and morals; and that therefore such definitions of the Roman Pontiff are irreformable of themselves, and not from the consent of the Church.

But if any one—which may God avert—presumes to contradict this our definition: let him be anathema.

Communism is completely opposed to the natural law itself, and its establishment would entail the complete destruction of all property and even human society.
Declaration, September 11, 1846, two years before publication of the Communist Manifesto

PIUS XI
(1857–1939)
Pope from 1922

"Casti Connubii" (1930)

Since the conjugal act is designed primarily by nature for the begetting of children, those who in exercising it deliberately frustrate its natural power and purpose, sin against nature and commit a deed which is shameful and intrinsically vicious.

However we may pity the mother whose health and even life is imperiled by the performance of her natural duty, there yet remains no sufficient reason for condoning the direct murder of the innocent.

"Quadragesimo Anno" (1931)

Socialism . . . is drifting toward truth which the Christian tradition has always supported. Indeed, it cannot be denied that its progress often comes close to the just demands of Christian reformers.

To suffer and to endure is the lot of humanity.

Through Christ and in Christ we are the spiritual descendants of Abraham. No, it is not possible for Christians to participate in anti-Semitism.

> Allocution, to Belgian pilgrims, September 1938, quoted in *Time,* November 14, 1938

The great scandal of the Nineteenth Century is that the Church has lost the working class.

> Quoted by Abbé Cardijn, founder of J.O.C.

PIUS XII (Eugenio Pacelli)
(1876–1958)
Pope from 1939

Apostolic Constitution (November 2, 1950)

We pronounce, declare, and define it to be a divinely revealed dogma: that the Immaculate Mother of God, the ever Virgin Mary, having completed the course of her earthly life, was assumed body and soul into heavenly glory.

> The Dogma of the Assumption

Individual liberty, freed from all bonds and all laws, all objective and social values, is in reality only a death-dealing anarchy.

> *Allocutions,* April 6, 1951

A correct organization of economic life requires the recognition and respect of the private ownership of the means of production. They are ordained by God . . .

> Address, quoted in *N.Y. Times,* September 23, 1956

MAX PLANCK
(1858–1947)
Originator of the Quantum Theory

The Philosophy of Physics (1936)

A new scientific truth does not triumph by convincing its opponents and making them see the light, but rather because its opponents eventually die out, and a new generation grows up that is familiar with it.

PLATO (né Aristocles)
(428–348 B.C.)
Athenian philosopher, disciple of Socrates*

*The Republic***

Mankind censure injustice fearing that they may be the victim of it, and not because they shrink from committing it.

> Bk. I, 334c

. . . let us begin and create in idea a State; and yet the true creator is necessity, which is the mother of our invention.

> Bk. II, 369c

Without determining as yet whether war does good or harm, this much we may affirm, that now we have discovered war to be derived from causes of almost all the evils in States, private as well as public.

> Bk. II, 373e

Then the first thing will be to establish a censorship of the writers of fiction, and let the censors receive any tale of fiction which is good, and reject the bad; and we will desire mothers and nurses to tell their children the authorized ones only.

> Bk. II, 377c

Then God, if he is good, is not the author of all things, as the many assert, but he is the cause of a few things only, and not of most things that occur to men. For few are the goods of human life, and many are the evils, and the good is to be attributed to God alone; of the evils the causes are to be sought elsewhere, and not in him.

> Bk. II, 379c

---

*"He cannot be separated from Socrates. Almost all Plato wrote professes to be a report of what Socrates said . . . and it is impossible to decide just what part belongs to each. Together they shaped the ideas . . . which the classical world lived by for hundreds of years and which the modern world has never forgotten."—Edith Hamilton, *The Greek Way,* ch. 14.
   "Plato is philosophy, and philosophy Plato." —Emerson.
   "All European philosophy is but a footnote to Plato."—Whitehead.
**"*The Republic,* the ideal commonwealth—the first Utopia in Literature"—J.D. Kaplan, editor of Pocket Book edition of Plato.

The rulers of the state are the only ones who would have the privilege of lying, either at home or abroad; they may be allowed to lie for the good of the State.

Bk. III, 389c

Let our artists rather be those who are gifted to discern the true nature of the beautiful and the graceful; then will youth dwell in a land of health, amid fair sights and sounds, and receive the good in everything; and beauty, the effulgence of works, shall flow into the eye and ear, like a health-giving breeze from a pure region, and insensibly draw the soul from earliest years into likeness and sympathy with the beauty of reason.

Bk. III, 401d

(Socrates) Has excess of pleasure any affinity to temperance?

(Glaucon) . . . pleasure deprives a man of the use of his faculties quite as much as pain. . . .

(Socrates) And is there any greater or keener pleasure than that of sexual love?

(Glaucon) No, nor a madder. . . .

(Socrates) Then mad or intemperate pleasure must never be allowed to come near the lover and his beloved; neither of them can have any part of it, if their love is of the right sort?

(Glaucon) No, indeed, Socrates, it must never come near them.

(Socrates) Then I suppose that in the city which we are founding you would have a law to the effect that a friend should use no other familiarity to his love than a father would use to his son, and then only for a noble purpose, and he must first have the other's consent; and this rule is to limit him in all his intercourse, and he is never to be seen going further, or, if he exceeds, he is to be deemed guilty of coarseness and bad taste.

Bk. III, 402e–403b

. . . but they cure the body with mind, and the mind which has become sick, can cure nothing.

Bk. III, 408e

The mere athlete becomes too much of a savage.

Bk. III, 410d

How then may we devise one of those needful falsehoods of which we lately spoke—just one noble lie which may deceive the rulers, if that be possible, and at any rate the rest of the city?

Bk. III, 414c

The audacious fiction, which I propose to communicate gradually, first to the rulers, then to the soldiers, and lastly to the people.

Citizens, we shall say to them in our tale, you are brothers, yet God has framed you differently. Some of you have the power to command, and in the composition of these he has mingled gold. . . . [O]thers he has made silver, to be auxiliaries; others again who are to be husbandmen and craftsmen, he has composed of brass and iron; and the species will generally be preserved in the children. . . . And God proclaims as a first principle to the rulers, and above all else, that there is nothing which they should so anxiously guard, or of which they are to be such good guardians, as of the purity of the race.

Bk. III, 414d–415c

Our object in the construction of the State is the greatest happiness of the whole, and not that of any one class.

Bk. IV, 420b

Any city, however small, is in fact divided into two, one city of the poor, the other of the rich; they are at war with one another; and in either they are many smaller divisions, and you would be altogether beside the mark if you treat them as a single state.

Bk. IV, 423

Sin is disease, deformity, weakness.

Bk. V, 444e

For I do indeed believe that to be an involuntary homicide is a less crime than to be a deceiver about beauty or goodness or justice as in the matter of laws.

Bk. V, 451b

A woman is only a lesser man.

Bk. V, 455e

Well, I said, the principle has been already laid down that the best of either sex should be united with the best as often, and the inferior with the inferior, as seldom as possible; and that they should rear the offspring of the one sort of union, but not of the other, if the flock is to be maintained in first-rate condition. Now these goings on must be a secret which the rulers know, or there will be further danger of our herd, as the Guardians may be termed, breaking out in rebellion.

Bk. V, 459e

And I think that our braver and better youth, besides their other honors and rewards, might have great facilities of intercourse with women given them; their bravery will be a reason, and such fathers ought to have as many sons as possible.

Bk. V, 460b

(Socrates) And the reason for this, over and above the general constitution of the State, will be that the guardians will have a community of women and children?

(Glaucon) That will be the chief reason. . . .

(Socrates) Then the community of wives and children among our citizens is clearly the source of the greatest good of the State?

(Glaucon) Certainly. . . .

(Socrates) Both the community of property and the community of families, as I was saying, tend to make them more truly guardians; they will not tear the city to pieces by differing about "mine" and "not mine," each man dragging any acquisition he has made into a separate house of his own, where he has a separate wife and children and private pleasures and pains because they are all of one opinion about what is near and dear to them, and therefore they will tend toward a common good.

Bk. V, 464d

Until philosophers are kings, or the kings and princes of the world have the spirit and power of philosophy, and political greatness and wisdom meet in one, and those commoner natures who pursue either to the exclusion of the other are compelled to stand aside, cities will never have rest from their evils—no, nor the human race, as I believe—and then only will this our State have a possibility of life and behold the light of day.*

Bk. V, 473c

He said: Who then are the true philosophers?

Those, I said, who are lovers of the vision of truth.

Bk. V, 475e

The true lover of learning then must from his earliest youth, as far as in him lies, desire all truth . . .

He whose desires are drawn toward knowledge in every form will be absorbed in the

pleasures of the soul, and will hardly feel bodily pleasures—I mean, if he be a true philosopher and not a sham one. . . .

Then how can he who has magnificence of mind and is the spectator of all time and all existence, think much of human life?

He cannot.

Or can such an one account death fearful?

No indeed.

Bk. VI, 485d–486b

(Socrates) Democracy comes into being after the poor have conquered their opponents, slaughtering some and banishing some, while to the remainder they give an equal share of freedom and power. . . .

And now what is their manner of life, and what sort of government have they? For as the government is, such will be the people. . . .

Democracy, which is a charming form of government, full of variety and disorder, and dispensing a sort of equality to equals and unequals alike.

Bk. VIII, 557–558c

(Socrates) Democracy has her own good, of which the insatiable desires bring her to dissolution.

(Adeimanthus) What good?

(Socrates) Freedom, I replied, which, as they tell you in a democracy, is the glory of the State—and that therefore in a democracy alone will the freeman of nature deign to dwell.

Bk. VIII, 562c

A tyrant . . . is always stirring up some war or other, in order that the people may require a leader.

Bk. VIII, 566e

. . . in all of us, even in good men, there is a lawless wild-beast nature, which peers out in sleep.

Bk. IX, 571d

. . . but a man is not to be reverenced more than the truth, and therefore I will speak out.

Bk. X, 595c

A man must take with him into the world below an adamantine faith in truth and right, that there too he may be undazzled by the desire of wealth or the other allurements of evil, lest coming upon tyrannies and similar villainies, he should do irremediable wrongs to others and suffer yet worse himself; but let him know how to choose the mean and avoid extremes on either side, as far as possible, not

---

*"That kings should become philosophers, or philosophers kings, can scarce be expected; nor is it to be wished, since the enjoyment of power inevitably corrupts the judgments of reason, and perverts its liberty."—Kant, Perpetual Peace.

only in this life but in all that which is to
come. For this is the way of happiness.
Bk. X, 619b

Laws

I think that the pleasure is to be deemed
natural which arises out of the intercourse between men and women; but that the intercourse of men with men, or of women with
women, is contrary to nature, and that the
bold attempt was originally due to unbridled
lust.
Bk. I, 636

But if you ask what is the good of education
in general, the answer is easy; that education
makes good men, and that good men act
nobly.
Bk. I, 641

But even God is said not to be able to fight
against necessity.
Bk. V, 741

But to be at once exceedingly wealthy and
good is impossible, if we mean by the wealthy
those who are accounted so by the vulgar, that
is, the exceptional few who own property of
great pecuniary value—the very thing a bad
man would be likely to own. Now since this is
so I can never concede to them that a rich
man is truly happy unless he is also a good
man, but that one who is exceptionally good
should be exceptionally wealthy too is a mere
impossibility.
Bk. V, 742e–743

No one has ever died an atheist.
Bk. X, 888

Do to others as I would they should do to
me.
Bk. XI, 913

Phaedo

Then tell me, Socrates, why is suicide held
to be unlawful?
(Socrates) The day may come when you will
understand. I suppose that you wonder why,
when other things which are evil may be good
at certain times, and to certain persons, death
is to be the only exception, and why, when a
man is better dead, he is not permitted to be
his own benefactor, but must wait for the hand
of another.
There is a doctrine whispered in secret that
man is a prisoner who has no right to open the
door and run away . . .
There may be reason in saying that a man
should wait, and not take his own life until
God summons him.
61e–62c

And the true philosophers, Simmias, are always occupied in the practice of dying, wherefore also to them least of all men is death
terrible.
64

Whence come wars and fightings, and factions? whence but from the body and the lusts
of the body? Wars are occasioned by the love
of money, and money has to be acquired for
the same and service of the body.
66c

For as there are misanthropists, or haters of
men, there are also misologists, or haters of
ideas, and both spring from the same cause,
which is ignorance of the world.
89d

Symposium

(Pausanius) Not every love, but only that
which has a noble purpose, is noble and worthy of praise. The Love which is the offspring
of the common Aphrodite is essentially common, and has no discrimination, being such
as the meaner sort of men feel, and is apt to be
of women as well as of youths, and is of the
body rather than of the soul. . . .
But the offspring of the heavenly Aphrodite
is derived from a mother in whose birth the female has no part—she is from the male only;
this is the love which is of youths. . . . Those
who are inspired by this love turn to the male,
and delight in him who is the most valiant and
intelligent nature; any one may recognize the
pure enthusiasm in the very character of this
attachment. For they love not boys but intelligent beings whose reason is beginning to be
developed, much about the time at which
their hearts begin to grow. And in choosing
young men to be their companions, they
choose to be faithful to them, to pass their
whole life in company with them. . . .

But the love of young men should be forbidden by law because their future is uncertain;
they may turn out good or bad, whether in
body or soul, and much noble enthusiasm
may be thrown away on them.
181e

[Diotima of Mantineia speaking] There is a
certain age at which human nature is desirous
of procreation—procreation which must be in
beauty and not in deformity; and this procreation is the union of man and woman, and is a
divine thing: for conception and generation are
an immortal principle in the mortal creature,
and in the inharmonious they can never

be. . . . Beauty then is the destiny or goddess of parturition who presides at birth. . . .

The love of generation and of birth is beauty.

206d

But why of procreation?

Because to the mortal creature, generation is a sort of eternity and immortality, she replied; and if . . . love is of the everlasting possession of the good, all men will necessarily desire immortality together with good: wherefore love is immortality.

207

This, my dear Socrates, said the stranger of Mantineia, is that life above all others which men should live, in the contemplation of beauty absolute, a beauty which if you once beheld, you would see not to be after the measure of gold, and garments, and fair boys and youths, whose presence now entrances you. . . . But what if man had eyes to see the true beauty—the divine beauty, I mean, pure and clear and unalloyed, not clogged with the pollutions of mortality and all the colors and vanities of human life—thither looking, and holding converse with the true beauty simple and divine? . . . and bringing forth and nourishing true virtue to become the friend of God and be immortal, if mortal man may. Would that be an ignoble life?

211c

Crito

(Socrates) In questions of just and unjust, fair and foul, good and evil, which are the subjects of our present consultation, ought we to follow the opinion of the many and to fear them; or the opinion of the one man who has understanding? Ought we not to fear and reverence him more than all the rest of the world; and if we desert him shall we not destroy and injure that principle in us which may be assumed to be improved by justice and deteriorated by injustice.

47d

Lysis

(Socrates) I affirm that the good is the beautiful.

216d

Phaedrus

(Socrates) Of madness there were two kinds; one produced by human infirmity, the other . . . a divine release of the soul from the yoke of custom and convention. . . . The divine madness was subdivided into four kinds, pro-

phetic, initiatory, poetic, erotic, having four gods presiding over them: the first was the inspiration of Apollo, the second that of Dionysus, the third that of the Muses, the fourth that of Aphrodite and Eros.

265b

Philebus

(Socrates) The three kinds of vain conceit . . . the vain conceit of beauty, of wisdom and wealth, are ridiculous if they are weak, and detestable if they are powerful.

48–49

Theaetetus

Wonder is the feeling of a philosopher, and philosophy begins in wonder.

155

Every man has had kings and slaves, barbarians and Greeks, among his ancestors.

175a

Timaeus

He who lived well during his appointed time was to return and dwell in his native star, and there he would have a blessed and congenial existence. But if he failed in attaining this, at the second birth he would pass into a woman . . .

42

(Pleasure) the bait of sin.

69d

Vice is ignorance. Virtue is knowledge.
Quoted in *Britannica*, 11th ed., vol. xxi

There is a written and unwritten law.

It is a man's goal to grow into the exact likeness of God.
Quoted in Diogenes Laërtius, "Plato"

The soul which has never perceived truth, cannot pass into the human form.
Quoted in Emerson, *Representative Men*

TITUS MACCIUS PLAUTUS
(254–184 B.C.)
Roman comic dramatist

Captivi

The gods play games with men as balls.
Line 23*

---

*Cf. Einstein, letter to Max Born.

Bacchides

He whom the gods love dies young.

Line 816

Mercator

I wish there were the same laws for the husband and the wife.

Line 823

Cistelaria

I do believe it was Love which first devised the torturer's profession here on earth.

Line 203

Aulularia

The facts speak for themselves.

Line 420

PLINY THE ELDER
(23–79 A.D.)
Roman naturalist, Stoic

Natural History

God has no power over the past except to cover it with oblivion.

It is ridiculous to suppose that the great head of things, whatever it be, pays any regard to human affairs.

Bk. 1

Nothing certain exists, and . . . nothing is more pitiful or more presumptuous than man.

Amid the miseries of our life on earth, suicide is God's gift to man.

Bk. 2

Man is the only animal that knows nothing, and can learn nothing without being taught. He can neither speak nor walk nor eat, nor do anything at the prompting of nature, but only weep.

Lions do not fight with one another, serpents do not attack serpents, nor do the wild monsters of the deep rage against their like. But most of the calamities of man are caused by his fellow-man.

Bk. 7

PLINY THE YOUNGER
(c.62–c. 113 A.D.)
Roman writer, governor

Panegyricus

No one has deceived the whole world, nor has the whole world ever deceived any man.

lxii

Epistulae

He who hates vice, hates mankind.

viii, 22

PLOTINUS
(205–270 A.D.)
Roman Neoplatonist

Knowledge, if it does not determine action, is dead to us.

First "Ennead," sixth tractate

Now everyone recognizes that the emotional state for which we make this "Love" responsible rises in souls aspiring to be knit in the closest union with some beautiful object, and that this aspiration takes two different forms, that of the good whose devotion is for beauty itself, and that other which seeks its consummation in some vile act.

Those who love beauty of person without carnal desire love for beauty's sake; those that have—for women, of course—the copulative love, have the further purpose of self-perpetuation: as long as they are led by these motives, both are on the right path, though the first have taken the nobler way.

Third "Ennead," fifth tractate

PLUTARCH
(46–120 A.D.)
Greek historian

Symposiacs

Anaximander says that men were first produced in fishes, and when they were grown up and able to help themselves, were thrown up and so lived upon the land.

Bk. 8

"On Moral Virtue"

Character is simply habit long continued.

"On Banishment"

Socrates said he was not an Athenian or a Greek, but a citizen of the world.

Lives

No beast is more savage than man, when possessed with power answerable to his rage.

"Cicero"

So very difficult a matter is it to trace and find out the truth of anything by history, when, on the one hand, those who afterwards write it find long periods of time intercepting their views, and, on the other hand, the contemporary records of any actions and lives, partly through envy and ill-will, partly through favor and flattery, pervert and distort truth.

"Pericles"

Of the Education of Children

Of all the advantages that accrue from philosophy, these I reckon the chiefest. To bear prosperity like a gentleman is the mark of a man, to deprecate envy the mark of a disciplined character, to rise superior to pleasure by reason the mark of a sage, to govern anger the mark of an extraordinary man. But perfect men I regard as those who are able to mingle and fuse political capacity with philosophy.

Nor is it always in the most distinguished achievements that men's virtues or vices may be best discovered; but very often an action of small note, a short saying, or a jest, shall distinguish a person's real character more than the greatest sieges, or the most important battles.

Consolatio and Apollonium

For an aching mind words are physicians.

Not even the gods can undo what has been done.

EDGAR ALLEN POE
(1809–1849)
American poet

"The Conqueror Worm"*

That motley drama—oh, be sure
  It shall not be forgot!
With its Phantom chased for evermore,
  By a crowd that seize it not,
Through a circle that ever returneth in
  To the self-same spot,
And much of Madness, and more of Sin,
  And Horror the soul of the plot.

St. 3

The curtain, a funeral pall,
  Comes down with the rush of a storm,
And the angels, all pallid and wan,
  Uprising, unveiling, affirm
That the play is the tragedy "Man,"
  And its hero the Conqueror Worm.

St. 5

---

*Originally published c.1838 as "Ligeie"; republished 1843 as "The Conqueror Worm."

"For Annie" (1849)

The fever called "Living"
  Is conquered at last.

St. 1

"A Dream within a Dream" (1827)

All that we see or seem
Is but a dream within a dream.

"Tamerlane" (1827)

O, human love! thou spirit given,
On Earth, of all we hope in Heaven!

"To Helen" (1831)

To the glory that was Greece,
And the grandeur that was Rome.

"The Poetic Principle" (1850)

I would define, in brief, the poetry of words as the rhythmical creation of Beauty.

"Eleanora" (1841)

Men have called me mad; but the question is not yet settled, whether madness is or is not the loftiest intelligence—whether much that is glorious—whether all that is profound—does not spring from disease of thought—from *moods* of mind exalted at the expense of the general intellect.

The Raven and Other Poems (1845)

The idea of God stands for the possible attempt at an impossible conception. We know nothing about the nature of God.

Preface

(Jules) HENRI POINCARÉ
(1854–1912)
French scientist

Value of Science (1904)

If we ought not to fear moral truth, still less should we dread scientific truth. In the first place it cannot conflict with ethics. . . . But if science is feared, it is above all because it can not give us happiness. . . . Man, then, can not be happy through science but today he can much less be happy without it.

Introduction

Science is facts. Just as houses are made of stones, so is science made of facts. But a pile of stones is not a house and a collection of facts is not necessarily science.

Pt. 3

POLYBIUS
(c. 208–126 B.C.)
Greek historian

Histories

Scrupulous fear of the gods is the very thing which keeps the Roman Commonwealth together. To such an extraordinary height is this carried among them, both in private and public business, that nothing could exceed it.

Many might think this unaccountable, but in my opinion their object is to use it as a check upon the common people. If it were possible to form a state wholly of philosophers, such a custom would perhaps be unnecessary. But seeing that every multitude is fickle, and full of lawless desires, unreasoning anger and violent passion, the only resource is to keep it in check by mysterious terrors and scenic effects of this sort. Wherefore, to my mind the ancients were not acting without purpose or at random, when they brought in among the vulgar those opinions about the gods, and the belief in punishment in Hades. *

Bk. 6

Jeanne Antoinette Poisson le Normant d'Etoiles, MARQUISE DE POMPADOUR
(1721–1764)
Chief mistress of Louis XV

Après nous le déluge.
After us, the deluge.
Attributed by Despres, *Mémoires de Madame de Hausset*

ARTHUR PONSONBY
(1871–1946)
British diplomat, writer

*Falsehood in Wartime** (1928)

When war is declared, Truth is the first casualty.

---

*Another translation: "Since the masses of the people are inconstant, full of unruly desires, passionate, and reckless of consequence, they must be filled with fears to keep them in order. The ancients did well, therefore, to invent gods, and the belief in punishment after death."
**An old German saying: *Kommt Krieg ins Land/ Gibt Lügen wie Sand*—When war comes to a country, lies are plentiful as sand.

ALEXANDER POPE
(1688–1744)
English poet

An Essay on Man (1733–1734)

Of Man in the abstract. I. That we can judge only with regard to our own system, being ignorant of the relations of systems and things.

II. That Man is not to be deemed imperfect, but a Being suited to his place and rank in the creation, agreeable to the general Order of things, and comfortable to Ends and Relations to him unknown.

III. That it is partly upon his ignorance of future events, and partly upon the hope of a future state, that all his happiness in the present depends.

IV. The pride of aiming at more knowledge and pretending to more Perfection, the cause of Man's error and misery. The impiety of putting himself in the place of God, and judging of the fitness or unfitness, perfection or imperfection, justice or injustice of his dispensations.

V. The absurdity of conceiting himself the final cause of the creation or expecting that perfection in the moral world, which is not in the natural.

VI. The unreasonableness of his complaints against Providence.

Argument of Epistle 1

Hope springs eternal in the human breast:
Man never is, but always to be, blest.
The soul, uneasy and confin'd from home,
Rests and expatiates in a life to come.

All Nature is but Art unknown to thee;
All chance direction, which thou canst not see;
All discord, harmony not understood;
All partial evil, universal good:
And spite of pride, in erring Reason's spite,
One truth is clear, *Whatever is, is right.*
Epistle I, *Of the Nature and State of Man with Respect to the Universe*

Know then thyself, presume not God to scan;
The proper study of mankind is Man.

With too much knowledge for the Sceptic side,
With too much weakness for the Stoic's pride,

He hangs between; in doubt to act or rest
In doubt to deem himself a God, or
   Beast; . . .

Great lord of all things, yet a prey to all;
Sole judge of Truth, in endless Error hurl'd;
The glory, jest, and riddle of the world!

Vice is a monster of so frightful mien,
As to be hated needs but to be seen;
Yet soon too oft, familiar with her face,
We first endure, then pity, then embrace.
   Epistle II, *Of the Nature and State of Man with*
   Respect to Himself, as an Individual

For forms of government let fools contest;
Whate'er is best administer'd is best.
   Epistle III, *Of the Nature and State of Man with*
   Respect to Society

Slave to no sect, who takes no private road,
But looks through Nature up to Nature's
   God.

An Honest Man's the noblest work of God.
   Epistle IV, *Of the Nature and State of Man with*
   Respect to Happiness

Epistle to Dr. Arbuthnot (1734)

Damn with faint praise, assent with civil
   leer,
And without sneering, teach the rest to
   sneer;
Willing to wound, and yet afraid to strike,
Just hint a fault, and hesitate dislike;
Alike reserved to blame or to commend,
A tim'rous foe, and a suspicious friend;
Dreading e'en fools, by flatterers besieged,
And so obliging, that he ne'er obliged.
   Line 200–207

"Who breaks a butterfly upon a wheel?"
   Line 308

The Dunciad (1728–1743, Bk. 4)

Art after art goes out, and all is night.
   Line 640

See skulking Truth to her old cavern fled,
Mountains of casuistry heap'd o'er her head!
Philosophy, that lean'd on Heaven before,
Shrinks to her second cause, and is no
   more.
Physic or Metaphysic begs defence,
And Metaphysic calls for aid on Sense!
See Mystery to Mathematics fly!
In vain! they gaze, turn giddy, rave, and die.
Religion, blushing, veils her sacred fires,
And unawares Morality expires.
   Lines 641–650

An Essay on Criticism (1711)

Trust not yourself; but your defects to know.
Make use of every friend—and every foe.
A little learning is a dangerous thing;
Drink deep, or taste not the Pierian spring:
There shallow draughts intoxicate the brain,
And drinking largely sobers us again.

Pride, the never-failing vice of fools.

Whoever thinks a faultless piece to see,
Thinks what ne'er was, nor is, nor e'er shall
   be.

To err is human, to forgive divine.

Moral Essays (1735)

Most women have no characters at all.
   Epistle II, line 2

The Ruling Passion, be it what it will,
The Ruling Passion conquers Reason still.
   Epistle III, line 153

"The Dying Christian to His Soul" (1712)

O Grave! where is thy Victory?
O Death! where is thy Sting?

"Elegy to the Memory of an Unfortunate Lady"
(1717)

Ambition first sprung from your blest
   abodes;
The glorious fault of Angels and of Gods.
   Lines 13–14

"Thoughts on Various Subjects" (1727)

Amusement is the happiness of those who
cannot think.

When men grow virtuous in their old age,
they only make a sacrifice to God of the devil's
leavings.

POPULIST PARTY OF AMERICA

Wealth belongs to him who creates it, and
every dollar taken from industry without an
equivalent, is robbery. "If they will not work,
neither shall they eat."
   First Party Platform, Omaha, July 4, 1892

EZRA POUND
(1885–1972)
American poet, fascist

"Ancient Music"

Winter is icummen in,
Lhude sing Goddamm.

E.P. Ode pour l'élection de son sepulchre (1920)

There died a myriad,
And of the best, among them,
For an old bitch gone in the teeth,
For a botched civilization.

IV

What is Money For? (a pamphlet, 1939)

USURY is the cancer of the world, which only the surgeon's knife of Fascism can cut out of the life of a nation.

Any man who could live in America is insane.

To judge, at treason trial

POWER
Variations on a theme by Lord Acton

Power corrupts the few, while weakness corrupts the many.

—Eric Hoffer

When power corrupts, poetry cleanses.

—John F. Kennedy

Power does not corrupt men; but fools, if they get into a position of power, corrupt it.

—G. Bernard Shaw

Power corrupts, but lack of power corrupts absolutely.

—Adlai Stevenson

Power does not corrupt. Fear corrupts, perhaps the fear of a loss of power.

—John Steinbeck

If power corrupts, weakness in the seat of power, with its constant necessity of deals and bribes and compromising arrangements, corrupts even more.

—Barbara Tuchman

PROGRESSIVE PARTY OF AMERICA
(Formed 1924)

Behind the ostensible government sits enthroned an invisible government owing no allegiance and acknowledging no responsibility to the people. To destroy this invisible government, to dissolve the unholy alliance between corrupt business and corrupt politics, is the first task of the statesmanship of today.

Party declaration, published in *LaFollette's Weekly*

SEXTUS PROPERTIUS
(54 B.C.–2 A.D.)
Umbrian-born Latin poet

Elegiae

May my enemies love women.

May my friends delight in boys.

Bk. 2, IV, 17

In mighty enterprises, to have willed success is enough.

Bk. 2, X, 5

No datur ad Musas currere lata via.
There is no royal road to the arts.

Bk. 3

PROTAGORAS OF ADERA
(c. 485–410 B.C.)
Greek Stoic philosopher

Man is the measure of all things, of things that are as they are, and of things that are not what they are not.

Fragment, I

Whether there are gods or not we cannot say, and life is too short to find out.

Quoted in Edith Hamilton, *The Greek Way of Life* (1930), ch. 15

PIERRE JOSEPH PROUDHON
(1809–1865)
Socialist, spiritual founder French Labor Movement

Qu'est-ce la propriété? [*What is Property?*] (1840)

If one were to ask the following question: *"What is slavery?"* and I should answer in one word, *"murder,"* my meaning would be understood at once.

Why, then, to this other question: *"What is property?"* may I not likewise answer, *"theft,"* with the certainty of being misunderstood; the second proposition being no other than a transformation of the first?

La propriété c'est le vol.
Property is theft.

Ch. 1

Communism is inequality, but not as property is. Property is the exploitation of the weak by the strong. Communism is the exploitation of the strong by the weak.

Individual *possession* is the condition of social life; five thousand years of property demonstrate it. *Property* is the suicide of society. Possession is a right; property is against right. Suppress property while maintaining possession, and, by this simple modification of the principle, you will revolutionize law, government, economy, and institutions; you will drive evil from the face of the earth.

Products are bought only by products . . . profit is impossible and unjust. Observe this elementary principle of economy, and pauperism, luxury, oppression, vice, crime, and hunger will disappear from our midst.

Politics is the science of liberty.

The government of man by man (under whatever name it be disguised) is oppression.

The ideal republic is a positive anarchy. It is liberty free from all shackles, superstitions, prejudices, sophistries, usury, authority; it is reciprocal liberty and not limited liberty; liberty not the daughter but the Mother of Order.

Ch. 5

The General Idea of the Revolution of the 19th Century

To be governed is to have every opinion, every transaction, every movement noted, registered, counted, rated, stamped, measured, numbered, assessed, licensed, refused, authorized, endorsed, admonished, prevented, reformed, redressed, corrected.

Principes d'organisation politiques ou la Création de l'ordre dans l'humanité (1843)

Man is destined to live without religion, but the moral law is eternal and absolute. Who would dare today to attack morality?

Les grands ne sont grands que parce que nous sommes à genoux; relevons-nous.
The great are only great because we are on our knees. Let us arise.

"Révolutions de Paris," motto

MARCEL PROUST
(1871–1922)
French novelist*

A la recherche du temps perdu [*Remembrance of Things Past*] (1913–1926)

Notre coeur change dans la vie, et c'est la pire douleur.
Our heart changes, and this is the greatest cause of suffering in life.
Vol. I, *Du côté de chez Swann* [*Swann's Way*]

Most of the time we are only partially alive. Most of our faculties go on sleeping because they rely on habit which can function without them.

The kind of fraud which consists in daring to proclaim the truth while mixing it with a large share of lies that falsify it, is more widespread than is generally thought.

Egoists always have the last word. Once and for all they establish the fact that their minds cannot be changed.
Vol. II, *Á l'ombre des jeunes filles en fleur* [*Within a Budding Grove*]

Everything great in the world comes from neurotics. They alone have founded our religions and composed our masterpieces. Never will the world know all it owes to them nor all that they have suffered to enrich us. [Boulbon speaking]**

It has even been said that the greatest praise of God lies in the negation of the atheist, who considers creation sufficiently perfect to dispense with a creator.

Each generation of critics does nothing but take the opposite of the truths accepted by their predecessors.

---

*Professor Ramon Guthrie, who taught Proust's work at Dartmouth, found Scott Moncrieff, the translator, not faithful to the text, making the English work partly his own. In his opinion, the volume translated for A&C Boni by F.A. Blossom is a truer work. Unfortunately, Blossom translated only Vol. II, so the Moncrieff translation is used here.
**This tribute to neurotics is frequently quoted. Dr. Guthrie has noted in my volume: "This passage was meant to show what fools people who are capable of uttering such idiocies are. . . . It is slap-stick irony that Proust puts into the mouth of a fool (Boulbon) in order to show what a fool he was."

We think and name in one world, we live and feel in another.

Vol. III, *Le côté de Guermantes* [*The Guermantes Way*]

In its early stage love is shaped by desire; later on it is kept alive by anxiety. In painful anxiety as in joyful desire, love insists upon everything. It is born and it thrives only if something remains to be won.

We love only what we do not completely possess.

Unconsecrated unions produce relationships that are just as numerous and complicated as those created by a marriage, but more solid.

L'adultère introduit l'esprit dans la lettre que bien souvent le mariage eut laissée morte.
Adultery introduces spirit into what might otherwise have been the dead letter of marriage.

Vol. V, *La prisonnière* [*The Captive*]

Those who practice the same profession recognize each other instinctively; likewise those who practice the same vice.

Vol. IV, *Sodome et Gomorrhe* [*Cities of the Plain*]

Man is a creature who cannot get outside of himself, and who knows others only in himself, and when he says the contrary he lies.

When we see ourselves on the edge of an abyss and it seems that God has abandoned us, we no longer hesitate to expect a miracle.

Desire is indeed powerful; it engenders belief.

Lies are essential to humanity. They are perhaps as important as the pursuit of pleasure and moreover are dictated by that pursuit.

Vol. VI, *Albertine disparue* [*The Sweet Cheat Gone*]

We like torturing people but without getting really into trouble by killing them.

Vol. VII, *Le temps retrouvé* [*The Past Recaptured*]

Nothing is more limited than sexual pleasure and vice. By changing the meaning of the phrase, it can truly be said that we move in the same vicious circle.

There is nothing like sexual desire to keep our words from having anything to do with our thoughts.

Attributed by Dr. Guthrie

WILLIAM PRYNNE
(1600–1669)
English Puritan pamphleteer

Historiomastix (1633)

It has ever been the notorious badge of prostituted strumpets and the lewdest Harlots, to ramble abroad to plays and to Playhouses, whither no honest, chaste or sober Girls or Women but only branded Whores and infamous Adulteresses did usually resort in ancient times.

PUBLILIUS (not Publius) SYRUS
(fl. 1st century B.C.)
Syria-born Latin writer

Maxims

All men are equal in the presence of death.
1

Honeste turpitudo est pro causa bona.
For a good cause crime is virtuous.
244

Those who plough the sea do not carry the winds in their hands.
(Cf. Bolivar)

Confession is the next thing to innocency.
1060

Speech is the mirror of the soul; as a man speaks, so is he.
1073

Sententiae

It is hardly granted by God to love and to be wise.
16

Rule your desires lest your desires rule you.
50

To ask a favor is a kind of slavery.

JOSEPH PULITZER
(1847–1911)
American newspaper publisher

. . . always fight for progress and reform, never tolerate injustice and corruption, always fight demagogues of all parties, never belong to any party, always oppose privileged classes and public plunderers, never lack sympathy with the poor, always remain devoted to the public welfare, never be satisfied with merely printing news; always be drastically independent; never be afraid to attack wrong, whether by predatory plutocracy or predatory poverty.

Statement of policy for the *N.Y. World* and St. Louis *Post-Dispatch,* on retirement, April 10, 1907

PYTHAGORAS
(fl. 6th century B.C.)
Greek philosopher, mathematician

The Golden Verses

Know this for truth, and learn to conquer these:
Thy belly first; sloth, luxury, and rage.
Do nothing base with others or alone,
And, above all, thine own self respect.

Let no man's word or deed seduce thee
To do or say aught not to thy best good.
Think first, then act; lest foolish be thy deed.

Do naught thou dost not understand.

Nor niggard be: in all the mean is best.

Ponder all things, and stablish high thy mind,
That best of charioteers. And if at length,
Leaving behind thy body, thou dost come
To the free Upper Air, then shalt thou be
Deathless, divine, a moral man no more.

Life . . . is like a festival; just as some come to the festival to compete, some to ply their trade, but the best people come as spectators (*theatai*), so in life the slavish men go hunting for fame (*doxa*) or gain, the philosophers for truth.

The soul of man is divided into three parts, intelligence, reason, and passion. Intelligence and passion are possessed by other animals, but reason by man alone.

Respect gods before demi-gods, heroes before men, and first among men your parents; but respect yourself most of all.

Friends have all things in common.
Quoted in Diogenes Laërtius, "Pythagoras"

There is a good principle which has created order, light and man; and a bad principle which has created chaos, darkness and woman.
Quoted in Simone de Beauvoir, *The Second Sex* (1953)

FRANCIS QUARLES
(1592–1644)
English poet

Enchiridion

Gaze not on beauty too much, lest it blast thee; nor too long lest it blind thee; nor too near, lest it burn thee; if thou like it, it deceives thee; if thou love it, it disturbs thee; if thou lust after it, it destroys thee; if virtue accompany it, it is the heart's paradise; if vice associate it, it is the soul's purgatory: it is the wise man's bonfire, and the fool's furnace.

SALVATORE QUASIMODO
(1910–1968)
Italian writer, Nobel Prize 1959

Indifference and apathy have one name—betrayal.
Quoted in *Saturday Review,* October 26, 1963

QUINTILIAN (Marcus Fabius Quintilianus)
(c. 35–c. 95 A.D.)
Iberian-born Roman rhetorician

Institutio Oratoria

The perfection of art is to conceal art.

Though ambition in itself is a vice, yet it is often the parent of virtues.

Bk. I

What in some is called liberty is called license in others.

Bk. 3

A liar should have a good memory.

Bk. 4

The Teacher and the Taught

The gifts of nature are infinite in their variety, and mind differs from mind almost as much as body from body.

FRANÇOIS RABELAIS
(c. 1494–1553)
French satirist

Gargantua and Pantagruel (1533–1535)

The Rule of their Order had but one clause: Do What Thou Wilt.

Bk. 1, ch. 57

Wisdom entereth not into a malicious mind, and science without conscience is but the ruin of the soul.

Bk. 2, ch. 8

One half of the world knoweth not how the other half liveth.

Bk. 2, ch. 32

The Devil was sick,—the Devil a monk
    would be;
The Devil was well,—the Devil a monk was
    he.

Bk. 3, ch. 24

Man has found remedies against all poisonous creatures, but none against a bad wife.
    Bk. 4, 1584, ch. 65 (a paraphrase of Euripides'
    "Andromache")

Speak the truth and shame the devil.

Bk. 5 (author's prologue)

———

I am going now to seek for a great perhaps.

Attributed death-bed statement*

———

*Another version concludes with the words *"tirez le rideau, la farce est jouée,"* ("draw the curtain, the farce is played out"). A third version has Rabelais saying "I am going to make a leap into the dark." Motteux in his *Life of Rabelais* wrote: "He left a paper sealed up, wherein were found three articles as his last will: 'I owe much; I have nothing; I give the rest to the poor.' "

I(sidor) I(saac) RABI
(1898–   )
American physicist, Nobel Prize 1944

The proper study of mankind is science, which also means that the proper study of mankind is man.
    Interview with Jeremy Bernstein, *The New Yorker*,
    October 20, 1975

SHEIKH MUJIBUR RAHMAN
(1920–1975)
Liberator of Bangla-Desh

In the war between falsehood and truth, falsehood wins the first battle and truth the last.
    Quoted in *Newsweek*, January 24, 1972

SIR WALTER RALEIGH
(1552–executed 1618)
English courtier, colonizer, writer

History of the World (1614)

Whosoever, in writing a modern history, shall follow truth too near the heels, it may haply strike out his teeth.

Preface

O eloquent, just and mighty Death! whom none could advise, thou has persuaded; what none hath dared, thou has done; and whom all the world hath flattered, thou only has cast out of the world and despised. Thou has drawn together all the far-stretched greatness, all the pride, cruelty, and ambition of man, and covered it all over with these two narrow words, *Hic jacet!*

Bk. V, pt. 1, ch. 6

"Affection and Desire"

Desire himself runs out of breath,
And getting, doth but gain his death.

"The Lie" (1608; manuscript copy 1595)

Go, Soul, the body's guest,
    Upon a thankless errand:
Fear not to touch the best,
    The Truth shall be thy warrant:
Go, since I needs must die,
    And give the world the lie.

Say to the Court it glows
    And shines like rotten wood,
Say to the Church it shows
    What's good, and doth no good:
If Church and Court reply,
    Then give them both the lie.

Tell zeal it wants devotion,
Tell love it is but lust;
Tell time it is but motion,
Tell flesh it is but dust;
And wish them not reply,
For thou must give the lie.

It is not truth, but opinion, that can travel the world without a passport.
Quoted in A.L. Rowse, *Sir Walter Raleigh*

FRANK PLUMPTON RAMSAY
(1903–1951)
British writer

The Foundations of Mathematics and Other Logical Essays (1931)

In time the world will cool and everything will die; but that is a long time off still, and its present value at compound discount is almost nothing. Nor is the present less valuable because the future will be blank.

AYN RAND
(1905–1982)
Russian-born American writer

For the New Intellectual (1961)

I am done with the monster of "We," the word of serfdom, of plunder, of misery, falsehood and shame. And now I see the free face of god, and I raise this god over the earth, this god whom men have sought since men came into being, this god who will grant them joy and peace and pride. This god, this one word: "I."

If any civilization is to survive, it is the morality of altruism that men have to reject.

The cross is the symbol of torture; I prefer the dollar sign, the symbol of free trade, therefore of a free mind.

Capitalism and altruism are incompatible . . . capitalism and altruism cannot coexist in man or in the same society.
Quoted in *Time*, February 29, 1960

JOHN RANDOLPH
(1773–1833)
American politician

So brilliant, yet so corrupt, which like a rotten mackerel by moonlight, shines and stinks.
A reference to Edward Livingston; attributed by W. Cabell Bruce

OTTO RANK
(1884–1939)
Vienna-born psychoanalyst

Art and Artist (1932)

If [the neurotic] seeks his salvation in artistic creation, instead of in the development of his personality, it is because he is still in the toils of old art-ideologies.
Ch. 3

For the only therapy is life. The patient must learn to live, to live with his split, his conflict, his ambivalence, which no therapy can take away, for if it could, it would take away with it the actual spring of life.
Attributed

GUILLAUME THOMAS FRANÇOIS RAYNAL
(1713–1796)
French Jesuit, writer

The Order of Jesuits is a sword whose handle is at Rome and whose point is everywhere.
Letter to Mlle. Volland (cf. Garibaldi)

SIR HERBERT READ
(1893–1968)
British writer*

The Realist Heresy (1952)

Art is an indecent exposure of the consciousness.

Art is not and never has been subordinate to moral values. Moral values are social values; aesthetic values are human values. . . . Morality seeks to restrain the feelings; art seeks to define them by externalizing them, by giving them significant form. Morality has only one aim—the ideal good; art has quite another aim—the objective truth . . . art never changes.

Art is a celebration of life.

All moral impulses, all feelings of goodness, all grace and truth, are but shadows cast from the dance of life; shadows cast, as Shelley said in his great poem, by the light of intellectual beauty.

*Inscription on his gravestone, by his order: "Herbert Read, Knight, Poet, Anarchist."

The Limits of Permissiveness in the Arts (1951)

Beauty is not necessarily the aim of the contemporary artist.

Art, in any meaningful sense of the word, must have three essential qualities: a formal correspondence in emotion and feeling, clarity . . . and a vital imagination. . . . The visual arts especially must exemplify this last quality, but it is the quality singularly lacking in the fragmented paintings and sculpture of recent years.

The Form of Things Unknown (1960)

The fundamental purpose of the artist is the same as that of a scientist: to state a fact.

Form is as mysterious as life itself. The artist is a man who reveals the mystery of form.
Quoted in *N.Y. Times Magazine*, April 17, 1960

His [Tolstoy's] definition of art is the inverse of the truth; the task of art is to transform not perception into feeling, but feeling into perception.
Contribution, *Saturday Review*, December 24, 1960

RONALD (Wilson) REAGAN
(1911–   )
Film actor, 40th President of the United States*

Belief in, and dependence on God, is absolutely essential. It will be an integral part of our public life as long as I am governor.
Contribution, *Esquire*, June 1967

Why should we subsidize intellectual curiosity?
Campaign speech, 1980

Government exists to protect us from each other. Where Government has gone beyond its limits is in deciding to protect us from ourselves.
Quoted in *N.Y. Times*, April 13, 1980

Concentrated power has always been the enemy of liberty.
Quoted in *New Republic*, December 16, 1981

---

*"Ronald Reagan is an ignoramus, a conscious and persistent falsifier of fact, a deceiver of the electorate, and, one suspects, of himself."—John Osborne, *New Republic*, June 12, 1980. "No reason to withdraw a word of that judgment."—Osborne, November 19, 1980.

RED JACKET (Sagoyewatha)
(c.1758–1830)
Seneca Indian Chief

You have got our country, but are not satisfied; you want to force your religion upon us. . . . Brother, you say there is but one way to worship and serve the Great Spirit. If there is but one religion, why do you white people differ so much about it?
Council of Chiefs of the Six Nations; reply to a missionary

THOMAS BRACKETT REED
(1839–1902)
Maine politician, Speaker of the House of Representatives

One of the greatest delusions in the world is the hope that the evils in this world are to be cured by legislation.
Speech, House of Representatives, 1886

The right of a minority is to draw its salaries, and its function is to make a quorum.
Quoted by William Safire, *N.Y. Times*, February 17, 1977

THEODOR REIK
(1888–1969)
Austrian-born American psychoanalyst

The Need to Be Loved (1963)

Women in general want to be loved for what they are and men for what they accomplish.
Pt. I, 1

Great innovators and original thinkers and artists attract the wrath of mediocrities as lightning rods draw the flashes.
Pt. I, 4

The last taboo of mankind, avoiding forbidden and dangerous thoughts, must be removed. There are no illegitimate thoughts.
Pt. I, 6

We are all in a race for dear life: that is to say, we are fugitives from death.
Pt. II, 159

Of Love and Lust (1957)

He [Freud] would often say three things were impossible to fulfill completely: healing, educating, governing. He limited his goals in analytic treatment to bringing a patient to the point where he could *work* for a living, and learn to *love*.

Is love thus an illusion? Of course it is. . . . Illusions are also physical realities. Freud called religion an illusion, but he did not deny that it was a great educational factor in the history of mankind.

To express unafraid and unashamed what one really thinks and feels is one of the great consolations of life.

Quoted in *N.Y. Times* obituary, January 2, 1970

ERICH MARIA REMARQUE
(1897–1970)
German writer

All Quiet on the Western Front.
Title of novel, 1929

(Joseph) ERNEST RENAN
(1823–1892)
French philologist, historian

Vie de Jésus (1863)

All history is incomprehensible without Christ.
Introduction

No miracle has ever taken place under conditions which science can accept. Experience shows, without exception, that miracles occur only in times and in countries in which miracles are believed in, and in the presence of persons who are disposed to believe in them.
Preface

Man belongs neither to his language nor his race; he belongs only to himself, for he is a free being, that is, a moral being.
Quoted in Benda, *Le Trahison des clercs*, 1927

THEODORE REPPLIER
(1900–   )
President, U.S. Advertising Council

People's Capitalism.
Term coined by Advertising Council, credited to him, and to Keith Funston, President, New York Stock Exchange

THE REPUBLICAN PARTY (GOP)
(Formed 1854–56)

Resolved: That in view of the necessity of battling for the first principles of Republican government, and against the schemes of aristocracy [the slave-holding South] . . . we will . . . be known as Republicans.
Cornerstone of platform, first convention, 1880

We cannot extend our trade further than we are able to defend it. Rivalries that begin in commerce end on battlefields.

Whatever the diplomatic excuse, every conflict in modern times had its origin in some question of property rights.
Statement in behalf of Hughes, signed by T. Roosevelt, Taft, and other GOP leaders, 1916

We deny the right to strike against the government.
National platform, 1920

PAUL DE GONDI, CARDINAL DE RETZ
(1613–1679)
French prelate, statesman

Memoirs (1655–1665?)

In the view of rulers, it is just as dangerous and almost as criminal to not do good as to intend evil.

That which is necessary is never a risk.

A man who never trusts himself never trusts anyone.

The most distrusting persons are often the greatest dupes.
Bk. II

JEAN-FRANÇOIS REVEL
(1924–   )
French writer, columnist for *L'Express*

Ni Marx, ni Jesus [*Without Marx or Jesus*] (1970)

It is no longer possible to maintain that there can be progress in socialism without equal progress in human freedom, and particularly in freedom of expression.

Socialism has not yet been realized anywhere in the world.
Ch. 3

Today in America—the child of European imperialism—a new revolution is rising. It is *the* revolution of our time. It is the only revolution that involves radical, moral, and practical opposition to the spirit of nationalism. It is the only revolution that, to that opposition, joins culture, economic and technological power, and a total affirmation of liberty for all in the place of archaic prohibitions. It therefore offers the only escape for mankind today: the acceptance of technological civilization as a means and not as an end, and—since we cannot be saved either by the destruction of civilization or by its continuation—the development of the ability to reshape that civilization without annihilating it.

Ch. 16 (concluding paragraph)

SIR JOSHUA REYNOLDS
(1723–1792)
English painter, writer

There is no expedient to which man will not resort to avoid the real labor of thinking.

Quoted in Mason, *Great and Mind-Liberating Thoughts*

CECIL RHODES
(1853–1902)
British colonial statesman

We [the Anglo-Saxons] are the first race in the world, and the more of the world we inherit the better it is for the human race.

Proclamation

The extension of British rule throughout the world . . . the ultimate recovery of the United States of America as an integral part of the British Empire . . . and finally, the foundation of so great a power as to hereafter render wars impossible and promote the best interests of humanity.

First will, 1877; quoted in Basil Williams, *Cecil Rhodes* (1921)

DAVID RICARDO
(1772–1823)
English political economist

Principles of Political Economy and Taxation (1817)

Labor, like all other things which are purchased and sold, and which may be increased or diminished in quantity, has its natural and its market price. The natural price of labor is that price which is necessary to enable the laborers, one with another, to subsist and to perpetuate their race, without either increase or diminution.

The market price of labor is the price which is really paid for it, from the natural operation of the supply to the demand. . . . However much the market price of labor may deviate from its natural price, it has, like commodities, a tendency to conform to it.

It is a truth which admits not a doubt, that the comforts and well-being of the poor cannot be permanently secured without some regard on their part, or some effort on the part of the legislature, to regulate the increase of their numbers, and to render less frequent among them early and improvident marriages.

Ch. V

On Protection to Agriculture (1820)

There is no way of keeping profits up but by keeping wages down.

SAMUEL RICHARDSON
(1689–1761)
English novelist

A Collection of the Moral and Instructive Maxims, Cautions, and Reflections, contained in the Histories of Pamela, Clarissa, and Sir Charles Grandison (1755)

Calumny. Censure. No one is exempt from calumny. Words said, the occasion of saying them not known, however justly reported, may be a very different construction from what they would have done had the occasion been told.

Were evil actions to pass uncensured, good ones would lose their reward; and vice, by being put on a foot with virtue in this life, would meet with general countenance.

Young folks are sometimes very cunning in finding out contrivances to cheat themselves.

Armand Jean du Plessis, DUC DE RICHELIEU
(1585–1642)
French Cardinal, statesman

Mirame (play, c. 1625)

If you give me six sentences written by the most innocent of men, I will find something in them with which to hang him.

"Les Thuileries"

To deceive a rival, artifice is permitted. One may employ everything against one's enemies.

Testament Politiques, Maxims (1645)

To know how to dissemble is the knowledge of kings.

VI

JEAN PAUL (Johann Paul Friedrich) RICHTER
(1763–1825)
German writer

Hesperus (1795)

The more weakness, the more falsehood, strength goes straight;   weaklings must lie.

4, cycle

Spring . . . makes everything young except man.

14, cycle

Titan (1800–1803)

Only a free soul never grows old.

Vol. 2, 140, cycle

Selina (1827)

This sorrow of the world he can bear only, so to speak, by gazing on soulfulness.

AMAURY DE RIENCOURT
Contemporary French historian

Sex and Power in History (1974)

The contemporary woman's liberation drive toward a *decrease* in sexual differentiation, to the extent that it is leading toward androgyny and unisexual values, implies a social and cultural death-wish and the end of the civilization that endorses it. The scientific and historical records show that all the way from unicellular organisms to human beings, progress in evolution has been stimulated by an *increase* in sexual differentiation.

Introduction

DAVID RIESMAN
(1909–   )
American social scientist

The Lonely Crowd (with Nathan Glazer and Reuel Denney) (1950)

Conversely, just as non-conformity in behavior does not necessarily mean non-conformity in character structure, so utter conformity in behavior may be purchased by the individual at so high a price as to lead to a character neurosis.

XIV

RAINER MARIA RILKE
(1875–1926)
German poet

Once there was God, now there is no God, some day there will be a God again.

Quoted in *Time*, May 2, 1969

ARTHUR RIMBAUD
(1854–1891)
French poet

"Une Saison en enfer" (1873)

Morality is the weakness of the mind.

FREDERICK WILLIAM ROBERTSON
("Robertson of Brighton")
(1816–1853)
English divine

Sermons (pub. 1865)

Women and God are the two rocks on which a man must either anchor or be wrecked.

MAXIMILIEN MARIE ISIDORE DE ROBESPIERRE
(1758–guillotined 1794)
French revolutionist*

Terror is nought but prompt, severe, inflexible justice; it is therefore an emanation of virtue; it is less a particular principle than a consequence of the general principle of democracy applied to the most pressing needs of the fatherland.

We desire to substitute morality for egotism, probity for honor, principles for usages, duties for functions, the empire of reason for the tyranny of fashions, the scorn of vice for the scorn of misfortune, pride for insolence, greatness of soul for vanity, the love of glory for the love of money, good citizens for good society, merit for intrigue, genius for cleverness, truth

*"The seagreen incorruptible."—Carlyle.

for splendor, the charm of happiness for the ennui of voluptuousness, the grandeur of man for the pettiness of the great, a magnanimous people, powerful, happy, for a people amiable, frivolous, and miserable; that is to say, all the virtues of a republic for all the vices and follies of a monarchy.

Address, National Convention, 1794

Declaration of the Rights of Man and Citizen (1792)

Society is under obligation to provide for the support of all its members either by procuring work for them or by assuring the means of existence to those who are not in condition to work.

Kings, aristocrats, and tyrants, whoever they may be, are slaves in rebellion against the sovereign of the earth, which is mankind, and against the legislator of the universe, which is nature.

EDWIN ARLINGTON ROBINSON
(1869–1933)
American poet

"John Brown"

I shall have more to say when I am dead.

"For a Dead Lady" (1910)

The grace, divine, definitive,
Clings only as a faint forestalling;
The laugh that love could not forgive
Is hushed, and answers to no calling;
The forehead and the little ears
Have gone where Saturn keeps the years;
The breast where roses could not live
Has done with rising and with falling.

"Miniver Cheevy" (1910)

Miniver loved the Medici,
Albeit he had never seen one;
He would have sinned incessantly
Could he have been one.

Miniver cursed the commonplace
And eyed a khaki suit with loathing;
He missed the medieval grace
Of iron clothing.

Miniver Cheevy, born too late,
Scratched his head and kept on thinking;
Miniver coughed, and called it fate,
And kept on drinking.

"Cassandra" (1916)

Your Dollar is your only Word,
And wrath of it your only fear.

Your Dollar, Dove and Eagle make
A Trinity that even you
Rate higher than you rate yourselves;
It pays, it flatters, and it's new.

You have the ages for your guide,
But not the wisdom to be led.

Think you to tread forever down
The merciless old verities?
And are you never to have the eyes
To see the world for what it is?

I have also been reading the Old Testament, a most bloodthirsty and perilous book for the young. Jehovah is beyond a doubt the worst character in fiction.

Letter to Mrs. Laura E. Richards, June 2, 1924

JAMES HARVEY ROBINSON
(1863–1936)
American historian

The chief strength of the ancient Greeks lay in their freedom from hampering intellectual tradition. They had no venerated classics, no holy books, no dead languages to master, no authorities to check their free speculation.

Quoted in Mason, *Great and Mind-Liberating Thoughts*

FRANÇOIS DE LA ROCHEFOUCAULD
(1613–1680)
French moralist

Réflexions, ou sentences et maximes morales (1664)

Our virtues are most often but our vices disguised.

1

We all have strength enough to endure the misfortune of others.

19

We need greater virtue to sustain good than evil fortunes.

25

Those who apply themselves too closely to little things often become incapable of great things.

41

If one judges love by most of its results, it is closer to hatred than friendship
72

It is with true love as with ghosts: the whole world speaks of it but few have seen it.
76

The mind is always the dupe of the heart.
102

The love of glory, the fear of disgrace, the incentive to succeed, the desire to live in comfort, and the instinct to humiliate others are often the cause of that courage so renowned among men.
213

Hypocrisy is the homage vice pays to virtue.
218

We often forgive those who bore us, but cannot forgive those we bore.
304

We would often be ashamed of our noblest actions if all their motives were known.
409

Few people know how to be old.
423

JOHN D. ROCKEFELLER (Sr.)
(1839–1937)
American capitalist, philanthropist

The good Lord gave me my money.
Address, first graduating class, University of Chicago, 1894

The growth of a large business is merely a survival of the fittest.
Quoted in Hofstadter, *Social Darwinism in American Thought* (1944, rev. ed. 1955)

AUGUST RODIN
(1840–1917)
French sculptor

Art is the only truth . . .

To the artist there is never anything ugly in nature.

There are no vices, there are only phases . . .
Quoted in Dorothy Dudley, *Forgotten Frontiers* (1932)

MME. JEANNE (Manon) ROLAND DE LA PLATIÈRE
(1754–guillotined 1793)
French Girondist

Liberty! It is for noble minds, who despise death, and who know how upon occasion to give it to themselves. It is not for those weak beings who enter in composition with guilt, who cover their selfishness with the name of prudence. . . . It is for wise people who delight in humanity, praise justice, despise their flatterers, and respect the truth.
As long as you are not such a people, O my fellow citizens, you will talk in vain of liberty.
Written at the Conciergerie the night before her cross-examination, 1793

O liberté! comme on t'a jouée.*
O liberty! how they have played with you.
Last words before her death on the guillotine

ROMAIN ROLLAND
(1866–1944)
French novelist

Jean-Christophe (1904–1913)

A hero is a man who does what he can.

To understand everything is to hate nothing.

What man more than the spiritual worker has to suffer more from the immorality of social conditions, from the scandalously unequal partition of wealth among men? The artist dies of hunger or becomes a millionaire for no other reason than the caprice of fashion and of those who speculate on fashion.

This thing must be put bluntly: every man who has more than is necessary for his livelihood and that of his family, and for the normal development of his intelligence, is a thief and a robber. If he has too much, it means that others have too little.

---

*Said on passing a statue of liberty. "Jouer" is also translated as "tricked" and "fooled."
The exclamation, "O liberté, liberté! que de crimes on commet en ton nom!" was years later attributed to Mme. Roland by Lamartine in *Histoire des Girondins* and quoted by Macaulay.

There is no joy but in creation. There are no living beings but those who create. All the rest are shadows, hovering over the earth, strangers to life.

To create in the region of the body, or in the region of the mind, is to issue from the prison of the body: it is to ride upon the storm of life: it is to be He who Is.

No man creates from reason but from necessity.

Truth is the same for each of us; but every nation has its own lie, which it calls its idealism; every creature therein breathes it from birth to death; it has become the condition of life; there are only a few men of genius who can break from it through heroic moments of crisis, when they are alone in the free world of their thoughts.

ELEANOR ROOSEVELT
(1884–1962)
American diplomat, writer

You Can Learn by Living (1960)

You gain strength, courage and confidence by every experience in which you really stop to look fear in the face . . . *You must do the thing which you think you cannot do.*

FRANKLIN DELANO ROOSEVELT
(1882–1945)
32nd President of the United States

Addresses, Speeches, Messages, etc.

. . . the forgotten man at the bottom of the economic pyramid.*
> Radio address, April 7, 1932

I pledge to you, I pledge myself, to a new deal for the American people.
> Acceptance speech, July 2, 1932**

---

*William G. Sumner published *The Forgotten Man* in 1883.
**FDR told Cyril Clemens he got that phrase from Mark Twain's *Connecticut Yankee*; *Time* credited Judge Samuel Rosenman with the term; the *New York Times*, February 20, 1975, credited Raymond Moley. Lloyd George's slogan for his 1919 election campaign was "A New Deal for Everyone."
FDR had numerous advisers and ghost-writers, notably Rexford Tugwell, Adolf Berle, Jay Franklin, Thomas Corcoran, and Stanley High, who coined the phrase "economic royalists."

No business which depends for existence by paying less than living wages to its workers has any right to continue in this country.
> June 16, 1933

[Business and finance are] unanimous in their hate for me—and I welcome their hatred. . . . I should like to have it said of my first Administration that in it the forces of selfishness and of lust for power met their match; I would like to have it said of my second administration that in it these forces met their master.
> Campaign speech, 1936; quoted by Justice Douglas

This generation of Americans has a rendezvous with destiny.
> Acceptance speech, June 27, 1936

I see one third of a nation ill-housed, illclad, ill-nourished.
> Second Inaugural, January 20, 1937

Remember always that all of us, and you and I especially, are descended from immigrants and revolutionists.
> Address, Daughters of the American Revolution, April 20, 1938

The liberty of a democracy is not safe if the people tolerate the growth of private power to a point where it becomes stronger than their democratic State itself. That, in its essence, is Fascism—ownership of government by an individual, by a group, or any controlling private power.
> Message proposing the Monopoly Investigation, 1938

A Radical is a man with both feet firmly planted—in the air.
A Conservative is a man with two perfectly good legs who, however, has never learned how to walk forward.
A Reactionary is a somnambulist walking backwards.
A Liberal is a man who uses his legs and his hands at the behest, at the command, of his head.
> Radio address, October 26, 1939

We look forward to a world founded upon four essential human freedoms.
The first is freedom of speech and expression—everywhere in the world.
The second is freedom of every person to worship God in his own way—everywhere in the world.
The third is freedom from want . . .
The fourth is freedom from fear . . .
> Message to Congress, January 6, 1941

We all know that books burn—yet we have the greater knowledge that books cannot be killed by fire. People die, but books never die. . . . No man and no force can put thought in a concentration camp forever. . . . Books are weapons . . . make them weapons for man's freedom.
Message to American Booksellers Association, April 23, 1942, anniversary of the Nazi book-burnings

We shall not be able to claim that we have gained total victory in this war if any vestige of Fascism in any of its malignant forms is permitted to survive anywhere in the world.
Message to Congress, September 14, 1943

The citizens of the United States must effectively control the mighty commercial forces which they have themselves called into being.
Quoted in R.E. Sherwood, *Roosevelt and Hopkins*, rev. ed. 1950

THEODORE ROOSEVELT
(1858–1919)
26th President of the United States

Addresses, Speeches, Etc.

No triumph of peace is so great as the supreme triumph of war.
Address, Naval War College, 1895

I wish to preach not the doctrine of ignoble ease, but the doctrine of strenuous life.
Address, Hamilton Club, Chicago, April 10, 1899

Wage workers have an entire right to organize. . . . They have a legal right . . . to refuse to work in company with men who decline to join in their organization.
Message to Congress, December 6, 1904

The men with the muckrakes are often indispensable to the well-being of society; but only if they know when to stop raking the muck.
Address, cornerstone laying, Gridiron Club, April 14, 1906

I am in every fiber of my body a radical.
Campaign speech, 1912

There can be no 50–50 Americanism in this country. There is room here for only 100 percent Americanism.
Speech, March 2, 1918

The New Nationalism (1910)

I believe in a graduated income tax on big fortunes, and . . . a graduated inheritance tax on big fortunes, properly safeguarded against evasion and increasing rapidly in amount with the size of the estate.
(cf. *Communist Manifesto*)

I believe in property rights; I believe that normally the rights of property and humanity coincide; but sometimes they conflict, and when this is so, I put human rights above property rights.
Contribution, *Outlook,* November 15, 1913

The things that will destroy America are prosperity at any price, peace at any price, safety first instead of duty first, and love of soft living and the get-rich-quick theory of life.
Letter to S. Stanwood Menken, January 10, 1917

The wealthier, or, as they prefer to style themselves, the "upper" classes, tend distinctly toward the bourgeois type of development, and an individual in the bourgeois state of development while honest, industrious, and virtuous, is also not unapt to be a miracle of timid and shortsighted selfishness.
Contribution, *Century Magazine*, 1886

Great, masterful races have been fighting races.
Quoted in Hofstadter, *The American Political Heritage*

A great democracy must be progressive or it will soon cease to be a great democracy.
Quoted by FDR at dedication of TR memorial

ALFRED ROSENBERG
(1893–1946)
German Nazi leader, editor

The Myth of the Twentieth Century (tr. F.L. Baumer, pub. 1952)

History and the mission of the future no longer mean the struggle of class against class, the struggle of church dogma against dogma, but the clash between blood and blood, race and race, people and people.

The Negro problem in the United States is vital to the country's existence. If means are not taken to suppress the Negroes . . . they, in their capacity as Bolshevik combatants, will prepare the doom of white America.

A new peace will make Germany master of the globe, a peace not hanging on the palm fronds of pacifist womenfolk, but established by the victorious sword of a master-race that takes over the world.

JULIUS ROSENWALD
(1862–1932)
American merchant, philanthropist

It is nearly always easier to make $1,000,000 honestly than to dispose of it wisely.

Quoted in *Saturday Review*, January 19, 1968

JEAN ROSTAND
(1894–1977)
French scientist

The Substance of Man (1962)

For the biologist there are no classes—only individuals.

Le Carnet d'un biologiste (1962)

Whatever an individual is—good or bad—has no causes other than the molecular make-up he received from his parents and the external influences that have worked on him. Our thanks or blame must fall on chemistry and luck.

Brief lightning flashes in the atheist's mind—they are perhaps worth more than the compact certitudes of the believer.

CLAUD JOSEPH ROUGET DE LISLE
(1769–1836)
French army officer

La Marseillaise (1792)

Allons, enfants de la Patrie!
  Le jour de gloire est arrivé!
Contre nous de la tyrannie
  L'étendard sanglant est levé.

Aux armes, citoyens!
  Formez les bataillions!
Marchons! marchons! Qu'un sang impur
  Abreuve nos sillons.

JEAN JACQUES ROUSSEAU
(1712–1778)
Swiss-born French philosopher*

The Social Contract (1762)

Man is born free, and everywhere he is in chains.

Bk. I, ch. 1

The first slaves were made so by force, the state of slavery was perpetuated by cowardice.

Bk. I, ch. 2

To renounce liberty is to renounce being a man, to surrender the rights of humanity and even its duties.

Bk. I, ch. 4

. . . the people is never corrupted, but it is often deceived . . .

Bk. II, ch. 3

Free people, remember this: You may acquire liberty, but once lost it is never regained.

Bk. II, ch. 8

If we ask in what precisely consists the greatest good of all, which should be the end of every system of legislation, we shall find it reduces itself to two main objects, liberty and equality.

By equality, we should understand, not that the degrees of power and riches are to be absolutely identical for everybody; but that power shall never be so strong as to be capable of violence and shall always be exercised by virtue of rank and law; and that, in respect to riches, no citizen shall ever be wealthy enough to buy another, and none poor enough to be forced to sell himself.

Bk. II, ch. 11

Were there a people of gods, their government would be democratic. So perfect a government is not for me.

In the strict sense of the term, a true democracy has never existed, and will never exist. It is against natural order that the great number should govern and that the few should be governed.

Bk. III, ch. 4

---

*"Rousseau produced more effect with his pen than Aristotle, or Cicero, or St. Augustine, or St. Thomas Aquinas, or any other man who ever lived."—Lord Acton.

As soon as any man says of the affairs of State, "What does it matter to me?" the State may be given up as lost.

Laws are always useful to those who own, and injurious to those who do not.

Laws give the weak new burdens, and the strong new powers; they irretrievably destroy natural freedom, establish in perpetuity the law of property and inequality, turn a clever usurpation into an irrevocable right, and bring the whole future race under the yoke of labor, slavery and money.

The first [religion of man] which has neither temples, nor altars, nor rites, and is confined to the purely internal cult of the supreme God and the external obligations of morality, is the religion of the Gospel pure and simple, the true theism, which may be called natural divine right or law.

But I am mistaken in speaking of a Christian republic; the terms are mutually exclusive. Christianity preaches only servitude and dependence. Its spirit is so favorable to tyranny that it always profits by such a regime. True Christians are made to be slaves, and they know it and do not much mind; this short life counts for too little in their eyes.

Bk. IV, ch. 8

An anti-social being . . .

Emile (1762)

The whole education of women should be relative to men. To please them, to be useful to them, to win their love and esteem, to bring them up when young, to tend them when grown, to advise and console them, and to make life sweet and pleasant to them; these are the duties of woman at all times, and what they ought to learn from infancy.

Everything is good when it leaves the hands of the Creator; everything degenerates in the hands of man. . . .

The way in which ideas are formed is what gives character to the human mind. The mind which forms its ideas on realities is a solid mind; that which is satisfied with appearances is superficial; that which sees things as they are is a just mind; that which appreciates them badly is a false mind; that which invents imaginary relationships having neither reality nor appearance, is a foolish one; that which does not compare is an imbecile. The attitude,

more or less great, of comparing ideas, and of finding a rapport and relationship is that which gives more or less character to the mind of man.

Always keep in mind that ignorance has never produced evil, that error alone is fatal.

He who eats in idleness that which he himself has not earned, steals it; and a capitalist whom the state pays for doing nothing differs little in my eyes from a brigand, who lives at the expense of passers-by.

The letter kills and the spirit makes alive.

Civilized man is born, lives, and dies in slavery; at his birth he is confined in swaddling clothes; at death he is nailed in a coffin. So long as he retains the human form he is fettered by our institutions.

Since we have to combat nature or society, we must choose between making a man or making a citizen—we cannot make both.

Teach him to live a life rather than to avoid death; life is not breath but action.

If we had the offer of immortality here below, who would accept this sorrowful gift?

A Discourse on the Origin of Inequality (1754)

The first man who, having enclosed a piece of ground, bethought himself of saying "This is mine," and found people simple enough to believe him, was the real founder of civil society. From how many crimes, wars and murders, from how many horrors and misfortunes might not anyone have saved mankind by pulling up the stakes, or filling up the ditch, and crying to his fellows, "Beware of listening to this imposter; you are undone if you once forget that the fruits of the earth belong to us all, and the earth itself to nobody."

Whatever moralists may hold, the human understanding is greatly indebted to the passions, which, it is universally allowed, are also much indebted to the understanding. It is by the activity of our passions that our reason is improved; for we desire knowledge only because we desire enjoyment; and it is impossible to conceive any reason why a person who has neither fears nor desires should give himself the trouble of reasoning.

The habit of living together soon gave rise to the finest feelings known to humanity, conjugal love and paternal affection.

The poet tells us it was gold and silver, but for the philosophers it was iron and corn which first civilized, and ruined humanity.

It is this desire for being talked about, and this unremitting rage to distinguish ourselves, that we owe the best and worst things we possess; both our virtues and our vices, our science and our errors, our conquerors and our philosophers; that is to say, a great many bad things and a very few good ones.

There is hardly any inequality among men in the state of nature.

The Confessions of Jean Jacques Rousseau (1781–1788)

I am commencing an undertaking, hitherto without precedent, and will never find an imitator. I desired to set before my fellows the likeness of a man in all the truth of nature, and that man shall be myself.
Bk. I (opening lines)

As long as the money in my purse lasts, it assures my independence. . . . The money which a man possesses is the instrument of freedom; that which we eagerly pursue is the instrument of slavery. Therefore I hold fast to that which I have, and desire nothing.

. . . we ought not to speak about religion to children, if we wish them to possess any, and further, . . . they are incapable of knowing God, even according to our ideas.
Bk. II

"Discours sur les sciences et les arts" (1750)

One can buy anything with money except morality and citizens.

Every useless amusement is an evil for a being whose life is so short and whose time is so pressing.
Letter to d'Alembert

Get rid of the miracles and the whole world will fall at the feet of Jesus Christ.
Quoted in Shaw, "Androcles and the Lion," preface

JOSIAH ROYCE
(1855–1916)
American philosopher

The Spirit of Modern Philosophy (1892)

Philosophy . . . has its origin and value in an attempt to give a reasonable account of our own personal attitude toward the more serious business of life.

Life involves passions, faiths, doubts and courage. The critical inquiry into what these things mean and imply is philosophy.
Lecture 1

The Philosophy of Loyalty (1907–1908)

Unless you can find some sort of loyalty, you cannot find unity and peace in your active living.
Lecture 1

RICHARD RUMBOLD
(1622–hanged and quartered 1685)
English rebel

I never could believe that Providence had sent a few men into the world, ready booted and spurred, to ride, and millions ready saddled and bridled to be ridden.
Spoken on the scaffold, quoted in Macaulay, *History of England*, ch. 1*

JALAODDIN RUMI
(1207–1273)
Founder of the Whirling Dervishes

I died as mineral and became a plant.
I died as plant and rose to animal.
I died as animal and I was man.
Why should I fear? When was I less by dying? . . .
I must pass on: all except God perish.
Quoted in *Anthology of Islamic Literature* (ed. James Kritzeck)

DAGOBERT D. RUNES
(1902–1982)
American philosophical writer

Treasury of World Literature (1966)

If God could make angels, why did he bother with men?

*Another version of Rumbold's last words reads, "I am sure there was no man born marked of God above another; for none comes into the world with a saddle upon his back, neither any booted and spurred to ride him." Rumbold was executed in Edinburgh; he was dragged to the scaffold although dying of wounds.

Millions have died for Him, but only a few lived for Him.

Morality is the observance of the rights of others.

Morality is always the same. However, immorality varies from generation to generation.

KARL RUDOLF GERD VON RUNSTEDT (1875–1953)
German Nazi General, World War II

One of the great mistakes of 1918 was to spare the civil life of the enemy countries, for it is necessary for us Germans to be always at least double the numbers of people of the contiguous countries. We are therefore obliged to destroy at least a third of their inhabitants. The only means is organized underfeeding, which in this case is better than machine guns.
Address, Reich War Academy, 1943

BENJAMIN RUSH (1745–1813)
American physician, signer of the Declaration of Independence

There is nothing more common than to confound the terms of the American Revolution with those of the late American war. The American war is over but this is far from being the case with the American Revolution. On the contrary, nothing but the first act of the great drama is closed.
Address, "To the People of the United States," 1789

Controversy is only dreaded by the advocates of error.
Quoted in Noyes, *Views of Religion*

JOHN RUSKIN (1819–1900)
British writer

Ethics of the Dust (1866)

I desire . . . to leave this one great fact clearly stated. THERE IS NO WEALTH BUT LIFE.

That country is the richest which nourishes the greatest number of noble and happy human beings.

Whereas it has been known and declared that the poor have no right to the property of the rich, I wish it also to be known and declared that the rich have no right to the property of the poor.

Time and Tide (1867)

Labor without joy is base. Labor without sorrow is base. Sorrow without labor is base. Joy without labor is base.
Letter 5

. . . to make your children *capable of honesty* is the beginning of education. Make them men first, and religious men afterwards, and all will be sound; but a knave's religion is always the rottenest thing about him.
Letter 8

Modern Painters (1856)

The simplest and most necessary truths are always the last believed.

All violent feelings . . . produce in us a falseness in all our impressions of external feelings, which I would characterize as the "Pathetic Fallacy."

I do not say therefore that the art is greatest which gives most pleasure, because perhaps there is some art whose end it is to teach and not to please. I do not say the art is greatest which teaches the most, because perhaps there is some art whose end it is to please and not to teach. I do no say that the art is greatest which imitates best, because perhaps there is some art whose end it is to create and not to imitate. But I say that the art is greatest which conveys to the mind of the spectator, by any means whatsoever, the greatest number of the greatest ideas, and I call an idea great in proportion as it is received by a higher faculty of the mind, and as it more fully occupies, and in occupying, exercises, and exalts, the faculty by which it is received.

If this then be the definition of great art, that of a great artist naturally follows. He is the greatest artist who has embodied, in the sum of his works, the greatest number of the greatest ideas.

The essence of lying is in deception, not in words; a lie may be told in silence, by equivocation, by the accent on a syllable, by a glance of the eye attaching a peculiar significance to a sentence; but all of these kinds of lies are worse and baser by many degrees than a lie plainly worded.

The greatest thing a human soul ever does in this world is to *see* something and tell what he *saw* in a plain way. Hundreds of people can talk for one who can think, and thousands can think for one who can see. To see clearly is poetry, prophecy and religion all in one.

Stones of Venice (1851–1853)

Remember that the most beautiful things in the world are the most useless: peacocks and lilies for instance.

Darkness and mystery, confused recesses of building, artificial light employed in small quantity, but maintained with a constancy which seems to give it a kind of sacredness, preciousness of material easily comprehended by the vulgar eye; close air loaded with sweet and peculiar odor associated only with religious services, solemn music, and tangible idols or images having popular legends attached to them,—these, the stage properties of superstition, which have been from the beginning of the world, and must be to the end of it, employed by all nations, whether openly savage or nominally civilized, to produce a false awe in minds incapable of comprehending the true nature of the Deity, are assembled in St. Mark's to a degree, as far as I know, unexampled in any other European church.

Vol. 1

Sesame and Lilies (1865)

If a book is worth reading, it is worth buying.

All books are divisible into two classes, the books of the hour, and the books of all time. . . . There are good books for the hour and good ones for all time; bad books for the hour, and bad ones for all time.

All these books of the house, multiplying among us as education becomes more general, are a peculiar possession of the present age: we ought to be entirely thankful for them, and entirely ashamed of ourselves if we make no good use of them. But we make the worst possible use if we allow them to usurp the place of true books; for, strictly speaking, they are not books at all, but merely letters or newspapers in good print.

You must get into the habit of looking intensely at words, and assuring yourself of their meaning, syllable by syllable—nay, letter by letter. . . . you might read all the books in the British Museum (if you could live long enough) and remain an utterly "illiterate," uneducated person; but if you read ten pages of a good book, letter by letter,—that is to say, with real accuracy—you are for evermore in some measure an educated person.

Lecture 1

The greatest efforts of the race have always been traceable to the love of praise, as the greatest catastrophes to the love of pleasure.

No nation can last, which has made a mob of itself, however generous at heart. It must discipline its passions, and direct them or they will discipline *it*, one day, with scorpion-whips. Above all, a nation cannot last in a money-making job; it cannot with impunity,—it cannot with existence—go on despising literature, despising science, despising nature, despising compassion, and concentrating its soul on Pence.

That thirst [for applause] if the last infirmity of noble minds, is also the first infirmity of weak ones.

Lecture 2

The Two Paths (1858–1859)

Fine art is that in which the hand, the head, and the heart of man go together.

Pre-Raphaelitism (1851)

No great intellectual thing was ever done by great effort; a great thing can only get done by a great man, and he does it *without* effort.

The Crown of Wild Olives (1866)

It is physically impossible for a well-educated, intellectual, or brave man, to make money the chief object of his thoughts.

Fors Clavigera (1876)

There are three Material things, not only useful, but essential to Life. No one knows "how to live" until he has got them.
These are Pure Air, Water, and Earth.
There are three Immaterial things, not only useful, but essential to Life. No one knows how to live until he has got them also.
They are Admiration, Hope, and Love.

I have seen and heard much of cockney impudence before now; but never expected to hear a coxcomb ask 200 guineas for flinging a pot of paint in the public's face.

Letter, July 2, 1877*

*This attack on Whistler was followed by a libel suit.

BERTRAND RUSSELL (Lord Russell)
(1872–1970)
British mathematician, philosopher*

Philosophical Essays (1903)

That man is the product of causes which had no provision of the end they were achieving; that his origin, his growth, his hopes, his fears, his loves and his beliefs, are but the outcome of accidental collocations of atoms; that no fire, no heroism, no intensity of thought and feeling, can preserve individual life beyond the grave; that all the labors of the ages, all devotions, all the inspiration, all the noonday brightness of human genius, are destined to extinction in the vast death of the solar system, and that the whole temple of Man's achievement must inevitably be buried beneath the debris of a universe in ruins—all these things, if not beyond dispute, are, yet so nearly certain, that no philosophy which rejects them can hope to stand. Only within the scaffolding of these truths, only on the firm foundation of unyielding despair can the soul's habitation henceforth be safely built.

To abandon the struggle for private happiness, to expel all eagerness of temporary desire, to burn with passion for eternal things— this is emancipation, and this is the free man's worship. And this liberation is effected by a contemplation of Fate, for Fate itself is subdued by this mind which leaves nothing to be purged by the purifying fire of Time.
                              "A Free Man's Worship"

Marriage and Morals (1929)

The psychology of adultery has been falsified by conventional morals, which assume, in monogamous countries, that attraction to one person cannot coexist with a serious affection for another. Everybody knows that this is untrue.

Love as a relation between men and women was ruined by the desire to make sure of the legitimacy of children.

To fear love is to fear life, and those who fear life are already three parts dead.

Morality in sexual situations, when it is free from superstition, consists essentially of respect

*All quotations dated 1903–1959 were confirmed by Lord Russell in a letter concluding, "I am glad to know that you are doing such a book as you mention and I like the selection of quotations from me."

for the other person, and unwillingness to use that person solely as a means of personal gratification, without regard to his or her desires.

The fact that an opinion has been widely held is no evidence that it is not utterly absurd; indeed in view of the silliness of the majority of mankind, a widespread belief is more often likely to be foolish than sensible.

The Conquest of Happiness (1930)

Boredom is a vital problem for the moralist, since at least half the sins of mankind are caused by the fear of it.
                              Ch. IV

Unpopular Essays (1950)

Empiricist Liberalism (which is not incompatible with *democratic* socialism) is the only philosophy which can be adopted by a man who, on the one hand, demands some scientific evidence for his beliefs, and, on the other hand, desires human happiness more than the prevalence of this or that party or creed.
                              "Philosophy and Politics"

Dogmatism and scepticism are both, in a sense, absolute philosophies; one is certain of knowing, the other of not knowing. What philosophy should dissipate is *certainty*, whether of knowledge or ignorance.
                              "Philosophy for Laymen"

If war no longer occupied men's thoughts and energies, we could within a generation, put an end to all serious poverty throughout the world.
                              "The Future of Mankind"

Portraits From Memory (1956)

It would now be technically possible to unify the world, abolish war and poverty altogether, if men desired their own happiness more than the misery of their enemies.

Education and the Good Life (1926)

The teacher should love his children better than his State or his Church; otherwise he is not an ideal teacher.
                              Pt. I, ch. 2

Men fear thought as they fear nothing else on earth—more than death. Thought is subversive, and revolutionary, destructive and terrible; thought is merciless to privilege, established institutions, and comfortable habits; thought is anarchic and lawless, indifferent to authority, careless to the well-tried wisdom of the ages. Thought looks into the pit of hell and is not afraid. . . . Thought is great and swift and free, the light of the world, and the chief glory of man.

But if thought is to become the possession of the many, and not the privilege of the few, we must have done with fear. It is fear that holds men back—fear that their cherished beliefs should prove delusions, fear lest the institutions by which they live should prove harmful, fear lest they themselves prove less worthy to the respect then they have supposed themselves to be.

Pt. II

Skeptical Essays (1928)

The fundamental argument for freedom of opinion is the doubtfulness of all our belief. If we certainly knew the truth, there would be something to be said for teaching it. . . . When the State intervenes to insure the indoctrination of some doctrine, it does so because there is no conclusive evidence in favor of that doctrine.

It is clear that thought is not free if the profession of certain opinions make it impossible to earn a living.

I am myself a dissenter from all known religions, and I hope that every kind of religious belief will die out. I do not believe that, on the balance, religious belief has been a force for good. . . . I regard it as belonging to the infancy of human reason, and to a stage of development which we are outgrowing.

XII

Understanding Human History

"Free thought" means thinking freely. . . . To be worthy of the name (freethinker) he must be free of two things: the force of tradition, and the tyranny of his own passions. No one is *completely* free from either, and in the measure of a man's emancipation he deserves to be called a free thinker.

Throughout a period of about 1200 years every Christian country in Europe condemned free thinkers to be burned at the stake. In Mohammedan countries . . . they were subject to abhorrence to the mob.

[F]or even now a *known* freethinker suffers serious disabilities, and has more difficulties making a living than the man who is reputed to accept the teachings of the Church.

God and Satan alike are essentially human figures, the one a projection of ourselves, the other of our enemies.

That they [the dogmas of religion] do little harm is not true. Opposition to birth control makes it impossible to solve the population problem and therefore postpones indefinitely all chance of world peace.

Practically all philosophers of any intellectual eminence are openly or secretly freethinkers.

The American Revolution . . . was led by freethinkers; Washington and Adams, just as much as Jefferson, rejected the orthodoxy that most of their followers accepted.

Heretical views arise when the truth is uncertain, and it is only when the truth is uncertain that censorship is invoked. . . . [I]t is difficult to find anything really certain outside the realm of pure mathematics and facts of history and geography.

"The Value of Free Thought"

Mysticism and Logic (1925)

Mathematics possesses not only truth, but some supreme beauty—a beauty cold and austere, like that of sculpture.

IV

What I Believe (1925)

I do not pretend to be able to prove that there is no God. I equally cannot prove that Satan is a fiction. The Christian God may exist; so may the Gods of Olympus, or of ancient Egypt, or of Babylon. But no one of these hypotheses is more probable than any other: they lie outside the region of even probable knowledge, and therefore there is no reason to consider any of them.

I

The Autobiography of Bertrand Russell (1967)

Three passions, simple but overwhelmingly strong, have governed my life: the longing for love, the search for knowledge, and unbearable pity for the suffering of mankind.

. . . the whole world of loneliness, poverty, and pain make a mockery of what human life should be.

Prologue

Man, even if he does not commit scientific suicide, will perish ultimately through the failure of water or air or warmth. It is difficult to believe that Omnipotence needed so vast a setting for so small and transitory a result.

Apart from the minuteness and brevity of the human species, I cannot feel that it is a worthy climax to such an enormous prelude.

"The Faith of a Rationalist," BBC broadcast, 1953

1. Do not feel certain of anything.

5. Have no respect for the authority of others, for there are always contrary authorities to be found.

6. Do not use power to suppress opinions you think pernicious, for if you do the opinions will suppress you.

7. Do not fear to be eccentric in opinion, for every opinion now accepted was once eccentric.
"The Ten Commandments," *The Independent*, 1965

The scientific attitude of mind involves a sweeping away of all other desires in the interest of the desire to know—it involves supression of hopes and fears, loves and hates, and the whole subjective emotional life, until we become subdued to the material, without bias, without any wish except to see it as it is, and without any belief that what it is must be determined by some relation, positive or negative, to what we should like it to be or to what we can easily imagine it to be.
"The Place of Science in a Liberal Education," *The New Statesman*, May 24, 1930

The argument that there must be a First Cause is one that cannot have any validity. . . . If anything must have a cause, then God must have a cause. If there can be anything without a cause, it may just as well be the world as God.

Science . . . has forced its way step by step against the Christian religion, against the churches, and against the opposition of the old precepts. Science can help us to get over this craven fear in which mankind has lived for so many generations.
Address, "Why I Am Not a Christian," Battersea Town Hall, March 6, 1927

The first dogma which I came to disbelieve was that of free will. It seemed to me that all notions of matter were determined by the laws of dynamics and could not therefore be influenced by human wills.

The basis of international anarchy is man's proneness to fear and hatred. This is also the basis of economic disputes; for the love of power, which is at their root, is generally an embodiment of fear. Men desire to be in control because they are afraid that the control of others will be used unjustly to their detriment. The same thing applies to the field of sexual morals: the power of husbands over wives and wives over husbands, which is conferred by the law, is derived from fear of the loss of possession.
Contribution, *Living Philosophies* (1931)

I admit that the love of God, if there were a God, would make it possible for human beings to be better than is possible in a Godless world.
Letter to Lowes Dickinson, September 22, 1904

ONLY PROTEST GIVES A HOPE OF LIFE.
Broadside, written for Trafalgar Square Meeting, Cuban missile crisis; printed in *Newsweek*, October 27, 1969

Patriotism is the willingness to kill and be killed for trivial reasons.

My own view of religion is that of Lucretius. I regard it as disease born of fear and as a source of untold misery.

There is therefore no escape from the choice that lies before us: Shall we renounce war, or shall we bring our species to an end?
These quotations, attributed to Russell, appeared after 1970 in the *New York Times*, *Saturday Review*, and *The Nation*

GEORGE W. RUSSELL
(1867–1935)
Irish poet, artist, essayist

The National Being (1917)

We have no more a real democracy in the world today. Democracy in politics has in no country led to democracy in its economic life. We still have autocracy in industry as firmly seated on its throne as theocratic kings ruling in the name of a god, or aristocracy ruling by military power; and the forces represented by these twain, superseded by the autocrats of industry, have become the allies of the power which took their place of pride. Religion and rank . . . are most often courtiers of Mammon and support him on his throne.

Race hatred is the cheapest and basest of all national passions, and it is the nature of hatred, as it is the nature of love, to change us into the likeness of that which we contemplate. We grow nobly like what we adore, and ignobly like what we hate. . . . All hatreds long persisted in bringing us to every baseness for which we hated others.

Nations hate other nations for the evil which is in themselves.

A Nation is dead where men acknowledge only conventions. We must find out truth for ourselves.

DONATIEN ALPHONSE FRANÇOIS COMTE DE SADE
(commonly called Marquis)
(1740–1814)
French writer*

La Philosophie dans le boudoir (1795)

Murder . . . like all destruction, is one of the first laws of nature.

Histoire de Juliette, ou les Prospérités du vice (1797)

Cruelty . . . is one of the most natural feelings of man, one of the sweetest inclinations, one of the most intense he has received from nature.**

No matter how this may shock mankind, the duty of philosophy is to say everything.

La Nouvelle Justine, ou les Malheurs de la vertu (1795)

In an absolutely corrupt age, such as the one we are living in, the safest course is to do as the others do.

It is infinitely better to take the side of the wicked who prosper than of the righteous who fail.

SA'DĪ (Musharrif-uddīn)
(c.1184–1291)
Persian poet

Gullistan [Rose Garden] (c. 1258)

Poverty borders on denial of God.

Ch. 7

---

*Although the *Britannica*, 11th ed., calls Sade a "licentious writer," Apollinaire paid tribute to him as "the freest mind that ever lived."
**This, and the three following quotations were used by the prosecution in the trial of Sade's publisher in 1956. Quotations, not the entire books, were the prosecution's main evidence.

Learning is the weapon with which Satan is combatted.

Ch. 8, maxim 44

CARL SAGAN
(1934–   )
American scientist

The Dragons of Eden (1977)

Civilization develops not from Abel, but from Cain the murderer. The very word "civilization" derives from the Latin word for city.

Ch. IV

Sceptical scrutiny is the means, in both science and religion, by which deep thoughts can be winnowed from deep nonsense.

Quoted in *Time,* October 20, 1980

ANTOINE DE SAINT-EXUPÉRY
(1900–1944)
French writer

Wind, Sand, and Stars (1939)

Let a man in a garret but burn with enough intensity and he will set fire to the whole world.

I know of but one freedom and that is the freedom of the mind.

Truth, for any man, is that which makes him a man.

LOUIS ANTOINE LÉON DE SAINT-JUST
(1767–guillotined 1794)
French revolutionary

It is never possible to rule innocently.

Address, National Convention, November 13, 1792, condemning Louis XVI

You must punish not only the traitors but also the indifferent.

Quoted in Djilas, *The New Class*

CLAUDE HENRI DE ROUVROY, COMTE DE SAINT-SIMON
(1760–1825)
Founder of French Socialism

Exposition de la doctrine de St. Simon (pub. posthumously 1829)

To each according to his capacity.
To each capacity according to his work.

cf. Marx

Nouveau christianisme [*New Christianity*] (1825, tr. Ronald Sanders)

God said: *All men must behave as brothers toward one another;* this sublime principle contains everything that is divine in the Christian religion.

One must make a distinction between what God Himself said and what the clergy has said in His name.

CHARLES AUGUSTIN SAINTE-BEUVE
(1804–1869)
French critic

If I had a device it would be the True, the True only, leaving the Beautiful and the Good to settle matters afterwards as best they could.
Letter to Durey, December 9, 1865

ANDREI DMITRIEVICH SAKHAROV
(1921–   )
Russian nuclear physicist

Progress, Coexistence, and Intellectual Freedom (secretly circulated in Moscow, 1968, tr. *N.Y. Times,* July 22, 1968)

The division of mankind threatens it with destruction. Civilization is imperiled by: a universal thermonuclear war, catastrophic hunger for most of mankind, stupefaction from the narcotic of "mass culture" and bureaucraticized dogmatism, a spreading mass of myths that put entire peoples and continents under the power of cruel and treacherous demagogues.
Ch. 1

Intellectual freedom is essential to human society. . . . Freedom of thought is the only guarantee against an infection of people by mass myths, which, in the hands of treacherous hypocrites and demagogues, can be transformed into bloody dictatorships.
Ch. 2

SALADIN (Salāh-al-Dīn)
(1138–1193)
First Aryubite Sultan of Egypt

Hold always the sign of blood in horror. Take care not to shed or stain thyself with it, for the mark is never washed away.
Advice to his son, Dhahir, on appointment as governor of Aleppo

SALLUST (Gaius Sallustius Crispus)
(86–34 B.C.)
First great Roman historian

The War with Catiline (c. 40 B.C.)

All men who would surpass the other animals should do their utmost not to go through life unheralded like the brutes whom nature made to face the ground, obedient to their bellies.
I

In public life, instead of modesty, incorruptibility, and honesty—shamefulness, bribery and rapacity hold sway.
III

It is the nature of ambition to make men liars and cheaters, to hide the truth in their breasts, and show, like jugglers, another thing in their mouths, to cut all friendships and enmities to the measure of their own interest, and to make a good countenance without the help of good will.
X

No mortal man has ever served at the same time his passions and his best interests.

All men who deliberate on controversial matters, should be free from hate, friendship, anger and pity.
LI

History

Few men desire liberty; most men wish only for a just master.
IV

They are content to pay so great a price as their own servitude to purchase dominion over others.
Fragment (published by Abraham Cowley)

GAETANO SALVEMINI
(1873–1957)
Italian professor of history

Prelude to World War II (1953)

Impartiality is either a delusion of the simple-minded, a banner of the opportunist, or the boast of the dishonest. Nobody is entitled to be unbiased toward truth or falsehood.
Preface

PAUL A. SAMUELSON
(1915–   )
American economist, Nobel Prize 1970

Profit is today a fighting word. Profits are the lifeblood of the economic system, the magic elixir upon which progress and all good things depend ultimately. But one man's lifeblood is another man's cancer.

> Address, Forum of European and American Economists, Harvard, quoted in *Time*, August 16, 1976

GEORGE SAND (Mme. Amandine Aurore Lucile Dudevant, née Dupin)
(1804–1876)
French writer*

Mauprat (1837)

We cannot tear out a single page of our life, but we can throw the whole book in the fire.

Jacques (1834)

No human creature can give orders to love.

To distrust the *flesh* cannot be good and useful except to those who are all *flesh*.

The magnet embraces the iron, the animals come together by the difference of sex. . . . Man alone regards this miracle which takes place simultaneously in his soul and his body as a miserable necessity, and he speaks of it with distrust, with irony, or with shame.

The result of this fashion of separating the spirit from the flesh is that it has necessitated convents and brothels.

> Quoted in Gamaliel Bradford's biography (January 1929)

Simplicity is the essence of the great, the true, and the beautiful in art.

> Attributed

CARL SANDBURG
(1878–1967)
American poet, Socialist

"The People, Yes" (1936)

Tell him too much money has killed men and left them dead years before burial:

---

* ". . . the most prolific authoress in the history of literature."—*Britannica*, 11th ed.

and quest of lucre beyond a few easy needs
has twisted good enough men
sometimes into dry thwarted worms.
9

When have people been half as rotten as what the
panderers to the people dangle before crowds?
20

Sometime they'll give a war and nobody will come.
23

To those who had ordered them to death
one of them said:
"We die because the people are asleep
and you will die because the people will awaken."
58

"Fog" (1916)

The fog comes
on little cat feet.

"Chicago" (1916)

Hog butcher for the world,
Tool maker, stacker of wheat,
Player with railroads and the nation's freight handler;
Stormy, husky, brawling,
City of big shoulders.

"Grass" (1918)

Pile the bodies high at Austerlitz and Waterloo,
Shovel them under and let me work—
I am the grass; I cover all.

"Cool Tombs" (1918)

When Abraham Lincoln was shoveled into the tombs,
he forgot the copperheads and the assassin . . .
in the dust, in the cool tombs.

"The Liars" (1919)

A liar lies to the nations.
A liar lies to the people.
A liar takes the blood of the people
And drinks this blood with a laugh and a lie.

EDWARD T. SANFORD
(1865–1930)
U.S. Supreme Court Justice

Freedom of speech and of the press do not protect disturbances to the public peace or the attempt to subvert the government. It does not protect publications or teachings which tend to subvert or imperil the government, or to impede or hinder it in the performance of its governmental duties. It does not protect publications prompting the overthrow of the government by force.
>Majority opinion, Gitlow v. The People of New York (1924)

MARGARET SANGER
(1884–1966)
Founder of Planned Parenthood Federation

Birth control.
>Coined phrase, first used in Woman Rebel (1914)

Love and attraction between men and women, in many cases, is the very finest relationship; it has nothing to do with bearing a child. That's secondary many, many times.
>TV Interview with Mike Wallace, 1958

Birth control, family planning and population limitation are most important in any effort to bring real peace into the world.
>Letter to the N.Y. Times, January 3, 1960

No woman can call herself free who does not own or control her body. No woman can call herself free until she can choose consciously whether she will or will not be a mother.
>Contribution, Parade, December 1, 1963

SANKARA ACHARYA
(c. 769–820)
Hindu theologian

Wisdom is not acquired save as the result of investigation.
>Quoted in Britannica, 11th ed.

GEORGE SANTAYANA
(1863–1952)
Spanish-born American skeptical philosopher

The Life of Reason (1905–1906)

Fanaticism consists in redoubling your effort when you have forgotten your aim.
>Introduction

Those who cannot remember the past are condemned to repeat it.

The true contrast between science and myth is more nearly touched when we say that science alone is capable of verification.

History is always written wrong, and so always needs to be rewritten.

Christianity persecuted, tortured, and burned. Like a hound it tracked the very scent of heresy. It kindled wars, and nursed furious hatreds and ambitions. It sanctified, quite like Mohammedism, extermination and tyranny. All this would have been impossible if, like Buddhism, it had looked only for peace and the liberation of souls. It looked beyond; it dreamt of infinite blisses and crowns it should be crowned with before an electrified universe and an applauding God. . . . Buddhism had tried to quiet a sick world with anesthetics; Christianity sought to purge it with fire.
>"Reason in Science"

That life is worth living is the most necessary of assumptions, and, were it not assumed, the most impossible of conclusions.

Character is the basis of happiness and happiness the sanction of character.
>"Reason in Common Sense"

The fact of having been born is a bad augury for immortality.

That fear first created the gods is perhaps as true as anything so brief could be on so great a subject.

Religions do not disappear when they are discredited; it is requisite that they should be replaced.

In spite of centuries wasted in preaching God's omnipotence, his omnipotence is contradicted by every Christian judgment and every Christian prayer.

In endowing us with memory, nature has revealed to us a truth utterly unimaginable to the unreflective creation, the truth of immortality.

The most ideal human passion is love, which is also the most absolute and animal and one of the most ephemeral.

It is easier to make a saint out of a libertine than out of a prig.

"Reason in Religion"

The life of reason is no fair reproduction of the universe, but the expression of man alone.

He who is not childless goes down to his grave in peace.

To fight is a radical instinct; if men have nothing else to fight over they will fight over words, fancies, or women, or they will fight because they dislike each other's looks, or because they have met walking in opposite directions. To knock a thing down, especially if it is cocked at an arrogant angle, is a deep delight to the blood. To fight for a reason and in a calculating spirit is something your true warrior despises.

To call war the soil of courage and virtue is like calling debauchery the soil of love.

Most men's conscience, habits, and opinions are borrowed from convention and gather continually comforting assurances from the same social consensus that originally suggested them.

The human race, in its intellectual life, is organized like the bees: the masculine soul is a worker, sexually atrophied, and essentially dedicated to impersonal and universal arts; the feminine is queen, infinitely fertile, omnipresent in its brooding industry, but passive and abounding in intuitions without method and passions without justice.

Friendship with a woman is therefore apt to be more or less than friendship; less, because there is no intellectual parity; more, because (even when the relation remains wholly dispassionate, as in respect to old ladies) there is something mysterious and oracular about a woman's mind which inspires a certain deference and puts it out of the question to judge what she says by masculine standards.

There can be no philosophic interest in disguising the animal basis of love, or in denying its spiritual sublimations, since all life is animal in its origin and spiritual in its possible fruits.

Not to believe in love is a great sign of dullness.

"Reason in Society"

The subject matter of art is life, life as it actually is; but the function of art is to make life better.

As to the word "God," all mutual understanding is impossible. It is a floating literary symbol, with a value which, if we define it scientifically, becomes quite algebraic.

Men have feverishly conceived a heaven only to find it insipid, and a hell to find it ridiculous.

"Reason in Art"

The Sense of Beauty (1896)

The sense of beauty has a more important place in life than aesthetic theory has ever taken in philosophy.

To feel beauty is a better thing than to understand how we come to feel it. To have imagination and taste, to love the best, to be carried by the contemplation of nature to a vivid faith in the ideal, all this is more, a great deal more, than any science can hope to be.

Introduction

The most economical arrangement which can be conceived, would be the one by which only the one female best fitted to bear offspring to a male should arouse his desire, and only so many times as it was well she should grow pregnant, thus leaving his energy and attention free at all other times to exercise the other faculties of his nature.

If this ideal had been reached, the instinct, like all those perfectly adjusted, would tend to become unconscious; and we should miss those secondary effects with which we are exclusively concerned in aesthetics. For it is precisely from the waste, from the radiation of the sexual passion, that beauty borrows warmth. . . . The capacity to love gives our contemplation that glow without which it might often fail to manifest beauty; and the whole sentimental side of our aesthetic sensibility—without which it would be perceptive and mathematical rather than aesthetic—is due to our sexual organization remotely stirred.

But sex endows the individual with a dumb and powerful instinct, which carries his body and soul continually toward another; makes it one of the dearest employments of his life to select and pursue a companion, and joins to possession the keenest pleasure, to rivalry the fiercest rage, and to solitude an eternal melancholy.

What more would be needed to suffuse the world with the deepest meaning and beauty?

Part II, 13

Love makes us poets and the approach of death should make us philosophers.

Part VI, 59

Beauty [is] the clearest Manifestation of perfection and the best evidence of its possibility. If perfection is, as it should be, the ultimate justification of being, we may understand the ground of the moral dignity of beauty.

Conclusion

Scepticism and Animal Faith (1923)

Scepticism is the chastity of the intellect, and it is shameful to surrender it too soon or to the first comer: there is nobility in preserving it coolly and proudly through a long youth, until at last, in the ripeness of instinct and discretion, it can be safely exchanged for fidelity and happiness.

Ch. IX

Soliloquies in England (1922)

My atheism, like that of Spinoza, is true piety toward the universe and denies only gods fashioned by man in their own image, to be servants of their human interests; and that even in this denial I am no rude iconoclast, but full of secret sympathy with the impulses of idolators.

"On My Friendly Critics"

There is no sure cure for birth and death save to enjoy the interval.

"War Shrines"

Some Turns of Thought in Modern Philosophy (1933)

If all the arts aspire to the condition of music, all the sciences aspire to the condition of mathematics.

III

Winds of Doctrine (1913)

The present age is a critical one. . . . We still love monarchy and aristocracy. . . . On the other hand the shell of Christendom is broken. The unconquerable mind of the East, the pagan past, the industrial socialist future confront it with their equal authority. Our whole life and mind is saturated with the slow upward filtration of a new spirit—that of emancipated, atheistic, international democracy.

Love must be spontaneous to be a spiritual bond in the beginning, and it must remain spontaneous if it is to remain spiritual . . . and those of us who do not believe in the possibility of free love ought to declare frankly that we do not, at bottom, believe in the possibility of freedom.

Interpretation of Poetry and Religion (1924)

The absence of religion in Shakespeare was a sign of his good sense; that a healthy instinct kept his attention within the sublunary world; and that he was in that respect superior to Homer and to Dante. . . . Shakespeare, however, is remarkable among the greater poets for being without a philosophy and without a religion. In his drama there is no fixed conception of any forces, natural or moral, dominating and transcending our mortal energies.

"The Absence of Religion in Shakespeare"

The Last Puritan (1936)

Originally . . . Christianity was partly poetry and partly delusion. The Roman Church clings to both parts equally; Protestantism has kept the delusion and destroyed the poetry; and only the Anglican tradition is capable of preserving the poetry, while sweeping the delusion away.

Pt. IV, ch. XI

Obiter Scripta (1936)

Man is a social rather than a political animal; he can exist without a government.

One of the assumptions of the pre-intelligent and pre-social soul is that it is immortal.

Words are weapons, and it is dangerous in speculation, as in politics, to borrow them from our enemies.

Persons and Places

It would repel me less to be a hangman than a soldier, because the one is obliged to put to death only criminals sentenced by the law, but the other kills honest men who like himself bathe in innocent blood at the bidding of some superior.

Vol. I (1944), ch. 2

Liberalism, Protestantism, Judaism, positivism all have the same ultimate aim and standard. It is prosperity, or as Lutheran theologians put it, union with God at our level; not at God's level. The thing all these schools detest is the ideal of union with God at God's level, proper to asceticism, mysticism, Platonism, and pure intelligence, which insist on seeing things under the form of truth and eternity. You must be content, they say, to see things under the form of time, of appearance, and of feeling.

Words are at least the tombs of ideas.
Vol. I, ch. 14

Catholicism is paganism spiritualized: . . . Religion is valid poetry infused into a common life. It is not revelation truer than perception or than science.
Vol. III (1953), ch. 5, "My Host the World"

The Ethics of Spinoza (1910)

The Bible is literature, not dogma.

Perhaps the only true dignity of man is his capacity to despise himself.
Introduction

It is not worldly ecclesiastics that kindle the fires of persecution, but mystics who think they hear the voice of God.
Contribution, *New Republic*, January 15, 1916

A child educated only at school is an uneducated child.
"Why I Am Not a Marxist," *Modern Monthly*

Music is essentially useless, as life is.
Quoted in *N.Y. Times*, April 23, 1967

SAON OF ACANTHUS
Ancient Greek poet

Asleep, not dead; a good man never dies.
Greek Anthology, tr. J.A. Symonds

SAPPHO OF LESBOS
(c. 612 B.C.)
Greek poet*

I loved thee once, Athis, long ago.

_____
*Known as "The Tenth Muse." "In antiquity her fame rivaled that of Homer."—*Britannica*, 11th ed. "Beyond all question and comparison the very greatest poet that ever lived."—Swinburne.

What is beautiful is good,
And who is good will soon be beautiful.

I know that in this world man cannot have the best; yet to pray for a part of what was once shared is better than to forget it.
Fragments

Someone, I tell you,
will remember us.
We are oppressed by
fears of oblivion
yet are always saved
by judgment of good men.
Quoted in *A Book of Women Poets from Antiquity*

JOHN SINGER SARGENT
(1856–1925)
American painter

Portrait painting is a pimp's profession.
Quoted in *Time*, April 17, 1964

JEAN-PAUL SARTRE
(1905–1980)
French writer, existentialist

Existentialism (1947)

The existentialist says at once that man is anguish.

There is no God and no prevenient design which can adapt the world and all its possibilities to my will. When Descartes said "Conquer yourself rather than the world" what he meant was, at bottom, the same thing.

Thus, there is no human nature, because there is no God to have a conception of it. Man simply is. . . . Man is nothing else but that which he makes of himself. That is the first principle of existentialism.

Nothing will be changed if God does not exist; we will rediscover the same norms of honesty, progress and humanity.

Man is condemned to be free. Condemned, because he did not create himself, yet is nevertheless at liberty, and from the moment he is thrown into this world he is responsible for everything he does.

Dostoyefsky said, "If God did not exist, everything would be possible." That is the very starting point of existentialism. Indeed, everything is permissible if God does not exist, and as a result man is forlorn, because neither within him or without does he find anything to cling to.

The Devil and the Good Lord (1951)

When the rich wage war it is the poor who die.

Les Mains sales [*The Dirty Hands*] (1948)

Hoederer: I'll lie when I must. . . . I wasn't the one who invented lying. It grew out of a society divided into classes, and each one of us has inherited it from birth. We shall not abolish lying by refusing to tell lies, but by using every means at hand to abolish classes.

Act V

Anti-Semite and Jew (1948)

There is no example of an anti-Semite claiming individual superiority over the Jews.

Anti-Semitism, in a word, is fear of man's fate. The anti-Semite is the man who wants to be a pitiless stone, a furious torrent, devastating lightning: in short, anything but a man.

To have accepted mediocrity does not mean to be humble, or even modest. Exactly the opposite in fact. The mediocre have their own passionate price, and anti-Semitism is an attempt to give value to mediocrity for its own sake, to create an elite of the mediocre.

If God exists, man does not exist; if man exists, God does not exist.

Quoted, CBS-TV, November 16, 1976

A writer must refuse to allow himself to be transformed into an institution.

On refusing the Nobel Prize, 1964; quoted in obituary, *Newsweek*, April 28, 1980

If you begin by saying, "Thou shalt not lie," there is no longer any possibility of political action.

Quoted in obituary, *Time*, April 28, 1980

Men are more easily taken in, more easily comic. Male society is a comic society. Women, as oppressed people, are almost more free in a certain sense than men. Women have fewer principles dictating their behavior, they are more disrespectful.

Quoted in obituary, *In These Times*, April 30, 1980

Existence precedes essence.

Quoted in obituary, *N.Y. Times*, April 16, 1980

(Johann Christoph) FRIEDRICH VON SCHILLER
(1759–1805)
German dramatist, poet, historian

Die Jungfrau von Orleans [*Joan of Arc*] (1801)

Against stupidity the very gods fight in vain.

Act III, sc. vi

Resignation (1786)

I too was born in Arcadia.

Demetrius (1798)

Sense has ever been centered in the few. . . . Votes should be weighed, not counted. The State must sooner or later be wrecked where the majority rules and ignorance decides.

I

Fiasco (1783)

Art is the right hand of Nature. The latter has given us only being, the former has made us men.

II

Wallenstein's Camp (1798)

The General's frequent saying was: live and let live.

Act VI

Wallenstein's Death (1798)

Man of destiny.

Act III

The World's Wise Men (1793)

Meanwhile, until philosophy maintains the working of the world, it [nature] maintains the machinery through hunger and love.

Essays, Aesthetical and Philosophical (1793)

Physical beauty is the sign of an interior beauty, a spiritual and moral beauty, which is the basis, the principle, and the unity of the beautiful.

Introduction

Love is at the same time the most generous and the most egotistical thing in nature; the most generous because it receives nothing and gives all—pure mind being only able to give and not receive; the most egotistical, for that which he seeks in the subject, that which he enjoys in it, is himself and never anything else.

"On Dignity"

Philosophical Letters

Egotism erects its center in itself; love places it out of itself in the axis of the universal whole. Love aims at unity, egotism at solitude. Love is the citizen ruler of a flourishing republic, egotism is a despot in a devastated creation.

IV, "Sacrifice"

World history is the world's judgment.
Inaugural lecture as professor of history, Jena, 1789

Dare to be wrong and to dream.
Quoted by Turgenev in dedicating a book to Flaubert

(August) WILHELM SCHLEGEL
(1767–1845)
German poet

Lectures (1807–1808)

Art cannot exist without nature, and man can give nothing to his fellow-man but himself.

Religion is the root of human existence.
"Democratic Art and Literature"

ARTHUR M. SCHLESINGER, JR.
(1917–   )
American educator, historian

Anti-intellectualism has long been the anti-Semitism of the businessman.
Contribution, *Partisan Review*, March 4, 1953

Those who are convinced they have a monopoly on The Truth always feel that they are only saving the world when they slaughter the heretics.

The only certainty in an absolute system is the certainty of absolute abuse. Injustice and criminality are inherent in a system of totalitarian dictatorship.
Address to the Indian Council of World Affairs, 1962

ARTHUR SCHOPENHAUER
(1788–1860)
German philosopher

The World as Will and Idea (1819)

Only through history does a nation become completely conscious of itself. Accordingly, history is to be regarded as the national conscience of the human race. . . . [O]nly by virtue of it does the human race come to be a whole, come to be a humanity. This is the true value of history.

But life is short and truth works far and lives long: let us speak the truth.

Bk. III

Life swings like a pendulum backward and forward between pain and boredom.

To desire immortality is to desire the perpetuation of a great mistake.

The greatest intellectual capacities are only found in connection with a vehement and passionate will.

Eros is the first, the creator, the principle from which all things proceed.

The relation of the sexes . . .is really the invisible central point of all action and conduct. . . . It is the cause of war and the end of peace; the basis of what is serious, and the aim of the jest; the inexhaustible source of wit, the key to all illusions, and the meaning of all mysterious hints.

Necessity is the constant scourge of the lower orders; ennui that of the higher classes.

Animals learn death first at the moment of death; . . . man approaches death with the knowledge it is closer every hour, and this creates a feeling of uncertainty over his life, even for him who forgets in the business of life that annihilation is awaiting him. It is for this reason chiefly that we have philosophy and religion.

Bk. IV

Supplements to the World as Will and Idea (ed. Richard Taylor)

With the exception of man, no being wonders at his own existence.

The majority of men . . . are not capable of thinking, but only of believing, and . . . are not accessible to reason, but only to authority.

The power by virtue of which Christianity was able to overcome first Judaism, and then the heathenism of Greece and Rome, lies solely in its pessimism, in the confession that our state is both wretched and sinful, while Judaism and heathenism were optimistic.

No truth is more certain than this, that all that happens, be it small or great, happens with absolute necessity.

For all love, however ethereally it may bear itself, is rooted in the sexual impulse alone, nay, it absolutely is only a more definitely determined, specialized, and indeed in the striot est sense, individualized sexual impulse.

The sexual impulse . . . next to the love of life . . . shows itself the strongest and most powerful of motives, constantly lays claim to half the powers and thoughts of the younger portion of mankind, to the ultimate goal of almost all human efforts, interrupts the most serious occupations every hour, sometimes embarrasses for a while even the greatest minds, does not hesitate to intrude with its trash, interfering with the negotiations of statesmen and the investigations of men of learning, knowns how to slip its love letters and locks of hair even into ministerial portfolios and philosophical manuscripts, and no less devises daily the most entangled and the worst actions, destroys the most valuable relationships, breaks the firmest bond, demands the sacrifice sometimes of life or health, sometimes of wealth, rank, and happiness, nay, robs those who are otherwise honest of all conscience, makes those who have hitherto been faithful, traitors; accordingly on the whole, appears as a malevolent demon that strives to pervert, confuse and overthrow everything.

That which presents itself to the individual consciousness as sexual impulse in general, without being directed toward a definite individual of the other sex, is in itself, and apart from the phenomenon, simply the will to live.

Egoism is so deeply rooted a quality of all individuals in general, that in order to rouse the activity of an individual being, egotistical ends are the only ones upon which we count with certainty.

I may here express my opinion in passing that the white color of the skin is not natural to man, but that by nature he has a black or brown skin, like our forefathers the Hindus; that consequently a white man has never originally sprung from the womb of nature, and that thus there is no such thing as a white race, much as this is talked of, but every white man is a faded or bleached one.

Every lover, after the ultimate consummation of the great work, finds himself cheated; for the illusion has vanished by means of which the individual was here the dupe of the species.

Happy marriages are well known to be rare; just because it lies in the nature of marriage that its chief end is not the present but the coming generation.

In the case of man the extinction of the generative power shows that the individual approaches death.

The life of a man, with its endless care, want, and suffering, is to be regarded as the explanation and paraphrase of the act of generation, i.e., the decided assertion of the will to live; and further, it is also due to this that he owes to nature the debt of death, and thinks with anxiety of this debt. Is this not evidence of the fact that our existence involves guilt?

Death is the true inspiring genius, or the muse of philosophy. . . . Indeed, without death man would scarcely philosophize.

To mourn for the time when one will be no more is just as absurd as it would be to mourn over the time when as yet one was not.

Death is the great reprimand which the will to live, or more especially the egoism which is essential to this, receives through the course of nature; and it may be conceived of as a punishment for our existence. It is the painful loosing of the knot which the act of generation had tied with sensual pleasure, the violent destruction coming from without of the fundamental error of our nature: the great disillusion.

The truth [is] that we have not to rejoice but rather to mourn at the existence of the world; that non-existence would be preferable to its existence.

The chief source of the serious evils which affect man is man himself: *homo homini lupus.*

The capacity for feeling pain increases with knowledge. . . . [A] degree which is the higher the more intelligent the man is.

Optimism is irreconcilable with Christianity.

If the world were a paradise of luxury and ease, a land flowing with milk and honey, where every Jack obtained his Jill at once and without any difficulty, men would either die of boredom or hang themselves; or there would be war, massacre, and murders; so that in the end mankind would inflict more suffering on itself than it has now to accept at the hands of Nature.

If children were brought into the world by an act of pure reason alone, would the human race continue to exist? Would not a man rather have so much sympathy with the coming generation as to spare it the burden of existence, or at any rate not to take it upon himself to impose that burden upon it in cold blood.

But that a God like Jehovah should have created the world of misery and woe, out of pure caprice, and because he enjoyed doing it, and should then have clapped his hands in praise of his work, and declared everything to be good—that will not do at all! In its explanation of the origin of the world Judaism is inferior to any other form of religious doctrine professed by a civilized nation; and it is quite in keeping with this that it is the only one which presents no trace whatever of any belief in the immortality of the soul.

Unrest is the mark of existence.

Human life must be some kind of mistake.

The only freedom that exists is of a metaphysical character. In the physical world freedom is an impossibility.

Man is the only animal which causes pain to others without any further purpose than just to cause it.

The world is itself the Last Judgment on it.

All disinterested kindness is inexplicable.

Hence, it will be found that the fundamental fault of the female character is that it has *no sense of justice*. This is mainly due to the fact, already mentioned, that women are defective in the power of reasoning and deliberation; but it is also traceable to the position which Nature has assigned to them as the weaker sex. They are dependent not upon strength, but upon craft, and hence their instinctive capacity for cunning, and their incredible tendency to say what is not true.

For the innate rule that governs women's conduct, though it is secret and unformulated . . . is this: We are justified in deceiving those who think they have acquired rights over the species but pay little attention to the individual, that is, to us. The constitution, and therefore, the welfare of the species has been placed in our hands and committed to our care through the control we obtain over the next generation, which proceeds from us.

It is only the man whose intellect is clouded by his sexual impulses that could give the name of *the fair sex* to that undersized, narrow-shouldered, broad-hipped, and short-legged race, for the whole beauty of sex is bound up with this impulse. Instead of calling them beautiful, there would be more warrant for describing woman as the unaesthetic sex. Neither for music, nor for poetry, nor for fine art have they really and truly any sense of susceptibility; it is mere mockery if they make a pretence of it in order to assist their endeavor to please.

There is no use arguing about polygamy; it must be taken as *de facto* existing everywhere, and the only question is how it shall be regulated.

We all live, at any rate for a time, and most of us always, in polygamy. And so, since every man needs many women, there is nothing fairer than to allow him, nay, to make it incumbent upon him, to provide for many women. This will reduce woman to her true and natural position as a subordinate being; and the *lady*—that monster of European civilization and Teutonico-Christian stupidity—will disappear from the world, leaving only *women*, but no more *unhappy women*, of which Europe is full.

The Christian System

Mankind cannot get on without a certain amount of absurdity.

It is only Protestants, with their obstinate belief in the Bible, who cannot be induced to give up external punishment in hell.

The Art of Controversy (tr. 1896)

To be alone is the fate of all great minds—a fate deplored at times, but still always chosen as the less grievous of two evils.
"Aphorisms"

Parerga und Paralipomena (1851)

Without women, the beginning of our life would be helpless, the middle devoid of pleasure, and the end, of consolation.
"Of Women," quoting Jouy

There is no absurdity so palpable but that it may be firmly planted in the human head, if only you begin to inculcate it before the age of five, by constantly repeating it with an air of great solemnity.

Hatred comes from the heart; contempt from the head; and neither feeling is quite within our control.
"Psychological Observations"

They tell us that suicide is the greatest piece of cowardice; . . . that suicide is *wrong*; when it is quite obvious that there is nothing in the world to which every man has a more unassailable title than to his own life and person.
"On Suicide"

The Art of Literature (tr. 1891)

No difference of rank, position, or birth, is so great as the gulf which separates the countless millions who use their head only in the service of their belly, in other words, look upon it as an instrument of the will, and those very few and rare persons who have the courage to say: No! it is too good for that, my head shall be active in its own service; it shall try to comprehend the wondrous and varied spectacle of this world, and then reproduce it in some form, whether as art or as literature, that may answer to my character as an individual.
"On Genius"

Counsels and Maxims (tr. 1892)

The mission of these great minds is to guide mankind over the sea of error to the haven of truth—to draw it forth from the abysses of barbarous vulgarity up into the light of culture and refinement.
"Our Relations to Ourselves"

Religion: A Dialogue, etc. (tr. 1890)

Still, instead of trusting what their own minds tell them, men have as a rule a weakness for trusting others who pretend to supernatural sources of knowledge.

The bad thing about all religions is that, instead of being able to confess their allegorical nature, they have to conceal it; accordingly, they parade their doctrine in all seriousness as true *sensu proprio*, and as absurdities form an essential part of these doctrines, you have the great mischief of a continual fraud.
"The Christian System"

"Personality, or What a Man Is"

The two foes of human happiness are pain and boredom.

————

A man can surely do what he wills to do, but he cannot determine what he wills.
Quoted in Einstein, *Living Philosophies*

If God made the world, I would not be that God, for the misery of the world would break my heart.
Quoted in Noyes, *Views of Religion*

Prostitutes are human sacrifices on the altar of monogamy.

The sexual organs are the true seat of the will, of which the opposite pole is the brain.
Quoted in Simone de Beauvoir, *The Second Sex*

DANIEL SCHORR
(1916–   )
American journalist

The casual anarchy which we call our way of life.
CBS-TV, September 22, 1959

CARL SCHURZ
(1829–1906)
American journalist, statesman

Our country, right or wrong! When right, to be kept right; when wrong, to be put right.
Address, Anti-Imperialistic Conference, Chicago, October 17, 1899

ALBERT SCHWEITZER
(1875–1965)
Alsatian-born physician, organist, philosopher

Out of My Life and Thought (1949)

Late on the third day, at the very moment when, at sunset, we were making our way through a herd of hippopotamuses, there flashed through my mind, unforeseen and unsought, the phrase, "Reverence for Life." The iron door had yielded: the path in the thicket had become visible. Now I had found my way to the idea in which affirmation of world- and life-affirmation and ethics are contained side by side! Now I knew that the world-view of ethical world- and life-affirmation, together with the ideals of civilization, is founded in thought.

Ch. XIII

The Philosophy of Civilization (1923)

Humanitarianism consists in never sacrificing a human being to a purpose.

The tragedy of man is what dies inside himself while he still lives.

Pt. I

A man is truly ethical only when he obeys the compulsion to help all life which he is able to assist, and shrinks from injuring anything that lives.

The good conscience is an invention of the devil.

Reverence for life is the highest court of appeal.

Pt. II

The future of a civilization depends on our overcoming the meaninglessness and hopelessness which characterizes the thought of men today.
Quoted in *Albert Schweitzer: An Anthology* (1955)

ROSIKA SCHWIMMER
(1877–1948)
American pacifist, feminist

Women's rights, men's rights—human rights—all are threatened by the ever-present spectre of war so destructive now of human material and moral values as to render victory indistinguishable from defeat.
Address, Centennial Celebration, Seneca Falls Convention on Women's Rights, July 1948

C(harles) P(restwich) SCOTT
(1846–1932)
Editor, *Manchester Guardian*

The newspaper is of necessity something of a monopoly, and its first duty is to shun the temptations of monopoly. Its primary office is the gathering of news. At the peril of its soul it must see that the supply is not tainted.

Comment is free, but facts are sacred.
Editorial, May 6, 1926

SIR WALTER SCOTT
(1771–1832)
English poet, novelist

Old Mortality (1816)

Sound, sound the clarion, fill the fife!
  To all the sensual world proclaim,
One crowded hour of glorious life
  Is worth an age without a name.
    (Attributed to Anonymous) Ch. XXXVI

"The Lay of the Last Minstrel" (1805)

Breathes there the man, with soul so dead,
Who never to himself hath said,
This is my own, my native land!

VI, 1

E(dward) W(yllis) SCRIPPS
(1854–1926)
American press lord

Damned Old Crank (pub. posthumously 1951)

In America the press rules the country; it rules its politics, its religion, its social practices.

The press of this country is now and always has been so thoroughly dominated by the wealthy few of the country that it cannot be depended upon to give the great mass of the people that correct information concerning political, economical, and social subjects which it is necessary that the mass of people shall have, in order that they shall vote and in all ways act in the best way to protect themselves from the brutal force and the chicanery of the ruling and employing class.

PUBLIUS POMPONIUS SECUNDUS
(fl. c. 50 A.D.)
Roman general, poet

Hadrian: What is woman?
Secundus: Man's damnation, an insatiable beast, a ceaseless fight, a continual solicita-

tion, the shipwreck of man's virtue, the manacles of the human race. *

Fragment, quoted in *Tragicorum Romanorum Fragmenta* (1897)

JOHN SELDEN
(1584–1654)
English jurist, Oriental scholar

Table-Talk (pub. posthumously 1689)

Scrutamini scriptura. [Let us look at the scriptures.] These two words have undone the world.

"Bible, Scripture"

Ignorance of the law excuses no man; not that all men know the law, but because 'tis an excuse every man will plead, and no man can tell how to refute him.

"Law"

Marriage is nothing but a civil contract.

"Marriage"

Pleasure is nothing else but the intermission of pain.

"Pleasure"

LUCIUS ANNAEUS SENECA (the Elder)
(c. 54 B.C.–39 A.D.)
Spanish-born Roman rhetorician

Controversiae

Some laws, though unwritten, are more firmly established than all written laws.

I, 1

LUCIUS ANNAEUS SENECA (the Younger)
(c. 4 B.C.–65 A.D.)
Spanish-born Roman statesman, philosopher

Epistolae Morales

Freedom can not be bought for nothing. If you hold her precious, you must hold all else of little value.

Leisure without study is death.

Wisdom, above all else, is liberty.

---

*"Only a few lines of his work remain, some of which belong to the tragedy *Aeneas*."—*Britannica*, 11th ed., vol. xxiv.

The primary sign of a well-ordered mind is man's ability to remain in one place and linger in his own company.

We are more wicked together than separately. If you are forced to be in a crowd, then most of all you should withdraw into your self.

This is the reason we cannot complain of life: it keeps no one against his will.

It is folly to die for fear of dying.

We are mad, not only individually, but nationally. We check manslaughter and isolated murders; but what of war and the much vaunted crime of slaughtering whole peoples?

Live with men as if God saw you; converse with God as if men heard you.

Most powerful is he who has himself in his own power.

Thou inquirest what liberty is? To be slave to nothing, to no necessity, to no accident; it means compelling Fortune to enter the lists on equal terms.

Drunkenness is simply voluntary insanity.

Life is warfare.

Our [the Stoic] motto, as you know, is live according to Nature.

Men learn while they teach.

In every good man a god doth dwell.

Show me a man who is not a slave. One is a slave to lust, another to greed, another to ambition, and all men are slaves to fear. . . . No servitude is more disgraceful than that which is self-imposed.

Life is a gift of the immortal gods, but living well is the gift of philosophy.

No man ever became wise by chance.

Begin at once to live, and count each separate day as a separate life.

There are a few men whom slavery holds fast, but there are many who hold fast to slavery.

To be feared is to fear: no one has been able to strike terror into others and at the same time enjoy peace of mind himself.

Why 'liberal studies' are so called is obvious: it is because they are the ones considered worthy of free men. But there is really only one liberal study that deserves the name—because it makes a person free—and that is the pursuit of wisdom.

Nothing is as deceptive as human life, nothing is as treacherous, not one of us would have accepted it, were it not given us without our knowledge.

Living is not the good, but living well. The wise man therefore lives as long as he should, not as long as he can. He will think of life in terms of quality, not quantity.

Dying early or late is of no relevance, dying well or ill is. To die well is to escape the danger of living well.

"To Polybius on Consolation"

A great fortune is a great slavery.

"To Marcia on Consolation"

If anyone pities the dead he must also pity the yet unborn.

"On Tranquility of Mind"

Nothing is less worthy of honor than an old man who has no other evidence of having lived long except his age.

It is extreme evil to depart from the company of the living before you die.

There never has been a genius without some touch of madness.*

"On Consolation"

Nothing is certain except the past.

"On the Shortness of Life"

Life, if thou knowest how to use it, is long enough.

A hungry people does not listen to reason.

"On Anger"

Hesitation is the best cure for anger.

---

*Seneca ascribed this thought to Aristotle; it is also found in the works of Petrarch, "De secreto conflictu." Seneca, according to *Born Under Saturn*, by Rudolf and Margot Wittkower, "referred to the Platonic fire of divine inspiration rather than to insanity."

Vice quickly creeps in; virtue is difficult to find. She requires rulers and guides. But vice can be acquired without a tutor.

Whom they have injured they also hate.

To strive with an equal is a doubtful thing to do; with a superior, a mad thing; with an inferior, a vulgar thing.

"On Providence"

Gold is tried by fire, brave men by adversity.

Scorn poverty; no one lives as poor as he was born. Scorn pain; it will either be relieved or relieve you. Scorn death, which either ends you or transforms you.

The highest good is immortal.

Hercules furens

Crime which is prosperous and lucky is called virtue.

Might makes right.

Hercules oetaeus

Courage leads to the stars, fear toward death.

Death is sometimes a punishment, often a gift, to many a favor.

Hippolytus

It is part of the cure to wish to be cured.

Troades

There is nothing after death, and death itself is nothing.

God is not to be worshipped with sacrifices and blood: for what pleasure can he have in the slaughter of the innocent? . . . Temples are not to be built for him with stones piled on high: God is to be consecrated in the breast of each.

Anyone can take life from man, but no one death: a thousand gates stand open to it.
                    Quoted in James Michener, *Iberia*

ERIC SEVAREID
(1912–   )
American journalist, TV commentator

Saints are usually killed by their own people.
                    CBS-TV, April 5, 1968

MARIE DE RABUTIN-CHANTAL, MARQUISE DE SÉVIGNÉ
(1626–1696)
French letter-writer

Fortune is always on the side of the largest battalions.
> A letter to her daughter, Countess de Grignan, 1690*

WILLIAM H. SEWARD
(1801–1872)
U.S. Senator, leader of the Republican Party

There is a higher law than the Constitution.
> U.S. Senate, March 11, 1850

It is an irrepressible conflict between opposing and enduring forces, and it means that the United States must and will, sooner or later, become either entirely a slave-holding nation or entirely a free-labor nation.
> Speech, Rochester, New York, October 25, 1858

BEN SHAHN
(1898–1969)
American artist

All art is based on non-conformity.
> Contribution, *Atlantic*, September 1957

The Shape of Content (1957)

The degree of non-conformity present—and tolerated—in a society might be looked upon as a symptom of its state of health.

LORD SHANG
(mid 4th century B.C.)
Prime Minister of the State of Ch'in

The Book of Lord Shang (tr. J.J.L. Duyvendak, Probsthain's Oriental Series, 1928)

A country where the virtuous govern the wicked, will suffer from disorder, so that it will be dismembered; but a country where the wicked govern the virtuous, will be orderly, so that it will be strong.

---

*See Voltaire and Tacitus. Napoleon replied: "Nothing of the kind: Providence is always on the side of the last reserve."

A country which is administered by the aid of odes, history, rites, music, filial piety, brotherly duty, virtue and moral culture, will, as soon as the enemy approach, be dismembered. . . . But if a country is administered without these eight, the enemy dares not approach.
> V. 27

SHANKARA
(9th century A.D.)
Hindu philosopher

Atma-Bodha

Knowledge alone effects emancipation.
As fire is indispensable to cooking,
So knowledge is essential to deliverance.

KARL SHAPIRO
(1913–   )
American writer

The good poet sticks to his real loves, those within the realm of possibility. He never tries to hold hands with God or the human race.
> Contribution, *N.Y. Times Magazine*, October 15, 1961

The artist's contribution to religion must in the nature of things be heretical.
> Contribution, *Saturday Review*, April 13, 1963

HARLOW SHAPLEY
(1885–1972)
American astronomer

The View From a Distant Star (1964)

That our planet is the one and only planet where life has emerged would be a ridiculous assumption. . . . Even if only one in a hundred of the ten billion suitable planets has actually got life well under way, there would be more than 100 million such planets. No, it is presumptuous to think that we are alone.

Which animal types will be here 10,000 years from now; which will be more likely to fall victim to fate or folly? The answer of course is too obvious, too painfully obvious. The fish has been here several hundred million years; man, but a few hundred thousand.

BORIS M. SHAPOSHNIKOV
(1882–1945)
Marshal of the U.S.S.R.

The Brain of the Army

War is a definite form of social relations and not merely an armed struggle for the annihilation of others.

In the final analysis, victory is gained or defeat is suffered, not by armies, but by peoples as a whole.

G(eorge) BERNARD SHAW
(1856–1950)
Irish dramatist*

Adventures of the Black Girl in Her Search for God (1932)

The best place to seek God is in a garden. You can dig for Him there.

Androcles and the Lion (1916)

Why not give Christianity a trial? The question seems a hopeless one after 2000 years of resolute adherence to the old cry of "Not this man, but Barrabas." . . . "This man" has not been a failure yet; for nobody has ever been sane enough to try his way.

No sooner had Jesus knocked over the dragon of superstition than Paul boldly set it on its legs again in the name of Jesus.

The followers of Paul and Peter made Christendom, whilst the Nazarenes were wiped out.

And to this day Pauline Christianity is, and owes its enormous vogue to being, a premium on sin.

Jesus was talking the most penetrating good sense when he preached Communism; when he declared that the reality behind the popular belief in God was a creative spirit in ourselves called by him the Heavenly Father and by us Evolution, Élan Vital, Life Force, and other names.

All prophets are inspired, and all men with a mission, Christs.

Preface

---

*The major works are quoted alphabetically.

Annajanska (1919)

All great truths begin as blasphemies.

Candida (1898)

We have no more right to consume happiness without producing it than to consume wealth without producing it.

Act I

Getting Married (1908)

Make divorce as easy, as cheap, and as private as marriage.

When two people are under the influence of the most violent, most insane, most delusive, and most transient of passions, they are required to swear that they will remain in that exalted, abnormal, and exhausting condition continuously until death do them part.

Place the work of a wife and mother on the same footing as other work: that is, on the footing of labor worthy of its hire.

Home life is no more natural to us than a cage is to a cockatoo.

Preface

The Irrational Knot (1905)

Money is indeed the most important thing in the world; and all sound and successful personal and national morality should have this fact for its basis.

Preface

John Bull's Other Island (1906)

Military service produces moral imbecility, ferocity and cowardice.

Preface

Major Barbara (1906)

The greatest of evils, and the worst of crimes, is poverty. Our first duty . . . is not to be poor.

Indeed, the religious bodies, as the almoners of the rich, become a sort of auxiliary police, taking off the insurrectionary edge of poverty with coals and blankets, bread and treacle, and soothing and cheering the victims with hopes of immense and inexpensive happiness in another world when the process of working them to premature death in the service of the rich is complete in this.

Not the least of its [money's] virtues is that it destroys base people as certainly as it fortifies and dignifies noble people.

Creeds must become intellectually honest. At present there is not a single credible established religion in the world. That is perhaps the most stupendous fact in the whole world-situation.

Preface

Nothing is ever done in this world until men are prepared to kill one another if it is not done.

The seven deadly sins. . . . Food, clothing, firing, rent, taxes, respectability and children. Nothing can lift these seven millstones from Man's neck but money; and the spirit cannot soar until the millstones are lifted.

Act III

Man and Superman (1903)

The world's books get written, its pictures painted, its statues modelled, its symphonies composed, by people who are free from the otherwise universal domination of the tyranny of sex.

"Epistle Dedicatory"

The true artist will let his wife starve, his children go barefoot, his mother drudge for his living at seventy, sooner than work at anything but his art.

Act I

Don Juan: Beauty, purity, respectability, religion, morality, art, patriotism, bravery and the rest are nothing but words which I or anyone else can turn inside out like a glove . . . [T]hey are mere words, useful for duping barbarians into adopting civilization, or the civilized poor into submitting to be robbed and enslaved. This is the family secret of the governing caste.

The Devil: This marvelous force of Life of which you boast is a force of Death. Man measures his strength by his destructiveness. . . . [T]he power that governs the earth is not the power of Life but of Death. . . . The plague, the famine, the earthquake, the tempest were too spasmodic in their actions; the tiger and crocodile were too easily satiated and not cruel enough: something more constantly, more ruthlessly, more ingenuously destructive was needed; and that something was Man, the Innovator of the rack, the stake, the gallows, the electric chair; of sword and gun and poison gas; above all of justice, duty, patriotism, and all the other Isms by which even those who are clever enough to be humanely disposed are persuaded to become the most destructive of all destroyers.

Don Juan in Hell, Act III

The Revolutionists Handbook

All who achieve real distinction in life begin as revolutionists. The most distinguished persons become more revolutionary as they grow older.

The only fundamental and possible Socialism is the socialization of the selective breeding of Man: in other terms, of human evolution. We must eliminate the Yahoo, or his vote will wreck the commonwealth.

We learn from history that we learn nothing from history.

Maxims for Revolutionists

Liberty means responsibility. That is why most men dread it.

A moderately honest man with a moderately faithful wife, moderate drinkers both, in a moderately healthy house: that is the true middle class unit.

Every man over forty is a scoundrel.

Marriage is popular because it combines the maximum of temptation with the maximum of opportunity.

The most revolutionary invention of the 19th century was the artificial sterilization of marriage.

The vilest abortionist is he who attempts to mould a child's character.

Mens sena in corpore sano is a foolish saying. The sound body is the product of the sound mind.

Never resist temptation; prove all things: hold fast that which is good.

Vice is a waste of life. Poverty, obedience, and celibacy are the canonical vices.

Whilst we have prisons it matters little which of us occupies the cells.

Life levels all men; death reveals the eminent.

Home is the girl's prison and the woman's workhouse.

Crime is only the retail department of what, in wholesale, we call penal law.

The reasonable man adapts himself to the world; the unreasonable one persists to adapt the world to himself. Therefore all progress depends on the unreasonable man.

The Man of Destiny (1897)

Tanner: But a lifetime of happiness! No man alive could bear it; it would be hell on earth.

The Quintessence of Ibsenism (1891)

First there was man's duty to God, with the priest as assessor. That was repudiated; and then came Man's duty to his neighbor, with Society as the assessor. Will this too be repudiated, and be succeeded by Man's duty to himself, assessed by himself?

Ch. 1

It is not surprising that our society, being directly dominated by men, comes to regard Woman, not as an end in herself like Man, but solely as a means of ministering to his appetite. The ideal wife is one who does everything that the ideal husband likes, and nothing else. Now to treat a person as a means instead of an end is to deny that person's right to live.

The sum of the matter is that unless Woman repudiates her womanliness, her duty to her husband, to her children, to society, to the law, and to everyone but herself, she cannot emancipate herself.

Ch. 3

The liar's punishment is, not in the least that he is not believed, but that he cannot believe any one else.

Ch. 4

Saint Joan (1923)

The exemption of women from military service is founded not on any natural inaptitude that men do not share, but on the fact that communities cannot reproduce themselves without plenty of women. Men are more largely dispensable, and are sacrificed accordingly.

Preface

Must then Christ perish in torment in every age to save those that have no imagination?

Epilogue

The Shewing-Up of Blanco Posnet (1909)

An attack on morals may turn out to be the salvation of the race.

No case whatever can be made out for the statement that a nation cannot do without common thieves and homicidal ruffians. But an overwhelming case can be made out for the statement that no nation can prosper or even continue to exist without heretics and advocates of shockingly immoral doctrines.

Preface

Sixteen Self-Sketches (1896)

All autobiographies are lies. I do not mean unconscious, unintentional lies: I mean deliberate lies. No man is bad enough to tell the truth about himself during his lifetime. . . . And no man is good enough to tell the truth to posterity in a document which he suppresses until there is nobody left alive to contradict him.

The Rejected Statement (1916)

Assassination is the extreme form of censorship.

Pt. 1

Karl Marx made a man of me. Socialism made a man of me.

Talk with guests, 80th birthday

I myself have been particularly careful never to say a civil word to the United States. I have scoffed at their inhabitants as a nation of villagers. I have defined the 100% American as 99% an idiot. And they just adore me.

Speech, New York City, April 11, 1933*

Patriotism is a pernicious, psychopathic form of idiocy.

Contribution, L'Esprit français, Paris, 1932

---

*Asked for a confirmation of this and other quotations, Shaw replied, December 10, 1937: "Dear Mr. Seldes: I cannot remember the exact wording of the statement to which you allude, but what I meant was that in my experience a man who calls himself a 100% American and is proud of it, is generally 150% an idiot politically. But the designation may be good business for war veterans. Having bled for their country in 1861 and 1918, they have bled it all they could consequently. And why not?—G. Bernard Shaw."

To me the sole hope of human salvation lies in teaching.

Power does not corrupt men; fools, however, if they get into a position of power, corrupt power.

Quoted in Stephen Winsten,
Days with Bernard Shaw

PERCY BYSSHE SHELLEY
(1792–1822)
English poet*

"Song to the Men of England" (1819)

Men of England, wherefore plough
For the lords who lay ye low?
Wherefore weave with toil and care,
The rich robes your tyrants wear?

St. 1

"The Masque of Anarchy" (1819)

"Men of England, Heirs of Glory,
. . .
Rise, like lions after slumber,
In unvanquishable number,
Shake the chains to earth like dew,
Which in sleep had fall'n on you—
Ye are many—they are few."

St. 37–38

"What are thou Freedom?
. . .
Thou art Wisdom—freedom never
Dreams that God will doom for ever
All who think those things untrue,
Of which priests make much ado."

St. 52–58

"Adonais" (1821)

The One remains, the many change and
    pass;
Heaven's light forever shines, Earth's
    shadows fly;
Life, like a dome of many-coloured glass,
Stains the white radiance of Eternity,
Until Death tramples it to fragments.

St. 52

---

*"A beautiful and ineffectual angel, beating in the void his luminous wings in vain."—Matthew Arnold, preface to Byron's poems.

No more let Life divide what Death can
    join together.

St. 53

"To a Skylark" (1820)

Hail to thee, blithe spirit!
    Bird thou never wert,
That from heaven, or near it,
    Pourest thy full heart
In profuse strains of unpremeditated art.

St. 1

Prometheus Unbound (1818–1819)

In each human heart terror survives
The raven it has gorged: the loftiest fear
All that they would disdain to think were
    true:
Hypocrisy and custom make their minds
The fanes of many a worship, now outworn.
They dare not devise good for man's estate,
And yet they know not that they do not dare.

The good want power, but to weep barren
    tears.
The powerful goodness want: worse need for
    them.
The wise want love; and those who love
    want wisdom;
And all best things are thus confused to ill.
Many are strong and rich, and would be
    just,
But live among their suffering fellow-men
As if none felt: they know not what they do.

Act 1

The loathsome mask has fallen, the man re-
    mains
Sceptreless, free, uncircumscribed, but man
Equal, unclassed, tribeless, and nationless.

Act 3

To suffer woes which Hope thinks infinite;
To forgive wrongs darker than death or
    night;
    To defy Power which seems omnipotent;
To love and bear; to hope till Hope creates
From its own wreck the thing it contem-
    plates;
    Neither to change, nor falter, nor re-
        pent;
This, like thy glory, Titan! is to be
Good, great and joyous, beautiful and free;
This is alone Life, Joy, Empire, and Vic-
    tory!

Act 4

Queen Mab (1810)*

And when reason's voice,
Loud as the voice of Nature, shall have
    waked
The nations; and mankind perceive that vice
Is discord, war, and misery; that virtue
Is peace, and happiness and harmony;
When man's maturer nature shall disdain
The playthings of its childhood;—kingly
    glare
Will lose its power to dazzle; its authority
Will silently pass by; the gorgeous throne
Shall stand unnoticed in the regal hall,
Fast falling to decay; whilst falsehood's trade
Shall be as hateful and unprofitable
As that of truth is now.

Power, like a desolating pestilence,
Pollutes whate'er it touches; and obedience,
Bane of all genius, virtue, freedom, truth,
Makes slaves of men, and of the human
    frame
A mechanical automaton.
                                        Act III

War is the statesman's game, the priest's de-
    light,
The lawyer's jest, the hired assassin's trade.
                                        Act IV

A brighter morn awaits the human day, . . .
When poverty and wealth, the thirst of
    fame,
The fear of infamy, disease and woe,
War with its million horrors, and fierce hell,
Shall live but in the memory of time.

Gold is a living god, and rules in scorn
All earthly things but virtue.
                                        Act V

Necessity! thou mother of the world.
                                        Act VI

"Rosalind and Helen" (1818)

"Fear not that the tyrants shall rule for ever,
Or the priests of the bloody faith;
They stand on the brink of the mighty river
Whose waves they have tainted with
    death: . . .
And their swords and their scepters I floating
    see
Like wrecks, on the surge of eternity.

---

*In 1841 Shelley's British publisher was found guilty of blasphemy for publishing *Queen Mab*. The judge ruled that certain lines were libels on God, and indictible. He was never sentenced.

Hellas (1821)

Another Athens shall arise,
    And to remoter time
Bequeath, like sunset to the skies,
    The spendour of its prime;
and leave, if naught so bright may live,
All earth can take or Heaven can give.

O cease! must hate and death return?
    Cease! must men kill and die?
Cease! drain not to its dregs the urn
    Of bitter prophecy.
The world is weary of the past,
O might it die or rest at last!

"Hymn to Intellectual Beauty" (1816)

Spirit of Beauty, that dost consecrate
    With thine own hues all thou dost shine
        upon
    Of human thought or form, where art
        thou gone?
Why dost thou pass away and leave our
        state,
This dim vale of tears, vacant and desolate?
                                        St. 2

"England in 1819"* (1819)

An old, mad, blind, despised, and dying
    king,— . . .
Rulers, who neither see, nor feel, nor know,
But leech-like to their fainting country
    cling,
Till they drop, blind in blood, without a
    blow.— . . .
Religion Christless, Godless—a book
    sealed; . . .
Are graves, from which a glorious Phantom
    may
Burst, to illumine our tempestuous day.

"Ode to the West Wind" (1819)

    Be thou, Spirit fierce,
My spirit! Be thou me, impetuous one!
    Drive my dead thought over the universe
    Like withered leaves to quicken a new
        birth,
And, by the incantation of this verse,
    Scatter, as from an unextinguishable
        hearth
    Ashes and sparks, my words among man-
        kind!

---

*The old, mad king was George III; the Phantom Shelley hoped for was Liberty.

Be through my lips to unawakened earth
  The trumpet of a prophecy! O wind,
  If Winter comes, can Spring be far be-
    hind?
                                              V

"Ode to Liberty" (1820)

A *glorious* people vibrated again
  The lightning of the nations: Liberty
From heart to heart, from tower to tower,
    o'er Spain,
  Scattering contagious fire into the sky,
Gleamed. My soul spurned the chains of its
    dismay.
                                            St. 1

O that the wise from their bright minds
    would kindle
  Such lamps within the dome of this dim
    world,
That the pale name of *Priest* might shrink
    and dwindle
  Into the hell from which it first was
    hurled,
A scoff of impious pride from fiends impure
  Till human thoughts might kneel alone,
  Each before the judgement-throne
Of its own aweless Soul, or of the power un-
    known!
                                           St. 16

"An Ode" (written October 1819)

Awaken, awaken, awaken!
The slave and the tyrant are twin-born foes.

"Political Greatness" (1821)

    Man who man would be,
Must rule the empire of himself! in it
Must be supreme, establishing his throne
On vanquished will, quelling the anarchy
Of hopes and fears, being himself alone.

The Cenci (1819)

    Worse than despair,
Worse than the bitterness of death, is hope.
                                     Act 5, sc. IV

"A Declaration of Rights" (Dublin, 1812)

Government has no rights; it is a delegation
from several individuals for the purpose of securing their own.
                                              I

The rights of man, in the present state of society, are only to be secured by some degree of
coercion to be exercised on their violator.
                                             VII

Government is never supported by fraud
until it cannot be supported by reason.
                                            VIII

A man has a right to unrestricted liberty of
discussion. Falsehood is a scorpion that will
sting itself to death.
                                             XII

Man has no right to kill his brother. It is no
excuse that he does so in uniform: he only
adds the infamy of servitude to the crime of
murder.
                                             XIX

No man has a right to be respected for any
other possessions but those of virtue and talents. Titles are tinsel, power a corrupter, glory
a bubble, and excessive wealth a libel on its
possessor.
                                           XXVII

The only use of government is to repress the
vices of man. If man were today sinless, tomorrow he would have a right to demand that
government and all its evils should cease.
                                            XXXI

Proposals for an Association of Philanthropists
(March 2, 1812)

A political or religious system may burn or
imprison those who investigate its principles;
but it is an invariable proof of their falsehood
and hollowness.

A man must have a right to do a thing before he can have a duty; this right must permit
before his duty can enjoin him to any act. Any
law is bad which attempts to make it criminal
to do what the plain dictates within the breast
of every man tell him that he ought to do.

Notes to Queen Mab (1813)

Necessity teaches us that . . . if God is the
author of good, He is also the author of
evil . . . God made man such as he is and
then damned him for being so.

A husband and wife ought to continue so
long united as they love each other, and any
law which would bind them to cohabitation
for one moment after the decay of their affection would be a most intolerable tyranny, and
the most unworthy of toleration.

Love is free; to promise for ever to love the same woman is not less absurd than to promise to believe that same creed; such a vow in both cases excludes us from all inquiry.

Wealth is a power usurped by the few, to compel the many to labour for their benefit.

A Defense of Poetry (1821)

Poetry is the record of the best and happiest moments of the happiest and best minds.

The rich have become richer, and the poor have become poorer; and the vessel of state is driven between the Scylla and Charybdis of anarchy and despotism.

A poem is the very image of life expressed in its eternal truth.

Poets are the unacknowledged legislators of the world.

A Philosophical View of Reform (1819)

War is a kind of superstition; the pageantry of arms and badges corrupts the imagination of man.

Reviewers, with some rare exceptions, are the most stupid and malignant race. As a bankrupt thief turns thief-taker in despair, so an unsuccessful author turns critic.
Preface to "Adonais," 1821, suppressed by publisher

WILLIAM SHENSTONE
(1714–1763)
English poet

"Essay on Men and Manners" (1764)

A man has generally the good or ill qualities which he attributes to mankind.

Dividing the world into an hundred parts, I am apt to believe the calculation might be thus adjusted: Pedants 15; Persons of Common Sense 40; Wits 15; Persons of a Wild Uncultivated Taste 10; Persons of original taste, improved by art 5.

RICHARD BRINDSLEY SHERIDAN
(1751–1816)
Irish dramatist, statesman

Give me a corrupt House of Lords, give me a venal House of Commons, give them a ty-rannical Prince, give them a truckling Court, and let me have but an unfettered Press, I will defy them to encroach a hair's breadth upon the liberties of England.
Address, Commons, February 8, 1810 quoted in Cobbett's Parliamentary Debates, 15

WILLIAM TECUMSEH SHERMAN
(1820–1891)
American general, Union Army

You cannot qualify war in harsher terms than I will. War is cruelty, and you cannot refine it; and those who brought war into our country deserve all the curses and maledictions a people can pour out.
Letter to Mayor Calhoun of Atlanta and others, September 12, 1864

There is many a boy here today who looks on war as all glory, but, boys, it is all hell. You can bear this warning voice to generations yet to come. I look upon war with horror.
Address, G.A.R. Convention, August 11, 1880*

HU SHIH
(1891–1962)
Father of the Chinese Renaissance

On the basis of biological, sociological, and historical knowledge, we should recognize that the individual self is subject to death and decay, but the sum total of individual achievement, for better or worse, lives on in the immortality of the Larger Self; that to live for the sake of the species and posterity is religion of the highest kind; and that those religions which see a future life either in Heaven or in the Pure Land, are selfish religions.
Contribution, *Living Philosophies*, 1931

---

*No evidence has been found that Sherman ever used the exact words "War is hell." This phrase was first attributed to him in 1914—it was then said, no evidence given, that Sherman had told the Michigan Military Academy, graduation day, June 19, 1879: "I am tired and sick of war. Its glory is all moonshine. It is only those who have neither fired a shot nor heard the shrieks and groans of the wounded, who cry aloud for blood. War is hell."

ABBÉ EMMANUEL JOSEPH SIEYÈS
(1748–1836)
French abbé, statesman, publicist

J'ai vécu.
I survived.*
Attributed by V. Mignet

La mort sans phrases.
Death; without any empty talk.
On casting a vote for death of Louis XVI,
January 19, 1793; attributed.

SIR PHILLIP SIDNEY
(1554–1586)
English writer

"Arcadia" (1580)

Who shoots at the mid-day sun, though he be so sure he shall never hit the mark, yet as sure as he is, he shall shoot higher than he who aims at a bush.

Hope is a fawning traitor of the mind, while under color of friendship, it robs it of its chief force of resolution.

"Astrophel and Stella" (pub. posthumously 1591)
"Fool!" said my muse to me, "look in thy heart, and write."

IGNAZIO SILONE (né Seconde Tranquilli)
(1900–1978)
Italian writer

"Emergency Exit" (1968)

No law, divine or human, can guarantee that man's revolt will end in victory. But this is one of the risks it is his duty and privilege to take.

Liberty isn't a thing you are given as a present. You can be a free man under a dictatorship. It is sufficient if you struggle against it.
Essay in *The God that Failed*
(ed. Richard Crossman, 1950)

The final struggle will be between the Communists, and the ex-Communists.
Quoted by Merle Miller, *N.Y. Herald*
Tribune, January 8, 1950

---

*Asked how he came through the Reign of Terror of the French Revolution, when he was in seclusion, he replied, "J'ai vécu."

SIMONIDES OF CEOS
(c. 566–468 B.C.)
Greek poet

Go tell the Spartans, thou that passeth by,
That here, obedient to their laws, we lie.*
Fragment 92, the Spartans at Thermopylae
(c. 480 B.C.)

Appearance overpowers even the truth.
Fragment 76

E'en the gods war not with necessity.
Quoted in Strobaeus, "Eclogues"

The race of fools is infinite.
Quoted in *Britannica*, 11th ed.

UPTON SINCLAIR
(1878–1968)
American reformer, writer, muckraker

The Profits of Religion (1918)

I can see how sincere, how passionately proletarian a religious prophet may be, that is the fate which sooner or later befalls him in a competitive society—to be founder of an organization of fools, conducted by knaves, for the benefit of wolves. That fate befell Buddha and Jesus, it befell Ignatius Loyola and Francis of Assisi, John Fox, and John Calvin, and John Wesley.

From the days of Constantine to the days of Bismarck and Mark Hanna, Christ and Caesar have been one, and the Church has been the shield and armor of predatory economic might.

ISAAC BASHEVIS SINGER
(1904–   )
American writer, Nobel Laureate

I don't think religion should be connected with dogma or revelation. Since He's a silent

---

*"Stranger, when you come to Lakadaimon, tell them that we lie here, obedient to her will."—Kenneth Rexroth version.

God, He talks in deeds, in events, and we have to learn his language.

The belief in God is as necessary as sex.
Quoted in *N. Y. Times,* October 23, 1968

JESUS BEN SIRA (or Sirach)
(fl. 2nd century B.C.)
Hebrew scholar

*Ecclesiasticus**

Call no man blessed before his death.
xi, 28

From a woman was the beginning of sin; and because of her we all die.
xxv, 24

SIR OSBERT SITWELL
(1892–1969)
British poet

"At the House of Mrs. Kinfoot"

Nothing exists which the British bourgeoisie
Does not understand
Therefore there is no death
—And, of course, no life.

POPE SIXTUS. *See* Xystus

THOMAS S. SKASZ
Hungarian-born American professor of
psychiatry

Law, Liberty and Psychiatry (1965)

If we are to respect human dignity and rights, the model for the rules of the psychiatric-diagnostic game must be our traditional maxim: Every person should be considered mentally healthy (innocent) until he is proved mentally sick (guilty).

Many modern psychotherapists have adopted as their credo, Socrates' declaration that "the unexamined life is not worth living." But for modern man that is not enough. We should pledge ourselves to the proposition that the irresponsible life is not worth living.

The Manufacture of Madness (1970)

It is one of the few "laws" of human relations that not only those who suffer from arbitrary authority, but also those who wield it, become alienated from others and thus dehumanized.

The Second Sin (1974)

There can be no humane penology so long as punishment masquerades as "correction." No person has a right to "correct" a human being; only God does.

THOMAS SKIDMORE
(1790–1842)
American laborer, labor leader

Inasmuch as great wealth is an instrument which is uniformly used to extort from others their property, it ought to be taken away from its possessors on the same principle that a sword or a pistol may be wrested from a robber, who undertakes to accomplish the same effect in a different manner.
Statement, proclaiming the formation of the
Working-Men's Party, 1829

B(urrhus) F(rederic) SKINNER
(1904–   )
Professor emeritus of psychology, Harvard

Beyond Freedom and Dignity (1971)

Better contraceptives will control population only if people will use them. A nuclear holocaust can be prevented only if the conditions under which nations make war can be changed. The environment will continue to deteriorate until pollution practices are abandoned. We need to make vast changes in human behavior.

ADAM SMITH
(1723–1790)
English economist*

The Wealth of Nations (1776)

Labor, therefore, is the real measure of the exchangeable value of all commodities.
Vol. I, bk. I, ch. 5

---

*This work is apocryphal. It is also known as *The Wisdom of Jesus the Son of Sirach.*

*"The father of political economy."—Prince Kropotkin, in *Fields, Factories and Workshops.*

Men, like all other animals, naturally multiply in proportion to the means of their subsistence.

The market price of every particular commodity is regulated by the proportion between the quantity which is actually brought to market, and the demand of those who are willing to pay the natural price of the commodity or the whole value of the rent, labor and profit which must be paid in order to bring it thither.
Vol. I, bk. I, ch. 7

People of the same trade seldom meet together, even for merriment and diversion, but their conversation ends in a conspiracy against the public, or in some contrivance to raise prices.
Vol. I, bk. I, ch. 10

Every individual endeavors to employ his capital so that its produce may be of greatest value. . . . He intends only his own security, only his own gain. . . . By pursuing his own interest he frequently promotes that of society more effectively than when he really intends to promote it.
Vol. II, bk. IV, ch. 2

But the mean rapacity, the monopolizing spirit of merchants and manufacturers, who neither are, nor ought to be, the rulers of mankind, though it cannot perhaps be corrected, may very easily be prevented from disturbing the tranquility of any body but themselves.

To found a great empire for the sole purpose of raising up a people of customers may, at first sight, appear a prospect fit only for a nation of shopkeepers.
Vol. II, bk. IV, ch. 7 (cf. Napoleon, c. 1795)

Science is the great antidote to the poison of enthusiasm and superstition.

Civil government, so far as it is instituted for the security of property, is in reality instituted for the defense of the rich against the poor, or of those who have some property against those who have none at all.

Wherever there is great property there is great inequality. For one very rich man there must be at least five hundred poor, and the affluence of the few supposes the indigence of the many.
Vol. II, bk. V, ch. 1

ALFRED E(manuel) SMITH
(1873–1944)
Governor of New York, Presidential candidate 1928

It is the right of our people to organize to oppose any law and any part of the Constitution with which they are not in sympathy.
Address, League of Women Voters, December 2, 1927

All the ills of democracy can be cured by more democracy.
Speech, June 27, 1935*

CAPTAIN JOHN SMITH
(1580–1631)
President, Colony of Virginia

And though you presume that authority here is but a shadow and that I dare not touch the lives of any, but my own must answer it, yet he that offendeth, let him assuredly expect his due punishment. You must obey this, now, for a law—"he that will not work shall not eat."
Statement to the Council, September 10, 1608

LOGAN PEARSALL SMITH
(1865–1946)
American-born writer

Afterthoughts (1931)

Those who serve both God and Mammon soon discover that there is no God.

Most people sell their souls and live with a good conscience on the proceeds.

SOFIA SMITH
(1796–1870)
Founder of Smith College

It is my opinion that by the higher and more thorough Christian education of women, what are called their "wrongs" will be redressed, their wages adjusted, their weight of influence

---

*"The doctrine that the cure for the evils of democracy is more democracy is like saying the cure for crime is more crime."—Mencken.

in reforming the evils of society will be greatly increased, as teachers, as writers, as mothers, as members of society, their power for good will be incalculably changed.

From her will, pub. 1875

REV. SYDNEY SMITH
(1771–1845)
English clergyman, writer

Peter Plymley's Letters (1807)

Every law which originated in ignorance and malice, and gratifies the passions from which it sprang, we call the wisdom of our ancestors.

When I hear any man talk of an unalterable law, the only effect it produces on me is to convince me that he is an unalterable fool.

In the four quarters of the globe, who reads an American book, or goes to an American play? or looks at an American picture or statue?

Contribution, *Edinburgh Review,* January 1820

EDGAR SNOW
(1905–1972)
American writer

Journey to the Beginning (1958)

No one can rule guiltlessly, and least of all those whom history compels to hurry.

In Russia religion is the opium of the people, in China opium is the religion of the people.

SOCIETY OF FRIENDS (Quakers)
(Founded c. 1650)
Sect formed by George Fox in England opposed to oath-taking and all war

The Christian faith, which we believe is the hope of our troubled world, is a revolutionary faith. It is rooted to inward experience, but, wherever it is genuine, it leads to radical changes in the ways in which men live and act.

We rejoice in the movements, appearing in many parts of the world at once, which are inspired by the desire for social justice, equal rights for all races, and the dignity of the individual person.

Declaration, World Conference, Oxford, 1952; commemoration of 300th anniversary

SOCRATES
(470?–399 B.C.)
Greek stonemason, general, philosopher*

Quoted in Plato's *Apology* (tr. Jowett)**

My plainness of speech makes them hate me, and what is their hatred but a proof that I am speaking the truth?

24

A man who is good for anything ought not to calculate the chance of living or dying; he ought only to consider whether in doing anything he is doing right or wrong—acting the part of a good man or a bad. . . . For the fear of death is indeed the pretense of wisdom, and not real wisdom, but a pretense of knowing the unknown; and no one knows whether death, which men in their fear apprehend to be the greatest evil, may not be the greatest good.

28–29

Are you not ashamed of heaping up in the greatest amount of money and honor and reputation, and caring so little about wisdom and truth and the greatest improvement of the soul, which you never regard or heed at all?

29e

For neither Meletus nor Anytus could injure me; that would be impossible, for I believe it is not God's will that a better man can be injured by a worse.

30d

---

*"Throughout his life and up to his very death Socrates did nothing other than place himself in this draft, this current [of thinking], and maintain himself in it. This is why he wrote nothing. For anyone who begins, out of thinking, to write must inevitably be like those people who run for shelter from a wind too strong for them. . . . Thinking becomes literature."—Heidegger.

**"It is significant that Plato is said to have been present at the defense. . . . Some of the topics may have been actually used by Socrates and the recollection may have rung in the ears of his disciple." —Jowett. Socrates is also quoted by Plato (q.v.) in *Crito* and *Phaedo,* and is the narrator of *The Republic.*

I am that gadfly which God has attached to the State, and all day long and in all places am always fastening upon you, arousing and persuading and reproaching you.

30e

And I have sufficient witness to the truth of what I say—my poverty.

31c

. . . I was really too honest a man to be a politician and live.

32

The unexamined life is not worth living.

38

The difficulty, my friends, is not to avoid death, but to avoid unrighteousness; for that runs faster than death.

39

Death is one of two things. Either it is annihilation, and the dead have no consciousness of anything; or, as we are told, it is really a change: a migration of the soul from this place to another.

40d

Therefore, O Judges, be of good cheer about death, and know of a certainty, that no evil can happen to a good man, either in life or after death.

41d

The hour of departure has arrived, and we go our ways—I to die, and you to live. Which is better only God knows.*

42

SOLON
(636?–558? B.C.)
Athenian statesman

Laws are like cobwebs, for if any trifling or powerless thing fall into them they hold it fast; while if it were something weightier it would break through them and be off.

Quoted in Diogenes Laërtius, *Lives of Emminent Philosophers,* bk. I, 58

Law and order make rough things smooth, stop insolence, weaken violence, wither the

growing blooms of sin, straighten crooked judgments, calm arrogant deeds, stop deeds of dissension, and stop the anger of painful strife; through law and order, all men's affairs are suitable and prudent.

Fragment 5

Keep thine eyes fixed upon the end of life.

Attributed

Make reason thy guide.

Attributed

ALEXANDER I. SOLZHENITSYN
(1918–   )
Russian writer, Nobel Prize 1970

The First Circle (1964)

For a country to have a great writer is like having a second government. That is why no regime has ever loved great writers, only minor ones.

The Gulag Archipelago (1918–1956)

If only there were evil people somewhere insidiously committing evil deeds and it were necessary only to separate them from the rest of us and destroy them. But the line dividing good and evil cuts through the heart of every human being. And who is willing to destroy a piece of his own heart?

Pt. I

Mankind's salvation lies exclusively in everyone's making everything his business, in the people of the East being anything but indifferent to what is thought in the West, and in the people of the West being anything but indifferent to what happens in the East. Literature, one of the most sensitive and responsible tools of human existence, has been the first to pick up, adopt, and assimilate this sense of the growing unity of mankind.

The simple act of any ordinary courageous man is not to take part, not to support lies! . . . Writers and artists can do more: they can VANQUISH LIES! In the struggle against lies, art has always won and always will. . . . Lies can stand up against much in the world, but not against art.

Nobel Lecture, 1970

Just the same, it is time to remember that the first thing we belong to is humanity. And humanity is separated from the animal world

---

*"And now the time has come when we must depart: I to my death, you to go on living. But which of us is going to the better fate is unknown to all except God."—tr. Kathleen Freeman.

by thought and speech and they should naturally be free. If they are fettered, we go back to being animals.
Letter to Writers' Union, Moscow; quoted in *N.Y. Times,* November 15, 1969

It is characteristic that Communism is so devoid of arguments that it has none to advance against its opponents. . . . It lacks arguments and hence there is the club, the concentration camp, the insane asylum. . . . Communism has never concealed the fact that it rejects all absolute concepts of morality, it scoffs at any consideration of "good" and "evil" as indisputable categories. . . . Communism is anti-humanity.
Address, AFL-CIO, New York City, July 1978

Hastiness and superficiality are the psychic diseases of the 20th Century, and more than anywhere else this disease is reflected in the press. Such as it is, however, the press has become the greatest power within the Western countries, more powerful than the legislature, the executive, and the judiciary.

Western thinking has become conservative; the world situation should stay as it is at any cost; there should be no changes. This debilitating dream of a status quo is the symptom of a society that has come to the end of its development.
Commencement address, Harvard University, June 1978

SUSAN SONTAG
(1933–   )
American novelist, critic

"Against Interpretation" (1961)

Sanity is a cozy lie.

Interpretation is the revenge of the intellect upon art.

To interpret is to impoverish.

The white race is the cancer of history. It is the white race and it alone—its ideologies and inventions—which eradicates autonomous civilizations wherever it spreads, which has upset the ecological balance of the planet, which now threatens the very existence of life itself.
Contribution, *Partisan Review,* 1967

The only interesting answers are those which destroy the questions.
Contribution, *Esquire,* July 1968

Lying is an elementary means of self-defense.
Contribution, *Saturday Review,* September 23, 1972

SOPHOCLES
(496?–406 B.C.)
Greek tragic poet

Ajax (c.409 B.C.)

Better to die, and sleep
The never-waking sleep, than linger on
And dare to live when the soul's life is gone.
Lines 392–394

In knowing nothing is the sweetest life.
Line 553

Laws can never be enforced unless fear supports them.
Line 1074

Antigone (c.442 B.C.)

None love the messenger who brings bad news.
Line 277

Of all the foul growths current in the world,
The worst is money. Money drives men
from home,
Plunders proud cities, and perverts honest
minds
to shameful practice, godlessness and crime.
Line 296

Numberless are the world's wonders,
but none
More wonderful than man.
Line 332 [Ode I]

Unwritten laws, eternal in the heavens.
Line 452

Dreadful is the mysterious power of Fate; there is no escape from it by wealth or war, by walled city, or dark, sea-beaten ships.
Line 952

Wisdom is the supreme part of happiness.
Line 1348

Electra (c. 414 B.C.)

The end excuses any evil.
Line 61

Death is not the greatest of evils; it is worse to want to die, and not be able to.
Line 1008

Oedipus at Colonus (406 B.C.)

In a really just cause the weak conquers the strong.

Line 880

Never to have been born is much the best;
And next the best, by far,
To return thence, by the way speediest,
Where our beginning were.

Lines 1224–1226

It is hope that maintains most of mankind.

Fragment

GEORGES SOREL
(1847–1922)
French engineer, syndicalist

Reflections on Violence (1906)

The strike is a type of warfare.

Syndicalists do not propose to reform the State, as the men of the 18th Century did; they want to destroy it, because they wish to realize this idea of Marx's that the Socialist revolution ought not to culminate in the replacement of one governing minority by another minority.

Proletarian violence, carried on as a pure and simple manifestation of the sentiment of the class war, appears thus as a very fine and very heroic thing; it is at the service of the immemorial interests of civilization; it is not perhaps the most appropriate method of obtaining immediate material advantages, but it may save the world from barbarism.

MURIEL SPARK
(1918–   )
British writer

It is impossible to repent of love. The sin of love does not exist.

Contribution, *The New Yorker,* July 10, 1965

THOMAS SPENCE
(1750–1814)
Scottish land reformer

If we really want to get rid of these evils from amongst men, we must destroy . . . the cause of them, which is private property in land. . . . The land shall no longer be suffered to be the property of individuals, but of parishes. *

Pamphlet

HERBERT SPENCER
(1820–1903)
English philosopher

Social Statics (1851)

An argument fatal to the communist theory, is suggested by the fact, that a desire for property is one of the elements of our nature.

Pt. II, ch. X

It is to the abnormal condition of the body politic that all evils arising from an unrestrained expression of opinion must be attributed, and not to the unrestrained expression itself. Under a sound social regime and its accompanying contentment, nothing is to be feared from the most uncontrolled utterance of thought and feeling.

Pt. II, ch. XIV

Liberty of each, limited by the like liberties of all, is the rule in conformity with which society must be organized. **

Government is essentially immoral.

The state employs evil weapons to subjugate evil, and is alike contaminated by the objects with which it deals, and the means by which it works.

The freest form of government is only the least objectionable form. The rule of the many by the few we call tyranny: the rule of the few by the many is tyranny also; only of a less intense kind.

Feudalism, serfdom, slavery, all tyrannical institutions, are merely the most vigorous kind of rule, springing out of, and necessary to, a bad state of man. The progress from these is in all cases the same—less government.

Pt. II, ch. XIX

If every man has freedom to do all that he wills, provided he infringes not the equal free-

---

*For publishing the above statement Spence was sent to prison for one year, on the charge of libel.
**The above, and several following quotations, were considered subversive, and omitted in Britain from the second and other editions for many years. The title of the chapter is "The Right to Ignore the State."

dom of any other man, then he is free to drop connection with the state—to relinquish its protection, and to refuse paying toward its support.

Pt. III, ch. XIX

So long as selfishness makes government needful at all, it must make every government corrupt, save one in which all men are represented.

Pt. III, ch. XX

First Principles (1862)

Religion has been impelled by science to give up one after another of its dogmas, of those assumed cognitions which it could not substantiate.

Principles of Biology (1864–1867)

Our lives are universally shortened by ignorance.

The survival of the fittest, which I have here sought to express in mechanical terms, is that which Mr. Darwin has called "natural selection, or the preservation of favored races in the struggle for life."*

If a single cell, under appropriate conditions, becomes a man in the space of a few years, there can surely be no difficulty in understanding how, under appropriate conditions, a cell may, in the course of untold millions of years, give origin to the human race.

Pt. III, ch. 12

The Man Versus the State (1884)

Be it or be it not true that man is shapen in iniquity and conceived in sin, it is unquestionably true that Government is begotten of aggression and by aggression.

The modifications of Nature in one way or other produced, are inheritable.

"The Sins of Legislators"

The belief, not only of Socialists but also of those so-called Liberals who are diligently preparing the way for them, is that by due skill an ill-working humanity may be framed into well-working institutions. It is a delusion. The de-

fective nature of citizens will show themselves in the bad acting of whatever social structure they are arranged into. There is no political alchemy by which you can get golden conduct out of leaden instruments.

"The Coming Slavery"

OSWALD SPENGLER
(1880–1936)
German philosopher*

The Hour of Decision (1934)

The age-old barbarism which for centuries lay bound and hidden under the severe discipline of a high culture, is again awakening that warlike healthy joy in one's own strength, which despises the age of rationalistic thought and literature, that unbroken instinct of a strong race which wishes to live otherwise than under the pressure of books and bookish ideas.

If few can stand a long war without the deterioration of soul, none can stand a long peace.

Ch. 3

Christian theology is the grandmother of Bolshevism.

It is from the intellectual "mob," with the failures from all academic professions, the spiritually unfit and the morally inhibited, at its head, that the gangsters of Liberal and Bolshevik risings are recruited.

Ch. 11

Socialism is nothing but the capitalism of the lower classes.

Ch. 14

Man is a beast of prey. I shall say it again and again. . . . Conflict is the original fact of life, is life itself, and not the most pitiful pacifist is able entirely to uproot the pleasure this gives the most inmost soul.

Ideas act irrationally through the blood.

Life is the alpha and omega, and Life is devoid of all systems, all progress, all reason. It exists simply for its own sake.

Contribution, *American Mercury,* v. 31**

*In *The Descent of Man* (1871), Darwin, using the phrase "the struggle for existence," writes: "The expression used by Mr. Herbert Spencer of the Survival of the Fittest is more accurate."

*Spengler was adopted by the Nazi ideologues.
**The *American Mercury* had been sold by H. L. Mencken to American editors who were attempting to form an American Fascist party.

BARUCH SPINOZA
(1632–1677)
Dutch philosopher*

Ethics (1677)

If this be denied, conceive, if it be possible, that God does not exist. Then it follows that His essence does not involve existence. But this is absurd. Therefore God necessarily exists.

I, 11

God is the absolutely first cause.

I, 16

Many errors, of a truth, consist merely in the application of the wrong names of things.

In the mind there is no absolute or free will.

II, 47

Love is nothing but joy accompanied with the idea of an eternal cause, and *hatred* is nothing but sorrow with the accompanying idea of an external cause.

III, 13

The love of a harlot, that is to say, the lust of sexual intercourse, which arouses from mere external form, and absolutely all love which recognizes any other cause than the freedom of the mind, easily passes into hatred, unless, which is worse, it becomes a species of delirium, and thereby discord is cherished rather than concord.

III, 29

There can be no hope without fear, and no fear without hope.

III, 59

Fear arises from impotence of mind, and therefore is of no service to reason, nor is pity, although it seems to present an appearance of piety.

IV, 16

The endeavor for self-preservation is the primary and only foundation of virtue.

IV, 17

---

*Also known as Benedictus de Spinoza, he was born in Holland of Portuguese-Jewish refugees from the Inquisition. He was excommunicated from the synagogue. *Ethics* was published after his death. Described as *"Ein Gott-betrunkener Mensch"* [A God-intoxicated man] by Novalis (Friedrich von Hardenberg).

If we live according to the guidance of reason, we shall desire for others the good which we seek for ourselves.

IV, 37

But the avaricious man who thinks of nothing else but gain or money, and the ambitious man who thinks of nothing but glory, inasmuch as they do harm, and are, therefore, though worthy of hatred, not believed to be mad. In truth, however, avarice, lust, etc., are a kind of madness, although they are not reckoned amongst diseases.

IV, 44

Envy, mockery, contempt, anger, revenge, and the other affects which are related to hatred or arise from it, are evil.

IV, 45

He who loves according to the guidance of reason strives as much as possible to repay the hatred, anger, or contempt of others toward himself with love and generosity.

IV, 46

In proportion, therefore, as we endeavor to live according to the guidance of reason, shall we strive as much as possible to depend less on hope, to liberate ourselves from fear, to rule fortune, and direct our actions by the counsels of reason.

IV, 47

The man who has properly understood that everything follows from the necessity of the divine nature, and comes to a pass accordingly to the eternal laws and rules of nature, will in truth discover nothing which is worthy of hatred, laughter, or contempt, nor will he pity any one, but, so far as human virtue is able, he will endeavor to *do well,* as we say, and to *rejoice.*

IV, 50

The crowd plays the tyrant, when it is not in fear.

IV, 63

If men were born free, they would, so long as they remained free, form no conception of good or evil.

IV, 68

No one can hate God.

V, 17

Blessedness is not the reward of virtue, but is virtue itself; nor do we rejoice in it because we restrain our lusts, but, on the contrary because we rejoice therein, we can restrain our lusts.

V, 42

There is no rational life, therefore, without intelligence, and things are good only in so far as they assist men to enjoy that life of the mind which is determined by intelligence. Those things alone, on the other hand, we call evil which hinder man from perfecting his reason and enjoying a rational life.

Appendix 5

With regard to marriage, it is plain that it is in accordance with reason, if the desire of connection is engendered not merely by external form, but by a love of begetting children and wisely educating them; and if, in addition, the love both of the husband and wife has for its cause not external form merely, but chiefly liberty of the mind.

Appendix 20

Theological-Political Treatise (1670)

Words can be treasonable as well as deeds.

Preface

We must necessarily permit what we cannot prevent, even though it often leads to harm. Things like extravagance, envy, greed, and drunkeness are a source of much evil; yet we put up with them because they cannot be prevented by legal enactment, vices though in fact they are.

Laws which prescribe what everyone must believe, and forbid men to say or write anything against this or that opinion, are often passed to gratify, or rather, to appease the anger of those who cannot abide independent minds.

Nothing is in itself absolutely sacred or profane, or unclean, apart from the mind, but only relatively thereto.

Philosophy has no end in view save truth; faith looks for nothing but obedience and piety.

The most tyrannical governments are those which make crimes of opinions, for everyone has an inalienable right to his thoughts.

XX

I do not know how to teach philosophy without becoming a disturber of the peace.

On being offered a Heidelberg professorship, 1670

BENJAMIN SPOCK
(1903–   )
American physician, writer

Inhibition is not unnatural . . . civilizations are built on restraints.

Interview, *N. Y. Times,* November 4, 1970

LYSANDER SPOONER
(1808–1887)
American lawyer, Libertarian

Trial by Jury

All restraints upon man's natural liberty, not necessary for the simple maintenance of justice, are of the nature of slavery, and differ from each other only in degree.

All governments, the worst on earth and the most tyrannical on earth, are free governments to that portion of the people who voluntarily support them.

MADAME DE STAËL (Anne Louise Germaine Necker, Baronne de Staël-Holstein)
(1766–1817)
Swiss-born French novelist

De l'Influence des passions (1796)

Love is the whole history of a woman's life; it is but an episode in a man's.

Corinne (1807)

Love is the emblem of eternity.

Tout comprendre rend très indulgent.
To understand all makes one tolerant.*

Once you have turned enthusiasm into ridicule, there is nothing left but money and power.

In life, you must choose between boredom and suffering.

Letter to Claud Rochet, 1800

*Frequently misquoted as *"Tout comprendre c'est tout pardonner"* ["To understand all is to forgive all"]. This saying is credited, by scholars, to Buddha.

The greatest things that man has done, he owes to the painful sense of incompleteness of his destiny.

Search for the truth is the noblest occupation of man; its publication is a duty.
Attributed by Dr. Ramon Guthrie, Head of French Dept., Dartmouth College

When woman no longer finds herself acceptable to men, she turns to religion.
Quoted in Noyes, *Views of Religion*

JOSEPH STALIN (Iosif Vissarionovich Dzhugashvili) (1879–1953) Ruler of the U.S.S.R.

Problems of Leninism (1940, tr. Max Eastman)

It is inconceivable that the Soviet Republic should continue to exist for a long period side by side with imperialist states—ultimately one or the other must conquer.

The press is the only weapon with whose aid the Party every day speaks to the working class in the language of the Party.
Contribution, *Pravda*, c.1917

"Three Years of Proletarian Dictatorship"

During the epoch of the dictatorship of the proletariat there can be no policy of universal freedom in our country, i.e., the freedom of speech, press, etc., for the bourgeoisie.
Speech, November 7, 1920

To put it briefly: the dictatorship of the proletariat is the domination of the proletariat over the bourgeoisie, untrammelled by the law and based on violence and enjoying the sympathy and support of the toiling and exploited masses.
Speech, April 24, 1924; International Publishers, New York, 1934

We guarantee the right of every citizen to combat by argument, propaganda and agitation, any and all religion. The Communist Party cannot be neutral toward religion. It stands for science, and all religion is opposed to science.
Declaration to American labor delegation, Moscow, September 7, 1927

We are in favor of the state withering away and at the same time we stand for the dictatorship of the proletariat. . . . Is it "contradictory"? Yes, it is "contradictory." But this contradiction is a living thing, and completely reflects Marxist dialectic.
Report to the 16th Congress of the CPSU, published in *Leninism*, 1942, vol. 2

Obsolete classes do not voluntarily abandon the stage of history. . . . Dying classes take to arms and resort to every means to save their existence as a ruling class. . . . I don't deny the role of the intelligentsia in revolutionary movements.

Education is a weapon, whose effect depends on who holds it in his hands and at whom it is aimed.
Stenogram of Stalin interview, July 23, 1934, from copy supplied by H. G. Wells

What can be the "personal freedom" of an unemployed person who goes hungry and finds no use for his toil?
Interview with Roy Howard, head of United Press, 1936

You cannot make a revolution with silk gloves.
Quoted in Gunther, *Soviet Russia Today*

How many divisions has the Pope?
Attributed by C. L. Sulzberger, *N.Y. Times*, October 8, 1958

ELIZABETH CADY STANTON (1815–1902) American reformer

The Bible and Church have been the greatest stumbling blocks in the way of women's emancipation.
Quoted in *Free Thought Magazine*, vol. xiv, September 1896

Throughout this protracted and disgraceful assault on American womanhood the clergy baptized each new insult and act of injustice in the name of the Christian religion, and uniformly asked God's blessing on proceedings that would have put to shame an assembly of Hottentots.
Public declaration; also signed by Mrs. Gage and Susan B. Anthony

The actual falsehood from which all forms of slavery originate is the doctrine of original sin, and woman as the medium for the machinations of Satan.
Quoted in Noyes, *Views of Religion*

LINCOLN STEFFENS
(1866–1936)
American journalist, muckraker

(Baruch) So you have been over into Russia?

(Steffens) I have been over there—and it works.
> Conversation, Hotel Crillon, Paris, 1919; as told to G. S. by Baruch*

The Christian churches would not recognize Christianity if they saw it.
> Quoted in Justin Kaplan, *Lincoln Steffens*

GERTRUDE STEIN
(1874–1946)
American writer

Vous êtes toute une génération perdue.
You are all a lost generation.**

Sacred Emily (1913)†

Rose is a rose is a rose. . . .

Brewsie and Willie (1946)

You'll be old and you never lived, and you kind of feel silly to lie down and die and to never have lived, to have been a job chaser and never have lived.

Lectures in America (1935)

The first hope of a painter who really feels hopeful about painting is the hope that the painting will move, that it will live outside its frame.

Sex and death are the springs of the most valid of human emotions. But they are not all; they are not even all emotions.

---

*Steffens frequently improved his remarks. The final version, in his autobiography: "I have been over into the future and it works."

**Gertrude Stein is not the author of this remark. She told Hemingway, who popularized it worldwide, that these exact words were said to her by her garage owner, who was referring to his post-war apprentices. The words first appeared as an epigraph in *The Sun Also Rises* (1926).

†A reference to a woman, not a flower, Miss Stein told the editor of *The Dial*.

Literature—creative literature—unconcerned with sex, is inconceivable.
> Quoted by J. B. Preston, "A Conversation," *Atlantic Monthly*

What is the answer? . . . In that case, what is the question?
> To Alice B. Toklas; from her deathbed

JOHN STEINBECK
(1902–1968)
American writer, Nobel Prize 1962

The Grapes of Wrath (1939)

A red is any son-of-a-bitch who wants thirty cents an hour when we're payin' twenty-five!

The Short Reign of Pippin IV (1957)

The King said, "Power does not corrupt. Fear corrupts, perhaps the fear of a loss of power."

Sweet Thursday (1958)

Man owes something to man. If he ignores the debt it poisons him, and if he tries to make payments the debt only increases, and the quality of his gift is the measure of the man.

America and Americans (1966)

I have named the destroyers of nations: comfort, plenty and security—out of which grow a bored and slothful cynicism, in which rebellion against the world as it is, and myself as I am, are submerged in listless self-satisfaction.

A dying people tolerates the present, rejects the future, and finds its satisfactions in past greatness and half-remembered glory.

I find it valid to understand man as an animal before I am prepared to know him as a man.
> Quoted by Daniel Aaron, *Saturday Review*, September 9, 1968

CHARLES P(roteus) STEINMETZ
(1865–1923)
American engineer, inventor

In the realm of science all attempts to find any evidence of supernatural beings, of metaphysical conceptions, as God, immortality, in-

finity, etc., thus far have failed, and if we are honest we must confess that in science there exists no God, no immortality, no soul or mind as distinct from the body.
Quoted in *American Freeman,* July 1941

STENDHAL (Marie Henri Beyle) (1783–1842) French writer

De l'Amour (1822)

There are four different kinds of love:
1. Passion-love, that of the Portuguese Nun, of Héloise for Abélard. . . .
2. Sympathy-love, such as . . . is found in the memoirs and romances. . . .
3. Sensual love.
4. Vanity love.

Ch. 1

Man is not free to refuse to do the thing which gives him more pleasure than any other conceivable action.

Ch. 5

Women prefer emotions to reasoning.

Ch. 7

Fragments

Prudery is a kind of avarice, the world of all.

5

Only great minds can afford a simple style.

28

One can acquire everything in solitude—except character.

92

The only unions which are always legitimate are those which are ordained by true passion.

115

Le Rouge et le noir [*The Red and the Black*] (1830)

The boredom of married life is inevitably the death of love whenever love has preceded marriage.

There is no such thing as "natural law": this expression is nothing but old nonsense. Prior to laws, what is natural is only the strength of the lion, or the need of the creature suffering from hunger or cold, in short, need.

STEPHEN I Pope 254–257

Let them innovate in nothing, but keep the tradition.
Letter to St. Cyprian (*Ep. Cyprian,* 74)

STEPHEN V Pope 885–891

The Popes, like Jesus, are conceived by their mothers through the overshadowing of the Holy Ghost. All Popes are a certain species of man-gods, for the purpose of being able to conduct the functions of mediator between God and mankind. All powers in Heaven, as well as on earth, are given to them.
Attributed

ALEXANDER H. STEPHENS (1812–1883) Vice-President, Confederate States of America

To maintain that Slavery is *in itself sinful,* in the face of all that is said and written in the Bible upon the subject, with so many sanctions of the relation by the Deity himself, does not seem to me to be little short of blasphemous! It is a direct imputation upon the wisdom and justice, as well as the declared ordinances, of God, as they are written in the inspired oracles, to say nothing of their manifestations in the universe around us.
Quoted in Pendleton, *Alexander H. Stephens,* vol. 2

JAMES STEPHENS (1882–1950) Irish writer

The Crock of Gold (1930)

Women are wiser than men because they know less and understand more.

Ch. 2

Some people think hunger is necessary for art. It is not. All that comes from hunger and the lower hardships, is dullness.
Letter, pub. 1975

WALLACE STEVENS
(1879–1955)
American poet

"Sunday Morning" (1923)

She says, "But in contentment I still feel
The need of some imperishable bliss."
Death is the mother of Beauty; hence from
  her,
Alone, shall come fulfillment to our dreams
And our desires.

St. 5

ROBERT LEWIS (Balfour) STEVENSON
(1850–1894)
British essayist, novelist, poet*

An Apology for Idlers (1877; reprinted in Virginibus Puerisque)

Idleness so called, which does not consist in doing nothing, but in doing a great deal not recognized by the dogmatic formularies of the ruling class, has as good a right to state its position as industry itself. It is admitted that the presence of people who refuse to enter in the great handicap race for sixpenny pieces, is at once an insult and a disenchantment for those who do.

Books are good enough in their own way, but they are a mighty bloodless substitute for life.

And if a man reads very hard, as the old anecdote reminds us, he will have little time for thought.

Extreme busyness whether at school or college, kirk or market, is a symptom of deficient vitality; and a faculty for idleness implies a catholic appetite and a strong sense of personal identity.

As if a man's soul were not too small to begin with, they have dwarfed and narrowed theirs by a life of all work and no play; until here they are at forty, with a listless attention, a mind vacant of all material of amusement, and not one thought to rub against another, while they wait for the train.

---

*Born in Edinburgh; christened Lewis—not Louis—according to Britannica, 11th ed.

Look at one of your industrious fellows for a moment. He sows hurry and reaps indigestion; he puts a vast deal of activity out to interest, and receives a large measure of nervous derangement in return. . . . I do not care how much or how well he works, this fellow is an evil feature in other people's lives. They would be happier if he were dead. . . . He poisons life at the well-head. It is better to be beggared out of hand by a scapegrace nephew, than daily hag-ridden by a peevish uncle.

There is no duty we underrate so much as the duty of being happy.

Virginibus Puerisque (1881)

In marriage a man becomes slack and selfish, and undergoes a fatty degeneration of his moral being.

Marriage is . . . a field of battle, and not a bed of roses.

I, Ch. 1

To marry is to domesticate the Recording Angel.

Ch. 2

The cruellest lies are often told in silence.
Ch. 4, "Truth of Intercourse"

Underwoods (1887)

Under the wide and starry sky,
Dig the grave and let me lie.
Glad did I live and gladly die,
  And I laid me down with a will.

This be the verse you grave for me:
Here he lies where he longed to be;
Home is the sailor, home from the sea,
  And the hunter home from the hill.
"Requiem"

Across the Plains (1892)

No man is useless while he has a friend.
"Lay Morals"

MAX STIRNER (Johann Kaspar Schmidt)
(1806–1856)
German writer, founder of theoretical anarchism

The Ego and His Own (1845)

Individually free is he who is responsible to no man.

A race of altruists is necessarily a race of slaves. A race of free men is necessarily a race of egoists.

The State seeks to hinder every free activity by its censorship, its supervision, its police; and holds this hindering to be its duty, because it is in truth a duty of self-preservation.

A fig for good and evil! I am I, and I am neither good nor evil. Neither has any meaning for me.

Property exists by force of the law. It is not a fact, but a legal fiction.

The State calls its own violence law, but that of the individual crime.

Before what is sacred, people lose all sense of power and all confidence; they occupy a *powerless* and *humble* attitude toward it. And yet no thing is sacred of itself, but by my *declaring it sacred,* by my declaration, my judgment, my bending the knee; in short, by my conscience.

The State rests on the *slavery of labor.* If *labor* becomes *free,* the State is lost.

The liberty of the press is always bound to favorable opportunities, and accordingly will never be an absolute liberty; Not *in* the State, but only *against* it can the liberty of the press be carried through.

Along with worldly goods, all sacred goods must be put away as no longer valuable.

Truths are phrases, ways of speaking, words; brought into connection, or into an articulate series, they form logic, science, philosophy.

The truth wears longer than all the gods; for it is only in the truth's service, and for love of it, that people have overthrown the gods and at last God himself. "The truth" outlasts the downfall of the world of gods, for it is the immortal soul of this transitory world of gods; it is Deity itself.

I will answer Pilate's question, What is truth? Truth is the free thought, the free idea, the free spirit.

WILBUR F. STOREY
(1819–1884)
Editor, Chicago *Times*

It is a newspaper's duty to print the news, and raise hell.
Statement, 1861

WILLIAM SCOTT, LORD STOWELL
(1745–1836)
Attorney General of England

A precedent embalms a principle.
Opinions, vol. 1; Disraeli's motto, attributed to him

GUSTAV STRESEMANN
(1878–1929)
German chancellor, Nobel Prize 1926

Sometimes you think you hear the voice of Almighty God, and it is only that of a Privy Councillor (*Geheimrat*).
To G. S., Foreign Office reception, 1925;
a reference to journalists

AUGUST STRINDBERG
(1849–1912)
Swedish writer

Married (1884)

The present attempt to liberate women is a revolt against nature.

There should be complete equality between the sexes, which will do away with that resulting form of hypocrisy called gallantry, or politeness to ladies.

Man and wife will conclude a contract, verbal or written, for a union of any length they may decide, which they will have the right to dissolve when they please, without reference to law or gospel.
Preface

ANDRÉ SUARÈS
(1868–1948)
French writer

Voici l'homme (1906)

As one wages war with the blood of others, so one makes a fortune with the money of others.

Péguy (1928)

Heresy is the lifeblood of religion. It is faith that makes heretics. In a dead religion there are no longer heresies.

SUETONIUS (Gaius Suetonius Tranquillus) (c.70–c.140 A.D.)
Roman historian

Lives of the Caesars

Make haste slowly.
"Augustus," 25

Hail, Emperor, those about to die salute you.
"Claudius," 21

ARTHUR HAYS SULZBERGER (1891–1968)
Publisher, *New York Times*

Man's right to knowledge and the free use thereof.
Theme for Columbia University bicentennial, 1968

A man's judgment cannot be better than the information on which he has based it. . . . [G]ive him no news or present him only with distorted and incomplete data, with ignorant, sloppy or biased reporting, with propaganda and deliberate falsehoods, and you destroy his whole reasoning process and make him something less than a man.
Address, N.Y. State Publishers Association, August 30, 1948

WILLIAM GRAHAM SUMNER (1840–1910)
American economist, sociologist

The Challenge of Facts (1880)

Nature is entirely neutral; she submits to him who most energetically and resolutely assails her. She grants her rewards to the fittest.

It is the utmost folly to denounce capital. To do so is to undermine civilization, for capital is the first requisite of every social gain, educational, ecclesiastical, political or other.

War (1903)

If you want war, nourish a doctrine. Doctrines are the most frightful tyrants to which men ever are subject, because doctrines get inside a man's reason and betray him against himself. Civilized men have done their fiercest fighting for doctrines.

Address, "The Forgotten Man" (1883)

The state, it cannot be too often repeated, does nothing and can give nothing which it does not take from somebody.

The Forgotten Man works and votes—generally he prays—but his chief business in life is to pay.

Wealth comes only from production, and all that the wrangling grabbers, loafers, and robbers get to deal with comes from somebody's toil and sacrifice—who then is he who provides it all? Go and find him and you will have once more before you the Forgotten Man.

WILLIAM A. (Billy) SUNDAY (1862–1935)
American evangelist

The rivers of America will run with blood filled to their banks before we will submit to them taking the Bible out of our schools.

When the consensus of scholarship says one thing and the Word of God another, the consensus of scholarship can go plumb to hell for all I care.
Revival meeting, Pittsburgh, Pa., 1912; reported by G. S.

America is not a country for a dissenter to live in.
Quoted in W. G. McLoughlin, *Billy Sunday Was His Real Name*

SUN TZU WU (fl. 500 B.C.)
Army commander of the King of Wu

Art of War (tr. Lionel Giles, London, 1910)

All warfare is based on deception.

There is no instance of a country having benefited from prolonged warfare.

Hence to fight and conquer in all our battles is not supreme excellence; supreme excellence consists in breaking the enemy's resistance without fighting.

DAISETZ T. SUZUKI
(1870–1966)
Japanese professor of philosophy

Zen Buddhism (1956)

Zen in its essence is the art of seeing into the nature of one's own being, and it points the way from bondage to freedom. By making us drink right from the fountain of life, it liberates us from all the yokes under which we finite beings are usually suffering in this world.

EMANUEL SWEDENBORG
(1688–1772)
Swedish theologian

Heaven and Hell (1758)

Hell and Heaven are near man, yes, in him; and every man after death goes to that Hell or that Heaven in which he was, or to his spirit, during his abode in the world.

Man is born to be intellectual, thus to think from the understanding; woman is born to be voluntary, thus to think from the will.

That love is the essence of heat is evident from the fact that the mind, and thence the body, becomes warm from love, and according to its degree and quality; and this man experiences in Winter as in Summer.

Infidelity has emanated chiefly from the learned.

Arcana Coelestia (1856)

Conscience is God's presence in man.

I have seen a thousand times that angels are human forms, or men, for I have conversed with them as man to man, sometimes with one alone, sometimes with many in company.
Vol. 1

Divine Providence (1764)

We are, because God is.

JONATHAN SWIFT
(1667–1745)
Irish satirist, Dean of St. Patrick's

Thoughts on Various Subjects (1706)

When men grow virtuous in their old age they are merely making a sacrifice to God of the devil's leavings.

Every man desires to live long; but no man would be old.

It is impossible that anything so natural, so necessary, and so universal as death should ever have been designed by Providence as an evil to mankind.

When a true genius appears in this world you may know him by this sign, that the dunces are all in confederacy against him.

We have just enough religion to make us hate, but not enough to make us love one another.

Arbitrary power is the natural object of temptation to a prince; as wine and women to a young fellow, or a bribe to a judge, or avarice to old age, or vanity to a woman.

"A Modest Proposal: For Preventing the Children of Poor People in Ireland From Being a Burden to Their Parents or Country" (1729)
I have been assured by a very knowing American of my acquaintance in London, that a young healthy child well nursed is at a year old a most delicious, nourishing and wholesome food, whether stewed, roasted, baked, or boiled, and I make no doubt that it will equally serve in a fricassee, or a ragout.

Gulliver's Travels (1726)

Whoever could make two ears of corn, or two blades of grass, to grow upon a spot of ground where only one grew before, would deserve more of mankind, and do more essential service to his country, than the whole race of politicians put together.
II, "Voyage to Brobdingnag," ch. 7

There is nothing so extravagant and irrational which some philosophers have not maintained for truth.
III, "Voyage to Laputa," ch. 6

A soldier is a Yahoo hired to kill in cold blood as many of his own species, who have never offended him, as possibly he can.
IV, "Voyage to the Country of the Houyhnhnms," ch. 5

The Battle of the Books (1697)

Instead of dirt and poison we have rather chosen to fill our lives with honey and wax; thus furnishing mankind with the two noblest of things which are sweetness and light. *

---

*Matthew Arnold appropriated the last phrase.

War is the child of Pride, and Pride the daughter of Riches. . . . The most ancient and natural grounds for quarrels are Lust and Avarice; which though we may allow to be brethren or collateral branches of Pride, are certainly the issues of Want.

A malignant deity, called Criticism. . . . At her right hand sat Ignorance, her father and husband, blind with age; at her left, Pride, her mother, dressing her up in scraps of paper herself had torn. There was Opinion, her sister, light of foot, hood-winked, and headstrong, yet giddy and perpetually turning. About her played her children, Noise and Impudence, Dullness and Vanity, Positiveness, Pedantry, and Ill-Manners. The goddess herself had claws like a cat, her head, and ears, and voice resembled those of an ass; her teeth fallen out before, her eyes turned inward, as if she also looked only upon herself; her diet was the overflowing of her own gall.

Preface

The Correspondence of Jonathan Swift

For life is a Tragedy, wherein we sit as Spectators awhile, and act out our own Part in it.

Self-love; as it is the Motive of all our Actions, so it is the sole Cause of our Grief. The dear Person you lament, is by no means an object of Pity, either in a moral or religious sense.

Philosophy always taught Men to despise Life as a most contemptible thing in itself, and Religion regards it only as preparation for a better.

Law is a bottomless pit; it is a cormorant, a harpy that devours everything.

That the universe was formed by a fortuitous concourse of the atoms, I will no more believe than that the accidental jumbling of the alphabet should fall into a most ingenious treatise on Philosophy.

Quoted in *New York Times Magazine*,
April 29, 1962

ALGERNON CHARLES SWINBURNE (1837–1909)
English poet

"The Garden of Proserpine"

I am tired of tears and laughter,
    And men that laugh and weep,
Of what may come hereafter
    For men that sow to reap.

St. 2

From too much love of living,
    From hope and fear set free,
We thank with brief thanksgiving
    Whatever gods may be
That no life lives forever;
That dead men rise up never;
That even the weariest river
    Winds somewhere safe to sea.

St. 11

"Atalanta in Calydon" (1865)

Before the beginning of years
    There came to the making of man
Time, with a gift of tears;
    Grief, with a glass that ran;
Pleasure, with pain for leaven;
    Summer, with flowers that fell;
Remembrance, fallen from heaven,
    And madness risen from hell;
Strength without hands to smite;
    Love that endures for a breath;
Night, the shadow of light,
    And life, the shadow of death.

"To Walt Whitman in America"

The earth god Freedom, the lonely
    Face lightening, the footprint unshod.
Not as one man crucified only
    Nor scourged with but one life's rod:
The soul that is substance of nations,
Reincarnate with fresh generations;
    The great god Man, which is God.

St. 17

"A Ballad of Francois Villon"

Bird of the bitter bright grey golden
    morn. . . .

Prince of sweet songs made out of tears and
    fire,
A harlot was thy nurse, a God thy sire.

Villon, our sad bad glad mad brother's
    name.

"Dolores" (1866)

Ah beautiful passionate body
That never has ached with a heart!

St. 11

For the crown of our life as it closes
Is darkness, the fruit there of dust;
No thorns go as deep as the rose's,
And love is more cruel than lust.

Time turns the old days to derision,
Our loves into corpses or wives;
And marriage and death and division
Make barren our lives.
                                                St. 20

Come down and redeem us from virtue,
    Our Lady of Pain.
                                                St. 35

"Hymn to Proserpine"

Thou has conquered, O pale Galilean; the
    world has grown grey from thy breath;
We have drunken of things Lethean, and
        fed on
    the fulness of death.
Laurel is green for a season, and love is
        sweet
    for a day.
And love grown bitter with treason, and
        laurel
    outlives not May.

"Hertha"

I am that which began;
Out of me the years roll;
I am equal and Whole;
God changes, and man, and the form of
    them bodily;
I am the soul.

"Dedication, 1865"

Change lays not her hand upon truth.

JOHN SWINTON
(1830–1901
Editor, *New York Sun*

There is no such thing as an independent
press in America. I am paid for keeping my
honest opinions out of the paper I am connected with. Any of you who would be so foolish as to write honest opinions would be out
on the street looking for another job.

We are the tools and vassals of the rich men
behind the scenes. We are the jumping jacks;
they pull the strings and we dance. Our talents, our possibilities and our lives are all the
property of other men. We are intellectual
prostitutes.
            Reply to the toast, "An Independent Press,"
        journalists' gathering, Twilight Club, New York
                            City, April 12, 1893

SYRUS, *see* Publilius Syrus

ALBERT SZENT-GYÖRGYI
(1893–   )
American biochemist, Nobel Prize 1937

Whatever a man does he must do first in his
mind.

Our species . . . probably has not changed
during the last 20,000 years. . . . Here we
stand in the middle of this new world with our
primitive brain, attuned to the simple cave
life, with terrific forces at our disposal, which
we are clever enough to release, but whose
consequences we cannot comprehend.
            Contribution, *Saturday Review,* July 7, 1962

You have only to wish it and you can have a
world without hunger, disease, cancer and
toil—anything you wish, wish anything and it
can be done. Or else we can exterminate ourselves . . . at present we are on the road to extermination.

Man is a very strange animal. In much of
the world half the children go to bed hungry
and we spend a trillion on rubbish—steel,
iron, tanks. We are all criminals. There is an
old Hungarian poem, "If you are among brigands and you are silent, you are a brigand
yourself."
            Contribution, *Paris Herald Tribune,*
                            February 23, 1970

It is sad that man is not intelligent enough
to solve problems without killing. . . . The
present world crisis can be solved only by a
general human revolution against outdated
concepts. . . . Man is not a blood-thirsty animal, and war is only due to the greed and lust
for power of relatively small groups, the conspiracy of the few against the many.
            Contribution, *The Churchman,* November 1978

CORNELIUS TACITUS
(c. 55–117 A.D.)
Roman historian

Life of Agricola (c. 97–98)

To robbery, slaughter, plunder they give the lying name of empire; they make a desert and call it peace.

Everything unknown is taken for something great.
Sec. 30 (quoting the "barbarian" chief Calgacus)

Histories (c. 115–116)

Gold and riches, the chief causes of war.

We are corrupted by prosperity.

There will be vices as long as there are men.
Bk. I

The desire for fame is the last infirmity cast off even by the wise.
Bk. IV

Annals (c. 115–116)

Nothing is so weak and unstable as a reputation for power not based on force.

Lust for power is the most flagrant of all the passions.

The desire for safety stands against every great and noble enterprise.

A race prone to superstition, opposed to religion. *
Ch. II

The more corrupt the State the more numerous the laws.

The chief duty of the historian is to judge the actions of men, so that the good may meet with the reward due to virtue, and pernicious citizens may be deterred by the condemnation

---

*Supposedly a reference to the Jews.

that awaits evil deeds at the tribunal of posterity. *
Ch. III

Christus . . . suffered the extreme penalty during the reign of Tiberius at the hands of one of our procurators, Pontius Pilatus.
Ch. XV (said to be the first historical reference to Jesus Christ)

ROBERT A. TAFT
(1889–1953)
American politician

Every Republican candidate for President since 1936 has been nominated by the Chase National Bank.
Statement to the press, after defeat in 1952 G.O.P. convention

---

WILLIAM HOWARD TAFT
(1857–1930)
27th President of the United States

One cannot always be sure of the truth of what one hears if he happens to be President of the United States.
Quoted in Archie Butt, *Taft and Roosevelt*, vol. II

RABINDRANATH TAGORE
(1861–1941)
Bengali philosopher, Nobel Prize 1913

"Prayer: Gitanjali" (1913)

Where the mind is without fear and the
head is held high,
Where knowledge is free; . . .
Where tireless striving stretches the arms
toward perfection;
Where the clear stream of reason has not
lost its way
into the dreary desert sand of dead
habits; . . .
My father,
let my country awake.

"Stray Birds"

Men are cruel, but Man is kind.

---

*"A strange conception, which turns history into a last judgment and the historian into a God."—Will Durant, *Caesar or Christ*.

Every child comes with the message that God is not yet discouraged of man.

It is cruel crime thoughtlessly to bring more children into existence than can be properly taken care of.
> Quoted on poster, Delhi Exposition, 1965

HIPPOLYTE TAINE
(1828–1893)
French critic, historian

Notes sur Paris (1868)

There are four kinds of people in the world: those in love, the ambitious, the observers, and the stupid. The most happy are the stupid.

S. G. TALLENTYRE (pen name of E. Beatrice Hall)
(1858–?)
British writer

The Friends of Voltaire (1906)

I disapprove of what you say, but I will defend to the death your right to say it.*

CHARLES MAURICE DE TALLEYRAND-PÉRIGORD
(1754–1838)
French statesman

It is no longer an event; it is only a news item.
> Comment on Napoleon's death

Without freedom of the press there can be no representative government.
> Address, Chamber of Deputies, 1822; quoted by J.F. Bernard

Mirabeau: he lacked the courage to be unpopular.

---

*Replying to the question, whether she or Voltaire was the author of this world-famous quotation, Miss Hall wrote Attorney Harry Weinberger of New York City, July 20, 1935: "I believe that I did use the phrase as a description of Voltaire's attitude. . . . I did not intend to imply that Voltaire used these words verbatim."

What clever man has ever needed to commit a crime? Crime is the last resort of political half-wits.
> Quoted in J.F. Bernard, *Talleyrand*

It is not man's fault but the malice and imposture of priests and kings which have everywhere destroyed truth.
> Quoted in Noyes, *Views of Religion*

War is much too serious a thing to be left to military men.
Attributed to Talleyrand by Briand, who quoted it to Lloyd George. Clemenceau claimed it was his own.

They have learned nothing and forgotten nothing.
> Attributed by Chevalier de Panat, 1796; a reference to the Bourbons (cf. Napoleon)

ROGER BROOKE TANEY
(1777–1864)
U.S. Supreme Court Justice

The question is simply this: Can a Negro, whose ancestors were imported into this country, and sold as slaves, become a member of the political community formed and brought into existence by the Constitution of the United States, and as such become entitled to all the rights and privileges, and immunities, guaranteed by that instrument?

The question before us is, whether the class of persons described in the plea in abatement compose a portion of this people, and are constituent members of this sovereignty. We think they are not.

Congress has no power to abolish or prevent slavery in any of its territories.
> Dred Scott v. Sanford, 19 Howard 393 (1858)*

TORQUATO TASSO
(1544–1595)
Italian poet

"Jerusalem Delivered" (1582)

O noble lie! was ever truth so good?
> ii, 22

Women have tongues of craft, and hearts of guile,

---

*"Probably the most unworthy, ill-advised opinion in its long history."—Justice Douglas on the Supreme Court's decision in the Dred Scott Case.

They will; they will not; fools that on
  them
trust;
For in their speech is death, hell in their
  smile.
                                    xix, 84

None merit the name of creator save God
and the poet.
           Quoted in Briffault, *The Mothers* (1927)

TATIAN
(fl. 2nd century)
Syrian-Christian apologist, heretic

Oratio ad Graecos (c. 150)

Nothing evil was created by God; we ourselves have produced all the wickedness.

RICHARD H. TAWNEY
(1880–1962)
British educator

Religion and the Rise of Capitalism (1926)

Capitalism was the social counterpart of
Calvinist Theology.

The interests of them who own the property
used in industry is that their capital should be
dear and human beings cheap.
                                    Ch. 2

In every human soul there is a socialist and
an individualist, an authoritarian and a fanatic
for liberty, as in each there is a Catholic and a
Protestant.
                                    Ch. 4

The certainties of one age are the problems
of the next.

Property is not theft, but a good deal of theft
becomes property.
                                    Ch. 5

BISHOP JEREMY TAYLOR
(1613–1667)
English prelate

Twenty-seven Sermons (1653)

Marriage hath in it less of beauty, but more
of safety, than the single life; it hath more
care, but less danger; it is more merry, and
more sad; it is fuller of sorrows, and fuller of
joys; it lies under more burdens, but it is supported by all the strengths of love, and charity,
and those burdens are delightful.

Hell could not be Hell without the despair
of accursed souls; for any hope were a refresh-
ment, and a drop of water, which would help
to allay those flames, which as they burn intol-
erably, so they must burn forever.

The Rule and Exercise of Holy Living (1650)

Husbands must give to their wives love,
maintenance, duty, and the sweetness of conversation; and wives must pay them all they
have or can, with the interest of obedience and
reverence.

A great fear, when it is ill-managed, is the
parent of superstition, but a discrete and well-
guided fear produces religion.

The Mysteriousness of Marriage (1651)

Let husband and wife infinitely avoid a curious distinction of mine and thine, for this hath
caused all the laws, and all the suits, and all
the wars in the world.

God that commanded us to forgive our enemies left it in our choice, and hath not commanded us to forgive an adulterous husband or
a wife.

JOHN TAYLOR
(1580–1653)
English pamphleteer

The Unnatural Father (1621)

As concerning lust or incontinency, it is a
short pleasure bought with a long pain, a hon-
eyed poison, a gulf of shame, a pickpurse, a
breeder of disease, a gall to the conscience, a
corrosive to the heart, turning man's wit into
foolish madness, the body's bane, and the
soul's perdition.

RICHARD TAYLOR
(1919–   )
American professor of philosophy

That we should cease to exist, that we
should live and so profoundly will our existence, only to face annihilation a few years
hence, is a thought from which men recoil,
not pausing to ask *why* such simple non-exist-

ence should be filled with such dread for them, but dreading it nonetheless. It is from this calamity that religion promises salvation, and upon this promise its strength and appeal entirely rest.

Introduction to Schopenhauer's The Will to Live, xv

SIR WILLIAM TEMPLE
(1881–1944)
Archbishop of Canterbury

The Faith of Modern Thought

The problem of evil. . . . Why does God permit it? Or, if God is omnipotent, in which case permission and creation are the same, why did God create it?

One of the best of the good things of life is victory and particularly moral victory. But to demand victory without an antagonist is to demand something with no meaning. If, then, goodness is to exist . . . there must at least be an antagonist to be overcome.

ALFRED, 1ST LORD TENNYSON
(1809–1892)
English poet laureate

Idylls of the King (1859–85)

For man is man and master of his fate.
"The Marriage of Geraint," line 352

. . . Men at most differ as heaven and
    earth,
But women, worst and best, as heaven and
    hell.
"Merlin and Vivien," line 812

The old order changeth, yielding place to
    new;
And God fulfills himself in many ways,
Lest one good custom should corrupt the
    world.
"The Passing of Arthur," lines 107–109

"Charge of the Light Brigade" (1854)

Theirs not to make reply,
Theirs not to reason why,
Theirs but to do and die.
St. 2

"Maud" (1855)

But the churchmen fain would kill their
    Church,
As the churches have killed their Christ.
Pt. II, v, 2

"Oenone" (1832)

Self-reverence, self-knowledge, self-control,
These three alone lead life to sovereign
    power.
Lines 142–43

"Locksley Hall" (1842)

Cursed be the social wants that sin against
    the strength of youth!
Cursed be the social ties that warp us from
    the living truth!
Cursed be the sickly forms that err from
    honest Nature's rule!
Cursed be the gold that gilds the straighten'd
    forehead of the fool!
Lines 59–63

I myself must mix with action, lest I wither
    by despair.
Line 96

Till the war-drums throbbed no longer and
    the battle flags were furled
In the Parliament of man, the Federation of
    the world.
Lines 127–28

"In Memoriam: A.H.H."* (1850)

Let knowledge grow from more to more,
    But more of reverence in us dwell;
    That mind and soul,
May make one music as before.
Prologue, st. 7

But, for the unquiet heart and brain
    A use in measured language lies;
The sad mechanic exercise,
Like dull narcotics numbing pain.
v, st. 2

I hold it true, whate'er befall;
    I feel it, when I sorrow most;
'Tis better to have loved and lost
    Than never to have loved at all.
xxvii, st. 4

There lives more faith in honest doubt,
Believe me, than in half the creeds.
xcvi, st. 3

*In memory of Arthur Henry Hallam.

The year is going, let him go;
Ring out the false, ring in the true.

cv, st. 2

Ring out the feud of rich and poor,
Ring in redress to all mankind.

cv, st. 3

Ring out old shapes of foul disease,
  Ring out the narrowing lust of gold;
  Ring out the thousand wars of old,
Ring in the thousand years of peace.

cv, st. 7·

"The Grandmothers" (1864)

That a lie which is half a truth is ever the
  blackest of lies,
That a lie which is all a lie may be met and
  fought with outright,
But a lie which is part a truth is a harder
  matter to fight.

St. 8

"Ulysses" (1842)

Tho' much is taken, much abides; and tho'
We are not now that strength which in old
  days
Moved earth and heaven; that which we are,
  we are;
One equal temper of heroic hearts,
Made weak by time and fate, but strong in
  will
To strive, to seek, to find, and not to yield.

Lines 44–49

"Tithonius" (1860)

The woods decay, the woods decay and fall,
The vapours weep their burden to the
  ground,
Man comes and tills the fields and lies be-
  neath,
And after many a summer dies the swan.

Lines 1–4

"The Lotos-Eaters" (1833)

Death is the end of life; ah, why
Should life all labour be? . . .
All things have rest, and ripen toward the
  grave
In silence—ripen, fall, and cease;
Give use long rest or death, dark death, or
  dreamful ease.

St. 4

The Princess (1847)

Dear as remembered kisses after death,
And sweet as those by hopeless fancy feigned
On lips that are for others; deep as love,
Deep as first love, and wild with all regret;
O Death in Life, the days that are no more.

"Tears, Idle Tears," st. 4

"Mariana" (1830)

She only said, "The night is dreary,
  He cometh not," she said;
She said, "I am aweary, aweary,
  I would that I were dead!"

Refrain

**TERENCE (Publius Terentius Afer)
(c. 190–159 B.C.)
Latin playwright***

Heauton Timorumenos [*The Self-Tormentor*] (163
B.C.)

*Homo sum, et humani nihil a me alienum
est.*
  I am a man, and nothing pertaining to man
is alien to me.

Line 77**

  The strictest justice is sometimes the greatest
injustice.

Line 796

  How many unjust and wicked things are
done from habit.

Line 970

Andria

  The golden rule is moderation in all things.

Line 61

The Eunuch (161 B.C.)

  Nothing is said nowadays that has not been
said before.

Line 41, prologue

  Facts speak for themselves.

Line 659

  When we will, they [women] won't; and
when we won't, they want to exceedingly.

Line 812

---

*Probably born in Carthage, date uncertain; brought
to Rome as a slave; disappeared at sea.
**Karl Marx's favorite maxim.

The Brothers

Old age brings this one vice to mankind, that we all think too much of money.

Line 833

Phormio (161 B.C.)

How unjust it is, that they who have but little should be always adding something to the wealth of the rich!

Line 40

Fortune favors the brave.

Line 203

So many men, so many opinions.

Line 454

TERTULLIAN (Quintus Septimus Tertullianus) (c. 160–240) Carthage-born Christian writer

De Carne Christi (c. 209)

It is certain because it is impossible.*

5

Apologeticus (c. 197)

The first reaction to truth is hatred.

7

For us murder is once for all forbidden; so even the child in the womb . . . it is not lawful for us to destroy. To forbid birth is only quicker murder. . . . The fruit is always present in the seed.

9

He [God] is invisible, although seen; incomprehensible, although revealed by grace; unfathomable, although fathomed by the human senses.

17

The Devil is God's ape.

23

The most ignorant peasant under the Christian dispensation possesses more real knowledge than the wisest of the ancient philosophers.

48

The more ye mow us down, the more quickly we grow; the blood of Christians is seed.

197

On Women's Dress (c. 220)

And do you not think that each of you women is an Eve? The judgment of God upon your sex endures even today; and with it inevitably endures your position of criminal at the bar of justice.

Bk. 1, ch. 1

A holy woman may be beautiful by the gift of nature, but she must not give occasion to lust. If beauty be hers, so far from setting it off she ought rather to obscure it.

Bk. II, ch. IV

A woman's appearance depends upon two things: the clothes she wears and the time she gives to her toilet. . . . Against the first we bring the charge of ostentation, against the second of harlotry.

Bk. II, ch. XI

Ad Uxorem (c. 202–203)

It is better to marry only because it is worse to burn. It is better neither to marry nor to burn.

Spectacles (c. 202–203)

Even those magistrates who abet the stage, discountenance the players. They stigmatize their characters and cramp their freedom. The whole tribe is thrown out of all honor and privilege.

X

There is no public entertainment which does not inflict spiritual damage.

XV

WILLIAM MAKEPEACE THACKERAY (1811–1863) English novelist

Vanity Fair (1848)

I think I could be a good woman if I had five thousand a year. [Becky Sharp]

Vol. II, ch. 1

---

*Probable origin of the phrase, *Credo quia impossibile,* "I believe because it is impossible"; condemned by Pius IX sixteen centuries later. "I can answer all the objections of Satan . . . with that odd resolution I learned of Tertullian, *Certum est quia impossible est.*"—Sir Thomas Browne, *Religio Medici.*

The Book of Snobs (1848)

People dare not be happy for fear of Snobs. People dare not love for fear of Snobs. People pine away lonely under the tyranny of Snobs. Honest kindly hearts dry up and die. Gallant generous lads, blooming with hearty youth, swell into bloated old-bachelorhood, and burst and tumble over. Tender girls wither into shrunken decay, and perish solitary, from whom Snobbishness has cut off the common claim to happiness and affection with which Nature endowed us all.

Ch. XXXIII

THALES OF MILETUS
(640?–c. 546 B.C.)
Semitic founder of Greek sciences, philosophy

Know Thyself.
Attributed by Diogenes Laërtius, also attributed to Solon and others

Nothing in excess.
Attributed; also attributed to Solon and Socrates

To the question, "What is the divinity?" he said, "That which has neither beginning or end."

When asked how men might live most virtuously and most justly, he said, "If we never do ourselves what we blame in others."

Hope is the only God common to all men; those who have nothing more, possess hope still.
Attributed

All things are full of gods.

Water is the principal, or the element, of things.
Attributed by Aristotle

Love thy neighbor.
Attributed by Stobaeus, *Floriletium*, iv, 79

U THANT
(1909–1974)
Burmese Secretary General, United Nations

In modern war there is no such thing as victor and vanquished. . . . [T]here is only a loser, and that loser is mankind.
Address, Economic Club, New York City, 1963

If we are not able to prevent a third world war, we shall go down in history—if history should survive—as the guilty generation, the generation which did nothing to prevent the annihilation of mankind itself.
Quoted in *N.Y. Times*, November 12, 1963

MARGARET THATCHER
(1925–   )
Tory leader, Prime Minister of Great Britain

I do regard the Russian threat as a worldwide thing. Their objective has never changed: it is the domination of the world by the Communist system.

There can be no liberty unless there is economic liberty.

Extinguish free enterprise and you extinguish liberty.
Interview, *Time*, May 14, 1979

THEMISTOCLES
(c. 528–462 B.C.)
Greek soldier, statesman

He who commands the sea has command of everything.
Quoted in Cicero, *Epistolae ad Atticum*, X, 8

ST. THERESA OF JESUS (Teresa de Cepeda)
(1515–1582)
Spanish nun, mystic, reformer

Whenever conscience commands anything, there is only one thing to fear, and that is fear.
Maxim, c. 1575

Let nothing disturb thee;
Let nothing dismay thee;
All things pass;
God never changes.

Patience attains
All that it strives for.
He who has God
Finds he lacks nothing;
God alone suffices.
Quoted by Longfellow

THOMAS À KEMPIS (Thomas Hammerken) (c. 1380–1471)
German Augustinian canon, writer

De Imitatione Christi [*The Imitation of Christ*, an ancient Latin saying popularized] (c. 1427)*

How swiftly passes the glory of the world!
Bk. I., ch. 3

Man proposes, but God disposes.
Bk. I, ch. 19

It is much safer to obey than to rule.

If ever I go among men, I come back less of a man.
Bk. I, ch. 20

Learning . . . a good conscience and a virtuous life are always preferred before it.
Bk. II, ch. 1

Little Alphabet of the Monks (pub. posthumously 1901)

Shun conversation with worldly men, for thou are not able to be satisfied with both God and men; with things eternal and things transitory.

The devil is continually tempting thee to seek high things, to go after honors.

Do not begin to wander after the various desires of the world, when the devil tempts thee. Listening to evil things is hurtful to the soul; the beholding of beauty is temptation.

DYLAN THOMAS (1914–1953)
Welsh poet

"Do Not Go Gentle Into That Good Night" (1953)

Do not go gentle into that good night,
Old age should burn and rave at close of
    day;
Rage, rage against the dying of the light.

And you, my father, there on the sad
    height,
Curse, bless, me now with your fierce tears I
    pray.
Do not go gentle into that good night,
Rage, rage against the dying of the light.

---

*The *Britannica*, 11th ed., vol. XIV, credits *De Imitatione Christi* to Thomas à Kempis but states controversy over authorship has lasted three centuries.

Selected Letters (pub. 1967)

There is always the one right word; use it, despite its foul or merely ludicrous associations.

NORMAN THOMAS (1884–1958)
American Socialist leader, presidential candidate

Dissent . . . is a right essential to any concept of the dignity and freedom of the individual; it is essential to the search for truth in a world wherein no authority is infallible.
Contribution, N.Y. Times Magazine,
November 15, 1959

FRANCIS THOMPSON (1859–1907)
English poet

"Mistress of Vision" (1897)

All things by immortal power,
Near or far, Hiddenly
To each other linkèd are,
That thou canst not stir a flower
Without troubling of a star.
St. XXII

"The Hound of Heaven" (1893)

I fled Him, down the nights and down the
    days;
I fled Him, down the arches of the years;
I fled Him, down the labyrinthine ways
Of my own mind; and in the midst of tears
I hid from Him, and under running
    laughter.
Line 1–5

ROY THOMPSON (Lord Thompson of Fleet) (1894–1977)
British press lord

I buy newspapers to make money to buy more newspapers to make money. As for editorial content, that's the stuff you separate ads with.
Attributed

JAMES THOMSON
(1700–1748)
English poet

Alfred: a Masque (1740)

Rule, Brittania, rule the waves;
Britons never shall be slaves.

Act 2, sc. V

JAMES THOMSON (signature: B.V.)
(1834–1882)
English poet

"The City of the Dreadful Night" (1874)

The City is of Night, but not of Sleep;
There sweet sleep is not for the weary brain;
The pitiless hours like years and ages creep,
A night seems termless hell. This dreadful
   strain
Of thought and consciousness which never
   ceases,
Or which some moments' stupor but in-
   creases,
This, worse than woe, makes wretches there
   insane.

I, st. 11

HENRY DAVID THOREAU
(1817–1862)
American libertarian writer

Walden (1854)

The mass of men lead lives of quiet desperation. What is called resignation is confirmed
desperation. From the desperate city you go
into the desperate country, and have to console yourself with the bravery of minks and
muskrats. A stereotyped but unconscious despair is concealed even under what are called
the games and amusements of mankind.
There is no play in them for this comes after
work. But it is a characteristic of wisdom not to
do desperate things.

Most of the luxuries and many of the so-
called comforts of life, are not only not indispensable, but positive hindrances to the elevation of mankind.

There are nowadays professors of philosophy, but not philosophers. . . . To be a philosopher is not merely to have subtle thoughts,
nor even to found a school, but so to love wisdom as to live according to its dictates, a life of
simplicity, independence, magnanimity, and
trust. It is to solve some of the problems of life,
not only theoretically, but practically.

Trade curses everything it handles; and
though you trade in messages from heaven,
the whole curse of trade attaches to the business.

There are a thousand hacking at the
branches of evil to one who is striking at the
root.

"Economy"

I went to the woods because I wished to live
deliberately, to front only the essential facts of
life, and see if I could not learn what it had to
teach, and not, when I came to die, discover
that I had not lived.

I wanted to live deep and suck out all the
marrow of life, to live so sturdily and Spartan-
like as to put to rout all that was not life, to cut
a broad swath and shave close, to drive life
into a corner, and reduce it to its lowest terms,
and, if it proved to be mean, why then to get
the whole and genuine meanness of it, and
publish its meanness to the world; or if it were
sublime, to know it by experience and be able
to give a true account of it in my next excursion.

Still we live meanly, like ants. . . . Our life
is frittered away by detail. . . . Simplicity,
simplicity, simplicity! I say, let our affairs be as
two or three, and not a hundred or a thousand
. . . simplicity of life and elevation of purpose.

Shams and delusions are esteemed for
soundest truths, while reality is fabulous. . . .
By closing the eyes and slumbering, and con-
senting to be deceived by shows, men establish
and confirm their daily life of routine and
habit everywhere, which still is built on purely
illusory foundations.

Let us settle ourselves, and work and wedge
our feet downward through the mud and slush
of opinion, and prejudice and tradition, and
delusion, and appearance, that alluvion which
covers the globe . . . till we come to a hard
bottom of rocks in place, which we can call
reality.

But I would say to my fellows, once for all,
As long as possible live free and uncommitted.

To be awake is to be alive. I have never yet
met a man who was quite awake.

A man is rich in proportion of the number of things he can afford to let alone.

"Where I Lived and What I Lived For"

How many a man has dated a new era in his life from the reading of a book!

"Reading"

I never found the companion that was so companionable as solitude.

"Solitude"

All sensuality is one, though it takes many forms; all purity is one. It is the same whether a man eat, or drink, or cohabit, or sleep sensually. They are but one appetite. . . . If you would be chaste, you must be temperate. What is chastity? How shall a man know if he is chaste? He shall not know it. We have heard of this virtue, but we know not what it is.

Chastity is the flowering of man; and what are called Genius, Heroism, Holiness, and the like, are but various fruits which succeed it. Man flows at once to God when the channel of purity is open.

No man ever followed his genius till it misled him.

"Higher Laws"

Why should we be in such a desperate haste to succeed and in such desperate enterprises? If a man does not keep pace with his companions, perhaps it is because he hears a different drummer. Let him step to the music which he hears, however measured or far away.

However mean your life is, meet it and live it; do not shun it and call it hard names. . . . Cultivate poverty like a garden herb, like sage. Do not trouble yourself much to get new things, whether clothes or friends. . . . Things do not change; we change. Sell your clothes and keep your thought. God will see that you do not want society.

"Conclusion"

On the Duty of Civil Disobedience (1849)*

I heartily accept the motto, "That government is best which governs least"; . . . Carried out, it finally amounts to this, which also I believe—"That government is best which governs not at all"; and when men are prepared for it, that will be the kind of government which they will have.

I think we should be men first, and subjects afterwards. It is not desirable to cultivate a respect for the law, so much as for the right. The only obligation which I have a right to assume is to do at any time what I think right.

How does it become a man to behave toward this American government today? I answer, that he cannot without disgrace be associated with it. I cannot for an instant recognize that political organization as *my* government which is the *slave's* government also.

Why does it [government] not cherish its wise minority? Why does it cry and resist before it is hurt? Why does it not encourage its citizens to be on the alert to point out its faults, and *do* better than it would have them? Why does it always crucify Christ, and excommunicate Copernicus and Luther, and pronounce Washington and Franklin rebels?

Moreover, any man more right than his neighbors constitutes a majority of one already.

Under a government which imprisons any unjustly, the true place for a just man is also a prison.

But the rich man—not to make any invidious comparison—is always sold to the institution which makes him rich. Absolutely speaking, the more money, the less virtue; for money comes between man and his objects, and obtains them for him.

Is a democracy, such as we know it, the last improvement possible in a government? Is it not possible to take a step further towards recognizing and organizing the rights of man? There will never be a free and enlightened State until the State comes to recognize the individual as a higher and independent power, from which all its own power and authority are derived, and treats him accordingly.

Life Without Principle (1863)

Business! I think that there is nothing, not even crime, more opposed to poetry, to philosophy, ay, to life itself, than this incessant business.

There is no more fatal blunderer than he who consumes the greater part of his life getting his living.

---

*"The Duty of Civil Liberties" was Gandhi's bedside book. The motto Thoreau quotes is Tom Paine's; it was used on the masthead of the publication *Democratic Review*, to which Thoreau contributed.

I believe that the mind can be permanently profaned by the habit of attending to trivial things. . . . Read not the Times, Read the Eternities.

A Week on the Concord and Merrimack Rivers (1849)

What man believes, God believes.

Not till we are lost, in other words, not till we have lost the world, do we begin to find ourselves.

Essays and Other Writings

Blessed are they who never read a newspaper, for they shall see Nature, and through her, God.

Journal (pub. 1906)

The man who is dissatisfied with himself, what can he not do?
November 23, 1850

The intellect of most men is barren. They neither fertilize or are fertilized. It is the marriage of the soul with Nature that makes the intellect fruitful, that gives birth to imagination.
August 20, 1851

Nothing is so much to be feared as fear.*
September 4, 1851

It is only when we forget all our learning that we begin to know.
October 4, 1859

The Living Thoughts of Thoreau, selected by Theodore Dreiser

There is no creed so false but faith can make it true.

At first blush, a man is not capable of reporting truth; he must be drenched and saturated with it first.

The gods can never leave a man in the world who is privy to their secrets. They cannot have a spy here.

If Christ should appear on earth he would on all hands be denounced as a mistaken, misguided man, insane and crazed.

---

*Emerson found this entry; and included it in Thoreau's complete works, which he published.

I believe that in this country the press exerts a greater and more pernicious influence than the church. We are not a religious people, but we are a nation of politicians. We do not care for, do not read the Bible, but we do care for and do read the newspapers.

The highest condition of art is artlessness.
October 4, 1859.

When will the world learn that a million men are of no importance compared with one Man?
Letter to Emerson, June 8, 1843

Do not be too moral. You may cheat yourself out of much life so. Aim above morality. Be not simply good, be good for something. . . . Let nothing stand between you and the light. . . . When you travel to the Celestial City, carry no letter of introduction. When you knock, ask to see God—none of his servants. In what concerns you much, do not think that you have companions, know that you are alone in the world.
Letter to Mr. B., March 7, 1848

PUBLIUS CLODIUS THRASEA PAETUS
(fl. reign of Nero, 54–68 A.D.)
Roman Senator, Stoic philosopher

He who hates vice hates mankind.
Attributed

THUCYDIDES
(c. 460–400 B.C.)
Athenian historian

History of the Peloponnesian War (431–413 B.C.)

Peace is an armistice in a war that is continuously going on.

I shall be content if those shall pronounce my History useful who desire to have a view of events as they did really happen, and as are very likely, in accordance with human nature, to repeat themselves at some future time—if not exactly the same, yet very similar.
Bk. 1

Wars spring from unseen and generally insignificant causes.

To admit poverty is no disgrace for a man; but, to make no effort to escape it is indeed disgraceful.

Bk. 2

Avoid the three errors which are most disastrous to empire, namely, pity, placability, and clemency.

Bk. 3

War is an evil thing; but to submit to the dictation of other states is worse. . . . Freedom, if we hold fast to it, will ultimately restore our losses, but submission will mean permanent loss of all that we value. . . . To you who call yourselves men of peace, I say: You are not safe unless you have men of action of your side.

Bk. 4

JUDAH ibn TIBBŌN
(c. 1120–c. 1190)
Spanish-born Hebrew translator

Property is theft. *

Attributed

PAUL (Johannes) TILLICH
(1886–1965)
German-born American theologian

Dynamics of Faith (1957)

The fundamental symbol of our ultimate concern is God. It is always present in any act of faith, even if the act of faith includes the denial of God.

Where there is ultimate concern, God can be denied only in the name of God. One God can deny the other one.

Atheism, consequently, can only mean the attempt to remove any ultimate concern—to remain unconcerned about the meaning of one's existence. Indifference toward the ultimate question is the only imaginable form of atheism.

All mythological elements in the Bible, the doctrine and liturgy, should be recognized as mythological, but they should be maintained in their symbolic form and not be replaced by scientific substitutes. For there is no substitute for the use of symbols and myths: they are the language of faith.

Doubt is not the opposite of faith; it is one element of faith.

On the Boundary (1962)

The courage to be is rooted in the God who appears when God has disappeared in the anxiety of doubt.

JOHN TILLOTSON
(1630–1694)
Archbishop of Canterbury

Sermons (pub. posthumously 1695–1704)

The Being of God is so comfortable, so convenient, so necessary to the felicity of mankind, that (as Tully admirably says) if God were not a necessary being of Himself, He might almost seem to be made on purpose for the use and benefit of man.

xciii

TIMON*
(fl. 5th century B.C.)
Athenian misanthrope

Here am I laid, my life of misery done,
Ask not my name, I curse you every one.
Epitaph, ordered inscribed on tomb at Halae

TITO (né Josip Broz)
(1892–1980)
President of Yugoslavia

The true socialist state must be built without compulsion, without terrorism.
Interview with G.S., 1948, following break with Stalin

Any movement in history which attempts to perpetuate itself becomes reactionary.
Talk with Vlado Dedijer and G.S.

---

*The French Socialist Proudhon appropriated this phrase in 1840 in his famous work *Qu'est-ce la propriété?*, q.v.

---

*"Timon of Athens, the noted misanthrope celebrated in Shakespeare's play, lived during the Peloponnesian War."—*Britannica*, 11th ed.

But we say that Socialism cannot be built with bayonets, cannot be built by administrative measures. It can be built only with the consciousness of the people.

Address, November 10, 1968; quoted in *N.Y. Times*, November 11

ALEXIS CHARLES HENRI MAURICE CLÉREL DE TOCQUEVILLE
(1805–1859)
French statesman

Democracy in America (1835)

I know of no country indeed where the love of money has taken a stronger hold on the affections of men, and where a profounder contempt is expressed for the theory of the permanent equality of property.

Vol. I, pt. 1, ch. 3

The Revolution of the United States was the result of a mature and reflecting preference for freedom, not of a vague or ill-defined craving for independence. It did not contract an alliance with the turbulent passions of anarchy, but its course was marked, on the contrary, by a love of order and law.

Than politics the American citizen knows no higher profession—for it is the most lucrative.

Vol. I, pt. 1, ch. 5

In America there are factions, but no conspiracies.

Vol. I, pt. 1, ch. 7

In America as in France it [the press] constitutes a singular power, so strongly composed of mingled good and evil that liberty could not live without it, and public order can hardly be maintained against it.

Vol. I, pt. 2, ch. 3

Democratic institutions awaken and foster a passion for equality which they can never satisfy.

In the principle of equality I discern two tendencies: the one leading the mind of every man to untried thoughts; the other prohibiting him from thinking at all.

Vol. I, pt. 2, ch. 5

I know of no country in which there is so little true independence of mind and freedom of discussion as in America. . . . The majority raises very formidable barriers to the liberty of opinion; within these barriers an author may write whatever he pleases, but he will repent it if he ever steps beyond them. Not that he is exposed to the terrors of an *auto-da-fé*, but he is tormented by the slights and persecutions of daily obloquy. His political career is closed forever.

What I find most repulsive in America is not the extreme freedom reigning there, but the shortage of guarantees against tyranny.

If ever the free institutions of America are destroyed, that event may be attributed to the unlimited authority of the majority, which may at some future time urge the minorities to desperation, and oblige them to have recourse to physical force. Anarchy will then result, but it will have been brought about by despotism.

Their life is so practical, so confused, so excited, so active, that little time remains for them for thought.

There is no country in the world in which the Christian religion retains a greater influence over the souls of men than in America. . . . In the United States religion . . . directs the manners of the community, and by regulating domestic life, it regulates the state.

If great writers have not at present existed in America, the reason is very simply given in the fact that there can be no literary genius without freedom of opinion, and freedom of opinion does not exist in America.

Vol. I, pt. 2, ch. 7

It may, however, be foreseen even now, that when the Americans lose their republican institutions, they will speedily arrive at a despotic Government, without a long interval of limited monarchy.

Vol. I, pt. 2, ch. 10

There are at the present time two great nations in the world—the Russians and the Americans. The American relies upon his personal interest to accomplish his ends and gives free scope to the unguided exertions and common sense of the people. The Russian centers all his authority of society in a single arm. The principal instrument of the former is freedom; of the latter, servitude. Their starting point is different and their courses are not the same; yet each of them seems marked by the will of Heaven to sway the destinies of half the globe.

I think in no country in the civilized world is less attention paid to philosophy than in the United States.

Among democratic nations, each new generation is a new people.

Vol. II, pt. 1, ch. 1

In the United States the majority undertakes to supply a multitude of ready-made opinions for the use of individuals, who are thus relieved from the necessity of forming opinions of their own. . . . Religion itself holds sway there much less as a doctrine of revelation than a commonly received opinion.

Vol. II, pt. 1, ch. 2

Americans are so enamored of equality that they would rather be equal in slavery than unequal in freedom.

Vol. II, pt. 2, ch. 1

I know of nothing more opposite to revolutionary attitudes than commercial ones. Commerce is naturally adverse to all the violent passions; it loves to temporize, takes delight in compromise, and studiously avoids irritation. . . . [I]t therefore prepares men for freedom but preserves them from revolution.

If we attentively consider each of the classes of which society is composed, it is easy to see that the passions created by property are keenest and most tenacious among the middle class.

Vol. II, pt. 3, ch. 21

The Old Regime and the French Revolution (1856)

The man who asks of freedom anything other than itself is born to be a slave.

ERNST TOLLER
(1893–1939)
German playwright, poet

History is the propaganda of the victors.
Quoted in Claud Coburn, *In Time of Trouble*

As a rule people are afraid of truth. Each truth we discover in nature or social life destroys the crutches on which we need to lean.

Many people have to surrender old privileges and everybody has to give up old customs without which life may seem hardly worth living. The old penalty for heretics was dramatic: death. The modern penalty is less drastic: boycott and social ruin.

Truth is a passion. One cannot learn it; one must possess it.

Fascism exploits the fear of reason which lives secretly in the conscious and subconscious minds of many people. Reason means facing life and its facts.
Quoted in *Saturday Review*, May 20, 1944

COUNT LEO NIKOLAEVICH TOLSTOY
(1828–1910)
Russian writer*

Anna Karenina (1875–1877)

All happy families resemble each other; each unhappy family is unhappy in its own way.

Without knowing what I am and why I am here, life is impossible.

Pt. 1, ch. 1

War and Peace (1865–1869)

But what is war? What is needed for success in warfare? What are the habits of the military? The aim of war is murder; the methods of war are spying, treachery, and their encouragement, the ruin of a country's inhabitants, robbing them or stealing to provision the army, and fraud and falsehood termed military craft. The habits of the military class are the absence of freedom, that is, discipline, idleness, ignorance, cruelty, debauchery, and drunkenness. And in spite of all this, it is the highest class, respected by everyone . . . and he who kills most people receives the highest awards.

Pt. X, ch. xxv [Prince Andrey speaking]

Man's mind cannot grasp the causes of events in their completeness, but the desire to find the causes is implanted in man's soul.

Pt. XIII, ch. i

When it is impossible to stretch the very elastic thread of historical ratiocination any further, when actions are clearly contrary to all that humanity calls right or even just, the historians produce a saving conception of "greatness." "Greatness," it seems, excludes the standards of right and wrong, there is no atrocity for which a "great" man can be blamed.

---

*"No man deserves more to be called a genius, no man is more complex, more contradictory, more admirable than he in all things, yes, in all things. . . . He is a man who envelops all men, a man—mankind."—Gorki.

And it occurs to no one that to admit a greatness not commensurate with the standard of right and wrong is merely to admit one's own nothingness and immeasurable meanness.

Pt. XIV, ch. xviii

The writers of universal history will only prove themselves of real value when they are able to answer the essential question of history: "What is power?"

Epilogue, Pt. II, ch. iii

The presence of the problem of man's free will, though unexpressed, is felt in every step of history.

If the will of every man were free, that is, if each man could act as he pleased, all history would be a series of disconnected incidents.

If in a thousand years even one man in a million could act freely, that is, as he chose, it is evident that one single free act of that man's violation of the laws governing human action would destroy the possibility of the existence of any laws for the whole of humanity.

All men's instincts, all their impulses in life, are efforts to increase their freedom. Wealth and poverty, health and disease, culture and ignorance, labor and leisure, repletion and hunger, virtue and vice, are all only terms for greater or less degree of freedom.

Epilogue, Pt. II, ch. viii

The only thing that we can know is that we know nothing and that is the highest flight of human wisdom.

The Kingdom of God is Within You (1893)

But Christ could certainly not have established the Church. That is, the institution we now call by that name, for nothing resembling our present conception of the Church—with its sacraments, its hierarchy, and especially its claim to infallibility—is to be found in Christ's words or in the conception of the men of his time.

But we know that laws are the offspring of party conflicts, false dealing, and the greed for gain; that they are not and can never be, the depository of true justice; and therefore it is impossible for people of the present day to believe that obedience to civil or state laws can ever satisfy the rational demands of human nature.

Physical violence is the basis of authority.

Government is an association of men who do violence to the rest of us.

The man who commits sin is the slave of the sin.

The Slavery of Our Times (1900)

Where there is a man who does not labor because another is compelled to work for him, there slavery is. And where, as in all European societies, men by force exploit the labor of thousands of men and regard it as their prerogative, while the latter submit to force and regard it as their duty, there we have slavery in terrible proportions.

Slavery exists. . . . Slavery has three fundamental methods: direct personal violence, militarism, land-taxes upheld by military power.

Slavery results from laws, laws are made by governments, and, therefore people can only be freed from slavery by the abolition of governments. . . . And it is time for people to understand that governments not only are not necessary, but are harmful and most highly immoral institutions, in which a self-respecting, honest man cannot and must not take part. . . . And as soon as people clearly understand this, they will . . . cease to give the governments soldiers and money. And as soon as a majority of people cease to do this, the fraud which enslaves people will be abolished. Only in this way can people be freed from slavery.

Reply to Synod's Edict of Excommunication (1901)

In the periodical absolution of sins at Confession I see a harmful deception which only encourages immorality and causes men not to fear to sin.

I believe in God, whom I understand as Spirit, as Love, as the Source of all.

The Kreutzer Sonata (1889)

To say that you can love one person all your life is just like saying that one candle will continue burning as long as you live.

If one has no vanity in his life, there is not sufficient reason for living.

The whole trade in the luxuries of life is brought into existence by the requirements of women.

What is Art? (1898)

Art is a human activity, whose purpose is the transmission of the highest and best feelings to which men have attained.

Art is not a pleasure, or an amusement; art is a great matter. Art is an organ of human life transmitting man's reasonable perception into feeling.

Ch. 8

On Life and Essays on Religion (first American pub. 1950)

All men know in their very earliest years that beside the good of their animal personality, there is another, a better, a good in life, which is not only independent of the gratification of the appetites of the animal personality, but on the contrary, the greater the renunciation of the welfare of the animal personality the greater the good becomes. . . . This feeling . . . is known to all. This feeling is love.

Freethinkers are those who are willing to use their minds without prejudice and without fearing to understand things that clash with their own customs, privileges, or beliefs. This state of mind is not common, but it is essential for right thinking; where it is absent, discussion is apt to become worse than useless.

What is Religion? (1885)

People today live without faith. On the one hand the minority of wealthy, educated people, having freed themselves from the hypnotism of the Church, believe in nothing. They look upon all faiths as absurdities or as useful means of keeping the masses in bondage—no more. On the other hand, the vast majority, poor, uneducated, but for the most part truly sincere, remain under the hypnotism of the faith. But this is not really faith, for instead of throwing light on man's position in the world it only darkens it.

What Are We to Do? (1891)

Money is a new form of slavery, and distinguished from the old simply by the fact that it is impersonal, that there is no human relation between master and slave.

Second Sketch from Sebastopol (1887)

The hero of my story . . . is The Truth. *

We must say what everybody knows but does not venture to say. We must say that by whatever name men may call murder—murder always remains murder. . . . They will cease to see the service of their country, the heroism of war, military glory, and patriotism, and will see what exists: the naked, criminal business of murder!
Address to the Swedish Government Congress Peace Conference, 1909

Anti-Semitism is . . . a pathological condition, a peculiar form of sexual perversion. . . . Among all disgraceful phenomena, it is the most disgusting and abominable.

We must repudiate one of the two, either Christianity with its love of God and one's neighbor, or the State with its armies and wars.
Letter to I. Tenoromo, 1880

The possibility of killing one's self is a safety valve. Having it, man has no right to say life is unbearable.
Letter to a friend, 1898

Yes, we will do anything for the poor man, anything but get off his back.
Quoted in Huntingdon, *Philosophy and Morality*

THEOBALD WOLFE TONE
(1763–1798)
Irish revolutionist

Manifesto to the Friends of Freedom in Ireland (written by Tone and others, June 1771)

The Greatest Happiness of the Greatest Number—on the rock of this principle let this society rest, and by this let it judge and determine every political question.

The Rights of Man are the Rights of God, to vindicate the one is to maintain the other.

ARNOLD TOYNBEE
(1852–1883)
English economist, social reformer

The Industrial Revolution.
Lecture, at Oxford, published 1884; coined term

*Quoted by Mary McCarthy, *Partisan Review*, Summer, 1960; Tolstoy was an army lieutenant at the time, also a war correspondent.

HEINRICH GOTTHARD VON TREITSCHKE
(1834–1896)
German historian, political writer

Politics (1896)

Those who preach the nonsense about ever-lasting peace do not understand the life of the Aryan race; the Aryans are before all brave.

To the historian who lives in the realm of the Will, it is quite clear that the furtherance of an everlasting peace is fundamentally reactionary. He sees that to banish war from history would be to banish all progress and becoming.

We have learned to recognize as the civilizing majesty of war precisely that which appears to the superficial observers to be brutality and inhumanity. . . . Man must not only be ready to sacrifice his life, but also the natural deeply rooted feelings of the human soul; he must devote his whole ego for the furtherance of a great patriotic idea: that is the moral sublimity of war.

Vol. I., bk. I

LEON TROTSKY (Lev Davidovich Bronstein)
(1870–assassinated 1940)
Soviet Russian leader, journalist

A new humanity will be born of this war.
Speech, November 16, 1917; reported by John Reed, *Ten Days That Shook the World*

Terror, as the demonstration of the will and strength of the working class, is historically justified, precisely because the proletariat was able thereby to break the political will of the intelligentsia, pacify the professional man of various categories and work, and gradually subordinate them to its own aims within the field of their specialties.
Contribution to *Izvesttia*, January 10, 1919

The New Course (1924)

As to the theory of the "permanent revolution," I see no reason for renouncing what I wrote on this subject in 1904. . . . The permanent revolution, in an exact translation, is the continuous revolution, the uninterrupted revolution.

Literature and Revolution (1923)

All the special illusions which mankind has raved about in religion, poetry, morals or philosophy, serve only the purpose of deceiving and blinding the oppressed.

What is Revolution if it is not a mad rebellion in the name of the conscious, national, purposeful and dynamic principle of life, against the elemental, senseless, biologic automatism of life, that is, against the peasant-roots of our old Russian history, against its aimlessness, its non-teleological character?

The Russian Revolution (1930)

The higher the political level of a revolutionary movement and the more serious the leadership, the greater will be the place occupied by conspiracy in a popular insurrection.

These solid people of capital, the press, the pulpit—where have they ever fought? They are accustomed to find out by telegraph and telephone the results of the battles which settle their fate.

Armed insurrection stands in the same relation to revolution as revolution as a whole does to evolution.

In comparison with monarchy and other heirlooms from the cannibals and cave-dwellers, democracy is of course a great conquest, but it leaves the blind play of forces in the social relations of men untouched.

Do the consequences of a revolution justify in general the sacrifices it involves? The question is teleological and therefore fruitless. It would be as well to ask in the face of the difficulties and griefs of personal existence: Is it worthwhile to be born?

In the last instance, the party is always right, because it is the only historic instrument which the working class possesses for the solution of its fundamental tasks.

Diary in Exile (1935)

Old age is the most unexpected of all the things that happen to a man.

HARRY S TRUMAN*
(1884–1972)
Haberdasher, Captain in the Rainbow
Division, 33rd President of the United States

Speeches, Addresses, Etc.

If we see that Germany is winning we ought to help Russia, and if we see Russia is winning, we ought to help Germany, and that way let them kill as many as possible.
> In the Senate, not generally reported; quoted in
> *U.S. Week,* June 5, 1941**

It is an atomic bomb. It is the harnessing of the basic power of the universe.
> Announcement about the Hiroshima bombing
> July 28, 1945

The seeds of totalitarian regimes are nurtured by misery and want. They spread and grow in the evil soil of poverty and strife. They reach their full growth when the hope of a people for a better life has died. We must keep that hope alive. The free people of the world look to us for support in maintaining their freedom.
> To Congress, March 12, 1947; The Truman
> Doctrine

McCarthyism . . . the meaning of the word is the corruption of truth, the abandonment of our devotion to fair play. . . . It is the use of the big lie and the unfounded accusation against any citizen in the name of Americanism. . . . This horrible cancer is eating at the vitals of America and it can destroy the great edifice of freedom.
> Radio-television address, November 17, 1953

If we do not abolish war on this earth, then surely, one day war will abolish us from the earth.
> Speech, Independence, Mo., 1966

. . . a man in his right mind would never want to be President, if he knew what it en-

tails. Aside from the impossible administrative burden, he has to take all sorts of abuse from liars and demagogues. . . . All the President is, is a glorified public relations man who spends his time flattering, kissing and kicking people to get them to do what they are supposed to do anyway.
> Letter to his sister, November 1947

I don't think the son of a bitch [Vice-President Nixon] knows the difference between telling the truth and lying.

All through history it's the nations that have given the most to the generals and the least to the people that have been the first to fall.
> Quoted in Merle Miller, *Plain Speaking: An Oral*
> *Biography*

I never give them hell. I just tell the truth, and they think it is hell.
> Quoted in *Look,* April 3, 1953

BARBARA W. TUCHMAN
(1912–   )
American historian, writer*

Books are the carriers of civilization. Without books, history is silent, literature dumb, science crippled, thought and speculation at a standstill. Without books, the development of civilization would have been impossible. They are engines of change, windows on the world, "lighthouses" (as a poet said) "erected in the sea of time." They are companions, teachers, magicians, bankers of the treasures of the mind. Books are humanity in print.
> Quoted in *Authors League Bulletin,*
> November–December 1979

Every successful revolution puts on in time the robe of the tyrant it has deposed.
> Attributed

---

*The initial S stands for nothing; it was added for euphony.
**The *N.Y. Times* version of June 23 reads: "Let's help the Russians when the Germans are winning and the Germans when the Russians are winning. So each may kill off as many as possible of the other."

---

*"Before the academic deluge this was what history was supposed to do—to teach philosophy by example—and few writers have performed this office more inspiritingly than Barbara Tuchman."—Jack Beatty, literary editor, *New Republic,* October 21, 1981.

BENJAMIN R. TUCKER
(1854–1939)
American philosophical anarchist

Instead of a Book (1893)

If there were more extremists in evolutionary periods, there would be no revolutionary periods.

Anarchism may be described as the doctrine that all the affairs of men should be managed by individuals or voluntary associations, and that the State should be abolished.

Individual Liberty (1926)

Nor does the Anarchistic scheme furnish any code of morals to be imposed upon the individual. "Mind your own business" is its own moral law. Interference with another's business is a crime and the only crime, and as such may properly be resisted.

"Sociology," I

IVAN TURGENEV
(1818–1883)
Russian writer

Fathers and Sons (1862)

Whatever a man prays for, he prays for a miracle . . . "Great God, let not two times two make four."

Nihilist.

[coined word] Ch. 5

I agree with no man's opinion.

Ch. 13

The courage to believe in nothing.

Ch. 14

Go and try to disprove death. Death will disprove you.

Ch. 24

I believe that love produces a certain flowering of the whole personality which nothing else can achieve.

Quoted in *Pages from the Goncourt Journal*

A(nne) R(obert) J(acques) TURGOT (Baron de l'Aulne)
(1727–1781)
French statesman, economist

Réflexions sur la formation et la distribution des richesses (1766)

The iron law of wages.

FREDERICK JACKSON TURNER
(1861–1932)
American writer

The Significance of the Frontier in American History (1894)

The result is that to the frontier the American intellect owes its striking characteristics. The coarseness and strength combined with acuteness and inquisitiveness; that practical inventive turn of mind, quick to find expedients; that masterful grasp of material things, lacking in the artistic but powerful to effect great ends; that restless, nervous energy; that dominant individualism, working for good and for evil, and with all that buoyancy and exuberance which comes from freedom—these are traits of the frontier.

JOSEPH MALLORD WILLIAM TURNER
(1775–1851)
English painter

Sun is God.

Attributed last words

TWAIN, Mark, *see* Clemens

JOHN TYNDALL
(1820–1893)
British physicist

Fragments of Science (1871)

Religious feeling is as much a verity as any other part of human consciousness; and against it, on the subjective side, the waves of science beat in vain.

Vol. II, "Prof. Virchow and Evolution"

The brightest flashes in the world of thought are incomplete until they have been proved to have their counterparts in the world of fact.
"Scientific Materialism"

Superstition . . . religion which has grown incongruous with intelligence.
"Science and Man"

TRISTAN TZARA
(1896–1963)
French poet and wit

Dadaist Manifesto (c. 1925)

Dada.
[Coined word]*

To destroy the drawers of the brain and those of social organizations; to sow demoralization everywhere.

TZE-SZE
(c. 335–c. 288 B.C.)
Chinese philosopher, grandson of Confucius

The Golden Mean of Tze-sze (tr. Ku Hungming)**

Truth means the fulfillment of our self; and moral law means following the law of our being. Truth is the beginning and end (the substance) of material existence. Without truth there is no material existence. It is for this reason that the moral man values truth.

Thus, the absolute truth is indestructible. Being indestructible it is eternal. Being eternal, it is self-existent. Being self-existent, it is infinite. Being infinite, it is vast and deep. Being vast and deep it is transcendental and intelligent.

What is God-given is what we call human nature. To fulfill the law of our human nature

is what we call the moral law. The cultivation of the moral law is what we call culture.

Confucius replied . . . "wisdom, compassion and courage—these are the three universally recognized moral qualities of man. It matters not in what way men come to the exercise of these moral qualities, the result is one and the same.

Confucius went on to say: "Love of knowledge is akin to wisdom." Strenuous attention to conduct is akin to compassion. Sensitiveness to shame is akin to courage."

"Being true to oneself is the law of God."
Trying to be true to oneself is the law of man

TZU-GUNG
Chinese sage

I have heard my teacher say that whoever uses machines does all his work like a machine. He who does his work like a machine grows a heart like a machine, and he who carries the heart of a machine in his breast loses his simplicity. He who has lost his simplicity becomes unsure in the strivings of his soul. Uncertainty in the strivings of the soul is something which does not agree with honest sense.
Quoted in Werner Heisenberg, *The Physician's Conception of Nature*

UMBERTO I
(1844–assassinated 1900)
King of Italy

Un incidente del metier.
It is an occupational hazard.
Attributed remark on escaping assassination

---

*Dada, which is based on the French word for hobbyhorse, was the name given to a popular artistic movement in the 1920s.
**"The Golden Mean (Chungyung) represents probably the best philosophical approach to Confucian moral philosophy."—Lin Yutang.

MIGUEL DE UNAMUNO
(1864–1936)
Spanish writer, rector of the University of
Salamanca

The Tragic Sense of Life (1913)

The Tragic Sense of Life.

Book Title

*Homo sum: nihil humani a me alienum
puto* said the Latin playwright [Terence]. And
I would rather say, *Nullus hominum a me alienum puto*: I am a man; no other man do I
deem a stranger.

Ch. I

For living is one thing and knowing is another; and . . . perhaps there is such an opposition between the two that we may say that
everything vital is anti-rational, not merely irrational, and that everything rational is anti-
vital. And this is the basis of the tragic sense
of life.

Science as a substitute for religion, and reason as a substitute for faith, have always fallen
to pieces.

Ch. II

True science teaches, above all, to doubt
and to be ignorant.

Ch. V

The most tragic problem of philosophy is to
reconcile intellectual necessities with the necessities of the heart and the will. For it is on
this rock that every philosophy that pretends to
receive the eternal and tragic contradictions,
the basis of our existence, breaks to pieces.

Philosophy and religion are enemies, and
because they are enemies they have need of
one another. There is no religion without
some philosophic basis, no philosophy without
roots in religion. Each lives by its contrary.

The truth? The truth, Lazarus, is perhaps
something so unbearable, so terrible, something so deadly, that simple people could not
live with it.

Faith is in its essence simply a matter of
will, not of reason, and to believe is to wish to
believe, and to believe in God is, before all
and above all, to wish that there may be a
God.

Note the greater part of our atheists and you
will see that they are atheists from a kind of
rage, rage at not being able to believe that
there is a God. They are the personal enemies
of God. They have invested Nothingness with
substance and personality, and their No-God
is an Anti-God.

Ch. VI

The most tragic thing in the world and in
life . . . is love. Love is the child of illusion
and the parent of disillusion; love is consolation in desolation; it is the sole medicine
against death, for it is death's brother.

In its essence, the delight of sexual love, the
genetic spasm, is a sensation of resurrection, of
renewing our life in another, for only in others
can we renew our life and so perpetuate ourselves.

Ch. VII

The satisfied, the happy, do not live; they
fall asleep from habit, near neighbor to annihilation.

Ch. IX

And perhaps the sin against the Holy Ghost
. . . is none other than that of not desiring
God, not longing to be made immortal.

Ch. X

At times to be silent is to lie. . . . You will
win because you have enough brute force. But
you will not convince. For to convince you
need to persuade. And in order to persuade
you would need what you lack: Reason and
Right.
Confrontation with fascist General Millan-Astray,
Salamanca, October 12, 1936*

UNITED NATIONS
(Established 1945)

United Nations Charter (1945)

We the people of the United Nations determined to save succeeding generations from the
scourge of war, which twice in our lifetime has
brought untold sorrow to mankind, and
to reaffirm faith in fundamental human
rights, in the dignity and worth of the human

---

*Millan-Astray shouted in reply, "Death to intelli-
gence. And long live Death," and drove Unamuno
out of the University at the point of a gun. Unamuno suffered a heart attack and died within a
week.

person, in the equal rights of men and women and of nations large and small,

to establish conditions under which justice and respect of the obligations arising from treaties and other sources of international law can be maintained, and

to promote social progress and better standards of life in larger freedom,

and for these ends

to practice tolerance and live together in peace with one another as good neighbors, and

to unite our strength to maintain international peace and security, and to insure by the acceptance of principles and the institution of methods, that armed force shall not be used, save in the common interest, and

to employ international machinery for the promotion of the economic and social advancement of all peoples,

have resolved to combine our efforts to accomplish these ends.

Preamble

Universal Declaration of Human Rights (1948)

All human beings are born free and equal, in dignity and rights.

Art. 1

Everyone is entitled to all the rights of freedom set forth in this declaration, without distinction of any kind, such as race, colour, sex, language, religion, political or other opinion, national or social origin, property, birth or other status.

Art. 2

Constitution of UNESCO (1946)

Since wars begin in the minds of men, it is in the minds of men that the defences of peace must be constructed.

UNITED STATES ARMY

The informed soldier fights best.
Army Orientation booklets, World War II

Fascism inevitably leads to war.

Fascism is government by the few and for the few.
The United States also has its native Fascists who say they are "100 per cent American."

The germ of Fascism cannot be quarantined in a Munich Brown House or a balcony in Rome. If we want to make certain that Fas-

cism does not come to America, we must make certain that it does not thrive anywhere in the world.
Army Orientation Fact Sheet 64, March 23, 1945*

UNITED STATES SUPREME COURT**

The law knows no heresy.
Madison v. Jones (December 1871)

There can be no equal justice where the kind of trial a man gets depends on the amount of money he has.
Griffin v. Illinois (1956)

Sex and obscenity are not synonymous.
Roth case (1957)

If one race is inferior to the other socially, the Constitution of the United States cannot put them on the same plane.
Plessy v. Ferguson (1890)

Separate educational facilities are inherently unequal. Therefore we hold that . . . [those segregated are] deprived of the equal protection of the laws.
Decision, Brown v. Board of Education (May 17, 1954); cf. Justice Warren

Neither a state nor the Federal Government can, openly or secretly, participate in the affairs of any religious organizations or groups and *vice versa*. In the words of Jefferson, the clause against establishment of religion by law was intended to erect "a wall of separation between Church and State."
McCullogh v. Board of Education of Champaign, Ill. (1948)

JOHN UPDIKE
(1932–   )
American writer

A true revolutionary despises the philanthropies whereby misery is abated and revolution delayed.
Contribution, *The New Yorker*, February 26, 1966

---

*Fact Sheet 64, explaining Fascism, was authorized by General Marshall; it was almost totally disregarded and usually destroyed.
**See also opinions and dissents under names of justices.

I was asked the question, "After Christianity, what?" Sex, in its many permutations, is surely the glue, ambience, and motive force of the new humanism.

Interview, *N.Y. Times,* April 7, 1968

URBAN II (Odo de Legary)
(1042–1099)
Pope from 1088

Christian warriors . . . go and fight for the deliverance of the holy places. . . . If you triumph over your enemies, the kingdom of the East will be your heritage; if you are conquered, you will have the glory of dying in the same place as Jesus Christ. . . . If you must have blood, bathe your hands in the blood of the infidel! . . . Soldiers of hell, become the soldiers of the Living God. *Dieu le veut.* (God wills it.)

Preaching the First Crusade, Clermont-Ferrand, France, November 26, 1095

HAROLD CLAYTON UREY
(1893–1981)
American scientist*

I am very unhappy to conclude that the hydrogen bomb should be developed and built.

There is no constructive solution to the world's problems except eventually a world government capable of establishing law over the entire surface of the earth.

Bulletin of the Atomic Scientists, March 1950

LEON URIS
(1924–   )
American novelist

To me a writer is one of the most important soldiers in the fight for the survival of the human race. He must stay at his post in the thick of fire to serve the cause of mankind.

Contribution, *N.Y. Herald Tribune,* August 16, 1959

---

*". . . whose discovery of heavy hydrogen opened the possibility of thermonuclear warfare."—*N.Y. Times* obituary, January 7, 1981.

U.S.S.R. (Union of Soviet Socialist Republics)

Constitution (1918)

1. The church is separated from the state.
3. Every citizen may profess any religion or none at all. Any legal disabilities connected with the profession of any religion are abolished.
18. The R.S.F.S.R. considers work the duty of every citizen of the Republic, and proclaims as its motto: He shall not eat who does not work.

Constitution of the U.S.S.R. (January 31, 1924; attributed partly to Stalin)

In conformity with the interests of the working people, and in order to strengthen the socialist system, the citizens of the U.S.S.R. are guaranteed by law: (a) Freedom of Speech; (b) Freedom of the Press; (c) Freedom of assembly, including the holding of mass meetings; (d) Freedom of street processions and demonstrations.*

In order to guarantee to all workers real freedom of opinion, the Russian Socialist Federated Soviet Republic [R.S.F.S.R., now U.S.S.R.] abolishes the dependence of the press on capitalism, and places at the disposal of the working class and the peasantry all the technical and material means for the publication of newspapers, pamphlets, books, and all other publications of the press, and guarantees free circulation for them throughout the country.

Comintern declaration, May 19, 1922

It is the historic mission of the Communist Internationale to be the gravedigger of bourgeois society.

Quoted in Kennan, *Russia and the West*

---

*Not one of the four freedoms mentioned in the 1924 Constitution exists today, 1985.

PAUL VALÉRY
(1871–1945)
French writer

Mauvaises pensées et autres (1941)

Every thought is an exception to the general rule that people do not think.

Two dangers constantly threaten the world: order and disorder.
> Contribution, *The Nation,* January 5, 1957

There are mistakes that are creative.

Disorder is the condition of the mind's fertility: it contains the mind's promise, since its fertility depends upon the unexpected, it depends rather on what we do not know . . . than what we know.
> Contribution, *Southern Review,* Winter, 1940; tr. Jackson Mathews

Tantôt je suis et tantôt je pense.
At times I think and at times I am.
> Quoted in *The New Yorker,* November 28, 1977

Great men die, once as men and once as great.
> Quoted by Malcolm Cowley, *Esquire,* June 1967

SIR JOHN VANBRUGH
(1664–1726)
English dramatist

The Relapse (1697)

O fortune, fortune, thou art a bitch!
> Act 1

MARTIN VAN BUREN
(1782–1862)
8th President of the United States

The second, sober thought of the people is seldom wrong.
> Letter, 1829; quoted in Schlesinger, *The Age of Jackson*

THEODORE H. VAN DE VELD
(1873–?)
Dutch physician

Ideal Marriage: Its Psychology and Technique

Sex is the foundation of marriage. Yet, most married couples do not know the A B C of sex.

MARK VAN DOREN
(1894–1973)
American poet, critic

Man's Right to Knowledge (1954)

An unexamined idea, to paraphrase Socrates, is not worth having; and a society whose ideas are never explored for possible error may eventually find its foundations insecure.

VINCENT VAN GOGH
(1853–suicide 1890)
Dutch painter

I can very well do without God both in my life and in my painting, but I cannot, suffering as I am, do without something which is greater than I, which is my life, the power to create.
> Letter to brother

BARTOLOMEO VANZETTI
(1888–executed 1927)
Italian-American fish peddler, anarchist

If it had not been for this thing, I might have lived out my life talking at street corners to scorning men. I might have died unmarked, unknown, a failure. Now we are not a failure. This is our career and our triumph. Never in our full life could we hope to do such work for tolerance, for justice, for man's understanding of man, as now we do by accident.
Our words—our lives—our pain: nothing! The taking of our lives—lives of a good shoemaker and a poor fish peddler—all! That last moment belongs to us—that agony is our triumph.
> Letter to his son, April 9, 1927

There is nothing, nowhere, neither on earth nor in heavens, that can make the true untrue or the untrue true.
> Found on prison tablet, after execution

MARCUS TERENTIUS VARRO
(116–27 B.C.)
Roman polymath, author of 500 books

On Agriculture

Divine nature made the country, human art built the cities.
Bk. III, i, 4

Antiquatum rerum humanarum et divinarum (c. 40 B.C.)

It is for the good of the state that man should be deluded by religion.

MATTHEW VASSAR
(1792–1868)
British-born American brewer, founder of Vassar College

Woman, having received from her Creator the same intellectual contribution as man, has the same right as man to intellectual culture and development.
Maiden speech, February 1861, to Vassar trustees

VATICAN COUNCIL

Dogmatic Constitution (1870)

We teach and define that it is a dogma divinely revealed: that the Roman Pontiff, when he speaks *ex cathedra,* that is, when in discharge of the office of pastor and doctor of all Christians, by virtue of his supreme apostolic authority he define a doctrine regarding faith or morals to be held by the universal Church, by the divine assistance promised him in blessed Peter, is possessed of that infallibility with which the divine Redeemer willed that his Church should be endowed for defining doctrine of faith and morals; and that therefore such definitions of the Roman Pontiff are irreformable themselves, and not from the consent of the Church. But if anyone presumes to contradict this definition of ours, which may God forbid, let him be anathema.
Session 4

HENRY VAUGHAN
(1622–1695)
English mystic poet

"The World" (1678)

I saw Eternity the other night,
Like a great ring of pure and endless light,
All calm, as it was bright;
And round beneath it, Time in hours, days, years,
Driv'n by the spheres,
Like a vast shadow mov'd: in which the world
And all her train were hurl'd.

"They Are All Gone" (1650)

Dear beauteous death, the jewel of the just!
Shining nowhere but in the dark;
What mysteries do lie beyond thy dust,
Could man outlook that mark!

O Father of eternal life, and all
Created glories under Thee!
Resume Thy spirit from this world of thrall
Into true liberty.

"The Retreat" (1650)

Before I taught my tongue to wound
My conscience with a sinfull sound,
Or had the black art to dispense
A sev'rall sin in ev'ry sence,
But felt through all this fleshly dresse
Bright shootes of everlastingnesse.

"Man" (1650)

Man is the shuttle, to whose winding quest
And passage through these looms
God order'd motion, but ordain'd no rest.

LUC DE CLAPIERS, MARQUIS DE VAUVENARGUES
(1715–1747)
French moralist

Reflections and Maxims (c. 1747)

Men are born truthful, and die liars.

All erroneous ideas would perish of their own accord if expressed clearly.

Commerce is the school for cheating.

There is nothing that fear or hope does not make men believe.

Those who do evil to others, hate them.

Servitude degrades people to such a point that they come to like it.

To accomplish great things we must live as if we were never going to die.

More are taken in by hope than by cunning.

FRANÇOIS DE LA VAYER MOTHE
French author

All respect is due to the living; to others nothing but the truth.
Adopted as the motto of the Biographie Universelle, Paris

THORSTEIN VEBLEN
(1857–1929)
American social scientist

The Theory of the Leisure Class (1899)

The office of the leisure class in social evolution is to retard the movement and to conserve what is obsolescent.

This conservatism of the wealthy class is so obvious a feature that it has even come to be recognized as a mark of respectability. Since conservatism is a characteristic of the wealthier and therefore more reputable portion of the community, it has acquired a certain honorific or decorative value. It has become prescriptive to such an extent that an adherence to conservative views is comprised as a matter of course in our notions of respectability; and it is imperatively incumbent on all who would lead a blameless life in point of social repute.

The accumulation of wealth at the upper end of the pecuniary scale implies privation at the lower end of the scale.

The institution of a leisure class hinders cultural development immediately (1) by the inertia proper of the class itself, (2) through its prescriptive example of conspicuous waste and of conservatism, and (3) indirectly through that system of unequal distribution of wealth and sustenance on which the institution itself rests.

Ch. VII

The enthusiasm for war, and the predatory temper of which it is the index, prevail in the largest measure among the upper classes, especially among the hereditary leisure class.

The ostensible serious occupation of the upper class is that of government, which, in point of origin and developmental content, is also a predatory occupation.

The addiction to sports, therefore, in a peculiar degree marks an arrested development of man's moral nature.

Ch. X

As a general rule the classes that are low in economic efficiency, or in intelligence, or both, are peculiarly devout—as, for instance, the negro population in the South, much of the lower-class foreign population, much of the rural population, especially in those sections which are backward in education, in the stage of development of their industry, or in respect to their industrial contact with the rest of the community.

Ch. XII

The Acquisitive Society (1920)

Militarism . . . is fetish worship. It is the prostration of men's souls before, and the laceration of their bodies to appease, an idol. What they do not see is that their reverence for economic activity and industry and what is called business is also fetish worship.

The Theory of Business Enterprise (1904)

The first duty of an editor is to gauge the sentiment of his reader, and then to tell them what they like to believe. . . . His second duty is to see that nothing is said in the news items or editorials which may discountenance any claims or announcements made by the advertisers, discredit their standing or good faith, or expose many weaknesses or deception in any business venture that is or may become a valuable advertiser.

LOPE DE VEGA
(1562–1635)
Spanish playwright

Corona Tragica (1627)

Though too much valour may our fortunes try,
To live in fear of death is many times to die.

VEGETIUS (Flavius Vegetius Renatus)
(fl. c. 375 A.D.)
Roman writer

*De Rei Militari III**

Qui desiderat pacem, preparet bellum.
Who desires peace should preparc for war.
Prologue

TOBIAS VENNER
(1577–1660)

Via Recta (1620)

Tobacco drieth the brain, dimmeth the sight, vitiateth the smell, hurteth the stomach, destroyeth the concoction, disturbeth the humors and spirits, corrupteth the breath, induceth a trembling of the limbs, exsiccateth the windpipe, lungs, and liver, annoyeth the milt, scorcheth the heart, and causeth the blood to be adjusted.

PIERRE VICTURNIEN VERGNIAUD
(1753–1793)
French revolutionist

There was a reason to fear that the Revolution, like Saturn, might devour every one of her children.
Quoted in Lamartine, *Histoire des Girondins,* 1847

VERGIL, *see* Virgil

PAUL VERLAINE
(1844–1896)
French poet

Romance sans paroles (1874)

Il pleure dans mon coeur
Comme il pleut sur la ville.
Tears fall in my heart
Like the rain falls on the city.
III

---

*"Maxims that have guided the leaders of professional armies in all countries at all times."—*Britannica,* 11th ed.

L'Art poétique (1884)

And all the rest is just literature.

GIOVANNI BATTISTA VICO
(1668–1744)
Italian jurist, philosopher

Principles of a New Science Concerning the Common Nature of Nations (1720–1725)

When men are unable to form an idea of distant and unknown things, they judge them by what is familiar and at hand. This axiom explains the inexhaustible source of all the errors about the principles of human nature. These errors are embraced by entire nations and by scholars.
Axiom 2

Philosophy considers man as he should be, and therefore is useful to but few; those who wish to live in Plato's Republic and not fall back into the scum of Romulus.
Axiom 6

Legislation views man as he is for the purpose of making him useful to human society. Out of savagery, avarice, and ambition, the three vices found in all parts of the human race, it creates the military, merchant, and governing classes, and thus the power, riches, and wisdom of the commonwealths. From these three great vices, which are capable of destroying all mankind on the face of the earth, it creates civil tranquility.
Axiom 7

Common sense is judgment without reflection which is shared by an entire class, a people, a nation, or the whole human race.
Axiom 12

This world of nations is the work of man, and its explanation therefore is only to be found in the mind of man.
Quoted in *Britannica,* 11th ed., vol. XXVIII

VICTORIA
(1819–1901)
Queen of Great Britain and Ireland from 1837, and Empress of India from 1876

We are not interested in the possibilities of defeat.
To A. J. Balfour, December 1899, during Boer War

GORE VIDAL
(1925–   )
American writer

To bring into the world an unwanted human being is as antisocial an act as murder.
Contribution, *Esquire,* October 1968

By the time a man gets to be Presidential material he's been bought ten times over.
Interview, *Newsweek,* November 18, 1974

ALFRED VICTOR, COMTE DE VIGNY
(1797–1863)
French poet

Servitude et grandeur militaires (1835)

An army is a nation within a nation; it is one of the vices of our age.
I, 2

La Bouteille à la mer

The true God, the all-powerful God, is the God of ideas.

FRANÇOIS DE MONTCORBIER VILLON
(1431–c. 1465)
French poet

"L'Epitaphe Villon"

Men, brother men, that after us yet live,
Let not your hearts too hard against us be
. . .
But pray to God that he absolve us all.

Le Testament (1461)

Mais où sont les neiges d'antan?
But where are the snows of yester-year?
"Ballade des dames du temps jadis"

In this faith I want to live and die.
"Ballade de l'homage à Notre Dame"

I know everything but myself.
"Ballade des menus propres"

HENRY VINCENT
English chartist leader

We believe that the only security against the corruption of the few and the degradation of the many, is to give the great body of the people their political and social rights.
Speech, Working Men's Association, February 2, 1837

RICHARD VINES
(c. 1585–1651)
English cleric

'Tis man's perdition to be safe,
When for the truth he ought to die.
Sermon for the House of Commons; quoted in Emerson, *Essays,* "Sacrifice" (1841)

VIRGIL (Publius Vergilius Maro)
(70–19 B.C.)
Roman poet

The Aeneid (19 B.C.)

Arma virumque cano.
Of arms and the man I sing.
Opening line

Forsan et haec olim meminisse iuvabit.
Perhaps even these things will some day be pleasant to remember.
Bk. I

Timeo Danaos et dona ferentes.
I fear the Greeks though bearing gifts.

Diis aliter visum.
The gods have judged otherwise.
Bk. II

Quid non mortalia pectora cogis,
Auri sacra fames.
To what cannot you compel the hearts of men,
O cursed lust of gold!

Malesuada fames.
Hunger persuades to evil.
Bk. III

At genus immortale manet.
But the race remains immortal.
Bk. IV

Possunt quia posse videntur.
They can because they think they can.
Bk. V

Facilis descensus Averno.
The road to hell is easy.

Mens agitat molem.
Mind moves matter.
Bk. VI

Audentes fortuna juvat.
Fortune helps the bold.
Bk. X

Georgics (37–30 B.C.)

Thrice they tried to pile Ossa on Pelion,
and to roll leafy Olympus upon Ossa.
I, 281

Felix qui potuit rerum cognoscere causas,
Quique metus omnes, et inexorabile fatum,
Subjecit pedibus, strepitumque Acherontis
avari.
Happy the man who has learned the causes
of things, and has put under his feet all fears,
and inexorable fate, and the noisy strife and
the hell of greed.
II, 490

Labor omnia vincit.
Work conquers all.
IV, 169

Varium et mutabile semper femina.
Woman is always a fickle, unstable thing.
IV, 569

Eclogues (43–37 B.C.)

Age steals away all things, even the mind.
IX, 51

Omnia vincit Amor.
Love conquers all.
X, 69

Epistulae

Does he advise you better who bids you
"Make money, money by right means if you
can, but if not, by any means make money?"

Sapere aude.
Have the courage to be wise.

He who lives in fear will never, in my judgment, be a free man.

VOLTAIRE (François-Marie Arouet)
(1694–1778)
French philosopher*

Letters

Quoi que vous faissiez, écrasez l'infâme.
Whatever you do, crush this infamy.
To Jean d'Alembert June 23, 1762**

---

*"He was more than a man, he was a century."
—Hugo.
". . . the first modern social historian."
—Beard, *The Rise of American Civilization*.
**L'infâme* translates into infamy, baseness, sordid-
ness; on November 28 Voltaire wrote d'Alembert he
meant "superstition." Biographers have interpreted
the word as meaning clericalism. Mencken: "He
sometimes used it in such a way that it unquestionably referred to Catholicism."

I detest what you write, but I would give my
life to make it possible for you to continue to
write.
To M. le Riche, February 6, 1770*

Doubt is not a pleasant condition, but cer-
tainty is absurd.
To Friedrich Wilhelm, Crown Prince of Prussia,
November 28, 1770

A wise and courageous prince, with money,
troops, and laws, can perfectly well govern
men without the aid of religion, which was
made only to deceive them; but the stupid
people would soon make one for themselves,
and as long as there are fools and rascals there
will be religions. Ours is assuredly the most ridiculous, the most absurd, and the most
bloody that has ever infected the world.
To Frederick the Great, January 5, 1767

The public is a ferocious beast; one must
either chain it up or flee from it.
To Mlle. Quinault, August 16, 1748

To hold a pen is to be at war.
To Mme. d'Angental, October 4, 1748

There are truths that are not for all men,
nor for all occasions.
To Cardinal de Bernis, April 23, 1761

Animals have these advantages over man:
they never hear the clock strike, they die without any idea of death, they have no theologians to instruct them, their last moments are
not disturbed by unwelcome and unpleasant
ceremonies, their funerals cost them nothing,
and no one starts lawsuits over their wills.
To Count de Schomberg, August 31, 1769

To worship God and to leave every other
man free to worship Him in his own way; to
love one's neighbor, enlightening them if one
can and pitying those who remain in error; to
dismiss as immaterial all questions that would
have given us no trouble if no importance had
been attached to them—this is my religion, it
is worth all your systems and symbols.
To an unknown correspondent, January 5, 1759

Philosophical Dictionary (1764)**

Without philosophy we should be little
above animals.
"Antiquity"

---

*It was not Voltaire, but his biographer, S. G. Tal-
entyre in *The Friends of Voltaire*, who originated
the famous remark, "I disapprove of what you say,
but I will defend to the death your right to say it."
She (E. Beatrice Hall) wrote Attorney Harry Weinberger of New York (July 20, 1935) that it was "a description of Voltaire's attitude."
**This book was publicly burned in Paris.

Atheist: A name given by theologians to whoever differs from them in their ideas concerning the divinity, or who refuses to believe in it in the form of which, in the emptiness of their infallible pates, they have resolved to present it to him. As a rule an Atheist is any or every man who does not believe in the God of the Priests.

"Atheist"

Auto de Fé: An act of faith. A dainty feast offered to the Divinity from time to time, and which consisted of roasting, in great pomp, the bodies of Jews or heretics for the salvation of their souls and the edification of the lookers-on.

"Auto de Fé"

Christianity: A religious system attributed to Jesus Christ, but really invented by Plato, improved by St. Paul, and finally revised and corrected by the Fathers, the councils, and other interpreters of the Church. Since the foundation of this sublime creed, mankind has become better, wiser, and happier than before. From that blessed epoch the world was forever freed from all strife, dissensions, troubles, vices, and evils of every kind; an invincible proof that Christianity is divine, and that it is to be possessed of the very devil himself to dare to commit such a creed or doubt its origin.

"Christianity"

Let the punishment of criminals be useful. A hanged man is good for nothing, and a man condemned to public works will serve the country, and is a living lesson.

"Civil Law"

Devil: The black sheep of the heavenly hosts, and the main prop of the Church. . . . Without the devil God would cut but a sorry figure at best. The love of God is frequently but the fear of the devil.

"Devil"

All men then would be necessarily equal, if they were without needs. It is the poverty connected with our species which subordinates one man to another. It is not the inequality which is the real misfortune, it is the dependence.

All men are born with a sufficiently violent liking for domination, wealth, and pleasure, and with a strong taste for idleness; consequently, all men covet the money, the wives, or the daughters of other men; they wish to be master, to subject them to all their caprices, and to do nothing, or at least to do only very agreeable things.

"Equality"

Fanaticism is to superstition what delirium is to fever, or rage to anger. Its most detestable example is provided by those bourgeois of Paris who in Saint Bartholomew's night ran to assassinate, butcher, defenestrate and chop to pieces those of their fellow citizens who did not go to Mass.

"Fanaticism"

One country cannot gain without another's losing. . . . Such then is the human state, that to wish greatness for one's country is to wish harm to one's neighbors. He who wishes that his fatherland might never be greater, smaller, richer, or poorer, would be a citizen of the world.

"Fatherland"

The will, therefore, is not a faculty that one can call free. A free will is an expression absolutely void of sense, and what the scholastics have called the will of indifference, that is to say a willing without cause, is a chimera unworthy of being combatted.

"Free-Will"

Friendship is the marriage of souls, and this marriage is subject to divorce.

The wicked have only accomplices; voluptaries have companions in debauch, self-seekers have partners, politicians attract partisans; the generality of idle men have attachments; princes have courtiers, and virtuous men alone have friends.

"Friendship"

Gospel: Signifies good news. The good news that the gospel of the Christians came to announce to them is that their God is a God of wrath, that he has predestined the far greater number of them to hell-fire, that their happiness depends on their pious imbecility, their holy credulity, their sacred ravings, on the evil they do to one another through hatred of one for another, . . . and on their antipathy for and persecution of all who do not agree with them or resemble them.

"Gospel"

Jews: A nation full of amenity and composed of lepers, misers, usurers, and scurvy rogues whom the God of the universe, delighted with their shining qualities, in former days fell in love with.

"Jews"

In general, the art of government consists in taking as much money as possible from one class of citizens and to give it to the other.

"Money"

Philosopher: a lover of wisdom, which is to say, truth.

All the philosophical sects have been stranded on the reef of moral and physical ill. We can only conclude and avow that God, having acted for the best, has not been able to act better.

"Philosopher"

Reason is, of all things in the world, the most hurtful to a reasoning human being. God only allows it to remain with those he intends to damn, and in his goodness takes it away from those he intends to save or render useful to the Church. . . . If reason had any part in religion, what then would become of faith?

"Reason"

Over the principal door [i.e., Zoroaster's] I read these words which are the sum of all moral philosophy, and which cut short all the disputes of the casuists: "When in doubt if an action is good or bad, refrain."

"Religion"

There are no sects in geometry.

One does not speak of a Euclidean, and Archimedean. When truth is evident, it is impossible for parties and factions to arise. There never has been a dispute as to whether there is daylight at noon.

All the philosophers of the world who had a religion have said in all ages: "There is a God; and one must be just." That, then is the universal religion established in all ages and throughout mankind. The point in which they all agree is therefore true, and the systems through which they differ therefore false.

"Sect"

Can there exist a people free from all superstitious prejudices? That is to ask: can there exist a nation of philosophers?

Superstition, born of paganism, and adopted by Judaism, has infested the Christian Church from earliest times. All the fathers of the Church, without exception, believed in the power of magic. The Church always condemned magic, but she always believed in it; she did not excommunicate sorcerers as madmen who were mistaken, but as men who were really in communication with the devil.

"Superstition"

If you have two religions in your land, the two will cut each other's throats; but if you have thirty religions, they will dwell in peace.

Of all religions, Christianity is without doubt the one that should inspire tolerance most, although, up to now, the Christians have been the most intolerant of all men.

If we were permitted to reason consistently in religious matters, it is clear that we all ought to become Jews, because Jesus Christ our Saviour was born a Jew, lived a Jew, died a Jew, and he said expressly that He was fulfilling the Jewish religion.

"Tolerance"

Humanly speaking, let us define truth, while waiting for a better definition, as *a statement of facts as they are.*

"Truth"

It is forbidden to kill; therefore all murderers are punished unless they kill in large numbers and to the sound of trumpets.

"War"

Man is not born wicked; he becomes so in the same way as he becomes sick.

"Wicked"

Eryphile (1732)

Superstitions are . . . the Kings of nations.

Act 3

Mahomet (1741)

My life is a warfare.

Mérope (1743)

Whoever serves his country well has no need for ancestors.

Act I, sc. III

Zadig (1747)

Passions are the winds which fill the sails of the vessel; sometimes they sink it; but without them it would be impossible to make way. . . . Everything is dangerous here below, but everything is necessary.

XX

Brutus (1748)

Man is free the moment he wants to be.

Act 2

Poème sur la vie naturelle (1756)

Prejudices are what fools use for reason.

Candide (1759)

All is for the best in the best of all possible worlds.*

Ch. I

In this country [England] it is well from time to time to kill an admiral to encourage the others.

Ch. XXIII

We must cultivate our garden.

Conclusion, ch. XXX

L'Ingénu (1767)

History is but the register of human crimes and misfortunes.

Ch. 10

Les Guebres (1769)

The poor man is never free; he serves in every country.

Act 3

Essai sur les mœurs et l'esprit des nations (1756–69)

This agglomeration which was called and which still calls itself the Holy Roman Empire is neither holy nor Roman, nor an empire.

La Béguède (1772)

The best is the enemy of the good.

(cf. Boccacio)

Pensées d'un philosophe

Marriage is the only adventure open to a coward.

Collection of Letters on the Miracles (1767)

Any one who has the power to make you believe absurdities has the power to make you commit injustices.**

In the midst of all the doubts which we have discussed for 4000 years in 4000 ways, the safest course is to do nothing against one's conscience. With this secret, we can enjoy life and have no fear of death.

Épître à l'auteur de livre des trois imposteurs (November 10, 1770)

If God did not exist it would be necessary to invent Him. But all nature cries aloud that He does exist; that there is a supreme intelligence, an immense power, an admirable order, and everything teaches us our own dependence on it.

I die adoring God, loving my friends, not hating my enemies, and detesting superstition.

Signed, February 28, 1788, quoted in Tallentyre,
Life of Voltaire

History is after all nothing but a pack of tricks which we play upon the dead.

Quoted in John Morley, *Voltaire,* 1828

You must have the devil in you to succeed in any of the arts.

Quoted in Tallentyre, *Life of Voltaire*

Needless to say; since Christ's expiation not one single Christian has been known to sin, or die.

Quoted in Noyes, *Views of Religion*

(Wilhelm) RICHARD WAGNER
(1813–1883)
German composer, poet, essayist

The Creative Force (1848)*

I will dissipate every illusion which has mastery over the human race. I will destroy the authority of the one over the many; of the lifeless over the living; of the material over the spiritual. I will break in pieces the authority of the great; OF THE LAW OF PROPERTY. Let the will of each be master of mankind, one's own desires fashion laws, one's own strength sublimer than he.

---

*This phrase, spoken by Dr. Pangloss, was Voltaire's ironic comment on the pollyanna philosophy of Leibnitz.
**Quoted in numerous books and the *N.Y. Times* as: "As long as people believe in absurdities they will continue to commit atrocities."

---

*Written before exile to France for participating in 1848 revolution.

Religion and Art

The Germans, of course, are by nature the flower of humankind: to fulfill their great destiny they have only to restore their sullied racial purity, or at all events to achieve "a real rebirth of racial feeling."

The Jewish race is "the born enemy of pure humanity and everything that is noble in it."

SELMAN A. WAKSMAN
(1888–1973)
"Father of Antibiotics," Nobel Prize 1952

My Life with the Microbes (1954)

It is usually not recognized that for every injurious or parasitic microbe there are dozens of beneficial ones. Without the latter, there would be no bread to eat nor wine to drink, no fertile soils and no potable waters, no clothing and no sanitation. One can visualize no form of higher life without the existence of the microbes. They are the universal scavengers. They keep in constant circulation the chemical elements which are so essential to the continuation of plant and animal life.

ALFRED RUSSELL WALLACE
(1823–1913)
English scientist

Darwinism (1889)

The theory of natural selection rests on two main classes of facts which apply to all organized beings without exception, and which thus rank as fundamental principles of laws. The first is, the power of rapid multiplication in geometrical progression; the second, that the offspring always vary slightly from the parents, though generally very closely resembling them. From the first fact or law there follows, necessarily, a constant struggle for existence; because, while the offspring always exceed the parents in number, generally to an enormous extent, yet the total number of living organisms in the world does not, and cannot increase year by year.

HENRY A(gard) WALLACE
(1888–1956)
Vice-President of the United States

The century on which we are entering can be and must be the century of the common man.
> Address, "The Price of Free World Victory,"
> May 8, 1942*

HORACE WALPOLE, 4TH EARL OF OXFORD
(1717–1797)
English politician, author

Letters to Sir Horace Mann

Our supreme governors; the mob.
> September 7, 1743

I have often said, and oftener think, *that this world is a comedy for those who think, and a tragedy for those who feel.*
> December 31, 1769

Sense makes few martyrs.
> February 7, 1772

SIR ROBERT WALPOLE, 1ST EARL OF OXFORD
(1676–1745)
Prime Minister of England

The balance of power.
> Address, House of Commons, February 13, 1741

All those men have their price.
> Quoted in W. Coxe, *Memoirs of Walpole* (1798),
> vol. IV

WILLIAM WALWYN
(fl. 1649)
English agitator

Shew me thy faith by thy workes; if I have all faith and have not luve, I am as sounding brass, or as a tinckling cymball, if faith workes, it workes by luve.
> Attributed

---

*This address was generally suppressed; it was printed in full in *In Fact,* and acknowledged by Mr. Wallace.

WILIAM WARBURTON
(1698–1779)
Bishop of Gloucester

Orthodoxy is my doxy; heterodoxy is another man's doxy.
Quoted by Joseph Priestley (1733–1804), *Memoirs*, vol. I

NATHANIEL WARD
(1578–1652)
English preacher

The Simple Cobbler of Aggawam in America (1647)

My heart hath naturally detested foure things: The standing of the Apocrypha in the Bible; Forrainers dwelling in my Countrey, to crowd out native Subjects into the corners of the Earth; Alchymized coines; Toleration of divers Religions, or of one Religion in segregant shapes: He that willingly assents to the last, if he examines his heart by daylight, his conscience will tell him, he is either an Atheist, or an Heretique, or an Hypocrite, or at best a captive of some Lust: Polypiety is the greatest impiety in the world.

EARL WARREN
(1891–1974)
Chief Justice, U.S. Supreme Court

We come to the question presented: Does segregation of children in public schools solely on the basis of race, even though the physical facilities and other "tangible" factors may be equal, deprive the children of the minority group of equal educational opportunities? We believe that it does.*
Unanimous decision, Brown *v.* The Board of Education of Topeka, 347 U.S. 483 (May 17, 1954)

All political ideas cannot and should not be channeled into the programs of our two major parties. History has amply proved the virtue of political activity by minority, dissident groups, who innumerable times have been the vanguard of democratic thought and whose programs were ultimately accepted.

*Justice Stanley Reed considered this one of the most if not the most significant judgment in the history of the Supreme Court.

Mere unorthodoxy or dissent from the prevailing mores is not to be condemned. The absence of such voices would be a symptom of grave illness in our society.
Sweezey *v.* New Hampshire (1957)

Investigations conducted solely for the personal aggrandisement of the investigators or to "punish" those investigated are indefensible.

The mere summoning of a witness and compelling him to testify against his will, about his beliefs, expressions or associations, is a measure of governmental interference. And when those forced revelations concern matters that are unorthodox, unpopular, or even hateful to the general public, the reactions in the life of the witness may be disastrous.
Watkins *v.* U.S., 354 U.S. 178 (1957)*

Liberty—not Communism—is the most contagious force in the world. It will permeate the Iron Curtain. It will eventually abide everywhere.
Address, Columbia University, 1954

JOSIAH WARREN
(1799–1874)
American inventor, philosophical anarchist**

Equitable Commerce (1855)

Liberty, then, is the sovereignty of the individual, and never shall man know liberty until each and every individual is acknowledged to be the only legitimate sovereign of his or her person, time, and property, each living and acting at his own cost; and not until we live in a society where each can exercise his right of sovereignty at all times without clashing with or violating that of others.

To require conformity in the appreciation of sentiments or the interpretation of language, or uniformity of thought, feeling, or action, is a fundamental error in human legislation—a madness which would be only equalled by requiring all to possess the same countenance, the same voice, or the same nature.

*This case involved abuses of civil rights by the House Un-American Activities Committee (HUAC)—which was eventually abolished.
**Credited by John Stuart Mill and Herbert Spencer with first proclaiming the sovereignty of the individual.

BOOKER T(aliaferro) WASHINGTON
(1856–1915)
American Negro leader

The American Standard (1896)

I beg of you to remember that wherever our life touches yours we help or hinder . . . wherever your life touches ours, you make us stronger or weaker. . . . There is no escape—man drags man down, or man lifts man up.

You can't hold a man down without staying down with him.

Up From Slavery (1901)

No race can prosper till it learns that there is as much dignity in tilling a field as in writing a poem.

―――――

In all things that are purely social we [black and white] can be as separate as the five fingers, yet one as the hand in all things essential to mutual progress.
> Public statement, known as "The Atlanta Compromise," September 18, 1895

The black man who cannot let love and sympathy go out to the white man is but half free. The white man who retards his own development by opposing the black man is but half free.
> Address, Boston, May 31, 1897

GEORGE WASHINGTON
(1732–1799)
1st President of the United States*

The fate of unborn millions will now depend, under God, on the courage and conduct of this army. . . . We have, therefore, to resolve to conquer or die.
> Address to troops, August 27, 1776

―――――

*"To the memory of the Man, first in war, first in peace, and first in the hearts of his countrymen."
—Henry Lee, eulogy of Washington, December 26, 1799.
"His mind was great and powerful, without being of the very first order; his penetration strong, though not as acute as that of a Newton, Bacon or Locke; and as far as he saw no judgment was ever sounder. It was slow in operation, being little aided by invention or imagination, but sure in conclusion." —Jefferson, letter to Walter Jones, January 1814.

Send me none but natives.
> Statement re bodyguard, April 30, 1777, after an attempt was made to poison him.*

It is a maxim founded on the universal experiences of mankind that no nation is to be trusted farther than it is bound by its interest.
> Letter to Henry Laurens, 1778

There is not a man living who wishes more sincerely than I do to see a plan adopted for the abolition of slavery. But there is only one proper and effectual mode by which it can be accomplished, and that is by legislative authority.
> Letter to Robert Morris, April 12, 1786

Mankind, when left to themselves, are unfit for their own government.
> Letter to Henry Lee, October 31, 1786; *The Writings of George Washington*, xxix, 34, ed. John C. Fitzpatrick

The period is not very remote, when the benefits of a liberal and free commerce will pretty generally succeed to the devastation and horrors of war.
> Letter to Lafayette, 1786

As mankind becomes more liberal, they will be more able to allow that those who conduct themselves as worthy members of the community are equally entitled to the protection of civil government. I hope ever to see America among the foremost nations in examples of justice and liberality.
> Message to American Catholics, 1789

To be prepared for war is one of the most effectual means of preserving peace.

There is nothing which can better deserve our patronage than the promotion of science and literature. Knowledge is in every country the surest basis of public happiness.
> Address to Congress, January 8, 1790

Happily the Government of the United States, which gives to bigotry no sanction, to persecution no assistance, requires only that they who live under its protection should demean themselves as good citizens in giving it on all occasions their effectual support.
> To the Jewish Congregation, New Port, Rhode Island, August 1790

―――――

*"Put none but Americans on guard" is apocryphal.

I have always given it as my decided opinion that no nation has a right to intermeddle in the internal concerns of another; that every one had a right to form and adopt whatever government they liked best to live under themselves; and that if this country could, consistently with its engagements, maintain a strict neutrality and thereby preserve peace, it was bound to do so by motives of policy, interest, and every other consideration.

Letter to James Monroe, August 25, 1796

"To the People of the United States," 1796*

Promote then as an object of primary importance, institutions for the general diffusion of knowledge. In proportion as the structure of a government gives force to public opinion, it is essential that public opinion be enlightened.

It is our true policy to steer clear of permanent alliances, with any portion of the foreign world.

The basis of our political system is the right of the people to make and to alter their constitutions of government.

Against the insidious wiles of foreign influence (I conjure you to believe me, fellow-citizens) the jealousy of a free people ought to be constantly awake; since history and experience prove that foreign influence is one of the most baneful foes of republican government.

Hence, likewise, they will avoid the necessity of those overgrown military establishments which, under any form of government, are inauspicious to liberty, and which are to be regarded as particularly hostile to republican liberty.

. . . that they may now and then recur to moderate the fury of party spirit, to warn against the mischiefs of foreign intrigue, to guard against the impostures of pretended patriotism; this hope will be a full recompense for the solicitude for your welfare by which they have been dictated.*

I would rather be in my grave than in the Presidency.

Quoted in John F. Kennedy, *Profiles in Courage*

JOHN B(roadus) WATSON
(1878–1958)
American founder of Behaviorist school of psychology

Behaviorism (1925)

Give me a dozen healthy infants . . . and I'll guarantee to take any one at random and train him to become any type of specialist I might select—doctor, lawyer, even beggarman and thief, regardless of his talents, penchants, tendencies, abilities, vocations and race of his ancestors.

THOMAS WATSON
(1557?–1592)
English poet

"The Passionate Century of Love" (1582)

Love is a sour delight, a sugar'd grief,
A living death, an ever-dying life;
A breach of Reason's law, a secret thief,
A sea of tears, an everlasting strife;
A bait for fools, a scourge of noble wits,
A deadly wound, a shot which ever hits.

SIDNEY WEBB, Lord Passfield
(1859–1947)
British socialist leader

The inevitability of gradualness cannot fully be appreciated.**

Presidential address, Labour Party, June 28, 1923

---

*Generally known as the Farewell Address, it was never delivered, but published, at Washington's request, in Claypool's *American Daily Advertiser,* Philadelphia, Monday, September 19, 1796.

At the end of his first term Washington had asked Madison to write a farewell address, which Madison did. Washington used it for his 1796 farewell, which he gave to Hamilton, asking him to "redress" it. Hamilton had the assistance of John Jay and Madison.

"Not withstanding suggestions from Madison and verbal and stylistic changes at the hands of Hamilton and Jay, the Address is essentially Washington's." —Commager.

*The paragraph, "Government is not reason, it is not eloquence—it is force! Like fire it is a dangerous servant and a fearful master . . ." although credited to the "Farewell" cannot be found in it. Lawson Hamblin, who owns a facsimile, and Horace Peck, America's foremost authority on quotations, informed me this paragraph is apocryphal. —G.S.
**The Fabian Socialists, of whom G.B. Shaw was one, believed in *gradual* Marxian Socialism, rather than immediate revolutionary change. "Gradualism" became the slogan of the Labour Party. Eventually it ruled the British Empire. "The phrase in which was summed up the Fabian Socialists' recipe for saving the world from the ills of capitalism," the *N.Y. Times* said editorially, October 20, 1947.

DANIEL WEBSTER
(1782–1852)
American statesman

An unlimited power to tax involves, necessarily, the power to destroy.
Argument, McCullough v. Maryland, Supreme Court (1819); cf. Justices Marshall and Holmes.

In the nature of things, those who have no property and see their neighbors possess much more than they think them to need, cannot be favorable to laws made for the protection of property. When this class becomes numerous, it becomes clamorous. It looks on property as its prey and plunder, and is naturally ready, at times, for violence and revolution.
Address, Massachusetts Convention, 1820

Labor in this country is independent and proud. It has not to ask the patronage of capital, but capital solicits the aid of labor. . . . If you divorce capital from labor, capital is hoarded, and labor starves.
Speech, April 2, 1824

It is, Sir, the people's Constitution, the people's government, made for the people, made by the people, and answerable to the people.

That other sentiment, dear to every true American heart—Liberty and Union, now and forever, one and inseparable!
Second speech on Foote's Resolution (reply to Sen. Hayne), January 26, 1830

There is no refuge from confession but suicide; and suicide is confession.
Trial of J. F. Knapp for murder of Captain Joseph White, April 6, 1830

America has proved that it is practicable to elevate the mass of mankind—that portion which in Europe is called the laboring, or lower class—to raise them to self-respect, to make them competent to act a part in the great right and great duty of self-government; and she has proved that this may be done by education and the diffusion of knowledge. She holds out an example a thousand times more encouraging than ever was presented before, to those nine-tenths of the human race who are born without hereditary fortune or hereditary rank.
The Bunker Hill Monument speech, June 17, 1843

JOHN WEBSTER
(c. 1580–c. 1625)
English dramatist

The White Devil (1612)

Religion, oh, how it commeddles with policy! The first bloodshed in the world happened about religion.

Fortune's a right whore:
If she give aught, she doth it in small parcels,
That she may take away all at one swoop.

The Duchess of Malfi (1623)

Cover her face; mine eyes dazzle; she died young.*
Act 4, sc. II

PELATIAH WEBSTER
(1726–1795)
American political economist

Strictures on Tender Acts (1780)

As money is the sinews of every business, the introduction of a doubtful medium—and forcing it into currency by penal laws—must weaken and lessen every branch of business in proportion to the diminution of inducement found in the money.
cf. Gresham's Law

SIMONE WEIL
(1909–1943)
French mystic writer, factory worker, teacher**

La Pesanteur de la grâce (1947)

God can only be present in the creation in the form of absence.

I can, therefore I am.
Quoted in Simone Pétrement, Simone Weil: A Life (1977)

---

*Considered by George Pierce Baker, professor of English at Harvard, the greatest line in Elizabethan drama. —Lecture, Boston, 1912.
**Died of starvation. The coroner's verdict: "The deceased did kill herself by refusing to eat. . . ."

OTTO WEININGER
(1880–1903)
German psychologist

Sex and Character

All genius is a conquering of chaos and mystery.

The genius which runs to madness is no longer genius.

ALBERT WEISBORD
(c. 1900–1977)
American labor leader

The Conquest of Power (1937)

The fact that in America the proletariat was represented in the beginning by the slave has colored the whole life of the American people. Since the working class was made up of a slave caste, no one not a slave would recognize himself as being part of a class with a fixed social status.

ORSON WELLES
(1916–   )
American actor, producer

An artist is always out of step with the time. He has to be.
Quoted in *N.Y. Times*, August 7, 1966

ARTHUR WELLESLEY, DUKE OF WELLINGTON
(1769–1852)
British military leader, statesman

Nothing except a battle lost can be half so melancholy as a battle won.
Dispatch, 1815, from the field of Waterloo

Beginning reform is beginning revolution.
Letter to Mrs. Arbuthnot, November 7, 1830

There is no such thing as a *little war* for a great nation.
Address, House of Lords, January 16, 1838

All the business of war, and indeed all the business of life, is to endeavor to find out what you don't know from what you do; that's what

I call "guessing at what is on the other side of the hill."
Letter to Mrs. Croker, September 3, 1852; quoted in *Croker Papers*, vol. 3

It was here that the Battle of Waterloo was won.*
Attributed by Montalembert, *De l'Avenir politique de l'Angleterre*

Take my word for it, if you had seen but one day of war you would pray to Almighty God that you might never see such a thing again.
Attributed

H(erbert) G(eorge) WELLS
(1866–1946)
British novelist, historian

The War That Will End War**
Book title, 1914

The Outline of History (1920)

Human history becomes more and more a race between education and catastrophe.
Ch. 41

Crux Ansata (1944)
Heresies are experiments in man's unsatisfied search for truth.

My idea of politics is an open conspiracy to hurry these tiresome, wasteful, evil things—nationality and war—out of existence; to end this empire and that empire, and set up one Empire of Man.

Man is immortal, but not men.
Contribution, *Living Philosophies* (1931)

The great trouble with you Americans is that you are still under the influence of that

---

*"Here," according to Robert Birley, headmaster of Eton, "was the classroom; Wellington did not say Waterloo was won 'on the playing fields of England.' "
"The remark is inapplicable historically and was never made by the Duke of Wellington."
—E. M. Forster, *Abinger Harvest* (1936).
**President Wilson used the phrase, "the war to end all wars," in 1917.

second-rate—shall I say, third-rate?—mind,
Karl Marx. *
> Statement to Sinclair Lewis, G. S., and friends,
> Bronxville, N.Y., 1935

FRANZ WERFEL
(1890–1945)
Austrian writer

Between Heaven and Earth (1944)

The basic formula of all sin is: frustrated or
neglected love.

JOHN WESLEY
(1703–1791)
English divine, founder of Methodism

Indeed, had there been no suffering in the
world, a considerable part of religion, yea, and
in some respects, the most excellent part,
could have had no place therein: since the
very existence of it depends on our suffering:
so that had there been no pain it could have
had no being.

The fall of Adam, first, by giving us an opportunity of being far more holy; secondly, by
giving us the occasions of doing innumerable
good works which otherwise could not have
been done; and, thirdly, by putting it into our
power to suffer for God, . . . may be of such
advantage to the children of men even in the
present life, as they will not thoroughly comprehend till they gain life everlasting.
> Sermon, "God's Love to Fallen Man"

Passion and prejudice govern the world;
only under the name of reason.
> Letter to Joseph Benson, October 5, 1770

We must exhort all Christians to gain all
they can and to save all they can; that is, in effect, to grow rich.
> Quoted in Herbert J. Muller, *The Uses of the Past*

Beware you be not swallowed up in books!
An ounce of love is worth a pound of knowledge.
> Quoted in Southey, *Life of Wesley*

---

*Mr. Wells proposed "Cosmopolitanism" as a sub-
stitute; it sounded very much like Marxism. —G. S.

REBECCA WEST (née Cicily Isabel
Fairfield)
(1892–1983)
British writer

The fear of Life which is the beginning of
all evil . . .
> Contribution, *Freewoman,* March 7, 1912

Motherhood is neither a duty nor a privilege, but simply the way that humanity can
satisfy the desire for physical immortality and
triumph over the fear of death.
> Contribution, *N.Y. Times,* May 8, 1960

RICHARD WHATELY
(1787–1863)
Scholar, Archbishop of Dublin

Elements of Logic (1826)

Post hoc, ergo propter hoc.
After this; therefore, on account of this.

Thoughts and Apothegms

"Honesty is the best policy"; but he who is
governed by that maxim is not an honest man.

JAMES (Abbott) McNEILL WHISTLER
(1834–1903)
American painter

The Gentle Art of Making Enemies (1890)

To the rare few, who, early in life, have rid
themselves of the friendships of the many.
> Dedication

Humanity takes the place of Art, and God's
creations are excused by their usefulness;
beauty is confounded with virtue, and, before
a work of Art, it is asked: "What good shall it
do?"

Listen! There never was an artistic period.
There never was an Art-loving nation.

That Nature is always right is an assertion,
artistically as untrue as it is one whose truth is
universally taken for granted. . . . Nature is
usually wrong . . .

Art happens—no hovel is safe from it, no
Prince may depend upon it, the vested intelligence cannot bring it about, and puny efforts

to make it universal end in quaint comedy, and coarse farce.

This one chord that vibrates with all—this "one touch of Nature" . . . this one unspoken sympathy that pervades all humanity, is— Vulgarity!

Ten O'Clock*

Art should be independent of all claptrap . . . as devotion, pity, love, patriotism, and the like.

Propositions, 2

BOUCK WHITE
(1874–1951)
American Congregationalist minister

Charity is twice cursed—it hardens him that gives and softens him that takes.

Quoted in Sinclair, *The Cry for Justice*

E(lwyn) B(rooks) WHITE
(1899–   )
American writer, editor

World Government and Peace

Democracy is the recurrent suspicion that more than half of the people are right more than half of the time.

Reprinted from *The New Yorker*, 1943–45

WILLIAM ALLEN WHITE
(1868–1944)
Editor, *Emporia Gazette*

Contentment is more wicked than red anarchy.

Review of Sinclair Lewis' *Main Street*

The facts fairly and honestly presented; truth will take care of itself. **

Formula for a free press; in conversation with G.S.

---

*When Ruskin published his attack on Whistler, saying, "I have seen and heard much of Cockney impudence before now, but never expected to hear a coxcomb ask two hundred guineas for flinging a pot of paint in the public's face," Whistler sued for libel; he won, was awarded a ha'penny damage, and went bankrupt. (Ruskin was a millionaire.) Whistler then assembled his followers and made this address on February 20, 1885.
**Mr. White believed that every newspaperman or editor who slanted the news or suppressed news, knew what he was doing; and all such reporters and editors should be fired.

ALFRED NORTH WHITEHEAD
(1861–1947)
British mathematician, philosopher

Adventures of Ideas (1933)

As society is now constituted a literal adherence to the moral precepts scattered throughout the Gospels would mean sudden death.

Part I, ch. II

But wherever ideas are effective, there is freedom.

Ch. IV

The recourse to force, however unavoidable, is a disclosure of the failure of civilization. . . . Thus in a live civilization there is always an element of unrest.

Ch. V

Routine is the god of every social system; it is the seventh heaven of business, the essential component in the success of every factory, the ideal of every statesman.

Ch. VI

An attack upon systematic thought is treason to civilization.

Must "religion" always remain a synonym for "hatred"?

Part II, ch. X

Every simplification is an over-simplification.

Part III, ch. XV

Truth is the qualification which applies to Appearance alone. Reality is just itself, and it is nonsense to ask whether it be true or false. Truth is the conformation of Appearance to Reality.

To know the truth partially is to distort the Universe.

It is an erroneous moral platitude, that it is necessarily good to know the truth. The minor truth may beget the major evil.

Part IV, ch. XVI

The perfection of art has only one end, which is Truthful Beauty. . . . In the absence of Beauty, Truth sinks to triviality. Truth matters because of Beauty.

The defence of morals is the battle-cry which best rallies stupidity against change.

Art can be described as a psychopathic reaction of the race to the stresses of its existence.

Ch. XVII

The Day of Judgment is an important notion: but that Day is always with us.

The merit of Art in its service to civilization
lies in its artificiality.

Art heightens the sense of humanity. It gives
an elation to feeling which is supernatural. . . . A million sunsets will not spur on
men towards civilization. It requires Art to
evoke into consciousness the finite perfections
which lie ready for human achievement.

In short art is the education of nature.
Thus, in its broadest sense, art is civilization.
For civilization is nothing other than the unremitting aim at the major perfections of harmony.

Ch. XVIII

Advance or Decadence are the only choices
offered to mankind. The pure conservative is
fighting against the essence of the universe.

Ch. XIX

Moral codes have suffered from the exaggerated claims made for them. The dogmatic fallacy has here done its worst. Each such code
has been put out by a God on a mountain top,
or by a Saint in a cave, or by a divine Despot
on a throne, or, at the lowest, by ancestors
with a wisdom beyond later question. In any
case, each code is incapable of improvement;
and unfortunately in details they fail to agree
either with each other or with our existing
moral intuitions. The result is that the world is
shocked, or amused, by the sight of saintly old
people hindering in the name of morality the
removal of obvious brutalities from a legal system. Some *Acta Sanctorum* go ill with civilization.

As soon as high consciousness is reached,
the enjoyment of existence is entwined with
pain, frustration, loss, tragedy.

The deepest definition of Youth is, Life as
yet untouched by tragedy.

Adventure belongs to the essence of civilization.

Ch. XX

Dialogues of Alfred North Whitehead (1953, as recorded by Lucien Price)

But the Jews, looking around them, saw always an Oriental despot, and so, looking over
the world at large, thought there must be a
despot over all, and the consequence was they
conceived one of the most immoral Gods ever
imagined.

XXVI

As for the Christian theology, can you
imagine anything more appallingly idiotic
than the Christian idea of heaven? What kind
of deity is it that would be capable of creating
angels and men to sing his praises day and
night to all eternity? It is, of course, the figure
of an Oriental despot, with his inane and barbaric vanity. Such a conception is an insult to
God.

XXXII

The Reformation was one of the most colossal failures in history; it threw overboard what
makes the Church tolerable and even gracious;
namely, its aesthetic appeal; but kept its barbarous theology.

XXXIV

There are no natural laws. There are only
temporary habits of nature.

XLII

Aims of Education and Other Essays (1929)

Culture is activity of thought, and receptive-
ness to beauty and humane feeling. . . . A
merely well-informed man is the most useless
bore on God's earth.

Ch. I

Knowledge shrinks as wisdom grows.

Morality, in the petty negative sense of the
term, is the deadly enemy of religion. . . .
The vitality of religion is shown by the way in
which the religious spirit has survived the ordeal of religious education.

Ch. III

The Concept of Nature (1926)

The guiding motto in the life of every natural philosopher should be, "Seek simplicity
and distrust it."

Religion in the Making (1926)

Religion is what the individual does with his
own solitariness.

Religions commit suicide when they find
their inspirations in their dogmas.

Science and the Modern World (1925)

Religion has emerged into human experience mixed with the crudest fancies of barbaric

imagination. Gradually, slowly, steadily, the vision recurs in history under nobler form and with clearer expression. It is the one element in human experience which persistently shows an upward trend. It recurs with an added richness and purity of content. The fact of the religious vision and its history of persistent expansion is our one ground for optimism.

God is the ultimate limitation, and His existence is the ultimate irrationality. . . . No reason can be given for the nature of God because that nature is the ground of rationality.

A clash of doctrines is not a disaster—it is an opportunity.

Ch. 12

Philosophy asks the simple question, What is it all about?

Contribution, *Philosophical Review*, vol. xlvi

WALT(er) WHITMAN
(1819–1892)
American poet

Leaves of Grass (1855–1892)

The United States themselves are essentially the greatest poem. In the history of the earth hitherto the largest and most stirring appear tame and orderly to their ampler largeness and stir. Here at last is something in the doings of man that corresponds with the broadest doings of the day and night. . . . Here is the hospitality which forever indicates heroes.

This is what you should do: love the earth and sun and the animals, despise riches, give alms to everyone that asks, stand up for the stupid and crazy, devote your income and labor to others, hate tyrants, argue not concerning God, have patience and indulgence toward the people, take off your hat to nothing known or unknown or to any man or number of men . . . re-examine all you have been told at school or church or in any book, dismiss what insults your own soul, and your very flesh shall be a great poem.

The art of art, the glory of expression and the sunshine of the light of letters is simplicity.

But to speak in literature with the perfect rectitude and insouciance of the movements of animals and the unimpeachableness of the sentiments of trees in the woods and grass by the roadside is the flawless triumph of art.

It is also not consistent with the reality of the soul to admit that there is anything in the known universe more divine than men and women.

Liberty is poorly served by men whose good intent is quelled from one failure or two failures or any number of failures, or from the casual indifference or ingratitude of the people, or from the sharp show of the rushes of power, or the bringing to bear of soldiers and cannon or any penal statutes. Liberty relies upon itself, invites no one, promises nothing, sits in calmness and light, is positive and composed, and knows no discouragement.

Whatever satisfies the soul is truth.

Preface, 1855 ed.

And I say to mankind, Be not curious about God. For I, who am curious about each, am not curious about God—I hear and behold God in every object, yet understand God not in the least.

Whoever degrades another degrades me.

Preface, 1872 ed.

If anything is sacred the human body is sacred.

"The Children of Adam"

Be not ashamed, woman—your privilege
    encloses the rest,
    and is the exit of the rest;
You are the gates of the body, and you are
    the gates
    of the soul.

"I Sing the Body Electric"

I see those who in any land have died for a
    good cause,
The seed is spare, nevertheless the crop shall
    never run out.
(Mind you, O foreign Kings, O priests, the
    common seed shall
    never run out.)

"Song of the Broad-Axe"

To the States or any one of them, or any city
    of the States.
Resist much, obey little.
Once unquestioning obedience, once fully
    enslaved,
. . . no nation, state, city or this earth ever
    afterward
    assumes its liberty.

"To the States"

I celebrate myself, and sing myself.
                    "Song of Myself," St. 1

I think I could turn and live with animals,
    they are so
placid and self-contained. . . .
They do not lie awake in the dark and weep
    for their sins,
They do not make me sick discussing their
    duty to God,
Not one is dissatisfied, not one is demented
    with the mania
of owning things,
Not one kneels to another, nor to his kind
    that lived
    thousands of years ago,
Not one is respectable or unhappy over the
    whole earth.
                                    St. 32

Behold, I do not give lectures or a little
    charity,
When I give I give myself.
                                    St. 40

I loafe and invite my soul.
I have said that the soul is not more than the
    body
And I said that the body is not more than
    the soul,
And nothing, not God, is greater to one
    than one's self is,
And whoever walks a furlong without sym-
    pathy walks to his
    own funeral drest in his shroud.
                                    St. 48

Do I contradict myself?
Very well then I contradict myself.
                                    St. 51

Come lovely and soothing death, . . .

Dark mother always gliding near with soft
    feet,
Have none chanted for thee a chant of full-
    est welcome?
Then I chant it for thee, I glorify thee above
    all,
I bring thee a song that when thou must in-
    deed come,
    come unfalteringly,
Approach strong deliveress,
When it is so, when thou has taken them, I
    joyously sing the dead. . . .
    "When Lilacs Last in the Dooryard Bloom'd"

I sit and look out upon all the sorrows of the
    world,
    and upon all oppression and shame. . . .

I see the workings of battle, pestilence, tyr-
    anny, I see
martyrs and prisoners, . . .
I observe the sights and depredations cast by
    arrogant
    persons upon laborers, the poor, and
    upon Negroes,
    and the like;
All these—all the meanness and agony with-
    out end
    I sitting look out upon,
See, hear, and am silent.
                        "I Sit and Look Out"

One's self I sing, a simple separate person,
Yet utter the word Democratic, the word
    En-Masse.
The Female equally with the Male I sing.

Of Life immense in passion, pulse, and
    power,
Cheerful, for freest action form'd under the
    laws divine,
The Modern Man I sing.
                        "One's-Self I Sing"

Nor is it you alone who know what it is to be
    evil,
I am he who knew what it is to be evil,
I too knitted the old knot of contrariety,
Blabb'd, blush'd, resented, lied, stole,
    grudg'd,
Had guile, anger, lust, hot wishes I dared
    not speak,
Was wayward, vain, greedy, shallow, sly,
    cowardly,
    malignant,
The wolf, the snake, the hog, not wanting
    in me,
The cheating look, the frivolous word, the
    adulterous wish,
    not wanting,
Refusals, hates, postponements, meanness,
    laziness, none of
    these wanting,
Was one with the rest, the days and haps of
    the rest . . .
                    "Crossing Brooklyn Ferry"

Shut not your doors to me, proud libraries. *
                        "Shut Not Your Doors"

Democratic Vistas (1871)

    The eager and often inconsiderate appeals of
reformers and revolutionaries are indispensa-

---

*Whitman was frequently suppressed or censored,
his books thrown out of libraries.

ble to counterbalance the inertness and fossil-ism making so large a part of human institutions.

The great poems, Shakespeare's included, are poisonous to the idea of the pride and dignity of the common people, the life-blood of democracy.

Specimen Days (1882)

The real war will never get in the books.
"The Real War"

Notes Left Over

To have great poets there must be great audiences.
"Ventures on an Old Theme"

The churches are one vast lie; the people do not believe them, and they do not believe themselves; the priests are continually telling what they know well enough is not so, and keeping back what they know is so. The spectacle is a pitiful one.
Letter to Emerson

I was a man. I suffered. I was there.
Quoted in Van Wyck Brooks, *The Confident Years*

I am a radical of radicals, but I don't belong to any school.
Quoted in Horace Traubel, *With Walt Whitman in Camden*

JOHN GREENLEAF WHITTIER
(1807–1892)
American poet, abolitionist

"Stanzas for the Times" (1835)

Rail on, then, brethren of the South,
Ye shall not hear the truth the less;
No seal is on the Yankee's mouth,
No fetters on the Yankee's press!
From our Green Mountains to the sea,
One voice shall thunder, We are free!

"Ichabod" (1850)*

All else is gone: from those great eyes
The soul has fled;
When faith is lost, when honor dies,
The man is dead!

*An attack on Webster, "the lost leader," who on March 7, 1850, appealing for Southern presidential votes, disillusioned his Northern abolitionist followers.

"The Preacher"

From the death of the old the new proceeds,
And the life of truth from the death of creeds.

"The Gallows" (1842)

Bear witness, O Thou wrong and merciful One,
That earth's most hateful crimes have in Thy name been done.

LANCELOT LAW WHYTE
(1896–1972)
Scottish physicist

Much of our failure to understand human nature arises from neglect of this need to have our faculties excited and our lives thereby enhanced. The human animal cannot be itself without this exciting enhancement. Excitement is not merely good; it is indispensable to a proper human life.
Contribution, *Saturday Review*, November 12, 1966

NORBERT WIENER
(1894–1964)
American scientist, "Father of Automation"

The Human Use of Human Beings (1950)

Any use of a human being, in which less is demanded of him and less is attributed to him than his full status, is a degradation and a waste.

Cybernetics
Book title, 1948

LADY JANE FRANCESCA WILDE
("Speranza")
(1826–1896)
Irish poet

"Ballad on the Irish Famine"

Weary men, what reap ye?—"Golden corn for the stranger."
What sow ye?—"Human corpses that await the Avenger."
Fainting forms, all hunger-stricken, what see you in the offing?
"Stately ships to bear our food away amid the stranger's scoffing."

"Despair"

> Day by day we lower sink, and lower,
>   Till the God-like soul within
> Falls crushed beneath the fearful demon
>   power
> Of poverty and sin.

OSCAR (Fingall O'Flahertie Wills) WILDE (1854–1900)
Irish writer

Lord Arthur Saville's Crime (1891)

Comfort is the only thing our civilization can give us.

The Critic as Artist (1891)

A little sincerity is a dangerous thing, and a great deal of it is absolutely fatal.

Nothing that is worth knowing can be taught.

There is no sin except stupidity.

Anybody can make history. Only a great man can write it.

Modern journalism by giving us the opinions of the uneducated, keeps us in touch with the ignorance of the community.

De Profundis (1905)*

I must say to myself that I ruined myself, and that nobody great or small can be ruined except by his own hand.

All great ideas are dangerous.

"The English Renaissance of Art"

Music is the art . . . which most completely realizes the artistic idea, and is the condition to which all the other arts are constantly aspiring.

One should never talk of a moral or an immoral poem—poems are either well written or badly written, that is all.

> Lecture, New York City, January 9, 1882

*So titled by Robert Ross; Wilde's title: "Epistola: In Carcere et Vinculus" (addressed to Lord Alfred Douglas).

An Ideal Husband (1895)

Morality is simply the attitude we adopt toward people whom we personally dislike.

There is only one real tragedy in a woman's life. The fact that the past is always her lover, and her future invariably her husband.

> Act iii

Intentions (1891)

It is always with the best intentions that the worst work is done.

We are never more true to ourselves than when we are inconsistent.

It is well for his peace that the saint goes to his martyrdom. He is spared the sight of the horror of his harvest.

The only difference between the saint and the sinner is that every saint has a past, and every sinner a future.

The public is wonderfully tolerant. They forgive everything except genius.

Lady Windermere's Fan (1892)

I can resist everything except temptation.
> Act I

(Cynic:) A man who knows the price of everything and the value of nothing.

Nowadays to be intelligible is to be found out.

Life is far too important a thing ever to talk seriously about.
> Act III

The Picture of Dorian Gray (1891)

All art is quite useless.

Death and vulgarity are the only two facts in the 19th century that one cannot explain away.

The one charm of marriage is that it makes a life of deception absolutely necessary for both parties.
> Preface

Conscience and cowardice are really the same things. Conscience is the trade-name of the firm.

To reveal art and conceal the artist is art's aim.

Women represent the triumph of matter over mind, just as men represent the triumph of mind over matter.

Ch. I

A Woman of No Importance (1893)

The history of woman is the history of the worst form of tyranny the world has ever known; the tyranny of the weak over the strong. It is the only tyranny that lasts.

One should always be in love. That is the reason one should never marry.

All thought is immoral. Its very essence is destruction. . . . Nothing survives being thought of.

Phrases and Philosophies for the Use of the Young (1894)

Religions die when they are proved to be true. Science is the record of dead religions.

The Decay of Lying

One touch of nature may make the whole world kin, but two touches of nature will destroy any work of art.

The more we study art, the less we care for nature. What art really reveals to us is nature's lack of design, her curious crudities, her extraordinary monotony, her absolutely unfinished condition.

The Soul of Man Under Socialism (1895)

In America the president reigns for four years, and journalism governs for ever and ever.

Socialism, Communism, or whatever one chooses to call it, converting private property into public wealth, and substituting cooperation for competition, will restore society to its proper condition of a thoroughly healthy organism, and ensure the material well-being of each member of the community. It will in fact give Life its proper basis and its proper environment.*

Disobedience, in the eyes of any one who has read history, is man's original virtue. It is through disobedience that progress has been made, through disobedience and through rebellion.

The recognition of private property has really harmed Individualism, and obscured it, by confusing a man with what he possesses. It has led individualism entirely astray. . . . *The true perfection of man lies, not in what man has, but in what man is.*

"Know Thyself" was written over the portal of the antique world. Over the portal of the new world, "Be Thyself" shall be written. And the message of Christ to man was simply "Be Thyself." That is the secret of Christ.

Individualism, then, is what through Socialism we are to attain to. As a natural result the State must give up all idea of government . . . there is no such thing as governing mankind. All modes of government are failures. . . . High hopes were once formed for democracy; but democracy means simply the bludgeoning of the people by the people for the people. . . .

The fact is, that civilization requires slaves. The Greeks were quite right there. Unless there are slaves to do the ugly, horrible, uninteresting work, culture and contemplation become almost impossible. . . . On mechanical slavery, on the slavery of the machine, the future of the world depends.

A map of the world which does not include Utopia is not worth even glancing at, for it leaves out the one country at which Humanity is always landing. And when Humanity lands there, it looks out, and seeing a better country, sets sail. . . .

With the abolition of private property, then, we shall have true, beautiful, healthy Individualism. Nobody will waste his life accumulating things and the symbols of things. One will live. To live is the rarest thing in the world. Most people exist, that is all.

The form of government that is most suitable to the artist is no government at all.

The Epigrams of Oscar Wilde (ed. Alvin Redman, 1954)

Starvation, and not sin, is the parent of modern crime.

Oscariana (1911)

A man who does not think for himself does not think at all.

---

*Wilde's Socialism is his own, not Marx's, according to British Socialists who accused Wilde of Utopianism and Anarchism.

To believe is very dull. To doubt is intensely engrossing. To be on the alert is to live, to be lulled into security is to die.

Every effect that one produces gives one an enemy. To be popular one must be a mediocrity.

Society often forgives the criminal, it never forgives the dreamer.

The things one feels absolutely certain about are never true. That is the fatality of faith and the lesson of romance.

Betwen men and women there is no friendship possible. There is passion, enmity, worship, love, but no friendship.

"Sonnet to Liberty"

And yet, and yet.
These Christs that die upon the barricades,
God know it I am with them, in some ways.

The Ballad of Reading Gaol (1898)

Yet each man kills the thing he loves,
    By each let this be heard,
Some do it with a bitter look,
    Some with a flattering word.
The coward does it with a kiss,
    The brave man with a sword!
                                    I, st. 7

Some kill their love when they are young,
    And some when they are old;
Some strangle with the hands of Lust,
    Some with the hands of Gold.

For he who lives more lives than one
    More deaths than one must die.
                                    III, st. 37

I know not whether laws be right,
    Or whether laws be wrong;
All that we know who lie in gaol
    Is that the wall is strong;
And that each day is like a year,
    A year whose days are long.
                                    V, st. 1

Ah! happy they whose hearts can break
    And peace of pardon win!
How else may man make straight his plan
    And cleanse his soul from Sin?
How else but through a broken Heart
    May Lord Christ enter in?
                                    St. 14

I sometimes think that God, in creating men, somewhat overestimated his ability.
                                    In conversation

I have nothing to declare except my genius.
    Attributed remark to customs officer on landing in New York.

It is indeed a burning shame that there should be one law for men and another law for women. I think there should be no law for anybody.

Creation for the joy of creation is the aim of the artist, and that is why the artist is a more divine type than the saint.
    Interview, *The Sketch,* January 9, 1895

Faithfulness is to the emotional life what consistency is to the life of the intellect—simply a confession of failure.

A man can be happy with any woman, as long as he does not love her.

Journalism justifies its own existence by the great Darwinian principle of the survival of the vulgarist.

Instead of monopolizing the seat of judgment, journalism should be apologizing in the dock.

The newspapers chronicle with degrading avidity the sins of the second-rate, and with the conscientiousness of the illiterate give us accurate and prosaic details of the doings of people of absolutely no interest whatever.

Sound English common sense—the inherited stupidity of the race.

When I think of all the harm that book [the Bible] has done, I despair of ever writing anything equal to it.

Every impulse we strive to strangle broods in the mind, and poisons us. . . . The only way to get rid of temptation is to yield to it.*

It is the confession, not the priest, that gives us absolution.

In this world there are only two tragedies. One is not getting what one wants and the

---

*"The core of Freud's doctrine." —Hesketh Pearson.

other is getting it. The last is much the worst, the last is the real tragedy.

I never came across anyone in whom the moral sense was dominant who was not heartless, cruel, vindictive, log-stupid, and entirely lacking in the smallest sense of humanity. Moral people, as they are termed, are simply beasts. I would sooner have fifty unnatural vices than one unnatural virtue.

Apathy is a vice.

How can a man who regards success as a goal of life, be a true artist. . . .

The poet's noblest verse, the dramatist's greatest scene, deal always with death: because the highest function of the artist is to make perceived the beauty of nature.

People fashion their God after their own understanding. They make their God first and worship him afterwards.

Quoted in Hesketh Pearson, *Oscar Wilde* (1946)

THORTON (Niven) WILDER
(1897–   )
American novelist, dramatist

The Skin of Our Teeth (1942)

Living is struggle. . . . Every good and excellent thing in the world stands moment by moment on the razor-edge of danger and must be fought for—whether it's a field, a home, or a country. All I ask is the chance to build new worlds and God has always given us that.

Antrobus's final speech

The Bridge of San Luis Rey (1927)

The whole purport of literature . . . is the notation of the heart. Style is but the contemptible vessel in which the bitter liquid is recommended to the world.

The public for which masterpieces are intended is not on this earth.

[Last lines:] There is a land of the living and a land of the dead and the only bridge is love, the only survival, the only meaning.

WILHELM II
(1859–1944)
German Kaiser

Smite them with your mailed fist.

To Prince Henry, expedition to China, 1897

Quarter will not be given, prisoners will not be taken. *

Address to personnel of the fleet, Bremerhaven, expedition to China, 1897

Remember, the German people are the chosen of God. On me the German emperor, the spirit of God has descended. I am his sword, his weapon, his vice-regent.

Address, from Palace, Unter den Linden, August 4, 1914

ROGER WILLIAMS
(c. 1603–1683)
Founder of Rhode Island

The Bloody Tenet of Persecution for Cause of Conscience (1644)

First, that the blood of so many hundred thousand souls of Protestants and Papists, spilt in the wars of present and former ages for their respective consciences, is not required by Jesus Christ the Prince of Peace.

Sixthly, it is the will and command of God that (since the coming of his Son the Lord Jesus) a permission of the most Paganish, Jewish, Turkish, or Antichristian consciences and worships be granted to all men.

The Bloody Tenet Yet More Bloody (1652)

No one tenet that either London, England, or the world doth harbor is so heretical, blasphemous, seditious, and dangerous to the corporal, to the spiritual, to the present, to the eternal good of all men, as the bloody tenet (however washed and whited) I say, as is the bloody tenet of persecution for the cause of conscience.

TENNESSEE WILLIAMS
(1914–1983)
American dramatist

Security is a kind of death.

Luxury is the wolf at the door and its fangs are the vanities and conceits germinated by success. When an artist learns this, he knows where the danger is.

---

*"You will give no quarter, you will take no prisoners. All who fall into your hands are at your mercy. Continue the reputation created by the Huns and Attila." —Another newspaper report.

A deaf, dumb and blind idiot could have made a better world than this.
Interview, *Esquire,* September 1971

Hell is yourself. When you ignore other people completely, that is hell.
Quoted in *Time,* March 9, 1962

WILLIAM CARLOS WILLIAMS
(1883–1963)
American poet

A Note on Poetry (1938)

By listening to the language of his locality the poet begins to learn his craft. It is his function to lift, by use of his imagination and the language he hears, the material conditions and appearances of his environment to the sphere of the intelligence where they will have new currency.

The commonplace, the tawdry, the sordid all have their poetic uses if the imagination can lighten them.

But all art is sensual and poetry particularly so. It is directly, that is, of the senses, and since the senses do not exist without an object for their employment all art is necessarily objective. It doesn't declaim or explain, it presents.

Times change and forms and their meanings alter. Thus new poems are necessary. Their forms must be discovered in the spoken, the living language of their day, or old forms, embodying exploded concepts, will tyrannize over the imagination, depriving us of its greatest benefits. In the forms of new poems will lie embedded the essences of future enlightenment.

WENDELL L. WILLKIE
(1892–1944)
American industrialist, presidential candidate

One World (1943)*

Freedom is an indivisible word. If we want to enjoy it, and fight for it, we must be prepared to extend it to everyone, whether they are rich or poor, whether they agree with us or not, no matter what their race or the color of their skin.
Ch. 13

___

*Written largely by William Blake.

COLIN WILSON
(1931–   )
British writer

Ritual in the Dark (1960)

If a man could kill all his illusions he'd become a god.

EDMUND WILSON
(1895–1972)
American writer, critic

Memoirs of Hecate County (1949)

Marxism is the opium of the intellectuals.
(also, *Letters,* p. 302)

In times of disorder and stress, the fanatics play a prominent role; in times of peace, the critics. Both are shot after the revolution.

All Hollywood corrupts, and absolute Hollywood corrupts absolutely.

To the Finland Station (1940)

The taking-over by the State of the means of production and the dictatorship in the interest of the proletariat can by themselves never guarantee the happiness of anybody but the dictators themselves.

Europe Without Baedecker (1947)

Socialism will not simply go on to its goal of making everybody healthy and happy, but will presently change its object to that of turning out better human beings.

___

[American radicals] must take Communism away from the Communists, and take it without ambiguities, asserting that their ultimate goal is the ownership by the Government of the means of production.
Quoted in obituary, *New York Times,* June 13, 1972

WOODROW WILSON
(1856–1924)
President of Princeton University, 28th
President of the United States

Addresses, Speeches, Etc.

The President is at liberty, both in law and conscience, to be as big a man as he can.
"Constitutional Government in the United States," 1908

By "radical" I understand one who goes too far; by "conservative" one who does not go far enough; by "reactionary" one who won't go at all.

Speech, New York City, January 29, 1911

Liberty has never come from government. Liberty has always come from the subjects of government. The history of liberty is the history of resistance.*

Address, N.Y. Press Club, May 9, 1912

No one can worship God or love his neighbor on an empty stomach.

Speech, New York City, May 23, 1912

The government of the United States at present is a foster child of the special interests.

There is no indispensable man.

The masters of the government of the United States are the combined capitalists and manufacturers of the United States.

American industry is not free, as once it was free; American enterprise is not free. . . . Why? Because the laws of this country do not prevent the strong from crushing the weak.

What I am interested in is having the government of the United States more concerned about human rights than property rights.

The government, which was designed for the people, has got into the hands of their bosses and their employers, the special interests. An invisible empire has been set up above the forms of democracy.

Speeches published as *The New Freedom,* 1913

The example of America must be an example, not of peace because it will not fight, but of peace because peace is the healing and elevating influence of the world, and strife is not. There is such a thing as a man being too proud to fight. There is such a thing as a man being so right that he does not need to convince others by force that he is right.

Speech, Philadelphia, May 10, 1915

The world must be made safe for democracy. . . . Civilization itself seems to be in the balance. But the Right is more precious than peace.

We have no selfish end to serve. We desire no conquest, no dominion. We seek no indemnities for ourselves, no material compensation for the sacrifice we shall freely make.

Address, asking Congress for a declaration of war, April 2, 1917

It must be a peace without victory. . . . Only a peace between equals can last.

Address to the U.S. Senate

Sometimes people call me an idealist. Well, that is the way I know I am an American. America is the only idealistic nation in the world.

Repeated in several 1919 speeches asking acceptance of the League of Nations

Why, my fellow Americans, is there any man here or any woman—let me say, is there any child here—who does not know that the seed of war in the modern world is commercial and industrial rivalry?

Address, St. Louis, September 5, 1919

The great monopoly in this country is the money monopoly. So long as it exists, our old variety of freedom and individual energy of development are out of the question.

Quoted in Brandeis, *Other People's Money*

The world is going to change radically . . . the government will have to take over the natural resources . . . all the water power, all the coal mines, all the oil fields, etc. They will have to be government-owned. . . . The only way we can prevent Communism is by some such action as this.

Quoted in Hofstadter, *The American Political Heritage*

GERRARD (or Jerrard) WINSTANLEY (1609–1661?)
English Leveler, "Spiritual Father of the Quakers"*

The True Levellers' Standard Advanced (1649)

For wherefore is it that there is such wars and rumors of wars in the nations of the earth? And wherefore are men so mad to destroy one another? But only to uphold civil property . . . which is the curse the Creation groans under, waiting for deliverance.

None has the right to be lord over another, but the earth is free to every son and daughter of mankind to live free upon.

Letter to Lord Fairfax

---

*Theodore Roosevelt picked up the last phrase and, apparently not knowing that Jefferson had made a similar declaration, attacked Wilson as a dangerous radical.

---

*"The first Socialist." —Charles H. George.

JOHN WINTHROP
(1588–1649)
Puritan, first Governor of Massachusetts

It will be a service to the Church of great consequence to carry the Gospell into those parts of the world, to helpe on the commings of the fullnesse of the Gentiles, & to raise a Bulworke against the kingdome of Antichrist wch the Jesuites labour to reare in thos parts.
  " 'Reasons' for going to America"; quoted in R. C. Winthrop, *Life and Letters of John Winthrop* (1864)

The woman's own choice makes such a man her husband; but being so chosen, he is her lord and she is to be subject to him, yet in a way of liberty not of bondage; and a true wife accounts her subjection her honor and freedom and would not think her condition safe and free but in her subjection to her husband's authority.
  Journal, 1645

Democracy is among most Civil nations accounted the meanest and worst of all forms of Government . . . and History does record that it hath always of least continuance and fullest of troubles.
  Quoted in Commager, *Living Ideas in America*

JOHN WISE
(1652–1725)
American preacher, libertarian

A Vindication of the Government of New England Churches (1717)*

Man's external, personal, natural liberty, antecedent to all human parts, or alliances, must also be considered. And so every man must be conceived to be perfectly in his own power and disposal, and not to be controlled by the authority of any other. And thus every man must be acknowledged equal to every man, since all subjugation and all command are equally banished on both sides; and considering all men thus at liberty, every man has a prerogative to judge for himself, viz. What shall be most for his behoof, happiness and well-being.

---

*"The first comprehensive argument for democracy in our literature." —Commager, *Living Ideas in America*.

The end of all good government is to cultivate humanity, and promote the happiness of all, and the good of every man in all his rights, his life, liberty, estate, honor, etc., without injury or abuse done to any.

LUDWIG WITTGENSTEIN
(1889–1951)
British philosopher

Tractatus Logico-Philosophicus (1922)

An atomic fact is a combination of subjects (entities, things).

The totality of existent atomic facts is the world.

For an answer which cannot be expressed the question too cannot be expressed.

If a question can be put at all, then it can also be answered.

The object of philosophy is the logical clarification of thought.

Philosophy is not a theory but an activity. . . .

Philosophy limits the disputable sphere of natural science.

Philosophy limits the thinkable and therefore the unthinkable.

Philosophy is language idling.

Everything that can be thought of at all can be thought of clearly. Everything that can be said can be said clearly.

Philosophy is a battle against the bewitchment of our intelligence by means of language.

The work of art is the object seen *sub specie aeternitatis;* and the good life is the world seen *sub specie aeternitatis.* This is the connection between art and ethics.
  Quoted in *N.Y. Times Magazine*, April 24, 1966

HUMBERT WOLFE
(1885–1940)
British poet

You cannot hope to bribe or twist
  (Thank God!) the British journalist;
But, seeing what the man will do
  Unbribed, there's no occasion to.
  Attributed

THOMAS WOLFE
(1900–1938)
American novelist

Look Homeward, Angel (1929)

Which of us has known his brother?
Which of us has looked into his father's
  heart?
Which of us has not remained forever
  prison-pent?
Which of us is not forever a stranger and
  alone?

Foreword

You Can't Go Home Again (pub. 1940)

You can't go back home to your family—
  to a young man's dream of fame and glory
  to the country cottage away from strife
    and conflict
  to the father you have lost
  to the old forms and systems of things
    which seemed
    everlasting but are changing all the
    time.

There is only one thing that a brave and
honest man—a gentleman—should be afraid
of. And that is death. He should carry the fear
of death forever in his heart—for that ends all
glory, and he should use it as a spur to ride his
life across the barriers.

Letter to his mother

I put the relation of a fine teacher to a student just below the relation of a mother to a
son, and I don't think I should say more than
this.

Contribution, *Unseen Harvests—A Treasury of*
Teaching (pub. 1947)

The whole conviction of my life now rests
upon the belief that loneliness, far from being
a rare and curious phenomenon, peculiar to
myself and to a few other solitary men, is the
central and inevitable fact of human existence.

Contribution, "The Anatomy of Loneliness,"
American Mercury, pub. October 1941

MARY WOLLSTONECRAFT (Godwin)
(1759–1797)
English writer, feminist

A Vindication of the Rights of Woman (1792)

Contending for the rights of women, my
main argument is built on this simple principle, that if she be not prepared by education to
become the companion of man, she will stop
the progress of knowledge, for truth must be
common to all, or it will be inefficacious with
respect to its influence on general practice.

The absurd duty, too often inculcated, of
obeying a parent only on account of his being
a parent, shackles the mind, and prepares it for
a slavish submission to any power but reason.

The two sexes mutually corrupt and improve each other.

THOMAS WOLSEY
(1475?–1530)
English Cardinal, statesman

Had I but served God as diligently as I have
served the King, he would not have given me
over in my grey hairs.*

To Sir William Kingston; quoted in Cavendish, *Life*
of Thomas Wolsey (1557)

We must destroy the press; or the press will
destroy us.

Quoted in Godwin, *An Inquiry Concerning*
Political Justice, bk. iv, ch. 2

WOMEN'S RIGHTS CONVENTION, 1848

*Declaration of Sentiments***

We hold these truths to be self-evident: that
all men and women are created equal.

The history of mankind is a history of repeated injuries and usurpation on the part of
man toward woman, having in direct object
the establishment of absolute tyranny over
her. . . . He has created a false public sentiment by giving to the world a different code of
morals for men and women, by which moral
delinquencies which exclude women from society, are not only tolerated, but deemed of little account in man. He has endeavored, in
every way that he could, to destroy her confidence in her powers, to lessen her self-respect,
and to make her willing to lead a dependent
and abject life.

Seneca Falls, New York

*Wolsey died on his way to London to answer a
charge of treason; see *Britannica,* 11th ed., vol.
xxviii.
**Sometimes called "Declaration of Independ-
ence."

C. VANN WOODWARD
(1908–   )
American historian

The history of intellectual growth and discovery clearly demonstrates the need for unfettered freedom, the right to think the unthinkable, discuss the unmentionable, and challenge the unchallengeable. To curtail free expression strikes twice at intellectual freedom, for whoever deprives another of the right to state unpopular views necessarily deprives others of the right to listen to those views.
Woodward Committee, Report on Free Speech,
N.Y. Times, January 28, 1975

LEONARD WOOLF
(1880–1969)
British writer, publisher

Nearly all good editors—like the great newspaper owners—become megalomaniacs and suffer from the hallucination that they control and exercise great power. The hallucination of power corrupts as efficiently as power.
Contribution, *Saturday Review*

VIRGINIA WOOLF
(1882–suicide 1941)
British writer

The Moment and Other Essays (pub. 1948)

If you do not tell the truth about yourself you cannot tell it about other people.

"I will not cease from mental fight," Blake wrote. Mental fight means thinking against the current, not with it. . . . It is our business to puncture gas bags and discover the seeds of truth.
Contribution, *New Republic,* October 21, 1940

There are no teachers, saints, prophets, good people, but the artists.
Letter to Gerald Brenan, Christmas Day, 1923

To admit authorities, however heavily furred and gowned, into our libraries and let them tell us how to read, what to read, what value to place upon what we read, is to destroy the spirit of freedom which is the breath of those sanctuaries. Everywhere else we may be bound by laws and conventions—there we have none.
Attributed

JOHN WOOLMAN
(1720–1772)
American Quaker

Journal (1774)

Every degree of luxury hath some connection with evil.

Journal and Essays

The creator of the earth is the owner of it.
"A Plea for the Poor"

JOHN M. WOOLSEY
(1877–1945)
U.S. District Court Judge

It is only with the normal person that the law is concerned. . . . *Ulysses* is a rather strong draught to ask some sensitive, though normal person to take. But considered opinion, after long reflection, is that whilst in many places the effect of *Ulysses* on the reader undoubtedly is somewhat emetic, no where does it tend to be an aphrodisiac.
Decision, December 6, 1933, allowing Joyce's
Ulysses to come into the U.S.*

WILLIAM WORDSWORTH
(1770–1850)
English poet

"Ode: Intimations of Immortality From Recollections of Early Childhood" (1803–1806)

Our birth is but a sleep and a forgetting:
The Soul that rises with us, our life's Star,
    Hath had elsewhere its setting,
        And cometh from afar.

But trailing clouds of glory do we come
    From God, who is our home.

Heaven lies about us in our infancy!
Shades of the prison-house begin to close
    Upon the growing Boy.
St. 5

---

*Printed in full in the American edition of the formerly banned novel.

Though nothing can bring back the hour
Of splendour in the grass, of glory in the
flower.

St. 10

"The World Is Too Much With Us" (1807)

The world is too much with us; late and
soon
Getting and spending, we lay waste our
powers;
Little we see in nature that is ours;
We have given our hearts away, a sordid
boon!

. . . Great God! I'd rather be
A Pagan suckled in a creed outworn;
So might I, standing on the pleasant lea,
Have glimpses that would make me less for-
lorn;
Have sight of Proteus rising from the sea,
And hear old Triton blow his wreathèd
horn.

The Excursion (1814)

Piety is sweet to infant minds.

"National Independence and Liberty"

We must be free or die, who speak the
tongue
That Shakespeare spake, the faith and morals hold
Which Milton held.

"Ode to Duty" (1805)

Stern Daughter of the Voice of god!
O Duty!

St. 1

"Lines Composed a Few Miles Above Tintern Ab-
bey" (1798)

. . . I have learned
To look on nature, not as in the hour
Of thoughtless youth; but hearing oftentimes
The still, sad music of humanity . . .

Lines 88–91

Knowing that Nature never did betray
The heart that loved her; 'tis her privilege,
Through all the years of this our life, to lead
From joy to joy: for she can so inform
The mind that is within us, so impress
With quietness and beauty, and so feed
With lofty thoughts, that neither evil
tongues,

Rash judgments, nor the sneers of selfish
men,
Nor greetings where no kindness is, nor all
The dreary intercourse of daily life,
Shall e'er prevail against us, or disturb
Our cheerful faith . . .

Lines 122–133

The Prelude (written 1799–1805)

Dust as we are, the immortal spirit grows
Like harmony in music; there is a dark
Inscrutable workmanship that reconciles
Discordant elements.

Bk. I

There is
One great society alone on earth:
The noble living and the noble dead.

Science appears as what in truth she is,
Not as our glory and our absolute boast,
But as a succedaneum, and a prop
To our infirmity.

Bk. II

There's not a man
That lives who hath not known his godlike
hours.

Bk. III

Bliss was it in that dawn to be alive.
But to be young was very heaven.

Not in Utopia,—in subterranean fields,—
Or some secreted island, Heaven knows
where!
But in the very world, which is the world
Of all of us,—the place where in the end
We find our happiness, or not at all!

Bk. XI

Lyrical Ballads

For all good poetry is the spontaneous overflow of powerful feelings: and though this be
true, Poems to which any value can be attached were never produced on any variety of
subjects but by a man who, being possessed of
more than usual organic sensibility, had also
thought long and deeply.

What is a Poet? To whom does he address
himself? And what language is to be expected
of him? —He is a man speaking to men: a
man, it is true, endowed with more lively sensibility, more enthusiasm and tenderness, who
has a greater knowledge of human nature, and
a more comprehensive soul, than are supposed
to be common among mankind; a man

pleased with his own passions and volitions, and who rejoices more than other men in the spirit of life that is in him; delighting to contemplate similar volitions and passions as manifested in the goings-on of the Universe, and habitually compelled to create them where he does not find them.

Poetry is the image of man and nature.

Poetry is the breath and finer spirit of all knowledge; it is the impassioned expression which is in the countenance of Science.

I have said that poetry is the spontaneous overflow of powerful feelings; it takes its origin from emotion recollected in tranquility; the emotion is contemplated till, by a species of re-action, the tranquility gradually disappears, and an emotion, kindred to that which was before the subject of contemplation, is gradually produced, and does itself actually exist in the mind.

Preface to the Second Edition, 1800

SIR HENRY WOTTON
(1568–1639)
British diplomat, writer

An ambassador is an honest man, sent to lie abroad for the good of his country.*
Written in Christopher Fleckmore's album, 1604; acknowledged in letter to Velserus, 1612

"Character of a Happy Life" (1614)

How happy is he born and taught
That serveth not another's will; . . .
This man is freed from servile bonds
Of hope to rise or fear to fall;
Lord of himself, though not of lands,
And having nothing, yet hath all.

FRANK LLOYD WRIGHT
(1869–1959)
American architect

A Testament (1957)

The insolence of authority is endeavouring to substitute money for ideas.

---

*The pun, "to lie abroad," is not evident in the original Latin. Plato wrote in The Republic: "The rulers of the State are the only ones who should have the privilege of lying, either at home or abroad . . . for the good of the State." Dr. Johnson wrote in The Idler, November 11, 1758: "A newswriter is a man without virtue, who lies at home for his own profit."

Ugliness is a sin.
Newspaper interview, 1955

What is needed most in architecture today is the very thing that is most needed in life—Integrity.
Quoted in N.Y. Times, January 29, 1957

Death is something you can do nothing about. Nothing at all. But youth is a quality, and if you have it you never lose it.
Interview, Mike Wallace, CBS-TV, 1958

Truth against the world.
Motto

WILBUR WRIGHT
(1867–1912)
American inventor

It is possible to fly without motors, but not without knowledge and skill.
Letter to Actave Chaneute, 1900

WILLIAM WYCHERLEY
(c. 1640–1716)
English dramatist

Plain Dealer (c. 1674)

With faint praise one another damn.
Prologue

Love in a Wood (1671)

Necessity, mother of invention.
Act III, sc. iii

JOHN WYCLIFFE
(c. 1320–1384)
English reformer*

This Bible is for the Government of the People, by the People, and for the People.
Preface, Bible, tr. Wycliffe and Nicholas Hereford, 1382; cf. Lincoln

Lords devour poor men's goods in gluttony and waste and pride, and they perish for mischief and thirst and cold, and their children also. . . . And so in a manner they eat and drink poor men's flesh and blood.
Attributed

---

*"The Morning Star of the Reformation."

ELINOR HOYT WYLIE
(1885–1928)
American poet

"The Eagle and the Mole" (1921)

Avoid the reeking herd,
Shun the polluted flock,
Live like that stoic bird
The eagle of the rock.

St. 1

If you would keep your soul
From spotted sight or sound,
Live like the velvet mole;
Go burrow underground.

St. 5

PHILIP WYLIE
(1902–1971)
American writer

Generation of Vipers (1942)

Ignorance is not bliss—it is oblivion.

The church has stood, a rock colossus of
bigotry, in the path of ten thousand reforms.
Sane efforts to legalize birth control, the dissemination of birth control information . . .
the publication of psychological and physical
sex information . . . myriad attempts by sane
men acting sanely on real problems—have
been fought down by church-frightened legis-
latures and church-dominated courts.

The Magic Animal (1968)

The Bible must be put away in libraries
where it belongs. Filed to gather dust beneath
appropriate labels: Mythology, Ancient History, Superstition, Folk-lore, Pre-scientific
Philosophy, and so on.

XENOCRATES OF CHALCEDON
(396–314 B.C.)
Greek philosopher

Men may commit theft as well as adultery
with the eye.

Maxim

XENOPHANES OF COLOPHON
(c. 570–c. 475 B.C.)
Reputed Founder of the Eleatic School of
Philosophy

Fragments

Even so, oxen, lions and horses, if they had
hands wherewith to grave images, would fashion gods after their own shapes and give them
bodies like their own.

No. 15

There is one god, greatest among gods and
men, neither in shape nor in thought like unto
mortals.

No. 23

Pure truth hath no man seen nor e'er shall
know.

No. 34

From earth all things are and to earth all
things return. From earth and water come all
of us.

All things are matter of opinion. . . . That
which I say is opinion like unto truth.

Quoted in *Britannica,* 11th ed.

To God everything is beautiful and good
and just; but men have posited this as unjust,
and this as just.

Quoted in Walter Kaufmann, *The Faith
of a Heretic* (1961)

XENOPHON
(430–355 B.C.)
Greek historian

Memorabilia

To want nothing is godlike; and the less we
want the nearer we approach the divine.

I, 6, 10

XYSTUS I (Sixtus)
(?–c. 125)
7th Bishop of Rome, Pope from c. 116

The Ring

Teachers are greater benefactors than parents.

Human punishment is execrable even when just.

Nothing good is engendered of the flesh.

Let the wedlock of the faithful be a rivalry in continence.

The chief aim of wisdom is to enable one to bear with the stupidity of the ignorant.

A scholar, possessing nothing of this world's goods, is unto God.

PHINEAS BEN YAIR
Hebrew scholar

The doctrines of religion are resolved into carefulness; carefulness into vigorousness; vigorousness into guiltlessness, guiltlessness into abstemiousness; abstemiousness into cleanliness; cleanliness into godliness.
Quoted by Rabbi A. S. Bettelheim

LEON R. YANKWICH
U.S. District Court Judge

There are no illegitimate children—only illegitimate parents.
Decision, Zipkin *v.* Mozon (1928)

BRUNO YASIENSKI
Contemporary Soviet novelist

The Plot of the Indifferent (1937) (unfinished work)

Do not be afraid of enemies; the worst they can do is to kill you. Do not be afraid of friends; the worst they can do is betray you. Be afraid of the indifferent; they do not kill or betray. But only because of their silent agreement, betrayal and murder exist on earth.

WILLIAM BUTLER YEATS
(1865–1939)
Irish writer,* Nobel Prize for Literature 1923

"The Lake Isle of Innisfree" (1893)

I will arise and go now, and go to Innisfree,
And a small cabin build there, of clay and
  wattles made:
Nine bean-rows will I have there, a hive for
  the honeybee,
And live alone there in the bee-loud glade.
                                          St. 1

And I shall have some peace there, for peace
  comes dropping slow,
Dropping from the veils of the morning to
  where the cricket sings; . . .
                                          St. 2

"When You Are Old" (1893)

How many loved your moments of glad
  grace,
And loved your beauty, with love false or
  true,
But one man loved the pilgrim soul in you,
And loved the sorrows of your changing
  face.

"The Land of Heart's Desire" (1894)

The land of faery,
Where nobody gets old and godly and grave,
Where nobody gets old and crafty and wise,

"Easter 1916"** (1921)
I have met them at close of day
Coming with vivid faces
From counter or desk among grey
Eighteenth-century houses.
I have passed with a nod of the head
Or polite meaningless words.

"The Second Coming" (1921)

Things fall apart; the centre cannot hold;
Mere anarchy is loosed upon the world,

---

*"The greatest poet of our time." —T. S. Eliot.
**The date of the Easter Rebellion in Ireland.

The blood-dimmed tide is loosed, and
everywhere
The ceremony of innocence is drowned;
. . .
St. 1*

Surely some revelation is at hand;
Surely the Second Coming is at hand.
St. 2

"A Prayer for My Daughter" (1921)

. . . the murderous innocence of the sea.
St. 2

Have I not seen the loveliest woman born
Out of the mouth of Plenty's horn,
Because of her opinionated mind
Barter that horn and every good
By quiet natures understood
For an old bellows full of angry wind?
St. 8

"Sailing to Byzantium" (1928)

An aged man is but a paltry thing,
A tattered coat upon a stick, unless
Soul clap its hands and sing.
St. 2

O sages standing in God's holy fire
As in the gold mosaic of a wall,
Come from the holy fire, perne in a gyre,
And be the singing-masters of my soul.
St. 3

"Crazy Jane Talks with the Bishop" (1933)

A woman can be proud and stiff
When on love intent;
But love has pitched his mansion in
The place of excrement.
St. 3

"Meru" (1935)

Civilization is hooped together, brought
Under a rule, under the semblance of peace
By manifold illusion.

"The Old Stone Cross" (1938)

A statesman is an easy man,
He tells his lies by rote;
A journalist makes up his lies
And takes you by the throat;
So stay at home and drink your beer
And let the neighbors vote.

---

*"With these words Yeats, in 1921, announced the dominant theme of the 20th century's consciousness and much of its serious literature." —Daniel Stern, *N.Y. Times.*

"Under Ben Bulben" (1936–1939)

Many times man lives and dies
Between his two eternities.

The Cutting of an Agate (1912)

Art bids us touch and taste and hear and see the world, and shrinks from what Blake calls mathematic form, from every abstract thing, from all that is of the brain only, from all that is not a fountain jetting from the entire hopes, memories and sensations of the body.

Dramatis Personae (Autobiography, 1936)

All empty souls tend to extreme opinion.

I am still of the opinion that only two topics can be of the least interest to a serious and studious mind—sex and the dead.
Letter to Olivia Shakespear, October 2, 1927

Man can embody truth but he cannot know it.
Attributed by Archibald MacLeish

I have certainly known more men destroyed by the desire to have a wife and child and to keep them in comfort than I have seen destroyed by drink and harlots.
Attributed

YEVGENY YEVTUSHENKO
(1933–   )
Dissident Soviet Russian poet

"Verses from the Log" (1967)

I believe in the stars, in women, the grass,
The boat's helm and the shoulders of a
friend . . .
Living people are my ikons.

Only he who feels that God is his rival
Can feel himself a man on this land.

One day posterity will remember
This strange era, these strange times, when
Ordinary common honesty was called courage.
Contribution, *Saturday Review,* November 8, 1969;
a rebuke to his critics

MELVIN B. YOKEN
Contemporary American professor of French

Biography of Claude Tillier (1976)

Love and death are linked inexorably in the Romantic imagination because they are both means of escape from the imperfections of life.

BRIGHAM YOUNG
(1801–1877)
American Mormon leader

Discourses of Brigham Young (1925)

The religion of Jesus Christ is a matter-of-fact religion, and taketh hold of the every-day duties and realities of this life.

In the mind of God there is no such thing as dividing spiritual from temporal, or temporal from spiritual; for they are one in the Lord.

Sin consists in doing wrong when we know and can do better, and it will be punished with a just retribution, in the due time of the Lord.

We want men to rule the nation who care more for and love better the nation's welfare than gold and silver, fame or popularity.

EDWARD YOUNG
(1683–1765)
English poet

Love of Fame (1725–1728)

One to destroy, is murder by the law;
And gibbets keep the lifted hand in awe;
To murder thousands takes a specious
    name,
War's glorious art, and gives immortal fame.
When angry sinners, to blot out their score,
Bequeath the church the leavings of a
    whore.

Resignation (1762)

Success, a sort of suicide,
Is ruin'd by success.

The Complaint, or Night Thoughts on Life, Death, and Immortality (1742–1745)

How poor, how rich, how subject, how august,
How complicate, how wonderful is
    man! . . .

From different natures marvelously mixt,
Connection exquisite of distant worlds!
Midway between Nothing and the
    Deity! . . .
An heir to glory! a frail child of dust!
Helpless immortal! insect infinite!
A worm! a god!
All men think all men mortal but them-
    selves.
Night 1

Time flies, death urges, knells call, Heaven
    invites,
Hell threatens.
Night 2

A God all mercy is a God unjust.
Night 4

By night an atheist half believes in God.
Night 5

JAN ZAMOYSKI
(1541–1605)
Polish statesman

The king reigns, but does not govern.
Speech, Parliament, 1605; referring to King
Sigismund III

YEVGENY ZAMYATIN
Contemporary Soviet Russian writer

A Soviet Heretic (1970)

Man ceased to be an ape, vanquished the ape, on the day the first book was written.

True literature can exist only where it is created, not by diligent and trustworthy officials, but by madmen, hermits, heretics, dreamers, rebels, and skeptics.

Explosions are not comfortable. And therefore the exploders, the heretics, are justly exterminated by fire, by axes, by words.

ISRAEL ZANGWILL
(1864–1926)
British writer

The Melting Pot (1920)

America is God's Crucible, the great Melting Pot where all races of Europe are merging and reforming. . . . Germans and Frenchmen and Englishmen, Jews and Russians—into the Crucible with them all! God is making the American

JOHN PETER ZENGER
(1697–1746)
Colonial American printer, publisher

The loss of liberty in general would soon follow the suppression of the liberty of the press; for it is an essential branch of liberty, so perhaps it is the best preservative of the whole.
*The New-York Weekly,** November 19, 1733

ZENO THE STOIC
(c. 335–c. 263 B.C.)
Cyprian-born Greek philosopher

No evil is glorious. But there are cases of glorious death. Death therefore is not evil.

Time is the extension of motion.

To live in accordance with nature is to live in accordance with virtue.
Quoted in More, *Hellenistic Philosophies*

Among the virtues some are primary, and some are subordinate to these. The following are the primary: Wisdom, courage, justice, temperance.

All good (they say) is expedient, binding, profitable, useful, serviceable, beautiful, beneficial, desirable, and just or right.

Only the morally beautiful is good.

Fear is an expectation of evil.
Under fear are arranged the following emotions: terror, nervous shrinking, shame, consternation, panic, mental agony. Terror is fear which produces fright; shame is fear of disgrace; nervous shrinking is a fear that one will have to act; consternation is fear due to a presentation of some unusual occurrence; panic is fear with pressure exercised by sound; mental agony is fear felt when some issue is still in suspense.

Now they [the Stoics] say that the wise man is passionless, because he is not prone to fall into such infirmity. But they add that in another sense the term apathy is applied to the bad man, when, that is, it means that he is callous and relentless.

Moreover, according to them not only are the wise free, but they are also kings.

But among the bad there is, they hold, no such thing as friendship, and thus no bad man has a friend.

It is a tenet of theirs that between virtue and vice there is nothing intermediate. . . . For, say the Stoics, just as a stick must be either straight or crooked, so a man must be either just or unjust. Nor again are there degrees between just and unjust.

It is also their doctrine that amongst the wise there should be a community of wives with free choice of partners, as Plato says in his *Republic.* . . . Under such circumstances we shall feel paternal affection for all the children alike, and there will be an end of the jealousies arising from adultery.
Quoted in Diogenes Laërtius, "Zeno"

EMILE ZOLA
(1840–1902)
French novelist

J'accuse.
I accuse.

My duty is to speak; I have no wish to be an accomplice.
Open letter to the President of France, *L'Aurore,**
January 15, 1898

Truth is on the march; nothing now can stop it.
Contribution, *Le Figaro,* November 25, 1897

---

*Four issues of this publication were burned by the public hangman and Zenger was arrested; he was defended by Andrew Hamilton, q.v.

L'Aurore was edited and published by Clemenceau, who wrote this headline to Zola's defense of Captain Dreyfus; Zola was sent to jail for this protest on February 23, 1898.

Paris (1898)

The *bourgeoisie,* wielding power, would relinquish naught of the sovereignty which it has
conquered, wholly stolen; while the people,
the eternal dupe, silent so long, clenched its
fists and growled, claiming its legitimate share.

Mes Haines (1866)

Art for me . . . is a negation of society, an
affirmation of the individual, outside of all the
rules and all the demands of society.

HULDREICH (or Ulrich) ZWINGLI
(1484–murdered, quartered, burned 1531)
Swiss reformation leader

In the things of this life, the laborer is most
like to God.
Written 1525; quoted in Tawney, *Religion and the
Rise of Capitalism* (1926)

The Mass, in which Christ is offered to God
the Father for the sins of the living and of the
dead, is contrary to Scripture and a gross affront to the sacrifice and death of the Saviour.

Marriage is lawful for all, to the clergy as
well as to the laity.
Propositions, quoted in *Britannica,* 11th ed., vol.
xxviii

INDEX